D0222719

# Texas Politics

## IDEAL AND REALITY

### Enhanced
### Thirteenth Edition

**Charldean Newell**
Regents Professor Emerita of Public Administration
University of North Texas

**David F. Prindle**
Professor of Government
University of Texas at Austin

**James W. Riddlesperger, Jr.**
Professor of Political Science
Texas Christian University

 CENGAGE

Australia • Brazil • Mexico • Singapore • United Kingdom • United States

***Texas Politics: Ideal and Reality,***
**Enhanced Thirteenth Edition**
**Charldean Newell, David F. Prindle,**
**James W. Riddlesperger**

Product Director: Laura Ross

Product Manager: Rich Lena

Product Assistant: Haley Gaudreau

Marketing Manager: Valerie Hartman

Content Manager: Dan Saabye

IP Analyst: Deanna Ettinger

IP Project Manager: Nick Barrows

Production Service: SPI Global

Compositor: SPI Global

Art Director: Sarah Cole

Text Designer: Cheryl Carrington

Cover Designer: Sarah Cole

Cover Image: DepositPhotos/Glow Images -
Sean Pavone/Alamy Stock Photo

© 2020, 2016, 2013 Cengage Learning, Inc.
Unless otherwise noted, all content is © Cengage.

ALL RIGHTS RESERVED. No part of this work covered by the copyright
herein may be reproduced or distributed in any form or by any means,
except as permitted by U.S. copyright law, without the prior written
permission of the copyright owner.

For product information and technology assistance, contact us at
**Cengage Customer & Sales Support, 1-800-354-9706** or
**support.cengage.com.**

For permission to use material from this text or product,
submit all requests online at **www.cengage.com/permissions**.

Library of Congress Control Number: 2019941600

Student Edition: ISBN: 978-0-357-12988-3
Loose-leaf edition: ISBN: 978-0-357-12995-1

**Cengage**
200 Pier 4 Boulevard
Suite 400
Boston, MA 02210
USA

Cengage is a leading provider of customized learning solutions with
employees residing in nearly 40 different countries and sales in more
than 125 countries around the world. Find your local representative at
**www.cengage.com**.

Cengage products are represented in Canada by Nelson Education, Ltd.

To learn more about Cengage platforms and services, register or access
your online learning solution, or purchase materials for your course, visit
**www.cengage.com**.

Printed at CLDPC, USA, 09-20

# Brief Contents

# Contents

# Fit your coursework into your hectic life.

Make the most of your time by learning your way. Access the resources you need to succeed wherever, whenever.

 Study with digital flashcards, listen to audio textbooks, and take quizzes.

 Review your current course grade and compare your progress with your peers.

 Get the free Cengage Mobile App and learn wherever you are.

Break Limitations. Create your own potential, and be unstoppable with *MindTap*.

## MindTap. Powered by You.

cengage.com/mindtap

# Texas Politics Helps You Meet the State Learning Outcomes for GOVT 2306

1. Explain the origin and development of the Texas constitution.
2. Demonstrate an understanding of state and local political systems and their relationship with the federal government.
3. Describe separation of powers and checks and balances in both theory and practice in Texas.
4. Demonstrate knowledge of the legislative, executive, and judicial branches of Texas government.
5. Evaluate the role of public opinion, interest groups, and political parties in Texas.
6. Analyze the state and local election process.
7. Describe the rights and responsibilities of citizens.
8. Analyze issues, policies, and political culture of Texas.

| Chapter in *Texas Politics* | | GOVT 2306 State Learning Outcomes (SLO) that are specifically addressed in the chapter |
|---|---|---|
| 1. | The Context of Texas Politics | SLO 2. Demonstrate an understanding of state and local political systems and their relationship with the federal government. |
| | | SLO 5. Evaluate the role of public opinion, interest groups, and political parties in Texas. |
| | | SLO 7. Describe the rights and responsibilities of citizens. |
| | | SLO 8. Analyze issues, policies, and political culture of Texas. |
| 2. | The Constitutional Setting | SLO 1. Explain the origin and development of the Texas constitution. |
| | | SLO 3. Describe separation of powers and checks and balances in both theory and practice in Texas. |
| | | SLO 4. Demonstrate knowledge of the legislative, executive, and judicial branches of Texas government. |
| 3. | Interest Groups | SLO 4. Demonstrate knowledge of the legislative, executive, and judicial branches of Texas government. |
| | | SLO 5. Evaluate the role of public opinion, interest groups, and political parties in Texas. |
| | | SLO 7. Describe the rights and responsibilities of citizens. |
| 4. | Political Parties | SLO 4. Demonstrate knowledge of the legislative, executive, and judicial branches of Texas government. |
| | | SLO 5. Evaluate the role of public opinion, interest groups, and political parties in Texas. |
| | | SLO 6. Analyze the state and local election process. |
| | | SLO 7. Describe the rights and responsibilities of citizens. |
| | | SLO 8. Analyze issues, policies, and political culture of Texas. |
| 5. | Voting, Campaigns, and Elections | SLO 4. Demonstrate knowledge of the legislative, executive, and judicial branches of Texas government. |
| | | SLO 5. Evaluate the role of public opinion, interest groups, and political parties in Texas. |
| | | SLO 6. Analyze the state and local election process. |
| | | SLO 7. Describe the rights and responsibilities of citizens. |
| | | SLO 8. Analyze issues, policies, and political culture of Texas. |
| 6. | The Legislature | SLO 3. Describe separation of powers and checks and balances in both theory and practice in Texas. |
| | | SLO 4. Demonstrate knowledge of the legislative, executive, and judicial branches of Texas government. |
| | | SLO 5. Evaluate the role of public opinion, interest groups, and political parties in Texas. |
| | | SLO 8. Analyze issues, policies, and political culture of Texas. |

| Chapter in *Texas Politics* | GOVT 2306 State Learning Outcomes (SLO) that are specifically addressed in the chapter |
|---|---|
| 7. The Governor | SLO 3. Describe separation of powers and checks and balances in both theory and practice in Texas. |
| | SLO 4. Demonstrate knowledge of the legislative, executive, and judicial branches of Texas government. |
| | SLO 5. Evaluate the role of public opinion, interest groups, and political parties in Texas. |
| | SLO 8. Analyze issues, policies, and political culture of Texas. |
| 8. The Administrative State | SLO 3. Describe separation of powers and checks and balances in both theory and practice in Texas. |
| | SLO 4. Demonstrate knowledge of the legislative, executive, and judicial branches of Texas government. |
| | SLO 7. Describe the rights and responsibilities of citizens. |
| 9. The Judiciary | SLO 3. Describe separation of powers and checks and balances in both theory and practice in Texas. |
| | SLO 4. Demonstrate knowledge of the legislative, executive, and judicial branches of Texas government. |
| | SLO 7. Describe the rights and responsibilities of citizens. |
| 10. The Substance of Justice | SLO 2. Demonstrate an understanding of state and local political systems and their relationship with the federal government. |
| | SLO 4. Demonstrate knowledge of the legislative, executive, and judicial branches of Texas government. |
| | SLO 5. Evaluate the role of public opinion, interest groups, and political parties in Texas. |
| | SLO 7. Describe the rights and responsibilities of citizens. |
| | SLO 8. Analyze issues, policies, and political culture of Texas. |
| 11. Local Government | SLO 2. Demonstrate an understanding of state and local political systems and their relationship with the federal government. |
| | SLO 6. Analyze the state and local election process. |
| 12. The State Economy and the Financing of State Government | SLO 2. Demonstrate an understanding of state and local political systems and their relationship with the federal government. |
| | SLO 3. Describe separation of powers and checks and balances in both theory and practice in Texas. |
| | SLO 4. Demonstrate knowledge of the legislative, executive, and judicial branches of Texas government. |
| | SLO 8. Analyze issues, policies, and political culture of Texas. |
| 13. Public Policy: People | SLO 2. Demonstrate an understanding of state and local political systems and their relationship with the federal government. |
| | SLO 4. Demonstrate knowledge of the legislative, executive, and judicial branches of Texas government. |
| | SLO 5. Evaluate the role of public opinion, interest groups, and political parties in Texas. |
| | SLO 8. Analyze issues, policies, and political culture of Texas. |
| 14. Public Policy: Resources | SLO 2. Demonstrate an understanding of state and local political systems and their relationship with the federal government. |
| | SLO 4. Demonstrate knowledge of the legislative, executive, and judicial branches of Texas government. |
| | SLO 5. Evaluate the role of public opinion, interest groups, and political parties in Texas. |
| | SLO 8. Analyze issues, policies, and political culture of Texas. |

# Letter to Instructors

The authors have observed and taught Texas politics for more than 125 years collectively. We remain fascinated by the foibles of Texas government and the dynamic changes that have occurred in the politics of the state since this book was first published in 1979. We write *Texas Politics: Ideal and Reality* because we think the governance of the second-largest state in the United States warrants close scrutiny and that instructors and students deserve a book that takes both a broad view and provides enough details to allow readers to evaluate their government. We are aware that most students take the Texas politics course only because the state says they must, but we hope that by emphasizing current events and recent history, we can pique the interest of both those who teach and those who learn.

## The Book's Themes

The dominant theme of this book is *ideal and reality*, that is, how democratic ideals of participation, majority rule, minority rights, and equality before the law are met by the realities of politics in a state that, through most of its history, has been a one-party state—not always the same party—and that emphasizes the values of individualism and traditionalism far more than a moralistic political culture. Two other themes help to shape the book: persistent but not unchallenged *conservatism* and *conflict* arising from various political factions and ethnic, racial, and economic diversity in the state. As political scientists, we are trained to be analysts, not apologists, for the system. Thus, in chapter after chapter, you will see questions raised about whether political processes and practices in Texas meet the test of democratic morality and suggestions about how to improve the Texas political system. We also examine the evolution of today's political conservatism and the state's political disagreements and their consequences for public policy.

## New to This Edition

In this edition, we have continued to focus on aligning our narrative with the state learning outcomes for GOVT 2306, to help students use higher-order thinking to master these objectives. New to this edition, we have introduced a strategy for addressing the skills-based core objectives required of the discipline, as defined by the Undergraduate Education Advisory Committee (UEAC) of the Texas Higher Education Coordinating Board (THECB). The enhanced edition has been designed to support students' development of these core objectives, prompting students to engage in critical thinking, develop communication skills, evaluate social responsibility, and reflect on their own sense of personal responsibility. Each of these exercises is designated by icons throughout the text:

In addition to refining our traditional analyses of Texas politics, and updating essential facts, for the Enhanced 13th edition we have provided new content, in the form of either adding new themes or expanding our coverage of previously mentioned subjects. For the text as a whole, we have introduced two topics that are discussed in several chapters: the politics of climate change and immigration. This edition also contains major substantive updates in the following chapters:

**Chapter 1:** In the historical section, we have added detail about slavery and secession, and provided a new "You Decide" box in which the reader is asked, "How Do You Remember the Alamo?"

**Chapter 2:** In our discussion of constitutional rights, we have added a box examining the conflict over the question of whether the state can force parents to vaccinate their children.

**Chapter 3:** This chapter contains our usual updates on major interest groups, including the conflict between the Christian Right and former speaker of the Texas house of representatives Joe Straus, the Christian Right's successes in persuading the legislature to pass anti-abortion laws, and the political flirtation of the League of United Latin American Citizens (LULAC) with President Donald Trump.

**Chapter 4:** We continue to recount the evolution of state parties through the election of 2018, including a box containing statements from the 2018 state platforms of the two major political parties. We also update and evaluate the changing role of partisanship in the state house versus the state senate.

**Chapter 5:** This chapter contains updates on the Texas Election Commission's efforts to enforce the election and campaign-finance laws; discussions of Russian interference in the 2016, and possibly 2018, elections, and a detailed analysis of 2018 campaigns in Texas.

**Chapter 6:** We report on the evolution of power in the state senate and house, especially the impact of lieutenant governor Dan Patrick on the Senate and Joe Straus on the house. We discuss the way that their differing viewpoints on policy, and institutional power, played out over the 85th legislative session in 2017. We have also added a new "You Decide" box on whether the legislature should be reformed, and if so, how.

**Chapter 7:** We have somewhat restructured the discussion of gubernatorial power by classifying the use of such power as "aggressive" (Rick Perry), "cooperative" (George W. Bush), or "deferential" (Dolph Briscoe).

**Chapter 8:** We have recast the analysis of the relations between the national and state governments after 1980 in terms of "devolution."

**Chapter 9:** We have updated the section on judicial selection to address the swing of the Harris County judiciary from Republican to Democratic in the election of 2018, including the election of 19 African American women to the county's benches. We consider how this change has renewed discussion of the use of partisan election as the process for the selection of judges.

**Chapter 10:** We update our discussion of chronic racism in Texas with the observation that while overt racism is now relatively rare, subtle forms of racism are still embedded in the state's culture. Additionally, we have included a new discussion box about the "new slavery" in Texas—human trafficking.

**Chapter 11:** In Gail Collin's book *As Texas Goes*, she dilates on the concept of "open space politics"—the idea that the state's citizens still see the state as dominated by the frontier. In this chapter, we apply and expand upon Collin's insight, especially in the way that the frontier myth has made governing a now-largely-urban state difficult.

**Chapter 12:** We have updated discussion of block grants and expanded the account of the Texas lottery as a source of state income.

**Chapter 13:** The "politics of immigration" is a major new topic in this chapter.

**Chapter 14:** In addition to updates in our previous discussions of water supply, energy supply, environmental protection, and transportation, we focus on the topic of global climate change, both as a subject in itself and as a theme that has an impact on the other four topics.

## MindTap

As an instructor, MindTap is here to simplify your workload, organize and immediately grade your students' assignments, and allow you to customize your course as you see fit. Through deep-seated integration with your Learning Management System, grades are easily exported and analytics are pulled with just the click of a button. MindTap provides you with a platform to easily add in current events videos and RSS feeds from national or local news sources.

## From the Authors

We hope you find *Texas Politics: Ideal and Reality* to be readable, thorough, and interesting. We welcome your comments and your reactions not only to the book itself but also to the new and exciting digital features designed to make your teaching job easier.

*Charldean Newell*

*David F. Prindle*
dprindle@austin.utexas.edu

*James W. Riddlesperger, Jr.*
j.riddlesperger@tcu.edu

Few students in Texas politics classes are political science majors, but every student is affected by the political processes common in the state and by the policy outcomes that are a result of the Texas political culture, the state's diversity, the attitude toward the national government, and the boom-and-bust economy. For those at a public college or university, how does diminishing support for higher education affect you personally? Most readers of this book will continue to live in Texas and be affected by its political decisions. Are the highways congested and rutted or nicely paved with free-flowing traffic lanes? Are the public schools adequate to prepare students for success in both college and the modern workforce? Is justice dispensed fairly and impartially or according to ethnicity, race, or wealth? Can the state attract employers offering high-end jobs, or is the quality of life in Texas inadequate to the task? As citizens, you need to not only vote in every election but also understand the issues and the candidates. Gaining that understanding can actually be a lot of fun once you begin to realize just how "crazy" the Texas political system really is.

## The Book's Themes

The dominant theme of this book is *ideal and reality*, with the themes of *conservatism* and *conflict* also appearing throughout the text. Texas politics so often presents two contrasting sides of a situation. For example, elected officials constantly rail against the national government, but also depend on it for a large share of the state's budget. Should a state always be a willing participant in the United States? Should it be consistent and either decline federal dollars or participate in all the programs available? The state has chosen not to expand Medicare and not to have a state pool under the Affordable Health Care Act even though Texas has the highest percentage of uninsured residents in the country. Yet this position is very popular with voters. Does the state meet the test of democratic morality—participation, majority rule, minority rights, and equality before the law—by the realities of its political practices? Similarly, the state is basically anti-tax, and, as the introduction to the finance chapter notes, a politician would rather handle a rattlesnake than suggest a tax increase. Resentment of taxes is a classic conservative position. Does the low-tax stance really save taxpayers money, or do they make their "contributions" in other ways such as college tuition, local utility rates, and borrowing?

Questions of democratic morality and conservatism exist in an environment of conflict. Politics is always about conflict, about disagreement, but Texas has extremes not only in its weather but also in its people—rich and poor, Anglo and non-Anglo, religious fundamentalists and non-religious humanists. Too often, these diverse groups play a "zero-sum" game, with the winner taking all and the loser receiving nothing. The room for compromise has grown smaller.

All of these conditions affect you now and will continue to affect you in the future. How much do you pay for tuition? Is there adequate student aid? Are there enough faculty members? Has a president or favorite faculty member been forced to resign because he or she disagreed with the politically appointed board of regents? How well are international students treated on your campus, especially those from the Middle East? Will you be paying college debt for the next twenty years? Did you miss a vital course due to campus cutbacks that will leave you ill-prepared for a future job? Has the college experience given you an appreciation of different cultures that will stand you in good stead in the future?

# Features of the Book

Some of the key features of this book are:

▶ **Learning objectives for each chapter** that guide the organization of and discussion of the chapter and are also summarized at the end of the chapter

▶ **Key term definitions in the margins** of each chapter as well as in the glossary

▶ **Critical thinking questions** for review

▶ **A "Texas Politics and You" feature in each chapter** that asks you to become directly involved in an often controversial issue, often through social media

▶ **A "You Decide" feature in each chapter** that poses a question, gives pro and con arguments, and then asks you to make a decision on the issue

▶ **Cartoons,** mainly by Pulitzer Prize winner Ben Sargent, designed to provoke your reaction and spur discussion

▶ **Digital tools and interactive media** are outlined below to help you master the course material

# MindTap

As a student, the benefits of using MindTap with this book are endless. With automatically graded practice quizzes and activities, an easily navigated learning path, and an interactive eBook, you will be able to test yourself in and outside of the classroom with ease. The accessibility of current events coupled with interactive media makes the content fun and engaging. On your computer, phone, or tablet, MindTap is there when you need it, giving you easy access to flashcards, quizzes, readings, and assignments.

# From the Authors

We hope that you will enjoy *Texas Politics: Ideal and Reality* and find it a useful tool to sparking your interest in state and local government and politics. At a minimum, we hope the book helps you to appreciate why you need to understand state and local politics and government and to vote regularly. Texas is a big, boisterous, sprawling state, and its politics follow suit. Think of Texas politics as a primetime soap opera.

*Charldean Newell*

*David F. Prindle*
dprindle@austin.utexas.edu

*James W. Riddlesperger, Jr.*
j.riddlesperger@tcu.edu

# Resources

## Students

Cengage Unlimited is the first-of-its-kind digital subscription that empowers students to learn more for less. One student subscription includes total access to every Cengage online textbook, platform, career and college success centers, and more—in one place. Learn across courses and disciplines with confidence that you won't pay more to access more. Available now in bookstores and online.

**\*Available only in select markets.** Details at **www.cengage.com/unlimited.**

## Instructors

*Access your Texas Politics, Enhanced 13e resources via*
**www.cengage.com/login.**
Log in using your Cengage Learning single sign-on user name and password, or create a new instructor account by clicking on "New Faculty User" and following the instructions.

## *Texas Politics, Enhanced 13e – Text Only Edition*

**ISBN: 9780357129883**
This copy of the book does not come bundled with MindTap.

## MindTap for *Texas Politics*

**ISBN for Instant Access Code: 9780357129913**
**ISBN for Printed Access Code: 9780357129920**
MindTap for *Texas Politics* is a highly personalized, fully online learning experience built upon Cengage content and correlating to a core set of learning out-

comes. MindTap guides students through the course curriculum via an innovative Learning Path Navigator where they will complete reading assignments, challenge themselves with focus activities, and engage with interactive quizzes. Through a variety of gradable activities,

MindTap provides students with opportunities to check themselves for where they need extra help, as well as allowing faculty to measure and assess student progress. Integration with programs like YouTube, Evernote, and Google Drive allows instructors to add and remove content of their choosing with ease, keeping their course current while tracking local and global events through RSS feeds. The product can be used fully online with its interactive eBook for *Texas Politics, Enhanced 13e,* or in conjunction with the printed text.

## MindTap Resource Center

**Thousands of primary and secondary sources at your fingertips!**
Access to Gale's authoritative library reference content is now available in every Political Science MindTap. Gale, part of Cengage, has been providing research and education resources for libraries for over 60 years.

Instructors have the option to choose from thousands of primary and secondary sources, images, and videos to enhance their MindTap course with the click of a button. This capability can replace a separate reader and conveniently keeps all course materials in one place. The selections are curated by experts, designed specifically for introductory courses, and can be accessed through MindTap's *Activity Builder* feature.

## Instructor Companion Website for *Texas Politics* Enhanced 13e

**ISBN: 9780357129890**

This Instructor Companion Website is an all-in-one multimedia online resource for class preparation, presentation, and testing. Accessible through Cengage.com/login with your faculty account, you will find available for download: book-specific Microsoft® PowerPoint® presentations; a Test Bank compatible with multiple learning management systems; and an Instructor Manual.

The Test Bank, offered in Blackboard, Moodle, Desire2Learn, Canvas, and Angel formats, contains learning objective-specific and core competency-specific multiple choice, short answer, and essay questions for each chapter. Import the Test Bank into your LMS to edit and manage questions and to create tests.

The Instructor's Manual contains chapter-specific learning objectives, an outline, key terms with definitions, and a chapter summary. Additionally, the Instructor's Manual features a critical thinking question, lecture launching suggestion, and an in-class activity for each learning objective.

The Microsoft® PowerPoint® presentations are ready-to-use, visual outlines of each chapter. These presentations are easily customized for your lectures. Access the Instructor Companion Website at www.cengage.com/login.

### Cognero for Texas Politics, Enhanced 13e
**ISBN: 9780357129944**

Cengage Learning Testing Powered by Cognero is a flexible, online system that allows you to author, edit, and manage test bank content from multiple Cengage Learning solutions, create multiple test versions in an instant, and deliver tests from your LMS, your classroom, or wherever you want. The test bank for *Texas Politics,* *Enhanced 13e* contains learning objective-specific and core competency-specific multiple choice, short answer, and essay questions for each chapter.

# Acknowledgments

Many people have helped in the preparation of the Enhanced Thirteenth Edition of this book. Our colleagues also offered constructive criticism and helpful hints. Sometimes we agreed with the reviewers but were unable to comply with their suggestions because of page limitations. Nevertheless, many changes in this edition are due to their comments and the comments of colleagues across the state who called our attention to points deserving coverage or correction. We are similarly indebted to students who raised provocative questions and pointed out places where greater clarity would be appreciated.

Additionally, many other individuals offered valuable assistance in helping us find specific information or documents. They include librarians and other faculty members, graduate students, legislative and state agency staff members, and journalists. We are especially grateful to two people who have been endlessly helpful to us over the course of the many editions of this textbook: Ben Sargent, who makes his editorial cartoons from the *Austin American-Statesman* and *Texas Observer* available to us. Additionally, political science undergraduate students at Texas Christian University were very helpful in the preparation of each chapter's "Texas Politics and You" feature. We would also like to thank Terri Wise for authoring this edition's Instructor's Manual and Powerpoint.

# Reviewers

We would also like to thank the instructors who have contributed their valuable feedback through reviews of this text:

For the Enhanced Thirteenth Edition:

Justin Moeller *WTAMU*
James Goss *Tarrant County College-Trinity River Campus*
Jeff Stanglin *Kilgore College*
Sarah Perez *University of Texas Rio Grande Valley*
Mary Louis *Houston Community College*
Mario Salas *UTSA*
Shannon Sinegal *Austin Community College*
Christopher Olds *Fort Hays State University*
Brenda Riddick *Houston Community College*
Reed Welch *West Texas A&M University*
Vinette Meikle Harris *Houston Community College*
Mohsen Omar *Alamo Community Colleges*

For the Thirteenth Edition:

Robert Ballinger *South Texas College*
Steven N. Tran *Houston Community College*
Tracy Cook *Central Texas College*
Blake R. Farrar *Austin Community College*
Mary Linder *Grayson College*

# About the Authors

## Charldean Newell

Charldean Newell was Richard Kraemer's co-author for the first edition of this textbook in 1979 and continued as the lead author when Kraemer retired from the project in 1992. She died in 2014, at the age of seventy-five.

A Fort Worth native, she earned her doctorate in Government at the University of Texas at Austin in 1965. In addition to this textbook, she was also the author *of The Effective Local Government Manager* (ICMA Press, 2004) and *City Executives* (SUNY Press, 1989), and editor of *Managing Local Government: Cases in Local Government Effectiveness* (ICMA Press, 2009). In her thirty-seven year career at the University of North Texas she won awards from students, colleagues, and alumni, as well as prizes from national public administration organizations. Her memorial service ended with the playing of "Singing Glory to the Green," the North Texas alma mater.

Despite her ferocious work ethic, Charldean was a cheerful and generous writing partner. Phone conversations about the next edition of this textbook were conducted amidst laughter, often including her continuing critiques of the travails of her beloved Texas Rangers baseball team, and generally included helpful advice. She always beat her deadlines, and invariably provided acute but respectful commentary on the chapter first drafts of her co-authors. Although she is no longer contributing new information to this book, many of her sentences and paragraphs continue to adorn its prose, along with continuing themes that reflect her passion for the subject matter. We are pleased that her name is still on the cover.

## David F. Prindle

David Prindle was born in Los Angeles and raised in Hermosa Beach, California. He earned a BA from the University of California, Santa Cruz in 1970, an MA from UCLA in 1972, and a PhD from the Massachusetts Institute of Technology in 1977. He was hired by the Government Department of the University of Texas at Austin in 1976.

He is the author of *Petroleum Politics and the Texas Railroad Commission* (University of Texas Press, 1981), *The Politics of Glamour: Ideology and Democracy in the Screen Actors Guild* (University of Wisconsin Press, 1987), *Risky Business: The Political Economy of Hollywood* (Westview Press, 1993), *The Paradox of Democratic Capitalism: Politics and Economics in American Thought* (Johns Hopkins University Press, 2005), *Stephen Jay Gould and the Politics of Evolution* (Prometheus Books, 2009), and *The Politics of Evolution* (Routledge/Taylor and Francis, 2015). He has won five teaching awards at the University of Texas. His hobbies include fly-fishing, reading detective novels, and getting lost in beautiful places.

## James W. Riddlesperger, Jr.

James W. Riddlesperger, Jr. (PhD, University of Missouri) is Professor of Political Science at Texas Christian University (TCU). A native of Denton, he has taught American politics, with interests in Texas politics, Congress, and the Presidency, at TCU since 1982.

Recipient of the TCU Chancellor's Award for Distinguished Achievement as a Creative Teacher and Scholar and the Honor's Professor of the Year award at TCU, his publications include *The Austin-Boston Connection: Five Decades of House Democratic Leadership, 1937–1989* (Texas A&M University Press, 2009), and *Lone Star Leaders* (TCU Press, 2011); he also co-edited *The Wright Stuff* (TCU Press, 2013), a collection of the writings of former House Speaker Jim Wright, and *Reflections on Rayburn* (TCU Press, 2017). A former president of the Southwestern Political Science Association, and Chief Reader for the U.S. Government Advance Placement exam, he enjoys reading, baseball, and walking.

The San Jacinto Monument near Beaumont commemorates the 1836 battle in which Texans won their independence from Mexico.

*iStock.com/PaulWolf*

# The Context of Texas Politics

M uch has changed in Texas between its entrance to the United States of American in 1845, and the present era in which journalist Erica Grieder, quoted below, described the state as a model for the nation. During the entire nineteenth century, and much of the twentieth century, the state was poor, agricultural, and sparsely settled. Today, it is the nation's second most populous state, four-fifths of the population lives in cities or suburbs, and it leads the country in consuming energy and producing semiconductors, among other distinctions. Yet, as we shall see, in some ways, Texas has changed little since 1845. The Lone Star State is a constantly developing mix of old and new.

Old habits of thought and behavior evolved to meet the problems of the nineteenth century, when Texas was settled by Americans of western European background. They persist today, despite serious new problems created in the latter decades of the twentieth and first decades of the twenty-first century. As Texans prepare themselves to meet the challenges of the future, they have to ask themselves if the habits and institutions they have inherited are up to the job.

In this chapter, the first topic is a summary of the history of Texas, with an emphasis on important political events and the development of the economy. Some of the most basic principles of

## Learning Objectives

After reading this chapter, you should be able to:

**LO1.1** Give a brief account of the causes and consequences of the major events in Texas history, such as the Texas Revolution, slavery, Civil War, Reconstruction, the cotton and oil industries, world wars and Depression, political changes from the Old South to modern Texas, and the state's evolution to a modern economy.

**LO1.2** Summarize democratic theory, and the standards that it supplies us in order to permit us to evaluate the democratic legitimacy of any state or country.

**LO1.3** Discuss whether it is desirable, or even possible, for Texas to have a "foreign policy."

**LO1.4** Give a brief description of the three political cultures, and explain how they apply to Texas.

**LO1.5** Summarize the overall pattern of the relationship of Texas government to the Texas economy, and explain why it is difficult to determine if Texas is or is not a good place to live.

**LO1.6** Discuss the ratio of Anglo, Latinos, and African Americans in the Texas population, and explain why these ratios matter to a book about state government.

TEXAS SOMETIMES LOOKS LIKE THE UNITED STATES TAKEN TO ITS LOGICAL CONCLUSION.

Erica Grieder,
*Big, Hot, Cheap, and Right: What America Can Learn from The Strange Genius of Texas 2013*

democratic theory are then discussed, along with an explanation of why it is vital to understand them, and a brief look at one of democracy's problems. Two discussions then situate Texas within the American federal system and the international arena. The focus then shifts to Texas's political culture and some historically crucial social and political attitudes. The next subject is the economy of Texas and the way it interacts with the state's political system. As an introduction to some discussions later in the book, the origin and distribution of the state's population are then considered. Finally, there is a brief outline of the agenda for the rest of the book.

## Texas History: A Chronology

Like a human being, a state is partly what it is because of what it has experienced. A review of Texas history will highlight the background and context of the themes, institutions, behaviors, and events we discuss in this book.

### The Earliest Days

Humans have inhabited Texas for much longer than there has been such a thing as a state. Skull fragments found near Midland (dubbed "Midland Minnie") and a complete female skeleton discovered near Leander have been dated at 10,000 to 13,000 years old; a larger Clovis period (10,000–9,000 B.C.) site has been excavated in Denton County. At the time of the first European exploration in the sixteenth century, perhaps 30,000 to 40,000 Native Americans inhabited what is now Texas, and some estimates run as high as 130,000. Among the major groups were the Caddo tribes of North and East Texas, Tonkawas in Central Texas, Karankawas along the coast, Coahuiltecans from the Rio Grande to what is now San Antonio, Lipan Apaches and Comanches in West Texas, and Jumanos in the Trans Pecos region. Determined to keep their lands, they violently resisted European settlement. Westward advancement in Texas cost seventeen White lives per mile. One can only guess at the cost to the Native Americans, although it was undoubtedly much higher.

As early as 1519, just twenty-seven years after the European discovery of the New World and a century before the English Pilgrims landed at Plymouth Rock, Spanish explorer Alonzo Alvarez de Pineda mapped the entire Gulf Coast. Several expeditions followed, but Spanish activity was not extensive until 1685, when the French explorer Rene Robert Cavaliere de Sieur La Salle built a small fort in what is now South Texas. This threat of competition from their imperial rivals spurred the Spanish to establish a series of missions beginning in 1690.

The purposes of these missions were to extend the sphere of Spanish domination and civil law and to convert Native Americans to Christianity. Spanish influence extended across South Texas from Louisiana to New Mexico, and by the time of the American Revolution in 1776, about 2,300 Native Americans had been baptized.

However, Spanish power was already waning as a result of economic and military factors. After one abortive attempt, Mexico achieved independence from Spain in 1821. By that year, despite the centuries of Spanish influence, there were only three permanent European settlements in Texas—San Antonio, Nacogdoches, and Goliad—and the European population had declined to 7,000 during the previous thirty years. Although their numbers were relatively small, Spaniards and Mexicans left rich and indelible influences on Texas through their language, law, religion, and culture.

## Anglo-American Colonization

Colonization from the south did not succeed in Texas because of shortsighted economic policies. The Spanish government exploited the few settlers by paying poor prices for their cattle and other products and, at the same time, by charging them high prices for trade goods. As a result, few settlers moved to the giant province.

Texas was potentially much more attractive to settlers from the neighboring United States. There, frontier land was sold to would-be settlers, but in Texas, land was free if one could get a government grant. Because the Spanish government had failed to persuade Mexican citizens to colonize the area, it was nervous about expansionist impulses in the United States. Spain decided to gamble that it could acculturate Anglo settlers and use them to protect Mexican interests against the growing, rambunctious democracy to the north.

Moses Austin, a native of Connecticut, abandoned his unsuccessful business activities in Missouri and turned his attention to Texas. Moses died after filing a formal application for settlement with the viceroy of Mexico in 1819. He was succeeded by his son, Stephen F. Austin, who received a generous land grant, as well as permission to bring in 300 families for colonization. The first settlements were at Columbus on the Colorado River and at Washington-on-the-Brazos. As impresario, or agent, Austin had wide powers over his colony to establish commercial activity, organize a militia, and dispense justice.

Other colonies quickly followed and the non-Native American population jumped from 7,000 to more than 35,000 between 1821 and 1836. The great majority of the settlers came in good faith, intending to take the oath of allegiance to Mexico and be good Mexican citizens. However, the cultural differences they encountered made this difficult. Not only was Spanish the official language, but the colonists, mostly Protestant, were required to accept Roman Catholicism.

There were also disagreements about the institution of slavery. The practice of one human being owning another was illegal in Mexico. But the Anglos who arrived from Southern states universally believed that they could not sustain an economy without owning slaves. Stephen F. Austin was typical. Although privately expressing moral qualms about the institution, he wrote in 1824, "The principal product that will elevate us from poverty is cotton, and we cannot do this without the help of slaves." The Anglo immigrants to the Mexican province brought their slaves with them, and the Mexican government, while officially forbidding them to do so, always found an unofficial way to tolerate the practice.[1]

Furthermore, the new Mexican nation was suffering from violent political instability, and policy toward Texas was both inconsistent and made 900 miles away in Mexico City by men who knew little about conditions in the area. Moreover, Anglos tended to regard themselves as culturally superior to Mexicans and vice versa. Alienation between Texas and Mexico grew, much as alienation between the colonists and the British had grown prior to the American Revolution two generations earlier.

## Revolution

The Mexican government now feared further Anglo-American settlement and acted to curtail it. The settlers responded with demands for concessions, including the right to use the English language in public business and the separation of Texas from the state of Coahuila. Austin was imprisoned in Mexico City for a time, and conditions degenerated. What followed is known to virtually every schoolchild in the state: Texas's war for independence. The most celebrated engagement was the battle in San Antonio during March 1836 in which a few Anglos and Texas-Mexicans held the Alamo against a much larger Mexican force for eleven days before being massacred. Nevertheless, although it makes a stirring story, the Alamo was not a decisive engagement. That distinction belongs to the Battle of San Jacinto, which took place between

The Alamo in San Antonio symbolizes the state's colorful political history.

Dennis Flaherty/Photodisc/Getty Images

**Competency Connection**
**CRITICAL THINKING**

How do you evaluate the phrase 'Remember the Alamo'?

the new Texas army, led by Sam Houston, and the Mexican army, led by General Antonio Lopez de Santa Anna, on April 21.

Surprising the Mexicans while they took a siesta in the afternoon, the Texans routed them in a mere eighteen minutes, captured Santa Anna, and ordered him to sign a document agreeing to their independence or be executed. Santa Anna signed, but repudiated the treaty as soon as he was safely across the border. Texans, however, considered themselves independent, and the Republic of Texas became a reality.

The history of the republic was eventful, but short. Independence brought sudden growth, with the population rising rapidly to about 140,000. The Mexicans invaded twice, capturing San Antonio both times before being repulsed. Resistant Native Americans continued to cause severe problems as well. The new nation soon found itself in debt and with a depreciating currency. Sentiment for annexation by the United States had always been strong, and on December 29, 1845, the U.S. Congress voted to admit Texas into the Union as the twenty-eighth state. This was one of those rare events in history in which an independent nation voluntarily gave up its sovereignty and became part of another nation. Unlike other states, Texas retained the title to all of its public lands when it accepted statehood.

## Early Statehood

A final peace treaty with Mexico had never been signed, and the Mexican government still considered Texas merely a rebellious province. Annexation of the area by the United States precipitated the Mexican War. This conflict was short and decisive. The first engagement took place at Palo Alto, near present-day Brownsville, on May 8, 1846, and Mexico City fell to United States troops less than a year and a half later, on September 14, 1847. Under the Treaty of Guadalupe Hidalgo, the defeated nation relinquished all claim to Texas and, in return for $15 million, ceded all territory west of Texas and south of Oregon to the United States. One can only wonder what the value of this vast tract is today.

No political parties, as such, existed in the Republic of Texas. Sam Houston, the hero of the Battle of San Jacinto, was the dominant political figure, and political debate generally divided along pro-Houston and anti-Houston lines. For the reasons outlined, to the extent that Texans thought about national politics, most were Democrats.

At the time of her independence in 1836, Texas was home to about 5000 Black slaves.[2] By joining the United States, however, the Lone Star State plunged into the political controversy over slavery. That issue simmered at higher and higher temperatures until it boiled over with the

# ISSUE SPOTLIGHT:
## Arguing about the Past, in the Present

More than a hundred and fifty years after it ended, Americans are still arguing about the meaning of the Civil War of 1861-65. One of the most contentious issues concerns the reasons that the Southern states seceded. Northern Whites, and African Americans in every state, assert that the cause of secession was Southern Whites' determination to preserve the institution of slavery. Southern Whites often insist that the cause was a desire to preserve the rights of states against the tyranny of the federal government.

The Southern viewpoint is on display in a plaque that the "Children of the Confederacy" placed in the Texas capitol building during the late 1950s. The plaque states that one of the "truths of history" is that "the war between the states was not a rebellion nor was its underlying cause to sustain slavery."

But the truth of history is better read in the secession document adopted by the Texas Secession Convention in early 1861, which proclaimed a "declaration of the causes which impel the State of Texas to secede from the Federal Union." That document asserts that it is the right of "white men" to preserve "the servitude of the African race," and that because the federal government threatens that right, secession is necessary.

The documentary evidence is thus clear: Texas seceded to preserve slavery. Any other view is an attempt to falsify history.

Many Texans would therefore like to see the Children of the Confederacy plaque removed. No less a personage than Joe Straus, former speaker of the state legislature, has argued that "We should not try to hide the fact that the Confederacy is part of our history. But in a public space like the Texas Capitol, we should also not promote falsehoods." Although many White Texans still cherished the memory of the Confederacy and wanted the plaque to stay, it was removed in January, 2019.

Source: Joe Straus, "Capitol's Plaque Lies About History. Let's Remove It," *Austin American-Statesman,* August 12, 2018, E2.

Competency Connection
**SOCIAL RESPONSIBILITY**

What is your opinion? Should the plaque have stayed or been removed?

election of an antislavery Republican, Abraham Lincoln, as president in 1860. Fearful that Republican control would mean a federal effort to emancipate their slaves, the southern states withdrew from the Union. Texas seceded in February 1861 and joined the new Confederacy in March.

Texans fought at home, on an expedition into New Mexico, and in large numbers in West Virginia, Tennessee, and elsewhere during the Civil War. Southern troops and southern generals were usually superior to their northern counterparts and won many battles. The agricultural South, however, was outgunned, outmanned, and outsupplied by the industrial North, and southern political leadership was inferior to Lincoln's. The U.S. president issued the Emancipation Proclamation, freeing the slaves, on January 1, 1863—an act that persuaded European powers not to enter the war on the South's behalf. As a consequence, the North ground down the South's ability to wage war over four years until the Confederacy fell apart in the spring of 1865. With the defeat of the rebellion, federal troops landed at Galveston on June 19, 1865, proclaiming the freedom of the state's 250,000 slaves. "Juneteenth" was originally celebrated by African-American Texans as Emancipation Day, and has now spread to the rest of the country as an informal holiday.

## Post–Civil War Texas

Confusion and bitterness followed the war. Despite President Lincoln's stated policy of "with malice toward none, with charity for all," the reaction in Texas, as in other parts of the South, was to continue to oppose national policy even though the war was over. Confederate officials and sympathizers were elected to state and local office; Black Codes that severely restricted the activities of the former slaves were passed by state legislatures. (It was Anglo refusal to grant full citizenship to Blacks, as much as the scorching Texas summers, that inspired a famous statement by Union General Phil Sheridan's in 1866, "If I owned hell and Texas, I'd rent out Texas and live in hell.")[3] This defiance by the defeated South strengthened the position of the Radical Republicans in Congress and caused a hardening of policy, and Lincoln's assassination prevented him from moderating their desire to punish the states of the defunct Confederacy for their rebellion. During the period known as Reconstruction, military government was imposed on the South, and former Confederate officials and soldiers were largely excluded from voting and from holding public office.

These actions by the federal government intensified the hostility with which most White Texans viewed the Republican Party. African Americans, as one might expect, voted for Republican candidates, giving White Texans even more reason to support the Democrats. Political activity by the freed slaves also spurred White citizens to form the Ku Klux Klan in Texas and throughout the South. Klan members met in secret, bound themselves by oath, and frequently wore hoods to conceal their identities. Their purpose was to keep African Americans in a position of great inferiority. Their methods included intimidation, violence, and sometimes murder.

The best remembered governorship of this Reconstruction period was that of E. J. Davis, one of a number of Texans who had fought for the Union during the war. A Republican, Davis held office from 1870 to 1874. Using the substantial powers granted by the state's Constitution of 1869, Davis acted like a true chief executive and implemented policies consistent with the philosophy of the Radical Republicans in Washington. To his credit, Davis reformed the penal system and greatly improved public education. To his discredit, during his tenure, state indebtedness increased considerably, and there were allegations of financial impropriety. But whatever the merits of his administration, to White Texans he was a traitorous agent of the hated Yankees.

In 1873, after political restrictions against former Confederate officials and soldiers were removed, a Democrat, Richard Coke, defeated Davis in his reelection bid by a two-to-one margin. Just as important as the return of the Democratic party to power was the repudiation of the Constitution of 1869 and its replacement with Texas's current basic law, the Constitution of 1876. The adoption of this document represented the end of Reconstruction and a substantial return to the traditional principles of the Jeffersonian Democrats, including very limited government and low taxes.

## The Late Nineteenth Century

Texas did not suffer the physical destruction that burdened other Confederate states, and economic recovery and development came quickly after the Civil War. The Hollywood version of this era in Texas is one of cowboys, cattle drives, and range wars. There is some basis for the mythical view of post–Civil War Texas as a land of ranches and trail drives, for between 1866 and 1880 four million cattle were driven "north to the rails."[4] Nevertheless, the actual foundation of the state's economy was King Cotton. In East Texas, the fields were worked largely by African Americans, and in West Texas, by Mexican Americans. Cotton remained the cash crop and principal export well into the twentieth century. However, in terms of the self-image of Texans, the myth of cow culture has been far more important than the reality of cotton farming.

Texas has few navigable rivers, and therefore transportation was a major problem. Because of the size of the state, thousands of miles of railroad track were laid. In 1888, railroad construction in Texas exceeded the total for all of the other states and territories combined.

In 1881, embarrassed officials discovered that the state legislature had given the railroads a million more acres of land for rights of way than were available, and the land-grant laws were repealed. In all, more than 32 million acres of land were given to the railroads, thus establishing early on the easy relationship between the state government and large corporations.

Race relations were difficult statewide, but particularly in East Texas. "Jim Crow laws," severely limiting the civil rights of African Americans, began to make their appearance, and violence against the former slaves was common and often fatal. Between 1870 and 1900, an estimated 500 African Americans died as a result of mob violence, much of it led by the Ku Klux Klan. Although citizenship is much more equal today than it was in the late nineteenth and early twentieth centuries, there is still ethnic conflict in Texas, and some parts of the state continue to display "Old South" racist patterns of behavior.

Throughout most of the final quarter of the nineteenth century, conservative Democrats maintained control of the state. Their rule was based on White supremacy and the violent emotional reaction to the Radical Republican Reconstruction era. But other political parties and interest groups rose to challenge them.

With the penetration of the state by railroads and the increase in manufacturing came organized labor. Most notable were the militant Knights of Labor, which struck the Texas & Pacific Railroad in 1885 and won concessions. Another strike a year later, however, turned violent. Governor John Ireland used troops, ostensibly to protect railroad property, and the strike was broken. In the optimistic and growing economy of the 1880s, labor unions were less acceptable in the South than elsewhere. In Texas, they were viewed as "Yankee innovations" and "abominations." Although a combination of capital was called a corporation and given approval by the state to operate under a charter, combinations of labor, called unions, were frequently labeled restraints of trade by the courts and forbidden to operate. Laws and executive actions also restricted union activities. These biases in favor of capital and against organized labor are still common in Texas.

More important than early labor unions was the agrarian movement. By the 1870s and 1880s, many of those who worked the land in Texas—whether White, African American, or Mexican American—were tenant farmers. Having to borrow money for seed and supplies, they worked all year to pay back what they owed and rarely broke even. Money and credit were scarce even for those who owned land, and railroad rates were artificially high.

The National Grange, or Patrons of Husbandry, was founded in 1867 in Washington, D.C., to try to defend farmers against this sort of economic hardship. The first chapter was established in Texas in 1872 and the organization grew quickly. Grangers were active in local politics, and the state organization lobbied the legislature on issues relevant to farmers. The Grange not only was influential in establishing Texas Agricultural & Mechanical College (now A&M University) and other educational endeavors but also played a significant role in writing the Constitution of 1876.

James S. Hogg, representing a new breed of Texas politician, was elected governor in 1890 and 1892. The first native Texan to hold the state's highest office, Hogg was not a Confederate veteran. He presided over a brief period of reform that saw the establishment of the Railroad Commission, regulation of monopolies, limitations on alien ownership of land, and attempts to protect the public by regulating stocks and bonds. Unfortunately, it was also an era that saw the enactment of additional Jim Crow laws, including the requirement for segregation of African Americans from Whites on railroads.

Both major political parties were in turmoil, and in the 1890s, opposition to the Democrats in southern states was most effectively provided by the new People's, or Populist, Party. Populists represented the belief that ordinary people had lost control of their government to rich corporations, especially the banks and railroads. Populists advocated monetary reform, railroad regulation, control of corporations, and other programs aimed at making government responsible to the citizens. Populists reached their peak strength in Texas in 1894 and 1896, but failed to unseat the Democrats in statewide elections. The dominant party adopted some

Populist programs, and most farmers returned to the Democratic fold. However, Populism, although not the dominant sentiment, is still influential in Texas. (Despite the fact that he is often labeled a "populist" in the media, President Donald Trump's governing philosophy is very different from historical Populism.) Texans who are usually political conservatives can sometimes be roused to vote for candidates who argue that government is making policy at the behest of wealthy insiders rather than ordinary people. The Populist streak makes Texas politics less predictable than it might otherwise be.

Jim Hogg left the governorship in 1895, and the brief period of agrarian reform waned, due in large measure to changes in the membership of the legislature. In 1890, about half the representatives were farmers, but by 1901, two thirds were lawyers and businessmen. The representation of these professions is similarly high today.

## The Early Twentieth Century

Seldom has a new century brought such sudden and important changes as the beginning of the twentieth century brought to Texas. On January 10, 1901, an oil well came in at Spindletop, near Beaumont. Oil had earlier been produced in Texas, but not on such a scale. In 1900, the state had supplied 836,000 barrels of oil—about 6 percent of the nation's production. The Spindletop field exceeded that total in a few weeks and, in its first year, gushed out 3.2 million barrels.

At first, Texas competed with Oklahoma and California for oil production leadership. However, with the discovery of the huge (6 billion barrels) East Texas field in 1930, the Lone Star State became not only the nation's leading producer, but the world's. Oil's abundance and low price led steamship lines and railroads around the country to abandon the burning of coal and convert to oil. Petroleum created secondary industries, such as petrochemicals and the well-service business. More large fields were discovered in every part of the state, except the far western deserts and the central hill country. Oil, combined later with natural gas, replaced cotton and cattle as the state's most important industry. Severance (production) taxes became the foundation for state government revenue.

The rise of the oil industry created considerable conflict, as well as prosperity. Through shrewd and ruthless means, the Standard Oil Company had made itself into a monopoly in the Northeastern states. Texans were determined to prevent the expansion of this giant

A cluster of oil derricks close together in the Spindletop oil field during the boom of the early 1900s near Beaumont.

AP Images/HO

corporation into their state. Beginning in 1889, the Texas attorney general began bringing "antitrust" suits against local companies affiliated with Standard Oil. After Spindletop, attorneys general were even more energetic in trying to repel the expansion of the monopoly. By 1939, the state had brought fourteen antitrust actions against oil companies.[5] People in other states often see Texas as dominated by the oil industry when in reality, as this brief summary illustrates, the state has had an ambivalent relationship with the industry. Texans generally celebrate small, independent firms. However, they are suspicious of the major corporations and state politicians sometimes reflect that suspicion. This is one expression of the Populist tradition in state politics.

The agrarian movement had ended, but the spirit of progressivism was not completely dead. In 1903, the legislature passed the Terrell Election Law, which provided for a system of primary elections rather than the hodgepodge of nomination practices then in use. The legislature also curtailed child labor by setting minimum ages for working in certain industries. National child labor legislation was not passed until thirteen years later. Antitrust laws were strengthened, and a pioneer pure food and drug law was enacted. Farm credit was eased, and the legislature approved a bank deposit insurance plan—a program not adopted by Washington until the 1930s.

Running counter to this progressive spirit, however, was the requirement that a poll tax be paid as a prerequisite for voting. Authorities differ as to whether African Americans, Mexican Americans, or poor Anglos were the primary target of the law, but African Americans were hit especially hard. Their voter turnout, estimated to be 100,000 in the 1890s, dropped to about 5,000 by 1906.

Even this small number, however, was too many for the advocates of White supremacy. In 1904, the legislature permitted, and in 1923 it required, counties to institute the "White primary," which forbade African Americans and Latinos to participate in the party contest to nominate candidates for the general election. Because in that era Texas was a one-party Democratic state (see Chapter 4), the winner of the Democratic primary was always the winner in the general election. Thus, even if minority citizens managed to cast a ballot in November, they could only choose among candidates who had been designated by an all-White electorate in April.[6]

Early efforts to ensure conservation of the state's natural resources enjoyed little success. Few attempts were made to extract oil from the ground efficiently. A large majority of the oil in most reservoirs was never produced, and some of the recovered oil was improperly stored so that it ran down the creeks or evaporated. Many improperly drilled wells polluted groundwater. The "flaring" (burning) of natural gas was commonplace into the 1940s. Fifteen million acres of virgin pine trees in East Texas were clear-cut, leading to severe soil erosion. By 1932, only a million acres of forest remained, and wood products had to be imported into the state. Conservation and environmental protection are still uphill battles in Texas.

## Wars and Depression

World War I, which the United States entered in 1917, brought major changes to Texas. The state became an important military training base and almost 200,000 Texans volunteered for military service. Five thousand lost their lives, many dying from influenza rather than enemy action.

America's native hatemongering organization, the Ku Klux Klan, flourished in the early 1920s. Originally founded to keep African Americans subjugated, after the war, the Klan expanded its list of despised peoples to include immigrants and Catholics. Between 1922 and 1924, the Klan controlled every elective office in Dallas, in both city and county government. In 1922, the Klan's candidate, Earle Mayfield, was elected to the U.S. Senate. Hiram Evans of Dallas was elected imperial wizard of the national Klan, and Texas was the center of Klan power nationwide.

When Alfred E. Smith, a New Yorker, a Roman Catholic, and an anti-prohibitionist, was nominated for the presidency by the Democrats in 1928, Texas party loyalty frayed for the first time since Reconstruction. Texans voted for the Republican candidate, Herbert Hoover, a Protestant and a prohibitionist. Because of such defections from the formerly Democratic "Solid South" and because of the general national prosperity under a Republican administration, Hoover won. Democrats continued to win at the Congressional and state levels however.

Partly because the state was still substantially rural and agricultural, the Great Depression that began with the stock market crash of 1929 was less severe in Texas than in more industrialized states. Further, a year later C. M. "Dad" Joiner struck oil near Kilgore, discovering the supergiant East Texas oil field. This bonanza directly and indirectly created jobs for thousands of people. Houston became so prosperous because of the oil boom that it became known as "the city the Depression forgot."

The liquid wealth pouring from the earth in East Texas, however, also created major problems. So much oil came from that one field so fast that it flooded the market, driving prices down. The price of oil in the middle part of the country dropped from $1.10 per barrel in 1930 to $0.25 a year later, and some lots sold for as little as $0.05 per barrel. With their inexpensive overhead, the small independent producers who dominated the East Texas field could prosper under low prices by simply producing more. However, the major companies, with their enormous investments in pipelines, refineries, and gas stations, faced bankruptcy if the low prices continued. The early 1930s was therefore a period of angry conflict between the large and small producers, with the former arguing for production control and the latter, resisting it.

The Railroad Commission attempted to force the independents to produce less, but they evaded its orders, and millions of barrels of "hot oil" flowed out of the East Texas field from 1931 to 1935. There was confusion and violence before the state found a solution to the overproduction problem. After much political and legal intrigue, the Railroad Commission devised a formula for the "**prorationing**" of oil that limited each well to a percentage of its total production capacity. By restricting production, this regulation propped up prices, and the commodity was soon selling for more than $1 per barrel again.

As part of this system of controlling production and prices, in 1935, Texas Senator Tom Connally persuaded Congress to pass a "Hot Oil Act," which made the interstate sale of oil produced in violation of state law a federal crime. The major companies thus received the state-sanctioned production control upon which their survival depended. Meanwhile, the Railroad Commission was mollifying the independents by creating production regulations that favored small producers. For four decades, the Railroad Commission was in effect the director of the Texas economy, setting production limits, and therefore price floors, for the most important industry in the state. Because Texas was such an important producer, the commission's regulations exerted a powerful effect on the world price of oil. The commission's nurturing of the state's major industry was a major reason the Depression did not hit Texas as hard as it had many other states.

Most Texans were thus able to weather the Depression, but there were still many who were distressed. Unemployment figures for the period are incomplete, but in 1932, Governor Ross Sterling estimated that 300,000 citizens were out of work. Private charities and local governments were unprepared to offer aid on this scale, and in Houston, African Americans and Hispanics were warned not to apply for relief because there was only enough money to take care of Anglos. The state defaulted on interest payments on some of its bonds, and many Texas banks and savings and loans failed. A drought so severe as to create a dust bowl in the Southwest made matters even worse. Texans, with their long tradition of rugged individualism and their belief that "that government is best which governs least," were shaken and frustrated by these conditions.

**prorationing**
Government restraint, suppression, or regulation of the production of oil and/or natural gas resources, with the dual purpose of conserving the resources and propping up prices.

Relief came not from state or local action but from the national administration of the new liberal Democratic president, Franklin D. Roosevelt. Texas Democrats played prominent roles in Roosevelt's New Deal (1933–1945). Vice President John Nance Garner presided over the U.S. Senate for eight years, six Texans chaired key committees in Congress, and Houston banker Jessie Jones, head of the Reconstruction Finance Corporation, was perhaps Roosevelt's most important financial adviser and administrator. The New Deal poured more than $1.5 billion into the state in programs ranging from emergency relief to rural electrification to the Civilian Conservation Corps.

As it had during the first global conflict, Texas contributed greatly to the national effort during World War II from 1941 to 1945. The state was once again a major military training site; several bases and many out-of-state trainees remained after the war. More than 750,000 Texans served in the armed forces and thirty-two received Congressional Medals of Honor. Secretary of the Navy Frank Knox claimed that Texas contributed a higher percentage of its male population to military service than did any other state.

## Post-World-War II Texas

By 1950 profound changes had occurred in Texas society. The state's population had shifted from largely rural to 60 percent urban in the decade of the 1940s, the number of manufacturing workers had doubled, and Texas had continued to attract outside capital and new industry. Aluminum production, defense contracting, and high-technology activities were among the leaders. In 1959, Jack Kilby, an engineer employed by Texas Instruments, developed and patented the microchip, a tiny piece of technology that was to transform the state, the nation, and the world.

Texas politics continued to be colorful, however. In 1948, Congressman Lyndon B. Johnson opposed former Governor Coke Stevenson for a vacant U.S. Senate seat. The vote count was very close in the primary runoff which, with Texas still being dominated by the Democratic Party, was the only election that mattered. As one candidate would seem to pull ahead, another uncounted ballot box that gave the edge to his opponent would be conveniently discovered in South or East Texas. The suspense continued for three days, until Johnson finally won by a margin of eighty-seven votes. Historical research has left no doubt that the box that put Johnson over the top was the product of fraud on the part of the political machine that ruled Duval County. Among students of American politics, this is probably the most famous dirty election in the history of the country. The circumstances surrounding the election have attracted so much attention because "Landslide Lyndon" Johnson went on to become majority leader of the U.S. Senate, vice president, and then in 1963, the first Texas politician to attain the office of president of the United States.

After the war, the state's politics was increasingly controlled by conservative Democrats. As a former member of the Confederacy, Texas was one of the twenty-two states that had laws requiring racial segregation. The 1954 U.S. Supreme Court decision (*Brown* v. *Board of Education*, 347 U.S. 483) declaring segregated public schools unconstitutional caused an uproar in Texas. State leaders opposed integration, just as their predecessors had opposed Reconstruction ninety years earlier. Grade-a-year integration of the schools—a simple and effective solution—was rejected. Millions of dollars in school funds were spent in legal battles to delay the inevitable.

Also in the postwar period, Texas experienced an influx of immigrants. Immigration in the nineteenth century had been primarily from adjacent states, Mexico, and west, central, and southern Europe. Today, immigrants come not only from all fifty states, but also from all of Latin America and a variety of other areas, including those of the Middle East and Asia.

## Gradual Political Change

Since the 1950s, Texas has become increasingly diverse politically as well. Politicians such as U.S. Senator Ralph Yarborough (1957–1971), Commissioner of Agriculture Jim Hightower (1987–1991), and Governor Ann Richards (1991–1995) demonstrated that liberals could win statewide offices. Republicans also began winning, first with U.S. Senator John Tower (1961–1984) and later with Governor Bill Clements (1979–1983 and 1987–1991). Furthermore, candidates from formerly excluded groups enjoyed increasing success, especially after the passage of the Voting Rights Act of 1965. Morris Overstreet was the first African American elected to statewide office, gaining a seat on the Court of Criminal Appeals in 1990. That same year, Mexican Americans Dan Morales and Raul Gonzalez were elected attorney general and justice of the Supreme Court, respectively. Kay Bailey Hutchison broke the sex barrier in statewide elections to national office by being elected U.S. Senator in 1993.

## Late Twentieth-Century Texas

Texas entered a period of good times in the early 1970s. As worldwide consumption of petroleum increased dramatically, the demand for Texas oil outstripped the supply. The Railroad Commission removed market-demand production restrictions in 1972, permitting every well to produce any amount that would not damage ultimate recovery. The following year, the Organization of Petroleum Exporting Countries (OPEC) more than doubled world oil prices and boycotted the American market. Severe energy shortages developed, and the price of oil peaked at more than $40 per barrel. Consumers, especially those from the energy-poor Northeast, grumbled about long lines at gas stations and high prices, but the petroleum industry prospered and the state of Texas enjoyed billion-dollar treasury surpluses.

The 1980s, however, were as miserable for Texas as the previous decade had been agreeable. High oil prices stimulated a worldwide search for the black liquid, and by 1981, so many supplies had been found that the price began to fall. The slide was gradual at first, but the glut of oil was so great that in 1985, the price crashed from its peak of over $40 per barrel in the 1970s to under $10. As petroleum prices plunged, so did Texas's economy: For every $1 drop in world oil prices, 13,500 Texans became unemployed, the state government lost $100 million in revenue from severance taxes and the gross state product contracted by $2.3 billion.[7] Northern consumers smiled as they filled the gas tanks of their cars, but the oil industry and the state of Texas went into shock.

Economic poverty was only one of the miseries that visited Texas in the 1980s. The state's crime rate shot up 29 percent.[8] Most of the crimes committed were related to property and were probably a consequence of the demand for illegal drugs, which constantly increased despite intense public relations and interdiction efforts at the national level. Texans insisted upon better law enforcement and longer sentences for convicted criminals just as the state's tax base was contracting. The combination of shrinking revenues and growing demand for services forced Texas politicians to do the very thing they hated most: increase taxes. In 1984, the legislature raised Texas taxes by $4.8 billion. Then, faced with greatly reduced state income, it was forced to act again. First came an increase of almost $1 billion in 1986, and then in 1987, there was a boost of $5.7 billion, the largest state tax increase in the history of the United States up to that time. The system of raising revenue, relying even more heavily on the sales tax, became more regressive than ever. To make matters worse, the increase came just as Congress eliminated sales taxes as a deductible item on the federal income tax. By the end of the 1980s, Texans were battered, frazzled, and gloomy.

However, the situation reversed itself again in the 1990s. As the petroleum industry declined, entrepreneurs created other types of businesses to take its place. Computer equipment, aerospace, industrial machinery, and scientific instruments became important parts of the economy. The state began to export more goods. Despite the fact that Texas oil production reached a fifty-year low in 1993, by the mid-1990s the economy was booming, even outperforming the nation as a whole. The boom continued to the end of the century, at which point the state had the eleventh largest economy in the world. The entry into a new economic era was underscored by the fact that by 1997, more Texans were employed in high-tech industries than by the oil industry.

Prosperity brought another surge in immigration, and in 1994, the Lone Star State passed New York as the second most populous in the country, with 18.4 million residents.[9] Even the crime rate was down. The election of the state's governor, George W. Bush, to the presidency of the United States in 2000 seemed to guarantee a rosy future for Texas.

## Modern Times

The new century contained many surprises for Texans and Americans, however, many of which were unpleasant. The national economy began to stagger during the spring of 2001. Soon, the media were full of revelations of gigantic fraud in the accounting practices of many apparently successful corporations, including Enron, an energy-trading company based in Houston. Enron went belly-up during the Fall of that year. The news sent the stock market into a tailspin, and the high-tech sector so important in Texas was hit particularly hard. As high tech went into a recession, Texas lost thousands of jobs.[10]

Economic troubles were joined by political disaster on September 11, when radical Muslim terrorists highjacked four jet planes, flying two into, and in the process destroying, the World Trade Center in New York, flying another into the Pentagon building in Washington, D.C., and crashing another into farmland in Pennsylvania. The national grief and fury over the 3,000 murders resulting from these attacks were accompanied by many economic problems as the United States struggled to spend money to prevent such outrages in the future. Although not a direct target of the attacks, Texans were as much involved in their consequences as the residents of other states. Efforts to guard borders and protect buildings were hugely expensive, and conflicting ideas about the ways to interdict terrorists while protecting the civil liberties of loyal citizens were as intense in Texas as elsewhere. More than a dozen years after the attacks, Americans were still arguing about whether electronic surveillance of American phone calls and emails by the National Security Agency was a necessary protection against terrorist plotting or an unjustified invasion of citizens' privacy.

The 2000s were also fraught with perils created by nature rather than by human action. In August 2005, Hurricane Katrina flooded New Orleans in Louisiana, sending hundreds of thousands of refugees across the state border to Houston. Texas state government paid for housing many of the storm refugees in the Astrodome. Just two weeks later, Hurricane Rita roared ashore on the Texas-Louisiana border, causing major flooding in East Texas and draining the state government of more funds. Then, in 2008, Hurricane Ike devastated Galveston with a 16-foot storm surge and 110 mile-per-hour winds, and caused destruction and loss of life in Houston and the Beaumont-Port Arthur area. Two years later, the state's insurance bill for Ike's damage had approached $12 billion, on top of more than three dozen deaths.[11]

But the most spectacular example of nature's fury was the devastation visited on the Houston area in August, 2017 by Hurricane Harvey. In four terrible days, the storm dropped more than thirty inches of rain on an area of southeastern Texas the size of New Jersey, and more than fifty inches in some specific spots. Harvey tied with Hurricane Katrina as the costliest tropical cyclone in the U.S. history, inflicting at least $125 billion in damages. It killed at least 88 people (thankfully many less than the 6,000 who were lost to the 1900 Galveston hurricane). When the deluge finally moved north from Harris County and into other states as a tropical storm, a third of Houston was under water. Great numbers of people in the area lost their homes, their cars, their pets, and their jobs.[12]

# Texas Politics and You

Although it was not the decisive engagement of the Texas war for independence, the siege and battle of the Alamo from February 23 to March 6 is of far greater importance to modern Texans. It is, in fact, the most important incident in what historians call the "collective memory" of citizens of the state—the shared stories of past events that help to form their identities and values. But as a memory both factual and mythical, it has a different significance to different groups. To Anglos, as one historian put it, the Alamo represents "the ultimate story of sacrifice in the name of liberty." To others, especially to Texans of Mexican descent, it can have a more ambiguous meaning.

The perils of tinkering with collective memory are illustrated by the very different public reactions to two motion pictures about the siege. The 1960 film, directed by, and starring John Wayne as a fearlessly determined Davy Crockett, and depicting the doomed Anglo defenders as heroic freedom-fighters, was a box-office success. The 2004 version, starring Billy Bob Thornton as an emotionally-conflicted Crockett, and taking pains to show the Mexican perspective on the war, was one of the biggest flops in Hollywood history, losing more than a hundred million dollars at the box office.

Not just in movies, but in politics also, the way the events of the Alamo struggle are depicted touches deep nerves of state patriotism. When he became Commissioner of the State Land Office in 2015, George P. Bush took over the managing of the actual Alamo site in San Antonio from a private organization, the Daughters of the Republic of Texas. His office launched an ambitious project to update the memorial, make it more tourist-friendly, and to bring it more in line with known historical facts. In the words of one journalist, his office "brought in historical preservation experts from a Philadelphia design firm, who approached the Alamo as a historical site instead of a place of popular imagination."

The reaction was immediate, and furious. Conservative Anglos from all over the state objected, claiming that Bush's plan represented an attempt to impose liberal "political correctness" on Texas history. At one protest in October, 2017, "one speaker decried Bush as part of a cabal that 'wants to destroy our Western sense of identity.'" Running against Bush in the March, 2018 Republican primary, Jerry Patterson repeatedly accused him of failing to fulfill his obligation to preserve the glory of Texas history.

Bush quickly saw his mistake, backtracked, drastically changed the plans for updating Alamo Plaza, and started portraying himself as the steward of the state's collective memory. He survived Patterson's challenge in the primary, and was returned to office in the general election in November, 2018.

But the question remains for students of Texas history and Texas politics.

Sources: Keith J. Volanto, "Strange Brew: Recent Texas Political, Economic, and Military History," in Walter L. Buenger and Arnoldo De Leon, eds. *Beyond Texas Through Time: Breaking Away from Past Interpretations,*" (College Station: Texas A & M University Press, 2011, 110; Gregg Cantrell and Elizabeth Hayes Turner, "Introduction: A Study of History, Memory, and Collective Memory in Texas," in Gregg Cantrell and Elizabeth Hayes Turner, eds., *Lone Star Pasts: Memory and History in Texas,* (College Station: Texas A & M University Press, 2007), 4–5; Gregg Cantrell, "The Bones of Stephen F. Austin: History and Memory in Pre-Progressive Era Texas," in Ibid., 41; Randolph B. Campbell, "History and Collective Memory in Texas: The Entangled Stories of the Lone Star State," in Ibid., 275; Tom Dart, "George P. Bush's Struggle in Texas May Signal End of 70-Year Political Dynasty," *The Guardian,* March 3, 2018; Christopher Hooks, "George P. Bush's Last Stand at the Alamo," *Texas Monthly,* March, 2018; election and box-office results from various Websites.

**Competency Connection**
**PERSONAL RESPONSIBILITY**

**How do we remember the Alamo?**

The consequences for the state of these natural disasters did not just consist of mourning and disruption; even before Ike, many insurance companies had stopped writing policies for homes along the Gulf Coast.[13] In the aftermath of the destruction, the citizens of Texas began to re-examine their opposition to government regulation in the midst of a debate about the wisdom of legal restraints on building in areas of coastline that are vulnerable to major storms.[14]

Moreover, as the nation tried to deal with a threatened economic catastrophe caused by the popping of a real-estate bubble, the consequent crash of the stock market, and a severe recession beginning in 2008, Texans found the values of their homes and their stock portfolios declining with everyone else's. As the private economy contracted, state revenue plunged, causing severe pain as the legislature was forced to cut the budget during the 2011 session.

By 2013, however, the state's economy was doing better than the country's as a whole, and various Texans (including Erica Grieder, quoted at the beginning of this chapter) proclaimed that this improvement ratified the Lone Star State's traditional deference to business needs and suspicion of government activity.[15] By October of 2017, the state's unemployment rate had fallen to an all-time historical low of 3.9 percent, and a 2018 report by the Federal Reserve Bank of Dallas proclaimed that the state's economy was "firing on all cylinders."[16]

Meanwhile, Texas continued to face some old problems. More than 15 percent of its population lived in poverty in 2016, placing it behind thirty-seven other states in overall prosperity (number one on the list was New Hampshire, with poverty rate of just 7.3 percent).[17] Although the overall crime rate was lower, the tide of drugs coming into society showed no signs of abating. Additionally, as will be discussed in this book, Texas still had major problems with its society and political system. Whether its traditional political attitudes will be adequate to deal with the challenges of the new era is a question that will be considered in the course of the discussion.

## Texas as a Democracy

**democracy** The form of government based on the theory that the legitimacy of any government must come from the free participation of its citizens.

**legitimacy** People's belief that their government is morally just, and that therefore they are obligated to obey its laws.

In this book, one of the major themes will be the concept of **democracy** and the extent to which Texas approaches the ideal of a democratic state. A democracy is a system of government resting on the theory that political legitimacy is created by the citizens' participation. **Legitimacy** is the belief people have that their government is founded upon morally right principles and that they should therefore obey its laws. According to the moral theory underlying a democratic system of government, because the people themselves (indirectly, through representatives) make the laws, they are morally obligated to obey them.

Complications of this theory abound, and a number of them are explored in each chapter. Because some means to allow people to participate in the government must exist, free elections, in which candidates or parties compete for the citizens' votes, are necessary. There must be some connection between what a majority of the people want and what the government actually does; how close the connection must be is a matter of some debate. Despite the importance of "majority rule" in a democracy, majorities must not be allowed to take away certain rights from minorities, such as the right to vote, the right to be treated equally under the law, and the right to freedom of expression.

In a well-run democracy, politicians debate questions of public policy honestly, the media report the debate in a fair manner, the people pay attention to the debate, and then vote their preferences consistently with their understanding of the public interest. Government decisions are made on the basis of law, without anyone having an unearned advantage.

In a badly run or corrupt democracy, politicians are dominated by special interests, but seek to hide the fact by clouding public debate with irrelevancies and showmanship, the media do not point out the problem because they themselves are either corrupt or lazy, and the people fail to hold either the politicians or the media accountable because they do not participate or because they participate carelessly and selfishly. Government decisions are made on the basis of special influence, inside dealing, and ignorance of facts. A good democracy, in other words, is one in which government policy is arrived at through public participation, debate, and compromise, and based on an awareness of the real state of the world. A bad democracy is one in which mass apathy, private influence, and wishful thinking are the determining factors.

All political systems that are based on the democratic theory of legitimacy have elements of both good and bad. No human institution is perfect—no family, church, or government—but it is always useful to compare a real institution to an ideal and judge how closely the reality conforms to the ideal. Improvements come through the process of attempting to move the reality ever closer to the ideal. Although many of them could not state it clearly, the great majority of Americans, and Texans, believe in some version of the theory of democracy. It is therefore possible to judge our state government (as it is also possible to judge our national government) according to the extent to which it approximates the ideal of a democratic society and to indicate the direction that the political system must move to become more democratic. Chapters in this book will frequently compare the reality of state government to the ideal of the democratic polity, and ask readers to judge whether they think there is room for improvement in Texas democracy.

As indicated, one of the major causes of shortcomings in democratic government, in Texas as elsewhere, is *private influence over public policy.* Ideally, government decisions are made to try to maximize the public interest, but too often, they are fashioned at the behest of individuals who are pursuing their own special interests at the expense of the public's. This book will often explore the ways that powerful individuals try to distort the people's institutions into vehicles of their own advantage. It will also examine ways that the representatives of the public resist these selfish efforts to influence public policy. Part of the political process, in Texas as in other democracies, is the struggle to ensure that the making of public policy is truly a people's activity rather than a giveaway to the few who are rich, powerful, and well-connected.

## Texas and American Federalism

**federal system** A system of government that provides for a division and sharing of powers between a national government and state or regional governments.

This book is about the politics of one state. Just as it would be impossible to describe the functions of one of the human body's organs without reference to the body as a whole, however, it would be misleading to try to analyze a state without reference to the nation. The United States has a **federal system**. This label means that its governmental powers are shared among the national and state governments. A great many state responsibilities are strongly influenced by the actions of all three branches of the national government. Further, the states and the federal government frequently disagree, and often their disagreements become connected to larger political conflict.

Texas politics is thus a whole subject unto itself and a part of a larger whole. Although the focus of this book is on Texas, it contains frequent references to actions by national institutions and politicians. In Chapter 2, we will discuss in more detail the way that the Lone Star State fits into, or refuses to fit into, the federal system.

## Texas in the International Arena

Despite the fact that the U.S. Constitution forbids the individual states to conduct independent foreign policies, Texas's shared border with Mexico has long exercised an important effect on its politics. Not only are many Texas citizens of Mexican (and other Latin) background, but the common border of Texas and Mexico, the Rio Grande, flows for more than 800 miles through an arid countryside, a situation that almost demands cooperation over the use of water. Furthermore, with the passage of the North American Free Trade Agreement (NAFTA) in 1993, Texas became important as an avenue of increased commerce between the two countries. (In 2018, NAFTA was theoretically replaced by the United States–Mexico–Canada Agreement—USMCA—although as this textbook went to press, the agreement had

## You Decide: Should Texas Have a Foreign Policy?

**A**s the world has become more integrated, and especially as economies have become globalized, Texas leaders have attempted to establish institutions for dealing with foreign governments. Their efforts in this area have been particularly enthusiastic in regard to Mexico. The state opened a trade office in Mexico City in 1971, helped establish the Border Governors' Conference in 1980, began the Texas–Mexico Agricultural Exchange in 1984, has participated in the Border States Attorneys General Conference since 1986, and established the Office of International Coordination to deal with the problem of retrieving child support payments from fugitive fathers in 1993. Texas governors now have special advisers on the economy and politics of foreign countries, and they take trips to visit foreign politicians in hopes of increasing commerce between their state and foreign countries.

In its attempts to establish regular relationships with foreign countries, Texas comes close to having a state "foreign policy." However, is it wise for a state, as opposed to the United States national government, to be so deeply involved in foreign affairs?

### Pro ✅

⬆ The Constitution does not forbid states to enter into voluntary, informal arrangements with foreign governments, and the Tenth Amendment declares that anything not forbidden to the states is permitted.

⬆ Most state foreign policy initiatives, such as Texas's trade agreements with Mexico, deal with friendly relations, not disputes.

⬆ Since when is competition a bad thing? If citizens want to keep labor unions strong and the environment clean, they should vote for candidates who will support such policies.

⬆ As the example of Javier Suarez Medina illustrates, Texas's domestic actions already have an impact on relations with foreign countries. It would be better to acknowledge this fact frankly and make state policy with the conscious intent of furthering the state's interests.

### Con ❌

⬇ A major reason that the independent states came together to form the union in 1787 was so that they could stop working at cross-purposes in foreign policy and present a united front to the world. That is why Article I, Section 10 of the Constitution says that "No state shall. . .enter into any Agreement or Compact . . . with a foreign Power . . ."

⬇ The Logan Act of 1799 prohibits U.S. citizens from "holding correspondence with a foreign government or its agents, with intent to influence the measures of such government in relations to disputes or controversies with the United States."

⬇ If states (and cities) are allowed to compete for business with foreign countries, their rivalry will cause them to lower standards of labor and environmental protection.

⬇ If all fifty states have independent relations with foreign countries, it will cause confusion and chaos between the federal government and those countries.

Source: Julie Blase, "Has Globalization Changed U.S. Federalism? The Increasing Role of U.S. States in Foreign Affairs: Texas-Mexico Relations," PhD dissertation, University of Texas at Austin, 2003.

Competency Connection
**SOCIAL RESPONSIBILITY**

**Should Texas Have a Foreign Policy?**

not yet been ratified by Congress). Interstate Highway 35, which runs from the Mexican border at Laredo through San Antonio, Austin, and the Dallas/Fort Worth Metroplex, to the north to Duluth, Minnesota, has become so important as a passageway of international trade that it is sometimes dubbed "the NAFTA highway." As a result of their geographic proximity, Mexico is an important factor in the Texas economy and Texas politics, and vice versa.

One of many possible examples from the early years of the twenty-first century illustrates the interconnections of Texan and Mexican politics. In Chapter 14, we will discuss the political fights over water policy within Texas. Here, we will recount how the need for water causes trouble between Texas and Mexico.[18]

In 1944, the two countries signed a treaty to balance the availability of water with the needs of their populations and agricultural industries. Because much of the southwestern United States contains fertile land but is arid, it would be easy for American farmers to soak up every drop of the Colorado River (the one that flows from the state of Colorado through Utah and along the California-Arizona border, not the identically-named one in Texas) for their crops. But that would mean that the river, which flows through Mexico for its last few miles to the Gulf of California, would dry up, depriving Mexican farmers of their access to the water. So, in the 1944 treaty, the countries came to an agreement that the United States would permit a certain amount of Colorado River water to flow through to Mexico, and, in return, Mexico would send an equal amount from its Rio Grande tributaries to farmers in Texas.

The agreement worked for decades. But, as a severe drought gripped both Texas and northern Mexico for much of the first thirteen years of the twenty-first century, Texans needed the Rio Grande water more, just as Mexicans became unwilling to supply it (wanting to keep it for their own farms). Mexico began to cut back its shipment of water to Texas to about half of its agreed-upon volume.

In 2013, Texas politicians launched a campaign to persuade or pressure Mexican officials to release more Rio Grande water to Texas. In April of that year the Texas house of representatives voted unanimously on a resolution imploring the federal government to persuade Mexico to live up to its 1944 treaty obligations. At the same time, Governor Rick Perry sent a letter to President Barack Obama, asking him and Secretary of State John Kerry to apply diplomatic pressure to do the same thing. Shortly thereafter, Texas' two United States Senators attempted to induce the International Boundary and Water Commission, which is responsible for enforcing water treaties between the United States and Mexico, to get tough with the Mexicans.

As the drought eased after 2011, however, so did the diplomatic conflict. In 2017, the two countries signed a document extending the water-sharing agreement for another five years.[19] As we will discuss in Chapter 14, however, such agreements depend upon the cooperation of Mother Nature. When another bad drought descends upon the region, as it certainly will, the cross-border conflict will flare again.

Thus, what happens in Texas has an impact, not only on the rest of the United States, but also on foreign countries. The reverse is also true—events in other countries, and especially in Mexico, are vitally relevant to Texas government.

## The Texas Political Culture

**political culture** A shared framework of values, beliefs, and habits of behavior with regard to government and politics within which a particular political system functions.

Like the other forty-nine states, Texas is part of a well-integrated American civil society. It is also a separate and distinctive society with its own history and present-day political system. Our political system is the product of our political culture. **Political culture** refers to a shared system of values, beliefs, and habits of behavior with regard to government and politics. Not everyone in a given political culture accepts all of that culture's assumptions, but everyone is affected by the beliefs and values of the dominant groups in society. Often, the culture of the majority group is imposed on members of a minority who would prefer not to live with it.

Political scientist Daniel Elazar and his associates have extensively investigated patterns of political culture across the fifty states. Elazar identifies three broad, historically developed patterns of political culture.[20] Although every state contains some elements of each of the three cultures, politics within states in identifiable regions tend to be dominated by one or a combination of two of the cultures.

In the **moralistic** political culture, citizens understand the state and the nation as commonwealths designed to further the shared interests of everyone. Citizen participation is a widely shared value, and governmental activism on behalf of the common good is encouraged. This culture tends to be dominant across the extreme northern tier of American states. The states of Washington and Minnesota approach the "ideal type" of the moralistic culture.

In the **individualistic** political culture, citizens understand the state and nation as marketplaces in which people strive to better their personal welfare. Citizen participation is encouraged as a means of individual achievement, and government activity is encouraged when it attempts to create private opportunity and discouraged when it attempts to redistribute wealth. This culture tends to be dominant across the "middle north" of the country from New Jersey westward. Nevada and Illinois approach the ideal types of the individualistic culture.

In the **traditionalistic** political culture, citizens technically believe in democracy, but emphasize deference to elite rule within a hierarchical society. While formally important, citizen participation is not encouraged and the participation of disfavored ethnic or religious groups may be discouraged. Government activity is generally viewed with suspicion unless its purpose is to reinforce the power of the dominant groups. This culture tends to be dominant in the southern tier of states from the east coast of the continent to New Mexico. The ideal types of states with traditionalistic cultures are Mississippi and Arkansas.

Table 1-1 summarizes the three political cultures as they are expressed across a number of important political and social dimensions. It is important to understand that the general tendencies displayed in the table permit many exceptions. They only report broad patterns of human action; that is, they describe the way many people in the groups have often behaved through history. They do not apply to everyone, nor do they prescribe a manner in which anyone must behave in the future.

The research that has been done on Texas places it at a midpoint between the traditionalistic and individualistic political cultures.[21] Historically, the state's experience as a slave-holding member of the Confederacy tended to embed it firmly in traditionalism, but its strong business orientation, growing more important every decade, infused its original culture with an increasingly influential individualistic orientation. Many of the political patterns discussed in this book are easier to understand within the context of the Texas blend of cultures.

Not all Texans have shared the beliefs and attitudes that will be described here. In particular, as will be discussed in more detail in Chapter 5, African Americans and Mexican Americans have tended to be somewhat separate from the political culture of the dominant Anglo majority. Nevertheless, both history and present political institutions have imposed clear patterns on the assumptions that most Texans bring to politics.

There is one sense in which Texas has a well-earned reputation for uniqueness. All visitors have testified to the intense state patriotism of Texans. Whatever their education, income, age, race, religion, sex, or political ideology, most Texans seem to love their state passionately. Whether this state patriotism is due to the myth of the Old West as peddled by novels, schools, and Hollywood, or to the state's size and geographic isolation, or to its unusual history, or to something in the water, is impossible to say. This patriotism has little political relevance because native Texans show no hostility toward non-natives and have elected several non-native governors. But woe to the politician who does not publicly embrace the myth that Texas is the most wonderful place to live that has ever existed on the planet! As scholars rather than politicians, the authors of this book intend to look at the state through a more analytic lens.

**moralistic** The culture, dominant in the northern tier of American states, in which citizens understand the state and the nation as commonwealths designed to further the shared interests of everyone, citizen participation is a widely shared value, and governmental activism on behalf of the common good is encouraged.

**individualistic** The culture, historically dominant in the middle tier of American states, in which citizens understand the state and nation as marketplaces in which people strive to better their personal welfare, citizen participation is encouraged as a means of individual achievement, and government activity is encouraged when it attempts to create private opportunity and discouraged when it attempts to redistribute wealth.

**traditionalistic** The culture, historically dominant in the southern tier of American states, in which citizens technically believe in democracy but do not encourage participation, and government activity is generally viewed with suspicion unless its purpose is to reinforce the power of elites.

| TABLE 1-1 | The Three Political Cultures | | |
|---|---|---|---|
| **Type** | **Moralistic** | **Individualistic** | **Traditionalistic** |
| **Attitude toward Participation** | Encouraging | Encouraging | Supports if on behalf of elite rule; otherwise, opposes |
| **Attitude toward Political Parties** | Encouraging | Strong party loyalty | Discouraging |
| **Attitude toward Government Activity** | Supports if activity is on behalf of the common good | Supports if on behalf of individual activity; opposes if on behalf of redistribution of wealth | Supports if on behalf of elite rule; otherwise, opposes |
| **Attitude toward Civil Liberties and Civil Rights** | Strongly supportive | Ambivalent; support rights for themselves, but indifferent to rights of others | Indifferent; often hostile to the liberties and rights of minorities |
| **Religious Groupings Most Commonly Supporting** | Congregationalists, Mormons, Jews, Quakers | Lutherans, Roman Catholics, Methodists | Baptists, Presbyterians, Pentecostals |
| **Geographic Area of Strongest Impact** | Northernmost tier of states, plus Utah and Colorado | Middle north tier of states | Old South, plus New Mexico |

NOTE: These are descriptions of general historical patterns only. They do not necessarily apply to the behavior of any specific family, individual, or group.

SOURCES: Daniel J. Elazar, *American Federalism: A View from the States*, 3rd ed. (New York: Harper & Row, 1984), 109–173; Ira Sharkansky, "The Utility of Elazar's Political Culture: A Research Note," in Daniel J. Elazar and Joseph Zikmund II, eds., *The Ecology of American Political Culture: Readings* (New York: Thomas Y. Crowell, 1975), 247–262; Robert L. Savage, "The Distribution and Development of Policy Values in the American States," in Ibid., 263–286, Appendices A, B, and C.

Competency Connection
**PERSONAL RESPONSIBILITY**

**Does your own family fit into the categories of this table, or is it an exception?**

**ideology** A system of beliefs and values about the nature of the good life and the good society, and the part to be played by government in achieving them.

**conservatism** A political ideology that, in general, opposes government regulation of economic life and supports government regulation of personal life.

**laissez faire** A Frenchphrase loosely meaning "leave it alone." It refers to the philosophy that values free markets and opposes government regulation of the economy.

A discussion of political cultures is mainly a discussion about general attitudes. It is not always easy to understand how general attitudes are translated into specific policies. But political culture is also related to political **ideology**—the cluster of beliefs and values that applies to specific governmental actions.

Part of the larger American political tradition is a basic philosophy toward government and politicians that was most famously expressed in a single sentence attributed to President Thomas Jefferson: "That government is best which governs least." Jefferson's philosophy has had a powerful presence in the United States in contemporary times. The name usually given to that philosophy is **conservatism**, and it has dominated Texas politics since the end of the Civil War.

The term *conservatism* is complex, and its implications change with time and situation. In general, however, it refers to a general hostility toward government activity, especially in the economic sphere. Most of the early White settlers came to Texas to seek their fortunes. They cared little about government and wanted no interference in their economic affairs. Their attitudes were consistent with the popular values of the Jeffersonian Democrats of the nineteenth century: The less government the better, local control of what little government there was, and freedom from economic regulation, or "**laissez faire**" (a French phrase loosely translated as "leave it alone"). Conservatism is, in general, consistent with the individualistic political culture on economic issues (anti-welfare, for example) and consistent with the traditionalistic political culture on social issues (indifferent to civil rights, for example).

In general, Texas conservatism minimizes the role of government in society and in the economy, in particular. It stresses an individualism that maximizes the role of businesspeople in controlling the economy. To a Texas conservative, a good government is mainly one that does not regulate business very much, and keeps taxes low.

The resistance to government aid to the needy has resulted in many state policies that mark Texas as a state with an unusually stingy attitude toward the underprivileged. For example, among the fifty states and the District of Columbia, in the second decade of the twenty-first century, Texas ranked forty-sixth out of fifty-one in per-capita state and local government expenditures for public welfare programs.[22]

The policy areas discussed so far—regulations on business to protect workers and the environment, and spending to support society's less well-off—fall under the heading of what political scientists call "**economic issues**." On those issues, conservatives are anti-government. But there is another area of policy, called "**social issues**," in which conservatives tend to be pro-government. Social issues are those areas of potential government regulation of personal rather than economic life—abortion, prayers in public schools, and gay rights are three examples. Conservatives generally favor government activity to impose their version of moral behavior on people who would otherwise choose to behave differently than the conservatives would prefer them to.

There is another general attitude toward government, called either **liberalism** or **progressivism**, that accepts or even endorses government activity in regard to economic issues. Liberals support regulations on business to protect workers and the environment, and endorse government support of society's less fortunate. While being pro-government activity in the area of economic issues, however, liberals tend to oppose government activity in the area of social issues—they believe that whether or not a woman has an abortion should be up to the woman, not the government; they oppose official prayers in public schools; they believe that homosexuals should have the same rights to marry and otherwise participate in society as heterosexuals.

As a result of these contradictions in ideological beliefs, American political rhetoric can be confusing. Conservatives are loudly anti-government on economic issues, and loudly pro-government on social issues. Liberals are just as loud, but in defense of the opposite attitude toward government activity.

Although conservatives have dominated Texas politics through most of its history, liberals have occasionally been elected to public office, and liberal ideas have sometimes been adopted as state policy. The conflict between liberalism and conservatism underlies much political argument in the United States. The way these two ideologies have formed the basis for much of Texas politics will be explored in Chapter 4.

**economic issues** Disputes over government policy regarding regulation of business to protect workers and the environment, and types of and rates of taxes and support for poor people.

**social issues** Disputes over government policy in regard to personal life, such as abortion, sexual behavior, and religion in public arenas such as the schools.

**liberalism** A political ideology that, in general, supports government regulation of economic life and opposes government regulation of personal life.

**progressivism** An alternative way of labeling the political ideology also known as "liberalism."

Liberal editorial cartoonist Ben Sargent presents the progressive view of conservative political ideology, as represented by Governor Rick Perry.
Courtesy of Ben Sargent

**Competency Connection**
**SOCIAL RESPONSIBILITY**

Do you agree or disagree with Sargent?

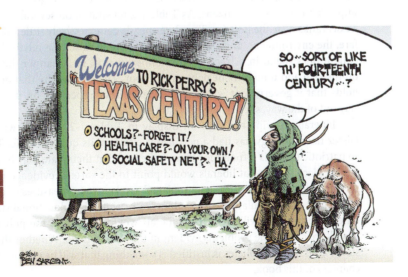

# Economy, Taxes, and Services

For much of the century after it won its freedom from Mexico, in 1836, Texas was poor, rural, and agricultural. As summarized earlier in this chapter, however, in the twentieth century, its economy was transformed: first by the boom in the oil industry that began at Spindletop in 1901, and then by its diversification into petrochemicals, aerospace, computers, and many other industries. Metropolitan areas boomed along with the economy, and the state became the second most populous in the nation.

The state's political culture, however, has not changed as rapidly as its population and its economy. Texas's basic conservatism is evident in the way the state government treats business and industry. In 2018, for example, cable television business-channel CNBC ranked Texas as the "America's Top State for Business." (Alaska came in last).[23] The ranking merely continued a tradition of the state being proclaimed as the best one for private industry. In 2013, for instance, an organization that surveys the opinions of corporate chief executives had ranked Texas as the "best state for business." (Florida was second, while New York and California were tied as the worst states).[24]

While in the short run, a favorable business climate consists of low taxes, weak labor unions, and an inactive government, however, in the long run these policies may create a fragile economy. Other observers are less admiring of the Texas economy and less optimistic about its future. For example, the Corporation for Enterprise Development (CED) is a private organization that sometimes grades each state in terms not only of its economic health at any one time, but also its capacity for positive growth in the future. In 2002 and again in 2007, the CED flunked the Texas economy as a whole, giving it Ds in "earnings and job quality," Fs in "equity," Fs in "quality of life," and Ds in "resource efficiency." The CED commented in 2002 that "a theme of inequality throughout the state . . . the disparity between the wealthy and the poor. . ." augured poorly for Texas's future.

Moreover, as the information in Table 1-3 illustrates, various rankings of quality of life do not paint Texas in such rosy tones. Whether or not the Lone Star State is a good place to live, in other words, depends on what is being measured.

Part of the substance of this textbook will be discussions of the way the politics of Texas reflects "a theme of inequality." Some chapters will analyze the sources of unequal politics; some will portray its consequences in terms of public policy. Always, the implications of inequality for democratic legitimacy will be a major topic.

Because of the Jeffersonian conservative philosophy underlying much of the activities of Texas government, it generally does little, compared to the governments of other states, to improve the lives of its citizens. As Table 1-2 illustrates, on several measures of state services, Texas ranks near the bottom. The state spends comparatively little on education, health, welfare, the environment, and the arts. Furthermore, it raises the relatively small amount of revenue it does spend in a "regressive" manner; that is, in a manner that falls unusually lightly on the rich and unusually heavily on the poor. The philosophy that dominates Texas politics holds that if government will just keep taxes low—especially on its wealthier citizens—and stay out of the way, society will take care of itself.

Liberals, viewing the facts on display in Tables 1-2 and 1-3, would argue that Texas's laissez faire ideology has had a pernicious effect on its quality of life. Texans, as a group, are so patriotic that it is difficult for them to believe that their state may be a comparatively undesirable place to live, but liberals would point to the sorts of evidence illustrated in Table 1-3. As the table emphasizes, the state ranks relatively low on measures of air cleanliness, the general health of its population, its freedom from crime, the educational status of its citizens, and other measures of civilized living. Liberals would argue that the policies evident in the first table have caused the problems evident in the second table. Whether the liberal critique of the state's conservative policies is justified is something that will be explored during the remaining chapters of this book.

| TABLE 1-2 | Texas Rank among States in Expenditure and Taxation | | |
|---|---|---|---|
| **Category** | | **Year** | **Rank** |
| a. Per-capita personal income | | 2016 | 25 (1 is richest) |
| b. State government per-capita spending | | 2015 | 47 (50 spends the least) |
| c. Per-capita state and local government expenditures for education | | 2015 | 24 (50 spends the least) |
| d. Average public-school teacher salary | | 2017 | 25 (1 pays the most) |
| e. Medicaid spending per enrollee | | 2014 | 29 (51 is lowest) |
| f. Average monthly benefit, Women, Infants, and Children (WIC) Special Nutrition Program | | 2017 | 50 |
| g. Average monthly payment, Temporary Assistance to Needy Families (TANF) | | 2015 | 38 (50 is lowest) |
| h. State spending on arts agency | | 2018 | 47 (50 is lowest) |
| i. Per-capita state spending on environmental protection | | 2008 | 45 (50 is least) |
| j. Regressivity of state and local taxes | | 2015 | 3 (1 is most regressive) |

SOURCES: a from Kathleen O'Leary Morgan and Scott Morgan, *State Rankings 2018: A Statistical View of America* (Sage: Thousand Oaks, California, 2018), 94; b from Ibid., 350; c from Ibid., 137; d from Ibid., 123; e from https://www.kff.org/Medicaid/state-indicator/Medicaid-spending-per-full-benefit-enrollee/?currentTimeframe=08LsortModel=%78"cold":"Location","sort":asc"%967D; g from Ibid., 546; h from Ibid., 164; i from David M. Konisky and Neal D. Woods, "Environmental Policy," in Virginia Gray, Russell L. Hanson, and Thad Kousser, eds., *Politics in the American States: A Comparative Analysis*, 10th ed. (Los Angeles: CQ Press/Sage, 2013), 483; j from *Who Pays? A Distributional Analysis of the Tax Systems in All 50 States*, 5th edition (Washington, D.C.: Institute on Taxation and Economic Policy, 2015).

| TABLE 1-3 | Texas Rank in Measures of Quality of Life | | |
|---|---|---|---|
| **Measure of Quality of Life** | | **Year** | **Rank** |
| a. Murder rate | | 2016 | 24 (1 is highest) |
| b. Overall crime rate | | 2016 | 17 (1 is highest) |
| c. Incarceration rate | | 2016 | 7 (1 is highest) |
| d. Percent of children living in poverty | | 2016 | 13 (1 is poorest) |
| e. Condition-of-children index | | 2016 | 43 (1 is best) |
| f. Total fossil fuel emissions | | 2015 | 1 (1 is dirtiest) |
| g. Total water pollution | | 2012 | 2 (1 is dirtiest) |
| h. Average composite ACT score | | 2017 | 28 (1 is best) |
| i. Overall education score | | 2016 | 41 (1 is best) |
| j. "Environmental quality" rank | | 2018 | 43 (1 is cleanest) |
| k. "Economic well-being" | | 2018 | 35 (1 is most livable) |

"SOURCES: a from Kathleen O'Leary Morgan and Scott Morgan, *State Rankings 2018: A Statistical View of America* (Thousand Oaks: Sage/CQ Press, 2018), 36; b from Ibid., 30 ; c from Ibid., 60; d from Ibid., 521; e "Kids Count Overall Rank," from the Website of the Annie E. Casey foundation, www.aecf.org; f from Morgan and Morgan, *State Rankings 2018*, 230; g from Sara Jerome, "Ten Worst States for Water Pollution," July, 11, 2014, data gathered from the Environment America Research and Policy Center; h from Morgan and Morgan, *State Rankings 2018*, 135; i from "Texas Earns a C-Minus on State Report Card, Ranks 41st in Nation," *Education Week*, December 30, 2016; j from WalletHub, 2018: https://wallethub.com/edu/greenest-states/11987/; k from Annie E. Casey Foundation, cited above.

## ISSUE SPOTLIGHT:
### Don't Worry, Be Happy

The measures of quality of life reported in Table 1-3 are *objective*. That is, they summarize how Texas ranks in the sorts of living situations that can be measured from the outside. On those measures, Texas looks like a comparatively poor place to live. But what about the *subjective*—the way people feel about themselves on the inside?

In 2009, researchers led by Professor Andrew Oswald of the University of Warwick published their conclusions after examining a 2005 survey of 1.3 million Americans' answers to questions about their satisfaction with their lives. On the basis of that subjective measurement, Texas was one of the happiest states, ranking number fifteen. Louisiana scored as the happiest state, while New York was the least happy.

So, is Texas a good place to live? The answer may depend on what measurements are used as evidence.

Source: "Louisiana the Happiest State, Study Says," *Austin American-Statesman*, December 18, 2009, A13.

Competency Connection
**SOCIAL RESPONSIBILITY**

**Which measurement do you prefer?**

# The People of Texas

In many ways, Texas is the classic American melting pot of different peoples, although it occasionally seems more like a boiling cauldron. The state was originally populated by various Native American tribes. In the sixteenth and seventeenth centuries, the Spaniards conquered the land, and from the intermingling of the conquerors and the conquered came the "mestizos," persons of mixed Spanish and Native American blood. In the nineteenth century, Anglos wrested the land from the heirs of the Spaniards, and the remaining Native Americans. They often brought Black slaves with them. Soon waves of immigration arrived from Europe and Asia, and more mestizos came from Mexico. After a brief outflow of population as a result of the oil price depression of the late 1980s, the long-term pattern of immigration resumed and brought many more thousands during the 1990s and beyond.

## The Census

At the end of each decade, the national government takes a census of each state's population. Table 1-4 shows the official Texas numbers for 1990 and 2010, and the estimated percentage of the population for the three major ethnic groups in 2017. Increases in population entitled Texas to three additional seats in the U.S. House in 1990, two more in 2000, and another four in 2010, bringing the state's total to thirty-six.

Besides the overall increase in population of 20.6 percent in the first decade of the twenty-first century, the most significant fact revealed by the 2010 census was the rapid increase in Texas's Hispanic population. Whereas Hispanics, the great majority of whom, in Texas, are either Mexican or Mexican American, constituted 21 percent of the state's population in 1980

| TABLE 1-4 | The Texas Population, 1990 to 2017 | | |
|---|---|---|---|
| **Ethnic Group** | **1990** | **2010** | **2017 Percent of total Estimated by Census** |
| Anglo (Non-Hispanic White) | 10,291,680 | 11,370,300 | 42.0% |
| African American | 2,021,632 | 2,866,500 | 12.7 |
| Hispanic or Latino* (of any race) | 4,339,905 | 9,538,000 | 39.4 |
| Other | 378,565 | 1,305,200 | 5.9 |

*The great majority of Hispanics in Texas are Mexican American or Mexican.

SOURCES: For 1990, *1992–93 Texas Almanac and State Industrial Guide* (Dallas: A. H. Belo Corp., 1991); for 2010, http://quickfacts.census.gov/qfd/states/48000. html; for 2017 estimate", https://www.census.gov/quickfacts/fact/table/tx,US/PST045217

and 26 percent in 1990; by 2010 they totaled almost 38 percent. The other important minority group, African Americans, comprised about 12 percent of the state's citizens, a percentage that has not changed appreciably over the last several decades.

The inevitable consequence of the increasing trend-line of the Latino population had arrived in 2005, when the Census Bureau announced an estimate that Texas's population consisted of 50.2 percent Black plus Latino.[25] The 2010 count merely confirmed that the falling Anglo percentage of the state population had continued, as that group, which used to be a large majority of the population, had dropped to 45.3 percent. In other words, there is now no "majority" ethnic group in the state; every group constitutes a minority of the population. If present population growth rates continue, however, a majority of Texas's population will be Hispanic by 2020.[26]

The distribution of population in Texas shows evidence of three things: the initial patterns of migration, the influence of geography and climate, and the location of the cities. The Hispanic migration came first, north from Mexico, and to this day is still concentrated in South and West Texas, especially in the counties that border the Rio Grande. Likewise, African Americans still live predominantly in the eastern half of the state. As one moves from east to west across Texas, annual rainfall drops by about five inches per 100 miles. East Texas has a moist climate and supports intensive farming, while West Texas is dry and requires pumping from underground aquifers to maintain agriculture. The overall distribution of settlement reflects the food production capability of the local areas, with East Texas remaining more populous. Cities developed at strategic locations, usually on rivers or the seacoast, and the state's population is heavily concentrated in the urban areas.

## The Political Relevance of Population

Our division of the Texas population into Anglos, Latinos (most of whom are Mexican Americans), and African Americans reflects political realities. All citizens are individuals, form their own opinions, and have the right to choose to behave as they see fit. No one is a prisoner of his or her group, and every generalization has exceptions. Nevertheless, it is a long-observed fact that people in similar circumstances often see things from similar points of view, and it therefore helps to clarify political conflict to be aware of the shared similarities.

In this book Anglos, Latinos (who are, in Texas, mainly Mexican Americans), and African Americans will often be discussed as groups, without an intent to be unfair to individual exceptions. Historically, both minority groups have been treated badly by the Anglo majority. Today, the members of both groups are, in general, less wealthy than Anglos. For example, according to a 2015 estimate by the U.S. Census, the mean household income of both Latinos and Blacks was about 62 percent of the figure for Anglos in the state. On the one hand, this represented a narrowing of the income gap between minorities and Anglos that existed in 1990. On the other hand, the difference in wealth was still very substantial and large enough to cause economic conflict.[27]

Political differences often accompany economic divisions. As will be discussed in Chapters 4 and 5, Mexican Americans and African Americans tend to hold more liberal political opinions than do Anglos and to vote accordingly. This is not to say that there are no conservative minority citizens and no liberal Anglos. Nevertheless, looked at as groups, Latinos, African Americans, and Anglos do display general patterns of belief and behavior that can be discussed without being unfair to individual exceptions. As a result, as the minority population increases in size relative to the Anglo population, its greater liberalism is likely to make itself felt, sooner or later, in the voting booth. Furthermore, Texans of Asian background are a relatively small, but growing proportion of the population (about 5 % according to a 2016 census estimate). As their population becomes larger, they may exert an independent influence percent on the political process. Texas's evolving mix of population is therefore constantly changing the state's politics.

## Summary

**LO 1.1**   **Texas history is filled with major events that are politically and economically relevant to the state today.**  The themes of this chapter are that parts of the Texas experience have changed a great deal—its transition from an rural, agricultural state to an urban, industrial one, for example—and parts have changed very little—the continuing political conservatism of its citizens, for example.

**LO 1.2**   **Democratic theory can be used to compare the reality of Texas politics to the democratic ideal.**  In a democracy, the major assumption is that the legitimacy of the government is based on the participation of the citizens. Other assumptions, almost as important, are the equality of citizens before the law and their retention of certain rights, such as the right to vote and to express their ideas freely. This textbook examines the way Texas actually functions, and compares it to the ideal democratic polity.

**LO 1.3**   **There are pro and con arguments about whether it is desirable, or even possible, for Texas to have a "foreign policy."**  But whether the "con" arguments are good or bad, Texas will go on interacting with foreign countries, because it is important for the state's economy to do so.

**LO 1.4**   **Three political cultures apply to Texas history and the state's politics today.**  Historically, the dominant Anglo culture has combined both the traditionalist and the individualist cultures into its own blend of values. This combination of political cultures has resulted in a state pattern of political conservatism in most eras, including the present.

**LO 1.5**   **There is an overall pattern to the relationship of Texas government to the Texas economy that influences whether the state is or is not a good place to live.**  There is a politically conservative culture that has resulted in a government that is almost always friendly to business, both in having very low tax rates and in refraining from passing regulations to protect the environment. Some evidence exists to support the claim that, objectively, Texas is a rather poor place to live compared to the other states, as well as the liberal claim that Texas's conservative public policies have caused the state to rank low on the indicators of the good life.

**LO 1.6**   **The ratios of Anglos, Latinos, and African Americans in the state's population matter to a book about Texas government.**  The percentage of Latinos in the state's population is growing, with several possible future consequences of that growth.

## Critical Thinking

1. If you were asked to evaluate the legitimacy of a state, or a national government, by the standards of democratic theory, what indicators would you look for? That is, what sort of observable measures would supply you with the kind of evidence you needed for an evaluation?

2. Would you say that the members of your family, in general, would fit into the moralistic, traditionalistic, or individualistic political cultures? What sort of examples of personal statements or behavior would you use to answer this question? Are their individual members of your family who seem to have a different "personal political culture" from the other members? Again, what sort of evidence would you use to answer this question?

The eighteen justices of the the Texas Court of Criminal
Appeals and Texas Supreme Court, who have the authority
to interpret the state constitution, attend the swearing-in
ceremony for Governor Rick Perry in February, 2011.

*Bob Daemmrich/Alamy Stock Photo*

# The Constitutional Setting

Since its ratification in 1789, the U.S. **Constitution** frequently has been used as a model by emerging nations. State constitutions, however, seldom enjoy such admiration. Indeed, the constitution of the state of Texas is more often ridiculed than praised because of its length, its obscurity, and its outdated, unworkable provisions.

Such criticism of state constitutions is common. The political circumstances that surrounded the writing of the national Constitution differed considerably from those that existed at the times when many of the fifty states—especially those of the old Confederacy—were writing their constitutions. State constitutions tend to be very rigid and include too many specific details. They do not follow the advice of Alexander Hamilton cited at the beginning of this chapter. As a result, Texas and many other states must resort to frequent **constitutional amendments**, which are formal changes in the basic governing document.

In federal systems, which are systems of government that provide for a division and sharing of powers between a national government and state or regional governments, the constitutions of the states complement the national Constitution. Article VI of the U.S. Constitution provides that the Constitution, laws, and treaties of the national government take precedence over the constitutions and laws of the states. This provision is known as the "supremacy of the laws" clause. Many states,

> CONSTITUTIONS SHOULD CONSIST OF ONLY GENERAL PROVISIONS; THE REASON IS THAT THEY MUST NECESSARILY BE PERMANENT, AND THAT THEY CANNOT CALCULATE FOR THE POSSIBLE CHANGE OF THINGS.
>
> Alexander Hamilton,
> American statesman and one of the authors of *The Federalist Papers* urging adoption of the U.S. constitution

**constitution** The basic law of a state or nation that takes precedence over all other laws and actions of the government.

**constitutional amendments** A change in a constitution that is approved by both the legislative body, and, in Texas, the voters. National constitutional amendments are not approved directly by voters.

including Texas, have constitutional and statutory provisions that conflict with federal laws, but these are unenforceable because of Article VI. Although the U.S. Constitution is supreme, state constitutions are still important because state governments are responsible for many basic programs and services, such as education, that affect citizens daily.

This chapter begins by describing federalism, and then examines purposes of constitutions. It outlines the development of the several Texas constitutions. It elaborates the principal features of the state's current document, and provides an overview of constitutional change, including both amendments and the movement for constitutional reform.

# American Federalism

The way in which the national constitution establishes the relationship between the nation and the states was unique when the U.S. Constitution was written. The only existing models were totally centralized governments and loose alliances of regions, clans, or tribes. As noted in Chapter 1, this system is known as federalism, which divides power between the central and regional governments. Twenty-six countries now have a federal system, but the dominance of the central government varies greatly across nations such as the United States, Australia, Canada, India, Mexico, and Venezuela.

## Division of Power

**reserved clause** Governmental powers reserved for the states and the people by the Tenth Amendment of the U.S. Constitution.

**dual federalism (layer cake)** A division of powers between the nation and the states that emphasizes each level operating independently.

**cooperative federalism (marble cake)** A concept of federalism emphasizing cooperative and collective interaction between the nation and the states.

**picket fence** A refinement of the concept of cooperative federalism that also emphasizes the role of the bureaucracy and of private interest groups in policy implementation.

The Tenth Amendment to the U.S. Constitution states, "The powers not delegated to the United States by the Constitution, nor prohibited by it to the States, are reserved to the States respectively, or to the people." This provision is known as the **reserved clause** because it assigns powers to the states and the people if they have not previously been reserved for the national government or legally prohibited. No such provision exists in state constitutions; the local governments—cities, counties, and special districts—are creatures of the state and have only the powers given to them by the state government.

How federalism is practiced in the United States has changed over time. Originally, federalism was seen as **dual**, resembling a **layer cake** with the national government as one layer and the states as the other layer.[1] Political analysts find it helpful to use metaphors, figures of speech that compare one thing to another, such as the layer cake. States, for example, were not expected to intervene in foreign policy, and the national government left education policy to the states. Each layer went about performing separate tasks. However, the reality was that the nation, states, and localities practiced **cooperative federalism** and often not only performed the same sorts of tasks but also did so together, a model more nearly resembling a **marble cake**. Today, while the dominant role in foreign relations belongs to the national government, both states and local governments actively pursue economic interests with foreign countries. Similarly, while state and local governments are still regarded as having primary responsibility for education, the national government has attempted to guide education standards for more than a half-century.

A variant of cooperative federalism in which all levels of government work cooperatively is **picket fence** federalism. The added element in picket fence federalism is the factor of the "pickets," which are the governmental functions involving complex bureaucratic and interest group relationships that affect policy implementation. The rails are the levels of government. For example, disaster relief involves national, state, and local governments as well as the Red Cross and other charitable organizations, and a variety of interest groups ranging from those concerned with public health to those concerned about economic interests get involved in disaster recovery.

# Federalism at Work

Federal-state and federal-state-local relationships are not always smooth ones. Policies involve political power, a cause of rivalry, and constant concerns for "who pays" for the policy as it is implemented. A good example of the tangled intergovernmental relations is the so-called Obamacare.

In 2009 the Democratic-controlled Congress passed, and President Obama signed, the Patient Protection and Affordable Care Act ("Obamacare").[2] The law had many provisions aiming to provide health insurance to the millions of Americans who were without such protection and to try to halt the increasing costs of medical care.

One federal law requires hospital emergency rooms to treat indigent patients—those without money or insurance. The cost of treating such patients is very high, and is borne by the paying patients who use the hospital's services. Lessening the number of indigent people who show up at emergency-room doors would go a long way toward lowering medical costs for the entire country.

Another federal program called Medicaid provides medical services to some of the poor, elderly, and disabled. (We will discuss the details of this program in Chapter 13.) Part of the purpose of the Obamacare law was to persuade the states to expand their administration of Medicaid to include every eligible person. The idea was that, with more poor people covered by this government health insurance, fewer of them would go to emergency rooms when they needed medical attention, and costs would come down all the way around. That is, implementation of the law would do two good things—it would provide health insurance to people who had none, and it would make the American health care system cheaper overall.

In 2012, the U.S. Supreme Court upheld the constitutionality of the Affordable Care Act.[3] However, it voided the part of the law that required states to participate in the Medicaid expansion program. If states were to cooperate with the federal government in expanding health insurance for poor people, their action would have to be voluntary.

In order to induce the states to go along with the expansion of Medicaid, the federal government offered to pay 90 percent of the cost. That is, for every dollar that the state of Texas spent in offering Medicaid coverage to the additional 1.5 million impoverished Texans who would be eligible for health insurance under the new program, the federal government would contribute nine dollars. Thus, to insure those one-and-a-half million poor people, Texas would have to spend $1.3 billion, and would receive almost $12 billion from Washington.

Nevertheless, governing officials in Texas, all of them Republicans, opposed the expansion for two reasons. First was the longtime Texan suspicion of government spending of any kind. Not only did many Texas leaders oppose the outlay of the first $1.3 billion, but they were also deeply skeptical that the federal government would come through with enough funds in the future. That is, they suspected that once the state was locked into the program, Washington would renege on the deal, leaving the Texas government with an obligation to spend ever more money on Medicaid for the unlimited future.

Second, as Governor Rick Perry wrote in a letter to Secretary Kathleen Sebelius, head of the federal Department of Health and Human Services, the new law was a "brazen intrusion into the sovereignty of our state." Texans do not mind receiving funds from Washington if they come with no strings attached, but they are intensely opposed to efforts by national politicians to tell Texans what to do. In 2013, the Republican majority in the legislature agreed with Perry's position, and rejected Texas participation in Medicaid expansion. It was more important to the leaders of the Texas government that they stay free of Washington's regulations than that they be able to provide health insurance to millions of their citizens.

Cartoonist Ben Sargent illustrates the ironic relationship that Texas politicians have with the federal government: While they despise and verbally abuse it often, they also rely on it for many vital resources.

Courtesy of Ben Sargent

**Competency Connection**
**SOCIAL RESPONSIBILITY**

Do you think that Texas politicians are justified in being suspicious of the motives of the federal government?

As a general theme, the state-versus-federal government argument arose before there was a state of Texas, during the 1790s, and will no doubt continue in some form long after this particular tiff between the Washington and Texas politicians is forgotten. For the present, the value of the controversy is that it illustrates the type of not-always-easy relationship that Texas experiences with the larger national government.

Health insurance is only one of the policy spheres in which the federal government is a constant and important influence—and sometimes an irritant—in the state's politics. Later chapters on the justice system and financial, social, and resource policy will demonstrate the many areas in which the state and the nation are intertwined. Among the other areas in which Washington makes an impact on Texas government are the following:

▶ Federal dollars that support the state budget
▶ Civil rights and liberties
▶ Accessibility of public buildings by the disabled
▶ Ways in which poverty is remediated
▶ Protection of the environment
▶ Effects on Texans of the deployment of federal troops to areas of conflict
▶ Economic impact of congressional legislation and presidential and bureaucratic decisions, including Federal Reserve policies to expand or contract the economy

Although this brief list may seem to describe the relationship between the states and the national government as one dominated by the central government, in fact, it is constantly changing, and thus, as the example of the Medicaid expansion illustrates, the subject of conflict. The nature of federalism, and therefore Texas's place within it, is the result of an ongoing argument.

Texas politics is therefore a whole subject unto itself and a part of a larger whole. Because the focus of this book is on Texas, the remainder of this chapter focuses on the Texas Constitution.

## Purposes of Constitutions

A constitution is the basic law of a state or nation that outlines the primary structure and functions of government. The purposes of all constitutions are the same.

## Legitimacy

The first purpose served by a constitution is to give legitimacy to the government. Legitimacy is the most abstract and ambiguous purpose served by constitutions. Legitimacy derives from agreed-upon purposes of government and from government keeping its actions within the guidelines of these purposes. The constitution contributes to this legitimacy by putting it down on paper. A government has legitimacy when the governed accept its acts as moral, fair, and just and thus believe that they should obey its laws.

This acceptance cuts two ways. On the one hand, citizens will allow government to act in certain ways that are not permitted to private individuals. For example, citizens cannot legally drive down a city street at sixty miles per hour, but police officers may do so when in the act of pursuing wrongdoers. Proprietors of private schools cannot command local residents to make financial contributions to their schools, but these local residents pay taxes to support public schools. On the other hand, citizens also expect governments not to act arbitrarily; the concept of legitimacy is closely associated with limiting government. If a police officer were to speed down a city street at ninety miles per hour just for the thrill of doing so, or if citizens were burdened with confiscatory school taxes, these acts probably would fall outside the bounds of legitimacy.

What citizens are willing to accept is conditioned by their history and their political culture. In Texas and the remainder of the United States, democratic practices including citizen participation in decision making, and fair processes are a part of that history and culture. Even within that broad acceptance of democratic principles, legitimacy varies from nation to nation and even from state to state. In England, for example, most police do not carry weapons; in California, pedestrians have absolute right of way in crossing streets. The traditionalistic/individualistic political culture that predominates in the South is even more dedicated to limiting government than the moralistic political culture; thus, southern constitutions, as a group, tend to be very restrictive.

## Organizing Government

The second purpose of constitutions is to organize government. Governments must be organized in some way that clarifies who the major officials are, how they are selected, and what the relationships are among those charged with basic governmental functions.

Again, to some extent, the American states have been guided by the national model. For example, both levels incorporate **separation of powers**—that is, a division into legislative, executive, and judicial branches. Also following the national Constitution's lead, the states have adopted a system of checks and balances to ensure that each separate branch of government can be restrained by the others. In reality, separate institutions and defined lines of authority lead to a sharing of powers. For example, passing bills is thought of as a legislative function, but the governor can veto a bill.

Each state has an elected chief executive. Each state, except Nebraska, has a legislative body composed of two houses, usually a house of representatives and a senate. Each state has a judicial system with some sort of supreme court. Just as the U.S. Constitution includes many provisions that establish the relationship between the nation and the states, state constitutions include similar provisions with respect to local governments.

Specific organizational provisions of state constitutions vary widely, and invariably reflect the political attitudes prevalent at the time the constitutions were adopted and various amendments added. In Texas, the traditionalistic/individualistic political cultures have dominated the constitutional process.

**separation of powers** A system of assigning specific powers to individual branches (or departments, in Texas) of government. In reality, the powers of the branches overlap, so that "separate institutions sharing powers" would be a more accurate term.

## Providing Power

Article I, Section 8, of the U.S. Constitution expressly grants certain powers to the national government and implies a broad range of additional powers through the "necessary and proper" clause. This clause, also known as the "elastic clause," enables Congress to execute all

# Texas Politics and You

A major issue on university campuses across Texas is whether the right to carry concealed handguns on campus would make campuses safer or more dangerous. In the aftermath of the shooting of elementary school children in Newtown, Connecticut, this student at the University of North Texas argues against concealed carry.

**Critical Thinking** *Is his argument persuasive or flawed?*

From "**Stop Gun Hysteria**," *North Texas Daily*, January 28, 2013, Joshua Knopp. A lot of people have said a lot of things about assault rifles in the wake of the Sandy Hook massacre. All of them are wrong:

"Assault rifles are designed specifically to kill people! We need to get them off the streets!"

The implication here is that bolt-action rifles are OK, because they are used for hunting, and that shotguns and pistols are OK because those are used for home and personal defense.

Let's assume assault rifles are banned. Let's even assume the civilian rifle Adam Lanza was carrying, which only looks like an assault rifle, is also made illegal. How does this prevent a massacre like Sandy Hook?

If Lanza had walked into that school with a bolt-action rifle or shotgun, nothing would change, since he was attacking unarmed children.

"We need to make it illegal for psychopaths like him to have guns!"

It is, in fact illegal for psychopaths like him to have guns. Lanza's mother, Nancy, was a gun enthusiast who acquired the weapons he used legally. Lanza stole these guns from her. Should we make stealing more illegal than it already is?

"We need to arm ourselves against these rampages! We should put more guns and armed guards in schools!"

The next time you're in class, look around at your classmates and ask yourself if you want them to have a weapon. College campuses already have their own special police force, and adding individuals with no training in crowd control or emergency management, no uniform and no understanding of how the real police are handling the situation isn't a solution, it's lunacy.

Instead of adding and subtracting gun owners to these situations, or giving them less potent weaponry, can we make them smarter?

In a perfect world, every gun owner would be a good marksman, could keep their weapon clean and wouldn't leave a round in the chamber. They would know to keep weapons in their homes where they were within easy reach but out of their children's hands.

The adage goes, "Guns don't kill people, people kill people." By the same token, guns don't keep people safe, people keep people safe. Guns are just tools, that's all. Instead of saying they're too dangerous, let's make sure everyone who has one knows how to use it.

I mean, everyone with a driver's license knows how to drive, right?

Source: Article, "Stop gun hysteria," *North Texas Daily*, January 28, 2013, Joshua Knopp

Do you agree with Joshua Knopp, or do you think that he has left something important out of his discussion?

---

its other powers by giving it broad authority to pass needed legislation. Thus, granting specific powers is the third purpose of constitutions. The Tenth Amendment reserves for the people or for the states powers not explicitly or implicitly granted to the national government.

As the U.S. Constitution has been developed and interpreted, many powers exist concurrently for both the federal and the state levels of government—the power to assess taxes on gasoline, for example. Within this general framework, which continues to evolve, the Texas Constitution sets forth specific functions for which the state maintains primary or concurrent responsibility. Local government, criminal law, and regulation of intrastate commerce illustrate the diversity of the activities over which the state retains principal control.

**incorporation** A historical activity by the U.S. Supreme Court that makes the protections of citizen rights established in the Constitution applicable to state and local governments.

**Bill of Rights** A section of a constitution that lists the civil rights and liberties of citizens and places restrictions on the powers of government.

A combination of factors has reduced the power of state officials, however. For example, the federal government's widespread use of its interstate commerce powers has limited the range of commercial activities still considered strictly intrastate. The **incorporation** of the **Bill of Rights**—the first ten amendments to the U.S. Constitution—has compelled changes in the criminal justice systems of the states. Incorporation means making the national protections, for example, the right to a fair and speedy trial by a jury of one's peers, applicable to state and local governments. In addition, the ability of individual states to deal with many socioeconomic matters such as energy use, civil rights, and urbanism is now seriously impaired. Thus, such matters are increasingly viewed as a responsibility of government at the national level.

Nevertheless, the fundamental law of the state spells out many areas for state and local action. Which, if any, of the broad problems the national government addresses depends on the prevailing Washington political philosophy, the party that controls Congress, the national administration, and who sits on the U.S. Supreme Court.[4] Resistance to perceived national power growth prompted Tea Party adherents (see Chapter 4) to urge a strong "states' rights" interpretation of the Tenth Amendment in 2010 and 2011.

## Limiting Governmental Power

American insistence on the fourth purpose of constitutions—limiting governmental power—reflects the influence of British political culture, our ancestors' dissatisfaction with colonial rule, and the extraordinary individualism that characterized national development during the eighteenth and nineteenth centuries.

In Texas, the traditionalistic/individualistic political culture resulted in a heavy emphasis on limiting government's ability to act. For example, the governor has only restricted power to remove members of state boards and commissions, particularly those appointed by a predecessor, except by informal techniques, such as an aggressive public relations campaign against a board member. This belief in limited government continues to wax strong in the new millennium. Citizens usually want less government regulation and more controls on spending.

Chief among the guarantees against arbitrary governmental action is the national Bill of Rights. It was quickly added to the original U.S. Constitution to ensure both adequate safeguards for the people and ratification of the Constitution. The Texas Bill of Rights, included as Article 1 in the Texas Constitution, resembles the national Bill of Rights.[5] Later amendments to the national Constitution have extended guarantees in several areas, especially due process and equal protection of the laws, racial equality, and voting rights.

In Texas, reactions to post–Civil War Reconstruction rule were so keen at the time the current constitution was written that the document contains many specific and picayune limitations. The creation of certain hospital districts and the payment of pensions to veterans of the war of independence from Mexico are examples. Such specificities have made frequent amendments necessary and have hamstrung legislative action in many areas.

## Texas Constitutional Development

The United States has had two fundamental laws: the short-lived Articles of Confederation and the present Constitution. Since independence from Mexico, Texas is currently governed by its sixth constitution, ratified in 1876.[6] The fact that the 1876 constitution had five predecessors in only forty years illustrates the political turbulence of the mid-1800s. Table 2-1 lists the six Texas state charters as well as the constitution when the state was part of Mexico.

Having been formally governed by Spain for 131 years and by Mexico for 15 years, Texans issued a declaration of independence on March 2, 1836. This declaration stated that "the people of Texas, do now constitute a Free, Sovereign, and Independent Republic, and are fully invested with all the rights and attributes which properly belong to independent nations."

| TABLE 2-1 | Constitutions of Texas |
|-----------|------------------------|
| **Constitution** | **Dates** |
| Coahulla y Tejas | 1824–1836 |
| Republic of Texas | 1836–1845 |
| Statehood | 1845–1861 |
| Civil War | 1861–1866 |
| Reconstruction | 1866–1869 |
| Radical Reconstruction | 1869–1876 |
| State of Texas | 1876–Present |

After a brief but bitter war with Mexico, Texas gained independence on April 21 of that year after the Battle of San Jacinto. Independence was formalized when the two Treaties of Velasco were signed by Mexican President Antonio López de Santa Anna and Texas President David Burnet on May 14, 1836. By September, the Constitution of the Republic of Texas, drafted shortly after independence was declared, had been implemented. Major features of this charter paralleled those of the U.S. Constitution, including a president and a Congress, but the document also guaranteed the continuation of slavery.

The United States had been sympathetic to the Texas struggle for independence. However, admission to the Union was postponed for a decade because of northern opposition to admission of a new slave state. After ten years of nationhood under the Republic of Texas Constitution, Texas was finally admitted into the Union. The Constitution of 1845, the Statehood Constitution, was modeled after the constitutions of other southern states. It was regarded as one of the nation's best at the time. The Constitution of 1845, which not only embraced democratic principles of participation but also included many elements later associated with the twentieth-century administrative reform movement, was a very brief, clear document.[7]

The Constitution of 1845 was influenced by Jacksonian democracy, named for President Andrew Jackson. Jacksonians believed in an expansion of participation in government, at least for White males.[8] Jackson's basic beliefs ultimately led to the spoils system of appointing to office those who had supported the winning candidates in the election ("to the victors belong the spoils"). Jacksonian democracy also produced long ballots, with almost every office up for popular vote, short terms of office, and the expansion of voting rights. Thus, while participatory, Jacksonian democracy was not flawless.

When Texas joined the Confederate States of America in 1861, the constitution was modified again. This document, the Civil War Constitution of 1861, merely altered the Constitution of 1845 to ensure greater protection for the institution of slavery and to declare allegiance to the Confederacy.

Texas was on the losing side of the Civil War and was occupied by federal troops. President Andrew Johnson ordered Texas to construct yet another constitution. The 1866 document declared secession illegal, repudiated the war debt to the Confederacy, and abolished slavery—although it did not provide for improving conditions for African Americans. In other words, the state made only those changes that were necessary to gain presidential support for readmission to the Union.

Radical postwar congressional leaders were not satisfied with these minimal changes in the constitutions of the southern states. They insisted on more punitive measures. In 1868–1869, a constitution that centralized power in the Texas state government, provided generous salaries for officials, stipulated appointed judges, and called for annual legislative sessions was drafted. It contained many elements that present-day reformers would like to see in a revised state charter. Because the constitution was forced on the state by outsiders in Washington and by *carpetbaggers*—northerners who came to Texas with their worldly goods in a suitcase made out of carpeting—White southerners never regarded the document as acceptable. They especially resented the strong, centralized state government and the powerful office of governor that were imposed on them. However, because all former rebels were barred from voting, the Constitution of 1869 was adopted by Unionists and African Americans. Ironically, this constitution least accomplished the purpose of legitimacy—acceptance by the people—but was the most forward looking in terms of power and organization.

The popular three-term governor, Elisha Pease, resigned in the fall of 1869 after the radical constitution was adopted. After a vacancy in the state's chief executive office lasting more than three months, Edmund J. (E. J.) Davis was elected governor and took office at the beginning of 1870. The election not only barred the state's Democrats and traditional Republicans, both conservative groups, from voting, but also exhibited a number of irregularities. Davis was an honest man, but the radical state charter, Davis's radical Republican ties, and his subsequent designation as provisional governor by President Ulysses Grant combined to give him dictatorial powers.[9]

## The Present Texas Constitution

**constitutional revision** Making major changes in a constitution, often including the writing of an entirely new document.

Traditionally Democratic, as well as conservative, Texans began to chafe for **constitutional revision**—changes to reform or improve the basic document—when the Democrats regained legislative control in 1872. An 1874 reform effort passed in the Texas Senate but failed in the House. This constitution would have provided flexibility in such areas as how tax dollars could be spent and terms of office. It also would have facilitated elite control and a sellout to the powerful railroads, which were hated by ordinary citizens because of their pricing policies and corruption of state legislatures.[10]

The legislature called a constitutional convention, and ninety delegates were elected from all over the state. The convention members were overwhelmingly conservative and reflected the "retrenchment and reform" philosophy of the Grange, which was one of several organizations of farmers.[11] This conservatism included a strong emphasis on the constitutional purpose of limiting government and a tolerance for racial segregation shared with other institutions of the time. As noted in Chapter 1, southern farmers were determined to prevent future state governments from oppressing them as they believed they had been oppressed under Reconstruction.

Accordingly, the new constitution, completed in 1875, curbed the powers of government. The governor's term was limited to two years. A state debt ceiling of $200,000 was established. Salaries of elected state officials were fixed. The legislature was limited to biennial sessions, and the governor was allowed to make very few executive appointments.

When this document went to the people of Texas for a vote in February 1876, it was approved by a margin of 136,606 to 56,652; 130 of the 150 Texas counties registered approval. All the ratifying counties were rural areas committed to the Grange and would benefit from the new constitution. The twenty counties that did not favor the new charter were urban areas that were heavily Republican, where newspaper criticism of the proposed document had been severe.[12]

### General Features

The Texas Constitution of today is very much like the original 1876 document in spite of 491 amendments by 2018 and some major changes in the executive article. It includes a preamble and sixteen articles, with each article divided into subsections.[13]

When the Texas Constitution was drafted more than a century ago, it incorporated protection for various private interests. It also included many details of policy and governmental organization to avoid abuse of government powers. The result is a very long, poorly organized document that does not draw clear lines of responsibility for government actions.

## ISSUE SPOTLIGHT:
### Independence Now and Then

**B**ecause Texas was an independent republic when the United States annexed it, the annexation agreement reflected compromises by both the state and national governments. For example, Texas gave up its military property, but kept its public lands. The national government refused to assume the state's $10 million debt. Texas, however, can carve four additional states out of its territory should the state want such a division.

However in the 1990s, a radical group calling itself the Republic of Texas contended that because Texas had been illegally annexed in 1845, it remained a nation. Pursuing this belief, members of the movement harassed state officials in a variety of ways, including filing liens against the assets of public agencies and regularly accusing state officials of illegally using their powers. Several of these individuals are still in prison for their violent actions.

In 2010, Governor Rick Perry suggested that Texas might secede from the United States. However, Texas did *not* enter the Union with any right of secession.

Competency Connection
**— SOCIAL —**
**RESPONSIBILITY**

**Do you think Texas would be better off as an independent country?**

As an example of details that might be contained better in legislation than in constitutional law, Article 5, Section 18, spells out procedures for electing justices of the peace and constables. These provisions have been amended four times; one amendment is so specific that it allows Chambers County the flexibility to have between two and six justice of the peace precincts. Besides having its own amendment, Chambers County (county seat: Anahuac) is best known for being one-third under water.

The Texas Constitution reflects the time of its writing, an era of strong conservative, agrarian interests, and of reaction to carpetbagger rule. Changes in the U.S. Constitution, both by amendment and by judicial interpretation, have required alterations of the state constitution, although provisions remain that conflict with federal law. These unenforceable provisions, along with other provisions that are so outdated that they will never again be enforced, are known as deadwood. Both the Sixty-fifth Legislature in 1977 and the Seventy-sixth Legislature in 1999 undertook to clean up the constitution by removing deadwood provisions through the formal amending process.

The frequent amendments have produced a state charter that is poorly organized and difficult to read, much less interpret, even by the courts.[14] Yet, the amendments are necessary because of the restrictiveness of the constitution. In recent years, voters have tended to approve virtually all proposed amendments. The Lone Star State can almost claim the record for the longest constitution in the nation. Only the constitution of Alabama contains more than the 87,000 words (as of 2017) in the Texas charter.[15]

### Specific Features

The Texas Constitution is similar in many ways to the U.S. Constitution, particularly the way in which the purposes of organizing and limiting government and legitimacy are addressed. Each government has executive, legislative, and judicial branches. Both are separation of powers systems; that is, they have separate institutions that share powers. Both include provisions against unequal or arbitrary government action, such as restricting freedom of religion. The two documents are less alike in terms of the purpose of providing power to government. The national Constitution is much more flexible in allowing government to act than is the state document. Texas legislators, for example, cannot set their own salaries.[16] Table 2-2 summarizes the key differences between the U.S. and Texas Constitutions.

**Bill of Rights** Like the national Bill of Rights, Article 1 of the Texas Constitution provides for equality under the law; religious freedom, including separation of church and state;[17] due process for the criminally accused; and freedom of speech and of the press. Among its thirty protections, it further provides safeguards for the mentally incompetent and provides several specific guarantees, such as prohibition against outlawing an individual from the state. It includes an equal rights amendment for all Texans.

Citizen opinion generally supports the U.S. and Texas Bills of Rights. However, just as the public sometimes gets upset with the U.S. Bill of Rights when constitutional protections are afforded to someone the public wants to "throw the book at"—an accused child molester, for example—Texans sometimes balk at the protections provided in the state constitution. Nevertheless, modern efforts toward constitutional revision have left the provisions intact.[18]

Chapter 10 discusses rights and liberties in greater detail, including interpretations of the right to keep and bear arms.

**Separation of Powers** Like the national Constitution, the state charter allocates governmental functions among three branches: the executive, the legislative, and the judicial. Article 2 outlines the separation of powers, including the "departments"—as the branches are labeled in the state constitution—of government. The national government divides power between the nation and the states, as well as among the three branches. Providing for a sharing of power should keep any one branch from becoming too powerful. Article 2 outlines the separation of institutions, and the articles dealing with the individual departments develop a system of **checks and balances** similar to those found in the national Constitution. Often, the same checks found in the U.S. Constitution are established in the state constitution.

**checks and balances**
An arrangement whereby each branch of government has some power to limit the actions of other branches.

A check on power results from assigning a function commonly identified with one branch to another. For example, the House of Representatives may impeach and the Senate may try—a judicial function—elected executive officials and judges at the district court level and above.[19] The governor has a veto over acts of the legislature and an item veto over appropriation bills—a legislative proceeding. The Texas Supreme Court may issue a writ of mandamus ordering an executive official to act—an executive function. These examples are applicable at the national as well as the state level and illustrate that powers are not truly separated, but overlapping and shared.

| TABLE 2-2 | Key Differences in U.S. and Texas Constitutions* | |
|---|---|
| **United States** | **Texas** |
| Powers are reserved to other states | Local governments are creatures of the state |
| Great flexibility | Great specificity |
| Provisions for strong chief executive | Provisions for weak chief executive |
| Relatively simple court system | Complex and confusing court system |
| Rarely amended | Frequently amended |

*There are also many similarities including separation of powers, checks and balances, provisions for both empowering and limiting government, and protections of individual rights.

## ISSUE SPOTLIGHT:
## When Individual Rights Conflict with the Public Interest

Freedom of religion is one of the most cherished of individual rights. It is the first right guaranteed in the First Amendment to the U.S. Constitution. The Texas Constitution also lists several types of passages promising protection from government intrusion on religious beliefs, the most general being "No human authority ought, in any case whatsoever, to control or interfere with the rights of conscience in matters of religion. . . ." (Article One). In addition, there is another right seemingly so basic that Texans in 1876 did not think that it needed to be protected in the document—the right of parents to raise their children as they see fit. (The U.S. Supreme Court, however, has recognized this right, in the *Wisconsin v. Yoder* decision of 1972).

Those are noble promises, in theory. The problem arises from the fact that religious beliefs often give rise to actual behavior, including the process of raising children. When that happens, religious practice sometimes collides with the public interest. Such is the case with childhood vaccinations and autism.

The rates of autism in children have been rising for several decades. Some parents, relying on one study published in *The Lancet* (the British medical journal) in 1998, and egged on both by contra-vaccination Websites and by public statements by some Hollywood celebrities, have concluded that school vaccinations are dangerous. Invoking a 2003 Texas law that permits parents to withdraw their children from the classic MMR (measles/mumps/rubella) series of shots administered by the public schools, a growing number of Texas parents are refusing to permit their children to be immunized. From 2003 to 2018, the number of parents invoking the religious-exemption law to prevent their children from being vaccinated rose from 3,000 to 57,000.

There are two problems with this action by parents. The first is that it is based on nonsense. The original anti-vaccine article from the 1990s has been declared fraudulent, and dozens of scientific studies since then have found no link between vaccinations and autism. The second problem is that it puts the public health at risk. Babies younger than six months cannot be vaccinated. If, during those vulnerable months, they come into contact with a non-vaccinated child who has contracted one of the diseases, they themselves could become sick and die. But it is not just infants; elderly people and others with compromised immune systems are in danger from unvaccinated children.

Public health experts say that, as a rule of thumb, 95 percent of the people in any given population should be vaccinated in order to provide "herd immunity"—the protection of the community in general from epidemics. As the number of unvaccinated children in the state rises, Texans lose that collective immunity, and the danger of mass sickness looms. And indeed, the latest statistics from the Texas Department of State Health Services show an alarming increase in childhood diseases. The number of cases of mumps in the state, for example, increased from 20 cases in 2015 to 191 in 2016. The Texas Constitution does not provide guidance about how to solve this problem.

Sources: Julie Chang, "Since 2008, Rate of Unvaccinated Kids Quadruples," *Austin American-Statesman*, September 2, 2018, A1; Jinny Suh, "Parents Must Speak Out About Rise in Dangerous Vaccine Exemptions,"

*Austin American-Statesman*, August 24, 2018, A9; "Texas Is No. 1 in 'Hotspots' for Vaccine Exemptions," and "Why Vaccine Opponents Think They Know More Than Medical Experts," both from the Texas Medical Association Website, www.texmed.org/immunizations; *Wisconsin v. Yoder*, 406 U.S. 205 (1972).

**Competency Connection**
**CRITICAL THINKING**

To invoke the rights to freedom of religion and freedom of parental judgment in the case of vaccines, therefore, is to put oneself at war with public health. Which is more important, the rights of parents to raise their children as they see fit, according to, among other things, their religious views, or the rights of everyone else to be free from epidemics?

**Legislative Branch** The Texas legislature, like the U.S. Congress, consists of a Senate and a House of Representatives. The legislative article (3) establishes a legislative body, determines its composition, sets the qualifications for membership, provides its basic organization, and fixes its meeting time. All these features are discussed in Chapter 6. The article also sets the salary of state legislators. Although a 1991 constitutional amendment provided an alternative method to recommend salaries through the Ethics Commission, the commission has never made a salary recommendation, and legislative salaries remain frozen at a surprisingly low $7,200 a year.

Rather than emphasizing the positive powers of the legislature, Article 3 spells out the specific actions that the legislature cannot take, reflecting reaction to the strong government imposed during Reconstruction. For example, the U.S. Constitution gives Congress broad powers to make any laws that are "necessary and proper." In contrast, rather than allowing lawmaking to be handled through the regular legislative process, the Texas Constitution sometimes forces state government to resort to the constitutional amendment process. For example, an amendment is needed to add to the fund maintained by the state to help veterans adjust to civilian life by giving them good deals on the purchase of land. Another example is the need for an amendment to change the percentage of the state budget that can be spent on public welfare.

The state constitution also provides the following limitations on legislative procedure:

1. The legislature may meet in regular session only every two years.
2. The number of days for introduction of bills, committee work, and floor action is specified. To permit early floor action, the governor can declare an emergency.
3. Salaries and the per diem reimbursement rate are described. Historically, this degree of specificity made an amendment necessary for every change in these figures. Although the Ethics Commission has made no recommendations about salaries, it has upgraded the per diem rate.
4. The legislature cannot authorize the state to borrow money. Yet, Section 23-A provides for a $75,000 payment to settle a debt to a contractor for a building constructed at the John Tarleton Agricultural College (now State University) in 1937.
5. The legislative article, not the municipal corporations article, includes provisions for municipal employees to participate in Social Security programs.
6. In spite of a stipulation that the legislature cannot grant public monies to individuals, exceptions are made for Confederate soldiers, sailors, and their widows.

These examples are taken only from the legislative article. A list of all similar idiosyncratic provisions in the constitution would be massive because limitations on legislative action are scattered throughout the constitution, especially in the General Provisions. Such detailed restrictions tie the hands of legislators and make it necessary for them to take many issues to the voters that are seemingly of little significance. Still, the legislature is the dominant institution in the state.

## Executive Branch

Little similarity exists between the provisions for the executive branch in the state charter and those in the national Constitution. The U.S. Constitution provides for a very strong chief executive, the president, and creates only one other elected official, the vice president, who since 1804 has run on a ticket with the presidential candidate. Tradition is that the presidential candidate selects the running mate, usually in an effort to pick up votes where the top candidate is weak. Article 4 provides that the governor will be elected statewide and will be the chief executive of the state. However, the state constitution requires that the following individuals also will be elected statewide:

1. The lieutenant governor, who presides over the Texas Senate
2. The comptroller (pronounced con-TROL-ler) of public accounts, who collects the state's taxes and determines who keeps the state's money on deposit
3. The commissioner of the General Land Office, who protects the state's environment and administers its vast public lands
4. The attorney general, who is the state's lawyer
5. Members of the Texas Railroad Commission, who regulate intrastate transportation and the oil, gas, and other mining industries

Furthermore, statutory laws require that the commissioner of agriculture and members of the State Board of Education be elected. Thus, quite unlike the president, who appoints most other key federal executives, the governor is saddled with five other elected executives and two key elected policymaking boards. He or she has no formal control over these individuals.

**plural executive**
A system of organizing the executive branch that includes the direct election of multiple executives, thereby weakening the chief executive, the governor.

Thus, Texas has a **plural executive**, with the result that the executive branch is "disintegrated" or "fragmented." Each elected executive is independent of the other. The governor must contend with a sprawling state bureaucracy, most of which receives policy direction from an administrative board or commission. The governor also has little power to reorganize executive agencies.

Like the legislative one, the executive article is overly specific and creates roadblocks to expeditious governmental action. Government cannot act when faced with too many restrictions, even when citizens need a fast response. More than the other articles, Article 4 reflects the period of its writing—the extreme reaction in the 1870s to the excesses of Reconstruction Governor E. J. Davis.

In a 2015 rating of the institutional power of governors in each state, Texas' chief executive was ranked as the ninth weakest.[20]

Governors, however, have learned how to use what constitutional powers they have. For example, through control of special sessions and through the veto power, the governor retains significant legislative power. Also, there is no restriction on the number of terms that a governor may serve.

Additionally, two modern amendments have strengthened the governor's position. In 1972, the governor's term of office was lengthened from two years to four years. In 1980, gubernatorial removal powers were strengthened by an amendment to Article 15. This amendment allows governors to remove, with the advice and consent of the Senate, individuals they have appointed. Legislation approved in 1993 further strengthened the office by giving the governor greater control over major policy boards, such as those dealing with insurance regulation and public education.

## Judicial Branch

The national judicial system is clear-cut—district courts, appeals courts, the U.S. Supreme Court—but the Texas judicial system is not at all clear. Like so many other articles in the constitution, the judicial article has various specific sections. These range from the requirement for an elected sheriff in each county to the restricted right of the state to appeal in criminal cases.[21]

Article 5, the judicial article of the state constitution, has three distinctive features. First, the constitution establishes a rather confusing pattern of six different types of courts. Further complicating the picture is the fact that Texas (along with Oklahoma) has two supreme courts, one each for civil (Supreme Court) and criminal (Court of Criminal Appeals) matters.

Second, each level of trial courts has concurrent, or overlapping, jurisdiction with another level; that is, either level of court may hear the case. Additionally, trial courts established by statute have different jurisdiction from those established by the constitution. For example, in civil matters, constitutional county courts have concurrent jurisdiction with justice of the peace courts in civil cases involving $200 to $5,000. County courts at law overlap district courts in civil matters involving up to $100,000. Although the legislature can adjust the jurisdiction of statutory courts, the authority of constitutional courts can be altered only by constitutional amendment. Furthermore, the minimum dollar amounts stated in the constitution reflect economic values of the nineteenth century. In an era of multimillion-dollar lawsuits, having a district court—the chief trial court of the state—hear a case in which the disputed amount is $1,000 or less hampers the more significant trial work of that court. The courts are fully discussed in Chapter 9.

Third, qualifications for Texas judges are so stated as to allow those with no legal training to be eligible for a trial court bench.[22] The resulting confusion increases the likelihood that someone without legal experience will be elected as a justice of the peace or county judge. The problem of judicial qualifications is aggravated by the fact that judges are elected in Texas so that, on occasion, vote-getting ability may be more important than the ability to render fair judgments.[23] The tradition of elected judges reflects the nineteenth-century passion for long ballots. In the national government, the president appoints all judges.

**Local Government** Local governments in Texas fall into three categories: counties, municipalities (cities and towns), and special districts. The state constitution, through Articles 3, 9, and 11, gives these governmental units varying degrees of flexibility.

Counties, which are administrative and judicial arms of the state, are most restricted. They are saddled with a commission form of government that combines executive and legislative authority and is headed by a judge. The powers vested in the county governments and the services they offer are fragmented. An amendment of some 2,000 words was passed in 1933 to allow larger counties to adopt a home-rule charter, but the provisions were so restrictive as to be inoperable.

**home rule** The ability of cities with populations of 5,000 or more to organize themselves as they wish within the constitution and laws of Texas.

**Home rule** allows a government to write its own charter and make changes in it without legislative approval. Had it been workable, this provision would have allowed counties to choose their own form of government and have more flexibility in day-to-day operations. The provision was deleted in 1969.

In contrast, cities enjoy a workable home-rule provision. Those with populations of more than 5,000 may become home-rule units of government. General-law cities, which are those without home-rule charters, must operate under statewide statutes. Cities, towns, and villages, whether operating under a home-rule charter or general law, are fairly free to provide whatever services and create whatever policies the citizens and governing bodies want, as long as there is no conflict with constitutional or statutory law. The major constitutional difficulties for cities are the ceilings imposed on tax rates and debt and limitations on the frequency of charter amendments.

Special districts are limited-purpose local governments that have taxing authority. The legislature generally authorizes the creation of special districts, although constitutional amendments have created some water and hospital districts. School districts are the best-known type of special district, but there are literally dozens of varieties. Because these types of government provide a way around the tax and debt limits imposed on cities and counties, they continue to proliferate.[24] (Chapter 11 discusses local government in detail.)

| TABLE 2-3 | Comparison of State Provisions for Amending the Constitution | | |
|-----------|-----------------------|-------------------|---------------------------|
| State(s) | Legislative Proposal | Initiative by Voters | Constitutional Convention |
| Texas | Yes | No | No |
| Number of other states | 49 | 18 | 41 |

SOURCE: *The Book of the States, 2013 Edition*, vol. 45 (Lexington, KY.: Council of State Governments, 2013), 14–18.

**Suffrage** The provisions on voting and the apportionment of legislative bodies are interesting because many of them have clearly conflicted with federal law, which itself continues to evolve as the legal/political philosophy of federal judges changes. As a result, Article 6 has been subject to frequent amendments to catch up with changes, such as the nationally established voting age and to allow participation in bond elections by voters who do not own property. The suffrage section of the constitution is shot through with "temporary transition provisions" to bridge the gap between state and federal law.

**Amendments** The framers of a constitution cannot possibly anticipate every provision that should be included. Consequently, all constitutions specify a procedure for amendment. Unlike the eighteen other states, most notably California, that allow citizens to initiate constitutional amendment proposals by petition and the forty-one states that provide for a constitutional convention (see Table 2-3), Texas has only one way to propose an amendment.

In Texas, proposals for amendments may be initiated during a regular or special session of the legislature, and an absolute two-thirds majority—that is, one hundred House and twenty-one Senate members—must vote to submit the proposed changes to the voters. The governor cannot veto a proposed amendment. The legislature also specifies the date of the election at which an amendment is voted on by the public. At least three months before the election, a proposed amendment must be published once a week for four weeks in a newspaper in each county. Whenever possible, amendments are placed on the ballot in general elections to avoid the expense of a separate, called election. Only a simple majority—that is, half plus one—of those citizens who choose to vote is needed for ratification, making it rather easy to add amendments. The governor officially proclaims the passage or rejection of amendments.

The public had voted on 669 amendments by 2018, with 491 passing. This number is vivid proof that the amendment process in the state has occupied considerable legislative time and that citizens have frequently confronted constitutional propositions at the polls.

The majority of amendments have been adopted since 1980, illustrating the relentlessness of the amendment phenomenon and the increasing reliance on amendments as a way to get something done in government. Some streamlining of the state charter ensued from a constitutional amendment passed in November 1997 that called for elimination of duplicate numbers in the Texas Constitution and of obsolete provisions.

## Constitutional Change

The framers of the U.S. Constitution were wise enough to provide only the essential structure of national government and to consign broad powers to governmental agents. The flexibility inherent in this approach has made possible the country's transition from a nation whose government was mainly concerned with fending off "hostile" Native Americans and delivering the mail to one whose government now shoulders the burdens of world leadership and myriad socioeconomic policies. State constitutions, on the other hand, tend toward an inflexibility that leads to frequent revision in the form of either a totally new document or many amendments. One need only compare the 27 amendments to the U.S. Constitution with the 491 amendments to the Texas Constitution.

## Overview of the Need for Reform

Americans are proud that their fundamental law, which has been amended only twenty-seven times, including the first ten amendments—the Bill of Rights—that were added almost immediately after ratification. At the national level, the admonition of Alexander Hamilton that opens this chapter has been heeded.

At the state level, however, constitutions have not fared as well. State charters tend to reflect the concerns of vested interests. These interests prefer the "security blanket" of constitutional inclusion to being left at the mercy of legislatures with changing party alignments, political persuasions, and political concerns.

By 2017, the average state constitution had been amended more than 150 times. The most-amended states were Alabama (926), California (535), and South Carolina (500). Texas came in fourth at 491. The least-amended state was Rhode Island, with 12 (Source: *Book of the States*, p. 10).

The ratification dates of state constitutions provide a clue as to what to expect in the way of content and, thus, number of amendments. Older state charters, unless they have been updated, tend to be more problematic than newer ones. For example, the two newest states—Alaska and Hawaii—have workable, sound constitutions that were modeled in part on the ideal document proposed by the National Municipal League.[25] These states have clearly profited from the mistakes of others.

Advocates of reform urge Texas to follow Hamilton's prescription by adopting a new document that is general, flexible, and streamlined in place of the specific, rigid, complicated constitution that hampers its government now. Reformers are not all of one mind and frequently differ on the details of their proposals. Nevertheless, reform advocates tend to agree on fundamentally important changes that should be made in the current constitution, as follows:

1. The biennial legislative session: As state politics and finance become more complex, the short legislative sessions held only every other year become more problematic in developing long-range public policy.
2. The judicial system: The Texas judicial system, as previously discussed, is characterized by multiple layers of courts with overlapping jurisdictions. Many reform advocates would like to see the establishment of a streamlined, unified judicial system.
3. The plural executive branch: The executive branch has many elected officials. Reformers suggest a state executive branch modeled on the national one—that is, a single elected official and a series of executive departments responsible to that official—to avoid the disintegrated, fragmented nature of the present structure.
4. County government: Especially in urban counties, the structure of county government and its lack of power to pass ordinances (local laws) mean that the counties cannot respond readily to urban problems. Reform advocates suggest that county government be streamlined and given at least limited ordinance power.
5. Detailed provisions in the constitution: For example, each time more funding is needed for welfare payments or the veterans' land program, a constitutional amendment must be passed. Thus, another area for reform is removing from the constitution details that are better left for statutory law, which can be changed more readily as situations demand.

Attempts have been made to modernize the Texas Constitution from time to time since its adoption in 1876. Serious interest in constitutional reform/revision was evident in 1957–1961, 1967–1969, 1971–1974, and to some extent, 1991–1993 and 1999. The only reform effort that resulted in an opportunity for the electorate to decide on a new document came in 1975.

Although three powerful legislators took an interest in constitutional reform in the 1990s, nothing came of their efforts. Neither other legislators nor citizens had much interest in constitutional revision. Both were more concerned about the issues that regularly beset the Texas political system—education, health care, highways, air quality, and so on. Only the League of Women Voters has shown a long-term concern for constitutional revision, joined by sporadic media interest in reform.[26]

Moreover, a pressing concern for constitutional reform is more likely to arise from a moralistic political culture than the traditionalistic/individualistic culture that characterizes Texas. Most Texans are politically conservative and prefer the basic governing document that they know to one that could cause social/political/economic changes that they might not like. Consequently, Texas has continued to use a patchwork approach to its basic document, relying on constitutional amendments and statutory law to alleviate some of the shortcomings of the constitution. The 1999 amendment that authorizes removal or rewording of outdated and repetitive parts of the state constitution is illustrative of the amendment approach to constitutional patching. Modifying the election code to ensure that the qualifications for voting in Texas conform to national requirements is one example of a statutory fix.

## Constitutional Politics

Making a constitution, like other lawmaking processes, is highly political. Whether the issue is general constitutional reform or an individual amendment, changing a constitution will benefit some groups and disadvantage others. Because the requirements of a two-thirds legislative vote and public approval make constitutional change more difficult than ordinary lawmaking, the political stakes are greater when alteration of a state's fundamental charter is an issue.

**Something for Everyone** Various special interest groups attempt to embody their political, social, economic, and/or moral viewpoints in the constitution by either advocating a particular change or working against it. If a group can embed its particular policy concern in the constitution, the issue is likely to remain there, perhaps forever. In other words, it is easier to "amend in" a provision than to "amend it out." The relative ease of amending the state charter contributes to this attitude of using the constitution as a security blanket. The constitution has become a political "goody" store that contains something for everyone.

One strategy used by these groups is to seek an authorizing provision in the constitution that will result in economic gains for the group. For example, a set of 1985 amendments about funding for water supply has given benefits to small cities, farmers, and ranchers, all of whom vigorously advocated passage of the proposals. Water interests also triumphed in 2013. Similarly, tax relief has been a frequent subject for constitutional amendment since 1978. Almost everyone—including farmers, ranchers, lumber interests, oil and natural gas producers, and residential property taxpayers—has gotten something from the amendments and the accompanying legislation.

Sometimes a group tries to prohibit a state from taking, or being able to take, a particular action. When the foes of parimutuel betting helped to destroy the efforts of the 1974 constitutional convention, their goal was to prevent the constitutional authorization of gambling in Texas. This issue was a political red herring dragged in by general opponents of constitutional reform, and it illustrates tactics that are used to defeat change. The proposed constitution did not specifically provide for parimutuel betting, but it did not prohibit it. Opposition to parimutuel betting has since lessened, and in November 1987, voters approved it in a referendum held at the time of a constitutional amendment election. A 1991 amendment authorized more gambling through a state lottery.

The strategy of getting something for everyone by opposition to particular policies has more recently focused on various proposed amendments that would prohibit a state income tax. In 1993, voters overwhelmingly approved an amendment that mandates a voter referendum if the legislature should ever pass an income tax. The amendment also requires that at least two-thirds of the revenue from an income tax be pledged to reduce property taxes that support public schools, with the remainder to go to support education. The importance of this provision has been evident in recent years when the legislature has been struggling to find funding sources for state programs.

At other times, a group seeks to advance some special interest that is already the subject of a constitutional guarantee. The periodic amendment of the legislative article on the Veterans Land Board is an example. This constitutional provision authorizes the state to sell bonds both to purchase land for veterans and to underwrite low-cost loans for home purchasers. It must be amended each time an authorization for more bond sales is needed.

Another example of the politics of constitution making concerns branch banking, which the Texas Constitution prohibited before a 1986 constitutional amendment. Larger banks wanted branch banking because they wanted to establish branches in other parts of a city or even in other cities. Smaller, independent banks, fearing the competition that a change would permit, opposed the practice. From 1987 through 1990, Texas banks and savings and loans suffered many failures. Because branch banking had been legalized, finding purchasers for the failed Texas financial institutions was easier. Larger, more stable banks both in Texas and in other states could acquire the troubled banks and make them branches. In 1997, financial institutions were major advocates of a proposal that would allow Texas homeowners, like the citizens of all other states, to take out a second mortgage on their residence. Voters, viewing home equity loans as a type of easy credit, went along with the banks and savings and loans.

Private interests are not always the only ones seeking constitutional change. Sometimes elected officials want changes in the constitution to enhance their power, but such ideas often do not fly with the general public. In 1980 and 1981, for example, the governor tried to gain greater control over the state's budgeting and spending processes through constitutional amendment, but the public defeated both of the proposed amendments. In 1999, voters defeated a proposal that would have allowed state employees who serve on local government boards to be paid the same as other compensated board members.

Public officials also may try to prevent constitutional change through fear of losing powers. Members of the Texas Association of County Officials (TACO) were a potent lobbying force against the proposed 1975 constitution. They were afraid of losing political control if county governments were modernized.

**The Political Process** The political process involved in constitutional change is essentially the same as it is in other activities designed to influence public policy. Elected officials, political parties, special interests and their lobbyists, and campaigning are all involved. A brief illustration of the political process is provided by a situation that began in 1979 and initially appeared to be resolved by an amendment approved by the voters in 1984—namely, the issue of building funds for the state's universities. The 1984 amendment, however, was not the end of the story.

The University of Texas at Austin and Texas A&M University at College Station, through provisions in Article 7 of the state constitution, were the sole beneficiaries of the Permanent University Fund (PUF). The PUF fund—which can be used for buildings, other permanent improvements, and enrichment activities—represents a large amount of money; it was worth over $11.4 billion in 2008 (the last full inventory of assets). The PUF money comes from the proceeds of the oil and gas leases on a million acres of public land granted to the two universities and from investment of these proceeds.

Seventeen other state universities originally received money for buildings directly from the legislature and then, beginning in 1947, from a dedicated fund fed by the state property tax. Institutions created after 1947 were dependent on legislative appropriations.

In 1979, as part of a general tax-relief movement, the legislature reduced the rate for the state property tax to almost zero. In the 1979 and 1981 sessions of the legislature, a variety of proposals to establish an alternative to financing college building programs were introduced. Neither the legislators nor the universities could agree on a proposal. The legislature subsequently proposed a constitutional amendment to abolish the state property tax altogether, and the voters approved the amendment in late 1982.

The 1983 legislature agreed on a basic plan that provided PUF coverage for other institutions in the UT and A&M systems, and established a separate fund (the Higher Education Fund) to cover the other state institutions. This separate fund would cover repairs and renovations, new construction, library and equipment purchases, and land acquisitions. They also agreed on a special infusion of funds to the two predominately African American institutions in the state, Texas Southern University and Prairie View A&M.

## You Decide: Should Texas Convene a Constitutional Convention?

The Texas Constitution was ratified in 1876. By 2018, it had been amended 491 times and is now 87,000 words in length. The average for all fifty states is 150 amendments and 39,644 words. California, the only state with a population larger than Texas', has a constitution with 535 amendments and 67,000 words.

### Pro ✓

⬆ Texas should convene a constitutional convention to draft a new state charter. The present state constitution

⬆ is antiquated.

⬆ conflicts with the national Constitution.

⬆ protects special interests.

⬆ reflects agrarian interests.

⬆ is far too specific.

⬆ needs frequent interpretation.

⬆ poorly organizes government, thus does not meet the needs of an urban state.

### Con ✗

⬇ The state constitution should not be revised to avoid

⬇ mistaking newness for quality; the U.S. Constitution is 89 years older than the Texas Constitution.

⬇ increasing partisanship that could create a political disaster.

⬇ "fixing something that ain't broke."

⬇ giving more authority to counties, which are already inefficient.

⬇ giving government, especially the governor, too much power.

⬇ a process likely to be an expensive exercise resulting in stalemates.

⬇ removing protection against arbitrary governmental action from those groups protected by the charter.

**Competency Connection**
**CRITICAL THINKING**

After having read our summary of the pros and cons of constitutional revision, would you vote pro or con if given the chance?

The UT and A&M representatives wanted to ensure that the PUF was not opened to other universities. They feared a significant reduction in the funds available to the two flagship institutions. Their willingness to include their branch campuses in the PUF avoided the need to include these branch campuses in the new construction fund. At the same time, UT and A&M also gained the agreement of the other universities not to seek inclusion in the PUF. In 1984, the issue of university construction was seemingly resolved as part of a broad solution to financing *capital* improvements (those of long-term duration).

In 2001, however, the legislature changed the system to begin reducing the amount of appropriated funds that went into the Higher Education Fund, and the difference was deposited in a new fund called the Texas Excellence Fund to spur research. No appropriation was made to the permanent Higher Education Fund for fiscal years 2004–2005. Then in 2003, a more conservative group of legislators, faced with a $10 billion deficit, pulled back general capital funding in favor of dollars designed to attract outside research funding. The Seventy-eighth Legislature in 2003 dictated that the Texas Excellence Fund and the University Research Fund would be repealed as of September 1, 2005. At that point, yet another fund, the Research Development Fund, was created.

This shift in emphasis to research-only funding had a major effect on every university student outside the University of Texas and Texas A&M systems. Because of the elimination of the special pot of funding for construction, repairs, libraries, equipment, and land that was not specially tied to external research funding, students found themselves saddled with the costs for these items in the form of assessments, such as special library fees and higher tuition that was in part pledged to construction bonds. At the same time, the PUF institutions were pointing out that they did not have adequate dollars to take care of all their building repair needs and that they were under similar pressures to emphasize their research missions.

This issue of capital funding for universities provides a portrait of how many varied interests can become involved in constitutional change. The saga of university construction has involved many people—legislators, universities, taxpayers, the Higher Education Coordinating Board, business and industry, and ethnic minorities. Different constitutional change issues have different casts of characters, but all are fraught with similar complex political relationships.

## Summary

**LO 2.1** **The United States has a federal system, which assigns powers to both the nation and the states.** Most of the time, the two levels work cooperatively in a model resembling a marble cake, but Texas often challenges national policy, even to the point of foregoing significant federal aid. The state constitution does not create a federal system; instead, local governments are creatures of the state.

**LO 2.2** **Constitutions have four purposes: legitimacy, organizing government, providing power, and limiting governmental power.** The six Texas constitutions have embodied these purposes in varying degrees. The 1876 state charter concentrated attention on legitimacy and limiting governmental power. Thus, the framers largely ignored the importance of assigning sufficient power to government officials, and they subverted the purpose of organizing government by creating a fragmented set of institutions and offices designed to diffuse authority. Although this approach limits government, it also makes citizen participation more difficult because state government is confusing to most people.

**LO 2.3** **The Texas Constitution reflects the traditionalistic and individualistic political culture of the state.** Lacking the farsightedness of the framers of the U.S. Constitution, the authors of the Texas charter produced a restrictive document that today sometimes impedes the development and implementation of needed policies and programs. As a result, by 2018, lawmakers and citizens had resorted to amending the Texas Constitution 491 times to make possible programs that otherwise would have been consigned to legislative dreamland. Dynamic public issues such as funding for water quality, welfare, and public education could be handled more smoothly without the necessity of proposing and ratifying a constitutional amendment.

**LO 2.4** **The most distinctive—and often the most cumbersome—provisions in the 1876 Texas Constitution are the following:**

1. The governor has limited direct control over most major policymaking offices, boards, and commissions.
2. The legislature must operate within the constraints of poverty-level salaries, short and infrequent sessions, and innumerable restrictions on legislative action.
3. Texas judges are virtually powerless to provide simpler, more uniform justice because of the overlapping and parallel jurisdictions of the state's courts.
4. County governments are restricted by their constitutional structure and scope.
5. The 483 amendments exacerbate the poor organization of the charter, making it even more difficult for the layperson to read and comprehend.

**LO 2.5** **The electorate still lacks sufficient understanding of the shortcomings of the present constitution to be receptive to revisions that involve increases in governmental power.** Also, citizens are far too concerned about state taxes, public education, social services, crime and punishment, and many other pressing issues to give constitutional revision much attention. Although the current constitution "creaks and groans," the state still takes care of its business. In addition, special interests have found it easy to amend the current document by influencing key legislators and then mounting serious campaigns to elicit voter support. They prefer the protection of a constitution to more easily changed statutes.

## Critical Thinking

1. What are the four purposes of constitutions? Which ones do you think are most reflected in the Texas Constitution? Which ones are least reflected? Why?

2. What similarities and differences do you see in the U.S. and Texas constitutions? Why do you think the differences exist?

The Capitol building in Austin is the focus of attention for many interest groups.

*Courtesy of Texas Department of Transportation*

# Interest Groups

3

Politics is concerned with the making of *public* policy, but a great many of its actions have *private* consequences. When government imposes a tax, begins to regulate an industry, or writes rules about the behavior of individuals, it makes an impact not just on the public in general but on citizens in particular. Human nature being what it is, people often tend to judge the action not so much on the basis of its value to their community as on the basis of its utility to themselves. Seeking to obtain more favorable policies, people organize to try to influence government. When they do, they create a problem for democracy. As citizens, we want our government to take account of the impact of its laws on individuals, but we do not want the special wishes of some people to be more important than the shared needs of us all. To the extent that public policy is made or modified at the behest of private interests, democracy is impaired.

In Texas as elsewhere in the United States, special organized interests are always busy trying to influence what government institutions do. Citizens have to decide whether these groups are merely presenting their point of view to public authorities or whether instead they are attempting to corrupt the process of self-government.

If the evaluation is negative, however, the solution cannot be that government should suppress some or all interest groups. The First Amendment to the

**LO 3.1**   Explain why interest groups create a dilemma for democracy, and why government cannot resolve the dilemma by outlawing such groups.

**LO 3.2**   Be able to define the term "interest group," list the types of groups that are relevant to politics, and describe the functions of such groups in the political system.

**LO 3.3**   Explain the biases in the formation of interest groups, and give the consequences of those biases in terms of who is more likely to be organized, and who is less likely.

**LO 3.4**   Recount the typical activities of political interest groups, and explain why some of those activities create a problem for democracy.

**LO 3.5**   Assess the effectiveness of efforts to regulate the activities of interest groups.

**LO 3.6**   List a half-dozen of the major interest groups in Texas, and explain why some of them are more, or less, influential in state politics, and why some have increased or decreased in influence over the last quarter-century.

MONEY DOESN'T TALK, IT SWEARS.

Bob Dylan,
*"It's Alright, Ma (I'm Only Bleeding)," 1965*

federal Constitution specifically protects "the right of the people peaceably to assemble, and to petition the Government for a redress of grievances," which has always been interpreted to mean that such groups must be left free to do and say what they like. Long ago, federal courts applied this rule to the states. So, good or bad, interest groups are here to stay.

In this chapter, the discussion first focuses on the definition and classification of interest groups. The chapter then describes and analyzes their activities and moves on to consider some efforts that have been made to regulate lobbying. There is then an examination of the history and recent activities of some of the major interest groups in Texas. The interest-group system in Texas is evaluated in the light of democratic theory.

## Interest Groups

The self-concept of Americans, and Texans, tends to be highly individualistic. The image of the lone cowboy riding across the range, who then cleans up the corrupt town single-handedly, summarizes the way many Texans think of themselves. But, in realistic terms, ordinary human beings do not have much influence on society unless they are organized into groups. When people join together to cooperate in defense of their interests, however, they become part of a powerful force in the politics of the state and the nation.

## Definition

An interest is something an individual or individuals have that has value and is therefore worth defending. It can be economic, religious, ethnic, or indeed, based on almost anything. People who produce oil have an interest, as do Catholics, and fans of Harry Potter novels. Interests affect politics in two general ways. One topic of Chapter Four will be the manner in which they form the basis for much of the battle between political parties. In this chapter, the subject is the direct effect of interests and interest groups on Texas government.

In the broad sense, an **interest group** is a private organization of individuals who have banded together because of a common cause or role. The focus here, however, is on **political interest groups**, those that try to influence politicians to make public policy in line with their preferences. When people join these groups, they exercise their right guaranteed by the **First Amendment** to the U.S. Constitution to "assemble" and "petition" the government.

Interest groups can be usefully contrasted with political parties. The focus of a party is broad, encompassing many different interests, whereas the focus of a group is narrow, comprising just one interest. Parties attempt to gain power by running candidates in elections, whereas groups try to affect power by influencing officeholders. Therefore, while parties are forced to appeal to the citizenry to marshal support, groups may work entirely behind the scenes. By joining groups, people gain the ability to affect government decisions beyond what they achieve with just their vote.

## Classification

Interest groups may be classified according to the types of interests they defend:

1. Economic groups, such as manufacturers' associations or labor unions. These represent the most common type of interest group and also, in general, the type with the most resources. Within this large category, there are many more specialized groups representing specific types of industries or occupations. An example of the former would be banking and financial organizations, represented by the Texas Bankers Association, among others. Examples of the

**interest group**
A number of people who are organized to defend an interest they share or wish to promote; the interest can be narrow (rice growers, for example) or broad (consumers, for example).

**political interest groups** A private organization that attempts to influence politicians—and through them public policy—to the advantage of the organization.

**First Amendment**
To the U.S. Constitution, containing a clause protecting the right of the people to "peaceably assemble, and to petition the government for a redress of grievances," among other protections.

latter would be professional associations, such as the State Bar of Texas, representing lawyers, or the Texas Medical Association, representing doctors. Like labor unions, these groups represent people who share a type of livelihood. Unlike most labor unions, they are composed of people who are generally well-educated and relatively wealthy.

2. Spiritual groups, such as church organizations or pro-life and pro-choice associations. These groups unite people who may be otherwise very different but who share a faith or a public policy position derived from their faith.

3. Artistic or recreational organizations, such as the local Symphony League or the Texas Association of Bass Clubs. This type of group includes people who share a hobby or other type of pastime.

4. Ethnic groups, such as the League of United Latin American Citizens (LULAC) or the National Association for the Advancement of Colored People (NAACP).

5. Associations of local governments, such as the Texas Municipal League and the Texas Association of Counties.

6. Public interest groups, such as Common Cause or the League of Women Voters. These groups try to pursue their understanding of interests common to all citizens rather than the individual interests of their members. The members of these groups can disagree about what constitutes the "public interest"—they can have opposing positions on whether school vouchers would be a good thing for education, for example—but those positions are based on their differing understanding of the broad-based needs of all citizens rather than on their own personal needs.

**Functions** Interest groups attempt to persuade both the public and individual government officials to take a particular point of view on specific public policies. In trying to be persuasive, they perform six important functions in the political process:

1. They furnish information to officeholders in all branches of government. This activity includes both communicating their collective opinion on public policy and supplying policymakers with their version of the facts.

## Texas Politics and You

A variety of public policies impinge on the lives of college students. For example, Congress sets interest rates on student loans, and state governments adopt various kinds of affirmative action programs. Although there is apparently no organization that represents the interests of Texas college students specifically, there are many national organizations. But because people disagree about what policies would best advance "student interests," student organizations tend to mirror the ideological differences in the larger society.

The largest and oldest college-student interest group in the country is the United States Student Organization, founded in 1947. Although it does not identify itself as a liberal or conservative organization, the issues it advocates on its Website place it squarely on the left, or liberal, side of the political spectrum.

Other organizations are more forthright about their ideological leanings. There is a number of national organizations representing the views of conservative students (The College Conservative, Young Americans for Freedom), liberal students (Democracy Matters, Young Democrats of America), and students who want to support specific causes (Students for a Free Tibet, Free Culture Foundation). All these groups encourage interested students to participate in their activities.

Sources: www.students.org/; http://thecollegeconservative.com/; www.yaf.org/; www.democracymatters.org/; www.yda.org/; www.studentsforafreetibet.org/; http://freeculture.org.

**Competency Connection**
**COMMUNICATION SKILLS**

What national student political organizations have chapters in your school? Are you a member of any of them?

2. They politicize and inform members of their groups as well as others.
3. They mediate conflict within their groups.
4. They engage in electioneering, especially the contribution of money to candidates, and possibly in other interventions in the governing process, such as filing lawsuits.
5. By disseminating information supporting their own policy stands to citizens, they help to form public opinion.
6. By providing institutions other than political parties that help people to participate in the process of governing, they help their members to become more involved democratic citizens.

**Interest Groups in the Political Process** The two most important points to understand about interest groups are that not all people who share an interest are organized and that organized interests are much more powerful than unorganized interests.

# Who Is Organized?

Although we might be tempted to believe that every potential interest spawns an interest group, in fact some interests are far more likely to be organized than others. Those that are organized are relevant to policymaking; those that are not organized are usually irrelevant.

For example, oil and gas producers are well organized and politically powerful in Texas. Oil and gas consumers, however, are not organized, except insofar as general consumers' groups (which theoretically represent everybody but never have a very large membership) include petroleum among the many products of interest to them. As a result, unless the price of gasoline at the pump rises steeply, thereby creating public anger, petroleum consumers are not usually of much concern to policymakers. Under ordinary conditions, government policymakers are likely to pay much more attention to petroleum producers.

There are three general rules of interest-group formation. First, economic producing groups are more likely to be organized than are consuming groups (as in the oil and gas example above). Second, regardless of the type of group, people with more education and income are more likely to join than are people with less education and income. (The Texas Medical Association, to be discussed shortly, is an example). Third, citizens who join groups out of personal involvement as opposed to economic stake tend to feel very strongly about the particular issue that is the group's reason for existence. (Both pro-choice and pro-life groups are examples). They are therefore much more likely to contribute money, write letters, attend rallies, and in other ways engage in actions that get the attention of government officials. Consequently, because they are more likely to be organized, producers tend to exert more political influence than consumers, the middle and upper classes more influence than the working classes, and passionate believers more influence than citizens who are less emotionally involved.

# Activities

Interest groups therefore enhance democratic government by supplying information to citizens, contributing to debates about issues, getting people involved in politics, and shaking up the established order by influencing institutions. But because they often attempt to skew the process of government to benefit themselves, these groups also can be a corrupting influence. A closer look at their activities will show the extent to which they deflect public policymaking into private channels.

**Information** Thousands of bills are introduced in the Texas legislature every session, and legislators can have no more than a passing knowledge of most of the policy areas involved. Even those legislators who may have specialized knowledge need up-to-date, accurate information. Therefore, in Texas as in other states, information ranks with money as one of the two most important lobbying resources. As two political scientists who have spent their careers studying interest groups in the states have written, ". . .there is one thing that virtually all state lobbyists have in common. They rely primarily upon information to make their case."[1] The information furnished is biased because it represents the group's viewpoint, but it also must be accurate. Getting and keeping a reputation for providing solid information are among the most important assets a lobbyist can develop.

Information is a tool of influence not only in relations with the legislature but also in dealing with the bureaucracy. State executive agencies have a constant need for information and sometimes no independent means of finding it. They may come to rely on lobbying groups to furnish them with facts. For example, since 1996, the state insurance commissioner has relied on the Texas Insurance Checking Office (TICO) to gather the data the commission uses to regulate insurance rates. The Checking Office is a subsidiary of an insurance industry lobbying group. An industry group is therefore supplying the information used to regulate the industry it represents. Consumers might suspect that such data will not show that insurance companies are charging too much.[2]

When the legislature is in session, lobbyists are always thronging the Capitol.

AP Images/Harry Cabluck

Competency Connection
**SOCIAL RESPONSIBILITY**

Is this activity good or bad for Texas democracy?

# Electioneering

One of the most common ways interest groups try to ensure that their future efforts at persuasion will be more effective is by supporting candidates for public office. Interest groups that have helped elect a politician can be confident that they will not be forgotten when the politician enters government.

Usually, the most effective way to help candidates is to give them money. Because campaigning demands the purchase of advertising in expensive media, all candidates but the few who are personally rich need to beg wealthy individuals and groups for large contributions. Various types of groups have come into being since the 1970s, partly to make it easier to combine many people's money so as to apply it to one organized purpose, and partly to evade the campaign finance laws. (We will discuss those laws later in this chapter). The three major kinds of groups that collect money from individuals and use it to influence campaigns are:

**political action committees (PACs)**
A group formed by a corporation, trade association, labor union, or other organization or individual for the purpose of collecting money and then contributing that money to one or more political candidates or causes.

**527s** An organization that collects money and uses it to try to influence public opinion, mainly through the media, and mainly during election campaigns.

**501(c)(4)** An organization that collects money and uses it to try to influence public opinion, mainly through the media, and mainly during election campaigns, but differs from "527s" in that it does not have to publicly reveal the names of its donors.

1. **Political Action Committees (PACs)**. A PAC is a committee formed by an organization, industry, or individual for the purpose of collecting voluntary contributions and then distributing that money to selected political candidates and causes.
2. **527s**. Named after the section of the federal tax code that applies to political contributions, these organizations collect money and mostly use it to influence public opinion through the media.[3] As long as they do not formally endorse specific parties or candidates in elections, they are subject to less regulation than an organization that does advocate a specific vote. 527 electoral media campaigns, therefore, are typically full of implications and innuendos, but not actual appeals for identifiable actions.
3. **501(c)(4)**. Also drawing their identity from the tax code, these are formally registered as civic or social welfare organizations. Their chief advantage, from the point of view of their contributors, is that they can keep the names of those contributors a secret. Like 527s, they are legally forbidden to endorse candidates for public office, but like 527s they nevertheless launch media campaigns of veiled rhetoric to try to persuade the public to vote one way or another, without actually saying so.

Because PACs, 527s, and 501(c)(4) coordinate and concentrate the financial clout of many individuals with a single interest, they can influence public policy far more effectively than can most ordinary, isolated citizens. Most states, including Texas, have tried to regulate the activities of these groups. In two decisions in 2006 and 2010, however (*Randall v. Sorrell* and *Citizens United v. Federal Election Commission*), the U.S Supreme Court made it more difficult to do so. The language of the rulings was unhelpful as to exactly what sort of regulation would be acceptable. The future of state efforts to control electioneering by interest groups is therefore unclear.[4]

There are many examples that might illustrate the impact of such spending by interest groups. One good example is the saga of Harold Simmons and Waste Control Specialists (WCS). Simmons (who died in 2013) was a billionaire businessman who owned a number of corporations, one of which had been angling for some time to build and operate a low-level nuclear waste depository in Andrews County, near the New Mexico border. In order to get state laws and permits for this activity, WCS and other businesses and organizations controlled by Simmons had been involved for some years in a campaign to acquire the loyalties of Texas politicians and institutions. During the 2012 election cycle, for example, one of Simmons' companies was the single largest contributor to Texas politicians, spending a total of $31,394, 818.[5]

In 2012, the Texas Ethics Commission fined Simmons $6450 for having made illegal campaign contributions to fifteen Republican and three Democratic state legislators in 2011. (The contributions were illegal because, although they allegedly came from a political action committee, he was its sole donor). Observers noticed the enormous difference between the amount of money that Simmons was willing to spend to influence state legislators, and the paltry amount—pocket change to a billionaire—that he was fined for breaking the law.[6]

More importantly, the campaign of influence-buying on behalf of WCS evidently was worth it. In 2009, the state issued two licenses to the company to permit it to bury the nuclear waste. In 2011, the state legislature passed a law opening up the dump site to accept deposits from thirty-six other states. In 2012, state officials gave final clearance to rules allowing the shipments. Trucks and trains carrying nuclear waste are now heading for Andrews County from other states and the federal government.[7]

In 2018, the investment firm J. F. Lehman and Company bought Waste Control Specialists. But that purchase will have no effect on what the company does, and will not change how it acquired its license to operate.

None of this discussion addresses the public-policy question posed by the possible development of nuclear power. In Chapter 14, we will discuss that conundrum in detail. Here, we are pointing out the ability of wealthy interest groups to influence the political process through the sustained application of campaign contributions.

There is no point in criticizing the integrity of public officials for being willing to accept large amounts of cash from groups and individuals that are pushing a narrow agenda. It is the reality of electoral financing and permissive lobbying laws, not personal dishonesty, that makes politicians overly sensitive to private, as opposed to public, interests.

## Lobbying

**lobby** To try to influence government policy through face-to-face contact.

**lobbyists** A person who attempts to influence government policy through face-to-face contact.

To **lobby** means to attempt to influence policymakers face to face. Everyone has the Constitutional right to try to make an impact on what government does, and it is obvious that a personal talk with a government official has more impact than one anonymous vote. Because of the rules of interest-group formation, however, some groups are much more likely than others to be able to afford to lobby. It is corporations and trade organizations that employ the most **lobbyists**—people whose profession is to try to influence government. Wealthy special interests may have good or bad arguments for their positions, but in either case, they employ the most people to make sure that their arguments are heard.

## Who Are the Lobbyists?

During the 2017 legislative session, there were 1,583 lobbyists registered with the Texas Ethics Commission—almost nine for each of the 181 members of the legislature. Together, these "hired guns" argued on behalf of 6,752 clients.[8] Lobbyists vary as much in their experience and competence as do the legislators they are trying to influence. In 2017, top-flight lobbyists could make as much as $2.6 million per session, according to reporting by *Texas Monthly* magazine.[9]

People do not have to be professionals to exercise their rights to freedom of speech and freedom to petition the government. Concerned citizens who want to express their views to government, especially to the legislature, can do so as individuals or as members of a group. Citizens who are willing to get organized, inform themselves, and spend the time talking to politicians can sometimes have an important impact on policy. But most of the time, on most issues, it is wealthy special interests that have the resources to hire the best lobbyists and thus have the most influence.

Many of the most successful lobbyists are former state legislators or executives. These individuals are able to parlay their knowledge of the governmental process and their friendship with many current officeholders into a personal influence that is rentable.

Not all lobbyists come from the ranks of the people they are hired to persuade, not all serve special economic interests, and not all earn fortunes from their work. Some "public interest" lobbyists serve their conception of the common good and take home a modest salary for their efforts. But the biases in the interest-group system mean that most of the people doing most of the lobbying will be serving narrow, wealthy interests.

## What Lobbyists Do and How They Do It

The best lobbying technique is direct personal contact. Lobbyists try to see as many legislators as possible every day, buying a lunch, chatting for a few minutes, or just shaking a hand. Most lobbyists are able to get on a first-name basis with each legislator they think might be sympathetic to their goals. The speaker of the House and the lieutenant governor are key figures in the legislature, and lobbyists try, above all else, to ingratiate themselves with these two powerful officials.

**Money** The best way to ensure personal access to politicians is to give them money or the equivalent. This money is contributed in a variety of ways. Groups spend some of it entertaining legislators and executives at parties, taking them to lunch, giving them awards, and attracting them to similar events that give lobbyists the chance to cultivate personal relationships and apply the arts of individual persuasion.

Another more direct way in which groups funnel money to politicians is by giving them campaign contributions. Few lobbyists are as brazen as East Texas chicken tycoon Lonnie "Bo" Pilgrim, who, during a fight over a new workers' compensation law in 1989, simply handed out $10,000 checks on the floor of the state senate.[10] But the state capital is thronged at all times, and especially when the legislature is in session, by representatives of interest groups who are eager to use money in a less public manner in the hope that their largesse will be rewarded with favorable laws, rulings, and interpretations.

Not all interest groups are wealthy, and not all use money to try to buy influence. Some that employ lobbyists to represent relatively poor groups rely on persistence, information, and the passion they feel for their cause. They sometimes score important victories. Nevertheless, despite the occasional influence of such general-interest groups, the power of money, day in and day out, to capture the attention of lawmakers makes wealth one of the great resources of politics and ensures that rich interest groups, over the long run, will tend to prevail over poor ones.

The power of money in the interest-group system brings up uncomfortable questions about democracy in Texas. Simply giving money to a politician for personal use is bribery and is illegal. Bribery is a danger to democracy because it substitutes money for public discussion in the making of public policy. When policy is made at the behest of a few rich interests working behind the scenes, then government is **plutocratic** (i.e., government for, although not necessarily by, the wealthy), not democratic. The disturbing fact is that the line between outright bribery (illegal) and renting the attention of public officials with campaign contributions, entertainment, gifts, and speaking fees (legal) is a very thin one. Money talks, and those with more of it speak in louder voices, especially in a state characterized by low legislative salaries and no public campaign finance.

**plutocratic** Adjective describing a government that mainly functions to advance the interests of rich people; as a noun, this would be a "plutocracy."

## Persuading the Public

Although most interest-group energy is expended in lobbying government directly, some organizations also attempt to influence public policy indirectly by "educating" the public. Sometimes they operate by buying television commercial time to argue their public policy case to citizens, who, they hope, will then pressure their representatives to support the groups' agendas. Sometimes they operate by attempting to persuade citizens to vote a certain way on a referendum.

The 2005 legislative sessions were good ones for observing the efforts of interest groups to persuade the public on behalf of their private causes. Especially noteworthy was a public-relations battle between giants SBC and Verizon Communications on one side and cable companies in alliance with Texas cities on another.[11]

Not so long ago, the telephone and television industries were separate entities. Telephones transmitted private conversations over lines owned by the phone company. Television sets received entertainment and news that had been broadcast over the airwaves via large transmitters owned by different corporations. Although both industries were partially regulated

## You Decide: Should Corporate Political Action Committees be Banned?

**A** political action committee (PAC) is an organization that collects voluntary contributions from citizens—generally, those who are affiliated with a particular organization such as a corporation, church, or labor union, or who believe in a particular cause—and distributes them to candidates. Reformers have often called for government to forbid corporations to form PACs. The logic of your decision on PACs would also apply to "527s" and "501(c)(4)," as discussed in the text.

### Pro ✓

⬆ Although "money talks," money is not speech. The First Amendment to the U.S. Constitution should not be interpreted so as to protect the power of money.

⬆ It is bad enough that individuals are able to corrupt the process of government by renting the allegiance of politicians with campaign contributions; it is much worse that corporate interests are able to do so.

⬆ Corporations already possess a great political advantage over ordinary citizens because of their ability to hire lobbyists and buy media advertising; the presence of PACs makes that advantage even more lopsided and unfair.

⬆ The political power of corporations has resulted in public policies that have contributed to the growing inequality of wealth in the United States; in order to permit the reversal of those policies, corporate power must be curtailed.

### Con ✗

⬇ The First Amendment protects individual freedom of expression, and citizens should be able to express themselves by contributing money to candidates or organizations.

⬇ A PAC is merely an organization that permits individuals with a shared interest to coordinate their political activity; shared economic interests are just as worthy of representation as religious, ideological, ethnic, or any other kind of interest.

⬇ The supposed political advantage possessed by corporations is a fiction in the mind of so-called reformers. In fact, corporations are over-taxed and over-regulated. They should have more political influence, not less.

⬇ Growing inequality of wealth has been caused by economic trends that are independent of government policies. Besides, differences in material equality reflect differences in merit, and are therefore good, not bad.

**Competency Connection**
**SOCIAL RESPONSIBILITY**

**Should Corporate Political Action Committees be Banned?**

by government agencies—the Federal Communications Commission in Washington and the Public Utility Commission in Austin—in each case the industry was under the authority of a different set of laws.

With the advent of personal computers in the 1980s, however, the phone business and the television business began to melt into one telecommunications industry. By 2005 most consumers watched television programs that had not been broadcast but had arrived at their homes over coaxial cable, and the cable companies were planning to begin offering telephone services. At the same time, telephone companies, having already merged with computer companies, were planning to get into the video industry, offering phone and television over the Internet. All these plans, however, were often impeded by communications laws that had been written during an earlier era, and all of them brought the two previously distinct industries into conflict.

During the regular and special 2005 legislative sessions two phone titans, SBC and Verizon Communications, attempted to persuade politicians to write a new set of regulations that would help them get into video and thereby compete with cable companies. The existing law ordered a cable company to negotiate franchise agreements with each city it served. The cities, for their part, exacted concessions from the cable companies, requiring them to carry a variety of public-access channels and pay a fee to the city each year. Since the cable companies enjoyed a virtual monopoly in the provision of clear video programming, they could charge high prices for their services. The arrangement was a win-win situation for both the companies and the municipal governments. Verizon and SBC asked the legislature to exempt their Internet video services from the requirement that they negotiate separate deals with each city. These phone companies lobbied legislators to pass a law allowing them to apply for a single statewide franchise that would enable them to pick and choose the cities, or neighborhoods within cities, where they would offer their new services.

The cable companies cried foul and launched their own lobbying effort in alliance with the Texas Municipal League (whose member cities stood to miss out on a fortune in franchise fees if cable lost this battle) to defeat the phone company bill.

The two coalitions also conducted a sustained public-relations campaign, each side trying to convince members of the public that their version of telecommunications policy was in the public interest. At first, cable companies attempted to bar the telephone companies' TV spots attacking them, but soon gave up that fight. The public was treated to an ill-tempered video brawl, with ads accusing the other side of being selfish, mean-spirited, and untruthful, and extolling their own side as being paladins of consumer interests. Meanwhile, various observers and spokespeople wrote op-ed pieces for the newspapers, arguing with their version of relevant arguments and evidence that one choice or the other should be the pick of good citizens in Texas. For a technical issue involving difficult questions of technology, economics, and law, it was a remarkably loud and unavoidable controversy on the state's television screens.

Cable and the cities prevailed in the regular session of the legislature, but in the second special session, the tide turned. Mired in indecision over school finance, legislators managed to pass a telecom bill that handed SBC and Verizon total victory. It is impossible to say whether this outcome was significantly affected by public opinion, was the result of lobbying, or illustrates the triumph of an idea whose time had come.

From the standpoint of democratic theory, the efforts of wealthy special interests to create public support through such public campaigns have both reassuring and troubling aspects. On the one hand, by expending their resources on propaganda aimed at ordinary citizens, interest groups greatly expand the amount of information available to citizens. Many thousands of people who would otherwise not have considered the issue of regulation of telecommunications were moved to think and act by the noisy campaign. Since an informed citizenry is a democratically competent citizenry, such campaigns are worthy additions to public debate. On the other hand, the arguments presented in the ads reflect a private, one-sided viewpoint. The cable and telephone industries could choose to express their positions on television, but no one can afford to buy television time to speak for the general public interest. On balance, such campaigns probably do more good than harm, but it is a close call.

## Influencing Administrators and Co-Opting Agencies

The executive branch of government also is an interest-group target. All laws are subject to interpretation, and most laws allow the administrator substantial leeway in determining not only the intent of the lawmakers but also the very meaning of their words. Interest groups attempt to influence the interpretation of laws that apply to them.

As society has become more complex, each individual has become less and less able to provide for her or his own needs. Where once people grew their own food, most must now buy it from large corporations. How can they be sure that it is pure, honestly labeled, and sold at a fair price? The wave of illness and death that swept the nation in 2006 as a result of the consumption of bagged spinach contaminated with *E. coli* bacteria, the similar problems with peanut butter containing Salmonella in 2009, the epidemic caused by contaminated cantaloupes in 2013, and the five dead and almost two hundred sickened by romaine lettuce in 2018 illustrate the problem of protecting public health in a large, complicated society in which a chain of business activities connect the people who grow food to the people who eat it.

To protect people's interests in those areas in which they cannot protect themselves, administrative agencies, or bureaus, have been created in the executive branch of government. Although many agencies provide public services, many others are regulatory. Their function is to protect the public by regulating various narrow, private interests. The concern here is with the regulatory agencies created to ensure that a particular industry provides good services at fair prices. Unfortunately, the history of these agencies is that, over time, they lose their independent role and become dominated by the interest they were created to control. This transition from guardian of the public interest to defender of private interests—called "**cooptation**"—has several causes.

**cooptation** The process by which industries and their interest groups come to dominate administrative agencies that were originally established to regulate the industry's activities.

First, people who serve on regulatory agencies tend to come from the industry being regulated and return to it after their stint in government is over. This oft-observed activity is called the **revolving door**. The Texas Commission on Environmental Quality (TCEQ), the state agency that is supposed to regulate industry to protect the quality of the air and water, is a good illustration of the revolving door. Four people were employed as executive director of the agency between 1994 and 2009. By 2009 each of them worked, in one way or another, for the industry they used to regulate. John Hall, for example, who had been chair of the Texas Natural Resource Conservation Commission, a TCEQ predecessor, was a lobbyist for utilities, landfill companies, and oil companies.[12] Because they come from the industry they are regulating and know that they may be employed there again after they leave government, regulators tend to share the perspective of that industry, to sympathize with its problems and share its values.

**revolving door** Informal term used by political scientists to describe the process in which government regulatory agencies hire their personnel from within the industry being regulated; after leaving government, former employees are typically hired once more by the regulated industry.

Second, although a serious problem may cause an initial public outcry demanding regulation of a private interest—railroads, meat packers, or insurance companies, for instance—once regulatory legislation is passed, the public tends to lose interest, and the spotlight of publicity moves elsewhere. From that point on, only the regulated industry is intensely interested in the activities of the government agency. Regulators find that representatives of the industry are constantly in front of them in person, bringing information, self-serving arguments, and the force of personality, while there is no one to speak up for the public.

## Interest Groups and the Courts

As with the legislative and executive branches, interest groups are active in the judicial arena of politics. Groups representing important economic interests make substantial contributions during judicial campaigns, hire lawyers to influence judges with legal arguments, and file suits. Money talks in courtrooms, as well as in legislatures and the executive branch.

Nevertheless, courts also can be an avenue of success for non-wealthy interest groups that have been unsuccessful in pressing their cases either through electoral politics or by lobbying the other two branches of government. An outstanding example is the National Association for the Advancement of Colored People (NAACP). Not only has this organization won such profoundly important national cases as *Brown v. Board of Education* (347 U.S. 483, 1954), in which segregated schools were declared unconstitutional, but it also has won vital victories at the state level. In *Nixon* v. *Herndon* (273 U.S. 536, 1927), the U.S. Supreme Court held that a Texas law excluding African Americans from the Democratic primary was unconstitutional. The Texas legislature attempted to nullify this decision by writing a new law authorizing party leaders to make rulings to the same effect, but this was struck down in *Nixon* v. *Condon* (286 U.S. 73, 1932). Later, in *Smith* v. *Allwright* (321 U.S. 649, 1944), the Texas NAACP won still another victory when the Court held that racial segregation in party primaries on any basis whatsoever is unconstitutional. Thus, although groups representing dominant interests may win most of the time, the history of the NAACP in Texas proves that any interest group can sometimes prevail if it organizes and knows how to use the court system.

# Regulation of Interest-Group Activity

It would be a violation of the rights of expression and association, protected by the First and Fourteenth Amendments, for government to *prevent* individual citizens from organizing to influence the political process. However, government has the authority to *regulate* the manner in which citizens attempt to exercise their rights. This distinction is especially apt in regard to the use of money, where the proper freedom to state one's case can easily evolve into an improper attempt to corrupt the system.

Nevertheless, aside from laws of general application regarding such crimes as bribery and conspiracy, Texas makes little attempt to regulate the activities of interest groups except in the area of lobbying. Early attempts at regulation in 1947, 1973, and 1981 were weak and ineffective because no state agencies were empowered to enforce the laws.

In 1991, however, the legislature passed a much-publicized Ethics Bill, which limited the amount of food, gifts, and entertainment lobbyists can furnish legislators and required lobbyists to report the name of each legislator on whom they spend more than $50. Most important, it created an **Ethics Commission** that could hold hearings on complaints of improper behavior, levy fines, and refer violations to the Travis County district attorney for possible prosecution. Texas seemed at last to have a lobbyist regulatory law with teeth.

The 1991 law was less forceful than it appeared, however. It failed to require legislators to disclose sources of their outside income and also neglected to ban the use of campaign contributions for living expenses. A three-quarters majority is required on the Ethics Commission for some important actions, which limits its activities. Finally, while the members of the commission are appointed by the governor, lieutenant governor, speaker of the House, and chief justice of the Texas Supreme Court, those who are chosen must come from a list of candidates furnished by the legislature.

By 2003, pressure was again building for a reform of the state's ethics laws. That legislature passed a new bill which made a variety of changes. Among the amended ethics law's provisions are the following:[13]

1. It requires candidates for public office, whether they win or not, to disclose cash balances in their campaign accounts and report the employer and occupation of larger donors.
2. Legislators who are lawyers now have to disclose when they are being paid to try to delay trials during a legislative session and their referral fees. Also, they are forbidden to represent a paying client in front of a state agency.
3. Candidates must file campaign finance reports via the Internet unless they raise or spend less than $2,000 a year and do not use a computer to keep their records.
4. Local officials in cities of more than 100,000 population and school districts with more than 5,000 students must file personal financial statements like those filed by other state officials.

Information is a useful resource in a democracy, and the 2003 Ethics Bill, because it ensures that more information will be available to the public, is a good thing. Furthermore, the provision that forbids legislators/attorneys to practice before state agencies is genuine reform that will make the outright buying of influence more difficult. The TEC now maintains a Website offering simple language "do's" and "don'ts" to politicians on such subjects as conflicts of interest, bribery, and abuse of office, so that honest Texas politicians can avoid falling into some of the legal pitfalls that accompany the profession of public servant.[14]

**ethics commission**
A Texas government agency created by the 1991 Ethics Bill and charged with the task of enforcing the provisions of that bill.

Nevertheless, the new law does no more than previous "ethics" bills to dilute the impact of private influence on public affairs. The history of campaign finance reform, in Texas and elsewhere, shows that politicians often devise creative ways to circumvent the laws that are supposed to keep their behavior within ethical boundaries. Without public determination to change the very basis of the political exchange of policy for money, wealth will continue to exercise great influence over Texas politics. As long as legislators' salaries remain below the poverty line, as long as private money dominates public elections, and as long as private information is used to make public policy, the prospects for effective control of lobbying are poor.

## Major Interest Groups in Texas

Interest groups want publicity for their programs and goals, but they tend to hide their operations. Political scientists have not done extensive research on interest groups in Texas, and the activities of such groups and the precise nature of their influence are difficult to discover. Nevertheless, we will try to describe some of the major interest groups in the state, explain their general success or weakness, and chart how their influence has changed over time.

### Texans for Lawsuit Reform

Scholars who study interest groups have identified "General Business Organizations" as the most influential types of lobbying groups in state capitols.[15] It is easy to see why business is so powerful: Business is by definition organized, and normally has more resources to put into politics than any other sector of society.

But the effectiveness of business lobbying varies with the situation. Not every business interest gets what it wants every time. Nevertheless, many business interests dominate policy-making much of the time.

A good example of a business group that has been spectacularly successful in Texas since 1994 is Texans for Lawsuit Reform (TLR). The group was formed by business leaders determined to change what they perceived as "Texas' Wild West Litigation Environment" by altering the state's tort laws.[16] Torts are wrongful acts; the loser of a civil lawsuit concerning such an act can be forced to pay an amount of money to compensate a victim and may be required to pay an extra amount as punishment (see the discussion of "tort reform" in Chapter 10). For decades before 1994, Texas businesspeople felt that they were often the victims of "frivolous" lawsuits, abetted by a state judiciary that was too beholden to campaign contributions from attorneys. In 1993 several business leaders founded TLR to try to wrench the policy process away from the lawyers.

TLR proceeded along two paths. First, it forged alliances with other groups attempting to make it harder to file and win tort lawsuits in the state, most notably the Texas Medical Association. Second, it used its deep pockets to earn the gratitude of lawmakers in the state, most of them Republican. According to followthemoney.org, a group that keeps track of contributions in state campaigns, from 1994 to 2018 TLR contributed more than $38 million to Texas politicians, 86% to Republicans. More than two-thirds of the candidates who received TLR money won their elections. TLR is an important reason that Republicans now control both houses of the state legislature, and members of the party are well aware of it.[17]

In 1994, George W. Bush ran for governor partly on a platform stressing tort reform. A law passed the 1995 legislature, but because the institution was then dominated by Democrats, it was a much-compromised, milder version of the bill than partisans of TLR hoped to see. In the intervening years, TLR kept spreading the campaign money to Republican candidates, and by 2003, with that party's accession to majority status in both houses of the legislature as well as the state house, its moment had arrived. The 2003 legislature gave the TLR about everything it wanted. As of 2003, it became much harder to sue anybody for anything in Texas.

Ben Sargent laments the fact that interest groups with many resources, especially those representing business, have disproportionate influence over politicians.

Courtesy of Ben Sargent

Competency Connection
**SOCIAL RESPONSIBILITY**

Do you think that money is too influential in Texas politics?

"Texas will be a better place to live," stated TLR president Richard Trabuisi Jr. triumphantly, "to raise a family, and work for a living once this historic legislation goes into effect."[18] Indeed, in 2006 the TLR bragged on its Website that a report from the Pacific Research Institute (which, on its own Website identifies itself as a "free market think tank") had ranked Texas "best in the nation" on its "U.S. Tort Liability Index."[19]

But, even after having achieved its goals, TLR was not finished. In 2018, Lee Parsley, TLR's general counsel, congratulated his organization for having persuaded the 2017 legislature to pass a law making it harder for "storm-chasing lawyers" to sue insurance companies in the wake of Hurricane Harvey.[20]

Others, of course, had contrary opinions about the value of the changes wrought by Parsley's organization. Nevertheless, as of 2018, Texans for Lawsuit Reform was king of the mountain among interest groups.

## Doctors

Sitting on the top of that mountain of influence with business is the Texas Medical Association (TMA).[21] Founded in 1853, the state's major doctors' interest group paid scant attention to state politics for most of its history. Its attitude changed in 1987 when, in the first battle of a fifteen-year war, it attempted to persuade the legislature to put a cap on damage awards in medical malpractice cases. Because such a limit would have cut into the income of plaintiffs' attorneys, it was opposed by the Texas Trial Lawyers Association (TTLA). With ten times the membership of the TTLA (38,000), the TMA was nevertheless soundly whipped in legislative infighting. Doctors then decided to pay more attention to politics.

The TMA turned its attention to acquiring political influence with great intelligence. Like Texans for Lawsuit Reform, it contributes large amounts of money to legislative and judicial candidates. It gave more than $5 million in Texas elections from 2003 to 2012, 69 percent to Republicans. Furthermore, TMA suggests to doctors that they lobby their patients on bills the TMA deems important. Its Web site offers physicians supplies of political posters, lapel stickers, and cards to pass out to "staff, patients, family and friends." It allies itself with other interest groups, joining forces with business tort reformers and even cooperating with its traditional rival, the Texas Trial Lawyers Association, on some lobbying efforts when the interests of doctors and lawyers ran parallel in 2001. Most important, it jumped on the bandwagon of history, allying itself with the Republican Party just as the GOP was poised to take over Texas politics.

As a result, the TMA is now one of the most effective political interest groups in the Lone Star State. According to the association's figures, it has succeeded in passing as much as 90 percent of the legislative agenda items it has sponsored. Most importantly, in the momentous 2003 legislative session, its alliance with Texans for Lawsuit Reform resulted in the TMA routing the opposition of the Texas Trial Lawyers Association, and obtaining legislation that severely limited malpractice lawsuits within the state. (We will discuss these large changes under the subheading "Tort Reform" in Chapter 10).

The TMA has not always been perfect in its political choices, however. After the 2001 legislature, when Governor Perry vetoed a bill requiring HMOs to pay medical claims promptly, doctors were furious. In retaliation, the group endorsed Democratic gubernatorial candidate Tony Sanchez in 2002. Perry's big victory in that election introduced considerable awkwardness between the governor and the association, and the TMA had to mend fences. It fired its chief political strategist and began giving even more money to Texas politicians, especially the governor. These efforts were successful. When Governor Perry staged a public signing of a new "prompt-pay bill" in June 2003, he was flanked in front of the news cameras by the TMA's board of directors. Perry made it clear he wanted bygones to be bygones. "Whether it's doctors or hospital administrators or any of a host of other individuals who are involved in the delivery of health care in Texas, we are very much open to bringing them back into the tent, so to speak," said the governor. Perry has never mentioned publicly the $174,926 that the TMA contributed to his campaign war chest from 2004 to 2010.

By 2008 the TMA was celebrating the five-year anniversary of the tort reforms, reporting, based on a survey of its members, that "the reforms have worked. Texans now have more doctors available to take care of them, especially the sickest and most badly injured patients," proving that Texas had "reined in the epidemic of lawsuit abuse."[22]

And so the Texas Medical Association, having strayed from the majority party coalition, has now bought its way back in. Having won its war with the Texas Trial Lawyers Association, the TMA, at present, concentrates its lobbying efforts on dealing with more technical problems. During the 2017 session of the legislature, for example, it obtained a law legally authorizing "telemedicine"—in which a doctor writes a prescription for a patient after examining him or her over the Internet (Skype), rather than in person.

## The Christian Right

In the late 1970s, a number of national organizations arose, calling for a return to "Christian values," as they defined them, in American government and in society.[23] The groups' purposes were to inform religious, politically conservative voters of a candidate's positions on certain issues and to persuade them to participate more actively in local politics. By the 1990s, these groups were a formidable presence at virtually every level of American politics. They have been especially important in the South.

Although Christian Right groups do not all place the same emphasis on each individual issue, they share a cluster of strongly conservative positions on important political issues. As Steve Hotze, one of Lt. Governor Dan Patrick's political allies, writes in his Website, "Christians need to rise up and join the cultural battle for the soul of Texas and America that is being waged fiercely against us by the godless, Marxist, Communist Alt-Left that wants to destroy any vestige of Biblical principles, Christian conservative values, and Constitutional First Amendment religious liberty and free speech rights from our society."[24]

Members of the Christian Right understand "a biblical worldview" to require them to be pro-life on the abortion issue, to oppose homosexual marriage, to fight against tax policies they view as subversive to families, to support school vouchers allowing public money to fund private schools, and to endorse a Constitutional amendment that would permit organized prayers in public schools.

During the 1990s, the Christian Right made a vivid impact on Texas politics and society. Whereas the influence of such interest groups as Texans for Lawsuit Reform rests on their ability to provide large quantities of money to campaigns, the influence of the Christian Right rests on its ability to strongly influence the voting decisions of millions of citizens and to mobilize thousands of activists to capture control of political organizations at the grassroots. Members of the Christian Right are concerned citizens in the best sense, organizing to pursue the public interest as they understand it.

The most dramatic flexing of the Texas Christian Right's muscles occurred in its capturing of the state Republican Party machinery in 1994 and its domination of the GOP's conventions through 2018. These events are discussed in detail in the next chapter.

The Republican coalition between business conservatives and Christian Rightists is sometimes an uneasy one, however. In the box "Republican Group Versus Republican Group," we detail the disagreements between the two groups in the State Board of Education. But in the legislature, also, the Christian Right and business conservatives sometimes clash.

A serious battle between the two wings of the party erupted in 2017, when Lieutenant Governor Dan Patrick, who describes himself as "a Christian first, conservative second, and Republican third,"[25] pushed the state senate hard to pass the so-called "bathroom bill," which would have required that people who identify with a sex other than the one created by their genetic identity must follow their genes, not their emotional reality, when using public toilets. Joe Straus, speaker of the Texas House of Representatives, and an "economic conservative" rather than a Christian Rightist, opposed the bill because he thought it would discourage businesses from locating in Texas. Without the support of the House, the bill did not pass.

Christian Rightists were furious with Straus. The outrage was so intense that Straus evidently calculated that he could no longer be an effective leader. Four months after the end of the legislative session, he announced that he would not seek re-election in 2018, which meant, of course, that he would also no longer be House speaker. To add to the issue, in January, 2018, the Texas State Republican Executive Committee voted to censure him for not being conservative enough.[26]

Although the "bathroom bill" made the most noise during 2017, the cause that Christian Rightists have embraced the longest, with the most fervor, is their intention to outlaw abortions. Because this issue does not, like evolution and gay rights, spur opposition from the business wing of the Republican Party, bills to limit the constitutional right of women to terminate their pregnancies tend to enjoy smooth sailing in the legislature. (On this point, see our discussion of the issue of abortion in Chapter 10).

The legislative session of 2017 saw a spate of anti-abortion bills passed, then signed by the governor. The most significant was a "fetal burial law," which required that health centers, including abortion clinics, bury aborted fetuses rather than disposing of them as is done with other tissue removed during medical procedures, through cremation. Like many other laws passed in Texas under the sponsorship of the Christian Right, this one was intended to make the act of having an abortion more expensive and emotionally burdensome for pregnant woman, thus discouraging them from going through with the procedure. And, as with several other such laws passed by the state legislature, this one was challenged in court by abortion providers, and tossed out by a federal judge.[27] The Christian Rightists, however, will keep trying.

## ISSUE SPOTLIGHT:
## Republican Group versus Republican Group

E ven though parties try to put together various groups to appeal to both voters and rich contributors, the coalitions they build are often uneasy and tension-filled. The tensions between the two most important interest groups in the Texas Republican coalition—the Christian Right (a source of voting support) and business (a source of financial support)—has long been on display in the State Board of Education, the agency responsible for setting curriculum standards for the public schools.

On the one hand, Christian Right activists tend to believe that God created humans fully-formed in six days less than ten thousand years ago. They thus reject the scientific theory of evolution, according to which human beings developed as part of the history of all life over about 3.8 billion years. As a result, they would like to replace the teaching of evolution in public-school biology classes with a "creationist" account, or at least teach both the scientific and the creationist story together.

On the other hand, business leaders tend to want to ensure that Texas students are scientifically literate, and thus ready to take their places in a modern economy. Most business leaders insist that science, and only science, should be taught in public-school science classes.

Republicans have held an easy majority on the fifteen-member state Board of Education since the early 1990s. In the late years of the first decade of the twenty-first century, creationist Republicans occupied seven seats. One creationist member, Chairman Don McLeroy, became nationally famous for his forthright style of expression ("Evolution is hooey!"). Yet a coalition of moderate Republicans and Democrats, maintaining an improbable majority of one, kept voting down creationist-inspired curriculum proposals.

After a while, business-oriented Republican contributors became tired of the series of near-misses with creationism. They recruited business-oriented, pro-evolution candidates to run against creationists in the 2010 Republican primary. This threat of a well-financed opponent persuaded one social conservative board member not to run for re-election. Don McLeroy, however, did run, and was defeated by his economic conservative opponent in the Republican primary.

Sources: Mariah Blake, "Revisionaries: How a Group of Conservatives is Rewriting Your Kids," *Washington Monthly*, Website accessed July 2, 2013; for an example of a McLeroy rant on YouTube, go to the site and insert "Don McLeroy on Stephen Jay Gould" into the search engine; "Texas State Board of Education Primary Delivers Upset," March 2, 2010, *Daily Kos* Website; Editorial, "Elect the Capable, Shun Ideologues," *Austin American-Statesman*, October 24, 2012, A10.

Competency Connection
**SOCIAL RESPONSIBILITY**

If it were up to you, would you teach only science in biology classes, or would you respect the wishes of many Texas parents by allowing creationist ideas to be added to the curriculum?

Since the future promises to supply many examples of the issues that galvanize its members, and since the Republican party is unlikely to lose its dominant position in state politics any time soon, the Christian Right is certain to be active in state politics for many years to come.

## Organized Labor

Many Texans think of organized labor, and its major organization, the American Federation of Labor and the Congress of Industrial Organizations (AFL-CIO) as a powerful interest group that has great influence on state policy, but there is little evidence to support this assumption. The primary explanation for this lack of power is cultural. As discussed in Chapter 1, the conservative political culture that dominates most of the southern states is hostile to labor unions. Texas is no exception. In 2017, 10.7 percent of the total national "wage and salary" work force was enrolled in labor unions, but only 5.8 percent of the Texas work force. Texas had only about one-fourth the unionized rate of New York.[28] This anti-union environment is undoubtedly one of the reasons that Texas is considered a state that is friendly to business.

Politically, unions have traditionally allied themselves with the Democratic Party nationally and with the liberal wing of that party within the state. (Although, in 2018, the AFL-CIO's political organization refused to endorse two Democratic legislative candidates who had been involved in an anti-labor lawsuit).[29] But the relative weakness of liberals in Texas has meant that labor unions are even less powerful than their membership figures would suggest. Their weakness is reflected in the relatively anti-labor nature of Texas's laws. Workers' compensation insurance, unemployment insurance payments, and other benefits are lower than those of most other industrial states, and the laws regarding unions are restrictive rather than supportive. Unions are forced to make public disclosure of virtually all their major activities. This requirement is not, of course, imposed on corporations. There are prohibitions against secondary boycotts, check-off systems for union dues, and mass picketing and other such activities, and the "right-to-work" law prohibits the closed shop and the union shop.[30]

Organized labor would like nothing better than to get rid of this array of restrictions, but it lacks the political power to do so. Although the state AFL-CIO political action committee puts money into political races, the rise of the traditionally pro-management, anti-labor Republican Party to power has given the workers' organization a set of discouraging alternatives: It can continue to give money to Democrats, who lose continuously, or it can give money to Republicans, who will, once elected, vote against its interests anyway.

The year 2003 was a good one in which to observe the futility of labor's political efforts in Texas. The AFL-CIO put its energies into three political causes. It tried to dissuade the legislature from passing a bill that would increase the governor's power and reorganize much of the state bureaucracy. It opposed the drawing of new redistricting maps that would favor Republican candidates for the U.S. House of Representatives (see Chapter 6). And it joined in a coalition with lawyers in attempting to persuade voters to defeat Proposition 12, which ratified the new Republican tort reforms championed by Texans for Lawsuit Reform and the Texas Medical Association. Its defeat in each campaign simply underscored its ongoing irrelevance to the state's politics.

Nationally, organized labor's fortunes wax and wane, depending on which party is dominant in Washington. When Democrats won a majority in Congress in 2006, and then the White House in 2008, the AFL-CIO's lobbyists enjoyed access to power, and a favorable hearing before legislators. When Republicans won back Congress in 2010, and then the White House in 2016, labor's effectiveness went into eclipse. Indeed, in 2018, Republican President Donald Trump specifically criticized the president of the national AFL-CIO in a tweet, suggesting that, with such incompetent leadership, ". . . it is easy to see why unions are doing so poorly."[31] The Democratic Party's capture of the U.S. House of Representatives in the November 2018 election was probably good news for organized labor, but the Republican Party's retention of its majority in the U.S. Senate rendered the relevance of the change ambiguous.

# ISSUE SPOTLIGHT:
## Sex, Power, and Money

There was a time within living memory when there were no women in the Texas legislature (see Chapter 6) and the only woman who had served as governor—Meriam "Ma" Ferguson, during the 1920s and 1930s (see Chapter 7)—was not taken seriously. That era is gone. Ann Richards, who occupied the governor's mansion from 1991 to 1995, was taken seriously by everyone, women now routinely serve in statewide offices and the legislature, and co-author Texas government textbooks.

Many liberal female activists, however, believe that their sex is still not fairly represented within the state's political establishment, and they believe they know why. It takes money to be elected, and women do not generally have access to the serious financing that is needed to make a political career successful. Thus, Annie's List was created.

Founded in 2003 and named for Annie Webb Blanton, the first woman to win a statewide office in Texas, as the Superintendent of Instruction in 1918, Annie's List is an interest group that both raises money, through its PAC, for female candidates who are pro-choice on the abortion issue, and recruits and trains women to run for office. (Its most famous protégé is Senator Wendy Davis of Fort Worth, the Democratic nominee for governor in 2014). Although the PAC does not make fine discriminations about the ideology of the candidates to whom it contributes, the fact that they are all pro-choice tends to give those who receive its money a liberal cast. "Ultimately," explained Bree Buchanan, its former executive director, "electing more women is a means to an end. What we really want is to promote a progressive agenda."

In its short life, the organization has proven itself to be a serious participant in Texas politics. In its early years, female Democrats backed by Annie's List were able to capture several Republican seats in the state legislature. As Democrats have been less successful in recent state elections, however, so have Annie's List–favored candidates.

Nevertheless, if Democrats ever create a new era in Texas politics, Annie's List will be one of the interest groups that will have helped to make it happen.

Sources: Luisita Lopez Torregrosa, "After Filibuster, a Star Rises in Texas," *New York Times*, July 23, 2013; *Texas Tribune* compilation of campaign finance data, www.texastribune.org/library/data/campaign-finance/filer/00053715-annies-list/; Bob Moser, "Bye-Bye Boys' Club," *Texas Observer*, January 23, 2009, 10; Annie's List Website, www.annieslist.com/.

**Competency Connection**
**SOCIAL RESPONSIBILITY**
Do you think that Texas government would or would not be improved if more female candidates were elected? Or do you think that it does not matter?

In Texas, however, because Republicans remain in control of the state's political machinery, there is no fluctuation in labor's political power. Labor has no power. If such organized efforts as those by labor unions and Annie's List (see box) every result in a Democratic takeover of the legislature and/or governor's office in Texas, labor will once again become influential. Until and unless such a day arrives, however, organized labor can only anticipate continuing futility.

## League of United Latin American Citizens

The most venerable of the Hispanic organizations, the League of United Latin American Citizens (LULAC) was formed in Corpus Christi in 1929.[32] Its founding members were much concerned about discrimination against Mexican Americans, especially in public education. In its first three decades, LULAC pursued the goal of equal education as both a private charitable organization and a public crusader. Privately, LULAC formed local self-help organizations to advance Latino education. Its "Little School of the 400" program of the 1950s, for example, which taught Spanish-speaking preschoolers the 400 English words they needed to know in order to survive in first grade in public schools, was so successful that it inspired the national program Head Start. Publicly, the organization persuaded the U.S. Supreme Court to forbid Texas to segregate Mexican Americans in public schools in 1948. Branching out to other issues, in 1953, LULAC won another suit against Texas's practice of excluding Mexican Americans from juries. Then, in 1959, it persuaded the state legislature to sponsor its program to teach Latino preschoolers English. Soon the Texas Education Agency was paying up to 80 percent of the program's funding. LULAC may have represented a struggling minority, but it had become part of the state's political establishment; it was a success.

Into the 1970s, LULAC continued to be the standard bearer for Mexican American aspirations for full citizenship in the United States in general and Texas in particular. But in that decade, it began to falter. As an organization dispensing millions of dollars in foundation grants, it attracted members who were more interested in advancing themselves than in advancing their ethnic group. Beginning in the mid-1970s, LULAC was rocked by a series of financial scandals. It was also racked by internal power struggles. Individuals and different Latino groups fought each other—Mexican Americans versus Puerto Ricans, for example—so that the organization no longer seemed to be a league of *united* Latin American citizens.

The cumulative effect of LULAC's troubles had a devastating effect on its prestige and membership. Once capable of mobilizing a quarter of a million citizens nationally, by the late 1990s, the organization could count on no more than 50,000 active members. Younger, better-run organizations such as La Raza and the Mexican-American Legal Defense Fund (MALDEF— created by LULAC itself in 1968) seemed to be on the verge of taking over the mantle of most respected Hispanic organization.

But LULAC was a resilient organization. Even while the leadership was faltering, the grassroots activists who worked in its local chapters always comprised a reservoir of good citizenship, available for mobilization. During the late 1990s and early 2000s, several honest and competent presidents put the organization's finances in order and then expanded and reorganized its staff.

Just as important, LULAC's leadership has been engaging in creative political activity. In its early decades, the organization avoided cooperation, or even communication, with African American organizations such as the NAACP. According to historian Neil Foley, LULAC's leaders refused to speak out publicly in favor of African American civil rights, believing that such activity would damage their own cause.[33]

But as the new millennium dawned, its leaders came to see this attitude as self-destructive. They began to forge a political alliance with the NAACP. In July 2002, LULAC's president, Hector Flores, addressed the NAACP's national convention, the first time a person in his position had given a speech to that organization. His remarks cemented an agreement of cooperation that had been working for a year, featuring a joint and bilingual voter mobilization project.

LULAC also expanded its area of activity to include lobbying in the nation's capital. After the Democrats regained majorities in both houses of Congress during the 2006 elections, the organization's influence broadened. During the maneuvering that accompanied Congress' consideration of the Comprehensive Immigration Reform Act of 2007, LULAC's representatives exercised "virtual veto power," according to one press report. Latinos objected to the bill's guest worker program, believing that it would create a group of underclass workers without benefits. In alliance with other Hispanic organizations, and various politicians from across the political spectrum, LULAC was able to block consideration of the legislation in the U.S. Senate. It never came to a vote.[34]

In Texas, however, the widespread perception that Latinos are mostly Democrats has led to conflict between the ruling Republican leadership and all the Hispanic organizations. Republican efforts to gerrymander U.S. Congressional district lines after the 2010 Census were viewed by LULAC as being an effort to dilute the impact of the Hispanic vote (see Chapter 6). Similarly, a Republican-passed state law to require photo identification at the polls on election day was interpreted as a measure to suppress the vote of minorities (see Chapter 5).[35]

Hopelessly outgunned within Texas' political system, LULAC's strategy to fight these Republican measures has been to appeal to the federal government, especially the courts, for help. It has filed numerous lawsuits against Congressional districts drawn by the legislature between 2011 and 2018. Nine times, federal courts have ruled that the district lines are gerrymanders, intended to discriminate against minority voters. The Republican establishment continues to fight the rulings, and the legal battles go on. Whether LULAC and the NAACP will ultimately win equal representation for their constituents cannot be predicted at this writing.[36]

By reaching out to other politically progressive groups, therefore, LULAC, once a more-or-less nonpartisan organization, has adopted a Democratic identity. But that partisan tilt has not gone smoothly. In 2018, in an effort to position his organization as willing to work with politicians on both sides of the party divide, LULAC president Roger Rocha sent a letter to Republican President Donald Trump, endorsing his administration's proposed immigration plan. This proposed policy would provide a pathway to citizenship for 1.8 million youths who were brought, illegally, to this country by their parents, in exchange for Democratic support for the allocation of $25 billion for construction of a wall along the border between the United States and Mexico.

Rocha's letter caused an explosion of opposition within the Latino community in general, and LULAC in particular. In a typical reaction, Montserrat Garibay, a long-time LULAC member, complained that "It's disgraceful that the president of LULAC puts his personal agenda before the families that LULAC represents." A social-media petition using the hashtag #Fuera Rocha (Fire Rocha) was attracting signatures. Within a few days, Rocha had rescinded his letter, but the calls for his resignation continued.[37] (He declined to resign, but chose not to run for re-election during LULAC's national convention in July 2018. He was replaced by Domingo Garcia, who had been harshly critical of Rocha's letter to Trump).

In the heated, politically polarized atmosphere of American and Texas politics in the 21st century, LULAC leaders and members are thus attempting to find their way to success, and finding the path bumpy. Whether the organization will hold to its historically nonpartisan strategy of persuasion, or keep along its newer, more militant and partisan direction, is a question that cannot be answered now. The future of LULAC contains both dangers and opportunities.

## Teachers

In a 2016 ranking of the fifty most successful interest groups in the fifty states, political scientists judged teachers to be the second most influential, after business.[38] Teachers do not, like business, possess the resource of wealth, for nowhere are they very well paid. Instead, teachers resemble the Christian Right in illustrating the power that can come from use of another resource: organization. In some states, a high percentage of public school teachers belong to a union or some other advocacy organization, and many belong to several. Teachers can usually be counted on to march, rally, write letters, contribute to political action committees, and vote in an informed manner. It is because they are such good citizens, willing to put in the time and trouble to act together, that teachers are generally so effective in advancing their interests.

In Texas, however, the effectiveness of teacher participation is diluted by a number of cultural and political difficulties. The traditionalistic political culture that has been so important in Texas history has never been particularly friendly to public education, and the state generally does not place in the higher ranks of educational funding. In 2017, for example, it stood thirty-fifth among the states in spending per pupil, and right in the middle—twenty-fifth—in average teacher salary.[39]

Politically, Texas's teachers are marked more by disorganization and competition than by coordination and cooperation. Like Texas's other white-collar workers, many of the state's teachers resist unionization, and many belong to no professional organization. As Table 3-1 illustrates, the membership of the two largest organizations declined noticeably in the period from 2000 to 2018. Those teachers who are members of organizations are divided among seven statewide and dozens of local groups, all fiercely competitive and sometimes recommending different strategies to their members (see the table for a summary of the differing approaches of Texas's four largest teacher organizations).

Moreover, teachers share with organized labor the current disadvantage of being members of the Democratic Party coalition. This problem does not arise only from a mistake in coalition building. A high percentage of teachers are ideologically liberal (see Chapter 4). They have become a favorite rhetorical target of conservatives, who love to blame teachers for the poor quality of some American schools, and blame teachers' unions for opposing some of the conservatives' favorite proposed reforms, especially school vouchers.

In a voucher system, instead of the state establishing and financing public schools, state money—indirectly, in the form of a voucher—would go to parents. The parents could then choose

| TABLE 3-1 | **Comparison of Four Largest Texas Teacher Organizations, 2000 and 2018** |
|---|---|

**TSTA:** Texas State Teachers Association (Affiliated with National Education Association)

**TAFT:** Texas American Federation of Teachers (Affiliated with AFL-CIO)

**TCTA:** Texas Classroom Teachers Association

**ATPE:** Association of Texas Professional Educators

| | TSTA | TAFT | TCTA | ATPE |
|---|---|---|---|---|
| Founded | 1880 | 1974 | 1927 | 1980 |
| Membership, 2018 | 68,000 | 65,000 | 50,000 | 100,000 |
| Membership, 2000 | 80,000 | 85,000 | 40,000 | 110,000 |
| Endorses candidates? | Yes | Yes* | Yes* | No |
| Supports pay raises? | Yes | Yes | Yes | Yes |
| Supports collective bargaining? | Yes | Yes | No | No |
| Supports publicly funded vouchers for private schools? | No | No | No | No |
| Lobbies legislature? | Yes | Yes | Yes | Yes |

*Indirectly, through a political action committee.

SOURCES: Compiled by David Prindle in August 2000 and September 2018, from organization Websites and interviews with organization officers.

among all possible schools to which to send their children, paying with the vouchers. Parents would not be forced to enroll their children in the local public school. Economic conservatives like the idea of such a system because it would mean that schools would be forced to compete with each other for students, making public education much more of a "free market" than it is now. Social conservatives like the idea because it would mean that many parents could send their children to schools with much more of a religious orientation than is available in today's public schools.

Teachers, however, detest the idea of vouchers, partly because it would give school administrators the power to lower their salaries and remove the job-protection guarantees that are available in the public education system. Many teachers also worry that the religiously oriented schools that would prosper under a voucher system might well get away with teaching supernatural creation myths, rather than scientific theories and evidence, in their biology classes.[40]

The teachers' organizations are, therefore, fundamentally at odds with the state's current power structure. As Mary Ann Whiteker, president of the Texas Association of Mid-Size Schools, remarked to a reporter in 2005, "The difficult thing is not to take this personally. You just walk through the Capitol thinking, 'Why do they hate me so much?'"[41] Therefore, when teachers' lobbyists attempt to persuade Texas legislators to back their policy proposals, they tend to get a mixed reception. They start from a position of weakness but can manage to make some headway by using information intelligently and by reminding politicians, however tacitly, that teachers are knowledgeable voters. As a result of this combination of political opposites—weak ideological position but strong organizational position—the teachers' organizations tend to be more successful with the legislature than might be expected, given typical Republican rhetoric.

All the legislative sessions from 2013 to 2017 were good ones to illustrate the sorts of political forces threatening teachers, and the way they have managed to score partial victories in a difficult environment.[42] Typically, in each session, Republicans in the senate would submit various bills, each of which would, if passed, directly or indirectly create a statewide school-voucher system. In each session, the senate, which is more responsive to urban areas, would pass one or more bills. And in each session, in the House, a coalition of Republicans representing rural areas, which fear that a state system of vouchers would devastate their public schools without creating a good substitute, plus all Democrats, would defeat the plan. Thus, for teachers, every recent session has been like a spy thriller novel, with disaster looming overhead, but featuring a hair's-breadth escape just before the end.

As long as teachers' basic professional and ideological positions do not change, and as long as Republicans dominate state politics, every legislative session will be much like those of 2013–2017. Each session will bring a spate of potential laws that threaten the very existence of public-school teachers. Each session, they will organize, lobby, appeal to the media, and work behind the scenes with politicians who are more sympathetic in their private actions than they are in their public rhetoric. Each session, they will defeat some attacks, mitigate some others, and lose some painful battles. The political life of Texas teachers will continue to be dangerous and painful, but never quite defeated.

## Summary

**LO 3.1** **Interest groups create a dilemma for democracy, but government cannot resolve the dilemma by outlawing such groups.** Because the First Amendment to the U.S. Constitution protects people's right to organize and communicate their wishes to government, the political process is full of individuals and groups who are trying to influence public policy from advancement of the public good to advancement to their private advantage. Thus, this chapter has dealt with a major them of this textbook—private influence over public policy.

**LO 3.2** **Interest groups—people organizing themselves to try to influence government—can be divided into some important classes, and perform several functions in a democratic society.** Some groups attempt to forward their vision of the public interest, and thereby add to the vitality of democracy. But even groups that seek to advance private interests add to democracy by providing information to officials, their members, and their fellow citizens, and by organizing people to engage in the peaceful conflict of democratic governance.

**LO 3.3** **There are biases in the formation of interest groups, and consequences of those biases, in terms of who is more and who is less likely to be organized.** Because they are more likely to be organized, producers tend to exert more political influence than consumers, the middle and upper classes more influence than the working classes, and passionate believers more influence than citizens who are less emotionally involved.

**LO 3.4** **The typical activities of interest groups can create a problem for democracy.** The two major resources possessed by interest groups are information and money. Because wealthier groups usually have more influence than poorer groups, the interest-group system seems to create an inequality of citizenship that contradicts the ideal of equal rights for everyone.

**LO 3.5** **Efforts to regulate the activities of interest groups have not been very successful.** Groups have managed to evade many of the statutes enacted at both the federal and state levels to try to control the amounts of money that groups and individuals use to influence politicians. In addition, they use their lobbying clout to prevent stronger regulatory laws from being passed.

**LO 3.6** **Turning from the general to the specific, the chapter concludes with an examination of a half-dozen of the major interest groups in Texas and an explanation as to why some of them are more, or less, influential in state politics, and why some have increased or decreased in influence over the past three decades.** Those groups that have affiliated themselves with the Republican Party, such as Texans for Lawsuit Reform, have grown in influence, whereas those that are affiliated with he Democratic party, such as teachers and organized labor, have fared poorly.

## Critical Thinking

1. Why do some people who believe in democracy have mixed feelings about the interest group system?

2. If you wanted to influence your state government in terms of some policy area, what would be the three most effective actions you could take?

This urban wired Latina executive and Anglo cowboy in rural Texas symbolize the vast differences in lifestyles that political parties must try to bridge.

(Top) Terry Vine/Blend Images/Corbis
(Bottom) Courtesy of Texas Department of Transportation

# Political Parties

4

**B**oth Schattschneider's favorable assessment of **political parties** and the anonymous cynical disparagement of their value are justified. Parties are, indeed, the only organizations capable of holding together many fractious interests so that governing is possible. At the same time, in Texas and elsewhere, parties frequently serve democracy badly.

This chapter opens with an examination of the major functions of political parties. It proceeds to a discussion of ideology and interests, the two bases for much party conflict. It then gives a brief history of the state's political parties, and an outline of party organization in Texas. The "four-faction system" that has recently emerged, and which can make the Texas two-party system confusing, is then explained,

## Learning Objectives

**LO4.1**  List the functions that political parties perform in a democracy.

**LO4.2**  Understand liberal and conservative political ideologies, and identify which ideology has been dominant, historically, in Texas.

**LO4.3**  Discuss the nature of political socialization in Texas, and the reasons why some Texans are exceptions to the general rules of socialization.

**LO4.4**  Identify which interests typically support which parties, and why.

**LO4.5**  Describe the historical process by which Texas has come to have two parties with at least three, and possibly four ideological factions, and explain why the two major parties are sometimes supplemented by third parties or independent candidates.

**LO4.6**  Describe party organization in Texas, and explain why organization is not as important as it might first appear.

**LO4.7**  Discuss the "three-faction" system, and speculate on its future development.

**LO4.8**  Briefly recount the history of third parties in Texas.

THE POLITICAL PARTIES CREATED DEMOCRACY AND MODERN DEMOCRACY IS UNTHINKABLE SAVE IN TERMS OF THE PARTIES. . .THE PARTIES ARE NOT THEREFORE MERELY APPENDAGES OF MODERN GOVERNMENT; THEY ARE THE CENTER OF IT AND PLAY A DETERMINATIVE AND CREATIVE ROLE IN IT.

E. E. Schattschneider,
*Party Government, 1942*

A POLITICAL PARTY IS AN ORGANIZATION THAT TAKES MONEY FROM THE RICH AND VOTES FROM THE POOR UNDER THE PRETEXT OF PROTECTING ONE FROM THE OTHER.

*Anonymous*

**political party** An organization devoted to winning public office in elections, and thus exercising control over public policy.

followed by a discussion of the state's occasional third-party efforts. At several points, the reality of Texas's party politics is contrasted with the democratic ideal.

## Functions of Political Parties

From the perspective of activists and candidates, the basic purpose of parties is to win elections and thus gain the opportunity to exercise control over public policy. While pursuing this goal, however, they often fulfill several functions that make them valuable institutions from the perspective of democratic theory. These functions include the following:

▶ Involving ordinary people in the political process, especially persuading them to vote and teaching them the formal and informal "rules of the game."
▶ Recruiting political leaders and persuading them to restrain their individual ambitions so that the party can achieve its collective purposes.
▶ Communicating to the leaders the interests of individuals and groups.
▶ Adding factual information and persuasive argument to the public discussion of policy alternatives.
▶ Structuring the nature of political conflict and debate, including screening out the demands of certain people and groups (usually fringe individuals or groups of very small minorities.)
▶ Moderating differences between groups, both within the party and in the larger society.
▶ Partially overcoming the fragmented nature of the political system so that gridlock can be overcome and coherent policy made and implemented.

Political parties in any democracy can be judged according to how well or badly they perform these functions. How do Texas parties measure up? We will address this question as the chapter proceeds.

## Ideology

**ideology** A system of beliefs and values about the nature of the good life and the good society, and the part to be played by government in achieving them.

In Texas as elsewhere, party rivalry is often based on differences in ideology. **Ideology** is a system of beliefs and values about the nature of the good life and the good society, about the relationship of government and the economy, about moral values and the way they should be achieved, and about how government is to conduct itself. The two dominant, and contesting, systems of beliefs and values in American and Texas life today are usually referred to as "liberalism" and "conservatism."

## Conservatism

**conservatism** A political ideology that, in general, opposes government regulation of economic life and supports government regulation of personal life.

**pseudo laissez faire** A French phrase referring to the tendency of entrepreneurs to oppose government involvement in the economy at the philosophical level, but to seek government assistance for their particular business.

The basic principle underlying **conservatism**, at least in economic policy, is "laissez faire"—or, to loosely translate from the French phrase, "leave it alone." In theory, conservatives prefer to allow free markets, not government, to regulate the economy. In practice, conservative governments often pursue **pseudo laissez faire** in that they claim to cherish free markets but actually endorse policies that deeply involve government in helping business to overcome problems in the marketplace. The $700 billion "Wall Street bailout" in 2008 sponsored by the Republican Bush administration (and eventually passed by a Democratic Congress) is a vivid example of the way that supposedly conservative politicians sometimes abandon laissez faire in the face of economic difficulties. Nevertheless, at the level of ideology, and certainly at the level of their argument with liberals, conservatives believe that economies run best if governments leave them alone. When contemplating economic problems such as poverty, pollution, unemployment, or healthcare, conservatives argue that government has caused most of them through over-regulation and that the best way to deal with them is for government to stop meddling and allow the market to work. It is common to speak of conservatives as being on the "right wing" of the political continuum.[1]

Activists in both major political parties argue constantly about what policy positions they should adopt. One of the common arguments, illustrated here, is that the party should be ideologically pure—that is, completely and uncompromisingly liberal or completely and uncompromisingly conservative.

Courtesy of Ben Sargent

Competency Connection
**CRITICAL THINKING**

In your judgment, would ideologically pure parties be good or bad for Texas government?

## Liberalism

**liberalism** A political ideology that, in general, supports government regulation of economic life and opposes government regulation of personal life.

**Liberalism** is the contrary ideology. Liberals are suspicious of the workings of unregulated markets and place more faith in the ability of government to direct economic activity. When thinking about economic problems, they are apt to blame "market failure" and suggest government activity as the solution. The 2008 Wall Street bailout was thus not contrary to liberal philosophy, although liberals also advocated a bailout of poor people who were losing their homes because of the economic crisis. It is common to speak of liberals as being on the "left wing" of the political spectrum.

All this is relatively clear. When dealing with issues of personal belief and behavior, such as religion, sexual activity, or drug use, however, liberals and conservatives often switch sides. Conservatives are generally in favor of more government regulation; liberals are in favor of less. Liberals oppose prayer in school, whereas conservatives favor it; liberals oppose laws regulating sexual behavior, whereas conservatives endorse them; and so on. An exception to this rule would be the issue of private gun ownership. Conservatives generally want less regulation of guns; liberals want more.

Finally, on foreign policy issues, liberals and conservatives tend to follow partisan rather than ideological cues. That is, liberals tend to endorse whatever a Democratic president wants to do and oppose the wishes of a Republican president, while conservatives support Republicans and oppose Democrats. Since the 1960s, there has been a slight tendency among liberals to emphasize "human rights" in foreign policy and a slight tendency among conservatives to emphasize military force, but these long-term positions are easily scrambled by the short-term partisan struggle. For example, liberals generally supported, and conservatives generally opposed, Democratic President Bill Clinton's air attack on Iraq in 1998, but liberals generally opposed, and conservatives generally supported, Republican President George W. Bush's ground invasion of the same country in 2003.

In summary, American ideological arguments are often confusing because liberals usually favor government activity in the economic sphere but oppose it in the personal sphere, whereas conservatives usually oppose government activity in the economic sphere but favor it in the personal sphere. Confusing or not, this ideological split is the basis for a great deal of rhetorical argument and many intense struggles over public policy (see Table 4-1).

## Ideology in Texas

As discussed in Chapter 1, Texas has historically been dominated by a combination of the traditionalistic and individualistic political cultures. The particular mix of those cultures within the state has generally produced an ideology that has been hostile to government activity in general and especially in regard to providing help for society's poorer and less educated citizens. The basic attitudes associated with cultural values have thus translated, in the Texas case, into an ideology of political conservatism.

| TABLE 4-1 | Policy Differences between Liberals and Conservatives | |
|---|---|---|
| **Issue** | **Conservative Position** | **Liberal Position** |
| **Economic Issues** | | |
| Taxation | As little as possible, and when necessary, regressive taxes such as sales taxes* | More to cover government spending; progressive preferred* |
| Government spending | As little as possible, except for military and anti-terrorism | Acceptable to provide social services or homeland security |
| Nature of government regulation | More in personal sphere; less in economic | Less in personal sphere; more in economic |
| Organized labor | Anti-union | Pro-union |
| Environment | Favors development over environment | Favors environment over development |
| **Social Issues** | | |
| Crime | Supports more prisons and longer sentences; opposes gun control | Favors social policies to attack root causes; favors gun control |
| Abortion | Pro-life | Pro-choice |
| Affirmative action | Opposes | Supports |
| Prayer in public schools | Favors | Opposes |
| Homosexual marriage | Opposes | Favors |
| **Foreign Policy Issues** | | |
| Human rights as large component of foreign policy? | Generally, no | Generally, yes |
| Free trade | More likely to favor (although President Trump is an exception) | Less likely to favor (although both Bill and Hillary Clinton were exceptions) |
| Military spending | More | Less |
| U.S. military intervention abroad | More likely to favor** | Less likely to favor** |

*A progressive tax is one that increases proportionately with income or benefit derived, such as a progressive income tax. A regressive tax, such as the sales tax, is a flat rate—the same for everyone. It is termed "regressive" because it places proportionately less of a burden on wealthy taxpayers and more of a burden on those with lower incomes.

**However, liberals tended to support the U.S./NATO bombing war against Serbia in 1999, while conservatives tended to oppose it; the ideologies reverted to form in regard to the invasion of Iraq in 2003.

NOTE: Two words of caution are in order. First, this table presents only a brief summary of complex issues, and thus, some distortion is inevitable. Second, it would be inaccurate to assume that every liberal agrees with every liberal position or that every conservative agrees with every conservative position. Even the most devout ideologues have inconsistencies in the beliefs and hitches in their logic, and personal interests (see discussion in this chapter) sometimes affect the way ideologies are applied to specific issues.

The distribution of opinion in the present-day population suggests that, when it comes to ideology, not much has changed in Texas since frontier days.

A survey conducted in 2018 reported that only 17 percent of Texas adults were willing to label themselves liberals, while 34 percent called themselves moderates, and 37 percent claimed the label "conservative."[2] The meaning of these simple self-reports is not completely clear because, by calling themselves conservative, people might be referring to economic issues, social issues, foreign policy issues, or all three. Moreover, national public opinion research over many years has shown that a significant percentage of American citizens label themselves conservative in general but endorse many specific liberal government domestic programs. Still, the self-reported percentages are sufficiently dramatic to emphasize the weakness of the liberal ideological tradition in the Lone Star State.

In Texas as elsewhere, the contradictory nature of political ideologies—sometimes recommending government activity, sometimes opposing it, and not always in a logically coherent manner—often makes the arguments of politicians and journalists difficult to understand. Nevertheless, ideologies form the basis for much of the party battle. In general, the Democratic Party is controlled nationally by liberals, and the Republican Party is controlled by conservatives. In Texas, however, the picture is more complicated. Both common observation and scholarly research lead to the conclusion that, historically, both the Democratic and Republican Parties in Texas have been unusually conservative.[3] The Democrats are more liberal because they, unlike the Republicans, harbor a large and active liberal faction. To understand how this situation has come about, it is helpful to have some knowledge of the way ideologies are learned and of the history of Texas as a Southern state.

## Political Socialization

As analyzed in Chapter 1, the attitudes and values of the traditionalistic/individualistic political culture that dominates Texas results in ideological conservatism: a basic hostility to government action, pseudo laissez faire, social Darwinism, and the trickle-down theory of economics. How is this ideology perpetuated? How is it transmitted from one generation to another?

The process by which we teach and learn our political knowledge, beliefs, attitudes, values, and habits of behavior is called **political socialization**. In this process, we are influenced by many things—peer groups, political leaders, and a variety of experiences—but the basic agents of political socialization seem to be family, schools, churches, and the media. An extensive discussion of the process of socialization is beyond the scope of this book, but some attention should be paid to these four agents, particularly as they operate in Texas.

**political socialization** The process by which we learn information, values, attitudes, and habits of behavior about politics and government.

### Family

The family is the most important agent of socialization. The first things a child learns are the basics: attitudes toward authority, others, oneself, and the community outside the family. Although scholarly studies of the process of political socialization in Texas are rare, it is fair to say that most parents in the state pass along their attitudes and philosophy to their children. Parents transfer political ideas along with religious beliefs and attitudes toward other people almost unconsciously as their children hear their conversations and observe their behavior throughout the many hours of association at home. Many Texans can be generous in making personal contributions to private charities, but as heirs to the Texas political culture, the attitudes most parents transmit to their children are opposed to *government* activity on behalf of the poor. By the time other social institutions begin to "teach" children consciously, they have already learned fundamental attitudes. For this reason, basic political orientations are difficult to alter, and the ideas of the population, in Texas as everywhere else, change only slowly.

## Schools and Churches

The public school system, and in some cases the churches, can be very influential in shaping political attitudes and beliefs. Again, the influence is strongly conservative.

Many Texans regularly attend religious services, and most houses of worship teach acceptance of religious theology, an acceptance that often spills over to include acceptance of prevailing social and political institutions as well.

Among Whites, the religious establishment is probably more conservative than most, since the type of Protestantism that dominates Anglo religion in the state stresses the responsibility of individuals for their own fate rather than the communitarian (government) responsibility of everyone for everyone else. Other religious traditions are also important in Texas, most notably Roman Catholicism among Mexican Americans. The Catholic Church has historically been more encouraging of government activity on behalf of society's underdogs than have Protestant churches. However, Protestantism, the dominant religion among the historically dominant social group, has been associated with attitudes that reinforce political conservatism. As Latinos, who are almost always Catholic, increase their percentage in the Texas population, they may dilute the dominant conservatism of Texas.

The overall influence of churches, however, may not be as intense or pervasive as that of the public schools, where students spend six or more hours a day, five days a week, for up to twelve years. There is little indication that schools in Texas educate children about politics or encourage them to participate in the political process in any way other than voting.

The essence of politics is conflict, but Texas public education does not recognize this. Instead, the schoolchild is taught to value the free enterprise system but not to be aware of its potential deficiencies, to be patriotic, and to respect authority. The nature of politics is distorted. The child is educated to passivity rather than to democratic participation.

In the most thorough study of socialization by public schools in Texas, anthropologist Douglas Foley spent sixteen months in a small South Texas town (which he called "North Town") during 1973 and 1974; he then returned during the summers and some weekends in 1977, 1985, 1986, and 1987. After interviewing students, teachers, administrators, politicians, and townspeople, and observing many activities, including sporting events, classroom teaching, social dating, and ethnic confrontations, Foley came to definite conclusions about the sorts of ideas passed along by North Town's schools:

> "After a year in North Town . . . I came to see that the school simply reflected the general conservatism of the community. The town's social and political environment did not demand or encourage a highly open, imaginative, critical curriculum. North Towners did not want their children reading avant-garde literature or critiques of corporation polluters or revisionist accounts of President Johnson's political corruption. They wanted their schools to discipline and mold their children into hard-working, family-oriented, patriotic, mainstream citizens.[4]

North Town is only one small place in a big state, but Foley's conclusions are consistent with common observations about Texas schools in general. The conservatism he found in North Town, while not found in every classroom or every school district, is generally representative of Texas public education.

## Media

As with other institutions in the state, most of the mass media in Texas are conservative. Most newspapers and TV and radio stations are profitable businesses that depend on other economic interests for their advertising revenues. Consequently, there is a tendency among these institutions to echo the business point of view on most issues. As Everett Collier, former editor of the *Houston Chronicle,* used to put it, "We are not here to rock the boat."[5]

As historical forces are constantly modifying Texas society, however, they are also changing the media. Just in the span of years since the first edition of this textbook was published, established patterns of media influence have suffered the shock of new technology. When this book first appeared in the 1979, newspapers and television dominated the political media. In the late 1980s, however, talk radio became important in the public arena. Because most talk radio programs are conservative, they certainly reinforced the traditional Texas pattern of socialization.

In the 1990s, however, personal computers, and therefore the Internet, offered a whole new medium of influence over politics. And in the 2000s, Internet technology mutated into a variety of innovative ways of communication with which Texas, like the nation, is just beginning to come to grips. Now, Texans, like other Americans, can encounter a variety of ideological viewpoints on Websites, on Facebook, on blogs, on Twitter, and, no doubt, soon on new cyber-inventions that do not even exist yet. As the new media replace the old, they create uncertainty as to their effects. Social scientists have long studied the impact of television and newspapers, but newspapers are in rapid decline and TV is not as important as it used to be. Yet scholars are just beginning to understand the impact of the new media on people's thoughts and habits.

Whether the new computer-based media will, like talk radio, merely supplement the basic Texas politically conservative socialization, or alter it in surprising and radical ways, is a question that cannot be answered now. The future, as always, contains the promise of both stability and change.

## Evaluation

After reviewing the socializing effects of families, schools, churches, and the media, one might wonder how any view other than the conservative ideology exists in Texas. It does exist, however, for several reasons: Some people adopt a personal point of view that is contrary to the opinion-molding forces around them; liberal families, churches, schoolteachers, and news outlets do exist in Texas, although they are in the minority; the national, as opposed to local, news media often display a liberal slant; and millions of non-Texans have moved to the state in the last few decades, bringing different political cultures with them. Moreover, the new Internet-based media are so personal, numerous, and pervasive that they may have startling effects on people's values and worldviews. Or they may turn out to be just flashy time-wasters, without political relevance. Thus, political conservatism continues to dominate, but as both the Texas population and media technology increase and become more diverse, the ideology is being challenged and modified by competing cultural values.

Ideology, however, is not the only basis for political party support. Equally important are people's interests and the way parties attempt to recruit citizen loyalty by endorsing those interests.

## Interests

**interest** Something of value or some personal characteristic that people share and that is affected by government activity; interests are important both because they form the basis of interest groups and because parties attempt to form many interests into an electoral coalition.

**coalition** A group of interests and individuals supporting a party or a candidate for office.

An **interest** is something of value or some personal characteristic that people share and that is affected by government activity—their investments, their race, their jobs, their hobbies, and so on. When there is a question of public policy on which political parties take differing positions, people often line up behind the party favoring their interests, whether or not their political ideology is consistent with that party's. Moreover, parties often take positions that will attract the money and votes of citizens with clashing interests. Thus, parties put together **coalitions** of interests to attract blocs of voters and campaign contributions. Party positions are therefore almost always much more ambiguous and confusing than they would be if they were simply based on ideology.

For example, since the early 1990s Republican Party candidates in Texas have tended to criticize the state's tort laws—the statutes that allow people who believe that they have been injured by someone else to sue for damages. Republicans have argued that the state makes it too easy to file "frivolous" lawsuits and allows juries to award damages that are too large to injured parties. They have supported "tort reform" by the state legislature. On the other hand, Democrats have tended to side with plaintiffs in lawsuits, arguing that injured people should have easy access to the courts and should be entitled to large amounts of money as compensation for injuries. They have usually opposed tort reform.

As a result, the types of people who tend to be the target of tort lawsuits (doctors and business owners, for example) have been inclined to support Republican candidates. Those who tend to benefit from such suits (plaintiff's attorneys, for example) have tended to side with Democrats. This alignment has very little to do with ideology and a great deal to do with who gets what from government. (This subject is also discussed in Chapters 3 and 11.)

Not all interests are economic. Since the 1960s, for example, Mexican Americans and African Americans have tended to support the Democratic Party because they have perceived the Republicans as less tolerant of ethnic diversity. Whether an interest arranges people in a politically relevant manner depends on what sorts of questions become issues of public policy.

Interests and ideologies tend to combine in different ways in different people, sometimes opposing and sometimes reinforcing one another. For example, a Latino doctor in Texas would be drawn to the Republicans by her professional interest and drawn to the Democrats by her ethnic interest. She might have had trouble making up her mind about how to vote in the 2018 election. On the other hand, an Anglo oil company executive or a Black labor union president would probably have experienced no such conflict. In each case, the citizen's personal ideology may either reinforce or contradict one or more of his or her interests. The way interests and ideologies blend and conflict, and interact with candidates and parties, is one of the things that makes politics complicated and interesting to study.

Interests thus help structure the party battle. They are politically important for other reasons as well. See Chapter 3 for a detailed discussion of the organizing and lobbying efforts of interest groups.

The partisan coalitions that have characterized recent Texas politics are summarized in Table 4-2. It is important to understand that not every person who has an interest agrees with every other person with the same interest, and so citizens who share interests are not unanimous in their partisan attachments. For example, although most of the people in the computer business who contributed large amounts to a political party during the 1990s and 2000s gave to the Republicans, not all did. Similarly, although the great majority of African Americans voters supported the Democrats, thousands did not. Table 4-2 describes how people with certain interests lean in general, not how every person with that interest behaves.

| TABLE 4-2 | Interests Generally Supporting the Two Major Parties | |
|---|---|---|
| **Type of Interest** | **Democrats** | **Republicans** |
| *Economic class* | Poor, lower middle | Wealthy, upper middle |
| *Economic structure* | Workers, esp. labor unions | Management |
| *Professions* | Plaintiff's attorneys, public employees, artists | Physicians, business entrepreneurs |
| *Development vs. environment* | Environmentalists | Developers, rural landowners |
| *Industry* | Entertainment | Oil and gas, computers |
| *Ethnicity* | African American, Mexican American | Anglo |

Politics would be fascinating enough if, once ideologies and interests had arranged themselves into a party coalition, they stayed that way. In fact, however, the party battle evolves as history changes the way people live. A hundred years ago, the Democratic Party was the more conservative party and dominated Texas almost completely. Today, the Republican Party is more conservative and has achieved at least temporary dominance over the Democrats.[6] It is not too much of an exaggeration to say that the history of Texas is written in the story of the two major parties.

## Texas Political Parties: A Brief History

Prior to joining the Union, Texas had no political parties. In the early days of settlement, the free spirits who came to Texas were happy to leave government and politics behind them. During the period of the Texas Republic (1836–1845), Texas politics was dominated by Sam Houston, the hero of the war for independence from Mexico. Although there were no political parties, pro-Houston and anti-Houston factions provided some discussion of public policy.

Texas entered the United States in 1845 as a slave state. Nationally, the Democrats were proslavery, while their opponents, the Whigs, ignored the issue. Moreover, the Democrats had endorsed the admission of Texas to the Union in the 1844 election, whereas the Whigs had waffled. Thus, most Texans were Democrats.

Party divisions became intense after the Civil War ended in 1865. The Republican administration of Abraham Lincoln had defeated the Confederacy, of which Texas was a member, and freed the slaves. Reconstruction, or federal government occupation, settled on all the southern states. White southerners found themselves under the rule of northerners, the military, and African Americans. Rightly or wrongly, they believed themselves to be subject to tyranny by a foreign conqueror. They identified this despotic occupation with the Republican Party. As a result, when Reconstruction ended in 1874, Texas, like the other former members of the Confederacy, was a solid one-party Democratic state. It kept the **one-party system** until the 1970s, with telling effects on politics and public policy.

At the national level, the United States has a competitive two-party system. For example, between 1924 and 2016, the Republicans and Democrats each won twelve Presidential elections. Competitive party systems are characterized by a great deal of public dialogue between the parties. Although personal attacks are made and inaccurate statements are common, intelligent discussion and genuine debate also occur. Emerging groups of voters—African Americans, Latinos, and women, for example—and emerging issues such as the environment and abortion find receptive ears in one or more of the competitive parties. In this way, these concerns become known throughout the political system.

Citizens are relatively active in a healthy two-party system, and voter turnouts are therefore fairly high. A one-party system is very different, and Texas furnished a good example in the first three quarters of the twentieth century. Because there was no "loyal opposition," elections were decided in the Democratic primary, and nominees usually ran unopposed in the November general election. The party label is the most important guide the American voter has at election time, but in Texas, it was of no value. Texas's voters usually had a choice of several candidates for each elective office, but they all ran as Democrats. There was some debate on public policy between liberal Democrats and conservative Democrats, but only a little.

Without party competition to foster debate and spur voter interest, most White citizens (in most areas of the state, minorities were prevented from voting) were apathetic, and voter turnout was very low. Candidates of all ideological persuasions, from Ku Klux Klansmen to liberals, ran as Democrats. Traditional party functions such as recruiting, financing, and conducting campaigns were performed not by the party but by informal, unofficial organizations, campaign committees, and other groups. Voters were uninformed about these groups and knew little, if anything, about who controlled them or what their goals were.

**one-party system** A state that is dominated by a single political party, characterized by an absence of party competition, inadequate debate of public policy, low voter turnout, and usually conservative public policy.

One result of this one-party system was that when voters elected Democrats to the offices of Governor, Lieutenant Governor, Attorney General, Railroad Commissioner, and so on, they were not sending a Democratic "team" to Austin. They were sending independent officials who were frequently rivals and had little in common except personal ambition and a Democratic label. The parties acted to emphasize, not overcome, the fragmentation of power created by the state constitution.

Under these conditions of splintered power, because there was no unified team, there was no unified program. Each politician went his or her own way. The act of holding together disparate interests, which is the basis for E. E. Schattschneider's praise of parties at the beginning of the chapter, was not performed.

In other words, one-party politics in Texas was really no-party politics. Instead of the vigorous debate and citizen involvement that characterize well-run democracies, confusion and apathy reigned.

The transition to two-party politics in Texas, as in most of the South, occurred gradually. Beginning in 1928, Texans sometimes voted for Republican presidential candidates. In 1961, Republican John Tower cracked the Democratic monopoly at the state level by winning a special election for a U.S. Senate seat. Republicans began to win a few local elections in Dallas and Houston soon thereafter, but conservative Democrats continued to dominate state politics into the 1970s. In 1978, Bill Clements beat John Hill for the governorship and became Texas's first Republican governor in 104 years. But Clements could not win reelection in 1982, in spite of spending a record $13.2 million during his campaign.

Republican President Ronald Reagan's landslide reelection in 1984 seemed to finally break the Democrats' hold on Texas. Dozens of Republican candidates rode Reagan's coattails to victory in local elections, as did Phil Gramm, the Republican candidate for U.S. senator. Some of the local officeholders subsequently lost their reelection bids, but by then, Texas could no longer be considered a Democratic monopoly.

Seen against this historical background, the election of 1994 appears to be truly a watershed. Republicans defeated an incumbent Democratic Governor, retained a second U.S. Senate seat, pulled almost even in the state Senate, and saw hundreds of local offices fall to their candidates.

By 2004, Texas could just barely be considered a two-party state. Every statewide elective official, including all eighteen members of the two top courts, was Republican, as were both U.S. senators and majorities in both houses of the state Legislature. Moreover, Texans gave decisive majorities of their major-party vote to Republican candidates in the seven Presidential elections from 1992 to 2016. The last Democratic bastion—the party's slim majority in the state's thirty-two-member delegation to the U.S. House of Representatives— had been destroyed by the legislature's redistricting bill in 2003. Democrats began to make inroads on complete Republican rule in local elections in some big cities in 2006 and 2008, but the state as a whole remained staunchly Republican. Observers anticipated that Texas might become as much a one-party state in the twenty-first century as it had been through most of the twentieth, but with different parties in command.

Table 4-3 displays the growth in the number of Republican officeholders in Texas from 1974 to 2017.

Patterns in Texas public opinion, however, suggest that the state is not quite as Republican as its recent voting history would suggest. In a survey taken in 2018, Democrats and Republicans were tied, with 39 percent claiming to "identify" with each party, while 22 percent picked "neither."[7] These figures suggest either that a large number of Democrats have been

| TABLE 4-3 | Growth of Republican Officeholders in Texas, 1974–2017 | | | | | |
|---|---|---|---|---|---|---|
| Year | U.S. Senate | Other Statewide | U.S. House | Texas Senate | Texas House | Total |
| 1974 | 1 | 0 | 2 | 3 | 16 | 22 |
| 1982 | 1 | 0 | 5 | 5 | 36 | 47 |
| 1990 | 1 | 6 | 8 | 8 | 57 | 80 |
| 1994 | 2 | 13 | 11 | 14 | 61 | 101 |
| 1998 | 2 | 27 | 13 | 16 | 72 | 130 |
| 2004 | 2 | 27 | 21 | 19 | 87 | 156 |
| 2008 | 2 | 27 | 20 | 19 | 76 | 144 |
| 2017 | 2 | 27 | 25 | 21 | 95 | 170 |

NOTE: Neither the Republican Party nor the Texas secretary of state keep track of the total number of electoral offices within Texas. As a result, it is impossible to count the number of local offices held by each party.

SOURCES: Republican Party of Texas, October, 2005; W. Gardner Selby, "Benkiser Seeking a National Perch, Touting GOP Gains," _Austin American-Statesman_, January 29, 2009, BI; Wikipedia for 2017.

voting Republican for many elections, or that they have not been participating in elections. We will explore these possibilities in the next chapter.

Nevertheless, the voting results over the past three decades suggest that, during the last two decades of the twentieth century, Texas went through a political **realignment**—a change in the standing decision, by many of its citizens, to vote for a given party. Until the 1980s, enough Texans had adopted a standing decision to vote for Democrats that the party's candidates could count on winning most of the time. By the twenty-first century, however, enough Texans had changed their habits so that Republicans were normally victorious in statewide, although not necessarily local, elections. Once solidly Democratic, Texas had realigned to be generally Republican.

**realignment**
A change in the standing decision to support one party or another by a significant proportion of the electorate, resulting in a change in which party has a "normal" majority on election day.

The growth of two-party competition in Texas has been good for democracy. Instead of the confused jumble that characterized Texas politics when Texas was a one-party state, in recent years there has been robust debate between the parties on many issues of importance to the citizens. Whether the democratic dialogue can last if the Republicans continue their statewide dominance is another question.

The public debate is so loud because policy differences between the parties are quite substantial. Table 4-4 displays some summary statements from the state Democratic and Republican Party platforms of 2018. As the table illustrates, the differences between the activists who write these platforms are of two kinds. First, on some issues—for instance, abortion, the minimum wage, climate change, and the Affordable Care Act ("Obamacare")—party activists are clearly and firmly on opposing sides. Second, the parties are concerned about different issues and therefore talk about different subjects. For example, the Republicans, but not the Democrats, talk about the fluoridation of the water supply, whereas the Democrats are the only party to mention the responsibility of government to provide affordable child care. Nevertheless, the parties occasionally agree completely on an issue. Both, for example, clearly oppose the Trans-Pacific Partnership, a free-trade treaty negotiated by the Obama administration, but never passed by Congress.

| TABLE 4-4 | 2018 Texas State Political Party Platforms | |
|---|---|---|
| **Issue** | **Republican** | **Democratic** |
| **Abortion** | We call upon the Texas legislature to enact legislation stopping the murder of unborn children . . . <br><br>We are resolute in our support of the reversal of Roe v. Wade. | Texas Democrats . . . trust Texans to make personal and responsible decisions about whether and when to bear children . . . Texas Democrats oppose any and all attempts to overturn Roe v. Wade. |
| **Affirmative action** | We support Texas college admissions based solely on merit. | Texas Democrats support innovative approaches to ensure diversity . . . in every Texas institution of higher education. |
| **Childcare** | Not mentioned. | Texas Democrats support child care initiatives that encourage both private and non-profit providers to expand the availability of quality child care services. |
| **Church and state** | We believe in "The laws of Nature and Nature's God," and we support the strict adherence to the original language and intent of the Declaration of Independence and the Constitutions of the United States and of Texas. | . . . entangling government with religion is dangerous to both government and religion . . . religion should not be invoked to supersede the rights of others. |
| **Climate change** | "Climate change" is a political agenda promoted to control every aspect of our lives. | . . . climate change is a real and serious threat . . . we recommend statewide and national . . . policies that will spur economic development and reduce carbon emissions in Texas and the nation . . . |
| **Evolution** | We support objective teaching of scientific theories . . . These should be taught as challengeable scientific theories subject to change as new data is produced. | Texas Democrats believe the State Board of Education should . . . adopt and teach the methods and content of professional science . . . |
| **Guns** | We support constitutional carry legislation . . . so that law-abiding citizens may carry any legally owned guns . . . [Calls for the repeal of the section of the Texas constitution that reads], "but the Legislature shall have the power, by law, to regulate the wearing of arms . . ." | We strongly support . . . Enacting sensible gun laws to curtail the availability of weapons with extended ammunition magazines . . . Repealing laws that allow the open carry of handguns and assault rifles . . . |
| **Healthcare** | We demand the immediate repeal of the . . . Affordable Care Act ["Obamacare"]. | Texas Democrats [advocate that the federal government] expand the advances made by the Affordable Care Act. |
| **Minimum wage** | We believe the Minimum Wage Act should be repealed. | We support requiring a minimum wage that is at least $15-an-hour. |
| **Public school vouchers** | Texas families should be empowered to choose from public, private, charter, or homeschool options for their children's education, using tax credits . . . | Texas Democrats oppose the misnamed "school choice" schemes of using public tax money for the support of private and sectarian schools. |
| **Immigration** | We demand that state and federal law enforcement officers enforce our immigration laws . . . Any form of amnesty with regard to immigration policy should not be granted. | We . . . strongly oppose the Trump Administration's so-called "zero tolerance" approach to immigration . . . strongly oppose efforts to build a border wall . . . |
| **Fluoridation of public water supply** | The Republican Party of Texas supports banning the fluoridation of the Texas water supply. | Not mentioned. |
| **Trans-Pacific Partnership** | We strongly oppose the TPP. | We categorically oppose the Trans-Pacific Partnership. |

SOURCES: 2018 Democratic and Republican state platforms, downloaded from the state party Websites.

# Party Organization

All parties are organizations, but they follow many different patterns of structure. In general, we can say that American parties, compared to those in foreign democracies, are weakly organized. They are not structured so that they can function easily as a cohesive team. The parties in Texas are especially weak in an organizational sense. As a result, they often do not perform the function of overcoming gridlock and making coherent policy very well, nor do they structure conflict to make it sensible to most ordinary citizens. A review of state party organization will suggest why this is so.

Figure 4-1 shows that in Texas, as in most states, parties are divided into a permanent organization and a temporary one. The **permanent party organization** consists of little more than a skeleton force of people who conduct the routine but essential business of the party. The party's primary purpose of winning elections requires far more people and much greater activity. The party comes alive in election years in the form of a **temporary party organization** geared to capturing power.

**permanent party organization** The small, fixed group of people that handles the routine business of a political party.

**temporary party organization** The large group of people formed during election years to mobilize the party's potential electorate and win an election.

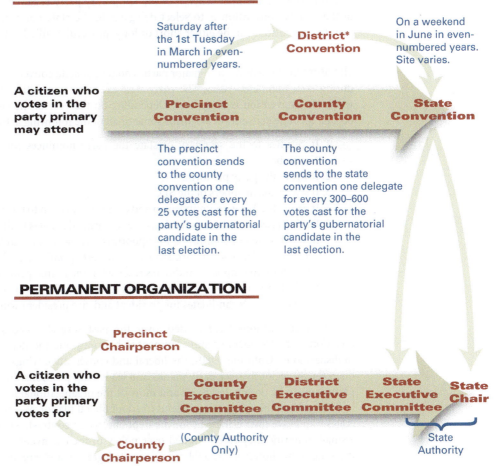

Figure 4-1 Major Party Organization in Texas

*District conventions are held in counties with more than one senatorial district.

SOURCE: State Democratic and Republican headquarters.

## The Temporary Party Organization

The temporary party organization is focused on the spring primary and the fall general election. It attempts to choose attractive candidates and mobilize voters to support them.

In Texas, party membership is determined by the act of voting; there are no permanent political party rolls. When citizens vote in the Democratic Party primary, for example, they are considered "affiliated Democrats" until the end of the calendar year. They may vote only in the Democratic runoff, if there is one, and participate only in Democratic conventions. The next year, however, they may legally change their affiliation and participate in Republican Party activities.

**Precinct and County Conventions** In the 254 counties of Texas, there are more than 6,000 precincts, each having from 50 to as many as 3,500 voters. Each voter is entitled to have a voice in choosing the precinct chairperson and proposing and voting on resolutions that will establish party policy, but voter participation in party affairs is low. Normally, only a small fraction of those who vote in the primaries—who are themselves only a fraction of the total number of registered voters and a smaller fraction of the citizens of voting age—participate in conventions or other party affairs.

The main function of the precinct convention is to select delegates to the county convention, which is the next echelon of the temporary party organization. The main function of the county convention is to select delegates to the state convention. Both precinct and county conventions can be either short or long, peaceful or filled with conflict, productive of resolutions or not.

**The State Convention** Both major parties hold their state conventions on a weekend in June during even-numbered years. The party state executive committee (SEC) decides when and where the convention is to be held. Depending on the year of the election cycle in which it occurs, the June convention performs some or all of the following activities:

1. It certifies to the secretary of state the party nominees for the general election in November.
2. It writes the party platform.
3. It selects the members of the SEC.
4. It names the Texas committeeman and committeewoman to the national party committee.
5. During presidential years, it selects the "at-large" delegates to the national party convention (who are not committed to supporting any particular candidate, as opposed to the "pledged" delegates who are sworn to support specific candidates and whose identity depends on the support candidates received in the March primary election).[8]
6. It selects a slate of presidential electors to serve in the national electoral college in the event the party's candidates for president and vice president win in Texas.

Party conventions have tended, over the past several decades, to travel in opposite directions—the Democrats from argument to harmony and the Republicans from agreement to disharmony. Until the 1980s, the liberal and conservative wings of the Democratic Party often fought viciously over party planks and leadership positions. In the 1990s, however, the party came to be dominated more and more at the organizational level by the liberal faction. In conventions, the delegates now tend to adopt liberal platforms—at least in regard to social issues—and save their criticisms for the Republicans. In contrast, when the Republicans were a small minority, they rarely argued over policy in their conventions. As their influence in the state grew, however, Republicans generated greater and greater internal disagreement, especially between social and economic conservatives.

The new pattern was set in 1994, when delegates from the Christian Right dominated the convention. The socially conservative platform and the convention's choice of a party chair sparked vigorous but futile opposition from delegates who were economically conservative but more moderate on social issues.

From 1994 to 2018, the Christian Right dominated Republican state conventions. In 1994, 1996, and 1998, Republican state platforms began with the words, "We believe in you! We believe that you are a sacred being created in the image of God." In each succeeding platform, the words varied slightly, but the message was the same. The 2018 platform, for example, began with the phrase, "Affirming our belief in God . . ." By 2000, those Republican delegates who were economic conservatives but social liberals had stopped making hopeless objections to Christian Right positions at the state convention, although the intra-party battle continued to be waged on other fronts.

Although events in the Democratic and Republican state conventions engender much publicity, their importance should not be exaggerated. Because candidates for public office in Texas are nominated in primaries rather than in caucuses or conventions (see Chapter 5), and because candidates typically raise their own campaign funds independently of the party, the state convention and platform are of little importance to what nominees say and do. Candidates typically run to gather support from the large number of potential voters, not the

Ordinary citizens can get involved in politics by participating in their state party conventions. These photographs show the Democratic (top) and Republican (bottom) conventions of 2018.

AP Images/Richard W. Rodriguez

Tamir Kalifa/The New York Times/Redux

tiny number of party activists who write the platforms. For example, in 2002 Governor Rick Perry publicly opposed twenty-three of the forty-six planks in his party's platform, distanced himself from sixteen others, and endorsed only seven.[9] His successor, Greg Abbott, has been more accommodating to the state platform, but the potential disagreement between activists and candidates remains unchanged.

By 2002, social conservative delegates to the Republican convention were so frustrated with the economic conservative officeholders they termed "RINOs" (for "Republicans in Name Only") that they sponsored Rule 43 as a floor amendment to the platform. This "RINO Rule" would have denied party funds to any candidate who refused to swear to endorse and attempt to implement every party plank if elected. Party Chair Susan Weddington, presiding at the convention, managed to squelch the Rule 43 movement, but the conflict between the two wings of the party continued.[10] In 2018, for example, the state Republican Executive Committee voted to censure their own speaker of the house, Joe Straus, for having pursued an insufficiently conservative (on social issues) agenda during the 2017 legislature.[11]

In summary, if students want to know what candidates plan to do if elected, they may want to ignore platforms and instead pay attention to the positions of the candidates themselves. The platform positions and rhetoric reproduced in Table 4-4 are good indications of the values and beliefs of the major party activists as groups but are not reliable guides to the issue positions of candidates as individuals.

## Permanent Party Organization

**Precinct Chairpersons** The citizen who votes in the primary has an opportunity to participate in the selection of the precinct and county chairpersons of his or her party. The precinct chairperson is the lowest ranking permanent party official. Elected for a two-year term, he or she is expected to be the party leader at the precinct level, recruiting candidates, arranging for the precinct convention, getting out the vote, and in general, beating the drum for the party.

**County Executive Committee** Together, the precinct chairs form the county executive committee, which is charged with two major responsibilities: (1) conducting the party primary elections and (2) conducting the county convention. It is presided over by the county chairperson, the most important official at the local level. Elected for two years to a demanding job, this official is unpaid, although some receive private donations.

County chairs are compensated by the state for the expense of conducting their party's primary elections. After the primary election has been held, the county executive committee canvasses the vote and certifies the results to the state executive committee.

**District Executive Committee** The Texas Election Code also provides for district executive committees. Their membership varies according to the number of counties and sections of counties that make up the senatorial district. These committees are supposed to perform party primary duties related to the district. In practice, however, few district executive committees are functional. Most district duties are performed by county executive committees.

**State Executive Committee** The highest permanent body in the state party is the state executive committee, and the highest state party official is the party chair. Both are elected by the state convention. If the party controls the governorship, the chair of this party is likely to be a friend and political ally of the governor. Normally, the governor and the party chair work together to advance the party campaign during an election year.

The Republicans in 1996 and 1998 were a notable exception. The rancor between social conservatives, as represented by Tom Pauken, the party chair, and economic conservatives, as represented by Governor George W. Bush, caused a split in campaign duties. Bush ran the fund-raising and campaign efforts for GOP presidential candidate Bob Dole in 1996 and congressional candidates both years, while Pauken oversaw money-raising efforts for "down-ballot" state candidates.[12] With the departure of both Bush and Pauken by 2000, harmony returned to the Republican camp. GOP Governors Perry and Abbott cooperated smoothly with their party chairs during the first two decades of the new millennium.

In a similar fashion, the chair of the state committee of the party out of power usually has a close relationship with the party's top leaders. By law, the executive committee of each party is responsible for staging the state convention, for certifying the party's candidates, and for coordinating a general party campaign over and above the efforts made by each individual candidate.

## The (Un)Importance of Party Organization

American political parties are not "responsible parties"—that is, they have neither centralized control over nominations and financing nor the power to impose the party platform on members. In Texas, parties are especially weak because it is in fact the primary election, not the party organization, that is important in determining who is nominated to office. Furthermore, candidates normally rely on their own fund-raising and organizing ability more than they rely on their party to help them get elected.

As a result, when candidates succeed in capturing an office, they mostly have themselves and the individuals and groups who contributed to their campaign fund to thank for their achievement. They therefore have very little loyalty to the party; they are more likely to feel beholden to some wealthy interest group. Officeholders are often ideologically friendly with others of the same party, but they are not obligated to cooperate with one another. The parties have no discipline over them.

Texas party organizations have some ability to fashion a "party attitude" on public policy because they are centers of information flow and personal interaction, but they are incapable of forging a disciplined governing team. Therefore, the party platforms summarized in Table 4-4 are in fact largely irrelevant to candidates' positions. They are a good indication of the sentiments of the party activists as a group, but they say little about the policy stands of candidates as individuals.

The unimportance of party organization in Texas is illustrated by the fact that the GOP was victorious in elections from 1994 to 2018 despite its internal squabbling. In a similar fashion, the Democratic Party won elections in the Lone Star State in previous decades despite the fact that it contained two battling factions.

The consequence of their organizational weakness is that Texas parties often fail to perform many of the functions that make parties elsewhere useful to democracy. By and large, they cannot recruit political leaders or overcome the fragmented nature of the political system by forming officials into disciplined organizations. Instead of thinking of parties in Texas as two stable, cohesive teams, it would be more realistic to imagine them as two (or as discussed in the next section, three or even four) loose confederations of citizens, interest groups, and officeholders that sometimes cooperate because of occasional ideological agreement and temporary parallel interests.

Lack of party cohesiveness also has important consequences in the legislature. Scholarly research has established the importance of party organization in state lawmaking bodies. According to Gerald Wright and Brian Schaffner, when the legislature has parties structured into two teams, political conflict is ordered so that issues tend to fall on either side of a clear, stable, voting cleavage in the legislature. Under such conditions, citizens are able to make sense of the political struggle. When Republicans and Democrats have no institutionalized divisions and organization, "It seems almost as though each bill is considered anew rather than in the context of established sides and coalitions."[13] Under these circumstances, lawmaking is confused and confusing, and citizens have difficulty holding politicians accountable for their actions.

Traditionally, Texas's weak parties have been reflected in the disorganization of its legislature. All through the 1990s and until 2017, the presiding officers (see Chapter 6) appointed members of both parties to chair important committees. The parties did not even caucus as separate groups until 1989, and afterward, those caucuses met only rarely during the legislative session.[14] Even in 2005, after the bruising and bitter partisan gerrymander of 2003, Republican Speaker Tom Craddick appointed Democrats to chair ten of forty-three House committees, and Republican Lieutenant Governor David Dewhurst chose Democrats to chair six of the fifteen Senate committees.

But this pattern of bi-partisan government is in the process of changing. Over the past several decades, parties in the United States Congress have become more ideologically polarized and less cooperative.[15] It has taken a while for this fierce party hostility to filter down to the Texas legislature, but the process of polarization is now clearly visible.

In 2014, the Republican candidate for Lieutenant. Governor, Dan Patrick, campaigned on the promise to be a more partisan presiding officer. He was elected, and for the 2015 session, he appointed only 2 Demos to chair committees out of 14 (17 percent). In 2017, Patrick again named only two Demos to chair the 14 committees. Meanwhile, the Speaker of the House, Joe Straus (also a Republican), followed the traditional pattern by appointing 13 Demos to chair committees out of a total of 40 (33 percent); in 2017 he appointed 13 Demo chairs out of 38 committees (34 percent).

After the 2017 legislature, however, GOP activists forced several changes in the house of representatives, to bring it in line with Lieutenant Governor Patrick's more partisan vision. In a house party caucus in December, 2017, representatives adopted a new party by-law. Before, every member of the House voted for Speaker at the beginning of a session, meaning that Straus had been chosen by winning the support of moderate Republicans and all Democrats. After the 2017 change, the Republicans will caucus and pick a Speaker candidate, and all members of the party will be bound to support that candidate. The Demos will have nothing to say about who becomes Speaker. This change will guarantee that the new Speaker will be more conservative than Straus, and less likely to appoint members of the minority party to chair committees.[16]

The changes of 2017 signal that Texas politics is headed in a somewhat different direction. Future legislatures will probably witness fewer minority party appointments to committee chairs, stronger legislative party organizations, and much more cohesive party voting. Such changes will undoubtedly produce more stress for legislators, but they might be good for democratic politics because the functioning of state government will be more coherent and responsible.

# ISSUE SPOTLIGHT:
## Both Sexes But Only One Profession

A s party interests and ideologies evolve through history, so does their leadership. Texas passed some sort of a milestone in the late 1990s when both parties, for the first time, elected women as leaders. Republican Susan Weddington was a former businesswoman from San Antonio. Democrat Molly Beth Malcolm was a former teacher and drug counselor from East Texas. Malcolm was a rarity in modern Texas politics—a former Republican who became an important Democrat.

Weddington and Malcolm each resigned as party chairs in 2003. Since that year, leadership in the state parties has not shown any particular pattern. In 2018, the Republican chair was James Dickey, an Anglo with a career in business. The vice-chair was Alma Perez-Jackson, a Latina who also has a career in business. The Democratic chair was Gilberto Hinojosa, a Latino lawyer who is also a former judge. The vice-chair was Dr. Carla Brailey, an African American sociology professor.

Sources: Texas Republican and Democratic Party Websites.

**Competency Connection**
**SOCIAL RESPONSIBILITY**

Do you think it matters if a party chair is of a particular ethnicity, religion, or sex?

## You Decide: Should Texas Have Responsible Parties?

In 1950, the American Political Science Association (APSA) sponsored a report entitled "Toward a More Responsible Two-Party System," in which it stated its organizational position that democracy would work better in the United States if the country's parties were more disciplined and coherent. In 2002, there was a movement within the ranks of the Texas Republican Party to force its candidates to endorse every plank in the party platform, on the theory that democracy would work better if Republicans, at least, were disciplined and coherent. Both APSA in 1950 and many Republican activists in 2002 endorsed the idea that disciplined party teams are better for democratic governance than the disorganized, candidate-centered system that prevails in both the United States and Texas.

Should such disciplined parties be the Texas institutions of the future?

### Pro ✓

⬆ **When** different candidates from the same party take differing positions on issues, it confuses the voters. If candidates were all forced to stand for the same things, citizens would be more able to understand the choices available to them, which would make for more intelligent voting.

⬆ **Many** foreign democracies have disciplined, responsible parties. Probably because politics in those countries makes sense, those typically have higher voter turnout than the U.S. and still higher turnout than Texas.

⬆ **Disciplined** parties would prevent wealthy special interests from secretly buying the loyalty of candidates. Once candidates got into office, there would be no betrayals of the public's trust.

⬆ **Once** candidates were forced to endorse a single set of principles in order to run, they would form a cooperating team when in office, and public policy would be both easier to enact and more self-consistent.

### Con ✗

⬇ **Election** campaigns are often confusing because politics itself is complicated and ambiguous. The solution to confusion is for citizens to better inform themselves, not for parties to impose a false clarity on voting choices.

⬇ **Almost** all those foreign democracies have multi-party systems, so citizens have more choices on election day. There is no evidence that any of those countries is better governed than the U.S. or Texas.

⬇ **If** wealthy special interests were denied access to candidates, they would simply corrupt parties. The problem is the power of money, not the lack of party discipline.

⬇ **One** of the major reasons that candidates vary in their policy positions is that constituencies vary from place to place. Any party that forced its candidates to say the same thing everywhere would soon discover that most of its candidates lost. Losers do not enact public policy.

Sources: "Toward a More Responsible Two-Party System: A Report of the Committee on Political Parties. American Political Science Association." *American Political Science Review*, vol. 44 (September 1950), 15; Austin Ranney, *Curing the Mischiefs of Faction: Party Reform in America* (Berkeley: University of California, 1975); Jake Bernstein, "Elephant Wars: The Christian Right Flexes its Muscles at the Republican Convention," *Texas Observer*, July 5, 2002, 8–9.

**Competency Connection**
**SOCIAL RESPONSIBILITY**

**Should Texas Have Responsible Parties?**

An early indication of the future, more party-conscious Texas political environment, had been on display in the primary election of 2004. Democrat Ron Wilson, an African American politician from Houston, had been conspicuously independent of his party's organizational needs since his election to the state House of Representatives in 1976. His willingness to vote with Republicans had made Wilson one of the few Democrats who retained internal power in the legislature as the party balance changed. He publicly supported the election of the new House speaker, Tom Craddick, and received many favors in return, being one of the minority-party representatives that Craddick appointed to chair a committee.

Wilson's lack of party loyalty was for many years of no concern to his constituents, who regularly reelected him by large margins. But by completely deserting the Democrats and endorsing the Republican redistricting plan in 2003, he went too far. In the March 2004 Democratic primary, Wilson was challenged by Alma Allen, a professional educator, member of the state board of education, and incidentally, also a Black candidate. During the primary campaign, Allen steadily pounded Wilson for his support of redistricting as well as his vote for Republican budget cuts. State Democratic leaders, including party chair Charles Soechting, publicly backed Allen. The voters got the message and nominated Allen by an eleven-point margin (because there was no Republican candidate running in this largely African American district, a victory in the primary ensured election in November). They made it clear that, in the new world of Texas politics, party loyalty mattered.[17]

## Two Parties, Three Factions (or Perhaps Four)

**faction** A group of citizens within a political party who differ in some important issues from the members of other groups within the same party.

Although the Republican and Democratic parties dominate Texas and national politics, the fact that candidates and voters participate under one or the other label does not guarantee that they always agree with others who share that label. Each party has **factions**—groups of citizens who differ on some important issues from other groups within the same party. Part of the function of party leadership is to smooth over differences within each party so that its members can concentrate their criticisms on politicians of the other party. Knowledge of the factional makeup of each party can foster a better understanding of the ways that the parties may evolve in the future.

### Republicans

Ideologically, the Texas Republican Party tends to be strongly conservative, usually opposing government involvement in the economy but sometimes endorsing such involvement in personal life. Although the party holds two recognizable factions, the social conservatives (most of whom are members of the Christian Right) and the economic conservatives, it is not quite accurate to speak of two opposed groups within the Republican Party. Many Republican office-holders manage to embody both wings of the party as they endorse social conservatism in their *intangible*, symbolic public statements but concentrate on passing *tangible* conservative economic policies while in office.

Both recent Texas governors, Rick Perry (2000–2015) and Greg Abbott (2015–), are good examples of Republican politicians who successfully appeal to the two halves of their party's coalition. Rick Perry, lieutenant governor who took office when governor Bush resigned to run for president, was elected on his own in 2002. In 2006, looking toward another re-election campaign, he publicly endorsed the teaching of "intelligent design" (a euphemism for Christian creationism) rather than the scientific theory of evolution by natural selection in the state's public-school biology classes. Since "intelligent design" is a religious doctrine, it would be unconstitutional to teach it in public schools, as courts have held several times.[18] There is consequently very little chance that such a doctrine could be taught in the state's biology classes. Even if such an unlikely event came to pass, the governor would have virtually nothing to do with it because his office does not have the power to set school curriculum for the state. By endorsing the teaching of "intelligent design," therefore, Perry was not making a genuine proposal for a realistic policy option. He was expressing symbolic solidarity with Christian conservatives.

Meanwhile, during his tenure in office, Perry concentrated on urging the legislature to pass tangible, business-oriented policies such as tort reform, tax relief, and lightening of regulation. He thus managed to appeal to both halves of his party's coalition, the social conservatives through symbolism and the economic conservatives through policies.

His successor, Greg Abbott, has adopted a slightly different strategy to cement the loyalty of both halves of the coalition. Not mentioning evolution directly, he has championed vouchers for the public education system. Christian Right activists would prefer a voucher system because it would allow parents to remove their children from the state-run schools, which are, under the law, secular, and put them into religious schools, which are free to substitute the creation story in the book of Genesis in the Bible for the scientific theory of evolution. Abbott has also strongly endorsed the right of individual Americans to possess firearms, a favorite social-conservative cause. Meanwhile, he endorses the low-tax, low-services policies of the economic conservatives.

## Geographic Distribution

Because the Republicans are the clearly dominant party in Texas, it is easier to describe the areas where they are weak than the areas where they are strong. They are weakest in the areas of the state where Mexican Americans are in the majority or nearly so—along the Rio Grande. They are also less dominant in central Texas, in the "Golden Triangle" of cities in the extreme southeastern part of the state, and in a few counties in the piney woods near the Louisiana border. As a rule, they are less important in the central cities (where minorities are numerous) than in the suburbs or small towns. Everywhere else, their advantage ranges from decisive to overwhelming.

## Socioeconomic and Ethnic Distribution

GOP activists come from a relatively narrow socioeconomic and ethnic base. Most candidates and party activists are Anglo, middle or upper class, businesspersons or professionals (although vice-chair of the party, Alma Perez-Jackson, is Latina, and Robin Armstrong, one of the national committeemen, and Corey Tabor, chaplain, are African American). Since 1994, they have tended to be evangelical Protestants, even though Tom Pauken, the party chair whose battles with Governor Bush have already been described, was Catholic. A sprinkling of African Americans and Latinos can be found among active Republicans, but the party has not appealed to significant numbers of minorities at the electoral level since the 1960s. Furthermore, the party's traditional opposition to policies such as welfare and job-training programs aimed at helping the poor has generally ensured that its activists and voters would be fairly wealthy.

## Conservative Democrats

Despite the fact that Texas has a "two-party system," it has for several decades actually offered its citizens three voting options, for the Democrats historically have been split into two factions. This "three-faction system" has the advantage of making more choices available to voters and the disadvantage of making Texas politics more confusing and chaotic than it might otherwise be.

Conservative Democrats are the representatives of habits of thought and behavior that survive from when Texas was part of the Old South. This traditionalist culture is very conservative on social issues but tends to be conflicted and inconsistent on economic issues. Many southerners are normally conservative economically but can be aroused to a fervent belief in the ability of government to protect the little people of society from wealthy individuals and corporations—an attitude that has historically been known as **populism**. The Populist (People's) Party was strong in Texas during the 1890s, and candidates who make populist-type appeals, such as Jim Ferguson (governor from 1915 to 1917) and W. Lee "Pappy" O'Daniel (1939–1941), have sometimes been elected. This populist streak makes the Old South part of Texas hard to predict on economic issues. (Although President Donald Trump is sometimes described as a Populist, his ideology does not really fit the historical description. Elaborating his set of beliefs and values would take us far beyond the scope of this book).

At the level of the party activists and officeholders, the conservative faction of the Democratic Party is slightly less devoted to laissez faire than Republicans but much more so than the liberal faction. It tends to be conservative on social issues, although conservative Democratic candidates have been known to bend to the left on social issues in an attempt to persuade minority citizens to vote for them. During the 2002 campaign, three of the Democrats' major candidates, Tony Sanchez (governor), Ron Kirk (U.S. senator), and John Sharp (lieutenant governor), were so conservative on economic issues that they were virtually indistinguishable from their Republican opponents, differing from the GOP candidates primarily by being more liberal on such social issues as affirmative action and abortion. The party's candidates for governor in the elections of 2006, 2010, 2014, and 2018, however, were clearly liberal on most issues.

**populism** The political belief or mass movement based on faith in the wisdom and virtue of the common people, and on the conviction that they are being cheated by elites.

## Geographic Distribution

The historical base of conservative Democrats is the piney woods of East Texas, where the traditionalist political culture is strongest. As Republicans have made major inroads among White conservatives, this base has shrunk considerably.

Small cities and rural areas in other parts of the state sometimes remain conservative Democratic in their affiliation, although they are steadily evolving toward greater Republican strength. Conservative Democratic candidates now have to court Hispanic voters to have any hope of success, a necessity that causes them to moderate their issue positions, especially on social issues.

## Socioeconomic and Ethnic Distribution

Representing the historically dominant wing of the party, until the 1980s conservative Democrats drew support from all classes in Texas, but that pattern has changed, for two reasons. First, Republicans have appealed to the wealthy for so long that it is now difficult to find any rich Democrats. Those who remain in Texas tend to be liberals. Second, the arrival of Donald Trump on the national political scene in 2015, and his election to the presidency in 2016, partially on the basis of his White-nationalist and anti-immigrant attitudes, has attracted a significant number of White working-class citizens to his populist/conservative banner, and repelled others. The result has been a scrambling of the political coalitions at both the national and state levels.

Nevertheless, public-opinion research makes it clear that there is still a reservoir of conservative Democratic sentiment in Texas. According to a Texas Lyceum poll in 2018, although only 17 percent of the state's population claimed to be liberals, 39 percent volunteered that they considered themselves to be Democrats—exactly as many as identified as Republican.[19] It seems unlikely, of course, that these citizens will ever be attracted again by an increasingly liberal Democratic party.

## Liberal Democrats

Liberals usually recommend policies that depend on government's being active in economic affairs, especially on behalf of those who have less wealth and power. They tend, however, to oppose government intervention in personal life. Former Governor Ann Richards (who died in 2006) and former mayor of San Antonio (and also former U.S. Secretary of Housing and Urban Development) Henry Cisneros are good examples of Texas liberal Democrats. The most famous and successful of all Texas Democratic politicians, Lyndon Johnson, was mainly, although somewhat inconsistently, a liberal. While a member of the U.S. House of Representatives, from 1937 to 1949, he sided with the left wing of the national party. While U.S. senator, from 1949 to 1961, he leaned more toward the conservative side. As president, from 1963 to 1969, however, he provided vigorous liberal leadership to the country.

## Geographic Distribution

In recent elections, liberal Democrats have been most successful in the areas of Texas where Hispanics are most numerous, in southern and far western areas of the state along and near the border with Mexico. Liberals are also strong where labor unions are a factor: in far East Texas, in East Central Texas, and along some of the Gulf Coast. Liberals can usually rely on doing well in Austin, the Beaumont–Port Arthur–Orange complex, San Antonio, Corpus Christi, and El Paso. They are few and weak in all of North Texas, the Panhandle, and the south plains; they win very small percentages of the vote in the suburbs around the state's large cities, and they are noticeably absent in the cities of Amarillo, Lubbock, and Midland–Odessa.

## Socioeconomic and Ethnic Distribution

Identifying the socioeconomic components of liberal Democratic strength in Texas is more complex than in the case of Republicans or conservative Democrats. Liberals form, at best, an uneasy coalition. While it can be said that liberal strength comes mostly from labor unions, African Americans, Mexican Americans, and certain educated Anglos, the mix is a volatile one that does not make for stable cooperation. White middle- and upper-class liberals can support African Americans and Mexican Americans in their quest for equal treatment, but labor unions have sometimes been cool in this area. African Americans and Mexican Americans usually give little support to reform legislation—of campaign spending and lobbying, for example—or to efforts to protect the natural environment, which energize Anglo liberals. Many Mexican Americans have sometimes been reluctant to vote for African American candidates, and vice versa.

Liberal leadership comes largely, but not exclusively, from the legal, teaching, and other professions. In earlier years, union officials provided leadership for the liberal faction, and in some areas, they still do. But leading the liberal Democrats is an uncertain business, especially after the electoral disasters the party has experienced since 1994.

## The Future of the Three-Faction System

The future does not look bright for Texas conservative Democrats. They are being drained from the right and squeezed from the left. The national party long ago became dominated by a moderate-to-liberal philosophy. Within Texas, Republicans steadily draw away conservative voters, while liberals continue to dominate the party organization. In 2002, the Democratic party offered a "dream team"—a slate of economically conservative candidates for governor, U.S. senator, and lieutenant governor—that differed from its Republican opposition not so much in ideology as in diverse ethnicity. This strategy of running a conservative but multicultural team failed badly, as all three Democrats lost. Since 2006, the Democrats have nominated White liberals for governor, and have been decisively defeated each time. In contemporary Texas, therefore, it may seem that the candidates and issues endorsed by Democrats are irrelevant, because in statewide races they are a hopeless minority.

Yet, as Texas evolves toward a population in which minorities constitute the majority, Democrats are almost certain to continue to nominate many Mexican American and African American candidates. Predictions are always risky, but it is possible to imagine Democratic strategists concluding from demographic trends that their party is destined by history to start winning elections, and that the way to hasten that outcome is to become ever-more-liberal, and to nominate more minority candidates.

It may be realistic, therefore, to foresee a day in the not-too-distant future when Texas has only a conservative Republican Party and a liberal Democratic Party. If voter turnout rates continue to favor conservative Anglos (see Chapter 5), then this arrangement along the ideological spectrum will ensure that Republicans will dominate the state for a long time. If liberal-leaning minorities begin to turn out to vote at higher rates, however, they will alter the party balance decisively. One of the few predictions that can confidently be made about party politics in Texas is that things will change.

## Third Parties in Texas

**third party** A minor political party that fails to achieve permanence but frequently influences the major parties and, through them, public policy.

Texas has had its share of **third parties**. The Know-Nothing Party, representing those who objected to Roman Catholics and immigrants, made a brief appearance before the Civil War. After the Civil War, the Greenback Party, which advocated inflation of the dollar, made an equally brief visit.

More important was the Populist (People's) Party, which reflected widespread discontent among farmers and other "little people." The Populists advocated an extensive program of government regulation of big business and economic policy reform. In particular, the party's 1892 national platform recommended government ownership and operation of railroads, confiscation of all land owned by corporations "in excess of their actual needs," and an income tax for individuals.[20] The fact that the Populist candidate for president drew 100,000 votes in Texas in 1892—almost 20 percent of the votes cast—illustrates the point that Texas's normal political conservatism can be credibly challenged.

New parties cannot get on Texas ballots by simply announcing their intention to run candidates. To allow every splinter group to call itself a party and thereby grab a line on the ballot would make for confusing, chaotic elections with dozens of candidates running for each office. In addition, of course, the major parties are not eager to make it easy for upstart competitors to grab the attention of voters. As a result, every democratic country, and every American state, has laws that discriminate in some manner against new parties.

Texas has some of the toughest ballot access laws in the nation. A person nominated for statewide office by one of the major parties is automatically accorded a spot on the ballot. But in the days following the April primary runoffs, an independent candidate must collect signatures totaling 1 percent of all the votes cast in the last gubernatorial election. These signatures must come from registered voters who did not participate in a primary or runoff that year. All signatures must be accompanied by the voter's registration identification number. The rules vary somewhat for candidates for federal offices and local offices, and for parties as opposed to individuals, but none of them are permissive. If a party manages to collect enough signatures to get its candidates on a ballot, it can ensure itself a place for the next election by garnering 5 percent of the vote for any statewide office or 2 percent of the gubernatorial vote. Needless to say, these rules prevent most independent and third-party candidates from ever getting on the ballot. The Reform Party, riding the popularity of its first presidential candidate, Texan Ross Perot, managed to make the ballot in 1992 and 1996 but has since faded.

Libertarians have qualified for the ballot in every election since 1986. They are the consistent antigovernment party, opposing any regulation of the economy (which makes them more conservative than the Republicans on economic issues) and equally opposing regulation of personal life (disapproving of the war on drugs, for example, which makes them more liberal than the Democrats on social issues). Although their candidates attract only a small percentage of the vote in any given election, the leaders of this parties have hopes of becoming a major force in the future.

Generally, candidates must be the nominees of some party in order to even think about running for statewide office. After 1859, when Texas revolutionary hero Sam Houston, running on his own ticket, beat Democrat H. R. Runnels for the governorship, there were no significant statewide independent candidates for almost a century and a half. In 2006, however, citizens disgruntled with the major parties were offered two candidates who were independent of all party backing.

The first 2006 independent, comptroller Carole Keeton Strayhorn, exemplified the dilemma of the "tweeners," the people who are more-or-less in the middle of the ideological spectrum. During the early 1980s, she had been the conservative Democratic mayor of Austin. In 1985 she became a Republican and ran successfully for a series of offices. Always more liberal than most Republicans but more conservative than the typical Democrat, she was as uneasy in her new party as she had been in her former party. As the Republicans consolidated their grip on state government in the early 2000s, she grew increasingly vocal in her criticisms of the policies pursued by her party, especially in regard to education and welfare. In 2006 she obtained the 45,540 signatures (from registered voters who did not vote in either major party's primary) necessary to put her on the November ballot as an independent candidate. She came in third in the election for governor.

The other 2006 independent was difficult to describe in ordinary political language. A musician, novelist, and humor columnist, Kinky Friedman had had very little to say about politics his entire life when he decided to run for governor in 2005. His campaigning did not do much to dispel the mystery of where he stood on issues, for his "speeches" consisted mainly of comedic one-liners interspersed with clever insults of ruling Republicans. He seemed to appeal mainly to people who were generally disgusted with politics in Texas or to liberals who despaired of voting for a forthright Democratic candidate. He brought a lightness of tone, but no realistic political alternatives, to the campaign of 2006, and only managed to come in fourth.

African Americans have never established a separate political party in Texas, although their main interest group, the National Association for the Advancement of Colored People (NAACP), often functions as a sub-faction of the liberal Democrats. Mexican Americans have established several well-known political interest groups aimed at improving the lot of Spanish-speaking Texans. In the 1970s, however, Mexican Americans formed their first true political party named La Raza Unida (la raza means "the race"), which won some local elections—notably in Crystal City—and even ran candidates for governor and other state offices. But infiltrated by the FBI for alleged radicalism and beset by personal and factional feuds, the party was out of existence by the early 1980s. Mexican Americans in Texas are currently represented by a number of organizations, including LULAC (see Chapter 3) and the Mexican American Legal Defense and Educational Fund (MALDEF), and by two organizations within the Democratic Party, Mexican American Democrats (MAD), and Tejano Democrats. What organizational patterns future Mexican American politics will take is not clear, but it seems certain that Mexican Americans will be of growing importance in Texas politics, as they form an increasingly large percentage of the state's population.

# Summary

**LO4.1**    **Political parties perform several functions in a democracy, and Texas parties can be evaluated according to how well they perform them.**

**LO4.2**    **Ideology is generally one of the most important bases for political parties, and in Texas, where parties have historically been weak, ideology has often been more important than party affiliation.** The major ideological conflict has been between conservatives and liberals. Liberals tend to favor government regulation of the economy but oppose it in personal life, whereas conservatives tend to favor regulation of personal life but oppose it in the economy. These basic differences lead to differences in many areas of public policy, from taxation to abortion. The Texas Republican Party is consistently strongly conservative, but the Democratic Party is split, at least temporarily, into a conservative and a liberal faction. Historically, conservative ideology has dominated Texas politics most of the time.

**LO4.3**    **The best explanation for the dominance of conservative ideology in Texas is that most of the state's institutions, such as families, churches, and schools, are entities that socialize (teach, persuade, indoctrinate) young citizens, who then carry on the ideological traditions.**

**LO4.4**    **Parties appeal to interests, as well as to ideology, to mobilize voter support and campaign contributions.** In attempting to form winning coalitions by putting together groups of voters and contributors, they sometimes reinforce their ideological leanings and sometimes violate them. We supply a list of interests that typically support each party.

**LO4.5**    **From 1874 to the 1970s, Texas was a one-party Democratic state. One-party states are characterized by an absence of party competition, inadequate debate about public policy, low voter turnout, and usually conservative public policy.** For a while in the 1980s and 1990s, Texas appeared to have established vigorous two-party competition, but in retrospect, those decades witnessed a transition to what has recently been one-party Republican rule.

**LO4.6**    **Texas's political parties have both temporary and permanent party organizations.** Nominations are made in primaries, and party leaders have no control over candidates or officeholders. Thus, party organization is much less important than ideology and interests in explaining the politics of the state. This lack of organizational strength means that Texas's parties are not "responsible" and are incapable of fulfilling some of the functions that they would perform in an ideal democracy. Nevertheless, in today's political situation, there is at least robust and spirited debate of public policy. Furthermore, the increasing partisan intensity in the legislature that is visible since 2003 may be a sign that Texas's parties are becoming more organized, disciplined, and coherent.

      Texas has given birth to a number of third parties, none of which achieved permanence but several of which influenced public policy in the state.

**LO4.7**    **Cautious speculations on the future development of the three-faction system.**

**LO4.8**    **Through Texas history, third parties have sometimes arisen to challenge the two major parties, but none have won statewide office, and most have lasted for only a brief period.**

# Critical Thinking

1. What are the basic ideological differences between liberals and conservatives? What are the more important policy differences between them?

2. Are you a liberal or a conservative? Are there any policy areas in which you disagree with what would otherwise be your ideological tendency?

3. Are you a Democrat, a Republican, or an independent? Why?

Governor Greg Abbott, first elected in 2014, re-elected in 2018. Lupe Valdez, the Democratic candidate for governor in 2018.

*(Top) Ron Jenkins/Fort Worth Star-Telegram/MCT/Tribune News Service/Getty Images*
*(Bottom) AP Images/Richard W. Rodriguez*

# Voting, Campaigns, and Elections 5

## Learning Objectives

**LO5.1** Explain the importance of voting in a democracy, the reasons why Texas has low voter turnout, and the major consequences for public policy of this low turnout.

**LO5.2** Summarize the history of the franchise—the right to vote—in Texas.

**LO5.3** Discuss the problem of low voter turnout in Texas, in the light of democratic theory.

**LO5.4** Explore the nature of election campaigns in Texas. Recount the basic facts about primary, general, and special elections. Identify the two most important campaign resources, outline the history of efforts to control campaign contributions, and describe the consequences for democracy of "negative campaigning."

**LO5.5** Describe the pattern of election results in Texas from 1994 to 2018, and explain what change in citizen behavior might cause a change in that pattern.

**LO5.6** Compare the reality of Texas elections to the democratic ideal, and evaluate how close the state comes to the ideal.

Nothing is more basic to the concept of democratic government than the principle of elected representatives freely chosen by the majority of the people, with each person's vote counting equally. In an ideal democracy, election campaigns are contests conducted by rival candidates for the people's support. Candidates debate public policy rather than engaging in a competition of personal insult and insinuations. On the official voting day, citizens cast their ballots on the basis of their evaluation of the debate, with almost everyone participating. On the other hand, in a bad democracy, election campaigns deal in trivialities, evasions, and slanders, candidates pay more attention to the wants of special-interest contributors than to the needs of the public, and very few citizens bother to participate on election day. Is Texas close to or far from the democratic ideal of campaigns and elections?

It is the overall purpose of this chapter to provide readers with information that will allow them to begin to answer this question for themselves. The chapter begins with a consideration of the reasons that voting is important to democracy. The topics that follow include the history of the suffrage (the right to vote) in Texas, the state's registration procedures, and its disturbingly low voter turnout. The focus next turns to election campaigns, with special attention given to the impact of money on the outcome. Afterward, the various types of

SUPPOSE THEY GAVE AN ELECTION AND NOBODY CAME?

*Bumper sticker from the 1960s*

POLITICS HAS GOTTEN SO EXPENSIVE IT TAKES LOTS OF MONEY JUST TO GET BEAT WITH.

*Will Rogers, American humorist, 1931.*

public elections in Texas are described. Next, the election campaigns and voting results of 1994 through 2018 are chronicled. Last comes a comparison of the reality of Texas elections with the democratic ideal and an argument that there is much room for improvement.

# Voting

Because voting is such an important activity, it is useful to discuss both its relevance to democratic theory and the way it is practiced in Texas.

## Why Vote?

As is the case with many important questions, the answer to this one is, "It depends." It depends on whether voting is viewed from the perspective of the individual voter, of the candidates, or of the political system.

From the perspective of the individual voter, there may seem to be no logic in voting, for public elections are almost never won by the margin of a single vote, except perhaps in small towns and special districts. The individual voter has very little hope of affecting the outcome of an election. Why, then, do so many people bother to register and vote? The main reason is that people do not think of voting in completely logical terms. Like other political behavior, voting is governed not only by reason but also by personal loyalties, ideological fervor, custom, and habit. Most people vote primarily because they have been taught that it is their duty as citizens (as, in fact, it is). And even though a single vote is unlikely to affect the outcome of an election, participation in the governing of the community is important to the self-development of each individual.

From the perspective of the candidate, voting is extremely important. There is a saying among politicians that "votes are counted one by one by one." It expresses the insight that although citizens may seem to be part of a mass, it is a mass of individual personalities, each with his or her own motivations, ideology, interests, and hopes for the future. Politicians who forget that each potential supporter is an individual soon find themselves forcibly retired.

From the perspective of the political system, elections are crucial. In democratic theory, it is the participation of the citizens that makes government legitimate (i.e., morally right and worthy of support). When large numbers of citizens neglect or refuse to vote, this raises questions about the most basic underpinnings of political authority.

Voting also performs other functions in a democratic society. The act of participating in an election decreases alienation and opposition by making people feel that they are part of the system. Further, the electorate does have an effect on public policy when it chooses one set of candidates who endorse one set of policies over another. Although one vote is unlikely to determine the outcome of an election, groups of like-minded citizens who vote the same way can be decisive.

Finally, large-scale voting has the added virtue of helping to prevent corruption. It is relatively easy to rig an election when only a few people bother to go to the polls. One of the best guarantees of honest government is a large turnout on election day.

So, despite the fact that one vote almost never matters, democracy depends on each citizen acting as if it does. When people take their right to vote seriously and act as responsible citizens, the system works. When they refuse to participate and stay home on election day, they abdicate control over government to the elites and special interests who are only too happy to run things. We can at least partly judge the extent to which a country or state has a legitimate government by the level of voter turnout among its citizens. How does Texas stack up? This question will be addressed shortly. First, however, must come a look at the legal context of the voting act. The most important parts of that context are suffrage and the system of registration.

## Suffrage

**suffrage** The legal right to vote in public elections.

One of the most important historical developments in American politics has been the expansion of the **suffrage**—the right to vote. The writers of the U.S. Constitution delegated to the states the power to determine voter eligibility in both national and state elections. At the time the Constitution was written, each state decreed the qualifications for voting within its boundaries, and limitations on the suffrage were widespread. Generally, states restricted the suffrage to adult White male property owners who professed a certain religious belief, which varied with the state. As a result of these restrictions, only about 5 percent of the 3,939,214 persons counted in the first national census in 1790 were eligible to vote. An even lower percentage actually went to the polls.

Since that era, a series of democratic reform movements has slowly expanded the suffrage. In the 1820s and 1830s, church membership and property ownership were removed as qualifications for voting in most elections. After the Civil War, the Fourteenth and Fifteenth Amendments to the Constitution were enacted in an attempt to guarantee full political rights to the freed slaves. At first, African Americans voted in substantial numbers. But the southern states, including Texas, retaliated with a series of legal and informal restrictions that succeeded in withdrawing the suffrage from African American citizens in most parts of the old Confederacy by 1900. (It is partly because of persistent southern resistance to Black suffrage that the region is said to have a "traditionalistic" political culture.) It was not until 1965, when Congress passed the Voting Rights Act, that the federal government began to enforce the right of African Americans to vote. In subsequent years, federal court decisions expanded the protection of Black suffrage. Women were enfranchised with the ratification of the Nineteenth Amendment in 1920, and in 1971, the Twenty-sixth Amendment lowered the minimum voting age to eighteen.

Several points stand out in this two-century evolution of the right to vote. First, it is not exclusively Texan but part of a national, even a worldwide, movement toward expanded suffrage. Within the United States, suffrage has been substantially nationalized. States still enact laws, but they do so within guidelines set down by the Constitution, Congress, and the Supreme Court and enforced by the federal Justice Department.

Second, an important part of the story of the struggle to include all citizens in the suffrage has been the fact that well into the 1970s, Texas and other southern states attempted to evade and obstruct the post–Civil War amendments and, later, the Voting Rights Act. They came up with various gimmicks such as poll taxes, White-only primaries, literacy tests, and more to keep African Americans from exercising the franchise.[1] These obstructions also successfully discouraged many Mexican Americans and poor Whites from voting. As a result, voter turnout in the South was far below the levels prevailing in the North.

Third, however, an equally important part of the story is that the federal government, supported by concerned citizens in both the North and South, gradually defeated these anti-democratic schemes, so that by the mid-1970s, all adult Americans had the legal right to vote. As will be discussed shortly, not all of them exercised that right, but at least state governments were no longer preventing them from going to the polling booth. The legal battle for democratic suffrage has been won.

## Registration

**voter registration** The formal action, by government, of making an official decision as to who is legally eligible to vote.

**poll tax** A tax levied on citizens before they are permitted to vote, forbidden by the Twenty-fourth Amendment to the U.S. Constitution in 1964.

Every democratic political system has a **voter registration** procedure to distinguish qualified voters from those who are ineligible because of immaturity, lack of citizenship, mental incapacity, or other reasons. In most countries, registration is easy; in some nations, the government goes to great lengths to make sure that all citizens are registered before every election.

Like the other former slaveholding states of the old Confederacy, however, for most of its history, Texas used a series of legal devices to deliberately limit registration and thus voting. The most effective and longest lasting of the anti-registration schemes was the **poll tax**. This was a $1.50 fee that served as the state's system of registration during the first part of the twentieth century. Those who paid it by January 31 were registered to vote in that year's elections. It discouraged less affluent citizens from registering, for back before inflation had eroded the value of the dollar, the fee represented a substantial portion of a poor person's income. Because people had to be registered in order to vote, this tax was a convenient way for the more affluent to ensure that they would not have to share power with their fellow citizens. Moreover, because minority citizens were usually poor, this device had the deliberate effect of keeping the ballot box a White preserve.

## ISSUE SPOTLIGHT:
## Anti-Fraud or Anti-Democrat?

**D**uring the 2005, 2007, and 2009 legislative sessions, Republican representatives introduced legislation, which, if they had passed, would have required citizens to show a photo identification, such as a driver's license, before they could be issued a ballot at a polling booth on election day. The bills were defeated in those sessions, but in 2011, a "voter identification" bill passed, and was signed by Governor Perry.

Democrats, however, immediately filed suit in the federal court, which overturned the law. Republicans passed similar bills in 2013 and 2015, but those, also, were voided by the courts. Finally, in 2017, a bill passed, and was signed by Governor Abbott, that still required voters to prove who they were, but allowed for several different ways, besides showing a photo identification, for citizens to prove they were eligible to vote. In 2018, this law was accepted by the courts, and is now in force.

Before being passed, these proposed photo ID laws sparked heated debate between the parties, both in and out of the legislature. What were the reasons that each party gave to either recommend or condemn these bills?

Republicans argued that under the present system of voter identification, fraud is too easy and has become too common. People need a driver's license to rent a movie or a DVD, they argued, and it is at least as important to prevent dishonest voting as to prevent dishonest film renting.

Democrats countered that there was no evidence of widespread voter fakery, and that the real purpose of the measure was to disenfranchise people who tended not to have photo identification—older, minority citizens who tend to vote Democratic. The voter identification bill, they charged, was actually a new form of poll tax. Until 2018, this is the reasoning that was accepted by the federal courts. The 2017 law, however, which provided a variety of ways to prove one's citizenship, and which did not insist that all of them include a photograph, satisfied the courts that they were not discriminatory.

Meanwhile, ONE person was convicted of fraudulent voting in Texas during the 2016 election.

Sources: Jason Embry and Corrie MacLaggan, "Key Bills Left for Dead Amid House Slowdown," *Austin American-Statesman*, May 27, 2009, A1; Mark Lisheron, "A Dewhurst Promise, and Voter ID Bill Dies," *Austin American-Statesman*, May 24, 2007, B7; Tom Aldred and Brent Connett, "ID Rule Will Bolster Integrity of Elections," *Austin American-Statesman*, May 1, 2007, A7; Nathanael Isaacson, "Call ID Rule What It Is—A New Kind of Poll Tax," *Austin American-Statesman*, April 28, 2007, A21; Tina Benkiser, "Democrats Are Blocking a Bill to Halt Voter Fraud," *Austin American-Statesman*, May 16, 2005, A13; Leticia Van de Putte, "Texans Shouldn't Need Driver's Licenses to Vote," *Austin American-Statesman*, May 18, 2005, A11; Chuck Lindell, "Abbott Signs More Lenient Voter ID Bill into Law," *Austin American-Statesman*, June 2, 2017, B5; Chuck Lindell, "Final Step: Judge Dismisses Texas Voter ID Challenge," *Austin American-Statesman*, September 18, 2018, B1.

Competency Connection
**CRITICAL THINKING**

**Which do you believe is a bigger problem, voting fraud or voter suppression?**

In 1964, the nation adopted the Twenty-fourth Amendment to the Constitution, outlawing the poll tax. Two years later, the U.S. Supreme Court threw out Texas's tax. The state legislature then devised a new system of voter registration. Although no tax had to be paid, the period of annual registration was identical: October 1 through January 31. Since most poor people (especially minorities) had little education, they were not apt to follow public affairs as closely as those with more education. By the time they became interested in an upcoming election, they had often missed their chance to register. The new law, then, was another ploy to reserve the ballot box for the White and wealthy.

**Equal-Protection Clause** The passage in the Fourteenth Amendment to the U.S. Constitution that guarantees all citizens the same rights as all other citizens.

In January 1971, a federal district court struck down this registration law as a violation of the **Equal Protection Clause** of the Fourteenth Amendment to the U.S. Constitution.[2] Declaring two provisions of the law—the annual registration requirement and the very early deadline for registration—to be discriminatory, the court expressed the opinion that 1.2 million Texans were disenfranchised by them. Later that year, the legislature responded with a new law that made registration much easier. Its major provisions, as amended, are as follows:

1. Initial registration. The voter may register either in person or by mail. A parent, child, or spouse who is registered may register for the voter.
2. Permanency. The voter remains registered as long as he or she remains qualified. A new voter registration card is issued every two years.
3. Period of registration. Voters may register at any time and may vote in any election, provided that they are registered thirty days prior to the election.

To vote in Texas today, one must:

a. Be a United States citizen eighteen years of age by election day.
b. Be a resident of the state and county for thirty days immediately prior to election day.
c. Be a resident of the election precinct on election day.
d. Have registered to vote at least thirty days prior to election day.
e. Not be a convicted felon, or, if convicted, have finished serving one's sentence.

# Texas Turnout

It is not just *voting choice* that is important. Whether or not citizens actually "turn out" to vote on election day is equally important in a democracy.

## Government by the People?

**voter turnout** The proportion of eligible citizens who actually cast ballots in an election.

Despite the fact that registration has been relatively easy in Texas for more than three decades, **voter turnout**, while climbing erratically, is still below national levels. Voter turnout means the proportion of the eligible citizens who actually cast ballots—not the proportion of those registered, but the proportion of adult citizens.

Table 5-1 shows that the percentage of Texans voting in both presidential and off-year congressional elections is considerably lower than the percentage voting nationally. An average of 48.1 percent of eligible Texans turned out for presidential balloting in the most recent twelve elections, and an average of 29.7 percent turned out for off-year congressional elections. In the 2016 presidential balloting Texas voter turnout was about eight percentage points below the turnout level in the country as a whole, and in the 2018 Congressional contest it was about two points below. In only the four most recent presidential elections did the state's turnout rise as high as 50 percent—although the trend is comforting in this regard.

Turnout for state offices is usually even lower than for these national elections, and turnout for local offices is poorer still. Many mayors have been elected with the votes of fewer than 10 percent of their city's electorate.

| TABLE 5-1 | Percentage of Voting-Age Population Voting in National Elections, 1972–2018 | | | | | | | | | | | |
|---|---|---|---|---|---|---|---|---|---|---|---|---|
| **Presidential Elections** | | | | | | | | | | | | |
| | 1972 | 1976 | 1980 | 1984 | 1988 | 1992 | 1996 | 2000 | 2004 | 2008 | 2012 | 2016 |
| U.S. | 55.5 | 54.3 | 51.8 | 53.1 | 50.2 | 55.2 | 50.8 | 52.2 | 60.3 | 61.7 | 57.5 | 59.3 |
| Texas | 45.4 | 47.3 | 44.7 | 47.2 | 44.2 | 49.0 | 43.0 | 45.0 | 53.4 | 53.7 | 53 | 51.6 |
| **Off-Year Congressional Elections (House of Representatives)** | | | | | | | | | | | | |
| | 1974 | 1978 | 1982 | 1986 | 1990 | 1994 | 1998 | 2002 | 2006 | 2010 | 2014 | 2018 |
| U.S. | 36.1 | 35.1 | 38.0 | 36.4 | 35.0 | 38.9 | 37.6 | 39.0 | 39.5 | 40 | 36.7 | 50.1 |
| Texas | 18.4 | 24.0 | 26.2 | 29.1 | 26.8 | 35.0 | 28.0 | 32.0 | 30.1 | 30.1 | 28.5 | 48.3 |

SOURCES: Statistical Abstract of the United States, 101st ed. (Washington, D.C.: U.S. Department of Commerce, Bureau of the Census, 1980), 517; 106th ed. (1989), 259; Federal Elections Commission, Washington, D.C., "Political Intelligence," *Texas Observer*, November 27, 1992, 8; "Voter Turnout Higher Than in '98, Survey Says," *Dallas Morning News*, November 7, 2002, A15; Walter Dean Burnham, Department of Government, University of Texas at Austin; for 2012, 2016, and 2018, from the United States Election Project, online.

Competency Connection
**CRITICAL THINKING**

**Is the long-term trend evident in these percentages good or bad for Texas democracy?**

In other words, government in Texas is never "by the people." At best, it is by a smidgen more than half the people; often, it is by a quarter of the people or even fewer.

## Why Don't Texans Vote?

Americans in general are not known for high voter turnouts, but Texans seem to vote even less than the residents of many other states. Why?

Texas is a rather poor state with a very uneven distribution of wealth. (Despite the increase in overall state prosperity because of the surge in petroleum production during the second decade of the century, Texas still ranked eighth poorest in the country in 2016 in terms of the percentage of its families living in poverty.[3]) The poverty rate is important because the poor and less educated, in the absence of strong parties to persuade them to go to the polls on election day, have a tendency to stay home. When the poor don't vote, the overall turnout rate is low.

The differences between rich and poor citizens are strongly related to differences between turnout rates for ethnic groups. Consider, for example, the national voter turnout rates for Hispanics, Anglos, and African Americans in the presidential and congressional elections from 2006 to 2016, as illustrated in Table 5-2.

As in the nation as a whole, minorities in Texas tend to go to the polls at lower rates than Anglos. (African Americans voted at relatively high rates in the presidential years of 2008 and 2012, undoubtedly because an African American, Barack Obama, was the Democratic candidate. In other years, their turnout was noticeably lower than that of Non-Hispanic Whites). As a result, the low overall state turnout rate is at least partly caused by the tendency of its Black and Latino citizens to stay home on election day. Thus, those who vote tend to be richer, better educated, and White; those who abstain tend to be poorer, uneducated, and minority. This does not mean that all Anglos vote, or that all minorities stay home on election day. But in democratic politics, statistical probabilities have major consequences.

## The Consequences of Nonvoting

The participation differences between ethnic groups in Texas have an important impact on public policy. Minority citizens tend to have more liberal opinions about what government should be doing, at least partly because they are more likely to be poor than Anglos. When they fail to go to the polls, however, their views become irrelevant. Because the more conservative

| TABLE 5-2 | Self-Reported Voter Turnout, 2006–2016 | | |
|---|---|---|---|
| | White, Non-Hispanic | Black, Non-Hispanic | Hispanic |
| 2006 (Congress) | 52% | 40% | 32% |
| 2008 (President) | 66.1 | 65.2 | 49.9 |
| 2010 (Congress) | 48 | 43 | 31 |
| 2012 (President) | 64.1 | 66.6 | 48 |
| 2014 (Congress) | 45.8 | 40.6 | 27 |
| 2016 (President) | 65.3 | 59.6 | 47.6 |

NOTE: The source for this table is self-reported voter turnout compiled by the U.S. Census Bureau. It has long been known that people tend to exaggerate the extent of their past participation because voting is a socially desirable activity. Thus, these figures inevitably contain an upward bias to an unknown extent.

SOURCES: For presidential years, www.census.gov/newsroom/blogs/random-samplings/2017/05/voting-in-america.html; for Congressional years, "Thom File, "Who Votes? Congressional Elections and the American Electorate, 1978–2014," at www.census.gov/content/dam/census/library/publications/2015/demo/p20-577.pdf

Competency Connection
PERSONAL
RESPONSIBILITY

If you personally fit into one of the reported categories, has your participation been like others of the group, or are you an exception?

White citizens vote at higher rates, their preferences usually determine which candidates win and therefore which policies are pursued by government. Low minority turnout is thus one of the major explanations for conservative public policy in Texas.

For example, minorities as a whole are far more Democratic than are Anglos. According to a 2014 Texas survey, only 28 percent of the state's Anglos identified themselves as Democrats, but 44 percent of Hispanics, and 76 percent of Blacks did so.[4] (A national survey in 2017 came up with a very similar distribution.[5]) Nothing is permanent in politics, and rising incomes or some other circumstance may change the balance of party identification among ethnic groups in the near future. But for the present, when minorities don't vote, it hurts Democrats.

Furthermore, it is not just any Democrats who suffer from low minority turnout. The liberal wing of the party needs minority support to win. As Tables 5-3 and 5-4 illustrate, African Americans and Hispanics often hold views on public policy that are clearly more liberal than the opinions of Anglos. Once again, the future may differ from the past and present. For now, however, it seems clear that if African American and Hispanic Texans had higher turnout rates, liberal Democrats would win elections much more often. Such an outcome would mean that government policy in Texas would be more liberal. As it is, the liberals rarely go to the polls, so state government remains conservative.

The crucial part played by different turnout rates is illustrated for the 2002 United States Senate race in Table 5-5. (We are reaching back to the 2002 race because it is the most recent one in which a Democratic candidate had even the slightest chance of winning). Blacks and Mexican Americans voted overwhelmingly for the Democratic candidate Ron Kirk, while Whites supported Republican candidate John Cornyn by a substantial margin. If members of each of the three major ethnic groups had gone to the polls at the state average of 32 percent, Kirk would have won. Because Whites turned out to vote at higher rates than minorities, however, Cornyn won. Ever since, Texas has had two Republican senators instead of one from each party.

The importance of different ethnic turnout rates compels the conclusion that the description of trends in Texas party success in Chapter 4 must be modified. Chapter 4 presented a portrait of a state undergoing a "realignment" from a normal Democratic majority to a normal Republican majority. Now it can be seen that the realignment scenario depends on a continuation of ethnic differences in voter turnout. Further, Texas's Latino population is rapidly growing (see Chapter 1), and because Mexican Americans generally vote Democratic when they do participate, they present the Democratic Party with a so-far-unrealized

| TABLE 5-3 | White and African American | |
|---|---|---|
| **Public Opinion, 2000–2018** | | |
| | **Percent Agreeing Among** | |
| Issue | White | African American |
| Support capital punishment: 2000 (Texas) | 81 | 44 |
| Support school vouchers: 2001 (entire U.S.) | 53 | 46 |
| Agree that the federal government should ensure everyone a job and a good standard of living: 2004 (entire U.S.) | 26 | 45 |
| Support affirmative action programs: 2005 (entire U.S.) | 44 | 72 |
| Teach "Intelligent Design" in public-school biology classes, either along with, or instead of, Darwinism: 2009 (Texas) | 62 | 36 |
| Strongly support an English-only amendment to state constitution: 2009 (Texas) | 59 | 24 |
| Favor building a wall along the US–Mexico border 2016 (Texas) | 52.6 | 9.1 |
| Would prefer universal health insurance program to current system 2017 (Texas) | 41 | 54 |
| Agree that gun control laws should be stricter 2018 (Texas) | 42.3 | 73.1 |
| Approve of President Trump 2018 (Texas) | 59 | 13 |

SOURCES: First item from Christopher Lee, "Majority Think Innocent Have Been Executed," *Dallas Morning News*, June 22, 2000, A1; second item from Karen O'Connor and Larry J. Sabato, *American Government: Continuity and Change* (New York: Pearson, 2004), 411; third item from *The ANES Guide to Public Opinion and Electoral Behavior*, Ann Arbor, Michigan, University of Michigan, Center For Political Studies, accessed on the Web on October 1, 2006: www.umich.edu/~nes/nesguide; fourth item from *The Gallup Poll: Public Opinion 2005* (New York: Rowman and Littlefield, 2007), 314; fifth item from UT-Austin Poll, October, 2008; sixth and seventh items from UT-Austin Poll, February–March, 2009; 2016 data from Texas Lyceum Poll, September, 2016; 2017 data from October, 2017 Texas Poll; 2018 data from June, 2018 Texas Poll.

Competency Connection
PERSONAL RESPONSIBILITY

If you personally fit into one of the reported categories, do your own opinions coincide with those of the other members of 'your' group?

| TABLE 5-4 | Anglo and Hispanic Public Opinion, 2001 to 2018 | |
|---|---|---|
| Question | Anglos | Hispanics |
| Are you satisfied with the way immigrants are treated? 2001 (Entire U.S.) Percent saying yes | 58 | 36 |
| Support school vouchers: 2001 (Entire U.S.) | 53 | 44 |
| Energy policy should emphasize: 2008 (Texas) Increased drilling and building nuclear plants | 28.6 | 7.5 |
| Wind, solar, conservation | 22.7 | 39.0 |
| Oppose English-only amendment to state constitution: 2009 (Texas) | 19 | 57 |
| Favor building a wall along the US–Mexican border 2016 (Texas) | 52.6 | 18.5 |
| Would prefer universal health insurance program to current system 2017 (Texas) | 41 | 50 |
| Agree that gun-control laws should be stricter 2018 (Texas) | 42.3 | 60 |
| Approve of President Trump 2018 (Texas) | 59 | 38 |

SOURCES: First item from *The Gallup Poll 2001* (Wilmington, Del.: Scholastic Resources, 2002), 158; second item from Karen O'Connor and Larry J. Sabato, *American Government: Continuity and Change* (New York: Pearson, 2004), 411; third and fourth items from UT-Austin Poll, October, 2008; fifth item from UT-Austin Texas Poll, February–March, 2009; 2017 data from October, 2017 Texas Poll; 2018 data from June, 2018 Texas Poll.

Competency Connection
PERSONAL RESPONSIBILITY

If you personally fit into one of the reported categories, do your own opinions coincide with those of the other members of 'your' group?

| TABLE 5-5 | Projected Vote in 2002 U.S. Senate Race, Assuming Ethnically Equal Voter Turnouts | | | | | | |
|---|---|---|---|---|---|---|---|
| Ethnicity | % of Population | % of Vote for Kirk | % of Vote for Cornyn | Projected Kirk Vote at 32% Turnout | Projected Cornyn Vote at 32% Turnout | Projected % for Kirk (D) | Projected % for Cornyn (R) |
| White | 52 | 30 | 69 | 705,624 | 1,622,935 | | |
| Black | 11.5 | 97 | 3 | 500,715 | 15,486 | | |
| Hispanic | 32 | 66 | 33 | 948,014 | 474,007 | | |
| Asian | 2.7 | 67 | 33 | 81,201 | 39,994 | | |
| Total Vote | | | | 2,235,554 | 2,152,422 | | |
| Total % | | | | | | 50.1 | 49 |

SOURCES: Calculations by Brian Arbour from exit poll data supplied by Daron Shaw and Mike Baselice. We are grateful to all three for their help.

**Competency Connection**
**CRITICAL THINKING**

If turnout among ethnic groups had been equal in 2002, who would have won the election for U. S. Senate?

## Texas Politics and You

Voting turnout tends to be low among students. Nevertheless, it is very easy for students to register and vote if they want to. Campus political clubs often hand out voter-registration forms, school newspapers frequently list polling areas in advance of election day, and schools themselves commonly provide venues for early voting. Individuals can also access voter registration information by logging on to the state Secretary of State's office. Go on the Web to www.sos.state.tx.us/ and click on the "Am I Registered to Vote?" icon at the top left of the page, then the "Not Registered to Vote?" label, and finally the "Register" label.

**Competency Connection**
**COMMUNICATION SKILLS**

Try it. Was it easy or difficult?

potential to resume its majority status among Texans. In the near future, it can be said with some confidence that the Republicans will continue to dominate Texas *as long as its minority citizens continue to stay away from the voting booths.* The Republican trend, which seems so solid when viewed from the perspective of election results since 1994, is actually quite fragile and could easily be upset if only the Democrats learned how to inspire their partisans to vote.

## Election Campaigns

Democracies do not hold elections unannounced. There is a period of time before the voting day in which the candidates attempt to persuade potential voters to support them. This period is the **election campaign**. In Texas, would-be officeholders run initially during the spring primary campaign. Those who win nomination in the primary then campaign to win the November general election.

**election campaign**
The activities of candidates and parties, trying to persuade citizens to vote for them, in the period of time before an election.

## Campaign Resources

Whatever their strategies, candidates must have two essential resources: people and money.

## People

The people who are needed to work in campaigns are both professionals and volunteers. The professionals plan, organize, and manage the campaign, write the speeches, and raise the money. Volunteer workers are the active amateurs who distribute literature, register and canvass voters, attend the phone banks, and transport supporters to the polls on election day. No major election can be won without competent people who are brought together early enough to plan, organize, and conduct an effective campaign, or without a sufficient number of volunteers to make the personal contacts and get out the vote.

The act of volunteering to work on a campaign not only is useful to the candidate but also is of great importance to the volunteers and to the democratic process. People who work on a campaign learn about the stupendous exertions, the difficult choices, and the painful blunders that make up public life in a free society. They learn tolerance for other points of view, how to argue and evaluate the arguments of other people, and why the media are important. Finally, they learn that when they win, the faults of the republic are not all corrected and that, when they lose, civilization does not collapse. They learn, in other words, to be good citizens. In Texas as elsewhere, political campaigns are the most intense means of creating the truly participatory society.

Professional and voluntary participation, the first major resource of campaigns, is thus entirely uncontroversial. Everyone endorses it. But about the second resource, money, there is great controversy.

## Money

Except in many municipal elections, where volunteers are most important, money is the most important campaign resource. Politicians need money to publicize their candidacies, especially over television. Even in the age of the Internet, with massive quantities of information, persuasion, and propaganda available to most citizens at the click of a mouse, television is still the most important source of campaign news for most Americans. Because statewide candidates have to buy ads in Texas' many media markets, from El Paso to Orange and Dalhart to Brownsville, costs can quickly mount into the millions.

For example, Tony Sanchez spent more than $67 million (62 percent of it for television advertising) attempting to defeat Rick Perry and win the governorship in 2002, while Perry spent almost $28 million (73 percent of it for TV) successfully defending his hold on the office. The two major-party candidates for lieutenant governor, David Dewhurst and John Sharp, spent about $12 million between them, while the major-party candidates for attorney general, Greg Abbott and Kirk Watson, spent roughly $4.5 million.[6] (We are not using figures from later campaigns because the Democratic candidates in those campaigns tended to be underfunded).

This money must come from somewhere. Very few candidates, such as H. Ross Perot, who tried to win the presidency as an independent in 1992 and 1996, and Sanchez, are so rich that they are able to finance their own campaigns. The great majority of candidates, however, must get their money from a source other than their own pockets.

**publicly-funded campaigns** A system in which the government pays for the candidates campaign expenses, either directly or through parties.

The United States is one of the few democracies that does not have **publicly-funded campaigns**. In many other countries, the government gives the parties tax money to cover part of the expenses of campaigning.

This means that the parties, if their candidates are successful, are relatively free of obligation to special interests. In the United States, however, we mostly rely on **privately-funded campaigns**. Candidates and parties must persuade private citizens to part with checks, or their campaigns will fail.

**privately-funded campaigns** A system in which candidates and parties must rely on private citizens to voluntarily donate money to their campaign chests.

The candidate with the most money does not win every election. In 1990, for example, Republican gubernatorial candidate Clayton Williams outspent Democratic candidate Ann Richards two to one and still lost, and in 2002, Tony Sanchez paid out more than two-and-a-half times Rick Perry's total, yet failed to defeat him.[7]

But the best financed candidate does win most of the time. And just because a victorious candidate spent less than the loser does not mean that money was unimportant to his or her campaign. Ann Richards's expenditure of more than $10 million in 1990 and Rick Perry's expenditure of $28 million in 2002 are large chunks of cash by anyone's accounting. Further, scholarly research has established that financial share is positively correlated to vote share, or in other words, the more money candidates spend, the more votes they tend to attract, especially in primary elections.[8]

In sum, although money may not be a *sufficient* resource to ensure political victory, it is still a *necessary* resource. People who are willing to contribute large amounts of money to campaigns, therefore, are extremely important to candidates

### Where Does the Money Come From?

Most of the money contributed to candidates comes from wealthy donors who represent some sort of special interest. For example, of the four major gubernatorial candidates in 2006, Democrat Chris Bell received a quarter of his contributions from people who wrote checks for $25,000 or more; Kinky Friedman received 30 percent of his contributions from checks of the same size, Carole Keeton Strayhorn 45 percent , and Rick Perry 47 percent.[9] In all state campaigns in 2006, 140 Texans contributed at least $100,000, for a total from those contributors of $52 million.[10] (Again we use older information because Democratic candidates in more recent campaigns have been woefully underfunded).

Employing such large contributions, people and organizations with wealth or access to wealth are able to rent the gratitude of candidates by helping to fund their campaigns. Ordinary people who have to worry about paying their bills are not able to contribute nearly as much and therefore cannot ensure candidates' attention to their concerns. In this way, private funding of campaigns skews public policy in favor of special interests.

Therefore, when it comes to money and political campaigns in Texas, the following summary seems justified: Money is very important, but it is not the only resource. Volunteers, imagination, ideology, partisanship, and personality also play a part, as do such things as the state of the economy, the presence or absence of a scandal, and the popularity or unpopularity of national political figures. The 1994 elections demonstrated that on those unusual historical occasions when the voters are particularly angry at the incumbent party, money is relatively unimportant. Nevertheless, because economic wealth is so unequally distributed, it seems particularly dangerous to democratic government. It gives a very few citizens access to a very large political resource. For that reason, journalists and textbook authors are always worrying about its potential power.

As a rule, politicians dislike the system of private campaign financing, finding it time consuming and demeaning. Many retired officeholders have written in their autobiographies that they hated having to ask people for money, both because it made them feel humiliated and because they would rather have been working at crafting public policy. When former astronaut John Glenn retired as United States Senator from Ohio in 1997, for example, he grumbled to a reporter, "I'd rather wrestle a gorilla than ask anybody for another fifty cents."[11] A survey of Texas candidates taken by Common Cause in 1990 revealed that 65 percent of them supported public financing of campaigns.[12] Yet the opposition of the special interests who benefit from the current system has thus far stymied efforts to introduce reform.

### Control of Money in Campaigns

The power of money in campaigns disturbs partisans of democracy because it seems to create an inequality of citizenship. Everyone has only one vote, but some people are multimillionaires. Those with more money to contribute seem to be "super citizens" who can wield influence denied to the rest. For this reason, many people have for decades been trying to control the impact of money in both state and national races. Their success at both levels is spotty at best.

In Texas, several laws have been passed to control the use and disclosure of the money collected by candidates. These laws have been made steadily tougher over the years, but they still allow wealthy individuals to purchase more political influence than is available to their fellow citizens.

## You Decide: Should Texas Have Publicly Funded Campaigns?

Although there is a system of public financing in place for state legislative campaigns in Maine, Arizona, and Connecticut, and a system of partial funding in eleven others, the remaining states permit their elections to be financed entirely from private sources. In Texas, candidates must either pay their own way or accept contributions from private individuals and organizations. There have been many suggestions, over the years, for some sort of plan for Texas to use tax money to support the campaigns of at least the major-party candidates in whole or in part.

### Pro ☑

⬆ State support of candidates would free them from dependence on special interests

⬆ It would not be difficult to devise a system of citizen-contributions that was non-coercive. In Arizona, for example, the program is financed through a 10 percent surcharge on civil penalties and criminal fees.

⬆ Granted that the program should be limited to general elections, are we going to refuse to clean up part of Texas politics because we cannot clean up all of it?

⬆ As with ballot-entry laws, some test of a party's appeal in the previous election could be applied to for state support. Besides, perhaps a few fringe parties arguing their "extremist" views might be a good thing for Texas.

### Con ☒

⬇ Unless all private contributions were outlawed, candidates would still feel beholden to those who contributed. If all private contributions were prohibited, then all candidates would become dependent on state largesse. The state would not be able to resist making "regulations" that would inevitably either favor one party or suppress vigorous debate.

⬇ Use of tax money to support candidates would mean that the coerced contributions of citizens were being used to subsidize candidates whose views many of them might abhor.

⬇ State contributions would almost certainly be limited to candidates in the general election. This would leave candidates in primaries still dependent on wealthy special interests. If the program were extended to primaries, then dozens of candidates would have an incentive to enter, and the costs would grow huge.

⬇ If the program were to be limited to candidates of the two major parties, it would suppress the expression of alternative political opinions. If it were expanded to all parties, it would provide incentives for small fringe parties to claim public subsidies to publicize their extremist views.

Sources: Elizabeth Daniel, "Public Financing: Making It Work," *The National Voter*, June/July 2001, 8–14; Jim Hightower, "The Hard and the Soft," *Texas Observer*, July 18, 2003, 15; Center for Governmental Studies, *Investing in Democracy: Creating Public Financing of Elections in Your Community* (Los Angeles: Center for Governmental Studies, 2003); Public Campaign Website, accessed October 2, 2006: www.publiccampaign.org/; Cato Institute Website, accessed October 2, 2006: www.cato.org/campaignfinance/; on Maine, Arizona, and Connecticut: www.ncsl.org/research/elections-and-campaigns/public-financing-of-campaigns-overview.aspx; information current as of 2015.

**Competency Connection**
**CRITICAL THINKING**

**Have you been persuaded by either of these arguments?**

**The Revenue Act of 1971** This is a federal law intended to broaden the base of financial support and minimize the dependence of candidates on large donations from a few contributors. It provided that taxpayers may stipulate that $1 of their U.S. income tax ($2 on a joint return) be put into the Presidential Election Campaign Fund to provide for the partial public funding of these national campaigns. The amount that taxpayers can contribute has since been raised to $3 for an individual and $6 for a joint return.

**The Federal Election Campaign Act of 1972** This law applies only to campaigns for federal offices—president, vice president, and members of Congress. It establishes a Federal Election Commission, requires candidates to make periodic reports of contributions and expenses, and places certain limits on contributions. Individuals may donate up to $1,000 in each primary or general election and a maximum of $25,000 in a given year. Groups may contribute up to $5,000 per candidate.

**The Texas Campaign Reporting and Disclosure Act of 1973** As amended, this act outlines procedures for campaign reporting and disclosure. It appears to strengthen the election code in several areas where previously it was deficient. As amended, the act's major provisions are:

1. Every candidate for political office and every political committee within the state must appoint a campaign treasurer before accepting contributions or making expenditures.
2. Contributions exceeding $500 by out-of-state political committees can be made only if the names of contributors of $100 or more are disclosed.
3. Detailed financial reports are required of candidates and managers of campaign committees. They must include a list of all contributions and expenditures over $50.
4. Violators face both civil action and criminal penalties.

The 1973 law sounds like a genuine attempt to force public disclosure of the financial sponsors of candidates. Its great flaw, however, was that it contained no provision for enforcement. Since laws do not enforce themselves, the public reporting of private contributions was at best a haphazard affair. Moreover, the law failed to impose any limits on the amount that individuals or organizations can contribute to campaigns; as long as they reported the amount, they could attempt to buy as much influence as they could afford.

**1991 Ethics Law** In 1991, the legislature passed another ethics bill designed to regulate and moderate the impact of private wealth on public policy in campaigns and at other levels of Texas politics. This law created an Ethics Commission that could hold hearings on public complaints, levy fines, and report severe violations to the Travis County (Austin) district attorney for possible prosecution. There are eight Texas Ethics Commissioners, who are appointed by the governor, the lieutenant governor, and the speaker of the state house of representatives.

Again, however, the law failed to place limits on campaign contributions. Furthermore, it required a "supermajority" of six of eight commissioners for important actions, a provision that was practically guaranteed to prevent the vigorous investigation of violators. As John Steiner, the commission's executive director, stated publicly in 1993, "There's very little in the way of real enforcement . . . in most of the laws we administer. It's just an unenforced statute except that if people don't [obey the law], it gets some bad press."[13]

When the Sunset Commission (SC) began evaluating the Texas Ethics Commission (TEC) in 2002 (see Chapter 7 for a discussion of the SC), the supposed ethics watchdog itself came in for some bad publicity. Journalists reported that in its decade of existence the TEC had never issued a subpoena, audited a file, or referred a complaint for criminal prosecution. Further, the commission could not compel targets of an investigation to respond, and therefore, campaign organizations had little incentive to provide complete information. Indeed, members of the public were unable to discover if financial disclosure reports were accurate because the TEC did not thoroughly check the reports that were filed.[14]

All this resulted in bad publicity for the TEC, and embarrassed the commissioners. In 2003, legislators amended the ethics law to make it apply more rigorously to lobbying but did not change the provisions that applied to campaigning. (See Chapter 3 for a discussion of the details of the new provisions of this law). Nevertheless, stung by the public criticism, the commissioners began to be more energetic in investigating and punishing candidates who violated the state's campaign finance laws.

For example, in 2008 the TEC fined state representative Rob Eissler (Republican from the Woodlands) $10,600 and ordered him to repay his campaign organization $18,600 for illegally spending donated money for personal use. Eissler had paid his wife from campaign funds to run his legislative office, which violated a law intended to prevent legislators from living off their campaign donors. These and other such actions showed that the TEC was no longer a completely useless institution.[15]

Nevertheless, as an agency that is supposed to expose the misbehavior of powerful people, the TEC, weak as it is, can still get itself into trouble. In the 2010s, the TEC took on Empower Texans, a conservative organization specializing in dirty tricks, deceptive campaign tactics, and violations of the campaign-finance laws. (Empower Texans is so unscrupulous that two reporters for *Texas Monthly* once referred to the man who runs it, Michael Quinn Sullivan, as "the skunk at the garden party" of Texas politics.") As an organization that has acquired a great deal of influence because of its giving of money and ruthless political actions, however, Empower Texans pushed back. In a 2016 state senate hearing, some of its friendly senators brutally criticized the TEC's representatives. The same year, Empower Texans sued the TEC in state court, arguing that the institution actually does not have the authority to carry out its core functions, including enforcement and oversight of campaign finance rules, and that, therefore, all of its activities should be shut down. (At the writing of this textbook in 2018, this lawsuit was still winding its way through the courts.)[16] In other words, when the TEC does nothing, politics-as-usual proceeds on its unreformed way; when the TEC does something, whatever corrupt person or organization it annoys proceeds to counterattack.

Thus, despite the TEC's efforts to police campaign contributions, there is still virtually no control over, and very little effort to ensure the public disclosure of, the influence of money in Texas political campaigns. As a consequence, people with money have more influence over politicians than do ordinary citizens. For observers who take democratic theory seriously, this situation is the single most disturbing fact about Texas politics.

*Hard* **v.** *Soft* The Federal Election Campaign Act (FECA) of 1972 originally set limits on the amount of money individual candidates could contribute to their own campaigns. But in the case of *Buckley* v. *Valeo* (424 U.S. 1, 1976), the U.S. Supreme Court held that these limits were unconstitutional suppressions of the freedom of speech guaranteed by the First Amendment. It is this decision that allowed Texas billionaire H. Ross Perot to spend millions of dollars of his own money to finance his independent candidacies for the presidency in 1992 and 1996.

*Buckley* v. *Valeo* also extended the right of free speech to political action committees (PACs) for "party building" at the national level. PACs were permitted to spend unlimited amounts on political activities such as get-out-the-vote campaigns or to contribute as much as they wanted to the party organizations, as long as these contributions were not directly coordinated with an individual candidate's election campaign. In the jargon of campaign financing, contributions that go directly to a candidate are "hard money," while those that go to parties, and therefore presumably benefit candidates only indirectly, are "soft money." The effect of *Buckley* v. *Valeo* was not limited to federal elections. Shortly after the case was decided, the attorney general of Texas ruled that the decision voided similar provisions in the state's 1973 campaign finance law as well (Texas Attorney General Opinion H864, 1976). As a

Cartoonist Ben Sargent points out that there is more than one way to corrupt democratic government.

Courtesy of Ben Sargent.

**Competency Connection**
**SOCIAL RESPONSIBILITY**

Do you agree with Ben Sargent that campaign contributions should be controlled?

result, Clayton Williams and Tony Sanchez were able to spend millions of dollars of their own wealth in their runs for governor in 1990 and 2002, and corporate, labor, and trade association PACs were permitted to contribute whatever they wished to state campaigns.

In the legislatures meeting after 2008, there have been a few attempts to impose more controls on campaign contributions, but they have either gone nowhere or been so watered-down as to be pointless.[17] In summary, at the national level, and even moreso in Texas, there is very little control over the ability of rich individuals and interests to buy influence over candidates.

## Negative Campaigning

In addition to the influence of money, another disturbing characteristic of contemporary campaigning is the use of personal attacks on candidates by their opponents, generally in television spots. Candidates are accused of everything from drug addiction to mental illness to marital infidelity to financial dishonesty to Satanism. Mainly, they are accused of being liars.

Personal attacks now dominate the airwaves during election years. According to a study by the Center For Responsive Politics in the Annenburg Public Policy Center at the University of Pennsylvania, 80 percent of the TV campaign spots aired during the Fall of 2006 by the Republican and Democratic campaign committees of the U.S. House of Representatives were negative.[18] It does not take a quantitative study to observe that campaigns have not changed much since that year.

Negative campaigning has a corrosive effect on democracy for four reasons. First, although political science research has not clearly answered the question as to how much influence negative ads have in a typical campaign, it seems clear that at least some elections are decided on the basis of inaccurate or irrelevant charges.[19] Second, discussions of public policy and how to solve national or state problems are shunted aside in everyone's eagerness to throw mud. Third, many good people may decide not to enter political life so that they can avoid becoming the targets of public attack. Fourth, negative campaigning disheartens citizens, who are thus more apt to stay home on election day. Research by political scientists has concluded that such campaigns may depress voter turnout by as much as 5 percent.[20]

Texas has had its share of negative campaigns and, thus, its share of damage to the democratic ideal. A large part of the gubernatorial race in 1990, during both the Democratic primary and the general election, consisted of accusations of illegal drug use by Ann Richards (who won both races despite the charges). The campaign of 2002, to be discussed shortly, broke all records for viciousness and distortion. Negative campaigning in Texas seems no worse than it is in most states, but that is bad enough.

# Public Elections

A public election is the only political activity in which large numbers of Texans (although, as we have seen, usually not a majority) are likely to participate. The state has three types of elections: primary, general, and special elections.

## Primary Elections

A **primary** is an election held within a party to nominate candidates for the general election or to choose delegates to a presidential nominating convention. It is because primaries are so important in Texas that parties are weak. Because they do not control nominations, party "leaders" have no control over officeholders and so, in reality, cannot lead.

Under procedures begun in 1988, the primary election in Texas occurs on the second Tuesday in March in even-numbered years, prior to the general election. The Texas Election Code provides that any political party whose candidate for governor received 20 percent or more of the vote in the most recent general election must hold a primary to choose candidates for upcoming elections. Parties whose candidates polled less than 20 percent may either hold a primary or choose their candidates by the less expensive method of a nominating convention. In effect, Republicans and Democrats must hold primary elections, while smaller third parties may select their candidates in conventions.

Under Texas law, a candidate must win the nomination with a majority vote in the primary. If there is not a majority winner, as there frequently is not if there are more than two candidates, the two leading vote getters meet thirty days later in a general runoff election.

## Texas's "Open" Primary

There are three types of primary election:

**open primary**
An election held within a party to nominate candidates for the general election, in which any registered voter may participate in any party's primary.

1. A blanket primary, used in only two states, is like a general election held before the general election. All candidates of all parties run on one list, and any registered voter can participate.
2. An **open primary** is one in which any registered voter may participate in any party's primary.
3. A **closed primary** is one in which only registered members of a party may participate in that party's primary.

**closed primary**
An election held within a party to nominate candidates for the general election, in which only voters who are registered members of that party may participate.

Technically, Texas laws provide for a closed primary. In practice, however, voters may participate in any primary as long as they have not already voted in the primary of another party during the same year. The only realistic sense in which Texas has a closed primary is that once voters have recorded their party affiliation by voting in one party's primary, they cannot participate in the affairs of the runoff primary or the convention of another party during that year.

Aspiring candidates obtain a place on the primary ballot by applying to the state executive committee for statewide office or to the county chairperson for local office. Drawings are held for position on the ballot, and filing fees discussed below must be paid before the ballot is printed.

## When Held

For most of the twentieth century, Texas and many of the other southern states held primaries in May. Several small northern states, most famously New Hampshire, held their primaries very early in a presidential year—often in January. Both candidates and the media concentrated on these early primaries, making it seem to the public that the New Hampshire winner was certain to win the party nomination. As a result, candidates who won in the early primaries often had achieved so much momentum that they had, in effect, wrapped up their party's nomination before most of the states' primaries had even been held.[21]

Feeling that their own importance was being unfairly neglected, other states, especially in the South, began moving up the dates of their own primaries during presidential years. As all the state primaries began to crowd into the early months of the crucial year, officials of the two major national parties started to make rules about which states could hold parties in which month. The result was an ongoing tussle, in which states were always lobbying the parties to be permitted to hold earlier primaries, and party officials were always trying to resist the pressure. The result of this continuous jostling was that Texas held its 2008 presidential primary on March 4th. Amidst a struggle between the Texas political system and the federal courts, the 2012 primary date slipped back to May 29. In 2016, however, the state managed to move its primary date up to an earlier date of March 1, and kept it in the first week of March during the non-presidential year of 2018.

## Administration and Finance

In Texas, primary elections are administered entirely by political party officials in accordance with the provisions of the Texas Election Code. The process is decentralized. Most of the responsibilities and work fall on the shoulders of the county chairperson and the members of the county executive committee, in cooperation with county clerks.[22] They must arrange for the polling places, provide the voting machines and other equipment, print the ballots, and determine the results. The election is supervised by a presiding judge and an alternate appointed in each precinct by the county chair, subject to approval by the county committee. The presiding judge appoints two or more clerks to actually conduct the election—checking registration rolls, issuing ballots, and settling occasional disputes.

Conducting a primary election is expensive, especially in a state as large as Texas. Clerks are paid a salary, albeit a modest one. Polling places and voting machines must be rented, ballots printed, and other expenses paid. Prior to 1972, the costs were met by charging each aspiring candidate a filing fee. In 1973, the Sixty-third Legislature enacted a permanent primary election finance bill, which provides for a combination of state and private funding. Filing fees are still in use, but the amounts are reasonable, ranging, in 2018, from a high of $5,000 for U.S. senator to $500 for justice of the peace.[23] Expenses beyond those that are covered by the filing fees are paid by the state. County political party chairs pay the costs of the primary and are then reimbursed by the secretary of state.

## General Elections

**general election** An election in which voters choose government officeholders.

The purpose of a **general election** is to choose state and national executives and legislators and state judges. General elections are held in even-numbered years on the Tuesday after the first Monday in November. In 1974, Texas joined the group of states that elect their governors and other state officials in the "off year," the even-numbered year between presidential election years. At the same time, the state adopted a constitutional amendment that extended the terms of office for the governor and other state officials from two to four years.

Unlike the case in primary elections, general and special elections are the responsibility of the state. The secretary of state is the principal election officer, although the election organization is decentralized and most of the actual work is performed at the county level. The county commissioners court appoints election judges, chooses the method of voting—paper ballots or some type of voting machine—and pays the bills. The county clerk conducts absentee balloting and performs many of the functions charged to the commissioners court.

Nominees of established parties are placed on the ballot when they win a party primary or are chosen by a party convention. New parties and independent candidates get on the general

## ISSUE SPOTLIGHT: "Nyet" to Democracy

American, and Texas, election campaigns, imperfect as they are, at least allow American citizens to register their honest opinions at the ballot box. But in 2016, a sinister new force invaded the United States from abroad. Computer experts stationed in Russia, and probably directed from the top of that country's political leadership, attempted to interfere in the American election process. They spread "disinformation" on social media platforms, especially Facebook, with the intention of making all American political conflicts more intense, and disheartening American citizens about the viability of their democracy. They hacked into Democratic computers, then publicized the private information contained in them, in order to embarrass Democratic Presidential candidate Hillary Clinton and aid the cause of Republican candidate Donald Trump. Although it does not appear that Russian efforts actually changed the outcome of the election, the fact that they might have done so adds a chilling new element to American—and Texas—government.

Amidst reports from U.S. intelligence agencies that Russians were again attempting to sew mischief via the Internet in 2018, various American institutions fought back. Facebook shut down dozens of pages and accounts it suspected of having ties to Russia. The states scrambled to make their campaigns, and, especially, their voting machines, more secure. News media reported that only Colorado, Rhode Island, and Virginia had made their voting systems completely impervious to outside meddling. Within Texas, Travis County (Austin) was the only county to achieve what experts called the "gold standard" of ballot security, while the remaining 253 counties tried to catch up.

This is a new kind of "cold war," aimed at disrupting national and state democracy from within. Will Texas be up to the challenge?

**Competency Connection**
**SOCIAL RESPONSIBILITY**

If the candidate that you supported wins an election, does it matter to you if he or she had help from a foreign government?

Sources: Taylor Goldenstein, "Travis Approves New Voting System," *Austin American-Statesman*, August 8, 2018, A1; Editorial, "Travis Paper-Trail Balloting Needs Voters to do Their Party," *Austin American-Statesman*, August 11, 2018, A15; Editorial, "How Are We Stopping Election Interference?" *Austin American-Statesman*, August 12, 2018, A21; James Anderson, "Colorado Tops U.S. in Vote Security, Government Says," *Austin American-Statesman*, September 16, 2018, A20; and dozens of print and electronic media news reports, 2016 to 2018; Associated Press Report, "Is There Interference in the 2018 Midterm Elections?" *Austin American-Statesman*, October 21, 2018, A4.

election ballot by presenting a petition signed by a specified number of qualified voters who have not participated in the primary election of another party. The number of required signatures varies with the office. At the local level, it may be no larger than 500; at the state level, it is 1 percent of the votes cast in the last gubernatorial election.

There is no standard election ballot in Texas. Primary ballots vary from party to party, and general election ballots vary from county to county. Whatever its form, the ballot lists the offices to be filled, beginning with the President (in an appropriate year) and proceeding down to the lowliest local position. Candidates' political party affiliations are listed beside their names, and candidates of the party that polled the most votes in the most recent gubernatorial election are listed first. Other parties' candidates appear in descending order of that party's polling strength in the preceding election. A space is provided for write-in candidates. Constitutional amendments, if any, are listed separately, usually near the bottom of the ballot, followed by local referendum questions.

A somewhat different form of the general election is held in cities. Elections for mayors and city councils are usually held in the Spring, and are always technically nonpartisan. Party labels do not appear beside the candidates' names, and no party certification is needed to get on the ballot. It is custom abetted by city charter provisions, not state law, that prevents partisan politics at the local level (see Chapter 12). By denying the voters the guidance provided by a party label, nonpartisan elections are even more confusing for them than are general elections, and voter turnout tends to be even lower.

## Special Elections

In Texas, a number of special elections are held in addition to primary and general elections. They may be called at the state level to fill vacancies in Congress or in the state legislature or to vote on proposed constitutional amendments. Because special elections are held at irregular times, they, like municipal contests, generally feature very low voter turnout. A special election held in September, 2003 in which the voters were asked if they wished to ratify Proposition 12, which capped medical lawsuit awards at $750,000, generated a barrage of op-ed newspaper columns, and engaged such wealthy interest groups—doctors vs. lawyers—that spending on television spots and mailed flyers topped $13 million. Yet all the loud publicity managed to persuade only about 13 percent of the eligible citizens to go to the polls. (Proposition 12 passed narrowly). Thus do small fractions of the population often determine state policy through special elections.[24]

## Absentee or Early Voting

While voters who register their preferences in the conventional manner must get to a polling place between 7 A.M. and 7 P.M. on election day, Texas citizens may vote absentee in any election. Voting may be done for a period of two weeks before the election at the county clerk's office or at a variety of polling places throughout the county. In the past, one needed a reason to vote absentee, such as a planned trip from the county or illness. In 1987 the legislature removed the restrictions, and anyone can now vote early. Typically, in the twenty-first century, two-thirds of those who vote cast their ballots prior to the official election day.[25]

# Recent Elections in Texas

As is the case with every state, the recent history of elections in Texas displays some clear trends, but also contains hints of possible changes in the future.

## Elections of 1994 through 2016

The political realignment toward which Texas had been inching since the 1960s finally arrived in 1994. Republicans successfully defended a U.S. Senate seat, picked up two seats in the U.S. House of Representatives, increased their representation in the Texas legislature, and garnered more than 900 local offices. They won both vulnerable railroad commission seats and captured minorities on the state Supreme Court and the state board of education. George W. Bush defeated incumbent Democrat Ann Richards to become Texas's governor. Until 1984, Texas had been a one-party Democratic state. After 1994, it increasingly looked like a one-party Republican state.

The patterns of voting evident in 1994 provided a template for interpreting Texas elections for at least the next quarter-century. The Republican victory was based on a clear pattern of ethnic and economic class cleavages and on differences in voter participation. Democratic candidates drew support from lower income Anglos, Mexican Americans, and African Americans. Republicans were supported by the wealthy in general and wealthy Anglos in particular. Because voter turnout was higher in the areas and among the people who tend to support Republicans, they were the winners.

It was perhaps at the level of the judiciary that the Republican Party made the most significant gains in 1994. GOP candidates won every seat they contested on the state Court of Criminal Appeals and Supreme Court, gaining their first majority on the latter since the days of Reconstruction. Republicans captured nineteen local judgeships from the Democrats in Harris County alone. The major long-term result of the Republican court victories was to replace plaintiff-oriented, pro-lawsuit judges with business-oriented, anti-lawsuit judges.

The fact that the 1994 results inaugurated a lasting pattern rather than a temporary perturbation was illustrated by the results of 1996 through 2016. Republicans continued to win every statewide electoral contest as well as all of Texas's electoral votes for president.

The only one of these contests in which the state Democratic party made any credible effort was in 2002. The party, with some difficulties in the primaries, managed to nominate an African American, Ron Kirk, as its candidate for U.S. Senate, a Mexican American, Tony Sanchez, as its standard-bearer for governor, and an Anglo, John Sharp, as its aspirant for lieutenant governor. The Democratic leadership hoped that each candidate would draw voters of his own ethnic group, all of whom would vote for the other candidates of the party. Moreover, by persuading multimillionaire Sanchez to be the nominee, Democrats hoped to overcome the absence of funding that had sunk Gary Mauro, their gubernatorial candidate in 1998.

Sanchez came through with the funding, contributing more than $60 million to his own campaign, but otherwise, the Democratic "dream team" flopped. Ethnic and economic voting followed familiar patterns, with Democrats capturing large majorities of minority voters and those lower on the income scale, and Republicans commanding the allegiance of Anglos and those with higher incomes. The Democratic strategy depended on their dream team inspiring a large turnout among its supporters. In fact, although turnout in some Latino and African American districts was up slightly from previous off-year elections, it did not rise nearly enough to offset the overwhelming advantage all Republican candidates enjoyed with Anglo voters. GOP candidates not only won every statewide office—executive, legislative, and judicial—but captured control of the state House of Representatives for the first time since Reconstruction.

As far as the tone of the 2002 campaign was concerned, all observers agreed that it was the sleaziest, the most vicious, and the least democratically informative contest that anyone could remember. The most deplorable contest among a host of negative campaigns was the one between Sanchez and Perry for the governorship. Sanchez's TV ads were tough, mean, and personal, but at first, they at least dealt with public policy. They blamed Perry for the state's troubled schools, ridiculed him for accepting contributions from energy and insurance interests, and mocked him for being an "unelected" governor (because, as lieutenant governor, he had become the chief executive when George W. Bush had resigned that office to run for President). Toward the end of the contest, however, still behind in the polls, Sanchez made an attack on Perry that was unconnected to any issues before the electorate. Perry's chauffeur had been stopped for a traffic violation by a police officer one day in 2001 as he drove the governor to the capitol building. Not aware that there was a camera and voice recorder on the hood of the police car, Perry had gotten out of the limousine and said to the officer, "Why don't you just let us get on down the road?" Sanchez's campaign got hold of the tapes and played them frequently in television ads, adding: "Rick Perry. Why don't we just let him get on down the road?"

It was unfair and unworthy of a hopeful public servant, but it was not the bottom of the barrel. That was supplied by Perry's campaign. For months, Perry had been running ads informing the electorate that, during the 1980s, one of Sanchez's banks had been discovered to have been knowingly laundering illegal drug money from Mexico. Although the federal judge who had been in charge of the case was happy to tell anyone that he had found that Sanchez had not known about the source of the money, the Perry campaign ignored the facts and kept running the misleading ad.[26]

This was bad enough. But after Sanchez's embarrassing "get on down the road" ad, the Perry campaign retaliated with what was perhaps the most noxious spot in the history of negative advertising. Perry put on camera two former federal Drug Enforcement Administration agents, who insinuated that Sanchez had somehow been involved in the slaying of DEA agent Enrique "Kiki" Camarena in 1985. There was neither evidence nor reasoning to support the charge. If Sanchez had not known about the drug laundering, he certainly could not have known of the drug traffickers' intention to kill an undercover agent. But the Perry campaign played the ad over and over in every media market anyway. Although candidates have asserted many reprehensible things about one another over the years, this was probably the first time that one has accused another of being a murderer. The fact that the charge was a fiction made it all the more indefensible.[27]

Most elections after 2002 were quieter, possibly because Democratic candidates were so underfunded that they could not buy much television advertising, positive or negative. Republican presidential candidates received huge margins in Texas, and their party continued to win every statewide election. There were, in some years, a few local Democratic wrinkles in the statewide Republican triumphs. Austin continued to give its votes to the now-minority party. In Dallas and Houston, Democrats began to win local contests, largely by running minority candidates in minority-majority districts. For example, in Dallas County in 2006, Craig Watkins defeated Toby Shook to become the county's first African American district attorney. Political scientists attributed the trends in the state's two largest cities to continuing demographic changes. Minorities, especially Latinos, had been moving to those cities, while Anglos had been moving to the suburbs in outlying counties. Because minorities tended to vote Democratic, the Democratic vote in the cities was increasing. But, through the election of 2016, these small-scale adjustments had not led to any large-scale changes in the pattern of Texas voting.[28]

Democrats continued to hope that, some day, a combination of minorities becoming a majority of the state's population, and minorities finally deciding to turn out to vote, and vote Democratic, would tip the electoral balance and turn Texas into a "blue state."[29] But, as the Democratic candidate for governor, Wendy Davis, complained after her defeat by Greg Abbott in 2014, "Texas is not a red state. It is a nonvoting blue state."[30]

## Election of 2018

Nationally, in the voting for the United States House of Representatives, the 2018 election was what many journalists and scholars termed a "blue wave."[31] On the basis of a national increase in voter turnout, from 2014 (the last mid-term election) of almost 15 percent, and an 8.6 percentage-point lead in the popular vote, Democrats picked up forty seats, winning their first majority-control since 2011. All observers agreed that the increased turnout and Democratic surge were based on the opposition of various groups and individuals to President Donald Trump's personality and policies. Nevertheless, because of the way the constitutional system distributes U.S. Senate seats across the country, the Republican party actually picked up two extra senators, to increase its majority to 53 out of 100.

Despite a similar surge in voting turnout in Texas, however, especially among minority citizens, the Democratic surge was not quite enough to turn the state blue. Statewide Republican majorities were down from previous elections, but they were still high enough to deny victories to the minority party. In the race that drew the most national interest, U.S. Senator Ted Cruz barely squeaked by his charismatic Democratic challenger, Beto O'Rourke, with 50.9 percent of the vote. Other Republicans won with slightly larger margins. Governor Greg Abbott fended off his Democratic opponent, Lupe Valdez, with almost 56 percent of the vote. In perhaps the most surprising Republican victory, state attorney general Ken Paxton, under indictment for securities fraud, managed to garner 50.6 percent to fend off Justin Nelson.

Democrats picked up two seats in the U.S. House of Representatives, but Republicans kept their solid margin in that institution, winning 22 of 36 seats. Democrats also made inroads in the state legislature, garnering ten extra seats in the state House of Representatives (with two still undecided at this writing) and two in the state Senate. They were still not close to winning a majority in either house, however.

The era of Republican dominance is thus not over in Texas. But the demographic and political trendlines suggest that, other things being equal, the Democrats can be optimistic about their future. Other things are often not equal in history, so nothing can be predicted with confidence. Texas elections, however, can be expected to be colorful, rough-and-tumble, and surprising.

All in all, a survey of voters, campaigns, and elections in Texas is not very encouraging to people who take democratic theory seriously. If the legitimacy of government in a democracy depends on the participation of citizens, then the very low voter turnout in state elections raises serious questions about the legitimacy of Texas government. Moreover, the great disparity in turnout between ethnic groups most certainly biases public policy away from the patterns that would prevail if all citizens voted. Looking beyond voting, the great impact of money on political campaigns and elections suggests the possibility, if not the certainty, that wealthy elites control the policy process, rendering whatever citizen participation exists irrelevant. A cynical view of democracy finds much support in Texas electoral politics.

There is, however, some cause for optimism. The old barriers to participation that kept people from exercising their citizenship are gone, and in fact voter turnout has been rising slowly and unsteadily in recent decades. It is possible that time and education will bring more people to fulfill their potential as citizens. Further, the gubernatorial campaigns of 1990 and 2002 proved that money is not the only thing that counts in Texas politics, and the Republican surge of 1994, together with the Democratic surges of 2006 and 2018, demonstrated that the electorate is capable of making informed choices in the polling booth.

The system, then, is imperfect but not completely depraved. For anyone trying to make a better state, there are both many flaws to try to correct and reason to hope that they may be correctable.

## Summary

**LO5.1** **Voting, campaigning, and elections are important to study because in a democracy the legitimacy of the government depends on the people's participation.** Thus, despite the fact that single votes almost never determine the outcome of elections, voting is important to the individual, the candidate, and the political system.

**LO5.2** **Consistent with its traditionalist history and culture, Texas until recently attempted to suppress voting by all but wealthy Whites.** Today, voter turnout is still below the national average, which is itself comparatively low. This pattern of anemic voter turnout is a problem for governance because, in democratic theory, it is the participation of the citizens that creates the moral underpinning of authority.

**LO 5.3** **Turnout of African Americans and Mexican Americans is generally lower than the turnout of Anglos.** This disparity makes public policy more conservative than it would be otherwise. Nevertheless, voter turnout has been rising in recent elections, and if the trendline continues all Texans may at some point begin to register their true policy preferences via the voting booth.

**LO5.4** **In campaigns, candidates attempt to persuade voters to support them.** To do so, they are forced to spend large amounts of money, which means that they become dependent on wealthy special interests that contribute to their cause. This dependence has consequences for public policy. At both the national and state levels, efforts of reformers to regulate campaign contributions in order to prevent money from dominating democracy have been only partially successful. Money is not absolutely decisive in campaigns, however, and candidates who are outspent by their opponents sometimes win.

There are three kinds of elections in Texas. Primary elections are held to choose candidates for general elections. In general elections, the electorate determines who will serve in public office. Special elections are held when they are needed between general elections, often to either fill unexpected governmental vacancies or to ratify constitutional amendments.

One of the more disturbing trends in election campaigns is the prevalence of negative personal attacks in television advertising. Recent historical experience is somewhat mixed in regard to negative campaigning. On the one hand, the gubernatorial campaigns of 1990 and 2002 were paradigms of sleazy viciousness. On the other hand, several of the most important state campaigns in the 1990s and 2000s were fought cleanly, which gives some reason to hope that future elections may be more issue oriented than those in the past.

**LO5.5** **A state dominated by Democrats until about 1984, Texas became dominated by Republicans starting in 1994.** The statewide victories of Republican candidates are at least partly based on the fact that citizens who are Democrats—primarily minorities—tend to go to the polls in low numbers on election day.

**LO5.6** **A comparison of the reality of Texas electoral politics with the ideal of the democratic polity thus suggests that Texas falls very far below the ideal but offers some reason for optimism.**

## Critical Thinking

1. In the days when Texas deliberately suppressed the voter turnout of everyone but wealthy Whites, was its government legitimate?
2. What are the consequences of differences in turnout among ethnic groups in Texas?
3. What effects does money have on campaigns? Are these good or bad for democratic government?

Dennis Bonnen of Angleton became the speaker of the
Texas house of representatives at the beginning of the 2019
session of the legislature.

*AP Images/Eric Gay*

# The Texas Legislature

6

## Learning Objectives

**LO 6.1** Understand the functions of legislative bodies.

**LO 6.2** Know the general and personal characteristics of legislators.

**LO 6.3** Discuss the structure of the Texas legislature, including size, terms, sessions, legislative districts, and compensation.

**LO 6.4** Understand the nature of power and influence in the legislature, including the roles of the presiding officers, the committee system, and staff agencies.

**LO 6.5** Trace how a bill becomes a law in Texas.

**LO 6.6** Be able to evaluate both the strengths and weaknesses of the Texas legislature, as well as some of the reforms that have been proposed to improve it.

**T**he Texas legislature is not easy to understand because it operates under complicated procedural rules as well as informal norms of behavior for its members. Additionally, state services and the quest to find revenue to fund them grow more complex every session. Nevertheless, because the state constitution vests the legislature with considerable power, understanding at least the basics of legislative operations is important.

This chapter examines the functions of legislative bodies, characteristics of members of the Texas legislature, and legislative compensation. It describes the constitutional, statutory, and informal aspects of legislative structure and the politics of redistricting. The chapter outlines the internal organization of the two houses, including presiding officers, committees, and staff. It then reviews the legislature in action as it goes about the business of making public policy, including the political dynamics influencing legislators. Taking all this information into account, the chapter evaluates the institution and suggests reforms. Finally, there is a narrative and evaluation of the accomplishments and failures of the 86th legislative sessions in 2019.

WHY ARE OUR LEADERS IN AUSTIN SO DETER-
MINED THAT TEXAS BE A MEDIOCRE STATE?

Former Lieutenant Governor Bill Hobby,
*How Things Really Work, 2010*

# Functions of Legislative Bodies

Among the great philosophers who first proposed the idea that a democracy was the only legitimate—morally defensible—kind of government, the legislature was the crucial institution.[1] Because it was the closest to The People, who were the "fountain of legitimacy," it was the part of government that deserved the most power.[2] The first and greatest function of a legislature in a state or nation, therefore, is to make government legitimate by translating citizen participation into government policy. As a result, in both the American and Texas constitutions, the legislature is the first institution discussed.

Nevertheless, the authors of both the United States and Texas constitutions were conflicted in their view of their fellow citizens. While never wavering in their plan to make government power derive from The People, they were also aware that people in general, and specific people in particular, could often be selfish, short-sighted, irrational, cruel, intellectually lazy, and sometimes bigoted, envious of the rich, and apt to be influenced by unscrupulous politicians up to no good. Therefore, the legislature, with both the ability to make laws and the "power of the purse" (authority to raise money through taxes), was the branch of government the most to be feared. It was, then, also the branch of government that most needed to be restrained.[3]

Thus, in both the United States, and in Texas (as we have explained in greater detail in Chapter 2) the first and most important function of the legislature is a paradox: making policy on behalf of The People, but in a manner that is hemmed in and weakened by various checks and balances. The halting, complicated, and sometimes infuriating way that both legislatures function is partly the result of the self-contradictory way that they were intended to create legitimacy by serving The People.

Another function of a legislature is **representation** of the various individuals, groups, and interests in the state, so that their opinions can be heard and their desires respected. Until fairly recently, the Texas legislature represented only a relatively narrow slice of the state's population: Anglo, mostly male, and relatively wealthy. As we shall see, this pattern of representation has been changing, and diversity is now a desired goal. It is a matter of controversy as to whether there has been enough change in this regard.

In terms of activities, the most obvious and understandable function of a legislature is lawmaking. But a focus on just the passing of individual laws—that is, submitting, thinking about, arguing about, and voting on proposed legislation—can be misleading. It is an incomplete approach because legislators generally do not pass laws simply one-by-one, without considering how they relate to other laws. Often, many different laws, over many years, are passed in service to some overall vision, philosophy, or ideology. The unifying philosophy that holds laws together is called *policy*.

Legislative bodies have several other functions as well, most of which arise from the separation of political institutions and the system of checks and balances that underlie our system of government. In addition to lawmaking, **reapportionment** and **redistricting**, which refer to the way that a legislative body determines the geographic area any given legislator will represent, and the constituent function of proposing constitutional amendments are all activities traditionally associated with legislative bodies.

In contrast, activities such as **legislative oversight**, the supervision of the administration, or doing **casework**—favors—for constituents may at first blush seem to belong to the executive rather than to the legislative branch. Conducting investigations also may seem to be an activity more readily associated with the executive branch, but legislators have broad powers to gather information and hold hearings in order to make informed policy judgments. Similarly, when the activity at hand is accusations and trial (impeachment), the details of court organization or procedures, or the settling of disputes such as those over elections, one may think first of the judiciary. Educating and informing the electorate may seem to be a function well suited to the schools or to private groups. In fact, the legislature is involved in all these functions.

**representation** The capacity of one person to act in the interests of another person, a group, an ideology, or all the people in a legislative district; each representative in a legislative body acts in place of a large number of other people

**reapportionment** To reallocate legislative seats by adding seats to areas with heavy population growth and taking away seats from areas without growth.

**redistricting** The designation of geographic areas that are nearly equal in population for the purpose of electing legislators—national, state, and local.

**legislative oversight** The legislature's supervision of the activities of state administrative agencies. Increasingly, the emphasis of oversight is on increasing efficiency and cutting back management—doing more with less.

**casework** A legislator's doing favors for constituents, such as troubleshooting or solving a problem.

Because the legislature is such an important institution, a major goal of this chapter will be to evaluate how well the Texas senate and house of representatives fulfill the functions of a good democratic assembly. Before getting to that bottom line, however, we must discuss fundamental facts about the institution.

# Basic Facts About the Legislature

As with any other institution—football, college, a church, etc.—there are basic rules about who can be in the Texas legislature, and how it must be organized.

## Size, Elections, and Terms

**bicameral** For a legislative body, divided into two chambers or houses.

With the exception of Nebraska, which has a unicameral (single-house) legislature, the American states have patterned themselves on the **bicameral** model of the U.S. Congress. Article III of the Texas Constitution stipulates that the legislature is composed of a senate and a house of representatives.

The two institutions have approximately equal power, but the senate has more prestige and is considered the upper chamber. One reason is its smaller size. Another is that each senator represents nearly five times as many citizens as does a member of the house. Still another factor is the senate's power to ratify or reject executive appointments. In addition, the senate's presiding officer, the lieutenant governor, is elected by the entire state. The senate's less formal procedures permit more extended—and sometimes highly publicized—debate than in the house, and a senator's term of office is longer than that of a member of the house. At both the state and national levels, when a member of the house seeks and wins a senate seat, this achievement is regarded as a political promotion.

The Texas constitution fixes the number of state senators at 31 and the maximum number of representatives at 150. The U.S. Congress has 100 senators and 435 representatives. In the national government, the number of senators is determined by the number of states; the number of members of the House, by statute (legislation). Among the fifty state legislatures, only the term *senate* is used consistently; the lower house is known variously as the assembly, house of representatives, and general assembly.[4] Although the terms *house* and *senate* are used by both national and state governments, and the term *legislator* refers to a lawmaker at any level, *Congress* and *congressman/woman* are exclusively national.

Key features of the system for electing legislators include the following:

1. Selection in the November general election in even-numbered years
2. Election from **single-member districts**
3. Two-year terms for house members and four-year staggered terms for senators, without limit as to the number of terms that can be served
4. A special election called by the governor to fill a vacancy caused by death, resignation, or expulsion from office

**single-member districts** A designated geographic area from which only one representative is elected.

Newly elected legislators take office in January. Whenever reapportionment to establish districts of approximately equal population size occurs—at intervals of no more than ten years—all senators are elected in the same year. They then draw lots to determine who will serve for two years and who will serve the full four-year term. This phenomenon last occurred in 2011, and will take place again in 2021.

If a vacancy occurs because of death, resignation, or expulsion from office, the governor calls a special election to fill it. The most common reason for a vacancy is resignation, usually occurring when a representative runs for higher office or a senator moves to the U.S. Congress or into an executive office. Deaths do occur, but rarely. Often a spouse will be designated to serve as a temporary member if an elected legislator is called to active duty in the armed services.

## Sessions

Two types of legislative sessions may be called—regular and special. Regular sessions are legally required.

**Regular Session**  The constitution provides for regular biennial sessions, beginning on the second Tuesday in January of odd-numbered years. These sessions may run no longer than 140 calendar days. Three other states (Montana, Nevada, and North Dakota) also have biennial sessions; the rest have either annual or continuous sessions or the authority to extend a biennial session across two years.

The short biennial legislative session accentuates all the formal and informal factors that influence legislation in Texas. For example, insufficient time for careful consideration of bills heightens the power of the presiding officers, the lobbyists, and the governor. Also, the brief biennial session prevents issues from being raised in the first place so that the state sometimes delays dealing with problems until a crisis occurs. Although there have been a number of changes in the specifics of the legislative sessions over the years, voters have consistently rejected amendments providing for annual sessions. Their fear of increased governmental power and spending is, in part, a reflection of the antigovernment attitude implicit in a conservative political culture and, in part, an acknowledgment of the $40-plus million price tag for a regular session.

**Special Sessions**  The governor can call the legislature into special session for a maximum of thirty days. The governor determines the agenda for this session. If a legislator wishes to add items to the agenda for a special session, the governor must agree. Thirty-four other state legislatures have mechanisms for calling themselves into special session. In Texas, only in the extraordinary situation that resulted in the impeachment of Governor Jim "Pa" Ferguson in 1917 for suspected corruption has the legislature ever convened a special session on its own. The senate, under the 1999 succession amendment to the constitution, can meet as a committee of the whole to elect an acting lieutenant governor.

The governor may call one special session after another if necessary. However, because the voting public has rejected annual sessions several times, Texas governors usually try to avoid calling numerous special sessions that might appear to function as annual sessions. The average price tag—about $800,000 per special session—is another disincentive. Nevertheless, governors sometimes have little choice about calling a special session because too much legislative business—often including the state budget—is unfinished. It is particularly difficult in a post-census year to complete both redistricting and the budget.

## Legislative Districts

One of the most contentious issues faces the legislature at least once a decade. Disputes over redistricting are strident and partisan.

**Mechanics**  Only one senator or representative may be elected from a particular district by the people living in that district. Although some districts are 300 times larger than others in geographic size (see www.tlc.state.tx.us/redist/maps&reports/maps&reports.html for official maps on the Texas Legislative Council site), each senatorial district had approximately 840,619 residents, and each house district had approximately 173,728 as of 2013.[5] These numbers will increase, of course, after the 2020 census. Achieving equally populated districts does not come easily, because the task is a highly political one carried out by the legislature, and the Texas population continues to grow.

If the legislature fails to redistrict itself, the Legislative Redistricting Board (LRB) comes into play. The LRB is composed of five *ex officio* state officials; that is, they are members by virtue of their holding another office. These five are the lieutenant governor, the speaker of the house, the comptroller of public accounts, the general land commissioner, and the attorney general. If both the legislature and the LRB fail in the reapportionment and redistricting task, the matter goes to the federal courts for resolution. Also, until 2013 the redistricting handiwork of the legislature and the LRB was subject to review not only by the courts but also by the U.S. Department of Justice because Texas, as a state that formerly discriminated against ethnic minorities in the voting process, was subject to the Voting Rights Act of 1965. The *Shelby County* decision by the U.S. Supreme Court, however, eliminated this requirement.

**History** Prior to the mid-1960s, legislative districts were a hodgepodge based partly on population, partly on geography, and largely on protecting rural interests. Members of the senate have always been elected in single-member districts, but in the past, those districts reflected land area, not population. Indeed, the Texas constitution once prohibited a single county, regardless of population, from having more than one senator. House districts were constitutionally based on population, but with limitations that worked against urban counties.[6] In addition, **gerrymandering**—drawing district lines in such a way as to give one faction or one party an advantage—was the norm. (*Gerrymander* is correctly pronounced with the sound of "g" as in gate, not "g" as in gentry.)

> **gerrymandering** The practice of drawing electoral districts in such a way as to advantage one party or one faction.

The federal courts changed the ability of the state to artificially limit representation from urban areas and forced the drawing of legislative districts according to population. In 1962, in *Baker* v. *Carr*[7]—the one-person, one-vote case—the U.S. Supreme Court overturned a legislative districting system that gave one group substantial advantages over another. In 1964, in *Reynolds* v. *Sims*,[8] the Court laid down its first guidelines on conditions that would necessitate redrawing district lines, including a mandate that the membership of both houses be based on population. The Texas house of representatives continued to use multimember legislative districts until the courts forced some counties to abandon them in 1975, and others volunteered to do so.[9]

Citizens in urban areas, Republicans, and ethnic minority groups have all been prominent in redistricting suits. The predominant ethnic minorities in Texas—Hispanics and African Americans—have made some gains through population-based districting. Texas is on the short list of states in which a majority of its population comprises ethnic minorities (the others are Hawaii, California, and New Mexico).[10] Ethnic minority groups made up 21.7 percent of the legislature in 1989. The percentage of "people of color," as journalists had begun to label them, had risen to 35.9 percent in the 2017 legislature.[11]

But because Republicans are mainly Anglo, and representatives from that party dominate the legislature, the percentage of minority representatives is likely to stay well below 50 percent unless Democrats begin to win elections. Indeed, the most dramatic change in the membership of the legislature over the past four decades has been the rise of the Republicans from small minority to robust majority. Table 6-1 shows the gains made by the GOP ("Grand Old Party"—a nickname that dates back to the nineteenth century) through the 2019 legislature. (We have discussed this important change in Texas politics in Chapters 4 and 5.)

As Republicans have transitioned from minority to majority status, conflicts over redistricting have grown intense. Legislators fight over redistricting because how district lines are drawn can powerfully influence who gets elected. How many Republicans or Democrats, how many Anglos versus African Americans or Latinos, and how many liberals or conservatives go to the legislature, can all be affected by the shape and position of districts. As a result, politicians pay as much attention to district line-drawing as to any policy issue they face, and the battles over redistricting that are touched off every ten years by the U.S. Census can be epic.

The biggest redistricting fight of the twenty-first century, in any state, occurred over congressional districts in Texas in 2003. The determination of Republicans, newly empowered by their takeover of the state house of representatives in the 2002 elections, to redraw every district line to benefit their party, sparked a nasty, intensely partisan series of special sessions. These sessions featured, among other dramatic actions, walkouts by Texas democratic state senators to the neighboring states of Oklahoma and New Mexico, abandonment of traditional

| TABLE 6-1 | | | **Political Party Membership in the Texas Legislature, 1977–2019, Transitional Years and Most Recent Years, by Percentage** | | | | |
|---|---|---|---|---|---|---|---|
| | Senate (N = 31) | | House (N = 150) | | Both Houses (N = 181) | |
| Year | Democrat | Republican | Democrat | Republican | Democrat | Republican |
| 1977 | 90.3% | 9.7% | 87.3% | 12.7% | 87.9% | 12.1% |
| 1987 | 80.6 | 19.4 | 62.7 | 37.3 | 71.3 | 28.7 |
| 1997 | 45.2 | 54.8 | 54.7 | 45.3 | 53.0 | 47.0 |
| 2003 | 38.7 | 61.3 | 41.3 | 58.7 | 40.9 | 59.1 |
| 2007 | 35.5 | 64.5 | 45 | 55 | 44.2 | 55.8 |
| 2009 | 38.7 | 61.3 | 49.3 | 50.7 | 47.5 | 52.5 |
| 2019 | 38.7 | 61.3 | 44.7 | 55.3 | 43.6 | 56.4 |

SOURCE: By count, using official records of the House of Representatives and the Senate and Legislative Reference Library, "Membership Statistics for 83rd Legislature," available at http://www.senate.state.tx.us/75r/Senate/Facts.htm and http://www.lrl.state.tx.us/sessions/sessionyears.cfm; 2019 figures from Wikipedia

Competency Connection
**CRITICAL THINKING**

**What is the most important historical trend that you see in these percentages?**

rules, and great rancor.[12] The media branded the walkout Democrats as the Killer Ds; the Republicans had a less kind name and called the walkers Chicken Ds. Senate efforts to prevent such disputes in the future by establishing a bipartisan commission to oversee congressional redistricting died in the lower house. In the end, Republicans got their way, but Democrats have been challenging district lines in court ever since.

# ISSUE SPOTLIGHT:
## No Invitation to the Party

How important political party is and how much the Republicans dominated the legislature were evident in the drawing of two adjacent house districts in the Rio Grande Valley in 2011. Aaron Pena, elected as a Democrat, had switched parties before the legislative session began. He was rewarded with a district that packed virtually every potential Republican vote into his district. That generosity meant destroying the district of the three-term Democrat Veronica Gonzales, chair of the Border and Intergovernmental Affairs Committee, who retained only 1.5 percent of her former district. In the senate, Wendy Davis, a first-term Democrat who represented a substantial portion of the minority population of Tarrant County, found her district redrawn to be more heavily Republican. The African American and Latino parts of her district were then dispersed to three other districts and their votes thus diluted. Davis was re-elected anyway and subsequently ran for governor.

Sources: "There's a Map for That," *Texas Observer*, May 20, 2011, 2; and "Wendy Davis Says Districting Plan an Insult to Her Constituents," *Fort Worth Star-Telegram*, May 12, 2011, available at http://www .star-telegram.com/2011/05/12/3072037/davis-says-redistricting-plan.html on May 19, 2011.

Competency Connection
**SOCIAL RESPONSIBILITY**

**Do you think that drawing district lines to benefit one party or the other is a good or bad thing for Texas democracy?**

## Compensation

Since 1975, members of the Texas legislature have received a salary of $7,200 each year; this figure was established by constitutional amendment. (Texas is one of only six states that set legislative salaries by constitution.) Legislators also receive a per-diem (daily) allowance when the legislature is in regular or special session to cover lodging, meals, and other expenses; for the Eighty-sixth Legislature in 2019, the per-diem rate was $190. In contrast to salary, the per-diem rate is among the highest in the nation. When they serve on a state board or council or conduct legislative business between sessions, legislators also are entitled to per-diem expenses for up to twelve days a month. In addition, they receive a travel allowance. The presiding officers receive the same compensation and are also entitled to apartments provided by the state.

As of 2017, California, the largest state in population, paid legislators $104,118 a year, more than fourteen times what Texas, the second-largest state, pays.[13] The low level of Texas salaries, which voters have repeatedly refused to change, makes legislators simultaneously more susceptible to lobbying tactics—at $7,200, a free lunch is important—and more likely to divert their attention to finding ways to earn a decent living. The latter task has become more difficult with the increase in committee work between legislative sessions and occasional special sessions.

Under a 1991 state constitutional amendment, the Ethics Commission can convene a citizen advisory board to recommend changes in legislative salary; the proposal must then be submitted to the voters. However, as of 2019, no such board had been formed. The Ethics Commission also is empowered to increase the per-diem expense money and has done so regularly.

The "bottom line" on legislative compensation is that the salary is very low, especially for a high-population state with a complex legislative agenda. The fringe benefits are rather generous, however. Some legislators have manipulated salary, the per diem, and travel reimbursements to bring in more than $75,000 during a regular session year. On average, a legislator receives about five times the constitutional salary when all forms of compensation are considered. The fundamentally undemocratic aspect of legislative compensation is that citizens have authorized only the $7,200 salary and might be surprised at the total compensation package. Nevertheless, the reality that confronts Texans is that only Texas, Alabama, and New Hampshire have not increased legislative salaries for more than thirty years.

Legislators also receive an allowance for operating an office both during the session and in the interim between sessions. These allowances compare favorably with those granted by other states. Additionally, legislators are entitled to retirement benefits if they serve at least twelve years if the retirement age is under fifty or eight years if the age is sixty or over. Joining the retirement system is optional; participants have 8 percent of their monthly salaries deducted. The retirement is based on the annual salary of a district judge, which was $140,000 in 2018.[14]

# Membership Characteristics

As is true with all officeholders, legislators have both formal and informal qualifications for the job.

## Formal Qualifications

The formal qualifications necessary to become a member of the Texas legislature are stipulated in Article 3 of the constitution. They are those commonly listed for elected officials: age, residency, U.S. citizenship, and voting status. Members of the senate must be twenty-six years of age or older, qualified voters for five years, and residents of the senatorial district from which they are elected for one year. Members of the house must be at least twenty-one years old, qualified voters, legal residents of the state for two years, and residents of the district from which they are elected for one year.

## Personal Characteristics

The formal qualifications are so broad as to make a substantial portion of the Texas citizenry eligible to run for legislative office. However, individuals with certain types of personal characteristics tend to get elected more readily than individuals who lack the characteristics. These characteristics reflect political, social, and economic realities and traditions and confirm the state's conservative political tradition. That they exist does not mean that they are desirable. Indeed, they indicate that certain groups may be underrepresented in the Texas legislature.

In general, Texas legislators tend to be middle-aged, White, male Protestant lawyers or businessmen who are married, have college educations, belong to a number of civic organizations, have considerable personal money, as well as access to campaign funds, and have the support of the local media. Not every legislator has all of these personal characteristics, but an individual elected without having any of them would be extraordinary indeed. Selected characteristics are shown in Table 6-2.

**Race, Ethnicity, and Sex** Race, ethnicity, and sex are all factors in politics. Both ethnic minorities and women are considerably underrepresented in the Texas legislature in terms of numbers, though not necessarily ideologically. Although Texas's total minority population exceeds 50 percent, minority membership in the legislature in 2019 was only 33.7 percent. The first Asian American member was elected in 2002, and three were members of the legislature in 2019. No Native American is a member. Although there are about 100 women for every 97 men in society, only 23.6 percent of the Eighty-sixth Texas Legislature was women. An important contextual fact about ethnic representation is that most ethnic minority members are Democrats, and the Democrats have been the minority party in both houses since the 2002 elections.

**Occupation** Legislators tend to be white-collar professionals and businesspersons. Other fields, such as farming and ranching, also have fairly strong representation, given their small numbers in the general population. Law traditionally has been seen as preparation for politics. In fact, aspiring politicians often attend law school as a means of gaining entry into politics. The result is that attorneys, who make up less than 4 percent of the state's total population,

| TABLE 6-2 | Selected Characteristics of Members of the Eighty-Sixth Texas Legislature, 2019 | |
|---|---|---|
| **Category** | **Senate = 31** | **House = 150\*** |
| Republicans/Democrats | 19/12 (61.3%/38.7%) | 84/64 (57%/43%) |
| Ethnicity | 7 Hispanic, 2 African American (29% minority) | 31 Hispanic, 17 African American, 3 Asian American (34.7% minority) |
| Women | 22 men, 9 women (29% women) | 114 men, 33 women (22.4% women) |
| Median Age | 50–59 | 50–59 |
| Professions | At least 12 different ones, led by law, fields of business | * |
| Tenure | 25 returning, 6 freshmen (19.3% turnover) | 118 returning, 27 freshman (18.4% turnover) |

*At the time of the writing of this chapter, three seats in the house were open. As a result, percentages are based on a membership of 147, not 150.

*The house did not provide summary information on professions. Usually, house members reflect more types of careers than the members of the smaller senate do.

SOURCE: By count, using official records of the House of Representatives and the Senate and Legislative Reference Library:
https://senate.texas.gov/facts.php
https://lrl.texas.gov/sessions/memberStatistics.cfm
https://house.texas.gov/members
https://senate.texas.gov/members.php

Competency Connection
**CRITICAL THINKING**

After having read our discussions in Chapters 4 and 5, can you explain why ethnic minorities are under-represented in the Texas legislature?

## Texts Politics and You

# Texas Politics and You

Go to the Web site of the Texas legislature: *www.capitol.state.tx.us/*. If you do not know who represents you in the legislature, fill in the "Who Represents Me" address lines and click. You will get a list of both national and state representatives. Once you know the name of your representative or senator, click on "Members" under either the house or the senate, then on the name of your representative or senator, then on his or her home page and biography. Legislators no longer furnish links to their Twitter and Facebook accounts on their biographical pages, although most of them have both. Thus, go to a search engine such as Google or Yahoo or Bing and look for the legislator's name. Find a link to a social medium,

then communicate a message to the legislator on any issue—college tuition, poor condition of the highways, lack of adequate health care in the state, fracking. You can also use the search function on Facebook to connect with your legislators.

Some questions you might ask yourself before communicating with a representative are: What are you planning to write to your legislator about? What expectations do you have for a response? How might engaging in a dialogue with your representative or senator influence your participation in state politics?

**Competency Connection**
**COMMUNICATION SKILLS**

**Who Represents You?**

typically hold one-third of Texas legislative seats. Their numbers have been slowly waning in recent years, reflecting a national trend away from lawyers as legislators. The most frequent business fields are real estate, insurance, finance, and various forms of consulting. In addition, there are several former college professors in the legislature, including some with political science or government degrees.

**Age** The house and senate no longer list the age of individual members, but instead provide summary statistics. Their Websites then indicate the average, which is calculated by adding up all the ages of each member, then dividing by the total membership. In 2019, the average age in the senate was 60, while the average in the house was slightly younger. The growing numbers of young adults are especially underrepresented, but the statistics are a bit misleading because two-thirds of the population under 40 are children. Senior citizens are somewhat overrepresented, which may reflect the reality that the paltry salary of legislators dictates that most individuals wait until they are financially secure to consider running for office.

**Other Factors** Education, marital status, religion, organization, money, and the media are additional factors in legislative elections. Since the late 1970s, virtually all members of the legislature have some college education, and slightly over half hold more than one degree—especially in law or business. The preponderance of legislators is married, although each year more members decline to state whether they are married. In 1991, the legislature had its first acknowledged gay man as a member.

Legislators no longer include religious preference in their biographical information, and it is increasingly difficult to find current information about the religious preferences of Texas citizens. This reality may reflect a greater sensitivity to religious freedom in the state. The most recent information is from the 1990s, when about two-thirds of both houses were Protestant, a little over a quarter of each house was Roman Catholic, and a small number of members were Jewish; several members provided no information about their religion. Those preferences were roughly in keeping with the preferences of the state's residents as a whole, and one can assume that legislators continue to look a great deal like the general public in their religious preferences.

Legislators tend to be members of the "right" groups. Memberships in civic associations, business and professional groups, and social clubs all help convince voters that the candidate is a solid citizen. Such memberships also provide contacts with potential campaign donors. Campaigning for office is expensive. (See Chapters 4 and 5 on this topic).

## Power and Influence in the Texas Legislature

**seniority** In a legislative body, the amount of time spent in continuous service in one house or committee.

**turnover** The proportion of the legislature that consists of first-term members because previous members retired, died, or were defeated at the polls.

**Seniority** has long been of great importance in the committee structure of the U.S. Congress, and Texas voters in many districts were accustomed to reelecting members of the Texas congressional delegation, at least until new district lines were drawn in 2003. In contrast, rapid **turnover** of 20–25 percent traditionally characterized the Texas legislature, with the result that state legislators have been accused of being inexperienced and amateurish. Recently, the rate of turnover has dropped slightly; 19.3 percent of Senators were freshman in 2019 and 18.4 percent of house members. These percentages are still higher than those that usually prevail in Congress, however.

What causes legislative turnover? Running for higher office, retirement, moving into the more profitable private sector, and reapportionment/redistricting are among the causes. Other causes of legislative turnover include tough urban reelection races, changing party alignments, and voter perception.

Although, as we will discuss shortly, seniority in the state legislature is not as important as it is in the U.S. Congress, it is not entirely irrelevant. Not only does long experience increase the probability that a legislator will be knowledgeable about policy issues, but it also means that the legislator will understand how the system works. In the senate, especially, the more-senior members tend to chair committees.

# Legislative Officers, Committees, and Staff

The presiding officers and committee chairs are the dominant players in the Texas legislature. The presiding officers usually vote only in case of a tie, although the speaker of the house is an elected member of the house and could vote should he or she desire to do so. Legislators are assisted by three key staff agencies that are discussed later in this chapter.

## Presiding Officers

The presiding officers of any legislative assembly have more power and prestige than do ordinary members. In Texas, however, the lieutenant governor and the speaker of the house have such sweeping procedural, organizational, administrative, and planning authority that they truly dominate the legislative scene.

Because the legislative session is so short and infrequent, and because the legislators themselves are forced by inadequate pay to be amateurs, the legislature as an institution is always faced with a huge problem of organization. With so little time, and so little information, legislative sessions could easily degenerate into chaotic futility. This large, wealthy, dynamic state would, in essence, be ungoverned. Texas politicians have met this organizational problem by concentrating power in the hands of the presiding officers. With two legislators, each in charge of one house, who are able to direct, discipline, reward, unite, and sometimes bully the individual members to make a united effort to get things done, the legislature usually avoids failure and manages to pass laws and produce a state budget.

By constitutional mandate, the presiding officer in the senate is the lieutenant governor, and the presiding officer in the house of representatives is the speaker of the house. The speaker and the lieutenant governor have both procedural and institutional powers. The first has to do with the organization of the legislature and legislative procedure. In varying degrees, all presiding officers exercise procedural powers of the chair. The second sort of power is institutional, and it has to do with the maintenance of the legislature as a vital organ of government.

Procedurally, the presiding officers:

1. Appoint half or more of the members of substantive committees and all members of procedural and conference committees (the house reserves half of the positions for seniority appointments; the senate requires only that some members have prior experience).
2. Appoint the chairs and vice chairs of all committees.
3. Determine the jurisdiction of committees through the referral of bills.
4. Interpret procedural rules when conflict arises.
5. Schedule legislation for floor action (especially important in the senate, which lacks a complex calendar system).
6. Recognize members who wish to speak, or refrain from recognizing them and thus prevent them from speaking.

The speaker and the lieutenant governor also have important powers to maintain the legislature as an institution, including:

1. Appointing the members of the Legislative Budget Board and serving as the cochairs thereof.
2. Appointing the members of the Texas Legislative Council and serving as the cochairs thereof.
3. Appointing the members of the Legislative Audit Committee and serving as the cochairs thereof.

Because of the historical one-party tradition, the tendency to have bipartisan leadership, and the domination of the presiding officers, party positions such as whip do not reach the same importance as they do in the U.S. Congress. The committee chairs hold the secondary positions of power, after the presiding officers. But because chairs are appointed by the presiding officers, they only rarely offer any threat to the power of either the speaker or the lieutenant governor.

**Lieutenant Governor** The lieutenant governor is elected independently by the citizenry, serves as president of the senate but is not a member of it, and does not run on a ticket with the gubernatorial candidate. The lieutenant governor rarely performs any executive functions and is chiefly a legislative official. The term of the office is four years.

Twenty-seven other states use the lieutenant governor as the presiding officer of the upper house. But these states (usually) also look to the governor for policy recommendations; their chamber rules are such that the lieutenant governor, far from exercising any real power, is generally in a position similar to that of the vice president of the United States—neither an important executive nor a legislative force. Such is not the case in Texas, where the lieutenant governor is a major force in state politics and one of the dominant figures during legislative sessions.

The ability of a determined lieutenant governor to impose his will on the senate was on display early in the 2019 legislative session. Senator Kel Seliger, who represented Amarillo and the state's panhandle, was the second-longest serving senator, and, although a Republican, known for not always following the requests of the party leadership. In particular, Seliger typically voted the wishes of his rural constituents, rather than the policy preferences of most party leaders, in opposing the creation of a "voucher" system to replace the state's public-school system. (For a detailed discussion of this issue, see Chapter 13). Under Republican Lt. Governor David Dewhurst, a rather mild personality, Seliger had not been punished for this deviation from the party line; indeed, Dewhurst had appointed him chair of the Higher Education Committee, and a member of the Finance Committee.

But Dan Patrick, who beat Dewhurst in the 2014 Republican primary, and was chosen lieutenant governor in the general election that year, was a sterner character. In the first two sessions in which he ran the senate, 2015 and 2017, Patrick deferred to Seliger's intelligence and competence, and, like Dewhurst, appointed him chair of Higher Education. In both sessions, however, Seliger refused to go along with several of Patrick's policy preferences, including the school-voucher plan. By 2019, Patrick had decided to impose his will. He appointed Seliger to neither Higher Education, nor Finance, instead, making him chair of the Agriculture Committee.

Seliger, no meek character himself, complained publicly, and made the politics of the situation perfectly clear. "This is a warning to other Republicans," he told an interviewer, "that if you stray from the Lieutenant Governor's agenda, there will be a price to pay." Indeed, and there was also a price to pay for complaining. The day after the interview appeared, Patrick removed Seliger from the Agriculture Committee. "We have a lot of serious business to do, and I need people who are on the team, pulling together," he explained to the media.[15]

In this one incident is a good illustration of the potential power of the presiding officer of the senate. If he insists that the senators be loyal to "the team," they had better comply, or find themselves bench-warmers.

**Speaker of the House** In contrast to the lieutenant governor, who is chosen by the voters statewide, the speaker of the Texas house of representatives is an elected member of the house who is formally chosen as speaker by a majority vote of the house membership at the opening of the legislative session. The results of the election are rarely a surprise; by the time the session opens, everyone usually knows who the speaker will be. Candidates for speaker begin maneuvering for support long before the previous session has ended. And during the session interims, they not only campaign for election to the house in their home districts, but also try to secure from fellow house members written pledges of support in the race for speaker. If an incumbent speaker is seeking reelection, usually no other candidates run.

Until 1951, speakers traditionally served for one term; between 1951 and 1975, they served either one or two. The house has abandoned the limited-term tradition, however. Billy Clayton served four terms as speaker (1975–1983), and his successor, Gib Lewis, served five (1983–1993). James E. (Pete) Laney, a West Texas cotton farmer, bested eight other house members to become speaker in 1993 and was elected to a fifth term in 2001.

Although the speaker has the same powers within the house that the lieutenant governor has within the senate, the fact that he (or, possibly in the future, she) is chosen by his colleagues within the legislature means that he must be more respectful of their opinions. Theoretically, a lieutenant governor could be tyrannical in behavior and contemptuous in attitude toward the other senators, without fear of losing his job. No matter how he treated them, they could not remove him.

But because the speaker is chosen by other members within the house, he (or, again, potentially, she) must be careful how he treats them. If he alienates too many of them, he could be replaced as presiding officer before the next legislative session.

A good example is representative Tom Craddick. He served as speaker for three terms (2003–2009) during which he became known as an authoritarian and oppressive leader. His heavy-handedness created resentment among the other house members. As a result, he was almost overturned in 2007, and by 2009, a movement known as ABC ("anyone but Craddick") made it obvious that he would not be re-elected to a fourth term.

The ABC rebellion created a situation that was highly unusual. As we have discussed in Chapter 4, the ruling Republican party has two factions, one whose members emphasize economic issues ("business conservatives"), and one whose members emphasize issues having to do with sex, religion, immigration, and guns ("populist movement conservatives" or "social conservatives"). Prior to the house 2009 session, in which the Republicans held a slim 76-to-74 majority, a group of eleven business conservatives, led by Joe Straus of San Antonio, met with the leaders of the Democrats to plan a rebellion against Craddick.

Although the Democrats held only a minority of seats in the house, and the business conservatives were a minority within the ruling Republicans, together they constituted a majority of all the seats. They struck a deal. Just before the 2009 session opened, Straus announced that he had pledges of support for the speakership from eighty-five members of the house, a comfortable majority. At this point, all other contenders, including Craddick, withdrew from consideration, and Straus was elected. Observers of Texas politics witnessed the bizarre spectacle of a Republican speaker, in a Republican-dominated institution, owing his office to Democratic votes.[16]

Straus was re-elected speaker in the sessions from 2011 to 2017. As we have discussed in Chapter 4, his moderation on social issues led to an intra-party rebellion against him in 2018, and he chose not to run for re-election to his state legislative seat in the general election of that year. But by then, the point had been made clearly: Unlike the situation in the senate, the presiding officer of the house must take care to remain popular, or at least tolerable, to his colleagues.

The different situations of the two presiding officers, one dependent upon his colleagues for his office, the other independent of them, may account for the differences in the way committee chairs have been distributed in recent years. Traditionally, the representatives from minority party were given roughly a third of committee chairs in both houses. When Dan Patrick campaigned against David Dewhurst for the Republican nomination for lieutenant governor in the 2014 primary, however, he promised to be a more partisan presiding officer of the senate. He was as good as his word, appointing only two Democratic chairs out of the fourteen senate committees (17 percent). By 2019 he had not slackened the partisanship of his appointments, as Democrats began the session running just two of the sixteen committees (12.5 percent).

Meanwhile, Joe Straus, as might be expected, was much less partisan in awarding committee chairmanships in the house. In 2015, thirteen Democrats, 33 percent of the forty available, became committee chairs. Given the circumstances under which Straus departed, it might have been expected that when Dennis Bonnen replaced Straus as speaker in 2019, he would emulate Patrick and freeze out the members of the minority party. Instead, however, Bonnen was at least as non-partisan as Straus had been in handing out chairmanships. Twelve of the thirty-four committees went to Democrats, or 36 percent.[17] Our conclusion must be that the relation between the parties in the house is thus different than it is in the senate.

## Centralized Power?

Because the lieutenant governor is so powerful in the senate, and the speaker is so powerful in the house, the question arises as to whether the institution as a whole is basically a tyranny, with two people creating Texas public policy, and almost everyone else a spectator. The answer is that, despite their undoubted control over the proceedings of the legislature, the two presiding officers do not qualify as co-tyrants. This evaluation is based on several generalizations.

First, the very fact that there are two presiding officers, who are very likely to be ambitious, dominating personalities, means that their cooperation cannot be guaranteed even when they represent the same party. Speaker Joe Straus and Lieutenant Governor Dan Patrick, in 2017, are perfect examples of the dysfunction and paralysis that can result when the presiding officers disagree on policy. On a host of issues, from whether or not to pass a law requiring that all people use the public restroom that would be appropriate according to their sex (a social issue), to how to reform the state's property-tax system (an economic issue), Patrick and Straus frustrated each other for the whole session. Two presiding officers may get along with perfect harmony in the future, of course. But, given the nature of the political personality, two separate institutions can be expected to clash through much of history.

Second, the two presiding officers are not the only players in the game. As we will discuss in Chapter 7, the governor has a very important, if largely negative, potential power over all legislation. As we will point out in Chapter 8, the comptroller is crucial in determining the size of the single most important piece of legislation passed each session, the state budget. At various

## ISSUE SPOTLIGHT:
## Whose Bill Is It, Anyhow?

An Austin lawyer-lobbyist remarked on his twenty years as a legislator by noting, "Here at the legislature, if you ask the question, 'Whose bill is it?' what you mean is, 'Which lobby wrote it?' If you want to know which legislator is sponsoring the bill, you ask, 'Who's carrying the bill?' That'll give you some idea of how influential lobbyists are."

**Competency Connection**
**CRITICAL THINKING**

After reading Chapters 3 and 5, can you explain why lobbyists are so influential in the Texas legislature?

times in Texas history—and especially in regard to education policy, which we will examine in Chapter 13—the state courts have been major players. And finally, in recent decades the federal courts have played an active role in blocking various policies that the socially-conservative wing of the Republican party enacted into state law, especially in regard to the Constitutional right of a woman to have an abortion.

Third, legislation does not take place in a vacuum. Although most Texas citizens do not follow the workings of the legislature closely, some issues draw intense public scrutiny. (An example would be the "bathroom bill" of 2017, mentioned earlier). And some individual citizens pay a great deal of attention to what goes on in a legislative session, because they are members of the media, because some proposed piece of legislation affects them personally, or because they are active in an interest group that lobbies legislators (See Chapter 3).

As we discussed in Chapters 3 and 5, some of those citizens give a great deal of money to politicians who please them, which means that they can withhold those campaign contributions if they are displeased. The presiding officers in the legislature, as professional politicians, are always thinking, not just about how to make good public policy, but about how to keep their public support. In a democratic political system such as the one in Texas, the ultimate check on the actions of a presiding officer is the voting public.

In summary, then, the two presiding officers are the most important, but by no means the only, actors in the process of enacting legislation in Texas.

### Legislative Committees

Legislative bodies in the United States have long relied on committees to divide up their work because the alternative is trying to accomplish detailed legislation, planning, and investigation by the whole house. "Everybody does everything" is not a formula for success in any institution. Thus, committees are critical to the legislative process in Texas. The five basic types of committees in the state legislature are listed here. Note that these categories are not mutually exclusive.

1. Standing committees are established by the rules of the two houses as permanent mini-institutions. They deal with designated areas of public policy. Because their chairs are appointed by the presiding officers, they are likely to pursue the policies that those officers prefer. But because many legislators are intelligent, energetic people with strong opinions, and because the presiding officers cannot pay attention to everything at once, committee members can often pursue independent lines of inquiry and legislation.

The state struggled with public school funding, children's health, and other issues from 2003 on, but the legislature often focused on political questions such as immigration and voter identification instead of pressing policy needs. This Ben Sargent cartoon sums up legislative and executive leadership during the period as an empty gas tank.

Courtesy of Ben Sargent

**Competency Connection**
**CRITICAL THINKING**

Why do you think that the legislature has such trouble with issues involving the expenditure of money?

2. Subcommittees are subdivisions of standing committees. They consider specialized areas of their standing committees' general jurisdiction.

3. Conference committees are formed for the purpose of arriving at acceptable compromises on bills that have passed both houses, but in different forms. These temporary committees include members from both houses, and also usually include a select number of members of the standing committees that originally had jurisdiction over the bills in question. Ad hoc committees are temporary and are appointed to consider specific issues or problems. Conference committees are a type of ad hoc committee. So are select committees appointed to deal with a specific item of legislation. A few of the best-known select committees have addressed public education, tax equity, public schools, the Texas Youth Committee, voter identification, transportation funding, and redistricting.

4. Interim committees continue the work of the legislature after the session ends, to study a particular problem and/or to make recommendations to the next legislature. Interim committees are frequently joint committees—that is, they have members from both houses.

## Legislative Staff

Although Texas legislators enjoy better office budgets and staff allowances than their counterparts in some other states, they still must rely on information furnished by outside groups. For example, the Texas Research League, a private business-oriented group, performs numerous studies and makes recommendations to the legislature. The Legislative Budget Board (LBB), an internal agency of the legislature, makes recommendations on the same appropriations bills that it helps to prepare. The Legislative Reference Library, while a valuable tool, is limited to maintaining a history of legislation in Texas and furnishing information on comparable legislation in other states.

Legislative committees also have limited budgets and professional staff, although a presiding officer may give his or her favorite committees liberal spending privileges. Accordingly, committees often must rely on assistance from the institutional staff of the legislature, such as the LBB, and from other state agencies, such as the attorney general's office or the comptroller's office. In addition, from time to time, legislators with compatible views form study groups to work on issues.

The lack of adequate staffing is of major importance to Texans. It means that legislators, in committee or individually, cannot easily obtain impartial, accurate information concerning public policy. Nonetheless, citizen interest in supporting larger budgets for legislative operations seems to be nil. Indeed, some Texans see any move on the part of legislators to eliminate their dependence on private groups and state administrators for information as a ploy to "waste" more tax money. This attitude, fully encouraged by lobbyists, keeps staffing low, although the National Conference of State Legislatures notes that the strength of a legislative body rests with its staff.[18]

**Legislative Budget Board** At the national level, in most states and even in most cities, the chief executive bears the responsibility for preparing the budget. In Texas, both the governor and the legislature prepare a budget, and state agencies must submit their financial requests to each. The legislative budget is prepared by the Legislative Budget Board (LBB), a ten-member senate-house joint committee that operates continually, whether the legislature is in session or not. In addition to the presiding officers, there are four members from each house appointed by the presiding officers. By tradition, these include the chairpersons of the committees responsible for appropriations and finance. Because of the importance of these "money" committees, their chairpersons sometimes develop power bases within the legislature that are independent of the presiding officers.

A professional staff assists the board in making its budget recommendations and then often helps defend those recommendations during the session. The staff recommendations on state agency requests are crucial to an agency's appropriations. Executives in administrative agencies therefore work closely with LBB staff in an effort to justify their spending requests. Additionally, the staff assists the legislature in its watchdog function by overseeing state agency expenditures and agency efficiency. This function increases in importance whenever the state has budget "crunches," most recently in 2011. Both the LBB and the Governor's Office of Budget and Planning now oversee agency planning and monitor agency performance in meeting state goals and objectives.

**Texas Legislative Council** The membership of the Texas Legislative Council was modified in 2003 to reduce the domination by the house of representatives. Today, its fourteen members consist of the speaker and the lieutenant governor, who each appoint six additional members from the house and six members from the senate.

The council oversees the work of the director and professional staff. During the session, the council provides bill-drafting services for legislators; between sessions, it investigates the operations of state agencies, conducts studies on problems subject to legislative consideration, and drafts recommendations for action in the next session. In short, it is the legislature's research office, similar to the Congressional Research Service.

**Legislative Audit Committee** In addition to the presiding officers, the other four members of the Legislative Audit Committee are the chairpersons of the Senate Finance, House Ways and Means, House Appropriations, and Senate State Affairs committees. The state auditor, appointed by the committee for a two-year term subject to two-thirds confirmation of the senate, heads the professional staff. This committee oversees a very important function of all legislative bodies, namely, checking that agencies properly spent money budgeted to them (the *post-audit*). The auditor and the auditor's staff also check into the quality of services and duplication in services and programs provided by state agencies. The highly detailed work of the professional staff involves a review of the records of financial transactions. In fact, the larger state agencies have an auditor or team of auditors assigned to them practically year-round.

# How a Bill Becomes a Law in Texas

The Texas Constitution specifies that a bill be used to introduce a law or a change in a law. Bills that pass both houses successfully become acts and are sent to the governor for his or her signature or veto. In addition to bills, there are three types of resolutions in each house:

1. Simple resolutions are used in each house to take care of housekeeping matters, details of business, and trivia. Examples include procedural rules adopted by each house—serious business, indeed—and trivia, such as birthday greetings to a member.
2. Concurrent resolutions are similar to simple resolutions but require the action of both houses. An example would be their use for adjournment.
3. Joint resolutions are of major interest to the public because they are the means of introducing proposed constitutional amendments. They require no action by the governor.

Each bill or resolution is designated by an abbreviation that indicates the house of origin, the nature of the legislation, and a number. For example, S.B. 1 is Senate Bill 1; S.J.R. indicates a joint resolution that originated in the senate.

Bills may originate in either house or in both simultaneously, with the exception of revenue bills, which must originate in the house, according to the Texas Constitution. During a typical session, legislators introduce several thousand (4,333 in 2017) bills, of which only 15 to 30 percent are passed.[19] After each census, when the legislature must also deal with reapportionment and redistricting, the number is reduced by several hundred as a concession to the time redistricting will take. Because lawmakers must consider so many proposals in such a limited time, originators of a bill often mark a bill "By Request" and drop it in the hopper—the traditional legislative "in-basket." This is their way of indicating that they were asked (probably by a constituent or a campaign contributor) to introduce the legislation but do not expect it to receive serious consideration.

These are the major differences in the procedures of the two houses:

1. The house has about twice as many committees as the senate; therefore, the speaker has a greater choice in determining where to refer a bill.
2. The calendars are different (as explained later in this chapter).
3. Debate is unlimited in the senate, whereas house debate is usually limited to ten minutes per member and twenty minutes for the bill's sponsor.

To be enacted into law, a bill must survive as many as four legislative steps and a fifth step in the governor's office (see Figure 6-1). Because the smaller size of the senate enables it to operate with less formality than the house, we use the senate to trace the path of a bill through the legislative process.

## Step One: Introduction and Referral

Every bill must be introduced by a member of the legislature, who is considered the sponsor. If a bill has several sponsors, its chances of survival are greatly enhanced. Bills can be introduced in two ways: (1) The member, after being recognized by the lieutenant governor as president of the senate, may introduce it from the floor; or (2) the member may deposit copies of the bill with the secretary of the senate (in the house, with the clerk), including prefiling a bill in November. The secretary assigns a number to the bill that reflects the order of submission. The reading clerk then gives the bill the first of the three readings required by the constitution. The first time, only a caption is read, which is a brief summary of the bill's contents. The second method of introducing bills is the one more commonly used. Legislation can only be introduced in the first sixty days of the session; as the deadline draws near, the number of bill filings increases exponentially.

## SENATE

**Step 1.** Bill is introduced, numbered, given first reading, referred to committee.

**Step 2.** Committee holds hearings, deliberates, and either pigeonholes the bill, reports it unfavorably, or reports it favorably. Favorable report may include amendments or be a substitute bill. Committee report is printed and distributed to senate.

**Step 3.** Senate has second reading, holds debate, amends bill, possibly has a filibuster. Senate then has third reading, debate, amendments only by two-thirds vote. Passed bill is sent to house.

## HOUSE

**Step 1.** House has first reading, and bill is referred to committee.

**Step 2.** Committee action is the same as in senate.

**Step 3.** Floor action is similar to senate except that no filibuster is possible and scheduling the bill for debate is more complex. Amended bill is returned to senate.

## SENATE AND HOUSE

**Step 4.** Conference committee irons out differences in house and senate versions of the bill. Both houses vote on conference compromise bill. Clean copy of the conference bill is prepared. Bill is enrolled and certified in both houses, and sent to the governor.

## GOVERNOR

**Step 5.** Governor may sign the act, let it become a law without his or her signature, or veto it.

Figure 6-1  How a Bill Becomes a Law in Texas.

This figure traces the passage of a bill that originated in the senate. Steps 1 to 3 for the senate and house would be reversed if the bill originated in the house. The example presumes the need for a conference committee.

The lieutenant governor (in the house, the speaker) then refers the bill to a committee. Because committees have life or death power over a bill, if the bill is to survive, it must be assigned to a friendly committee. The bill's sponsor will have been on "good behavior" in the hope that the lieutenant governor will give the bill a favorable referral. The large number of committees in both houses gives the presiding officers some discretion in the assignment of bills and resolutions to committees, and lobbyists will actively try to influence the choice. The lieutenant governor (or speaker) will consider: (1) the positions of their own financial supporters and political backers on the bill; (2) the effect of the bill on other legislation, especially the availability of funding for other programs; (3) his or her own ideological commitment to the bill; (4) the past record of support or nonsupport of the bill's backers, both legislators and special interests; and (5) the bargaining in which the bill's backers are willing to engage, including promises of desired support of, or opposition to, other bills on which the presiding officers have strong positions, as well as a willingness to modify the bill itself.

## Step Two: Committee Action

Standing committees are really miniature legislatures in which the nitty-gritty of legislation takes place. Legislators are so busy—particularly in Texas, with the short, infrequent sessions—that they seldom have time to study bills in detail and so must rely heavily on the committee reports. A bill's sponsor, well aware of the committee's role, will do everything possible to ensure that the committee's report is favorable. It is particularly important to avoid having the bill *pigeonholed* (put on the bottom of the committee's agenda, with or without discussion, never to be seen again) or totally rewritten, either by the committee or, if the bill is referred to a subcommittee, by the subcommittee. If the bill can escape being pigeonholed, its sponsor will have a chance to bargain with the committee in an effort to avoid too many changes in the bill.

The standing committees hold hearings on proposed legislation. Major bills will generate considerable public, media, and lobbyist interest. The large number of committees and the volume of proposed legislation sometimes mean that these hearings are held at odd hours, such as 11 P.M.

**tag** A means by which an individual senator can delay a committee hearing on a bill for at least forty-eight hours.

A senator, but not a representative, can **tag** a bill, indicating that the lawmaker must get a forty-eight-hour written notice of the hearing. If the senator does not receive notice or if the bill was not posted publicly seventy-two hours in advance, a senator can use a tag to object to the bill and delay the committee hearing. Tagging is sometimes an effective practice to defeat a bill late in the legislative session.

The committee may report the bill favorably, unfavorably, or not at all. An unfavorable report or none at all will kill it. Unless there is a strong minority report, however, there is little reason for the committee to report a bill unfavorably; it is easier to pigeonhole it and avoid floor action completely.

## Step Three: Floor Action

Once reported out of committee, a bill must be scheduled for debate. The senate calendar is rarely followed; instead, senators list their bills on the Intent Calendar, which in essence is a declaration of intent to ask for a suspension of the rules to take up a bill out of order. (See Table 6-3 for a comparison of legislative calendars of the Texas legislature and U.S. Congress.) Three-fifths (60 percent) of those present and voting must vote yes on the suspension. (Suspension of the rules used to require two thirds—67 percent—of the senate, a much higher hurdle to leap. Dan Patrick persuaded his fellow senators to lower the threshold at the beginning of the 2015 session.[20]) Before filing intent to ask for a suspension, the bill's sponsors generally get an assurance from the presiding officer that they will be recognized, and thus given an opportunity to make the motion. The three-fifths rule allows legislators to proceed smoothly because most members have agreed to consider it. The lieutenant governor can force a vote without a three-fifths majority by using another rule that allows house bills to be taken up on certain days of the week without the supermajority,[21] a tactic that David Dewhurst used several times in 2011.

When the bill receives the necessary three-fifths vote, it can proceed to its second reading and debate. If the second reading has not occurred by the time the legislature is within seventy-two hours of adjournment, the bill dies. The sponsor of the bill is relieved because only a simple majority of votes is required for passage. (In the house, the Calendars Committee establishes a schedule for debate.) Senators have unlimited privileges of debate: They may speak as long as they wish about a bill on the floor. Sometimes senators use this privilege to

| TABLE 6-3 | Comparison of the Legislative Calendars in the Texas Legislature and the U.S. Congress |
|---|---|
| **Texas Legislative Calendars** | |
| **Senate** | **House** |
| Senate | Daily House |
| Intent | Supplemental House |
| | Local, Consent, and Resolutions |
| | Congratulatory and Memorial |
| | Categories for grouping legislation on the Supplemental House Calendar, which is the major calendar, are: emergency; major state; constitutional amendments; general state; local, consent, and resolutions; resolutions; and congratulatory and memorial resolutions |
| **Congressional Calendars** | |
| **Senate** | **House** |
| Senate | House |
| Executive | Union |
| | Consent |
| | Private |
| | Discharge |

**filibuster** An effort to kill a bill in a legislature by unlimited debate; it is possible in the Texas and U.S. Senates, but not in the houses of representatives.

**filibuster**—that is, to try to kill a bill by talking at length about it and anything else that will use up time. By tying up the floor and preventing other bills from being considered, the senator or group of senators hopes to pressure enough of the membership to lay aside the controversial bill so that other matters can be debated. The filibuster is most effective at the end of the legislative session when time is short and many bills have yet to be debated. Shutting off debate ("cloture"), however, requires a simple majority vote. Despite their potential effectiveness, filibusters do not occur frequently because so much senate business is conducted off the senate floor in bargaining sessions. The presiding officer, incidentally, has the power to ask the intention of a member when the member is recognized for debate and thus knows when a filibuster will occur. Tradition also dictates that a member who plans to filibuster notify the press of the forthcoming event.

If a bill is fortunate enough not to become entangled in a filibuster, debate proceeds. During the course of debate, there may be proposed amendments, amendments to amendments, motions to table (i.e., to lay aside the bill), or even motions to send the bill back to committee. However, if a bill has succeeded in reaching the floor for discussion, it is usually passed in one form or another. A vote is taken after the third reading, again by caption, of the bill. At this stage, amendments require a two-thirds vote. It is more or less routine for three-fifths of the senate to vote to suspend the rules and proceed immediately to the third reading.

## In the House: Steps One Through Three Repeated

If it was not introduced in both houses simultaneously, a bill passed in the senate must proceed to the house. There, under its original designation (e.g., S.B. 341), it must repeat the same three steps, with the exceptions noted earlier. It has little chance of passing if a representative does not shepherd it through. (This situation is true in reverse also, when a bill passes the house and is then sent to the senate.) In addition, the Laney reforms of 1993 included a series of deadlines concerning the final seventeen days of a legislative session, and a bill must comply

# ISSUE SPOTLIGHT:
## Four Ways to Block a Bill

### The Filibuster and Chubbing

Former Senator Bill Meier, who talked for forty-three hours straight in 1977, holds the Texas and world records for filibustering. He successfully blocked consideration of a workers' compensation bill. More recently, in 1993, Senator Gonzalo Barrientos stopped just short of eighteen hours in an unsuccessful effort to protect Austin's Barton Creek and its popular swimming hole. In 2013, Senator Wendy Davis received national attention for an eleven-hour filibuster protesting proposed tightening of the antiabortion laws. The house does not allow filibusters, but has experienced "chubbing," which is a term that describes minority efforts to block a bill by offering needless amendments to and discussion on other bills in an effort to prevent the offending bill from reaching the floor. It has been a tactic of last resort for House Democrats since 2009.

### The Technicality

One of the most bizarre events in the history of the Texas legislature occurred in 1997, when conservative Representative Arlene Wohlgemuth, angry at the blockage of a bill regarding parental notification before girls under eighteen could get an abortion, raised a point of order about the calendar for May 26. The effect was to kill fifty-two bills that were scheduled for debate because the point of order concerned the calendar itself. Her fellow legislators referred to the incident as the "Memorial Day Massacre" and were irate that months of work, including the delicate negotiations between house and senate members to achieve compromise bills, apparently had been for naught. After tempers cooled, legislators found ways to resurrect some of the bills by tacking them onto other bills that had not been on the calendar for Memorial Day and by using resolutions.

### Pocketing

The presiding officers can also block bills by pocketing them; that is, they can decline to send a bill to the floor for debate even though a committee has given it a favorable report. Often, a presiding officer will pocket a bill because it virtually duplicates one already in the legislative pipeline or to keep an unimportant bill from cluttering up the agenda near the end of the session when major legislation is pending.

**Competency Connection**
**CRITICAL THINKING**

Why do you think that the rules of the legislature make it so easy to block a bill?

---

with those house rules. For example, after 135 days of a regular session, the house cannot consider a senate bill except to adopt a conference report, reconsider the bill to remove senate amendments, or override a veto; the deadlines for various types of house bills are earlier.[22]

## Step Four: Conference Committee

**conference committee** A temporary joint committee of both houses of a legislature in which representatives attempt to reconcile the differences in two versions of a bill.

Our explanation of the conference committee assumes that the bill being followed passes the house, but with one amendment added that was not part of the senate's version. Because the senate and house versions of the bill differ, it must go to a **conference committee**, which consists of ten members: five appointed from each house by the presiding officers.

Appointees to conference committees usually share the viewpoints of the presiding officers on what should be done with the bill in question. Representatives of special interests often become involved in conference committee deliberations in an attempt to arrange trade-offs, or bargains, with the presiding officers, making one concession in exchange for another. However, sometimes the main proponents of the two versions of the bill are able to work out a compromise without the committee even meeting.

If the house and senate versions of the bill exhibit substantial differences, the conference committee may attach several amendments or rewrite portions of the bill. It may even be pigeonholed. On a bill with only one difference between the versions passed by the two houses, the single vote of the committee members from the senate and the single vote of those from the house may be obtained without too much wrangling.

The bill is then reported back to the senate and the house for action in each chamber. The report of the conference committee must be voted on as it stands; neither house can amend it. It must be accepted, rejected, or sent back to the conference committee. If it fails at this stage—or indeed, at any stage—it is automatically dead. No bill can be introduced twice during the same session, although a bill can be rewritten and introduced as a new piece of legislation.

If the bill receives a majority of the votes in each house, the engrossing and enrolling clerk prepares a correct copy of it, first for the house where the bill originated, then for the other house. Its caption is read a final time, and it is signed by the presiding officers, the house chief clerk, and the senate secretary. The vote of passage is certified, and the engrossed (officially printed) bill, now an act, is sent to the governor for action. A record of these steps is printed in the journal of each house.

## Step Five: The Governor

The governor has ten days (excluding Sundays) to dispose of enacted legislation. If the legislature adjourns, the ten-day period is extended to twenty days. The governor has three options available to deal with an act. The first is to sign it, thus making it law.

The second option is to allow the act to become law without signing it. If the governor does not sign it, an act becomes law in ten days if the legislature is in session, and in twenty days if it is not. By choosing this rather weak course of action, the governor signifies both opposition to the legislation and an unwillingness to risk a veto that could be overridden by a two-thirds vote of both houses or that would incur the disfavor of special interests supporting the bill.

Third, the governor may veto the act. Although it is possible for the legislature to override a veto, the governor often receives legislation so late in the session that the act of vetoing or signing it can be deferred until the session has ended. A veto then is absolute because it must be overridden during the same legislative session in which the act was passed and the legislature cannot call itself into special session. At any time, the legislature may have difficulty mustering the two-thirds vote necessary to override a veto. Because recent legislative sessions have been faced with one crisis after another and have had too little time to deal with issues, the governor's powers have been strengthened through use of the veto and threats of a veto.

**item veto** The governor's constitutional power to strike out individual items in an appropriations bill.

If the governor chooses to veto, the veto applies to the entire act, except in the case of appropriations bills—that is, a bill that authorizes the state to spend money, for one purpose, or many purposes. On an appropriations act, the governor has the power of **item veto**; that is, specific items may be vetoed. This is a powerful gubernatorial tool for limiting state spending, but in recent years, the legislature has blunted this tool by making lump-sum appropriations to agencies such as colleges and universities.

When the governor signs an act, it becomes one of the few proposals that manage to survive. It is entered in the statute books by the secretary of state. If it contains an emergency clause, it becomes effective as law either immediately or whenever designated in the bill. If it does not, it becomes effective ninety days after the session ends. Again, there are special circumstances for appropriations acts. They always become effective September 1 because the state's fiscal year (its budget period) is from September 1 through August 31 of the following year.

## Legislative Dynamics

The public often thinks that the legislature accomplishes very little. It is in fact amazing that the legislature accomplishes as much as it does, given the limitations under which the institution must labor. The forces influencing legislation are complex and varied: interest groups, the powers of the presiding officers, the governor, constitutional limitations, political parties, the role of committees, short and infrequent sessions, inadequate salaries, and the prerogatives of individual members.

### Handicaps

Consideration of thousands of bills and resolutions each session means the legislative workload is very heavy. Very few of these proposals are substantively important, and many are trivial matters that could more easily be left to administrative agencies. Nevertheless, in the short 140-day session, legislators must acquaint themselves with the proposals, try to push their own legislative programs, attend to a heavy burden of casework, spend countless hours in committee work, meet with hometown and interest-group representatives, and hear the professional views of state administrators who implement programs. Although some legislators are personally wealthy, those who are not must also try to avoid going into debt because their salaries are inadequate and their personal businesses or professions cannot be attended to when the legislature is in session.

Lenient lobbying laws, lack of public support for adequate information services for legislators, and the need for continuous campaigning make the average legislator easy prey for special interests. On many issues, the interests of a legislator's district and of special interest groups often overlap and are difficult to distinguish. Even when the interests are not so closely aligned, legislators may have to depend on lobbyists for much of their information. Certainly, they depend on them for campaign help.

The legislators' frustrations are especially evident when the biennial budget is considered. Appropriations are the major battleground of legislative sessions. There are always more programs seeking support than there is money available to support them. Power struggles over money continue because each individual who promotes a program—be it for highways, public schools, utilities rates, environmental protection, lending rates, tort reform, law enforcement, or welfare administration—believes in either its moral rightness or its economic justification. Who wins the struggles is determined not only by the power and effectiveness of the groups backing a program, but also by the political preferences of the legislators. Furthermore, the winners largely determine public policy for the state because few government programs can operate without substantial amounts of money. Chapter 12 examines the politics of the budgetary process in detail.

Lack of public understanding and support is another handicap for legislators. The public often criticizes politicians for being unprincipled and always willing to compromise. But compromise is an essential activity in a democracy. History suggests that when politicians refuse to compromise, violence is the outcome. The American Civil War of 1861–65 is an example of the disastrous consequences of a refusal to compromise. The essence of the legislative process is the mutual, peaceful accommodation of antagonistic interests and strong-willed individuals who disagree about the public interest. When citizens hold the process of accommodation in contempt, they display their lack of knowledge about the workings of a peaceful, democratic society.

## Changing Alignments

Recent sessions of the legislature have been especially interesting because of shifting alliances. While the lineup of interests for each party that we discussed in Chapter 4 hold most of the time, for most issues, the constant maneuvering of individuals and groups can result in some surprising temporary coalitions. The situation that we discussed earlier in this chapter, in which the Republican speaker of the house, Joe Straus, was kept in his office for five legislative sessions by Democratic votes, is an example of the way that short-term maneuvering can sometimes cut across long-term agreements. There is an old saying that sums up this view of the governing process: "Politics makes strange bedfellows."

Thus, an additional difficulty that legislators face is adjusting to the shifting trends within the legislature. Long dominated by rural, Democratic conservatives, in recent years, the legislature has become more urban and more Republican. When urban issues are at stake, temporary bipartisan alliances among big-city legislators sometimes are formed against rural legislators.

Compounding the problem of party and geographic transition is the fact that the two houses have not changed in the same way. Although Republicans are the majority in both houses, the degree of partisanship, the sharpness of the ideological divisions, and the traditions surrounding the operation of the two houses are quite different. The senate often seems to be driven by the ideological fervor of "populist movement conservatives"; the house usually seems to be more amenable to deal-making and compromise.

## Nonlegislative Lawmaking

The responsibility for lawmaking was intended to rest with the legislature; however, executive, administrative, and judicial officials also make public policy that has the force of law. This overlap of functions, rather than being described with the traditional phrase as a "separation of powers," should more correctly be defined as a separation of roles and institutions with a sharing of powers.

**Governor** The governor is involved in lawmaking in two ways. First, by presenting messages to the legislature giving actual recommendations on legislation, the governor influences its outcome. The governor may also rally the support of political cronies and lobbyists for or against a bill. Besides vetoing bills, the governor can threaten to veto and so force changes in appropriations and other bills.

Second, the governor can indirectly influence how, or even if, legislation will be administered through appointments to state boards and commissions. Because the bureaucracy interprets general legislation and thus determines how it is to be applied in specific instances, gubernatorial appointees may have tremendous influence on how the public does (or does not) benefit from state laws. Often, though, the ties between an agency's permanent bureaucracy and legislators are so strong that the board members appointed by the governor have only limited influence.

Another way the governor influences legislation indirectly is by being the major liaison between Texas and other states, and between Texas and the federal executive establishment. In this capacity, the governor can affect interstate and federal-state relationships and policies. This aspect of the governorship was evident in 2009 and 2013 when Rick Perry did not want to accept all the economic stimulus money available from Washington or increased Medicaid funding. Texas thus refused the federal largesse, and thousands of uninsured poor people are the result.

**Administration** In addition to the governor and lieutenant governor, the state executive branch includes four other elected executives and two elected state boards. There also are dozens of policymaking boards and their staffs. As noted earlier, the administration (or bureaucracy) has a tremendous effect on how legislation is carried out. Because statutes are written in rather general terms to avoid unnecessary rigidity and specificity, administrative policies, rules, and regulations are a must. Each board policy made and each staff rule or regulation written supplement the statutes enacted by the legislature and constitute lawmaking.

Individual administrators also interpret statutes, an action that is a type of lawmaking. In addition, by functioning as expert advisers to members of the legislature during the session, administrators can directly influence the outcome of bills. Indeed, they often use their bureaucratic skills in conjunction with special interest groups that are concerned with similar issues. Perhaps no executive agency is as influential as the attorney general's office, which can issue opinions on the constitutionality of legislation. These opinions have the force of law unless they are successfully challenged in court.

The rule-making of federal agencies can also be a factor and create the need for subsequent legislative action. In 2013, following a long federal-state battle, the U.S. Environmental Protection Agency was forced by the Fifth Circuit Court of Appeals to back away from stringent air-quality control rules, much to the delight of Texas policymakers, but the U.S. Supreme Court ultimately decided against the state (*Texas* v. *Environmental Protection Agency*, Docket No. 12-1260, 2014).

**Courts** The judiciary, too, has a role in lawmaking. The courts are frequently asked to determine whether a statute is in conflict with higher law. Both federal and state courts can review legislative acts that have been challenged on the grounds of unconstitutionality. In 2014, for example, the federal courts invalidated the state's ban on same-sex marriages. Federal and state judges also spend considerable time hearing challenges to administrative interpretations of laws. In fact, most of the civil dockets of the courts are taken up with administrative matters—for example, whether an agency has jurisdiction over the matter at hand or whether an administrative interpretation is correct.

## Evaluation and Suggested Reforms

How does the Texas legislature stack up in terms of efficiency, effectiveness, and democratic theory? Both the structure of the legislature and its operations warrant criticism, as well as the courtesy of suggested changes.

**Criticisms** Extensive efforts to revamp state legislative structures have been made by organizations such as the National Legislative Conference, the Council of State Governments, the Citizens Conference on State Legislatures, and the National Municipal League. This last organization even produced a Model State Constitution as a "companion piece" for its Model City Charter. But state legislatures have been universally non-innovative. As Alexander Heard observed, "State legislatures may be our most extreme example of institutional lag. In their formal qualities, they are largely 19th-century organizations, and they must, or should, address themselves to 20th- [and now 21st-] century problems."[23] Although that sentence was written in 1966, state legislatures in general, and Texas' in particular, have changed surprisingly little since Heard made his analysis.

The Texas legislature seems to be caught in the proverbial vicious circle. Low salaries and short terms force legislators to maintain other sources of income, a necessity that leads to inattentiveness to legislative business, especially between sessions. On salary alone, a legislator would be far below the federal poverty line. The $190 a day allowance, not counting the travel and mileage allowances, does help raise the total compensation to at least $40,000 a

## You Decide: Should the Texas Legislature Be Reformed?

**M**any people have suggested that Texas would be better served by a legislature that would be quite different than the one it has now. The most commonly recommended reforms would be: 1. The legislature be in session every year, for most of the year; 2. Legislators be paid a salary commensurate with the importance of their job, at least as much as the legislators in California; 3. Legislators be forbidden to take any benefit from lobbyists; instead, the state would finance their election campaigns; and 4. Staff allowances should be generous, so that legislators could afford to hire intelligent, public-spirited people to give them information and analyze bills in terms of costs-and-benefits.

What is your opinion?

### Pro ✅

⬆️ The Texas legislature is full of amateurs; as a result, the state's schools are terrible, the roads are clogged, and nothing is being done about such crucial problems as climate change.

⬆️ In several recent sessions (2006, 2017), ideological fighting caused gridlock and frustration; the process needs to be streamlined so that government can govern.

⬆️ The presiding officers are too powerful; changes should be made to open up the process to more democratic procedures.

⬆️ The power of campaign contributors needs to be reined in by freeing candidates from needing to rely on private contributions.

⬆️ With a staff that was adequately compensated, legislators would be able to make more intelligent policy.

### Con ❌

⬇️ The Texas economy is booming, a thousand people move to the state every day to take advantage of the opportunity found here; if it ain't broke, don't fix it.

⬇️ As witnessed by the U.S. Congress, legislative gridlock is caused by the deep fissures in American society, not by a problem with the legislature.

⬇️ In the senate, the presiding officer represents the wishes of the state's voters at large; in the house, the speaker represents the wishes of the majority of the other representatives; in either case, the presiding officer is a perfect representation of democracy in action. Besides, centralized organization is necessary if the short session is not to dissolve into complete ineffectiveness.

⬇️ This suggestion merely represents the desires of liberals to damage conservatives' chances to be elected; it would be a partisan power-grab, not a genuine reform.

⬇️ Texas policy is intelligent now; indeed, thousands of families are fleeing the liberals' ideal, California, to move to Texas; Texans should follow the advice of the bumper sticker that reads "Don't Californicate Texas."

SOURCE: Vanessa Romo, "Texas Becoming a Magnet for Conservatives Fleeing Liberal States Like California," NPR Politics Newscast, August 27, 2017; www.npr.org/2017/08/27/546391430/Texas-becoming-a-magnet-for-conservatives-fleeing-liberal-states-like-california

**Competency Connection**
**SOCIAL RESPONSIBILITY**

**What is your opinion?**

year for the average legislator during a regular session, and to more than $50,000 when the summer is filled with special sessions. But, considering that they are, in effect, directing the operations of an economy with one of the largest Gross Domestic Products in the world, and deciding how to spend a state budget that greatly exceeds $100 billion a year, their responsibilities are far out of proportion to their monetary rewards. Human nature being what it is, the only way to explain the willingness of legislators to do so much for so little is either that they feel an intense need for public service, or that they hope to profit from corrupt actions. The way the legislature is set up, in other words, means that Texans who hope for good state government must have faith that a 181 elected officials are highly intelligent, exceptionally energetic, wholly public-spirited, and completely honest. The historical record suggests that these hopes are too often disappointed.

Legislative process has also received its share of criticisms from public-spirited observers. The two most frequent criticisms are of the number of legislative committees and the dominance of lobbyists. For example, in the senate, during the 2019 legislature, a mere thirty-one members had to serve on sixteen standing committees. Overwhelmed by the number of issues with which they must deal, and the constricted amount of time with which they must think about those issues, senators frequently turn to lobbyists for advice and information. During a session, the bill that survives may be one drafted and urged by lobbyists, not one carefully crafted by a legislator. The short session, the volume of legislation, and the dependence on lobbyists often make representatives and senators less a reflection of the democratic ideal of representativeness and more a demonstration of the practical reality of getting legislative work done.

**Suggested Reforms** Interest in changing the structure of the Texas legislature has centered on sessions, size and salaries, and terms. The focus of process change is on the number of committees and uncontrolled lobbying. In reality, none of these elements is likely to change.

**Sessions** The institution of annual legislative sessions has been a major reform proposal in all recent constitutional revision efforts. Annual sessions would allow legislators time to familiarize themselves with complex legislation, permitting them, for example, to bring a little more knowledge to the chaotic guessing game that produces the state's biennial budget. Annual sessions would virtually eliminate the need for special sessions when a crisis arises between regular sessions. They would allow time for the continual introduction of all those special resolutions, such as declaring chili the official state dish, that have negligible importance for the general public, but take up so much valuable legislative time. They also would provide an opportunity for legislative oversight of the state bureaucracy. Coupled with adequate staff support, annual sessions would allow legislators to engage in more long-range planning of public policy.

The legislature also needs to be empowered to call itself into special session. At present, if legislative leaders see the need for a special session and the governor is reluctant to call it, the legislature is helpless. In thirty-two other states, legislators can initiate a special session either independently or in conjunction with the governor, and efforts to gain that privilege for Texas legislators continue to be pressed. At a minimum, legislators need more freedom to add to the agenda of special sessions. Even though a session is called for a specific purpose, other significant items could be entered on the agenda and dispensed with, thus reducing the clutter of the next regular session's agenda.

The restrictions on both regular and special legislative sessions result in a high concentration of political power. The presiding officers dictate the flow of business during regular sessions, and the governor dominates special sessions. Many observers would like to see the legislator become less centralized, with more responsibilities given to each individual legislator. But such a reform would have to wait until the problems of the constricted schedule and inadequate pay are solved.

**Size** Some advocates of reform have recommended that the Texas house be reduced in size to 100 members. Others have suggested that, because both houses are now elected on the basis of population distribution, one house should be eliminated altogether and a unicameral legislature adopted. But tradition strongly militates against such a change. The physical size of the state poses another risk to reducing the size of the legislature. As population and thus district size continue to grow, citizens will increasingly lose contact with their representatives. A reduction in the number of legislators would be a trade-off between legislative efficiency and representativeness. Although efficiency is important to citizens, so is being represented by someone from a small enough geographic and population area to understand the needs of the people in the district.

**Salaries** More serious are recommendations for salary increases. The $7,200 salary is insufficient to allow legislators to devote their full energies to state business. A salary in the range of the average among the nine other largest states—about $68,000—would not, of course, guarantee that legislators would be honest and conscientious and devote all of their working time to the business of the state.[24] A decent salary level, however, would ensure that those who wished to could spend most of their time on state business. Moreover, it might also eliminate the retainer fees, consultant fees, and legal fees now paid to many legislators. In addition, it would guard against the popular suspicion that only the rich or the corrupt are able to run for public office. However, a livable wage for legislators also flies in the face of the fiction that the state has a citizen legislature filled with individuals serving only because of their civic-minded nature.

**Terms** If senate members had staggered six-year terms and house members had staggered four-year terms, legislators could be assured of having time to develop expertise in both procedures and substantive policy. Moreover, the virtually continuous campaigning that is required of legislators who represent highly competitive urban districts would be greatly reduced, leaving them more time to spend on legislative functions. Less campaigning also might serve to weaken the tie between legislators and the lobbyists who furnish both financial support for campaigning and bill-drafting services.

**Committees** The twenty-one house standing committees of 1973 had grown to thirty-four for the 2019 session. The senate managed to operate with only nine standing committees from 1973 until 1985, but now has sixteen. These numbers do not count subcommittees or select committees in either house. Thus, both houses need to be wary of further committee expansion.

Having substantially fewer committees would result in less ambiguity over committee jurisdiction. In addition, both houses could make more use of joint committees instead of submitting every issue for separate study and hearings. A joint budget committee is particularly needed. Fewer committee meetings would give legislators more time to familiarize themselves with the issues and the contents of specific bills. Fewer committees also might increase the chance for adoption of uniform committee rules throughout the two houses. Better meeting facilities for committees and more professional committee staff also are needed. Currently, chairs can hire staff or elect to use their own, so that independence is also a political issue.

**Uncontrolled Lobbying** Until legislators are able to declare their independence from lobbyists and state administrators, it will be impossible for the legislature to be truly independent of all interests but the public interest. Such a change depends on many factors: citizen attitudes, such as public willingness to allow adequate legislative sessions, pay, and staff support for legislators; public financing of election campaigns; and a commitment on the part of legislators to give up the social and economic advantages of strong ties to the lobby. The likelihood of total independence from the lobby is not high: All legislative groups everywhere have some ties to special interests. At a minimum, however, Texas needs to abandon such blatant practices as allowing lawyer-legislators to accept retainer fees from corporations that subsequently send lobbyists to Austin to influence these same legislators. A starting point in reform was Speaker Laney's rule prohibiting members of his own staff from accepting a job as a lobbyist for a year after leaving the speaker's office. That rule, however, is not binding on the staff members hired by other speakers, and the legislature has failed to pass a bill institutionalizing restrictions.

## Assessing a Legislative Session

After a legislative session ends, a variety of organizations rank the performance of the institution and its members. Many of the rankings merely reflect how closely the members adhered to the position favored by the organization, so it is difficult to use these lists except as measures of, say, pro-business or pro-labor votes. The press also joins in the rating game, but reflects publishers' viewpoints—for example, the liberal viewpoint of the *Texas Observer*'s annual legislative assessment. One effort to judge legislators on grounds other than political philosophy, however, is that of *Texas Monthly*, which includes both liberals and conservatives of both urban and rural persuasions in its biennial list of ten best and ten worst legislators. The criteria used by *Texas Monthly* are also suitable for use by the public in its evaluation, as follows:

> Our criteria are those that members apply to one another: Who is trustworthy? Who gets things done? Who brings credit upon the Legislature and who brings shame? Who does his homework? Who looks for ways to solve problems and who looks for ways to create them? Who is hamstrung by ideology and partisanship and who can rise above them? Politics is not just about conservatives and liberals and Republicans and Democrats. It is and always will be about personality and relationships and comportment—not that there's anything wrong with that.[25]

The session as a whole is even more difficult to evaluate. One's own political viewpoint and interest in specific issues can bias one's view of the actions of legislators. It is necessary to consider the bills and the votes, as well as the people. A sample of general criteria for such an assessment would include these questions:

1. Did the legislature deal with major issues facing the state or mainly with trivial issues?
2. Did the appropriations bill reflect genuine statewide concerns or only the interests of the large lobbies?
3. Did the leadership operate effectively, forcing the legislature to give attention to major issues and arranging compromises on stalled bills, or did it cater to the lobbyists or the personal agendas of the presiding officers?
4. Was the effect of current legislation on future social, economic, and physical resources considered, or did the legislature live for today?
5. Did the legislature address truly important topics, such as climate change and the frequent occurrence of mass-murder with firearms, in a serious-minded manner, or did it waste its time on hot-button, symbolic topics that pushed the electorate's emotional buttons but had no long-term relevance, such as who gets to use which bathroom?
6. Were basic tests of democracy—representation, transparency, fairness—met?

# THE 86TH LEGISLATIVE SESSION, 2019

The 86th session of the Texas state legislature illustrated the state's conservative political culture in its strengths and weaknesses. Under the direction of speaker of the house Dennis Bonnen and lieutenant governor Dan Patrick, and with the encouragement of governor Greg Abbott, the legislature featured some noteworthy successes, some surprising failures, and some predictable omissions.

Under the category of "success," the legislature passed a $250.7 billion two-year budget. The state's booming economy permitted a 16% spending increase from the previous biennium. Texas' prosperity thus permitted a total of $6.5 billion more money for schools than in the 2018-2019 biennium, and $5.1 billion for property tax relief. The relative generosity for schools did not mean that Republicans had suddenly become a group of liberals, however, for they also cut Medicaid funding for poor children by $900 million.

In regard to non-budgetary subjects, the legislature successfully passed bills to tighten the state regulation of day-care centers, expand gun rights for Texas citizens, force cities to dismantle "red-light cameras" that photograph motorists driving through intersections, and make cities and the state be more efficient in protecting women from sexual violence. In keeping with the intentions of the Religious Right, the legislature passed several bills to make it harder for a woman to have an abortion, although its efforts in this regard were not as drastic as the measures passed recently by other states.

Given the united conservative-Republican nature of the legislative session, however, there were some surprising failures. It has been a long-term goal of conservatives to funnel money away from the public-schools with a "voucher" program that would permit parents to use state funds to enroll their children in private schools. Given the emphasis on education in this session, it might have been expected that this was the year that such a program would finally pass. But there was no such effort from the state's leaders. Other bills that went down to defeat was one that would have started the process of eliminating Daylight Savings Time in Texas, another that would have toughened the penalties for committing such "election crimes" as voter fraud, and another that would have deregulated the barbering and cosmetology industries.

Just as important as what happened in the 86th legislature was what did not happen. Although a bill passed to protect public schools from the massacres that have become routine in the last two decades, Texas' leaders did not even consider the possibility of making it more difficult for murderous maniacs to get their hands on guns. And, faced with the greatest danger to Texans, Americans, and the human species—climate change—the governing Republicans refused to even utter the phrase, let alone pass a measure to prevent the looming catastrophe.

## Summary

**LO 6.1** **Legislatures have many functions.** Most importantly, they legitimate democratic government by providing a connection between the people's participation and the actions of government. At a more short-term level, legislators not only pass laws but also deal with reapportionment and redistricting, propose constitutional amendments, provide oversight of the bureaucracy, and do casework for constituents.

**LO 6.2** **The legislature is predominately Republican, Anglo, male, and middle-aged,** although the proportion of women and minorities has been slowly growing. Seniority is of limited importance in both houses, and turnover averages between 18 and 25 percent each session.

**LO 6.3** **The 181-member Texas legislature consists of a house of representatives and a senate.** It is restricted to one regular session every two years, although the governor can call special sessions of up to thirty days per call. Its members are elected from single-member districts of roughly equal population size, with senatorial districts averaging about five times the population size of house districts. Political battles over drawing district lines are fierce. Legislators have been increasingly partisan in recent years. The pay is only $7,200.

**LO 6.4** **Both the house of representatives and the senate are dominated by the presiding officers—the speaker of the house and the president of the senate (lieutenant governor)—who also control the committees and chair the boards overseeing staff agencies.** Although the speaker and lieutenant governor are the most important actors in any session, lobbyists, the news media, campaign contributors, public opinion, individual representatives, and committee chairs can be crucially influential in a given set of circumstances. Structurally, the committee system is crucial to the substance and flow of legislation.

**LO 6.5** **In both houses, passing a piece of legislation involves these steps: introduction, committee action, and floor action.** The two houses often disagree on major bills, making a conference committee necessary. Once enacted, the legislation goes to the governor who can sign it, veto it, or let it become a law without his or her signature.

**LO 6.6** **Legislators are handicapped by having too many bills and resolutions to consider in a short, biennial session, aggressive lobbying, little public support, and the need to campaign continuously.** They have to contend with constantly shifting political alignments in the legislature and with the policy preferences and edicts of other branches of government. Better salaries, an annual session, fewer committees, and increased staffing are among suggestions for improving the effectiveness of the Texas legislature.

## Critical Thinking

1. How closely does the Texas legislature approach the ideal institution of democratic theory? If you could change one thing about the legislature to make it a more democratic institution, what would you change? Why?

2. How representative do you think the legislature is of the general population in Texas? Do you think all groups are well represented? If so, describe the various groups and how they are well represented. If not, which groups are not well represented, and why not?

Rick Perry became the longest-serving governor in Texas history in December of 2008. Perry is shown here with his predecessor as Governor, George W. Bush. In November of 2014 Greg Abbott was elected governor after a combined 20 years in the office by Governors Bush and Perry.

*TIM SLOAN/AFP/Getty Images*

# The Governor

## Learning Objectives

**LO 7.1** Describe the structure of the Texas governorship, including how the governor is selected, the term of office and tenure possibility, the process of impeachment, compensation, and staffing.

**LO 7.2** Explain how the plural executive model is a basic characteristic of the governorship.

**LO 7.3** Discuss the personal characteristics that might lead to gubernatorial electoral success.

**LO 7.4** Assess the formal and informal roles that the governor plays, and their varying leadership styles.

**LO 7.5** Explain the limitations on gubernatorial power.

The Texas state Constitution, like the American Constitution, separates powers among three branches of government. Chief executives and administrative agencies are important components of politics, and must be evaluated against the ideal of democracy. In Texas, the Constitution created a strong legislature and a governor's office weak in formal powers. Accordingly, bargaining skills and persuasive ability are keys to gubernatorial leadership.

This chapter examines the basic structure of the governor's office, the formal qualifications for the office and personal characteristics of those who are typically elected to it, the roles that the governor plays, and the limitations on those roles, including the **plural executive** model. It is the story of a chief executive hampered by a restrictive state constitution and a state administration that is largely independent of the governor's control. Despite limitations, some individual governors have overcome the weaknesses of the office through their political skills and personal magnetism. Though some governor's powers have been enhanced in recent decades, they remain weak among governors in the United States.

> IT IS WIDELY REPORTED THAT THE GOVERNORSHIP OF TEXAS IS BY DESIGN A WEAK OFFICE. HOWEVER, THE STRENGTH OF AN INDIVIDUAL GOVERNOR'S PERSONALITY CAN OVERCOME MANY OF THE LIMITATIONS IMPOSED ON THE OFFICE.
>
> Brian McCall,
> *The Power of the Texas Governor, 2009*

**plural executive** A system of organizing the executive branch that includes the direct election of multiple executives, thereby weakening the chief executive, the governor.

# Basic Structure of the Governor's Office

## Election

In Texas, the governor and all statewide elected executives are chosen in statewide elections held in even-numbered years when there is no presidential election. Candidates are selected in party primaries held earlier the same year (see Chapter 5). Gubernatorial elections are held in the "off year," with the hope that national issues will not overshadow state issues, but election contests for the Texas governor's office often focus as much on personalities as issues. As a result, these elections attract fewer voters absent the presidential election as a drawing card. The last two cycles have shown how variable turnout can be in off-year elections, with very low turnout in 2014, when fewer than 25 percent of Texas adults voted. In 2018, national politics dominated the election cycle, and more than 42 percent of Texas adults voted—still lower than turnout in presidential election years, but high turnout for the mid-term. Unlike in national politics, where the vice-president is part of the "presidential ticket," in Texas the lieutenant governor runs independently of the governor.

## Term of Office

Gubernatorial influence was enhanced in 1974, when the governor's term of office was extended from two to four years. Under the Texas Constitution, governors are not limited in the number of terms they may seek, unlike the American president who is limited to two four-year terms. Table 7-1 summarizes some institutional characteristics of the governor's office compared with those of other states. The table shows the number of other states that share a particular characteristic with Texas, as well as the ranking of the Texas governor on a national scale of institutional power. The Texas governor, overall, ranks well below average in overall powers—tied for thirty-eighth among the states.

# ISSUE SPOTLIGHT:
## Abbott and Leadership During Crisis

**G**overnor Greg Abbott has faced a number of crises during his time as Chief Executive, including a major flood in central Texas, Hurricane Harvey, and mass shootings in a church in Sutherland Springs and in a school in Santa Fe. In each case, Abbott was quick to respond to the crisis, and in each instance, he went beyond expressing sympathy for families affected to calling for policy change to make less likely their recurrence.

Over the Memorial Day holiday in 2015, a massive flood hit central Texas, killing fourteen people and causing millions of dollars of damage to homes and property. Though that event was devastating, it paled in comparison to the damage caused by Hurricane Harvey in August of 2017, where 68 people were killed and up to $125 billion damage was inflicted. Both events pointed to property and environmental problems caused by low levels of regulation about where homes can be built and the ways in which corporations are allowed to store and dispose of environmentally hazardous materials.

The shootings in Sutherland Springs (where 26 people were killed and 20 others injured when a gunman invaded a sanctuary during a church service) and Santa Fe (where 10 people were killed and 13 injured in a public high school) presented anew the problems of gun violence in the state. These are the latest examples of mass shootings in Texas that have occurred periodically for many years. Governor Abbott expressed openness to a variety of solutions to the problems, concluding that we must "work together on putting together laws that will protect Second Amendment rights but at the same make sure our communities and especially our schools are safer places."

Abbott has said "I'm a person who's felt pain. I know personally what disaster is. Life-changing disaster. As a result, I can be very empathetic with people whose lives have been turned upside down." His ability to relate with people facing life-altering challenges has won high marks in each instance. Yet, Abbott's own conservatism normally is skeptical of government regulation and of limitations on gun ownership. Multi-pronged approaches that could lead to lessened susceptibility to these varied disasters are elusive.

Sources: Neena Satija, "Before Central Texas Flooding, Officials Sounded Alarm," *Texas Tribune*, May 26, 2015; Dave Harmon, "Four Months after Hurricane Harvey, Four Major Questions about Recovery for 2018," *Texas Tribune*, January 4, 2018; Anna Tinsley and Diane Smith, "Gov. Abbott Wants More Marshals, Increased Mental Health Screening to Make Schools Safer," *Fort Worth Star Telegram*, May 30, 2018; John C. Moritz, "Texas Gov. Greg Abbott: Overcoming Personal Adversity Shaped Leadership in Times of Crisis," *Corpus Christi Caller Times*, December 20, 2018.

**Competency Connection**
**CRITICAL THINKING**

Among the most challenging issues confronting Texas are reactions to natural disasters and to mass shootings. Beyond expressing empathy for victims, how might the governor use the powers of office to improve government response to such events?

### TABLE 7-1 — The Texas Governor's Institutional Powers among the States

| Texas Provision | Number of Other States with the Provision | Beyle's Ranking of Institutional Power |
| --- | --- | --- |
| Four-year term without restrictions on number of terms or number of consecutive terms* | 12 | 5 (high) |
| Public election of six or fewer state executives | 29 | 2 (fairly low) |
| Governor's appointment power** | | 1 (low) |
| Shares responsibility for budget preparation | 14 | 2 (fairly low) |
| Gubernatorial party control | | 4 (fairly high) |
| Item veto over appropriations*** | 42 | 5 (high) |
| Overall ranking among the states | | Tied for 40th |

*Only Vermont and New Hampshire have a two-year term.
**Beyle's ranking was of appointment power over major functional areas of state government.
***Beyle's ranking was of the whole veto power, including the Texas governor's advantage because of the short legislative session.

SOURCES: *The Book of the States, 2010*, vol. 42 (Lexington, KY.: Council of State Governments, 2010), 196–197, 201–206; Thad Beyle, "The Governors," in Virginia Gray and Russell L. Hanson, eds., *Politics in the American States: A Comparative Analysis*, 9th ed. (Washington, D.C.: CQ Press, 2008), 212–213.

**Competency Connection**
**CRITICAL THINKING**

Would Texas be well-served by a more powerful governor? If so, which of the powers in the table might be enhanced to help the governor serve the citizens?

## Tenure

Until after World War II, Texas governors were routinely elected for one or two two-year terms.[1] During and after the war, this precedent was supplanted by a trend to three terms, as indicated in Table 7-2. The precedent was broken when Governor Preston Smith, trying for a third term in 1972, was defeated in the wake of the Sharpstown Bank scandal. Smith, among other public officials, was alleged to have bought and then sold stock at a great profit in exchange for passing a bill benefiting the Sharpstown Bank.

| TABLE 7-2 | Texas Governors and Their Terms of Office, under the 1876 Constitution | | |
|---|---|---|---|
| Richard Coke* | 1874–1876 | Miriam A. Ferguson | 1933–1935 |
| Richard B. Hubbard | 1876–1879 | James V. Allred | 1935–1939 |
| Oran M. Roberts | 1879–1883 | W. Lee O' Daniel* | 1939–1941 |
| John Ireland | 1883–1887 | Coke R. Stevenson | 1941–1947 |
| Lawrence S. Ross | 1887–1891 | Beauford H. Jester* | 1947–1949 |
| James S. Hogg | 1891–1895 | Allan Shivers | 1949–1957 |
| Charles A. Culberson | 1895–1899 | Price Daniel | 1957–1963 |
| Joseph D. Sayers | 1899–1903 | John Connally | 1963–1969 |
| S. W. T. Lanham | 1903–1907 | Preston Smith | 1969–1973 |
| Thomas M. Campbell | 1907–1911 | Dolph Briscoe | 1973–1979 |
| Oscar B. Colquitt | 1911–1915 | William (Bill) Clements | 1979–1983 |
| James E. Ferguson** | 1915–1917 | Mark White | 1983–1987 |
| William P. Hobby | 1917–1921 | William (Bill) Clements | 1987–1991 |
| Pat M. Neff | 1921–1925 | Ann Richards | 1991–1995 |
| Miriam A. Ferguson | 1925–1927 | George W. Bush | 1995–2000 |
| Dan Moody | 1927–1931 | Rick Perry | 2000–2015 |
| Ross Sterling | 1931–1933 | Greg Abbott | 2015– |

*Coke and O'Daniel resigned from the governorship to enter the U.S. Senate. Jester died in office.
**James Ferguson was impeached and convicted.

SOURCE: Adapted from "Governors of Texas," prepared by the Texas Legislative Council and available at http:www.lrl.state.tx.us/.

Modern governors serving four-year terms have had mixed results in being reelected, in part due to the shifting party preferences of Texans. Bill Clements (Republican) lost to Mark White (Democrat) in 1982, but White lost to Clements in 1986. Ann Richards (Democrat) then served a single term after her 1990 election. On the other hand, George W. Bush (Republican) won a second term by an overwhelming majority, although he resigned to become president of the United States. Rick Perry (Republican) served three full terms after finishing Bush's unexpired term when he succeeded to the governorship from his lieutenant governor seat, and Greg Abbott was reelected to a second term in 2018. In recent decades, because Texas is the second most populous state in the Union, Texas governors have often been in the spotlight as future presidential or vice presidential candidates. Such was the case with Bush, who became president in 2001, and Perry, who was selected to serve as Energy Secretary in President Donald Trump's cabinet.

## Impeachment and Succession

If the legislature believes a governor has misused the office, it may begin action toward impeachment. The state's succession plan then goes into effect.

In Texas, a governor may be removed from office only through an **impeachment** proceeding. Impeachment is a formal accusation, similar to a grand jury indictment in criminal procedure. The state constitution does not define what constitutes an impeachable offense. By implication and by the precedents set in the impeachment of Governor James E. Ferguson in

**impeachment** The process of formally accusing an official of improper behavior in office. It is followed by a trial, and upon conviction, the official is removed from office.

# Texas Politics and You

One of the major issues in federalism is that different states, while part of a nation, also have different interests. Texas has been aggressive in giving companies tax incentives to move to Texas from other states. In this cartoon, cartoonist John Darkow of the *Columbia Daily Tribune* portrays Missouri as being victimized by the tactics of Governor Perry. Students, asked to respond to this cartoon, made the following observations:

"This artist is making a statement that Texas is stealing jobs from and ruining the economies of other states. This happens through the business appeal of Texas, and infers that Perry does not care about the national effects."

"The comparison of taking jobs from other states to poaching makes Texas look like a state of dumb hunters that doesn't understand economics."

"The way I see it, there is some incentive or reason that companies are funding jobs in Texas and moving there, and if other politicians want to complain about it, maybe they need to try implementing some of the concepts that Governor Perry has."

"A governor should be concerned with his state while still recognizing that all states are on the same team—the U.S. team. State success and growth should come from the creation of jobs, not the transferring and hunting of jobs from other states."

John Darkow/Tribune

### Critical Thinking

From your perspective, should Texas fund the governor's office to try to attract businesses to transfer to Texas from other states? Why do you think Texas creates more jobs than other states?

**Competency Connection**
**COMMUNICATION SKILLS**

Explain how a state might be a "good citizen" within the United States, creating job opportunities in their own state while not taking jobs from another state?

1917, however, the grounds would consist of official misconduct, incompetence, or failure to perform required duties.[2]

The impeachment procedure in Texas is similar to that at the national level, and has been successfully used only against Ferguson. The House of Representatives, by a majority vote of those present, must first impeach the executive. Once the formal accusation is made, the Senate acts as a trial court, with a two-thirds vote of the senators present being necessary to convict. Penalties for conviction are removal from office and disqualification from holding future governmental offices in the state.

If a governor is removed from office by impeachment and conviction, dies in office or before taking office, or resigns, the constitution provides that the lieutenant governor will succeed to office. A 1999 constitutional amendment further stipulates that, should the governor become disabled, the lieutenant governor will carry out the duties of the office; should the governor die or otherwise be unable to return, the lieutenant governor will become governor for the rest of the term. If the lieutenant governor is unable to serve, the president pro tempore of the Senate will carry out the duties. Once the lieutenant governor becomes governor, the lieutenant governor's position is vacant. No one can be governor and lieutenant governor simultaneously. Within thirty days, the Senate will elect one of its members to fulfill all of the duties of lieutenant governor until the next general election. The executive article states that the senator elected as presiding officer is also the lieutenant governor, but the legislative article is more ambiguous, stating only that the presiding officer will "perform the duties of the Lieutenant Governor."

## Compensation

A 1954 amendment allows the legislature to determine the salary of the governor and other elected executives. The legislature provided generous increments for many years, raising the governor's salary from $12,000 in 1954 to its current amount of $150,000 in 2009, ranking thirteenth among all governors in 2017. Interestingly, the governor's salary is less than nearly 1,900 other public officials in Texas, from county, to city, to school districts.[3] The lieutenant governor is paid as a legislator—$7,200 a year plus a per diem—although he or she receives a salary supplementation for acting as governor whenever the governor leaves the state.

**fringe benefits** Special considerations that the governor receives in addition to a simple paycheck.

The governor also receives numerous **fringe benefits**, including an official mansion. In 2012, Governor Perry moved back into the restored governor's mansion, which was badly damaged by an arsonist's fire in 2007.[4]

## Staff and Organization

The governor has a sizable staff to carry out his or her functions, including a personal staff and help from the professional staffs of the divisions that make up the Office of the Governor. Designated staff members serve to voice the governor's priorities with the legislature, attempting to persuade the legislature to adopt the governor's agenda and making known an impending threat to veto a particular piece of legislation. Other staff members recommend candidates for the hundreds of appointments the governor makes to state boards, commissions, and executive agencies. Governor's aides also prepare the executive budget requests, coordinate the various departments and activities of the governor's office, and schedule appointments and activities. Overall, the governor's staff provides assistance in performing the specific tasks assigned to the office by law and in promoting enactment of the governor's programs.

The Texas governor has a large and well-paid staff of professionals. Under Governor Ann Richards, the office swelled to over 400 members, though in recent years the number has been significantly lower, with Governor Greg Abbott having a staff of about 250 employees in 2018. To staff the office, however, Governor Abbott has had to pay his top advisors salaries significantly higher than his own, with five of his advisors having salaries of $265,000, more than $100,000 higher than his.[5]

Each governor organizes the office somewhat differently. Commonly, new program initiatives begin under the governor's auspices and then become independent or move to other agencies. The governor has a wide range of responsibilities. As of 2018, the governor's office consisted of offices that performed the following functions:

▶ Helping the governor with making the many appointments to boards and commissions in the state, and providing human resource programs for employees
▶ Working on state budget issues and economic development for Texas, including securing federal grants for the state through the Office of Federal/State Relations, promoting the state film and music industries, and providing a workforce for economic growth

▶ Providing for public safety within Texas and homeland security
▶ Overseeing military preparedness through supervision of the Texas military forces
▶ Promoting Texas as a travel destination
▶ Overseeing operations within the governor's office, including auditing of expenditures, constituent communication, legal advice through the general counsel, compliance with legal requirements, the governor's press office, and a scheduling office[6]

# Qualifications for Governor

Both legally mandated criteria and informal standards set by political interests and voters shape who is eligible to serve as governor.

## Formal Qualifications

As is true of the qualifications for members of the legislature, the formal qualifications for governor are minimal. Article 4 of the constitution stipulates that the governor must be at least thirty years old, be a citizen of the United States, and have been a resident of Texas for the five years immediately preceding the election. These qualifications also pertain to the lieutenant governor. Article 4 also mandates that the governor "shall be installed on the first Tuesday after the organization of the Legislature, or as soon thereafter as practicable." Article 3 gives the legislature the responsibility for settling any election disputes that might arise concerning the governor.

## Personal Characteristics

Formally qualifying for the governorship and actually having a chance at being considered seriously as a candidate are two very different matters. The social, political, and economic realities of the state dictate that personal characteristics, not stated in law, help determine who will be the victors in gubernatorial elections. Although some of these are based on personal accomplishments of gubernatorial aspirants, others represent traditions of economic and social class advantage.

Governors have overwhelmingly been White Anglo-Saxon Protestant (WASP) males who are politically conservative, involved in civic affairs, and wealthy. More than likely, but less inevitably, this individual will have held some other office, often that of attorney general or lieutenant governor, although being a professional politician is sometimes a liability among voters with a penchant for electing "good ol' boys."

The most atypical governor in more than a half-century was Ann Richards (1991–1995), a populist Democratic female (see Chapter 4 for a discussion of populism in Texas). Richards took strong stands against concealed weapons and environmental destruction, and urged reform of selected state agencies, such as the Insurance Commission and Department of Commerce, that had strong ties to business. Greg Abbott, a Republican, has a resumé that is consistent with Texas traditions. Before becoming governor after the election of 2014, he served as a state district judge from Houston, as a member of the Texas Supreme Court, and as Texas Attorney General. Abbott has a compelling life story, having overcome paralysis when a tree fell on him while jogging in 1984, and his family represents the multicultural heritage of Texas. His wife Cecilia, who spent many years as an educator in Catholic schools, is a descendent of Mexican immigrants to Texas. He handily defeated Democrats Wendy Davis and Lupe Valdez in his two elections to the governorship, and has been unfailingly conservative during his terms as governor. In his 2019 inaugural address, he sounded populist messages about allowing opportunity for all, regardless of their economic circumstances: "We must ensure destiny is not determined by zip code. Students from the most challenging circumstances can perform at the highest levels. But we have to give them the opportunity to succeed." And he sounded out conservative themes too, arguing that Texas taxes, and particularly, the property tax, are too high and that federal mandates are unfair: "Texas must limit the ability of taxing authorities to raise

## ISSUE SPOTLIGHT:
## Texas Version of Foreign Affairs

One major recent development has been the assertion of American state activity in international affairs. Although Article I, Section 10 of the U.S. Constitution forbids the states to enter into any agreement or compact with a foreign power, many states have begun to do so rather explicitly. For example, the Texas governor's Web site says Texas is "a globally-connected economic powerhouse" that "remains wide open for business—and welcoming to international companies of all sizes and industries."

Governor Abbott has taken numerous trips abroad to promote Texas business interests, though less aggressively than his predecessor. He made official visits to five countries as governor during his first term: Cuba, Mexico, Switzerland, Israel, and India. In India, he promoted the sale of crude oil and liquefied natural gas and in Japan, he encouraged Toyota to enhance its investments into the Texas economy. His visit to Cuba was to "build business ties with the Communist nation." And, of course, like other governors, he has continuous discussions with businesses in Mexico, a nation that shares 1,954 of border with the state. This demonstrates that Texas aggressively seeks business ties worldwide and that in an ever smaller world, traditional limits on states having "foreign policy" are less inviolate than in previous times.

Sources: Robert T. Garrett, "Abbott in India: Governor Declares Trip a 'Home Run,' Urges Texas Businesses to Work with Indian Companies," *Dallas Morning News*, March 30, 2018; Robert T. Garrett, "Texas Gov. Greg Abbott Vacations in Japan, Takes Time Out to Visit with Toyota's Top Executive," *Dallas Morning News*, December 27, 2018; Chris Tomlinson, "Abbott's Trip to Cuba Good for Texas Business," *Houston Chronicle*, November 30, 2015.

**Competency Connection**
**CRITICAL THINKING**

The United States Constitution denies states the right to make foreign policy, and yet, Texas and other states seek business relationships with other countries. Should state be allowed to compete with each other for foreign investment in their economies? Or would the nation be better served by having only the national government negotiate business ties?

your property taxes. At the same time, Texas must end unfunded mandates on cities and counties. And taxpayers should be given the power to fire their property tax appraiser."

## Conservative

Traditionally, a gubernatorial candidate had to be a conservative Democrat. E. J. Davis, a much-maligned Republican governor during Reconstruction, was the only Republican governor until Bill Clements was elected in 1978. Since 1978, Republicans have held the office most of the time, with only Mark White, elected in 1982, and Ann Richards, elected in 1990, breaking the Republican dominance.

In the 1990 Ann Richards–Clayton Williams race, Richards was elected perhaps despite her Democratic party affiliation when her opponent, Clayton Williams, proved to be an "open-mouth-put-foot-in" candidate. He seemed particularly adept at insulting women and ordinary taxpayers. In the first instance, he opined that rape was like bad weather so that, "If it's inevitable, [a woman should] just relax and enjoy it." In the second, Williams, a multimillionaire who financed much of his own campaign, bragged about not paying federal income taxes. George W. Bush entered the race in 1994 as a mainstream Republican, concerned with state control over state policy, the integrity of the family, the quality of education, and the rising incidence of juvenile crime. He and Richards differed little on those issues. He reflected more of a national Republican position in wanting to cut welfare and in openly advocating a freer operating climate for business, especially by placing many restrictions on lawsuits for such activities as professional malpractice and faulty products. Significantly, however, he talked about his conservatism, not his party affiliation. Because of the growth of the Republican Party, Bush won that election even though Richards remained personally popular among voters even at the time of the election.

Governor Rick Perry consistently earned his conservative credentials in the legislative sessions, pushing business interests, emphasizing tax cuts over solutions to the knotty school finance problem, and even enduring criticism from fellow Republicans for letting his industry ties dominate public policy. His major speeches often addressed the concerns of poor people, but his legislative agenda tended to address the desires of business. He ran against Senator Kay Bailey Hutchison in the Republican primary and Democrat Bill White in the general election of 2010 as a conservative alternative to each. Since Hutchison voted conservatively around 80 percent of the time in the U.S. Senate, and Bill White had been seen as a pro-business mayor of Houston, Perry's conservative credentials were impressive.

Greg Abbott became Perry's successor after having established his conservative credentials as Attorney General. He used his own personal popularity along with solidly conservative credentials to sail to two easy victories in his two elections. Texas continued to be dominated by Republicans in gubernatorial contests, though most analysts concluded that neither Wendy Davis nor Lupe Valdez were particularly strong candidates. In general, though Abbott won handily, Democrats pointed to closer margins of victory across the state in 2018 as a sign for possible competitiveness in the future.

### Wasp, Middle-Aged Male

Texas has not had a non-Anglo governor since it became independent of Spain and Mexico. Until the election of Greg Abbott, no Catholic had served as governor. The religious preferences of the governors had previously been confined to the mainstream Protestant churches, such as Methodist and Baptist.

Texas governors have tended to reach the top office shortly after their fiftieth birthday. Of the thirty-two individuals who have served as governor of Texas under the 1876 Constitution,

## ISSUE SPOTLIGHT:
## Good Ol' Girl

**A**nn Richards wanted to ensure that Texans understood the difference between her people's campaign (populism) and run-of-the-mill liberalism. She went to some lengths to look like a good ol' girl, including joining the boys for the opening of bird-hunting season. She also posed for the cover of *Texas Monthly* wearing a black leather jacket and sitting on a Harley-Davidson motorcycle.

**Competency Connection**
**CRITICAL THINKING**

To date, Ann Richards is the only woman to serve as Texas Governor in the modern era. Would the state be well served to have governors who might come from varying backgrounds that might bring new perspectives to state governance?

Ann Richards served
as governor from 1991
until 1995.

AP Images/Eric Miller

only two—Ann Richards and Miriam A. Ferguson—were female, though Democrats have nominated women, Wendy Davis and Lupe Valdez, as their candidates in 2014 and 2018.

## Attorney/Businessperson, Community Pillar

Governors, as well as legislators, are often attorneys. Since 1876, seventeen of the thirty-two Texas governors have been lawyers. Of the six most recent governors in the state, only Mark White and Greg Abbott were lawyers. Bill Clements and George W. Bush were businesspeople. Ann Richards, although she had been a public school teacher, was essentially a professional politician who went to work as a lobbyist for a Washington-based law firm when she left office. Rick Perry was a fifth-generation Texas farmer-rancher with more than twenty years spent in elected office.

The final personal characteristic that candidates must have is being a "pillar of the community." Governors are members of civic, social, fraternal, and business organizations and seem to be the epitome of stable family life. Richards, being divorced, was something of an exception, but she was frequently photographed with her children and grandchildren.

**formal roles** Duties that the governor performs that stem from the Texas Constitution, including chief executive, chief legislator, commander in chief/top cop, chief of state, and chief intergovernmental diplomat.

**informal roles** Duties that the governor performs that stem from the culture and traditions of Texas, including chief of party and leader of the people.

## Roles of the Governor and Limits on Those Roles

The office of governor consists of numerous leadership roles. Some are **formal roles**, prescribed by the constitution and supplementing statutes: chief executive, chief legislator, commander in chief/top cop, chief of state, and chief intergovernmental diplomat. Others are **informal roles**, deriving from the Texas political setting: chief of party and leader of the people. Governors of all states play similar roles, as does the U.S. president, who also has added responsibilities in the areas of international affairs and economics.

The personality of the governor and the political and economic circumstances that prevail during a governor's administration largely determine which roles are emphasized. Democratic theory dictates that the elected executive be accountable for the executive branch. In Texas, the governor has to rely heavily on informal means to gain the expected control over the state bureaucracy and to achieve his or her policy agenda.

To view the governor in action, this chapter looks briefly at the styles of the governors of the state during the modern era. These brief biographical sketches may help the reader understand the diverse personalities and operating styles of recent Texas governors.

Over the years, three different styles have characterized Texas governors: aggressive, cooperative, and deferential leadership. With the limitations on gubernatorial formal powers, and a bias toward the legislature as the dominant branch of government, powers of the governors are largely what they make of them. In the 1970s, two Texas governors, Preston Smith and Dolph Briscoe, allowed the legislature to take the lead in managing the policy agenda of Texas, perhaps representing the weak governorship envisioned by the framers of the 1876 Constitution. These two governors were seen as **deferential leaders**. Governors Bill Clements and Rick Perry tried to dominate Texas politics, including their relationship with the legislature, demonstrating an **aggressive leadership** style. Governors George W. Bush and Greg Abbott were more likely to engage with the legislative leaders in jointly framing the policy agenda, marking them **cooperative leaders**.

Mark White (1983–1987) oversaw comprehensive reform of the public school system and pushed for vigorous regulation of public utilities in Texas through a cooperative leadership style. His accomplishments could not overcome the faltering Texas economy and the growing Republican Party.[7] Bill Clements (1979–1983, 1987–1991) emphasized tax reform, a war on drugs and crime, long-range planning, and better ties to neighboring states and Mexico during his first term. During his second term, out of necessity, Clements's legacy was bringing "business principles and discipline to the state budget and government" by attempting to dominate decision-making through aggressive leadership.[8]

The governor acknowledged to be atypical, Ann Richards (1991–1995), got high marks for the quality and diversity of her appointments; for forcing changes in the controversial boards governing some state agencies, and for exerting executive control over other agencies, such as the Texas Department of Commerce. She also worked hard at economic diversification. However, Richards's approach to legislative relations was aggressive, partisan and heavy handed, and, although she was appreciated for her salty sense of humor and her reputation as "the thorny rose of Texas,"[9] she sometimes had difficulty pushing her policy agenda through the legislature. Though she was popular among Texans even at the end of her term, Richards lost handily to George W. Bush in 1994.[10]

George W. Bush (1995–2000), son of a former president,[11] used a nonpartisan, low-key, and cooperative approach to leadership. Bush saw himself as a deal maker. He campaigned on four issues: reform of the juvenile justice system, setting limits on civil lawsuits (tort reform), more flexible and better public education, and restrictions on welfare. These issues were common throughout the country in 1994. Once elected, Bush stuck with those issues and pushed each through the 1995 legislature. While he was successful in further expanding public school flexibility in the 1997 legislative session, his push for major changes in the Texas tax system was rebuffed. His popularity and bipartisan leadership led to reelection in 1998 by 69 percent of the vote.[12] By January 1999, Governor Bush was campaigning for the U.S. presidency. *The Wall Street Journal* noted that the Bush "'Yellow Rose Garden' strategy of having potential presidential supporters and advisers, along with world leaders, come to Austin" overshadowed "anything that was happening across the street at the state Capitol."[13] Rick Perry's conservative tenure as governor began on such a low key that

**deferential leader**
A governor who lets the legislature initiate policy, as the 1876 Constitution envisioned.

**aggressive leader** A governor who uses the status of his office to try to dominate Texas politics despite the structural weakness of the office.

**cooperative leader**
A governor who tries to be involved in decision-making at every stage through negotiation with legislative leaders.

The conservative nature of Texas politics has often led to the criticism that the government is often too eager to cut spending on essential social programs.

Courtesy of Ben Sargent

**Competency Connection**
**PERSONAL RESPONSIBILITY**

Which programs such as the ones listed in the cartoon that the state provides could be cut back if citizens were expected to show personal responsibility for their own needs?

*Texas Monthly* magazine rated him as "furniture" after the 2001 session. That designation indicated that he had little effect on the outcome of the session until after it was over. Then Perry used the veto power generously, killing eighty-two bills—some of vital concern to his own party.

Perry was reelected to an unprecedented third four-year term in 2010, even suggested that national politics, and especially the national health care reform law of 2009, were such an anathema that Texas could secede from the Union if it wanted to. He quickly added that he thought we had a great union and that "there is absolutely no reason to dissolve it." The legislative sessions of 2013 were Perry's swansong. The three sessions were more bipartisan than normal, but are best remembered for the successful filibuster of a restrictive abortion bill by Senator Wendy Davis, passage of the bill in a subsequent session, and Perry's signing the bill. Perry's strong leadership over his fourteen years and his suspicion of a dominant national government made him popular among conservatives, and he briefly ran for the Republican nomination for president both in 2012 and 2016 before accepting an appointment as President Trump's Secretary of Energy.[14]

The election of Greg Abbott in 2014 brought a new leadership style to Texas, and while he was as conservative as Rick Perry, his style was more befitting of someone who had served many years as a judge, and he soon earned a reputation as a cooperative leader working with the legislative leadership. He has pushed for education funding while reducing taxes, and he is often seen as a leader who "seldom was seen as a magnet for headlines even into his early tenure as governor." Abbott has been seen as an empathetic leader, with his physical disability and confinement to a wheelchair giving credibility to his claims that he knows what it is to feel pain and overcome adversity.[15]

# Formal Roles and Limitations

The Texas Constitution was written at a time when concentrated power in the hands of a single state official was viewed with great apprehension. E. J. Davis, the last Republican governor before Clements, held office from 1870 to 1874, and his administration was seen as representative of northern dominance during the period of Reconstruction after the Civil War. When the 1876 Constitution was drafted, the framers reacted against the Davis administration by creating a constitutionally weak governor's office (see Chapter 2).

Today, the governor still copes with a highly fragmented executive branch that results in a plural executive. The executive branch includes not only the governor, but also five other elected executives, two elected boards, and a complex system of powerful policymaking boards and commissions. Recent governors have sought greater institutional power with modest success. Under Governor Rick Perry, control of economic development, health and human services, and the chairmanship of many state boards was enhanced.[16]

## Chief Executive

**appointment and removal powers** The governor's constitutional and statutory authority to hire and fire people employed by the state.

As the "chief executive," the governor has control over the state bureaucracy and **appointment and removal**, budgeting, planning, and supervisory and clemency powers. Although this is one of the governor's most time-consuming roles, it traditionally has been one of the weakest, as the following discussion illustrates.

Texas uses a long ballot, indicating that a large number of state officials are elected by the people rather than appointed by the governor. The list of officials elected on a statewide basis includes the lieutenant governor, the attorney general, the comptroller of public accounts, the commissioner of the General Land Office, and the agriculture commissioner. In addition, members of the Texas Railroad Commission and the State Board of Education are elected. They are elected independently, so they feel no obligation to the governor. Absent direct influence on these elected officeholders, the governor must be highly skilled in the art of persuasion. One important consequence of these independently elected officials is that often the governor's most likely competitors have held statewide elective office. The most visible executive appointments that the governor makes are those of secretary of state, commissioner of education, commissioner of

## ISSUE SPOTLIGHT:
### How a Governor Can Get Things Done

George W. Bush, elected in 1994, observed that "the way to forge good public policy amongst the leadership of the legislative branch and executive branch is to air our differences in private meetings that happen all the time.... The way to ruin a relationship is to leak things and to be disrespectful of meeting in private."

Source: R. G. Ratcliffe, "Away from the Spotlight, Governor Makes His Mark," *Houston Chronicle*, April 15, 1995, 10A.

**Competency Connection**
**CRITICAL THINKING**

In recent decades, there has been a movement to keep government decisions from being made in private, among just a few elected officials. Governor George W. Bush suggests that some difficult decisions are best made in private. Can democracy be well-served by private decision making?

insurance, commissioner of health and human services, the executive director of the Economic Development and Tourism Division, the director of the Office of State-Federal Relations, and the adjutant general, who heads the state militia. The governor also fills any vacancy that occurs in one of the major elected executive positions, such as railroad commissioner, until the next election. The governor also appoints all or some of the members of about two dozen advisory councils and committees that coordinate the work of two or more state agencies.

Most state agencies are not headed up by a single executive making policy decisions. The result is a highly fragmented executive branch; power is divided among both elected executives and appointed boards. Nevertheless, the governor has a major effect on state policy through approximately 3,000 appointments to about 125 policymaking, multimember boards and commissions. Examples include the University of Texas System board of regents, the Public Utility Commission, and the Texas Youth Commission. In 2003, the legislature gave Governor Rick Perry greater control over the chairs of state boards, allowing him the ability to appoint the presiding officer, as long as the appointee had received Senate confirmation.[17]

The members of these boards are usually appointed for a six-year term, but with the following limitations:

1. The terms of board and commission members are overlapping and staggered to prevent the governor from appointing a majority of the members at the outset of his or her term.
2. The statutes establishing the various boards and commissions often specify both a certain geographic representation and occupational or other background characteristics of the members.
3. Appointments to some boards and commissions must be made from lists supplied by members of professional organizations and associations.[18]

One other important use of the appointment power is filling vacancies in the judiciary. Although Texas has an elected judiciary, vacancies occur through retirements or resignations. The governor makes appointments to these benches until the next election. Indeed, many district court judges in the state are first appointed and subsequently stand for election.

The governor must obtain a two-thirds confirmation vote from the Texas Senate for appointments. As in national politics, there is the practice of "senatorial courtesy": The Senate will usually honor the objection of a senator from the same district as the nominee for appointment by refusing to approve confirmation.

Texas's short biennial legislative session, however, permits the governor to make many interim appointments when the legislature is not in session. This practice gives these appointees a "free ride" for as long as nineteen months. These recess appointments must be presented to the Senate within the first ten days of the next session, whether regular or special.

Another aid to the governor is incumbency. If a governor is reelected, he or she will be able to appoint all members of the board or commission by the middle of the second term. The governor may then have considerable influence over policy development within the agency.

The Texas governor has only limited removal power. The governor can remove appointed political officials with the consent of the Senate. He also can remove personal staff members and a few executive directors, such as the one in the Department of Housing and Community Affairs. However, the governor cannot remove members of boards and commissions whom he did not appoint and obviously cannot remove elected state executives. This lack of removal power deprives the governor of significant control over state agencies. Because Article 15 of the Texas Constitution stipulates the right to a trial before removal from office, impeachment is likely to remain the chief formal removal procedure because it does involve a trial by the Senate. However, even its use is quite rare.

**Budgeting** By law, the governor submits a biennial budget message to the legislature within five days after that body convenes in regular session. The executive budget indicates to the legislature the governor's priorities and signals items likely to be vetoed. With the exception of the item veto, the Texas governor lacks the strong formal budgetary powers not only of the president, but also of many state executives (see Chapter 12).

Traditionally, the Legislative Budget Board (LBB), which also prepares a budget for the legislature to consider, has dominated the budget process. The legislature always has been guided more by the legislative budget than by the governor's. A significant exception occurred in the regular 2003 legislative session when the governor's staff was heavily involved in developing the final budget for floor consideration.[19]

**Planning** Both modern management and the requirements of many federal grants-in-aid emphasize substate regional planning, and the governor directs planning efforts for the state through the Budget, Planning, and Policy Division. When combined with budgeting, the governor's planning power allows a stronger gubernatorial hand in the development of new programs and policy alternatives. Although still without adequate control over the programs of the state, the governor has had a greater voice in suggesting future programs over the past two decades, mainly because many federal statutes have designated the governor as having approval power for federal grants.

During Ann Richards's administration, Comptroller John Sharp—in part at the request of the governor to allow a more rational appropriations act for fiscal years 1992–1993—developed an elaborate system for monitoring the performance of state agencies. This system, known as the Texas Performance Review (TPR), requires state agencies to engage in strategic planning. The TPR has continued as a vital part of state government, though it is largely overseen by legislative staff agencies.

**Supervising** The state constitution charges the governor with the responsibility for seeing that the laws of the state are "faithfully executed," but provides few tools for fulfilling this function. The governor's greatest supervisory and directive powers occur in the role of commander in chief. Governors can request reports from state agencies, appoint board chairs, remove their own appointees, and use political influence to force hiring reductions or other economies. But lack of appointment power over the professional staffs of state agencies and lack of removal power over a predecessor's appointees limit the governor's ability to ensure that the state bureaucracy performs its job.

## ISSUE SPOTLIGHT:
## Budget Growth in a Conservative Era

Although Governor Rick Perry frequently called for conservative revenue measures and restrictions on state spending, he saw the budget continue to grow during his administration, including a 5.1 percent increase from FY 2012–2013 to $200,421.1 billion for FY 2014–2015. This period also saw the state swing from a deep shortage to a generous surplus. Per-person spending actually declined in terms of national rankings. The budget continued to grow under Governor Greg Abbott, reaching $251 billion for the 2019-2021 biennium.

Sources: "Texas House Proposes Sweeping Cuts," *Texas Tribune*, January 19, 2011; *Fiscal Size-Up, 2014–2015 Biennium*, pp. 1–2.

**Competency Connection**
**CRITICAL THINKING**

Though conservatives often decry increases in government spending, the Texas government, dominated by conservatives, keeps growing. Why?

The governor thus falls back on informal tactics to exercise any control over the administration. In this respect, the governor's staff is of supreme importance: If staff members can establish good rapport with state agencies, they may extend the governor's influence to areas where the governor does not have formal authority. They are aided in this task by two factors of which agency personnel are well aware: the governor's leadership of the party and veto powers (both discussed in the "Chief Legislator" section).

**message power** The governor's means of formally establishing his or her priorities for legislative action by communicating with the legislature.

**session power** The governor's constitutional authority to call the legislature into special session and to set the agenda of topics to be considered in that session.

**veto power** The governor's constitutional authority to prevent the implementation of laws enacted by the legislature. The item veto allows the governor to delete individual items from an appropriations bill.

**Clemency** The governor's power with regard to acts of clemency (mercy) is restricted. The state's chief executive officer makes recommendations to the Board of Pardons and Paroles, which is part of the Department of Criminal Justice. Although empowered to refuse an act of clemency recommended by the board, the governor normally cannot act without its recommendation.

## Chief Legislator

Although the legislature tends to dominate Texas politics, the governor is a strong chief legislator who relies on three formal powers in carrying out this role: **message power**, **session power**, and **veto power**.

**Message Power** The constitution requires a gubernatorial message when legislative sessions open and when a governor retires. By law, the governor also delivers a biennial budget message. Other messages come when the legislature is in session to promote the governor's policy agenda. They also attract the attention of the media and set the agenda for state government, giving the governor a persuasive tool of influence.

**Session Power** As discussed in Chapter 6, the legislature is constitutionally limited to 140 legislative days each biennium. Only the governor may call special sessions. Called sessions are limited to a maximum duration of thirty days, but a governor who wants to force consideration of an issue can continue calling one special session after another, and there have commonly been special sessions in recent years.

## ISSUE SPOTLIGHT:
## Ma Ferguson and Clemency

The governor's clemency power was not always so restricted. Under the Constitution of 1876, it was actually quite extensive. During the 1920s and 1930s, however, Governor Miriam "Ma" Ferguson was suspected of selling pardons, in combination with other financial shenanigans. Critics complained that "Ma pardons criminals before they're indicted." In response to this perceived abuse of the governor's power, in 1936, the state adopted a constitutional amendment establishing the Board of Pardons and Paroles and severely limiting the governor's authority to pardon, especially in the area of prisoners condemned to die. Now, the only action the governor can take without the written recommendation of the board is to give a death row inmate one thirty-day reprieve.

Source: Dave McNeely, "What Bush Could and Couldn't Have Done," *Austin American-Statesman*, June 24, 2000, A15.

Competency Connection
**CRITICAL THINKING**

**Should the clemency powers of the governor be strengthened? Why or why not?**

The governor also sets the agenda for special sessions, although the legislature, once called, may consider other matters on a limited basis. As the complexity of state government has grown, legislators sometimes have been unable to complete their work in the short biennial regular sessions, requiring more frequent special sessions. The eight governors before Bush called a total of thirty-four special sessions. Bush called none, a reflection on the one hand of his ability to get along with the legislative leadership, and on the other hand of budget surpluses. Rick Perry, in part because of his party's dominance of state government, used the session power extensively, calling numerous special sessions during his time in office from 2003 to 2014, including three in 2013 to consider congressional redistricting, abortion, and a new highway program. Greg Abbott called a special session in 2017, and it had an ambitious twenty-item agenda.[20]

**Veto Power**  The governor's strongest legislative power is the veto. Every bill that passes both houses of the legislature in regular and special sessions is sent to the governor, who has the option of signing it, letting it become law without signing it, or vetoing it.[21] If the legislature is still in session, the governor has ten days in which to act. If the bill is sent to the governor in the last ten days of a session or after the legislature has adjourned, the governor must act within twenty days. If the governor vetoes a bill while the legislature is still in session, that body may override the veto by a two-thirds vote of both houses.

Because of the short legislative session, many important bills are often sent to the governor so late that the legislature has adjourned before the governor has had to act on them. The legislature cannot override if it is not in session, so in those instances, the veto power is absolute. Short biennial sessions thus make the governor's threat of a veto an extremely powerful political tool. Even during the sessions, the override of a veto takes a two-thirds vote in both houses of the legislature, a rare occurrence. The last bill overridden was under Governor Bill Clements in 1979. Some observers have argued that when a governor uses his or her veto power frequently, it is actually a sign of gubernatorial weakness. The reasoning for such a claim is that a powerful governor actually is able to negotiate with legislative leaders, thus ironing out compromises over legislation, while a weak governor, not having such persuasive abilities, is left only with the veto pen to exert his or her influence.

# ISSUE SPOTLIGHT:
## The Veto Record Book

Governor Rick Perry holds the record for the most bills vetoed in a single session (82) and for the most bills vetoed in the shortest time (132 in three years). Bill Clements holds the overall record for the most bills vetoed (190 in eight years). Perry was a Republican governor with a Republican legislature; thus, he vetoed the bills of his own party. He also used the veto to discipline wayward legislators—for example, his annulment of four noncontroversial bills sponsored by fellow Republican Charlie Geren, who failed to support his reorganization efforts. Clements was a Republican governor with a Democratic legislature who was trying to transform the state in terms of both policy and procedure. Governor Abbott vetoed 58 bills after the 2019 legislative session.

Competency Connection
— CRITICAL —
THINKING

How might the use of the veto signal weakness in a governor's leadership?

After serving six years on the Texas Supreme Court and twelve years as attorney general, Greg Abbott was elected governor in the 2014 election.

AP Images/Pat Sullivan

**Competency Connection**
**– COMMUNICATION –**
**SKILLS**

Governor Abbott had long experience in Texas government, first as a member of the Texas Supreme Court and then as Texas Attorney General. Is experience of this sort helpful, or are citizens better represented by people from outside who can bring a differing perspective to governance? Explain.

The governor has one other check over appropriations bills: the item veto.[22] The governors in forty-three other states have a similar power. This device permits the governor to delete individual items from a bill without having to veto it in its entirety. The item veto, however, may be used only to strike a particular line of funding; it cannot be used to reduce or increase an appropriation.

The item veto illustrates a reality of gubernatorial power in Texas. The governor's power over legislation is largely negative—he or she often finds it easier to say no than to get his or her own legislative agenda adopted. This truism particularly describes the budget process. Yet the timing of the appropriations act and the number of items that the legislature can cram into one line item are factors that affect the governor's use of the item veto as a fiscal tool to control spending.[23]

The use of the item veto was challenged in 2014 when an Austin grand jury indicted Governor Rick Perry, alleging abuse of executive authority in the use of his item veto. Perry had threatened to veto the $7.5 million budget for the Travis county public integrity unit, overseen by Austin District Attorney Rosemary Lehmberg. Perry wished Lehmberg to resign her position after an embarrassing drunk driving arrest, and when she refused, he vetoed the appropriation. The charges were later overturned.

## Commander in Chief/Top Cop

Though the state of Texas does not independently engage in warfare with other nations, the governor does have the power to declare martial law—that is, to suspend civil government temporarily and replace it with government by the state militia and/or law enforcement agencies. Although seldom used, this power was invoked to quell an oil field riot in East Texas in 1931 and to gain control of an explosive racial situation on the Gulf Coast in 1943.

Additionally, the governor is commander in chief of the military forces of the state (Army and Air National Guard), except when they have been called into service by the national government. The head of these forces, the adjutant general, is one of the governor's important appointees. The governor also may assume command of the Texas Rangers and the

Department of Public Safety to maintain law and order. These powers become important in the aftermath of natural disasters, or when the governor wishes to enhance border security. Following the terrorist attacks on the United States on September 11, 2001, the national government created a Department of Homeland Security and mandated security responsibilities for state and local governments in addition to their traditional function of disaster management. The Texas homeland security office, the Division of Emergency Management, reports to the governor. In routine situations, the governor is dependent on local law enforcement and prosecuting agencies to see that the laws of the state are faithfully executed. When evidence of wrongdoing exists, governors often bring the informal powers of their office to bear, appealing to the media to focus public attention on errant agencies and officeholders.

## Chief of State

Just as presidents use ceremonial pomp and circumstance to augment other roles, so also do governors. Whether presiding over a Veteran's Day ceremony or serving as host to a visiting dignitary, the governor's performance as chief of state enhances the more important formal roles of the office. In the modern era, governors use their high profile on television and social media to set the policy agenda through publicity.

More and more, Texas governors are using the ceremonial role of chief of state, sometimes coupled with the role of chief intergovernmental diplomat, to become actively involved

# ISSUE SPOTLIGHT:
## The Governor in Command

In 1985, Governor Mark White used the commander-in-chief powers in a controversial way. First, he authorized the state militia to participate in a military training exercise in Honduras, which borders on the politically volatile countries of Nicaragua and El Salvador. Then White joined the troops and oversaw the delivery of Texas barbecue to the militia over the Easter weekend—just as the legislature began to discuss the state budget.

In 1999–2000, Governor George W. Bush also used the commander-in-chief powers in an unusual way. In his bid for the Republican nomination for president, he traveled across the United States. During these campaign tours, he was protected by the Texas Department of Public Safety, which always guards the governor. Thus, for a change, a few state troopers and Texas Rangers got to see much of the country.

In 2005, Governor Rick Perry announced that Texas would need to guard its own borders because the federal government had failed to do so. He emphasized reducing crime along the Texas–Mexico border, training the National Guard to respond to emergencies, and generally relying on law enforcement for safety. Like President George W. Bush at the national level, he endorsed a sponsored immigrant worker program. With increased drug-related violence along the Texas–Mexico border in 2011 and a very tight state budget, Perry asked for 3,000 additional federal officials to patrol the border.

Greg Abbott used his commander-in-chief powers to call up the national guard in response to the devastation of Hurricane Harvey.

**Competency Connection**
**CRITICAL THINKING**

Should the governor be given broad powers in using the state's national guard or law enforcement agencies, or should those powers be restricted to using them in conventional ways?

in economic negotiations, such as plant locations. Efforts are directed toward both foreign and domestic investments and finding new markets for Texas goods. In such negotiations, the governor uses the power and prestige of the office to become the state's salesperson (see "Texas Version of Foreign Affairs").

## Chief Intergovernmental Diplomat

The Texas Constitution provides that the governor, or someone designated by the governor, will be the state's representative in all dealings with other states and with the national government. This role of intergovernmental representative has increased in importance for three reasons. First, federal statutes now designate the governor as the official who has the planning and grant-approval authority for the state. This designation has given the governor's budgeting, planning, and supervising powers much more clout in recent years, and federal budget philosophy (see Chapter 12) further enhances the governor's role.

Second, some state problems, such as water and energy development, often require the cooperation of several states, such as planning solutions for the water problems of the High Plains area. Additionally, although the U.S. Constitution precludes a governor from conducting diplomatic relations with other nations, Texas's location as a border state gives rise to occasional social and economic exchanges with the governors of Mexican border states on matters such as immigration and energy. The box entitled "Texas Version of Foreign Affairs" earlier in this chapter outlines the aggressive international role of the governor.

Third, acquiring federal funds is essential in modern times, with about a third of the state budget coming from federal aid. States and localities alone do not have nearly the resources necessary to provide the wide array of governmental services in a modern state. In 2009, during the economic downturn, the federal government offered states money to help stimulate the economy. Governor Perry, believing such stimulus might hurt the state in the long run, rejected $556 million in federal unemployment funds because they might have required Texas to expand the program to cover different kinds of workers, but accepted other stimulus funds.[24] Often, the governor works in concert with other governors to try to secure favorable national legislation, including both funding and limits on unfunded federal mandates (see Chapter 11).

A more traditional use of the governor's intergovernmental role is mandated by Article IV of the U.S. Constitution, which provides for the rendition (surrender) of fugitives from justice who flee across state lines. The Texas governor, like other governors, signs the rendition papers and transmits them to the appropriate law enforcement officials. Law officers are then in charge of picking up the fugitives and returning them to the appropriate state.

# Informal Roles and Limitations

In addition to the five roles just described, there are at least two informal powers. They have no basis in law, but they are nevertheless important to the job.

## Chief of Party

As the symbolic head of the Democratic or Republican Party in the state, the governor is a key figure at the state party conventions and usually is the leader of the party's delegation to national conventions. A governor may, however, have to compete with his or her party's U.S. senator. Governors are able to use their influence with the party's state executive committee and at party conventions to gain a subsidiary influence over candidates seeking other state offices. An active, skilled governor can thus create a power relationship with state legislators and bureaucrats that the more formal roles of the office do not permit. The governor also wins some political influence by campaigning for other party candidates who are seeking state or national offices.

Recent governors have shown contrasting party leadership styles. In 1995, George W. Bush operated on a cooperative basis and secured the support of both members and leaders of the Democratic majority legislature for his legislative program. He also made his own Republican Party angry by cooperating with the Democrats and by having a moderate position on a number of issues. For example, Governor Bush, a Republican, and Speaker of the House Pete Laney and Lt. Governor Bob Bullock, both Democrats, worked especially well together, and Bush told the state party bigwigs to back off from trying to defeat Laney in his 1996 reelection bid. In 1997, he fared somewhat less well with the legislature even though the Senate had become Republican, in part because of resistance to his tax plan by conservative members of the GOP. Rick Perry's approach was more aggressive. In 2001, the legislature was split between a Republican Senate and a Democratic House, and Perry had come to office by succession when Bush ran for president. Perry was not a significant factor in the legislative session until he angered his GOP colleagues by vetoing some of their pet bills after the session had ended. In 2003, Perry was emboldened by having been elected to office and by the Republican control of all branches of government and took a particularly partisan approach by forcing congressional redistricting. In 2007, Perry stormed into the legislative session with policy positions at variance not only from those of Democrats, but also his fellow Republicans. He conservative social policies such as a restrictive abortion law and resistance to federal laws, most notably the Affordable Care Act.

Governor Greg Abbott has been more like Bush, taking a cooperative approach to working with legislative leaders. His job has been easier than Bush's was in one sense because Republicans have controlled both of the legislative chambers during his tenure. However, during his first term, the Speaker of the House Joe Straus, a moderate Republican, and Lt. Governor Dan Patrick, a very conservative Republican, often had strong conflicts, particularly on social conservative issues such as transgendered bathrooms in public schools. Abbott often found himself mediating between the two. For the 2019 session, with Straus replaced by a more conservative speaker in Dennis Bonnen but Democrats picking up seats in both chambers in the 2018 elections, Abbott's judicial temperament may be challenged.

## Leader of the People

Most Texans, unaware of the limitations gubernatorial powers, look to the chief executive of the state for the leadership necessary to solve the state's problems and to serve as their principal spokesperson on major issues. A skilled governor can turn this role to substantial advantage when bargaining with key leaders in the legislature and the state's administration. For example, through the media, the governor can rally public support for programs and policies. Accepting invitations to speak is another way a governor can gain public support for programs and plans, including the budget. Public appearances usually serve as occasions for emphasizing gubernatorial accomplishments. They also allow a governor to show concern for ordinary citizens with extraordinary problems, such as visits to areas damaged by tornadoes or floods. In keeping with the traditionalistic tenor of the state, some governors use this role to show that they are "active conservatives."

Coupled with the strong legislative role, this informal role is critical to a governor's success. Leadership has been depicted as consisting of two parts: the ability to "transact" (i.e., to make things happen) and the ability to "transform" (i.e., to decide what things should happen).[25] The successful Texas governor is one who can both make things happen and decide what policies ought to happen.

## You Decide: Does the Texas Governor Need More Power?

The powers of the Texas governor used to be ranked almost at the bottom of gubernatorial powers in the fifty American states. More recently, the Texas governor's institutional powers—those established by constitution and statute—rank just about in the middle. Indeed, the powers of the governor of California are considered less than those of the Texas governor, although the New York governor has greater power. Thus, even among the very largest states, Texas stands in the middle.

### Pro ✓

⬆ Texas should, by statute or constitutional amendment, increase the power of the governor because:

⬆ Bureaucrats have far too much discretion to act when there is no clear executive authority.

⬆ The public is confused by the number of elected officials in Texas (the long ballot).

⬆ Texas needs someone with greater authority to show mercy to convicted felons facing the death penalty.

⬆ A governor needs to be able to control all boards and commissions soon after election to implement policies he or she favors.

⬆ A more powerful governor would mean that the legislature's power could be reduced.

⬆ Texas needs its governor to have meaningful budget authority.

### Con ✗

⬇ Texas should not, by statute or constitutional amendment, increase the power of the governor because:

⬇ The personal power of the governor—based on margin of electoral victory and personal persuasion—is already great.

⬇ The veto power is virtually absolute.

⬇ Dispersion of power is a good way to keep one person from gaining too much control.

⬇ The governor's clout is obvious when one considers the salary, the size of the staff, and the lack of effort over the years to remove the governor from office.

⬇ Democracy is better served when the legislature is the more powerful institution because the people are closer to their elected representatives than to the governor.

⬇ The dual budgeting system encourages fiscal control.

**Competency Connection**
**SOCIAL RESPONSIBILITY**

The governor is given a variety of formal and informal powers. Would enhancing those powers allow the governor the opportunity to be a better representative of the policy needs of the citizens of the state?

---

**populist** Someone who believes in appealing to the political wishes of the common people, and that those people should be protected from exploitation by corporations, the elite, and government.

Texas governors have often employed a **populist** approach to leadership, attempting to respond to the preferences of the common citizens. In Texas, populism often represents the conservative instincts of the people, and might involve support for gun rights, capital punishment, and limited taxation. In recent years, Texans have also advocated the improvement of public education, and Governors Ann Richards, George W. Bush, and Greg Abbott all have wanted to improve public education—though they employed different styles. Governor Perry pushed to strengthen the office of governor while at the same time limiting the powers of government in general, a preference that has continued under Governor Abbott.[26]

## Summary

**LO 7.1** **The Texas governorship is elected to a term of four years and has no limit on the number of terms he or she may serve.** Like the U.S. president, the governor can be removed from office through an impeachment process. Despite having relatively weak powers, the Texas governor has a relatively large staff.

**LO 7.2** **The Texas governor is limited in power due to the number of independently elected executives in the state, including the lieutenant governor, agriculture commissioner, the attorney general, the commissioner of the general land office, and the comptroller of public accounts.**

**LO 7.3** **Elected in a conservative state, Texas governors typically are White male Protestants of middle age, married, professionals, and pillars of their communities.**

**LO 7.4** **The Texas governor serves a four-year term and is paid fairly well. Nevertheless, the office is constitutionally weak, and the approval and successful implementation of gubernatorial budgetary and programmatic policies depend more on the governor's leadership skills than on formal powers.**

**LO 7.5** **The Texas governor has many important functions to perform, which are embodied in the various roles that make up the office of chief executive for the state. These roles, however, are restricted in the following major ways: Five other elected executives, an elected state policy board, and an elected regulatory commission make up the state's plural executive; the state bureaucracy is largely controlled by multimember boards and commissions; senatorial confirmation of appointees requires a two-thirds vote; the governor's power to remove appointed officials other than personal staff is quite restricted; and the state has both a legislative and an executive budget.** On the other hand, the governor does have some constitutional and statutory strengths including the following: an item veto over appropriations bills; command over the militia and law enforcement agencies; personal leadership opportunities; and control over the presiding officers of appointed boards and commissions.

## Critical Thinking

1. Although the Texas governor is the elected chief executive, the power of the office is quite limited compared to that of other governors. Identify two strengths of the Texas governor and two weaknesses. Explain how the identified powers enable or limit the governor in carrying out his or her responsibilities.

2. Discuss the leadership styles that recent governors have used; reflect on the consequences of those styles for gubernatorial success.

Speaking at the podium in front of the Alamo is Commissioner of the General Land Office in Texas George P. Bush.  Bush, the grandson of President George H.W. Bush and nephew of President George W. Bush, represents a new generation of leaders for the state.

*AB Forces News Collection/Alamy Stock Photo*

# The Administrative State

Citizens interact with government almost entirely through the administrative agencies of government. While the study of administration is often seen as tedious and boring, it is the full time professionals in government offices who are the faces of government and who make decisions regarding the enforcement of government regulations and the carrying out of political functions. Police on patrol, public school principals, highway workers, college registrars, clerks in state offices—they represent government in action.

Government bureaucracy is also the place of Americans' inconsistent views—we love the benefits of government programs but often hate "bureaucrats," who are viewed as inefficient and undemocratic barriers to program success. We simultaneously want less government, but more programs that benefit us. The political culture of a state directly affects what government programs the state provides. In states with a moralistic culture, greater emphasis is placed on programs for the common good, such as environmental protection, education, and social services. In states such as Texas, with a heritage of individualistic/traditionalistic political culture, policymakers often focus more on limiting government costs, on cutting taxes, and on providing a business environment with minimal regulations.

## Learning Objectives

**LO 8.1**  Understand the complexity of the administrative organization in Texas, including the plural executive.

**LO 8.2**  Trace the growth of government.

**LO 8.3**  Describe the characteristics of bureaucracy and bureaucratic survival techniques.

**LO 8.4**  Evaluate bureaucratic orientation and its effect on the public interest.

**LO 8.5**  Assess the bureaucracy's accountability to the governor, the legislature, and the public.

MANY PEOPLE CONSIDER THE THINGS WHICH GOVERNMENT DOES FOR THEM TO BE SOCIAL PROGRESS, BUT THEY CONSIDER THE THINGS GOVERNMENT DOES FOR OTHERS TO BE SOCIALISM.

Earl Warren,
*Chief Justice of the United States, 1953–1969*

**bureaucracy** A type of organization that is characterized by hierarchy, specialization, fixed and official rules, and relative freedom from outside control.

**hierarchy** Levels of authority in an organization, with the maximum authority on top.

This chapter begins with a description of the state administrative agencies and the **bureaucracy** that carries out its functions. It then addresses how the administrative state became so big. Bureaucracy is an organization associated with complicated rules, specialization, and **hierarchy**. Hierarchy refers to an arrangement that puts a few people with power at the top of the organization, and many people with little authority at the bottom of the organization. Finally, the chapter examines efforts to control the bureaucracy and ensure that it performs as the public and elected officials intend.

Administrators are responsible for enforcing *public policy* in forms such as laws, judicial rulings, and federal and state programs. While legislators write laws that give outlines of the goals of policy, bureaucrats determine what is to be done specifically because it is their job to *implement* policy—that is, to translate policy into action. Thus, some bureaucratic decisions are in themselves operational public policy—for example, determining the college tuition rate on a campus balancing broad statewide interest in providing affordable education with the sense that those who benefit from higher education should have a substantial role in paying for it. Policy is not always implemented successfully. For example, Texas state government and local school districts are charged with providing a high quality of education, yet often the reality falls far short of the ideal. Erratic funding, and disparities of funding between urban and suburban schools, does not help the situation.

Any state employee may be a *bureaucrat*, but the term most commonly is limited to administrators, executives, and lower-echelon white-collar office employees who are appointed politically or selected because of some test of their merit. Members of the traditional professions and also of the professions peculiar to government are more usually referred to by their professional titles, such as teacher, nurse, attorney, or game warden.

Implementing or executing the law is formally the responsibility of the executive branch of government; thus, the bureaucracy is nominally headed by the chief executive—in Texas, the governor. However, bureaucracy permeates all branches and its interests and powers crisscross the entire fabric of governmental structure. Furthermore, as the previous chapter demonstrated, the governor is a constitutionally weak chief executive. In fact, administrative powers are distributed among several elected executives and boards in the state who have independent organizations that do not report to the governor. Woven throughout this chapter is a concern for the democratic legitimacy of the administrative state. In a democracy, the participation of the citizens legitimates government action. However, administrators, or "bureaucrats," are not elected. Often, they cannot be removed by the governor, who is, of course, elected by the people. Yet, they often wield great power in Texas politics. What can justify such power?

## State Administrative Agencies

State bureaucracy is necessary to carry out government policy, but the Texas administration is complex and lines of authority are often confusing. Three essential characteristics of the state administration cause this confusion.

1. No single, uniform organizational pattern exists.
2. Texas administration features numerous exceptions to the traditional notions of bureaucratic hierarchy.
3. Some state agencies have narrow responsibilities while others have broad powers, and the number of agencies is impossible to define accurately.

There are at least five different types of top policymakers in state agencies: (1) elected executives, (2) appointed executives, (3) an elected commission and an elected board, (4) ex officio boards and commissions, and (5) appointed boards and commissions (see Table 8-1). Agencies headed by an elected or appointed executive follow traditional hierarchical principles in that a single individual clearly is the "boss" and thus is ultimately responsible for the operation of a particular department or office. But the agencies that are headed by a multimember board or commission have three or six or even a greater number of bosses—whatever the number of members on the board. Although there also is a hierarchical organization in these agencies, it begins with the professional staff of the agency, the level below that of the policy-setting board.

Another complication is that one office, board, or commission may be responsible for the general policies of a number of separate agencies. For example, the Board of Regents of the University of Texas is the policymaking board for the entire University of Texas System, which includes fifteen agencies that are separately funded. As of fiscal year 2018–2019, about 182 agencies, institutions, and independent programs, excluding the judicial and the legislative branches, were funded by general appropriations.[1] This list was not all-inclusive, however, because not all agencies appeared individually in the state budget. A rough count of just the *budgeted* policymaking boards, commissions, departments, institutions, and offices—excluding the courts and related agencies, the legislature and its staff agencies, and the offices of elected executives—yields

| TABLE 8-1 | Types of Administrative Agencies in Texas |
|---|---|
| **Agencies Headed by Elected Executives** | |
| Office of the Attorney General | |
| Department of Agriculture | |
| Office of the Comptroller of Public Accounts | |
| General Land Office | |
| **Agencies Headed by Appointed Executives** | |
| Office of the Secretary of State | |
| Health and Human Services Commission (see Chapter 13) | |
| **Multimember Boards and Commissions** | |
| Elected Board and Commission | |
| State Board of Education | |
| Texas Railroad Commission | |
| Ex Officio Board | |
| Bond Review Board | |
| Appointed Boards and Commissions | |
| Texas Higher Education Coordinating Board | |
| Public Utility Commission | |

a count of about 142 agencies, most of which are governed by a multimember board. Community/junior colleges are unusual in that their boards are local, and not appointed by the governor.

All of this discussion suggests why the number of state agencies is usually expressed in approximate terms. The sheer number of agencies precludes a systematic discussion of each. Therefore, a few of the most important state agencies are used to illustrate the various bureaucratic arrangements in the state.

## Agencies with Elected Executives

Five state officials, in addition to the governor, are elected on partisan ballots for four-year terms. They are, in theory at least, directly accountable to the citizenry for their performance and their integrity in office. All 2018 elected executives were Republican. One of them, the lieutenant governor, presides over the Texas Senate and does not head any executive office. In the elections of 2018, all five elected executives won reelection: Dan Patrick as lieutenant governor; Ken Paxton attorney general; Glenn Hegar, comptroller of public accounts; George P. Bush, land commissioner; and Sid Miller, agriculture commissioner.

**Attorney General** Along with the governor, the lieutenant governor, and the speaker of the House, the attorney general is one of the most powerful officers in Texas government. Although candidates for the position often run on an anticrime platform, the work of the office is primarily civil. As the attorney for the state, the attorney general and staff represent the state and its agencies in court when the state is a party to a case. The Office of the Attorney General also is responsible for such varied legal matters as consumer protection, antitrust litigation, workers' compensation insurance, organized-crime control, and environmental protection.

The attorney general's greatest power, however, is that of issuing opinions on questions concerning the constitutionality or legality of existing or proposed legislation and administrative actions. These opinions are not legally binding, but they are rarely challenged in court and thus effectively have the same importance as a ruling by the state's Supreme Court. Because the attorney general's opinions often make the headlines, and because the attorney general works with all state agencies, the office is second only to the governor's office in the public recognition it receives, a situation common in other states.[2] Because the position is regarded as one of the stepping-stones to the governor's office, attorneys general often encourage publicity about themselves, their agency, and their support groups with an eye to possible future election campaigns. The current attorney general, Ken Paxton, is an especially controversial incumbent. As of 2019, Paxton remains under indictment on three criminal charges: two counts of securities fraud (first-degree felonies) and one count of failing to register with state securities regulators (a third-degree felony). As a result, while he won reelection in 2018, it was by a narrower margin than other elected executives.

**Comptroller of Public Accounts** The comptroller (pronounced con-TROL-ler) is responsible for the administration of the state tax system and for performing preaudits of expenditures by state agencies, along with acting as the state's banker. In addition, as part of the budget process, the comptroller certifies to the legislature the approximate biennial income for the state. The Texas Constitution precludes the legislature from appropriating more funds than are anticipated in state revenues for any biennial period. Texas, like most other states, must have a balanced budget. The comptroller's office also issues the excise tax stamps used to indicate the collection of taxes on the sale of alcoholic beverages and cigarettes in the state. In short, the comptroller takes in the state's revenues, safeguards them, and invests them. In 2003, the legislature limited the power of the comptroller somewhat by placing primary responsibility for performance evaluations in the hands of the Legislative Budget Board. However, the comptroller's estimates of how much revenue will be produced by taxes still forms the basis for the amount of money the legislature can appropriate. First elected in 2014, the current comptroller is Glenn Hegar, a conservative Republican who previously served in both the Texas House and Texas Senate.

**Commissioner of the General Land Office** Only Texas and Alaska entered the Union with large amounts of public lands, and only they have land offices. About 22.5 million Texas acres are administered by the commissioner of the General Land Office. This acreage includes 4 million acres of bays, inlets, and other submerged land from the shoreline to the three-league marine limit (10.36 miles out). The land commissioner's land-management responsibilities include the following:

1. Supervising the leasing of all state-owned lands for such purposes as oil and gas production, mineral development, and grazing (more than 14,000 leases)
2. Administering the veterans' land program, by which veterans may buy land with loans that are backed by state bonds
3. Maintaining the environmental quality of public lands and waters, especially coastal lands

The current land commissioner is George P. Bush, the grandson of President George H. W. Bush, nephew of former Texas Governor and U.S. President George W. Bush, and son of former Florida Governor Jeb Bush. He is widely seen as having aspirations far above the land commissioner position, and as someone whose mother was born in Mexico and speaks fluent Spanish, he also personifies the ongoing diversification of ethnicity in Texas. Like all land commissioners, he must try to balance environmental interests with land and mineral interests. And, his highest profile activity has been bringing the Alamo under his supervision, and away from the Daughters of the Republic of Texas

**Commissioner of Agriculture** Farming and ranching are still important industries in the state, even though only about 1 percent of the population is engaged in agriculture. The Texas Department of Agriculture, like its national counterpart, is responsible both for the regulation and promotion (through research and education) of the agribusiness industry and for consumer protection, even though these functions may sometimes be in conflict. Departmental activities are diverse—for example, enforcing weights and measures standards, licensing egg handlers, determining the relative safety of pesticides, and locating export markets for Texas agricultural products. Pesticides illustrate the conflicting nature of the roles assigned to this office: Requiring that pesticides be safe for workers, consumers, and the environment may be detrimental to the profits of farmers.

Election to this office is specified by statute rather than by the state constitution. Sid Miller was elected agriculture commissioner in 2014. He had served in the state House of Representatives before losing in the Republican primary of 2012. Miller is a farmer and rancher who breeds and trains American Quarter Horses, and has successfully competed as a rodeo cowboy.

Cartoonist Ben Sargent portrays a preacher arguing in favor of programs that pursue the public good while the person in the congregation is thinking that the Texas government, represented by Attorney General Ken Paxton, wants to challenge such programs, particularly those that come from the national government.

Courtesy of Ben Sargent

Competency Connection
**PERSONAL RESPONSIBILITY**

Should the state of Texas aggressively pursue all money available from the national government for social programs—thereby keeping state taxes as low as possible and benefits greater than they are today, or should it refuse those programs when they seem to advocate more liberal goals than Texans have traditionally supported?

## Agencies with Appointed Executives

One example of an agency headed by an appointed executive is the Office of the Secretary of State. The state constitution stipulates that the governor shall appoint the secretary of state, whose functions include safeguarding the great seal of the state of Texas and affixing it to the governor's signature on proclamations, commissions, and certificates. In addition to this somewhat ceremonial duty, the duties of the secretary include certifying elections (verifying the validity of the returns), maintaining records on campaign expenditures, keeping the list of lobbyists who register with the state, administering the Uniform Commercial Code, issuing corporate charters, and publishing the *Texas Register*—the official record of administrative decisions, rules, regulations, and announcements of hearings and pending actions. The newest duty of the secretary is to serve as the state's international protocol officer. In his role as interim Secretary of State, David Whitley, named to the post in 2018 by Governor Abbott, claimed that up to 58,000 undocumented Texans illegally voted in Texas elections. That dubious claim led the legislature to fail to confirm Whitley's appointment during the 2019 session, and Whitley resigned from the position.

The secretary of state's office, though appointive, can sometimes be a springboard to elective office. Former Lieutenant Governor Bob Bullock and former Governor Mark White both held the position, as did former Comptroller John Sharp and former Mayor Ron Kirk of Dallas, appointed by President Barack Obama as his trade negotiator. Antonio (Tony) Garza continued in their footsteps by being elected to the Texas Railroad Commission in 1998; President George W. Bush then appointed him as ambassador to Mexico in 2002. Roger Williams, a former Perry appointee, was elected to the U.S. Congress.

## Boards and Commissions

Multimember boards or commissions head most state administrative agencies and make overall policy for them. These boards appoint chief administrators to handle the day-to-day responsibilities of the agencies, including the budget, personnel, and the administration of state laws and those federal laws that are carried out through state governments. Two of these boards and commissions have elected members. The others have appointed or ex officio members.

**Elected Boards and Commissions** The Texas Railroad Commission (TRC) is one of the most influential agencies in the state, and its three members are powerful indeed. The commission has tremendous political clout in the state because of its regulation of all mining

---

# Can Twitter Save Your Life?

Texas is infamous for its weather extremes, and from late spring through early fall, tornados are common. In other times of the year, flash floods or ice storms create problems for Texans. Acccess @TDEM or go to http://www.txdps.state.tx.us/dem/, the Web site of the Texas Division of Emergency Management, and click on the Twitter link at the bottom of the home page. Recent tweets are included on the Web page, but you may not always have ready access to the site. You can also sign on to become a follower of TDEM, an act that could save your life if you receive a "take shelter/tornado warning" alert or "avoid FM 35/flash flood" warning.

**Competency Connection**
**COMMUNICATION SKILLS**

Social media, such as Twitter, have often been criticized as leading to political polarization in the United States, but surely they can be used for the public good. How might Texas make better use of social media to serve its citizens?

and extractive industries, including oil, gas, coal, and uranium. Of growing importance is its control of intrastate road transportation—buses, moving vans, and trucks, including tow trucks—because of the importance of trucking rates to economic development. (Trucking is the number-one method by which goods are conveyed to market.) The TRC also regulates intrastate railroads. Its members are chosen in statewide elections for staggered six-year terms. In 1995, the TRC became all Republican for the first time and has remained so. The commissioners as of 2018 were Christi Craddick, the daughter of former House Speaker Tom Craddick (elected in 2012), along with Ryan Sitton (elected in 2014) and Wayne Christian (elected in 2016).

The fifteen-member State Board of Education (SBOE) was originally created as an elected body. As part of the public school reforms of 1984, it was made an appointive board. In 1987, the voters overwhelmingly approved returning it to elective status. Its fifteen members are chosen by the voters from districts across the state. A majority of the board's members are conservative Republicans, a fact that has reintroduced a long-standing controversy about content in the Texas history curriculum, with one recent controversy being whether "states' rights," along with other causes, should be listed as a cause for the Civil War. The Board voted, largely along party lines, with Democrats opposed and Republicans in favor, to retain the states' rights language, something many Democrats think does not accurately reflect the real cause of the war—protection of slavery.

**Ex Officio Boards and Commissions** There are many boards in the state administration whose members are all ex officio; that is, they are members because of another office they hold in the administration. When these boards were created, two purposes were served by ex officio memberships: The members usually were already in Austin (no small matter in pre-freeway days), and they were assumed to have some expertise in the subject at hand. An example is the Bond Review Board, which includes the governor, lieutenant governor, comptroller, and speaker of the House and ensures that debt financing is used prudently by the state.

**Appointed Boards and Commissions** Administration of most of the state's laws is carried out by boards and commissions whose members are appointed rather than elected and by the administrators the boards then appoint. The members of many boards are appointed

The State Board of Education, which oversees the Texas public schools, is an elected board that is well known for its ultraconservatism and lack of enlightenment. The SBOE has been particularly controversial when selecting science and social science textbooks.

Courtesy of Ben Sargent

Competency Connection
PERSONAL RESPONSIBILITY

Often, the State Board of Education has acted to preserve traditional interpretations of Texas history and to promote traditional values. At what points are students mature enough to examine the ideas of scholars and social critics who question Texas tradition?

by the governor, but some other boards have a combination of gubernatorial appointees, appointees of other state officials, and/or ex officio members. These boards vary in size and, as a rule, have general policy authority for their agencies. Members serve six-year overlapping terms without pay.

There are three broad categories of appointed boards and commissions: (1) health, welfare, and rehabilitation; (2) education; and (3) general executive and administrative departments. Examples of each category are: (1) the Health and Human Services Council, (2) the Texas Higher Education Coordinating Board, and (3) the Parks and Wildlife Department and the Public Utility Commission, respectively.

**Appointed Boards and Citizens** How do the 142 or so policymaking boards affect the ordinary citizen? Three examples will serve as an illustration.

**The Case of the Public Utility Commission** One example is the Public Utility Commission of Texas (PUC), which fosters competition and promotes a utility *infrastructure* (the basic physical structure for delivery of public utilities, such as pipelines, cables, and transformers). The PUC has been very busy since the legislature deregulated the electric industry in 1999, both overseeing procedures for deregulation and trying to ensure the availability of adequate and reliable electric power. A second focus is overseeing the telecommunications industry. Any Texas citizen can contact the PUC's Office of Customer Protection to complain about unreliable electric or telecommunications service, or seeming misdeeds on the part of providers of those utilities. For example, in 2019, there is worry that Texas' electricity generation might not be sufficient to get citizens through the hot summer, when energy consumption is at its peak. One of the duties of the Public Utilities Commission is to try to identify power reserves that might mitigate the problem.

**The Case of the College Governing Board** Whether one is in a public community college, a private university, or a public university, that institution has a board of trustees or a board of regents. These board members set policy for the college and appoint the president. In the case of a university system, such as the University of Texas or Texas A&M, the board is responsible for all institutions in the system. At one typical board of regents meeting, the board members (1) renewed the president's contract, (2) approved a resolution increasing tuition, (3) granted tenure to twenty faculty members, (4) approved the hiring of a new liberal arts dean, and (5) approved a contract for construction of additional classrooms in the environmental sciences building. Each of these actions affected students—directly in the case of tuition increases and classroom space, and indirectly in the case of the three types of personnel actions.

**The Case of the Parks and Wildlife Commission** If a person is "outdoorsy" and likes to camp, fish, or hunt, the annual decisions of the Texas Parks and Wildlife Commission (TPWC) on what fees will be levied for each of these activities are of interest. Texas traditionally has had very low parks and wildlife fees compared with other states. If a fishing license suddenly costs $200 instead of $30, the outdoors person might have second thoughts about this form of recreation. Sports people also are affected by decisions of this board as to what type of fish it will release into the lakes of the state, and how well state and sometimes local parks are managed. (The TPWC through the Parks and Wildlife Department often operates local parks, such as a lakeside recreational area, by agreement with the local government.) Once the pride of Texas, state parks have suffered from perennial underfunding and overcrowding. Their infrastructure is deteriorating at a time when more Texans than ever are seeking outdoor experiences. Attendance at the state parks was over ten million in 2017, a 20 percent increase from just five years earlier.

# Big Government: How Did It Happen?

Our country changed from an individualistic society that depended on government for very little to an urban, interdependent nation supporting a massive governmental structure. How did this change come about? And why?

The many, and complex, answers to these questions involve the Industrial Revolution, the mechanization of farms and ranches, and the technological revolution. These changes in turn led to urbanization. When workers followed job opportunities from farms to factories, much of the nation's population shifted from rural to urban areas. The American business philosophy was **pseudo laissez-faire**—that is, commerce and industry should be allowed to develop without government restraint but with governmental aid, and government's responsibility for the well-being of its citizens was minimal. American social philosophy was dominated by a belief in social Darwinism, which holds that those who are the most talented and hardest working should be rewarded according to the laws of natural selection—the survival of the fittest. Accordingly, the poor are poor because they are "supposed" to be that way due to their "naturally" inferior abilities or laziness, while the rich are rich due to their "naturally" superior abilities. American barons of industry—individuals earlier in our history and now usually corporate owners—grew rich and powerful, controlling not only the economy, but also the politics of the nation.

Eventually, the conditions resulting from these two philosophies, principally an unpredictable boom-and-bust economy and widespread poverty, caused a number of political developments. The expansion of voting rights, big-city ward politics, and a Populist movement that insisted on protection for workers and farmers are only a few examples. The outcry against the economic conditions brought about by pseudo laissez-faire finally became so great that the national government stepped in to curb the worst excesses of big business and to attempt to protect citizens who could not protect themselves. For example, the railroads so controlled state legislatures in the last quarter of the nineteenth century that state governments were powerless to protect their citizens. The Interstate Commerce Commission (ICC) was created in 1887 to regulate the railroads, which had been pricing small farmers out of business by charging exorbitant freight rates.

The creation of the ICC illustrates the beginning of an activist national government. During the thirty years just before and just after the turn of the twentieth century, the focus was on regulation of the economy. The second growth thrust came in response to the Great Depression of the 1930s, with the expansion of both government services and the administration necessary to implement them. For example, the Social Security, farm price support, and rural electrification programs all began in the 1930s. This expansion represented a major shift in political ideology from a conservatism that had advocated very limited government to a liberalism that held government intervention was required to protect the average citizen against the excesses of unregulated capitalism.

**pseudo laissez-faire**
A phrase referring to the tendency of entrepreneurs to oppose government involvement in the economy at the general philosophical level, but to seek government assistance for their particular business.

## Postwar Growth

After World War II, government continued to expand in scope. There were social concerns such as civil rights, newly recognized industrial problems such as environmental pollution, and technologies such as nuclear power, all requiring oversight. The federal government not only entered areas that traditionally had been left to state and local governments—education and health care, for example—but also fostered social change through such policies as equal opportunity and affirmative-action employment. By channeling funds for new programs at the state and local levels through state agencies, the federal government has served as the major catalyst for the increased role of the public sector. An expanding electorate and a more complex society both contributed to government growth.

The national government continued to expand its programs and their associated costs throughout the 1970s. State and local governments grew rapidly to take advantage of available federal dollars for new programs, to respond to mandatory federal initiatives, to promote economic expansion, and to develop new programs and services brought about by citizens' demands for an improvement in the quality of life. Each new service increased the number of people necessary to keep the wheels of government turning. In a state such as Texas, with a high population growth rate, it is inevitable that the combination of more programs and increased population would cause an increase in the size and scope of state and local governments.

Figure 8-1 shows the largest program areas in Texas as compared with all of the fifteen most populous states. Texas has the same or fewer employees per 10,000 population than the other states, except in the category of corrections and public welfare. Because these numbers already take into account the difference in population among the states, one is left to conclude that either Texas has proportionately more criminals than other states or more of a lock-'em-up attitude. The following two chapters help to explain that the reason for the large number of corrections employees is the lock-'em-up attitude. Chapter 13 explores poverty in the state, an indication of the larger number of public welfare workers. The lower numbers in the other major categories do not signal greater efficiency. Rather, they signal that Texans receive proportionately fewer government services than citizens in the other large states and that the state has a significant number of poor people requiring public hospital and public welfare services.

**devolution**
Redistributing power, responsibility, and funding from the national government to the states for many of the programs shared by the two levels of government.

## Devolution Politics Since 1980

The election of Ronald Reagan to the presidency in 1980 signaled a shift away from liberal ideology and a new stress on the **devolution**, or centering of greater responsibility, from the national to the state governments in the American federal system. Along with an erratic

Figure 8-1  State Employment in Texas and Fifteen Largest States, per 10,000 Population, by Function

SOURCE: *Fiscal Size-Up, 2014–2015 Biennium* (Austin: Legislative Budget Board, 2014), 58.

Competency Connection
SOCIAL RESPONSIBILITY

How do Texas expenditures in Texas vary from other large states in public higher education and in corrections? What do these differences suggest about Texas politics?

economy in the modern era, the new conservatism also brought about cuts in funding for federal programs, forcing reductions in state and local social programs that had previously been funded by the national government.

At the national level, two related phenomena particularly affected federal-state relations. First, the election to the presidency of a number of former governors who had great confidence in the ability of states to implement innovative programs, often at less cost than the national government could do. Presidents Jimmy Carter, Ronald Reagan, Bill Clinton, and George W. Bush have all come to office with chief executive experience at the state level, and while two were Democrats and two Republicans, they all had experienced success in state politics and saw value in allowing states to prosper, sometimes with less funding from the national government, and sometimes with reduced regulation. For example, President Clinton's agreement to change the nation's primary welfare program, Aid to Families with Dependent Children (AFDC) to a new program, Temporary Assistance to Needy Families (TANF). The new program gave states much more discretion in administering the program and limited lifetime benefits.

Second, the period since 1980 has been dominated at the national level by Republicans. Since 1981, the nation has had four Republican presidents compared to two Democrats, and one of the major initiatives common to all of the Republicans—Ronald Reagan, George H. W. Bush, George W. Bush, and Donald Trump—has been to devolve power from the national government to the states. There have been two elements to devolution: converting grants from the national government from categorical grants to block grants to give states more responsibility in the administration of programs and steadily diminishing federal contributions to social programs, hoping that efficiency at the state level might allow delivery of quality programs at reduced prices. Of course, the politics of these changes are but a few of the differences between the parties and have led to heated debates about how successful devolution has been. As a consequence of these changes at the national level, state and local governments continued to grow in size, programs, and expenditures, much to the regret of many taxpayers, who have often preferred less government and an end to state and local tax increases. Texans have always had a strong antigovernment streak, but the state has the additional burden of high population growth. A bias against government spending and growth and a burgeoning population do not mix well, as Chapter 12 will discuss.

Figure 8-2 shows relatively steady growth in state and local government since 1980, with a higher growth rate for local government, which includes public schools. Even when the economy is in the doldrums, government employment often holds steady or even grows as government responds to the needs of the people. The best example of this phenomenon is the Great Depression of the 1930s.

In Texas and many other states, a review of bureaucratic performance began, especially on the criterion of efficiency—the least expenditure of dollars and other resources per unit of output—in the early 1990s. President Bill Clinton assigned Vice President Al Gore to begin a similar initiative in the national government based on the models set by Texas and a half-dozen other states. These activities are known as **reinventing** or **reengineering government**.

**reinventing or reengineering government**

A national and state movement in the 1990s to improve government performance; sometimes called "reengineering."

Nationally, the Democrats took control of Congress in 2007 and the presidency in 2009. By 2009, they faced an existing deficit, international turmoil, and especially domestic economic woes that were addressed with massive expenditures, further increasing the national debt (see Chapter 12). The Democrats then lost control of the House in 2010. In the elections of 2010, the emergence of the Tea Party movement made it clear that voters thought there was too much government, at least in programs that did not benefit them. Winds of change continued in the elections of 2016 and 2018. In 2016, in a very close election, Republican Donald Trump was selected as president while the Republicans retained control of both chambers of Congress. This was thought to signal more devolution from the national government to the state, but relatively little legislative action took place following Trump's election. Then, in 2018, Democrats took control of the U.S. House of Representatives, making prospects for further devolution unlikely in the immediate future.

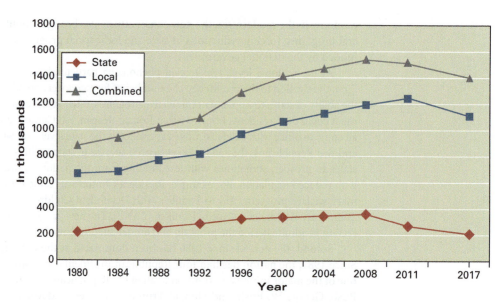

**Figure 8-2 State and Local Government Employment in Texas, 1980–2017**

SOURCES: *Texas Almanac, 1982–1983, 1986–1987, 1990–1991, 1994–1995, 1998–1999, 2002–2003, 2006–2007, 2008–2009* (Dallas: *Dallas Morning News,* 1981, 1986, 1989, 1993, 1997, 2001, 2006, 2008), 410, 597, 502, 467, 548, 548, 578, 603, respectively; *Texas Almanac, 2010–2011* (Denton: Texas State Historical Association, 2010), 607; and "State and Local Government Employment," *2012 Census of Governments* (Washington, D.C.: Bureau of the Census, 2013), available at http://www/2.census.gov/govs/apes/11loctx.txt; U.S. Census Bureau, 2017 Government Employment and Payroll Tables, https://www.census.gov/data/tables/2017/econ/apes/annual-apes.html

# Characteristics of Bureaucracy

Bureaucratic structure is traditionally viewed as the most efficient way to organize human endeavors so as to ensure competent, quick, and expert problem solving. It is used not just in government but also in businesses and other organizations. As so often happens, however, the ideal differs considerably from the reality. Indeed, experts on governmental organization and management frequently suggest alternatives to a strict bureaucratic organization.[3]

## Traditional Characteristics

Early in the 1900s, Max Weber, considered the father of modern sociology, listed the main characteristics of a bureaucratic organization as part of his examination of the phenomenon of authority. Weber's list is important because it has been the starting point for subsequent discussions of bureaucratic structures.

1. Authority is hierarchical; an organization chart of a bureaucracy looks like a pyramid. At the top, there are the fewest people but with the greatest authority. At the base of the pyramid are the most people but with the least authority.
2. Individuals are assigned specific tasks to perform, and a combination of training and the continual performance of these tasks results in expertise in the specific area.
3. Bureaucracies have defined jurisdictions; that is, they are created to accomplish definite and limited goals.
4. There are extensive rules and regulations to ensure that policy is implemented uniformly and consistently.
5. Bureaucrats, because they follow comprehensive and detailed rules that depersonalize administration, are politically neutral.[4]

## Modern Characteristics

Today's American bureaucracies deviate considerably from the classic European organizations that Weber observed. Boards and commissions, rather than a single chief executive, are often at the power peak of agencies; authority (and accountability) is thus diffused. Jurisdictions are broadly defined, meaning that limits on goals and authority are obscured. As a result, confusion and competition occur because of overlapping jurisdictions and authority. Agency staffers, especially executives and sometimes minor bureaucrats, far from being politically neutral, are very much involved in political processes. Moreover, bureaucracies hire, fire, and promote from within. It is often very difficult even for bureau managers to fire someone and usually impossible for the chief executive to dismiss an employee. Politically, it is often the case that legislators have few incentives to engage in systematic oversight. Modern bureaucracies can be largely immune to outside control.

The public interest sometimes becomes lost in the shuffle. We seemingly are overwhelmed by the administrative state, which Emmette Redford defines as a society in which "we are affected intimately and extensively by decisions in numerous organizations, public and private, allocating advantages and disadvantages to us."[5] The cumulative effect of these deviations from Weber's model is that the bureaucracy is relatively free from outside control. Administrators enjoy a substantial amount of independence. Politicians in most democracies complain about the difficulty of getting bureaucrats to do anything they do not want to do. When administrators do not fear being fired for refusing to cooperate with politicians, they may evade and even disobey the orders of the people they are supposedly working for. It is potentially a problem for democracy to have unelected bureaucrats that seem unaccountable to elected officials. At the same time, most bureaucrats are dedicated to professional standards that transcend the politics of the moment, insuring that recipients of public services may continue to receive benefits even while politicians running for office call for an end to various social programs. In other words, bureaucrats often assure continuity in government services when the ebb and flow of election politics might lead to fluctuation in government services and unpredictability in the administration of government.

## ISSUE SPOTLIGHT:
## Pushing the Cost of Government Downward

Citizens see the cost of government as rising even when one level of government brags about tax cutting. Examples of what happens when a higher-level government begins to retrench are seen all over Texas in the very practical matters of water runoff and solid waste (garbage) disposal. At one point, the national government provided considerable assistance with the costs of laying new sewer lines and acquiring landfill sites. The assistance is no longer forthcoming, but environmental standards have risen higher and higher. Small cities can ill afford the costs of disposing of their own wastes under the new standards and are dependent on contracts with larger communities to provide all or some of these services, as is the case, for example, with Graham and Fort Worth or Krum and Denton. While the higher-level government can boast of budget slashing and program reduction, citizens do not pay any less; they just transfer their dollars from one government to another. The situation for small cities and their residents has not changed.

Competency Connection
**CRITICAL THINKING**

**Is it fair for the national government to place restrictions on the states or for state governments to place restrictions on cities without providing funds for lower levels of government to pay for those restrictions? Why or why not?**

The rules designed to ensure consistency and fairness sometimes contradict one another. Equal opportunity requires absolutely equal treatment of all candidates for a job, for example, but affirmative action requires special measures for protected classes of citizens. Other rules create problems while trying to solve them. For example, regulations of the federal Occupational Safety and Health Administration (OSHA) require roofers to be tethered to the roof to avoid falling, but roofers contend that many injuries can occur because of tethering. However, rules or "red tape" have been a nuisance to citizens throughout much of history. In fact, the term *red tape* goes back to the sixteenth century when orders from the English king were bound in packets by red ribbons.

Today, the role of the expert is often uncertain. Traditionally, the expert was to carry out detailed functions—whether issuing a driver's license or testing water purity in the city's laboratory. But increasingly, experts, who often disagree with one another or have narrow views, dominate our organizations. Lawyers and accountants are prime examples in both business and government.

Another characteristic of modern bureaucracies is their reliance on managers not only to oversee policy implementation, but also to serve as brokers between citizens and elected officials. In both business and government, layers of management isolate the citizen-customer from key decision makers.

In the United States, size also is of concern, especially the relationship between the number of government employees and the number of citizens served. The number of federal civilian employees—about 195,000 of whom work in Texas—has changed little since the 1960s. In fact, state and local governments, contract employees, nonprofit organizations, and consultants administer many national programs. Major shifts in the numbers of federal government personnel have occurred only when the military was engaged in a buildup or during a downsizing. The size of the federal administration is, in 2019, about the same as it was in 1984. New federal spending initiatives often mean that state and local government workers will increase in number as implementation of national policy falls to these governments.

As in other states, the bureaucracy in Texas continues to grow, though the state does enjoy an economy of scale compared to states with lower populations. Generally, the larger the state, the lower is the ratio of state employees to citizens. The number of state employees per ten thousand citizens ranges from a high of 245 in Alaska to a low of 46 in Indiana. California, the most populous state, has a relatively low number of 61 full-time equivalent (FTE) employees per 10,000 population despite the fact that it is a high service state. That rate for Wyoming, a low service state and the state with the lowest population, is 160 employees per 10,000. Texas tends toward the low end, both because of its high population and relatively low state services at 65 public employees per 10,000 population. The number of FTE employees in Texas has been relatively constant.[6]

A final characteristic of modern bureaucracy is frequent reorganization. In trying to find the most efficient means of carrying out policies and, at the same time, coping with increased numbers of employees and the proliferation of programs, governments keep shuffling their internal organization. Many states, Texas among them, have enacted legislation that calls for periodic evaluations of state agencies. An example is the Sunset Act, discussed later in this chapter. Elected political leaders often argue that reorganization can eliminate unnecessary positions and increase government efficiency, both admirable goals. As a result, parts of the bureaucracy are combined, reorganized, and even sometimes eliminated each year.

## Bureaucratic Survival Techniques

Bureaucratic agencies share one characteristic with the rest of us: They need money. In the push and scramble of overlapping jurisdictions, authorities, and programs, agency staffers must fight for funds if they want their agency to continue. Agency people seek first survival and then growth for three principal reasons: (1) personal—their jobs; (2) programmatic—genuine commitment to the program administered by the organization; and (3) clientele—a sincere concern for the people who benefit from the agency's programs. Because the administrators operate in the arena of political activities, they use political tactics to achieve their goals, just as state legislators and the governor do. Administrators must develop their own sources of political power if they want policies favorable to them enacted into law, and they have done so.[7]

## Sources of Bureaucratic Power

The principal sources of bureaucratic power are clientele group(s), the legislature, the chief executive, the public, the agency's own expertise and information, its leadership, and the strength of its internal organization. Each of these categories is explored in the following sections.

**clientele group** The interest group or groups that benefit from or are regulated by an administrative agency.

**Clientele Groups** The cornerstone of an agency's political clout is its relationship with its **clientele** (interest) **group** or groups. This relationship is mutually beneficial. The agency and its clientele have similar goals, are interested in the same programs, and work together in a number of ways, including sharing personnel, information, and lobbying strategies. The greater the economic power of the clientele groups, the stronger the political ties between them and "their" agencies—so strong in fact that "regulation" often becomes promotion of the clientele group's interests.

Among the better-known agency–clientele relationships are those between the oil, gas, and transportation industries and the Texas Railroad Commission; the Texas Good Roads and Transportation Association (an interest group) and the Texas Department of Transportation; and the banking industry and the State Banking and State Depository Boards. The ties are not always economically motivated, however, as, for example, in the case of the support given to the Parks and Wildlife Department by local chapters of the National Rifle Association or to a state university by its alumni. During a legislative session, the competition for as large a share as possible of the state's financial resources can be fierce indeed, with phalanxes of agency-clientele group coalitions lined up against one another.

**The Legislature** Agencies' relationships with legislators are of two types: direct and indirect. First, agencies directly attempt to influence legislation and their budgets by furnishing information in writing and through testimony to legislative committees. In addition, agency executives work hard to get to know the speaker of the House, the lieutenant governor, and the members of the Legislative Budget Board and the Legislative Council, all of whom operate year-round, even when committee chairs and other legislators have gone home. Second, agencies use their clientele groups to try to influence legislation, budgets, and the selection of legislative leaders. During budget shortfalls in recent years, a number of state agencies—including higher education—became adept at finding powerful groups, such as chambers of commerce and specially formed support groups, to help them try to ward off agency budget cuts.

**The Chief Executive** As previously noted, the governor's power over state agencies has been strengthened, though it remains a weakness for the governor overall with so many departments having chief executives who are elected, as discussed earlier in the chapter. The governor usually appoints the agency head or members of the board or commission that oversees the agency, and for many agencies, he or she appoints the board chair. A governor who is a skillful chief legislator can help an agency get its budget increased or add a new program. The chief executive can also referee when an agency does not have the support of its clientele group and give an agency visibility when it might otherwise languish in obscurity. The governor's legislative and party roles can be used to influence neutral legislators to look favorably on an agency, and the governor can greatly affect an agency's success or failure through appointments to the policy board or commission that oversees it. To state administrators who are not elected, the chief executive is more powerful than the formal roles of the gubernatorial office would suggest.

Recently, Governor Greg Abbott has engaged in what some critics have called a "power grab," asking boards and commissions that he appointed to ask his office for approval before either making new rules and regulations or changing old ones. This is unprecedented, but is an attempt to exert more authority than previous governors have exercised. There is no clear line of authority for the governor to make such a demand, but Abbott insists that he is simply trying to exert executive authority and coordinate government programs.

**The Public** Some bureaucratic agencies enjoy considerable public recognition and support. Among these are the Texas Rangers, the Texas Department of Transportation, and the Parks and Wildlife Department. The Rangers are an agency founded by Stephen F. Austin and associated with the heroic narrative of Texas history, where, as the old saying goes, a Ranger could single handedly enforce the law ("One Ranger, One Riot"). The latter two agencies use the technique of news and information for gaining public attention: road maps, carefully labeled highway projects, mapped-out camping tours, and colorful signs. However, generally favorable opinion toward Parks and Wildlife has not saved the agency from disastrous budget reductions that have resulted in the closing of some state parks and related facilities.

Usually, however, agencies have little, if any, public support to help them gain legislative or gubernatorial cooperation. The public, diverse and unorganized, often is unaware of the very existence of many agencies, much less able to give them the concerted support necessary to influence top-level elected administrators. Such support, when forthcoming, depends largely on the public's awareness of the importance of the agency's programs to the general welfare.

**Expertise and Information** Expert information is a political commodity peculiar to bureaucrats, who enjoy a unique position in state government through their control of the technical information that the governor and legislators must have to develop statewide policies. Although all bureaucracies have this advantage, it is particularly strong in Texas because the state's legislative committee system does not produce the same degree of legislative expertise that is enjoyed by members of the U.S. Congress. Usually, the only alternative source for the legislator who does not want to use the information from an agency is the agency's clientele group. However, the more technical an agency's specialty, the greater is that agency's advantage in controlling vital information. For example, if the legislature is trying to determine whether the state is producing enough physicians, the Board of Medical Examiners and the Department of State Health Services, as well as the Texas Medical Association and the Texas Osteopathic Medical Association, are all ready to furnish the information. The public's ideas on the subject are seldom considered.

**Leadership** Another factor that determines the political power of bureaucracies is the caliber of leadership within the agency. Agency heads must be able to spark enthusiasm in their employees, encourage them toward a high level of performance, and convince elected officials and clientele groups that their agencies are performing effectively. A competent chief administrator will usually be retained by the members of the agency's governing board or commission, even though the board or commission membership changes over the years. The department benefits from continuity and stability at the top, and there is minimal disruption in the agency's relationship with clientele groups and legislators.

**civil service system**
A personnel system in a government administrative agency in which employees are hired, fired, and promoted based on merit.

**Internal Organization** Some agencies have a **civil service system** that protects agency workers from outside influence. In a civil service system, workers are hired on merit—that is, their performance on written tests and other forms of examination—and are evaluated on job performance. Agencies with a merit-based personnel system can resist the influence of, for example, a legislator trying to get his nephew hired for the summer or an aide to the governor who wants an agency employee fired because the two had a disagreement.

The adoption of a civil service system for hiring and promoting state workers introduces a paradox into the democratic nature of Texas government. The point of the "merit system" is to insulate agency workers from undue interference by politicians and from having to make decisions on a partisan basis. Yet those politicians are the people's representatives. When they cannot control state administrators, the people's will is obstructed. Part of the hostility that private citizens often express against bureaucrats may be due to the recognition on their part that "civil servants" are paid with taxes, yet are at best imperfectly accountable to the people. At the same time, we must consider the consequences if every administrative agency was forced to bend to the partisan will of elected officials.

## Bureaucratic Involvement in the Policymaking Process

Bureaucrats cannot directly lobby, but they have other ways of influencing public policy. These include the use of discretion and the way in which information is provided to the legislature.

**Implementation of the Laws**  The primary task of state bureaucrats is to enforce the laws of Texas, and that means they must make rules about their implementation. This gives them considerable **administrative discretion**, allowing them to use their own judgment as to how the laws will be carried out. Regulatory boards illustrate most clearly the power of administrative agencies. When the Texas Railroad Commission (even if efforts to reorganize it should ever be successful) determines the monthly oil allowable (the number of barrels of oil that can be pumped during a particular month), it is making (administrative) rules that, like legislative statutes, have the force of law. It is, therefore, performing a quasi-legislative function. When the Alcoholic Beverage Commission decides who will be issued a license to sell beer, wine, and distilled spirits, it is performing a quasi-judicial function by determining whether a person has the right to go into business.

**administrative discretion** The freedom that administrators (bureaucrats) have in implementing and interpreting laws.

Often, a statute passed by the legislature creates a general framework for implementing a service or regulatory program, but state agencies have considerable discretion in interpreting statutes. Consequently, the 120 or so policymaking boards, commissions, and authorities are very important in determining what government actually does. Especially in a state like Texas, which lacks a cabinet system and an integrated executive branch, the average citizen is affected on a daily basis by what these boards do, but that citizen may have little understanding of how they work or how to approach them. Recent changes that resulted in making the board chairs accountable to the governor may help because the public can more nearly determine "who's in charge here." The board and commission structure makes public participation more difficult.

Moreover, these boards usually appoint an executive director or college president to carry out their policies, and that executive officer has considerable influence over board policies. For example, a Texas State University student may wish to protest the abolition of a popular major. Determining how to make a protest requires information about how the decision was made. Was the change made by the system's board of regents on its own or upon recommendation of the president, or was it forced by policies of the Texas Higher Education Coordinating Board in Austin? Were the students consulted before the decision was made?

Although it can obscure how a decision was made, administrative discretion can be a positive factor in effective government. A common example is the decision of a Department of Public Safety law enforcement officer to allow one suspect to go free in the hope that he will lead criminal-intelligence agents to a more important suspect. Another example is that of professors at state universities, who have considerable freedom to design their classes. Each professor decides on the balance between lecture and discussion, textbooks, whether to include an online component to the course, what the mix of multiple-choice and essay tests will be, whether to use PowerPoint, and the basis of grading. Thus, by interpreting laws, making rules, and making judgments, administrators make public policy.

**Influencing Legislation**  Bureaucrats directly influence the content and meaning of statutes that are passed by the legislature, and they do so in three principal ways: by drafting bills, furnishing information to legislators, and lobbying.

During its short session, the Texas legislature is under great pressure to draft, consider, and dispose of needed legislation. State bureaucrats are eager to aid the lawmakers, and two ways in which they do so are mutually beneficial: furnishing specialized information to legislative committees and drafting bills that individual legislators may then present as their own. Legislators thus gain needed assistance, and administrators are able to protect their agencies by helping to write their own budgets and develop their own programs.

Bureaucrats also influence legislation by lobbying legislators for or against proposed bills. State employees cannot legally act as lobbyists, but they can furnish information. For the average citizen, it is splitting hairs to make that distinction. Agencies usually work closely with their clientele group or groups in the lobbying endeavor. The governor is also lobbied not only for support of legislation that is favored by agencies and their clients, but also for agency appointments that are acceptable to them and their clients. If successful, both of these lobbying activities can greatly influence the decisions of legislators, as well as the policies set by boards and commissions. In 2017, the 327,016 state employees, through such organizations as the Texas Public Employees Association, actively lobby the legislature on matters of salary and fringe benefits.

## What Happens to the Public Interest?

Public administration originally was created to serve and protect the public interest. Sometimes, however, the public interest can be forgotten in the shifting, complex kaleidoscope of hundreds of agencies, bureaus, departments, and commissions constantly striving for more money, more personnel, more programs, and more power. Bureaucrats are no more evil, incompetent, or venal than employees of privately owned companies. However, the bureaucracy is funded with public money—tax dollars—so people naturally are a little more concerned with the honesty and efficiency of the state's administration than those of AT&T, Dell Computers, or ExxonMobil.

Administrative scandals, such as the mistreatment of people with intellectual disabilities at state schools or public employees benefiting from state travel in the name of economic development, heighten that interest. Years ago, Paul Appleby drew the distinction between government and private administration by noting that the public administrator is continually subject to "public scrutiny and outcry" by "press and public interest in every detail of his life, personality, and conduct."[8] In short, public administrators live in the proverbial goldfish bowl. While publicity may not be as effective in instilling democratic accountability into administrators as it is with elected politicians, it is better than nothing.

## Bureaucratic Orientation

In any organization, the longer one remains in one agency or company, the more likely it is that one's perspectives narrow to those of the organization, thus adapting to the organization's way of doing things. In a public agency, this orientation often leads to a loss of concern for more general public goals and an inability to see different points of view. This shifting of bureaucratic orientation is known as *goal displacement*—that is, the replacement of one goal by another. In this case, the public interest is forgotten and the agencies' interests and those of their clientele groups become paramount. Many complex factors are involved in the displacement of publicly stated goals in agency priorities: (1) the rapid, piecemeal creation of new agencies that have overlapping jurisdictions and authorities; (2) the co-optation of regulatory agencies by their clientele groups; (3) the fact that most top-level administrators are appointed by an executive who has no power to remove them from office and that most career bureaucrats are protected in their jobs by tenure; (4) the fact that the public is generally bewildered about which government official or body is responsible for what governmental action or program; and (5) the fact that the publicly stated goals may not have been the "real" goals from the outset.

The vast majority of public managers and bureaucrats are conscientious, and most maintain a keen sense of public interest. Nevertheless, it can be difficult to reconcile bureaucracy and democracy.

## Overstepping the Law

In addition to the bureaucratic orientation that develops over time, some state administrators are further tempted toward inappropriate bureaucratic activities. In Texas, these temptations are due to (1) extremely strong special interest groups, (2) weaknesses in the governor's office, and (3) the handicapped legislature. State agencies and bureaucrats have run afoul of the law in a variety of ways, such as using state funds for personal travel, assigning contracts without bids, awarding high dollar consulting contracts as a means of hiring "unseen" staff, and causing injuries and deaths through failure to enforce safety regulations. These incidents involved irregularities, not simply inefficiencies.

How, then, can citizens ensure that the state bureaucracy performs honestly, efficiently, and effectively? How can public trust be earned? In short, how can accountability on the part of the state administration be maintained?

## Harnessing the Administrative State

As part of the state's system of checks and balances, the governor has a veto over legislative acts, and the legislature can impeach a governor or refuse to confirm gubernatorial appointments. As well as controlling various offices and agencies that report directly to them, all three traditional branches of government—executive, legislative, and judicial—have means of holding the bureaucracy, sometimes called the "fourth branch of government," in check. Democratic theory posits that government should be elected by the people, but most administrators are not. The governor and other elected officials have legitimacy (popular acceptance). State administrators must derive as much legitimacy as they can from these elected officials.

During the 1990s, the nationally recognized Texas Performance Review (TPR) system, administered first by John Sharp, later by Carole Keeton Strayhorn, and then by the Legislative Budget Board, was created. The TPR requires that, before agencies can submit their budget proposals, they must prepare strategic plans that emphasize quality of service, access to programs, and measures of agency performance. Citizen demand for accountability and government's response to it illustrate that both citizens and elective officials play a role in harnessing the administrative state. The 2015 TPR involved 49 agencies and made 106 recommendations that would enhance government efficiency, improve reporting of government activities, and result in significant cost savings.

### How Much Accountability to the Chief Executive?

It would seem logical to make the bureaucracy accountable to the governor, who is the chief executive and nominal head of the state administration. But the governor's powers were limited intentionally to avoid centralizing government power in any one office.

1. Appointment powers are restricted and removal powers are limited.
2. There is no true executive budget.
3. The executive branch is fragmented: Four departments, a major commission, and a major board are headed by elected officials, and many separate agencies deal with related

functional areas—including local community college boards (more than eighty policy-making boards are involved in the area of education alone). Instead of single-headed agencies, about 120 multimember boards and commissions officially make policy for their 142 or so state agencies. In reality, the executive director of the agency, who administers the affairs of the agency, is usually the most powerful person connected with the organization—and is partially insulated from elected officials by the board.

Even if there were a complete reorganization of the executive branch, including consolidated departments headed by officials who constituted a governor's cabinet—such as thirty-nine other states have—the sheer size and diversity of the bureaucracy, coupled with other demands on the governor's time and staff, would make executive control loose and indirect. Just as it is difficult to hold a president responsible for the actions of a Social Security clerk in Laramie, Wyoming, it would be difficult to hold a governor responsible for the actions of a college professor in Canyon or a welfare caseworker in El Paso. Some agencies have responded to the governor's urging to use an *ombudsman*—complaint department—to hear public complaints against administrative agencies in an effort to increase executive responsiveness to citizen problems.

Stronger supervisory control would allow the governor to exercise greater influence over major policy decisions. With a consolidated executive branch, unencumbered by other elected administrators, and with managerial control over the state budget, the chief executive would have more hope of implementing policy. The advantage of having a strong chief executive as the head of a more truly hierarchical administration would be having overall responsibility vested in a highly visible elected official who could not be so easily dominated by special interests.

Texas has been moving slowly toward a more integrated executive branch, at least with regard to agencies headed by appointed executives or appointed boards. Nevertheless, the governor relies heavily on the roles of chief legislator, chief of state, and leader of the people to influence state agencies. However, recent governors have succeeded in adding some clout to their chief executive role—more removal power, more appointments to the executive director positions in state agencies and to the chairmanships of boards, more budget clout, and mandatory strategic planning. They are aided by the Budget, Planning, and Policy Division. The most successful example of consolidating various boards and agencies is the Health and Human Service Commission.

## How Much Accountability to the Legislature?

To what extent can the legislature oversee the bureaucracy? It has two main tools: legislative oversight and the Texas Sunset Act.

**Legislative Oversight** Legislatures traditionally have been guardians of the public interest, with powers to oversee administrative agencies. These powers include budgetary control, the post-audit of agency expenditures to ensure legality, programmatic control through the statutes, investigation of alleged wrongdoing, and impeachment of officials.

Although traditional legislative oversight is somewhat effective in Texas, several factors militate against its total success. One is the tripartite relationship among legislators, bureaucrats, and special interest groups. Legislators may be reluctant to ruffle the feathers of groups that supply them with campaign contributions by pressing their oversight vigorously. These groups in turn often have strong connections to the bureaucracy. Another is the high turnover of legislative committee personnel. A third is the lack of ongoing supervision because legislators are on the job only part-time as a result of Texas's short biennial legislative sessions. Much of the burden of oversight falls on the Legislative Budget Board, the Legislative Council, and the Legislative Audit Committee, although historically none of these has adequate staff or time for a thorough job, and none is well known to the general public.

## You Decide: Does the Texas Governor Need Cabinet Government in the Executive Branch?

Thirty-nine other states have an executive branch that is organized like that of the U.S. government—that is, a chief executive who heads a cabinet made up of directors or secretaries of a limited number of broad-based departments. Examples of such possible departments include Public and Higher Education, Public Safety and Criminal Justice, and Health and Human Services.

### Pro ✓

⬆ Texas should pass the necessary statutory and constitutional provisions to establish a cabinet system because:

⬆ Citizens could more easily understand a government that was organized like that of the United States.

⬆ Greater economy and efficiency could be achieved with broad-based departments that could operate with economy of scale.

⬆ The heads of the broad-based departments would be clearly associated with their agencies, could more easily be held accountable, and would more likely carry out the governor's policy preferences.

⬆ The fact that a majority of states have a cabinet system is evidence in and of itself of the value of this type of organization.

### Con ✗

⬇ Texas should not pass the necessary statutory and constitutional provisions to establish a cabinet system because:

⬇ "Supersized" departments would concentrate power in the hands of too few people.

⬇ Many smaller programs that serve useful purposes—for example, medical help for children with kidney disease—would get lost in the bureaucracy of large departments.

⬇ The governor already has enough to do without directly supervising a cabinet.

⬇ There is almost no chance that voters would approve a constitutional amendment supporting cabinet government; thus, efforts to make this major change would be better aimed at improving state programs.

**Competency Connection**
**SOCIAL RESPONSIBILITY**
Would the public interest in Texas be better served by having an elected governor appoint the senior administrators in Texas? Or is the public interest better served by having most senior administrators elected directly by the people? Explain.

---

A substitute for direct legislative oversight is legislation that provides specific detail about its enforcement. Such specific laws tend to limit administrative discretion in rule-making. No amount of specific detail can completely offset the powers of bureaucrats, but it can curtail it to some degree. For example, the legislature has passed highly specific legislation that dictates the core curriculum, the admission standards, and the maximum number of credit hours at publicly assisted colleges and universities. The Texas Higher Education Coordinating Board is charged with enforcing these statutes, which affect every student at a public college or university in the state.

**sunset reviews**
The process by which the legislature reviews the performance of administrative agencies, and then renews, reorganizes, or eliminates them.

**Texas Sunset Act** With the passage of the Texas Sunset Act in 1977, Texas established a procedure for reviewing the existence of all statutory boards, commissions, and departments—except colleges and universities—on a periodic basis. More than 130 agencies and advisory committees are included, and new ones are added as they are created. These **sunset reviews** are conducted by a twelve-member Sunset Advisory Commission composed of five senators and five representatives appointed by their respective presiding officers, who also appoint two citizen members. The chairmanship rotates between the House and the Senate every two years. The Sunset Commission can determine the list of agencies to be reviewed before the beginning of each regular legislative session as long as all agencies are evaluated within a twelve-year period. The agencies must submit self-evaluation reports, and the Sunset Commission coordinates its information gathering with other agencies that monitor state agencies on a regular basis, such as the Legislative Budget Board, legislative committees, and the offices of the state auditor, governor, and comptroller. Following sunset review, the legislature must explicitly vote to continue an agency, and may reorganize it or force it to modify its administrative rules and procedures.

By the conclusion of the 2017 regular legislative session, the sunset process had resulted in the examination of some 25 departments and agencies, with recommendations that would result in savings of 5.8 million dollars. Illustrative recommendations included the following:

▶ Several changes aimed at keeping pressure on the Texas Department of Transportation to remain headed toward a more transparent, performance-based planning and project selection

▶ Transferring a small agency, the Texas State Board of Podiatric Medical Examiners to the Texas Department of Licensing and Regulation to ensure the agency's mission is carried out more effectively and efficiently

▶ Strengthening the State Bar's public protection mission and improving its slow and ineffective rulemaking process

▶ Dissolving the Central Colorado River Authority, reclassifying the Palo Duro River Authority as a local water district, and directing the Upper Colorado River Authority to better identify local priorities to stay relevant in its watershed

▶ Requiring practitioners to check the Prescription Monitoring Program, the state's key method of tracking all controlled substance prescriptions, including opioids, and reviewing a patient's prescription history before prescribing certain controlled substances

About twenty agencies were scheduled for sunset review in 2019.

## How much Accountability to the Public?

One might easily assume that the general public has no control over bureaucrats. However, a citizen can take measures to ensure effective and honest bureaucratic performance.

**Elective Accountability** American government is based on the premise that it will be accountable to the people it governs. If accountability cannot be achieved directly—all citizens of a political division meeting to vote directly on laws and policies—theoretically, it can be achieved through elected representatives who meet in government and report back to their citizen-constituents. But voters encounter difficulty when they try to make intelligent decisions regarding the multitude of names on the long ballot in Texas. Long ballots tend to lead to confusion, not accountability. Additionally, the vastness of the bureaucracy and the reality that incumbents can usually count on being reelected simply because the voters recognize their names mean that the elective process has become an unsatisfactory method of ensuring responsible administrative action. In view of these problems, Texas citizens need some way to check on the activities of particular administrators and agencies on which public attention, for whatever reason, is focused, a process made easier through regular posting of department activities on websites, but something still not done in a systematic way.

**Sunshine Law** A law that provides for public access to the records of administrative agencies.

**Open Records and Meetings** Under the Texas Open Records Act, originally passed in 1973, the public, including the media, has access to a wide variety of official records and to most public meetings of state and local agencies. Sometimes called the **Sunshine Law** because it forces agencies to shed light on their deliberations and procedures, this act is seen as a way to prevent or expose bureaucratic ineptitude, corruption, and unnecessary secrecy. An agency that denies access to information that is listed as an open record in the statute may have to defend its actions to the attorney general, and even in court.

Sunshine laws require the following:

▶ The 1987 Open Meetings Act strengthened public access to information by requiring government bodies to certify that discussions held in executive sessions were legal or to tape-record closed meetings.

▶ Closed meetings are permitted when sensitive issues, such as real-estate transactions or personnel actions, are under consideration, but the agency must post an agenda in advance and submit it to the secretary of state, including what items will be discussed in closed session.

▶ State agencies are required to write rules and regulations in understandable language.

▶ In 1999, the legislature strengthened open meetings provisions by placing firm restrictions on private staff briefings that could be made before governing bodies at the state and local level.[9]

Governments were still allowed to have closed meetings when competitive issues were the topic of discussion.

In 2005, the Seventy-ninth Legislature mandated that not only public officials but also members of all boards, including local ones, receive training in open government. The formats include online instruction, DVDs, and organized classes. While sunshine laws have had a salutary effect, they are not perfect by any stretch of the imagination. In recent times, there has been criticism that because public officials in Texas do not respect the media, they withhold information from them. One recent example is the charge brought against Attorney General Ken Paxton's office. His spokesman justified releasing information slowly in this way: "The problem with our culture today is that journalists and reporters no longer have ethical responsibilities, but they demand everybody else does."[10]

**Whistle-Blower Protection** The 1983 legislature passed an act affording job security to state employees who spot illegal or unethical conduct in their agencies and report it to appropriate officials. The national government established the precedent for **whistle-blower** legislation in 1978, and its purpose was to protect employees who report illegal acts. The implementation of this act has not been promising. Even settlements mandated by the courts have tended to be delayed as long as a decade.

**whistle-blower**
Someone who "blows the whistle," that is, informs on a government official who is guilty of misdeeds or malpractice.

## Is There Accountability?

The passage of sunshine and sunset laws in recent years has enabled the public, the press, and the legislature to harness the worst excesses of bureaucracy more successfully. In addition, routine audits often turn up minor violations, a forceful governor or attorney general can "shake up" a state agency, and the state budget can be a means of putting a damper on any agency that seems to be getting out of hand. Top-level officials also have to file financial disclosure forms as a check on potential conflicts of interest. These devices help guard against serious wrongdoing on the part of state officials and help ensure accountability.

Serious wrongdoing, however, is not usually the problem. Much more frequently, we see indifference or occasional incompetence. How can we minimize the indifference and incompetence that citizens sometimes encounter in state, federal, or local agencies? How can we reduce the amount of time-consuming red tape? There seem to be few formal means of ensuring that bureaucratic dealings with citizens are competent, polite, and thorough—until citizen reaction demands them. What little political attention is given to the administrative state is aimed primarily at the federal bureaucracy rather than at state or local bureaucracies. Yet, public managers may have come up with their own solution: the Citizens as Customers movement. This approach requires that public employees treat citizens as customers in the same way that a business treats its customers as valuable resources. State and local governments also have implemented Raising the Bar campaigns to signify a commitment to higher standards of service. Thus, we find that elected officials, with the assistance of the media, can ensure a fair measure of bureaucratic accountability and that they continue to seek ways to control the appointed bureaucracy. The current emphasis on government performance is merely the latest of these ways.

The most frequent change suggested to bring about greater accountability is consolidation of similar agencies into fewer than a dozen "cabinet" departments. Texans have shown little interest in such reorganization.

## Summary

**LO 8.1**  **Texas has a complicated state bureaucracy that includes both elected and appointed executives.** Many specialized agencies, the fact that some agencies do not report to the governor, and an absence of a state cabinet characterize the state bureaucracy, resulting in what is called a plural executive.

**LO 8.2**  **A combination of factors, including public reaction against a pseudo laissez-faire philosophy and social Darwinism, urbanization, and the enormous growth of federal funds available to the states in the past few decades have contributed to the growth of the administrative state.**

**LO 8.3**  **Much of the Texas state administration exhibits the traditional characteristics of bureaucracy—hierarchy, specialization, defined jurisdiction, rules and regulations, a dedication to rules—though other agencies operate with a decision-making board rather than a hierarchy headed by a single person.** Lines of jurisdiction are often blurred between agencies. Bureaucracies develop their own bases of power through their clientele groups, the legislature, the governor, the public, their expertise and unique information, agency leadership, and the way the organization is structured internally.

**LO 8.4**  **A major concern is always the possibility of a bureaucrat being more dedicated to the agency than to the public and even overstepping the law.** Because the public pays little attention to bureaucracy, sometimes bureaucracies are co-opted by their major interest groups. The boards and appointed executives hold political positions, and the sheer number of agencies and the dissonance between their stated and actual controls contribute to administrative independence. Strong interest groups, a lack of formal gubernatorial controls, and limits on the legislature make controlling the bureaucracy difficult.

**LO 8.5**  **A major challenge, then, is to find ways to harness the powerful state administration, a task that is far from easy. Two measures, however—the Open Records Act and the Sunset Act—have made strides in the direction of giving Texas citizens a responsible bureaucracy.** The combined efforts of the governor, the comptroller, and the legislative leadership to insist on a budget based on planning and on quantitative measures of agency performance—the Texas Performance Review—has been an important step. Traditional controls, such as the legislative audit and the legislature's power to investigate agency activities, also help promote accountability on the part of the administration.

## Critical Thinking

1. The numerous state agencies in Texas are complex. Evaluate whether the Texas administration reflects democracy in action, or whether it works against the ideal of democracy. Offer evidence to defend your answer.

2. Explain how the public can hold the bureaucracy accountable. Are the current systems in place adequate to assure the public interest is served? Provide examples to justify your answer.

The 2018 elections in Texas showed a changing face of the Texas Judiciary. In Harris County, 19 African American women were elected to judicial positions.

*Harris County Democratic Party*

# The Judiciary

**LO 9.1** Discuss the judiciary as a political branch of government.

**LO 9.2** Describe the major players in the judicial system, including the central roles of the attorney general, the bar, and lawyers in the process.

**LO 9.3** Understand the structure of the Texas court system from the lowest courts to the two "supreme" courts.

**LO 9.4** Compare the roles of grand juries and trial juries.

**LO 9.5** Evaluate major issues in the Texas judiciary, including problems with crime, problems with judicial selection, and issues of equality in the administration of justice.

A discussion of the **judiciary**—the system of courts, judges, lawyers, and other actors—brings up several problems for democratic theory. Judges are the arbiters of conflicts within society and the interpreters of the rules by which we govern ourselves. Some people argue that judges should be able to hold themselves above the dirty struggles of the political process and as independent as possible from the democratic necessities of elections, interest groups, and money. Other people have pointed out, however, that democracy requires important decision makers to be accountable to the public and therefore made to stand for election. Texas has a long tradition of colorful judges who defied stereotypes, such as the legend of Judge Roy Bean and "the law west of the Pecos." Judge Roy Bean was a real person—a saloon keeper who relied perhaps more on his own political agendas than law books in making his decisions in the frontier of far West Texas. Surely Judge Bean was a singular character, but his reputation brings up important questions.

Are judges part of the political process or not? If they are, how can they be installed in office in a manner that ensures they will be fair and impartial but still accountable to the public? In Texas, the constitution comes down on the side of democracy and makes judges answerable to the people through partisan election. However, when judges

> IF I ASKED YOU TO DESIGN A CRIMINAL JUSTICE SYSTEM AND YOU CAME UP WITH ONE LIKE WE HAVE HERE IN TEXAS, WE'D HAVE TO COMMIT YOU TO AUSTIN STATE HOSPITAL BECAUSE YOU'D BE A DANGER TO YOURSELF AND SOCIETY.
>
> Jim Mattox,
> *Attorney General of Texas, 1988*

**judiciary** A collective term referring to the system of courts and its judges and other personnel.

are treated like other politicians, they become vulnerable to the suspicion that they are allowing private interests to corrupt their views on public affairs.

Furthermore, the importance of money in the judicial system is also troubling: It creates doubts as to whether the courts are fulfilling the ideal to provide equal justice to all. If access to legal representation is expensive, and if the outcome of trials depends on adequate representation, do poor people have a fair chance in a courtroom?

Also complicating election of judges is that judicial elections are numerous—including judges from the Supreme Court all the way down to the justices of the peace—and they are "down ballot" elections that often draw little attention among average voters. As a result, when people come to the polls to vote on judicial elections, the judicial candidates are largely unknown to them, making informed voting much less frequent in judicial elections compared to elections for higher-profile offices.

The first subject of this chapter is an examination of the political nature of judges, followed by a summary of the important features of the judicial branch of government in Texas. The focus then considers the players in the state system of justice. The remainder of the chapter is devoted to discussions of vexing problems facing the state judiciary from the perspective of democratic theory.

## The Myth of the Nonpolitical Judiciary

"There ought to be a law…"

This expression reflects the faith many of our citizens have in laws as solutions to social problems. When a law is enacted, Americans tend to believe that the problem has been solved and promptly forget about it. The fact that the laws already on the books have not solved society's problems does not seem to shake our hope that a few more will do the trick.

**judge** A public official who presides over a court.

Along with this faith goes the American perception of **judges**—the government officials who preside over a courtroom and rule on the application of the laws—as officials who are somehow "above" the political process. One scholar describes this perception: "Scratch the average person's idea of what a judge should be and it's basically Solomon. If you had a benign father, that's probably what you envision. We demand more from them, we look for miracles from them. . . . It's romantic, emotional, unexamined, unadmitted, and almost undiscussable."[1]

Over the centuries, judges have attempted to live up to the romantic ideal of the wise rule-giver. They do so because they know that people are more likely to comply with the decisions of judges if those judges are perceived as nonpolitical. Judges wear black robes, are addressed as "Your Honor" in the courtroom, write opinions in a specialized language that is beyond the understanding of most citizens, and in general try to demonstrate that they are not part of the messy business of governing.

In the long history of the development of our legal system, great jurists in England and the United States have developed—and are developing—neutral, impersonal criteria to use in making decisions. The hope is that a judge acts in an impartial and incorruptible manner, ruling purely on the basis of fairness and established principles. Clearly, this ideal has some basis in reality. Judges are less moved by political bias and outside influence than are legislators or governors.

But the notion that what judges do is not political is mythical. Whenever judges apply a statute, and especially when they interpret a constitution, they make choices among competing rules, individuals, and groups. Even deciding not to decide a case is a decision.

When a judge makes a decision, somebody wins and somebody loses, and the rulings can be quite important for large groups of people. As a result, the coalitions of interests that tend to oppose each other in political parties also tend to adopt differing philosophies of judicial interpretation. Republican judges, in perfectly good faith, often interpret words so as to favor business interests while Democratic judges, also in good faith, often favor individuals suing businesses. Therefore, judges make laws, and the constitution, in the process of interpretation. Texas judges, and especially members of the Supreme Court and Court of Criminal Appeals are central components of the state's political system.

Former Texas Court of Criminal Appeals Judge W. A. Morrison made no bones about his personal contribution to the state's system of laws. "I have engrafted into the law of this great state my own personal philosophy," he stated. Claiming that every appellate judge does much the same thing, he explained that during his first day on the bench as a young man, the other two judges could not agree on more than a dozen cases, and so Morrison cast the deciding vote in each one. He attributed his having "engrafted" his personal philosophy into the state's law to a greater degree than most other judges to the fact that he came to the bench early in life and remained longer than most.[2]

More recently, Texas district judge John Dietz clarified the political aspect of his job: "I redistribute wealth. I decide whether someone can keep theirs or [must] give it to someone else."[3]

The fact that Texas judges are elected makes the political nature of their work even more obvious. As one state jurist proclaimed in the early 1970s, "This job is more politics than law; there's no two ways about it. Hell, you can have all kinds of dandy ideas, but if you don't get yourself elected, you can sell your ideas on a corner somewhere. Politics isn't a dirty word in my mouth."[4]

Although judges from the rival political parties frequently split in judicial philosophy, they can also strongly disagree with others of the same party in their analysis of individual cases. A case in point is a verbal brawl that erupted in the Texas Supreme Court in 2000 over the proper interpretation of a law requiring a doctor to notify the parents of a girl under the age of eighteen before performing an abortion on her.[5] All nine of the justices were Republicans, but the case reveals the important differences over judicial principles that can exist between nominal allies.

In 1999, a law requiring parental notification was enacted and signed by Republican Governor George W. Bush. Mindful of federal courts' history of voiding state antiabortion laws, however, the legislature had put in a judicial bypass clause, allowing an underage girl to get an abortion without informing her parents if she could convince a state judge that she met certain criteria. Among the criteria were that she was mature and well informed. In early 2000, a pregnant teenager ("Jane Doe" in court discussions) had asked a judge to give her a judicial bypass and had been turned down. She appealed the case to the state's highest civil court.

The case brought up important questions of interpretation. What did "mature" and "well informed" mean when applied to a teenager? Had the legislature intended to make judicial bypass a relatively easy and common process or something difficult and rare? By a 6–3 vote in March 2000, the court ruled that the legislature had intended the criteria to be relatively easy to meet and granted Jane Doe permission for an abortion.[6]

Although all nine justices were members of the same party, there was an ideological divide. The three dissenters expressed their outrage. "The plain fact is that the statute was enacted to protect parents' right to involve themselves in their children's decisions and to encourage that involvement as well as to discourage teen-age pregnancy and abortion," fumed Justice Nathan Hecht. "The court not only ignores these purposes, it has done what it can to defeat them." The majority's "utter disregard" for legislative intent was "an insult to those legislators personally, to the office they hold and to the separation of powers between the two branches of government." No less annoyed, Justice Priscilla Owen (later appointed to the Fifth Circuit Federal Appeals Court by President George W. Bush) charged that the majority had "manufactured reasons to justify its action" and "acted irresponsibly." Justice Greg Abbott (and later attorney general, and elected governor in 2014) accused the majority of practicing "interpretive hand-wringing."

In response, several members of the majority criticized Hecht's "explosive rhetoric," accusing him of having "succumbed to passion." To interpret the law as the dissenters urged, argued Justice Alberto Gonzales (later U.S. Attorney General under President George W. Bush) would be to misunderstand the new law and "would be an unconscionable act of judicial activism."

In this one episode, the true nature of the judiciary stood revealed. Fair-minded or not, judges bring as many ideological commitments to their work as do legislators or executives. They are politicians in black robes.

## The Players in the System of Justice

The judiciary is part of an entire system that attempts to interpret and apply society's laws. A summary of the parts of this system, and some of its subject matter, follows.

### The Attorney General (AG)

The attorney general is an independently elected executive (see Chapter 8) who has important functions within the judicial system. Indeed, although the governor may be the most important single politician in Texas, the attorney general is more directly relevant to the judicial functions of the state. As Texas's chief lawyer, the attorney general (helped by many assistant AGs) represents state agencies when they sue a private individual or another agency or when they are sued. The AG also represents the state as a whole when it becomes involved in the federal courts.

In addition, the AG has a highly significant, if somewhat informal, power: the authority to issue advisory opinions. The constitution established the attorney general not only as Texas's chief legal officer but also as legal adviser to the governor and other state officials. The legislature later expanded the scope of the AG's advisory activity. Out of this expansion has arisen the now firmly established practice that the legislature, agencies of the executive branch, and local governments will seek advice on the constitutionality of proposals, rules, procedures, and statutes. In 2018, Ken Paxton handed down forty-nine "Attorney General's Opinions" dealing with the constitutionality of proposed government laws or actions.[7] Rather than filing a court action that is expensive and time-consuming, Texas officials who go to the attorney general obtain a ruling on disputed constitutional issues in a relatively brief period of time and at almost no expense. The Texas judiciary and virtually everyone else in the state have come to accept these rulings, albeit sometimes with a good deal of grumbling.

The most publicized attorney general's ruling of modern times, and perhaps in history, dealt with the divisive subject of affirmative action. For some years prior to 1996, the University of Texas Law School had been favoring African American and Latino applicants in its admissions process. An Anglo woman, Cheryl Hopwood, had been turned down for admission to the law school despite the fact that her qualifications (grades and Law School Aptitude Test scores) were higher than those of some minority applicants who had been admitted. Hopwood sued in federal court. In 1996, the Fifth Circuit Federal Appeals Court ruled in Hopwood's favor, deciding that such "reverse discrimination" against Anglos was unconstitutional.[8]

The federal Fifth Circuit court's decision was significant as it stood because it applied to the state's premier law school. Nevertheless, its scope did not extend to other schools. On February 5, 1997, however, Attorney General Dan Morales dismayed Texas's university community by issuing Letter Opinion 97-001, in which he decreed that the federal court's ruling had outlawed race as a consideration in any admissions process or financial aid decision at any public school. Affirmative action was therefore forbidden in all Texas public colleges.[9]

Although the Supreme Court declined to hear Texas's appeal, in 2003 it in effect reversed the *Hopwood* decision when it upheld the affirmative action program at the University of Michigan. After seven years, therefore, Texas universities were again free to consider race in their admissions policies.[10]

The issue was revisited by the Supreme Court in another case arising from the University of Texas in 2013. In the case of *Fisher* v. *University of Texas,* the Supreme Court did not rule on the merits of the case brought by Abigail Fisher, but instead sent it to the Fifth Circuit court for further consideration. This court found that affirmative action could be used as part of a "holistic" admissions process, thus upholding the system used at the University of Texas. In reviewing the circuit court decision, in 2016 the Supreme Court upheld the admissions process for the University of Texas, saying that "Considerable deference is owed to a university in defining those intangible characteristics, like student body diversity, that are central to its identity and educational mission. But still, it remains an enduring challenge to our Nation's education system to reconcile the pursuit of diversity with the constitutional promise of equal treatment and dignity."[11]

Although the issue of affirmative action has not been finally settled, the essential point here is that in one of the most important and intensely conflict-ridden issues in Texas, policy has been set neither by the state legislature nor by the governor, but by the attorney general. Such is the power of that institution in state government.

## Lawyers

Law is a "profession," meaning that not just anyone can claim to be an attorney. Everyone who practices law for money must have passed the state bar examination and received a license; the overwhelming majority of licensed lawyers also have attended law school. In 2019, the state was home to 103,342 licensed attorneys, a number that has grown by 23 percent over the last decade. Although 84 percent of lawyers are white, and 64 percent are males, the pool of attorneys is becoming more diverse in its ethnic and gender background.[12]

## The State Bar of Texas

All lawyers who practice within the state are required to maintain membership in the State Bar and pay annual dues. The State Bar occupies a unique position: It is an agency of government, a professional organization, and an influential interest group active in state politics.

## The Court System

In 1972, the Texas Chief Justice's Task Force for Court Improvement noted that the Texas Constitution prescribes the basic organizational structure of the Texas court system, that the structure is essentially the same today as it was under the Republic of Texas, and that the rigidity of the constitutional structure has led to the development, of necessity, of one of the most complex and fragmented judicial systems of all the states.[13] Nineteen years later, the Texas Research League opened its study of the state's court system with the words, "The Texas judiciary is in disarray with the courts in varying parts of the state going their own way at their own pace.... Texas does not have a court *system* in the real sense of the word."[14]

These are not the only reformers' panels to have been dismayed by the Texas court system. Critics complain about the duplication of jurisdiction between types of courts, about the fact that not all courts keep records of their proceedings, about the fact that a single court may both try cases and hear appeals, and about the lack of standardization within the system, so that the jurisdiction of the sundry types of courts varies from county to county. Whether it functions well or badly, however, the court system does function.

The following sections present a brief description of the activities of Texas's 3,204 judges from the lowest to the highest levels of the courts (see Figure 9-1).[15]

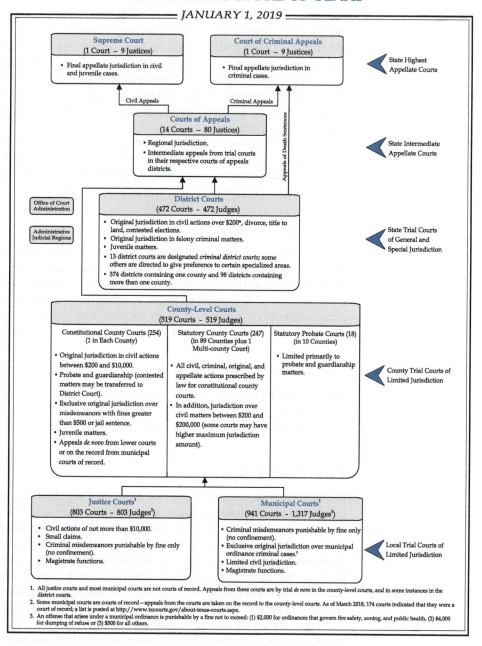

Figure 9-1 Court Structure of Texas

SOURCE: State of Texas, http://www.courts.state.tx.us/.

## Municipal Courts

City courts are authorized by the state constitution and by state laws to handle minor criminal matters involving a fine of no more than $500 with no possibility of imprisonment (Class C misdemeanors), where they have concurrent jurisdiction with justice courts. They also have exclusive jurisdiction over municipal ordinances and can impose fines of up to $2,500. Municipal courts have no civil jurisdiction and deal mainly with violations of traffic laws. They generally do not keep records of trials. In fiscal 2019, there were 1,317 municipal court judges in 940 cities, who disposed of more than 4.8 million cases, the overwhelming percentage of which were traffic violations (nearly always from city police).

Qualifications for municipal judges are decreed by the governing body of the city. Most municipal judges are appointed by the governing body, although in a few cities they are chosen in nonpartisan elections. Terms of office are usually two years. Their salaries are paid entirely by the city and are highly variable.

## Justice Courts

**original trial courts** Courts having the authority to consider and decide both criminal and civil cases in the first instance, as distinguished from appellate courts.

**criminal jurisdiction** The authority of courts that handle offenses punishable by fines, imprisonment, public service, or death. These offenses include murder, rape, assault, theft, embezzlement, fraud, drunken driving, speeding, and other acts that have been defined as criminal by the state legislature or municipal authorities.

Until recently known as "justice of the peace" courts, these are **original trial courts** with both civil and **criminal jurisdiction**. The Justice Courts deal with misdemeanor criminal cases when the potential punishment is only a fine. They have exclusive jurisdiction over civil cases where the amount in controversy is $200 or less and concurrent jurisdiction with both county and district courts when the amount in controversy is between $200 and $5,000. Their judges preside over small claims courts, act as notaries public, and, like other Texas judges, are authorized to perform marriages. In all but the largest counties, they may function as coroners, and in this role they may be required to certify cause of death, despite the fact that few if any justices have any medical training. In fact, there are no constitutional or statutory qualifications for justice court judges, who may therefore come from any background. As a result, only about 6 percent of Texas's justice court judges are lawyers.

Justice court judges are elected by the voters of the precinct and, like other county officials, serve for four years. Salaries are set by county commissioners, and can range from practically nothing to more than $60,000 per year, depending on the size of the precinct and the volume of activity. Texas's 803 justice courts dealt with 2,658,953 criminal cases and 532,330 civil cases in fiscal year 2018. As was the case with municipal courts, most of the criminal cases were traffic tickets (mostly from state troopers and sheriffs' departments) and most civil cases involved conflicts between tenants and landlords.

## County Courts

The Texas Constitution requires each county to have a *court of record*—that is, a court where a complete transcript is made of each case. Judges of these 254 "constitutional" courts need not be lawyers but only "well-informed in the law of the state."[16] They are elected for four-year terms, and their salaries are paid by the counties and are highly variable, ranging from $10,000 in rural counties to well more than $150,000 in urban counties. Vacancies are filled by appointments made by the county commissioners court. Not all constitutional county courts exercise judicial functions. In large counties, the constitutional county judge may devote full time to the administration of county government. Because county judges do not have to have a law degree, their training as judges, as little as 30 hours, leads to concerns that the rights of people accused of crimes might be diminished. Critics point out that jailers in the jails that house criminals might very well have more job training than the judges who send them there. This problem is perhaps especially acute in less urban counties, where there is only a county judge whose primary job is to supervise the commissioners court.

**appellate jurisdiction** The authority of a court to hear cases sent to it on appeal from a lower court. Appellate courts review only the legal issues involved and not the factual record of the case.

**original jurisdiction** The authority to hear a case first, usually in a trial.

When county courts do exercise judicial functions, they have both original and **appellate jurisdiction** in civil and criminal cases. Their **original jurisdiction** extends to all criminal misdemeanors where the fine allowed exceeds $500 or a jail term may be imposed. County courts also hear appeals in criminal cases from justice and municipal courts. In civil matters, constitutional county courts have concurrent jurisdiction with justice courts when the amount in controversy is between $200 and $5,000.

The volume of cases in eighty-eight of the state's larger counties has moved the legislature to establish a number of specialized statutory county courts, often called "County Courts at Law," with jurisdiction that varies according to the statute under which they were created. Some exercise jurisdiction in only civil, criminal, probate, or appellate matters, while others are in effect extra, generalist county courts. Judges for these 263 "statutory county courts" and "statutory probate courts" must be attorneys. The probate courts are in urban counties and deal with settling the estates of people who have died. They are paid the same amount as the judges in the constitutional county courts.

Appellate jurisdiction from the decisions of county courts rests with the courts of appeals. The "constitutional county courts" disposed of 53,622 cases and the "statutory county courts" disposed of 569,774 cases in 2018. Frequently, the criminal cases in county courts deal with family violence, assault, and driving while intoxicated (DWI) cases.

## State Trial Courts: The District Courts

In Texas, the 469 district courts are the principal trial courts. Each has a numerical designation and each court has one judge. Most district courts have both criminal and civil jurisdiction, but in the metropolitan areas, some specialize in criminal, civil, or family law cases.

District court judges must be attorneys who are licensed to practice in the state and who have at least four years' experience as lawyers or judges prior to being elected to the district court bench. The basic salary of $140,000 paid by the state is supplemented by an additional sum in many counties. Terms are for four years, with all midterm vacancies filled by gubernatorial appointment.

Cases handled by district court judges are varied. The district courts usually have jurisdiction over felony criminal trials, divorce cases, suits over titles to land, election contests, and civil suits in which the amount in controversy is at least $200, and share some of their civil jurisdiction with county courts. An additional complication for the allocation of jurisdiction is that at least one court in each county must be designated as the **juvenile court** to handle Texans younger than seventeen who are accused of crimes. These courts can be district, county courts at law, or constitutional county courts.

**juvenile court** Special state court that handles accused offenders under the age of seventeen.

District court cases are appealed to a court of appeals, except for death penalty criminal cases, where appeal is made directly to the Court of Criminal Appeals. In fiscal year 2018, district courts disposed of 865,231 major criminal and civil cases.

## Intermediate State Appellate Courts: The Courts of Appeals

The courts of appeals have intermediate civil and criminal appellate jurisdiction. Unlike the lower courts, appellate courts—the courts of appeals, the Court of Criminal Appeals, and the Supreme Court—are multi-judge courts that operate without juries. Appellate courts consider only the written records of lower court proceedings and the arguments of counsel representing the parties involved.

Texas's fourteen courts of appeals, each of which is responsible for a geographical district, have from three to thirteen justices per court, for a total of eighty judges statewide. Cases are usually considered by a panel of three justices, but the courts may hear cases *en banc* (together). All decisions are by majority vote. Justices are elected for staggered six-year terms and must have the same qualifications as justices of the state's Supreme Court: Each must be at least thirty-five years of age and have ten years' legal experience either as a practicing attorney or as a practicing attorney and judge of a court of record. Associate justices receive an annual salary of $154,000, and the chief justice, elected as such, receives $156,500.

Jurisdiction of the courts of appeals consists of civil and criminal cases appealed from district courts, county courts, and county courts at law. They both review the decisions of lower court judges and evaluate the constitutionality of the statute or ordinance on which the conviction is based. Decisions of the courts of appeals are usually final, but some may be reviewed by the Court of Criminal Appeals or the Texas Supreme Court. The courts of appeals had caseloads of 5,581 civil and 4,696 criminal cases in fiscal year 2018.

## Highest State Appellate Courts

**Supreme Court** The highest state appellate court with civil jurisdiction.

**Court of Criminal Appeals** The highest state appeals court with criminal jurisdiction.

Texas and Oklahoma are the only states to have split their highest appellate jurisdiction between two courts: a **Supreme Court** that hears only civil cases and a **Court of Criminal Appeals** for criminal cases. Each has responsibility not only for reviewing the decisions made by lower court trial judges but also for interpreting and applying the state constitution, making these courts of vital political importance.

The Court of Criminal Appeals is the state's final appeals court in criminal matters, although in rare instances its decisions may be appealed to the U.S. Supreme Court. It considers *writs of error*, filed by losing attorneys who contend that their trial judge made a mistake in applying Texas law and who wish to have the verdict overturned, and *writs of habeus corpus*, in which attorneys claim that a certain person has been unlawfully detained and should be released. In fiscal year 2018, the court wrote 448 opinions and disposed of 10 death penalty cases.

Qualifications for judges of the Court of Criminal Appeals and the justices of the Supreme Court are the same as those for justices of the courts of appeals. The nine judges of the Court of Criminal Appeals are elected on a statewide basis for six-year staggered terms, and the presiding judge runs as such. Vacancies are filled by gubernatorial appointment. Cases are normally heard by a three-judge panel. The salary is $168,000 per year, and the presiding judge receives $170,500.

The Supreme Court hears appeals only for civil and juvenile cases, but like its counterpart at the national level, it is the most prestigious court in the system. Qualifications for Supreme Court justices are the same as those for the judges of the courts of appeals and Court of Criminal Appeals. There are nine justices on the bench, including a chief justice. All are elected for six-year staggered terms, with three justices elected every two years. Salaries are the same as those for the Court of Criminal Appeals.

The Supreme Court's original jurisdiction is limited, and most cases that it hears are on appeal from the courts of appeals. In 2018, the Supreme Court issued 132 opinions.

However, the Supreme Court also performs other important functions. It is empowered to issue *writs of mandamus*—orders to corporations or persons, including judges and state officials other than the governor, to perform certain acts. Like the Court of Criminal Appeals, it spends much of its time considering applications for *writs of error*, which allege that the courts of appeals have ruled wrongfully on a point of law. It conducts proceedings for removal of judges and makes administrative rules for all civil courts in the state.

Although media portrayals depict criminal cases as being settled in trials, most cases are settled by plea bargains. Here, a lawyer discusses a plea offer with his client.

Halfdark/Getty Images

**Competency Connection**
**SOCIAL RESPONSIBILITY**

Are the interests of the public well-served by plea bargains? Explain.

**grand jury** A legal body of twelve or more individuals convened at the county seat. The grand jury considers evidence submitted by prosecutors and determines whether there is sufficient evidence to indict those accused of crimes.

**indictment** An official accusation that a person or organization has committed a crime, normally issued by a grand jury, and normally involving felonies rather than misdemeanors.

**felony** A major crime, punishable by at least a year in prison upon conviction. Capital felonies may involve the death penalty.

**misdemeanors** A small or moderate crime, punishable by fines or, at maximum, a year in jail.

The Supreme Court also plays a unique role within the legal profession in Texas. It approves new schools of law, appoints the Board of Law Examiners (which prepares the bar examination), determines who has passed the examination, and certifies who is entitled to practice law in Texas.

## Juries

Ordinary citizens have an important part to play in the judicial system and can be compelled to serve on one of two kinds of juries: grand juries and trial juries.

**Grand juries** meet in the seat of each county and are convened as needed. Grand jurors are chosen from a list prepared by a panel of jury commissioners—three to five persons appointed by the district judge. From this list, the judge selects twelve persons who sit for a term, usually of three months' duration. Grand jurors consider the material submitted by prosecutors to determine whether sufficient evidence exists to issue a formal **indictment**, that is, an official accusation. The process of indictment is intended to be a formal step to protect citizens from being charged with trivial evidence, but grand juries are often criticized for acting almost always in the way that prosecutors want them to act. For examples, prosecutors often back policemen who are involved in shootings while they are on duty, and it is relatively unusual for policemen to be indicted. Usually the cases considered by a grand jury are alleged **felonies**—serious crimes. Occasionally, persons are indicted for **misdemeanors**. In Texas, grand juries are frequently used to investigate such problems as drug trafficking within the community, increasing crime rates, alleged misconduct by public officials, and other subjects.

**trial juries** Six to twelve persons who determine the legal guilt or innocence of defendants in a criminal trial or the liability of defendants in a civil trial.

**Trial juries** make actual decisions about truth and falsehood, guilt and innocence. Under Texas law, defendants in civil cases and anyone charged with a crime may demand a jury trial. Although this right is frequently waived, thousands of such trials take place within the state every year. Lower court juries consist of six people, and district court juries have twelve members. The call to duty on a trial jury is determined through a list generated from the county voter registration, driver's license, and state identification card lists.

## Police

The state maintains an extensive organization primarily for the enforcement of criminal law. In addition to the judiciary and various planning and policymaking bodies, Texas had 41,912 full-time law enforcement officers staffing state and local police agencies as of October 31, 2017. Principal among these is the Texas Department of Public Safety (DPS). The DPS, with headquarters in Austin, employed 4,187 commissioned officers in 2017.[17] The other law enforcement officers include the 254 county sheriff's departments and more than 1,000 local police departments. Coordination and cooperation among these police agencies has become more sophisticated in recent years, but with so many agencies in the state, overlapping jurisdictions and complex organizational responsibilities can be challenging.

## Removal and Reprimand of Lawyers and Judges

The Texas State Bar is authorized by the legislature to reprimand or disbar any practicing attorney in the state for fraudulent, dishonest, or unethical conduct. Grievance committees have been established in each congressional district to hear complaints and to act against offending attorneys. In practice, reprimand and disbarment are uncommon and usually occur only after the offending lawyer has been convicted on some serious charge.

District and appellate court judges may be removed from the bench by impeachment after a vote of two-thirds majority of the legislature. District judges may also be removed by the Supreme Court, and lower court judges may be removed by action of a district court. A thirteen-member Texas State Commission on Judicial Conduct hears complaints against any judge in the state and can censure, reprimand, or recommend removal by the Texas Supreme Court. As with the disbarment of lawyers, punishment of judges is a rare occurrence.

## Issues Facing the Texas Judiciary

Too much crime, problems with the methods of selecting judges, and persistent issues of equality in the justice system are concerns for the Texas judicial system.

### Too Much Crime, Too Many Criminals

Even if the Texas court system were perfectly organized, the number of accused criminals would challenge the system. From 1982 to 1992, the state's crime rate increased dramatically, by more than 12 percent.[18] The crime rate generally declined in the period 2007–2017, the last year for which records are available. However, even with lower rates, there were 842,055 crimes committed in Texas during 2017.[19]

The high levels of street crime, leading to large numbers of arrests, have swamped the courts, stretching the ability of the courts to handle the case load. But the declining crime rate, along with a trend toward incarcerating fewer nonviolent criminals, means that, while the prison system is very large, the number of incarcerated Texans is also going down. In 2018, Texas held 140,086 prison inmates in its 108 facilities, more than any other state. Over the last dozen years, Texas has reduced its prison population significantly, by more than twelve thousand.[20] Here, the instincts of social conservatives to punish criminals harshly have lost out to fiscal conservatives. Fiscal conservatives want to avoid building more prison facilities and paying the high costs of keeping inmates incarcerated. The demand that public officials "lock 'em up and throw away the key" has been offset, to some degree, by the prohibitive cost of running the state's prison facilities.

The overwhelming caseload, along with incentives by defense attorneys to seek lesser punishment for their clients and for prosecutors to gain certain convictions, has led judges to do what they can to keep the system functioning. As a result, **plea bargains**—deals where defendants pleads guilty to a lesser charge (e.g., manslaughter instead of murder) and receives a lesser penalty (less time in prison or a probated sentence), thus avoiding a trial—account for more than nine of ten criminal convictions in Texas.[21]

Because a plea bargain puts the criminal back on the streets quickly, it does almost nothing to make society safer. Ordinary citizens are often appalled at the swiftness with which violent criminals are recycled into their neighborhoods, but the courts cannot handle the twin problems of a crushing caseload and overstuffed prisons in any other way. At the same time, occasionally, a person who is factually innocent may have incentives to plead guilty to a crime because of the assurance of a lower punishment than if a trial were held. This, too, becomes a challenge for creating a truly just system.

And so, despite the somewhat lower crime rate it has enjoyed over the past decade, Texas continues to be plagued by crime. As a result, its judicial system continues to be challenged by a large workload.

**plea bargain** The process in which an accused person agrees to plead guilty to a lesser crime and receives a lighter sentence. He or she avoids having to stand trial on a more serious charge, and the state saves the time and expense of a trial.

## ISSUE SPOTLIGHT:
## Justice Is not Cheap

The sheer number of crimes is a burden not only to the state as a whole but also to its individual parts. For example, in 2003, Hidalgo County in South Texas was struggling with the responsibility of conducting sixteen murder trials. Eleven of the accused killers were indigent, so the county had to appoint, and pay for, their defense counsels.

State law required that two lawyers to be appointed to represent such defendants. To be qualified to handle a death penalty case, the lead attorney had to have practiced in fifteen felony jury trials and tried two death penalty cases as first or second defense counsel. Only eleven lawyers in Hidalgo County were qualified to handle such cases. Furthermore, because court-appointed attorneys were paid $40 an hour for out-of-court work and $70 for in-court work, much less than the standard $200-per-hour fee schedule that prevailed among lawyers in 2003 for private representation, competent attorneys were often reluctant to take on such cases.

As a result, Hidalgo County was scrambling, first to find attorneys willing and able to defend accused murderers, and second to pay for them. The cost of the criminal justice system continues to vex rural counties.

Source: "Murder Cases Try County's Resources," *Austin American-Statesman*, May 12, 2003, B6.

**Competency Connection**
**SOCIAL RESPONSIBILITY**

Since the Sixth Amendment of the U.S. Constitution has been ruled to require that states provide an attorney to citizens accused of crime, should the state, and not local governments, be required to pay for such legal representation?

# Judicial Selection

The job of a judge is an inherently ambiguous one in a democratic society. Many people believe that judges serve society best if they are *independent*—that is, if they are at least partly insulated from outside pressures. The best way to insulate judges is to have them appointed for life. Yet democratic theory requires that all public officials be *accountable* to the public, which would seem to demand that they all be subject to frequent review through regularly scheduled elections. Although some scholars have tried to argue that judges should be both independent and accountable, the two concepts are inherently contradictory.[22]

In practice, various levels of government have tried to find compromises between the two desirable but incompatible goals in different ways. At the federal level, judges are appointed by the president and serve for life, whereas in many states, including Texas, their jobs must be periodically ratified by the voters in partisan elections. Whatever compromise is chosen, it is never satisfying to everyone. National politicians frequently argue that federal judges must be made more accountable, but in Texas, there are always some prominent people arguing that state judges should be granted more independence. There is no easy answer to the dilemma of accountability versus independence; citizens must make up their own minds. The following text presents a discussion about two of the ways the argument has surfaced in Texas.

**Partisan Elections?** In the fifty states, there are numerous systems used to select judges, and many states use differing systems for trial judges and appeals judges. Texas is one of only six states to use partisan election for all levels of its constitutional courts, though each state has its own quirks in selection. Four methods are used to select judges for the courts of final appeals:

1. Partisan election. Judges are chosen in elections in which their party affiliation is listed on the ballot. This is the system employed in Texas and five other states.
2. Nonpartisan election. Judges are chosen in elections, but no party labels appear on the ballot (sixteen states).
3. Appointment by the legislature or the governor (twelve states).
4. Missouri Plan (sometimes called the "merit plan"). The governor makes the appointments from a list submitted by a nominating commission. At regular intervals, judges must be approved by the voters in a referendum. If they fail to win a majority of the votes, they must leave office, and the governor appoints someone else (sixteen states). It is called the "Missouri Plan," because it was first adopted in that state.[23]

As indicated above, in Texas, all judges except municipal judges are popularly elected in partisan contests. Trial court judges serve for four years before having to face the voters again, and appellate judges enjoy a six-year term. The consequence of the state's system is that judges are like other politicians in that, although they do not campaign all the time, they must always be thinking about the next election. Like other politicians, they are aware that what they do or say today may affect their chances for reelection tomorrow. Unlike other politicians, however, judges are supposed to be fair and impartial when trying cases and to pay no attention to the possible partisan consequences of their decisions.

With the next election always just over the horizon, reelection politics can permeate a courthouse, and the struggle for advantage may taint the quest for impartial decisions. After the 2018 elections, one where Democrats swept out Republicans across the board in Houston, Harris County's longest serving state district judge, Michael McSpadden, commented on the election outcomes, reflecting on the complex realities of judicial elections:

▶ "Straight-ticket voting determines elections," he said. "It's happened to both sides over the years."
▶ "I have no regrets about losing," he said. "These are not our courts and everybody has a chance to run and a chance to win."

And Texas Southern Law Professor James M. Douglas commented that: "At the end of the day, you want to make sure that all judicial selections are informed decisions. And there are so many names on the ballot now that it's hard to know who everyone is. I don't know how you can make an informed decision."[24]

The Harris County elections had one other obvious change, the election of 19 new African-American women judges, a change that is significant symbolically but also one that will change judicial politics in Harris County. The elections of 2018 drew an endorsement of nonpartisan elections by the Chief Justice of the Texas Supreme Court Nathan Hecht. Frustrated that 20 Republican appeals judges lost reelection bids, he called the Texas system of partisan election "among the very worst methods of judicial selection." He went on to decry partisan politics: "When partisan politics is the driving force and the political climate is as harsh as ours has become, judicial elections make judges more political, and judicial independence is the casualty." Moreover, Hecht argued, the Democrats were not elected because they were superior candidates: "Qualifications did not drive their election. Partisan politics did."[25]

All systems have flaws, and the democratic appeal of partisan elections is strong, despite Chief Justice Hecht's complaints about the 2018 elections. Studies show that the most important factor in allowing citizens to predict how judges will decide cases is their political party. Republican judges tend to favor business and people with power and wealth; Democrats tend to favor labor unions, the poor, and social underdogs in general. In other words, Texas has the perfect system for allowing its citizens to select judges who share their ideologies.[26] Moreover, as the findings summarized in the "Is Reform Needed?" box illustrate, there is no good evidence that a different system of choosing judges would produce a more honest system than the one Texas has now. An appointive or nonpartisan system might not create a better judiciary and would be less democratic.

**Is Justice for Sale?** The practice of electing judges aligns with democratic theory. When judges must run for office at periodic intervals, they are kept accountable to the people's wishes. However, there is a problem with elections, a problem common to all offices but particularly troubling in regard to the judiciary. When judges have to run for office like other politicians, they also have to raise money like other politicians. When lawyers who practice in judges' courtrooms or others with a direct interest in the outcome of legal cases give judges campaign contributions, it raises the uncomfortable suspicion that those judges' court rulings might be affected by the money. Wealthy special interests may taint the administration of justice just as they deform the public policy made by other institutions.

James Andrew Wynne, Jr., is a judge in the North Carolina Court of Appeals. In 2002, Judge Wynne used a vivid metaphor to summarize the uneasiness of those who suspect that justice may be for sale in partisan election judicial systems. Suppose, he mused, that major-league baseball umpires had to run for office, and the players were allowed to contribute money to their campaigns: "Under that scenario, how can anyone have the confidence in the strike calls of an umpire if you know the pitcher contributed $10,000 to select that umpire to call the game?"[27] It is a fair question. Wealthy private interests may taint the administration of justice just as they deform the public policy made by other institutions.[28]

Texas judicial candidates finance their election campaigns with private funds. Not surprisingly, one of the chief sources of campaign contributions to judicial candidates is the very lawyers who will be practicing in their courts if they win office. In 2003, Texans for Public Justice (TPJ) analyzed the campaign finances of eighty-seven winning candidates for the intermediate courts of appeals. The conclusion reached by the TPJ was that attorneys contributed 72 percent of the total funding for those successful races.[29] A majority of the funding for the reelection races of five Supreme Court justices running in 2006 came from attorneys and law firms.[30] There is no reason to believe that these patterns have not recurred in recent elections. It is difficult to imagine that judges would be able to forget the source of their campaign resources when arbitrating the cases of attorneys and groups that have supported them.

## ISSUE SPOTLIGHT:
### Is Reform Needed?

In 2009, political scientists Chris Bonneau and Melinda Gann Hall published a systematic evaluation of the consequences of Supreme Court selection processes in the fifty states. Their conclusion was that, despite much criticism of judicial elections as politicizing what should be a neutral application of law, elections actually serve a positive purpose. They encourage citizen participation and create a link between the electorate and those elected to serve them. Further, state high court judges who are appointed are not, as a group, more independent from the political process than are judges who are elected in partisan races.

In a follow-up book in 2017, they conclude that "each system of recruiting and retaining the state court bench has advantages and disadvantages, and in large measure reflects fundamental beliefs about who should control access to the bench and supervise judicial performance." In other words, the Texas system has some advantages and there is no reason to believe Texans would find another system more advantageous.

Sources: Chris Bonneau and Melinda Gann Hall, *In Defense of Judicial Elections* (New York: Routledge, 2009); Chris Bonneau and Melinda Gann Hall, *Judicial Elections in the 21st Century* (New York: Routledge, 2017), p. 268.

**Competency Connection**
**CRITICAL THINKING**

**Should Texas move to nonpartisan elections? Or are the findings of Bonneau and Hall, reflected in this box, persuasive in concluding that changing selection systems might solve one problem but create others?**

In an analysis of the decisions of the Ohio supreme court aimed at addressing this very question, reporters for the *New York Times* compared the behavior of those justices to the sources of the funds for their campaigns. They came to two conclusions. First, Ohio supreme court justices almost always failed to withdraw from hearing cases in which lawyers and interests who had contributed to their campaigns appeared. Second, over the course of twelve years, supreme court justices voted in favor of those contributors 70 percent of the time.[31] There is no reason to think that Texas judges behave any differently.

Responding to the public perception that justice might be for sale, in 1995 the legislature passed the Judicial Campaign Fairness Act (JCFA). This legislation limited individual contributions to statewide judicial candidates to $5,000 each election and prohibited law firms from contributing more than $30,000 to individual Supreme Court candidates. Judicial candidates were also forbidden to accept more than a total of $300,000 from all political action committees.

Although the intent of the JCFA was clearly to stop the contamination of the Texas judiciary by money, events almost immediately proved it to be ineffective. In 1996, Texas Supreme Court Justice James A. Baker allowed an attorney with a case pending before him to participate in his fund-raising efforts.[32] When journalists reported this obvious conflict of interest, the bad publicity forced Baker to withdraw from the case. His withdrawal solved the immediate concern about one questionable case, but it did not address the basic problem. As long as attorneys are allowed to raise campaign funds for judges and to contribute money themselves, there will be public doubts about the impartiality of the judiciary. The JCFA, while it was well intentioned, does not address this fundamental problem.

In 2000, two consumer advocacy groups filed suit in federal court, arguing that when Texas allows judges to solicit campaign contributions from lawyers who may appear in their courts, the state violates its citizens' constitutional rights to fair trials. They lost the case, with U.S. District Judge James Nowlin writing, "The issue of limiting campaign contributions and/or potential contributions are questions for the citizens of Texas and their state representatives, not a federal court." Given this decision, if the Texas system of financing judicial elections is to be changed, the impetus must come from inside the state.[33]

As with elections to other offices, the suggestion is sometimes made that both the appearance and the reality of impropriety could be avoided if judicial campaigns were publicly, as opposed to privately, financed (see Chapter 5). Public financing, it is argued, would permit judges to be held democratically accountable, yet would soften the impact of special interests. Former Chief Justice Tom Phillips of the Texas Supreme Court, for one, has advocated this change in the state's judicial elections. Phillips points out that no additional tax money need be used for this reform because judicial campaigns could be bankrolled using an existing $200 lawyer occupation tax that raises $10 million annually.[34] So far, however, this suggestion has found no support among lawmakers.

## Equal Justice?

The dilemmas of too much crime and of judicial selection are not the only serious problems facing the Texas system of justice. The state has for some time been in the midst of another argument over the way it affords legal representation to poor people accused of crimes.

Before people are put in prison, they must be tried and convicted. Because one of the most important ideals of democracy is that everyone is equal before the law, Texans would like to think that all accused persons are treated fairly and impartially in this process. A well-functioning democracy features a judiciary that rigorously but fairly judges the guilt of everyone brought to trial. Nevertheless, there is substantial evidence that the Texas criminal justice system does not affect all citizens equally. It imposes severe burdens on the poor and

In this cartoon, Ben Sargent satirizes the fact that elected judges bow to the popular will of voters, and especially those who donate money to their campaigns, even when justice is compromised.

Courtesy of Ben Sargent

**Competency Connection**
**PERSONAL RESPONSIBILITY**

Is it too much to ask for judges to raise money from attorneys to fund an election campaign and then to be neutral professionals when those attorneys appear before them in trial? Or is it human nature to help those who helped finance in the election?

particularly on members of ethnic minorities—the same groups who are at a disadvantage in other areas of politics. Legal fees are expensive—in 2018, the standard lawyer's fee was more than $300 per hour—and the system is so complex that accused people cannot defend themselves without extensive and expensive legal help.

The result is that the prisons, and death row, are full of poor people. Wealthier defendants can afford to hire attorneys to help them try to "beat the rap," and in any case, they are often offered plea bargains that allow them to stay out of prison. But until recently, Texas lacked a system of *public defenders* to provide free legal assistance to accused criminals who were too poor to pay a lawyer, except in the case of defendants who had been convicted of capital murder and sentenced to death. Judges, using county rather than state funds, appointed private attorneys to represent indigent defendants. Frequently, they were inexperienced or already busy with paying clients.

In 1999, journalist Debbie Nathan spent time observing the way county-appointed attorneys interacted with their indigent clients. Her summary had to be troubling to citizens who thought that the poor, too, should be entitled to competent legal counsel when they are accused of a crime:

> What I witnessed was low-grade pandemonium. Attorneys rushed into court, grabbed a file or two, and sat down for a quick read; this was their first and often most lengthy exposure to their new client's case. Confused-looking defendants, mostly Hispanic or African American, met their counsel amid a hubbub of other defendants, defendants' spouses, and defendants' squalling babies.[35]

Reformers have argued that if justice is to be done, Texas should have a system of public defenders equal in number and experience to the public prosecutors; without such procedures, the system inevitably discriminates against poor defendants, who tend to be minority citizens.

## You Decide: At-Large or Single-Member District Elections?

State district judges in Texas are selected in at-large elections. All candidates receive their votes from the whole district, which in a metropolitan area is typically a county. Such elections tend to make it difficult for minorities to be elected. If, for example, a quarter of the population of a county is Hispanic, and there is more-or-less bloc voting by each ethnic group, then Hispanic candidates will be outvoted three to one every time. Although Hispanics represent 25 percent of the population in a given county, they will have 0 percent of the judges in that county.

Consequently, minority representatives almost always prefer single-member district elections to at-large elections. If the county is carved into a number of geographic districts, with each district electing a single judge, then (assuming that people of different ethnic groups tend to live in different areas) the proportion of judges from each group should be roughly proportional to that group's representation in the population of that county. Minority leaders, therefore, often argue that Texas should adopt a system of electing county judges in which all candidates run from single-member districts.

### Pro ✅

⬆ The 1965 Voting Rights Act forbids systematic discrimination against the voting rights of minorities. Because at-large districts make minority candidates unelectable, they are illegal.

### Con ❌

⬇ The Voting Rights Act forbids discrimination against *voters*. It does not guarantee that minority *candidates* must win.

(Continued)

## Pro ✅

🔼 In many counties, the proportion of minority judges is far below the proportion of minority citizens in the county.

🔼 Ever since 1994, very few minority judges have been elected in Texas. This fact is evidence that Anglo citizens refuse to vote for minority candidates.

🔼 When minority citizens see that there are no minority judges, it undermines their faith in the justice system; such a lack of faith cannot be good for society as a whole.

🔼 Minorities should be guaranteed some representation on the bench by the deliberate creation of some "minority-majority" districts.

🔼 Putting aside questions of minority politics, single-member districts provide better representation for discrete areas of a city or county.

🔼 Minorities should keep suing in federal court until Texas is forced to create a single-member-district judicial election system.

## Con ❌

🔽 The lack of minority judges is mainly caused by the lack of qualified minority attorneys. Therefore, it is not evidence of discrimination.

🔽 The lack of minority success at the polls is caused by the fact that almost all minority candidates are Democrats. Where Democrats do well, as in Dallas County in 2006, minority candidates do well.

🔽 Granted, this is a problem. The solution is for minorities to become Republicans, thereby increasing their chance to be elected.

🔽 Such a plan would amount to a "Democrat-protection scheme," which the Constitution does not oblige Republicans to endorse.

🔽 At-large election plans ensure that each candidate must consider the welfare of the entire county, whereas district plans create a system of jealous, quarreling pieces.

🔽 In *Houston Lawyers' Assoc. et al.* v. *Attorney General of Texas et al.* (501 U.S. 419, 1994), the federal courts already settled this question; more lawsuits would be futile.

Sources: James Cullen, "Lawyers Protect Their Own," *Texas Observer*, September 17, 1993, 4; Suzanne Gamboa, "Judicial Elections Proposal Rejected," *Austin American-Statesman*, August 25, 1993, A1; Lani Guinere, *The Tyranny of the Majority: Fundamental Fairness in Representative Democracy* (New York: Free Press, 1994); David Lubin, *The Paradox of Representation: Racial Gerrymandering and Minority Interests in Congress* (Princeton, NJ: Princeton University, 1997); David T. Canon, *Race, Redistricting, and Representation: The Unintended Consequences of Black Majority Districts* (Chicago: University of Chicago, 1999).

Competency Connection
**SOCIAL RESPONSIBILITY**

When judges are elected, are they elected to serve the interests of their constituents or the interests of justice? How might dividing counties into judicial districts change judicial behavior?

For example, in 1993, the Texas Bar Foundation sponsored a study by the Spangenberg Group of the state's system of appointing attorneys for indigents accused of murder. The group's conclusions about Texas justice were consistent and unambiguous:

> In almost every county, the rate of compensation provided to court-appointed attorneys in capital cases is absurdly low . . . the quality of representation in these cases is uneven and . . . in some cases, the performance of counsel is extremely poor.[36]

If such deficient legal representation was common for citizens accused of murder, which is a high-profile crime, then the representation afforded people accused of lesser crimes must have been even worse. The same problems have persisted over time, with a 2017 Pew Trust study showing that public defender caseloads are overwhelming, and juggling clients is a "Sysyphean task," referencing a Greek mythological job of doing an impossible feat of rolling a rock uphill for eternity. Liberals argue that such a problem should be addressed with increased funding to hire more public defenders to assure "that low-income people who have a constitutional

The democratic ideal of equal justice for all citizens faces a severe test when poor people are accused of crimes. If they cannot pay a private attorney, and the state refuses to provide them with competent counsel, they stand little chance of receiving an adequate defense.

Courtesy of Ben Sargent

**Competency Connection**
**PERSONAL RESPONSIBILITY**

Is it the responsibility of the state to make sure that individuals accused of crime should have competent representation or should individual citizens be responsible for their own defense? Does providing representation waste precious government resources or does it protect the precious equal right to justice? (see box, p. 226)

right to court-appointed counsel are represented by lawyers who have the skills and resources necessary to really test the government's case and counsel their clients about potential courses of action."[37] Conservatives such as Marc Levin, a vice president at the Texas Public Policy Foundation suggest that a reduction in the number of offenses that carry the potential of jail time would reduce costs and diminish the need for public defenders.[38] In short, the reality of unequal justice is a challenge to the democratic ideal of the Texas judicial system.

The problem of unequal justice is especially acute because Texas is a state with the death penalty. From the year 1982, when Texas resumed executions following a hiatus ordered by the U.S. Supreme Court, through February 2019, the state executed 558 people. Since 2014, over 70 percent of those sentenced to death are persons of color. And although African Americans comprise less than 13 percent of the prison population, a percent comparable to their representation in the general population of Texas, 43.7 percent of those on death row in Texas are African American.[39] In Chapter 11, the issue of whether capital punishment is defensible will be examined. Whether the death penalty is justifiable, however, it seems to be inflicted unequally on poorer and wealthier defendants. The problems of unequal justice for the poor continue up the judicial ladder to the most serious crimes. A troubling case came in 2007, when the presiding judge of the Texas Court of Criminal Appeals, Sharon Keller, turned away the last appeal of a death row inmate because the rushed filing was delayed past the court's 5 p.m. closing time.

The fact that poor defendants probably have a greater chance of being incarcerated, and executed, would not be so worrisome if there were reasons to have confidence in the fact that they were all guilty. However, recent history is not reassuring to partisans of the state's criminal justice system on that issue.

There is good reason to think that some of the people convicted of capital crimes in Texas have actually been innocent, the victims of a criminal justice system that often fails to ensure them an adequate trial. Furthermore, there are numerous examples of people who have been convicted of crimes and sentenced to prison, only to have later advances in investigative science prove them innocent. The ability of geneticists to analyze DNA, in particular, has led to the overturning of a remarkable number of convictions. From 1989 to February 2019,

## Texas Politics and You

Capital punishment has long been controversial. Rationales for it center on three issues: retribution against heinous criminals, removing a threat from society, and acting as a deterrent to crime. Yet, many argue against it, citing the possibility of making an error in conviction or the moral dilemma of having blood on society's hands. Asked about capital punishment, students responded with a variety of tweets, including the following:

"Necessary evil."

"Special offer: a one-4-one trade. Restrictions and termination costs may apply, see judge for details."

"Death penalty is dead wrong."

"I love sinking to other people's levels."

"We used to sell tickets to executions back in the day. Why not resume this practice? An eye for an eye."

"an unethical way to deal with crime."

"You know what they say, 'everything is bigger in Texas.'"

"CP has no repeat offenders."

Competency Connection
**CRITICAL THINKING**

In your view, on balance, is capital punishment a good or bad thing? Explain.

---

nationwide, 364 people were released from prison after DNA tests led to the nullification of their sentences, 18 of them in Texas.[40]

These wrongfully convicted people come from all across Texas. For example, consider these recent cases:

- ▶ In 2016, Sonia Cacy of Fort Stockton, was exonerated from a conviction of killing her father in a house fire to collect his life insurance money. The court concluded that Cacy had not set the fire, but that it was likely caused by her father falling asleep while smoking.

- ▶ In 2010, Governor Rick Perry issued a posthumous pardon to Timothy Cole, who had died in prison in 1999 after serving thirteen years for a rape in Lubbock that DNA evidence proved he did not commit.

- ▶ In 2011, Johnny Pinchback of Dallas was exonerated of rape by DNA evidence after having been behind bars for twenty-seven years.

- ▶ In 2016, the Court of Criminal Appeals exonerated Elizabeth Ramirez, Kristie Mayhugh, Cassandra Rivera, and Anna Vasquez, known as the "San Antonio Four," for a wrongful conviction for gang rape in San Antonio in 1998. "The trials turned on the false testimony from the alleged victims in the case, who had apparently been coached by adults, and the testimony of a physician who admitted that she misrepresented the facts."[41]

- ▶ In 2006 Governor Perry pardoned Greg Wallis and Billy Wayne Miller for similar reasons. They had been in prison eighteen and twenty-two years, respectively, and, if the ability to analyze DNA had not come along, would be there still.[42]

Perhaps the most unsettling case in recent years concerned Cameron Todd Willingham who was put to death in 2004. Willingham was convicted of starting a fire at his home in Corsicana, Texas, and purposely killing his three young children in 1999. Willingham refused to accept a plea bargain that would have allowed him to receive a life sentence instead of the death penalty, saying, "I ain't gonna plead to something I didn't do." The case against Willingham was circumstantial. Although Willingham had led a rough life and was not a particularly sympathetic character, the evidence was less compelling than one might ordinarily

Cameron Todd Willingham, shown here, was put to death after being convicted of murdering his children. Some have questioned whether the conviction was based upon good evidence and whether Willingham was actually an innocent man.

Lara Solt/Dallas Morning News/Corbis News/Corbis

**Competency Connection**
**PERSONAL RESPONSIBILITY**

Does the potential that Texas put an innocent man to death "haunt" you?

want to convict someone of a capital offense. One jailhouse witness who claimed originally that Willingham had confessed to the murders later recanted his testimony. Recent evidence uncovered by the Innocence Project suggests that the jailhouse witness testimony was obtained by prosecutors in exchange for a reduced sentence. And the forensic evidence about the fire was referred to by one scientist as "junk science." There is no definitive answer to whether Mr. Willingham was innocent of these murders, but at a minimum, as one columnist wrote, "The ghost of Cameron Todd Willingham is still haunting us, as well it should."[43]

## Summary

**LO 9.1** **The Texas judicial system is a huge part of the state government, and one of the most distinct in the country.** Although judges have traditionally been portrayed as "above politics," they are actually very much politicians. They are elected in partisan elections, and decisions that they make reflect political values.

**LO 9.2** **Texas has a complex judicial system, with judicial roles ranging from the two "supreme" courts—the Supreme Court and the Court of Criminal Appeals—through the courts of appeal, the district courts, county courts, justice courts, and municipal courts.** The courts handle everything from small claims to major civil cases and from traffic tickets to capital murder cases. The attorney general represents the interests of the state in courts, and members of the bar—licensed attorneys—represent citizens.

**LO 9.3** **The structure of the system includes small claims and minor criminal cases (justice courts and municipal courts), intermediate trial courts (county courts and county courts at law), major trial courts (district courts), intermediate appeals courts (courts of appeal), and supreme courts in civil matters (Supreme Court) and criminal matters (Court of Criminal Appeals).** All state judges are elected in partisan elections, and municipal court judges are selected in the manner prescribed by local city charters (mostly appointed by city councils).

**LO 9.4** **The two major types of juries in Texas are grand juries and trial juries. Grand juries determine if there is sufficient evidence to try citizens for crimes they are accused of committing by issuing indictments or failing to indict.** Trial juries hear evidence during trials and decide on guilt or innocence in criminal cases or which party to a suit has the preponderance of evidence on its side in civil cases.

**LO 9.5** **Although the judiciary processes the agenda of the state with regard to justice, and does so with fair success, various issues challenge the system.** The high number of crimes committed in Texas keeps the system very busy and forces many criminal cases to be resolved by plea bargains. Partisan election allows citizens to select judges who share their values, but leaves the appearance of judges being "politicians in black robes." The system gives advantages to citizens with resources and has the potential to convict people of crimes wrongfully on occasion.

## Critical Thinking

1. The judicial function is often seen as not being political, and yet politics is unquestioningly involved in the administration of justice. Evaluate whether judicial elections promote politics in the courtroom, whether plea bargains promote or hinder the fair application of the law, and whether Texas justice is "for sale."

2. Texas judges are elected in partisan elections. Discuss the advantages and disadvantages of the partisan election. Using the "You Decide" chart in the chapter, evaluate whether electing judges by district would be a positive or negative change in Texas.

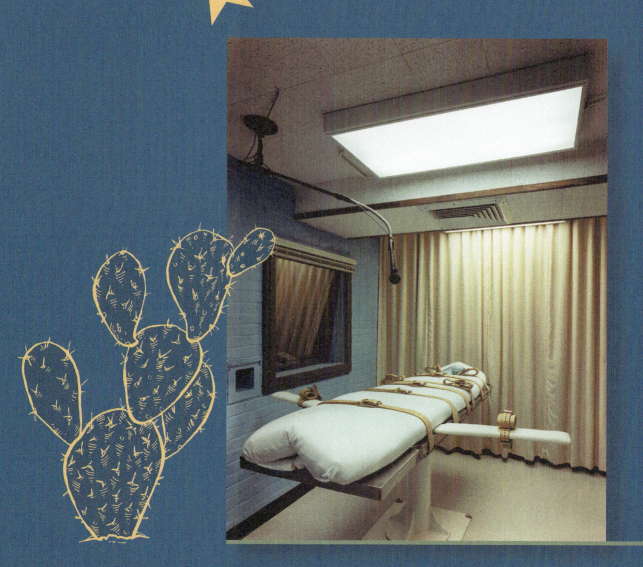

The gurney in Huntsville state prison where condemned murderers are strapped prior to being executed.

*Mark Jenkinson/Corbis*

# The Substance of Justice

**LO 10.1** Discuss issues in civil liberties in Texas, including freedom of expression, freedom of religion, the right to bear arms, and abortion.

**LO 10.2** Describe issues in civil rights in Texas, including school segregation, education, changing racial attitudes, and civil rights for convicted criminals.

**LO 10.3** Assess capital punishment in Texas.

**LO 10.4** Evaluate tort laws in Texas.

**D**ecisions of the judicial system are extraordinarily important to all of us. The system protects—or fails to protect—our rights in a democratic society and processes our case in the event we are accused of a crime. It also allocates large amounts of money and power by arbitrating between conflicting interests, especially those of a business nature.

Chapter 9 examined the structure and behavior of the Texas judiciary, suggesting that its relationship with democracy is complicated. That being so, it might be expected that the products of the system—the substance of justice—would also lead to ambivalent outcomes. Justice in Texas is complicated, and, in some cases, more admirable than knowledge of the judiciary's institutional weaknesses might lead us to believe.

The first topic of this chapter is an examination of the Texas judiciary's record on civil liberties and civil rights, followed by an evaluation of the manner in which it deals with accused criminals, and then a discussion of some of the issues surrounding the cry for "tort reform" in the area of lawsuits against business. The system's record is uneven; in

EVERY PERSON SHALL BE AT LIBERTY TO SPEAK, WRITE OR PUBLISH HIS OPINIONS ON ANY SUBJECT, BEING RESPONSIBLE FOR THE ABUSE OF THAT PRIVILEGE; AND NO LAW SHALL EVER BE PASSED CURTAILING THE LIBERTY OF SPEECH OR OF THE PRESS. TEXAS CONSTITUTION BILL OF RIGHTS, ARTICLE 1, SECTION 8, 1876 some areas, such as civil rights and liberties, it is dishearteningly backward. In other areas, especially the manner in which it has forced the state to equalize education, it is surprisingly progressive. When measured against the standards of democratic theory, Texas justice provides cause for both pessimism and optimism.

# Civil Liberties

**civil liberties** Individual freedoms such as speech, press, religion, and assembly. The protection of these liberties is essential to a vital democratic society. Generally, the protection of civil liberties requires forbidding government to take certain actions.

The phrase **civil liberties** refers to the basic individual freedom from government interference that is crucial to sustaining a democratic government. Democracy requires that citizens be free to speak, read, and assemble so that they may choose in an independent and informed manner among competing ideas, candidates, and parties. In addition, because a democratic society must respect individual autonomy of thought and conscience, government must not be allowed to interfere with freedom of religious choice.

The First Amendment to the U.S. Constitution declares that Congress may neither abridge the people's freedom of speech or of the press, nor their right to assemble peaceably, nor to petition the government for a redress of grievances. It also forbids Congress to "establish" religion—that is, support it with money and coercive laws—or prohibit its free exercise. The Fourteenth Amendment, passed after the Civil War in the 1860s, has gradually been held by the U.S. Supreme Court to apply most of these protections to the states—a process known as **incorporation**.

**incorporation** The judicial rule that applies civil liberties in the national Bill of Rights to the states because of the due process clause of the Fourteenth Amendment.

In addition, the states have similar guarantees in their constitutions. As the quotation at the beginning of the chapter shows, the Texas Constitution ensures freedom of speech and press. Beyond that, Section 27 promises that the state's citizens may assemble "in a peaceable manner" and petition the government "for redress of grievances or other purposes." Individual liberties are thus acknowledged in Texas, as in the federal government, to be of fundamental importance to a democratic society.

The words in both constitutions seem to protect individual freedoms, but the history of the documents teaches us that no political guarantee can be taken for granted. In the South, especially, the traditionalist political culture has never been eager to grant the individual freedoms promised by constitutions. Majorities in the South have often resisted the idea that African Americans and Mexican Americans should enjoy the same personal liberties as Anglo Americans. For all of the nineteenth and most of the twentieth century, Texas was quite reluctant to give its citizens the freedom its constitution guarantees. Even in the twenty-first century, there are hot disagreements about which exercises of government authority are legitimate and which violate someone's civil liberty.

Furthermore, some politicians and private citizens either do not understand the importance of civil liberties or do not value them, placing individual rights frequently under siege. The fear of terrorism and the challenges of immigration into Texas have sharpened disagreements about the balance between government authority and personal freedom. Sometimes the battle over civil liberties is fought in the legislature. Just as frequently, however, the struggle takes place in court.

## Freedom of Expression

Although "freedom of speech and press" seems to be an unambiguous phrase, only a little thought can create a variety of difficult problems of interpretation. Do constitutional guarantees of freedom of speech protect those who would incite a mob to lynch a prisoner? Teach terrorist recruits to make bombs? Tell malicious lies about public officials? Spout racist propaganda on a local cable TV access program? Publicly burn an American flag? Falsely advertise a patent medicine? These questions and others like them have sparked intense political and intellectual conflict.

In 1925, in *Gitlow* v. *New York*, the U.S. Supreme Court for the first time held that the U.S constitutional protections of freedom of speech and press were binding on state and local governments through the "due process of law" clause of the Fourteenth Amendment.[1] Since then, the Court's interpretation of the meaning of "freedom of speech and press" has constantly evolved so that American liberties are never quite the same from year to year. Since the 1960s, the First Amendment has come to contain protection for a "freedom of expression" that is larger than mere speech and press. Citizens may engage in non-speech acts that are intended to convey a political communication.

For example, at the 1984 Republican National Convention in Dallas, Gregory Lee Johnson and others protested the Reagan administration's policies by burning an American flag while chanting, "America the red, white, and blue, we spit on you." Johnson was arrested and charged with violating a Texas law against flag desecration. Johnson's attorneys argued that his act was "symbolic speech" protected by the First Amendment. The U.S. Supreme Court agreed. In its 1989 decision in ***Texas v. Johnson***, the majority held that "Johnson's burning of the flag was conduct sufficiently imbued with elements of communication to implicate the First Amendment,"[2] thus overturning the Texas law and freeing Johnson from the threat of jail time.

*Texas v. Johnson (1989)* A U.S. Supreme Court decision that ruled the Texas law against burning a U.S. flag in a political protest as an unconstitutional restriction of the freedom of speech.

This decision caused a national furor. A large majority of Americans, while supporting freedom of expression in the abstract, were not willing to grant it to someone whose ideas they found so obnoxious. In this way, they showed the inconsistency that people sometimes display when they discover that they dislike the specific consequences of general principles they otherwise endorse.

First Amendment freedoms are not designed to protect conventional or conformist views; rather they protect the expression of despised views such as Johnson's. Democracy requires not only majority rule, but also minority rights. Fashionable opinion does not need protection because its very popularity renders it immune from suppression. Freedom comes into play only when there is some danger to the speaker for expressing his or her thought—that is, when the thought is disagreeable to the majority. The American—and Texas—public missed this point.

The public being so aroused, the U.S. Congress was not about to stand in its way. Congress quickly passed the Flag Protection Act of 1989, mandating punishment for anyone who "knowingly mutilates, defaces, physically defiles, burns, maintains on the floor or ground, or tramples upon, any flag of the United States." A federal court quickly struck down this law for the same reason that the Supreme Court had invalidated the Texas statute. Because federal judges could not be removed, they were free to protect the liberty of an unpopular person such as Gregory Lee Johnson.

Perhaps the most divisive issues in Texas and across the nation in the last few years have been concerns expressed by African Americans and women. Protests about the disproportionate number of African Americans who have been killed by law enforcement agents, a movement often called "black lives matter," have been especially passionate. One particular march in Dallas on July 7, 2016, brought the intensity of this issue to a head. During a peaceful march, with Dallas policemen working to make sure there was no trouble as citizens expressed their views, a heavily armed man, an Army veteran and African American, opened fire on the policemen, killing five and injuring seven, explaining that he wanted to kill as many white policemen as he could. The event that had begun to peacefully bring focus to a divisive issue ended in a violent tragedy with policemen, ironically working to keep the peace, as victims.[3]

Women's marches in reaction to the Trump presidency and the "me too" movement against sexual harassment and assault of women have occurred across the state. The marches began as a protest against the inauguration of Donald Trump as president of the United States and have been repeated each January since then. Marches have taken place across the United States, but some notable ones have happened in large cities in Texas—in Austin, Dallas,

Houston, and Fort Worth. One protestor tweeted that "Progress & change isn't handed over on a neat, tidy platter. It's won through impassioned grit & determined collective struggles." Such a statement sounds like the very essence of First Amendment freedoms.[4]

## Freedom of Religion

The First Amendment provision that forbids Congress to pass laws "respecting an establishment of religion" has been interpreted to mean either (1) that there should be a "wall of separation" between church and state, and that government may not help or even acknowledge religion in any way, or (2) that government may aid religion, at least indirectly, as long as it shows "no preference" among the various religious beliefs. In practice, the U.S. Supreme Court has allowed the states to provide a variety of aids to religion—for example, school lunches and public facilities for church-run schools and tuition grants for church-run colleges—as long as government agencies do not show a preference for one church over another.

A First Amendment provision regarding religion that is frequently misunderstood forbids Congress to prohibit the "free exercise" of faith. The freedom to believe in a supreme being necessarily involves the freedom to disbelieve. The freedom to worship requires the freedom not to worship. As a majority of the U.S. Supreme Court ruled in 2005, "the touchstone for our analysis is the principle that the First Amendment mandates government neutrality between religion and religion, and between religion and nonreligion."[5] Under the U.S. Constitution, therefore, the atheist and the believer are equally protected. Thus, the provision of the Texas Constitution—Article 1, Section 4—that requires persons holding public office to "acknowledge the existence of a Supreme Being" is contradicted by the nation's fundamental law and is no longer enforced.

Because of the passion and prejudice that surround the subject of faith, government officials sometimes follow momentary convenience rather than timeless principles when making decisions about religious questions. As a result, the politics of religious freedom is often characterized by inconsistency and hypocrisy.

As Ben Sargent dramatizes in this cartoon, preventing people from expressing their opinion by burning the flag violates the freedom for which the flag stands.

Courtesy of Ben Sargent

**Competency Connection**
**PERSONAL RESPONSIBILITY**

While political protest is one of a number of basic American rights, what are the appropriate limitations to those rights? Or put another way, when do individuals have to consider the rights of others before they exercise their own?

# ISSUE SPOTLIGHT:
## Slavery Still Exists in Texas

One tragedy in Texas Human Rights is human trafficking, and government response to solving the problem is just now beginning to recognize the challenge. Human trafficking has become a topic about which more and more Texans are aware, and yet the problem persists. **Human trafficking** is the exploitation of men, women, and children for forced labor or sex by a third-party for profit or gain. It is estimated that this form of slavery is far more pervasive than many people think, and it is one issue that does not separate Texans by ideology or by political party. Yet the heartbreaking personal stories of tragedy and exploitation are far too common.

One example of this tragedy was reported in the *Dallas Morning News* in 2018. In West Dallas, for three years, a number of women were confined in a 672-square-foot home. They were drugged, raped, beaten, and forced to perform sex acts for money. Cameras were installed to monitor the women's movements, and one of the traffickers apparently stationed himself at the front door with a weapon to prevent escape.

A second example came in an operation that covered Dallas, Lewisville, and Commerce, Texas, where at least sixteen women were being housed in a commercial building in Dallas. The prostitution ring was run out of illicit massage businesses named "Jasmine," "Passion," and "Blue Star/Charming." The businesses were busted by federal, state, and local law enforcement agents in February 2019.

A third case comes from Houston, where a fourteen-year-old girl was forced into prostitution. She was a runaway who was rescued from a motel where her pimp had "groomed" her to become a prostitute.

These are but three of dozens of recent examples that could be reported. In all, it is estimated that there are more than 234,000 victims of sex trafficking in Texas at any given point in time and that there are more than 79,000 youth victims.

In 2019, Governor Abbott signed five bills aimed at combating human trafficking--enhancing tools for combating online trafficking, eliminating the backlog in checking rape kit results, creating a Sexual Assault Survivors' Task Force within the Office of the Governor, providing funds to aid victims of sex trafficking, and providing enhanced access for victims of trafficking to specially trained health professionals.

**human trafficking** A form of modern day slavery, it is the exploitation of men, women, and children for forced labor or sex by a third-party for profit or gain.

**Competency Connection**
**PERSONAL RESPONSIBILITY**

What can you, as an average citizen, do to help resolve the problem of human trafficking?

Sources: "Sex Slavery Bust in Dallas Reveals a Big Problem for the City, and Texas," *Dallas Morning News*, June 21, 2018; Domingo Ramirez, Jr., "Former College Assistant Basketball Coach Accused in Dallas Sex-trafficking Operation," *Fort Worth Star Telegram*, February 21, 2019; Julian Gill, "14-Year-Old Girl Rescued from Sex Trafficking at Harris County Motel, Constable Says," *Houston Chronicle*, February 22, 2019; Texas Attorney General Website, https://www.texasattorneygeneral.gov/initiatives/human-trafficking; Jane Nelson, "Human Trafficking Takes Up Residence, but Has No Home, in Texas," *Fort Worth Star Telegram*, January 26, 2019.

Nevertheless, courts have devised some tests with which to bring a measure of rationality to their decisions. On the one hand, the courts usually do not permit a general law protecting the public welfare to be violated in the name of religious freedom. For example, early in the twentieth century, Texas courts ruled that parents could not refuse to have their children vaccinated against smallpox on the grounds that it was contrary to their religious convictions. Similarly, Texas courts ruled that members of a church were not denied their freedom of religion by a zoning ordinance that restricted use of property surrounding the church to single-family dwellings.[6] (This particular principle may be due for a rethinking—see the box entitled "A Conflict of Good Causes.")

On the other hand, laws conflicting with religious beliefs may sometimes be overturned if the public interest is not seriously threatened. For example, in 1938, a Texas appellate court, anticipating a similar U.S. Supreme Court ruling five years later, held that a parent who refused to salute the flag as a matter of religious conviction could not be deprived of custody of his or her child.[7]

In Texas, as in other states, religious belief can be intense, and religious people can sometimes be intolerant of others who do not share their beliefs. Politicians responding to their constituencies sometimes take actions that threaten the religious rights of people whose views happen to be in the minority. When they do so, they come into conflict with the federal Constitution, and religious fervor is translated into political tension.

A major issue of this sort is the question of religious recitation in public schools. In 1962 and 1963, the U.S. Supreme Court ruled that a nondenominational prayer used in public schools,[8] the reading of the Bible, and the recitation of the Lord's Prayer[9] were unconstitutional. The basis of the decisions was that the prayer was a Christian ritual imposed upon all children of a school, many of whom might be non-Christian. Because the prayer takes place in a public school, it is an example of the "establishment" of religion outlawed by the First Amendment.

Although the reasoning of these decisions is difficult to refute, they have been controversial. Americans still support the idea of prayer in schools, but support has declined among Catholics and mainstream Protestants while remaining very strong among conservative evangelicals.[10] Many local politicians and school boards try to evade the Court's pronouncements by sneaking in prayer under some other name. As a result, the courts still deal with school prayer cases.

A good example is the situation in Santa Fe, on the Texas mainland north of Galveston. The population of this small town is about 90 percent Protestant with a significant representation of conservative evangelicals. In the 1990s, encouraged by the Santa Fe school board, teachers and students began pushing their variety of religion in the classrooms. For example, a teacher handed out flyers advertising a revival, schools invited representatives of the Gideon Bible society to campus to proselytize, and a Protestant chaplain was recruited to read prayers at school ceremonies.

Two sets of parents, one Catholic and the other Mormon, filed suit against such spiritual propaganda in 1995. Realizing the legal threat, the Santa Fe school board forbade most of the objectionable activities. It retained, however, the practice of allowing one student, elected by majority vote of the student body, to recite a "brief invocation and/or message" over the stadium's public address system before each high school football game. The parents sued again, pointing out that a majority of the student body would always pick a Protestant to speak the "message," which would invariably be a prayer, meaning that this state institution was being used to subject their children to a religious message. In other words, the parents argued, the Texas government was imposing an establishment of religion on their children, an action that violated the First Amendment.

Texas's Republican establishment, part of a political coalition that includes the Christian Right (see Chapters 3 and 4), supported the school board. The fact that a public opinion survey showed that 82 percent of Texans agreed that students should be allowed to lead prayers over public address systems before sporting events no doubt encouraged the politicians to endorse the Santa Fe majority.[11]

"Have we actually reached the point as a society where saying a prayer for the health and well-being of the players and the safe return home of the visiting team is no longer acceptable in Texas?" asked party chair Susan Weddington. Attorney General John Cornyn and Governor George W. Bush filed a "friend of the court" brief supporting Santa Fe's position. "The Santa Fe district's students have a constitutionally protected right to . . . offer a prayer before football games," wrote Cornyn.[12]

Because it dealt with a First Amendment issue, the Santa Fe lawsuit was decided by federal rather than Texas courts. In June 2000, the U.S. Supreme Court affirmed that the Santa Fe pre-game "message" was unconstitutional. At their next meeting, the school board eliminated the policy, and that particular squabble about civil liberties was over.[13]

The general issue, however, has shown no sign of exiting from Texas politics. In 2003, the Texas legislature passed a law requiring that all the state's schoolchildren must begin the day with a quasi-religious ritual. First they must recite the Pledge of Allegiance to the American flag, then the Texas Pledge, and then observe a minute of silence (during which, presumably, most of them would pray, although that activity was not required in the statute). The law was certainly intended to instill patriotism in children.[14] In 2007, the words "under God" were added to the Texas Pledge by the legislature. The bill's sponsor said that it was simply a "commonsense" move to bring the Pledge into conformity with the U.S. Pledge of Allegiance. On October 13, 2010, the federal Fifth Circuit court ruled that the Pledge did not constitute an establishment clause issue. There was no violation of separation of church and state. The court concluded that there was a **secular** justification for the addition of "under God," writing, "There can be no doubt that mirroring the national pledge and acknowledging the state's religious heritage are permissible secular purposes."[15]

Freedom of religion issues persist. As President Trump moves to build a wall along the Rio Grande as a barrier along the Southern Border of the United States, La Comita Chapel in Mission has challenged the right of the government to take its land to build a barrier, claiming religious freedom. The church has challenged the government's right to survey their property in preparation for building a barrier, arguing that any access to their property, according to a lawyer representing the church, "violates the sacred nature of the place, though a federal court has allowed the survey to proceed."[16]

Without question, however, the general issue remains unsettled. The future of Texas holds many more laws, and many more lawsuits, on the subject of church and state.

**secular** A term that means "apart from religion." Public policies must serve a secular, as opposed to a religious, purpose to avoid establishing a religion.

## A Right to Keep and Bear Arms?

Perennially, crime is an important political issue in the United States in general, and Texas in particular. One suggested way to reduce the number of homicides is to restrict access to guns. On the one hand, because firearms killed 39,773 people in the United States in 2017 (3,513 of them in Texas), it is logical to argue that the crime rate would be lower if fewer people had guns.[17]

On the other hand, there are about 14 million hunters in the country and millions more who own firearms, so there is also a great resistance to the idea of gun control. Many people believe that law-abiding citizens would be safer from crime if they were allowed to carry concealed weapons for self-defense. Although there were only 353 justifiable homicides (defense of persons or property) by private citizens in the United States in 2017, *protective* uses of guns against burglary, assault, and robbery as a deterrent to crime is, of course, far more prevalent.[18] Thus, rational arguments exist both for and against an armed citizenry.

The shadows of two recent mass shootings in Texas continue to shape discourse. One was a shooting at the First Baptist Church of Sutherland Springs, Texas on November 25, 2017. A gunman toting a semi-automatic rifle opened fire on the congregation during worship, killing 26 people and wounding 20 others in the deadliest church shooting in American history. Then, on May 18, 2018, a disturbed student entered his school, Santa Fe High School, carrying a pump-action shotgun, and killed ten people, injuring thirteen others. While these two events haven't changed Texas laws, they have put a new frame on the question of how to deal with gun violence in Texas. The Second Amendment to the U.S. Constitution reads: "A well-regulated Militia, being necessary to the security of a free State, the right of the people to keep and bear Arms, shall not be infringed." The National Rifle Association, an organization with a 2018 membership of nearly 5 million, is particularly tireless in arguing that the individual "right to keep and bear arms" is guaranteed by the Second Amendment. Although public opinion surveys consistently show that two thirds of the American people, and 51 percent of Texans, favor stricter gun control, many politicians echo the claim that the Second Amendment prohibits all regulation of firearms.[19]

Furthermore, a significant proportion of Texans evidently believe that they have a constitutional guarantee to own anything from a purse pistol to an assault rifle and that government does not have the legitimate authority to do anything about it. Many Texans agree with Lt. Governor Dan Patrick, who, two days after the Santa Fe High School tragedy, voiced that guns are not the problem but "are part of who we are as a nation."[20]

Traditionally, the Second Amendment was interpreted as protecting state militias—that is, official state military organizations, not private clubs or vigilante groups—from being disbanded by the federal government.[21]

In June 2008, the U.S. Supreme Court established a new view of the meaning of the Second Amendment, finding for the first time in history that it protected the rights of individuals to own firearms. This decision was extended in 2010 to apply the Second Amendment protections directly to the states in the case of *McDonald* v. *Chicago*.[22] The Court's reasoning in these cases clarified some issues, while leaving others open for future litigation. Both were 5–4 decisions. The reasoning of the decisions rested on three grounds: (1) that the second clause of the Amendment ("the right to keep and bear arms") is controlling, and is meant to ensure the right of self-defense as well as protection against tyranny; (2) that the first clause (calling for a "well-regulated militia") originally referred to "all males physically capable of acting in concert for the common defense" rather than an organized military force; and (3) that state constitutions in existence at the same time justify this interpretation (since the Bill of Rights was intended to extend provisions of state constitutions to the national government). These decisions, while clear on the right to bear arms, do not settle lingering questions about *which kinds of arms* will ultimately be deemed to be protected.

The Texas Constitution, in Section 23 of the Bill of Rights (Article 1), guarantees that "Every citizen shall have the right to keep and bear arms in the lawful defense of himself or the State, but the Legislature shall have power, by law, to regulate the wearing of arms, with a view to prevent crime." Because of strong support in Texas, the state's public policy has long been permissive of private gun ownership.[23] In 1995, the state legislature passed a law allowing Texans who have undergone ten hours of training to carry concealed handguns, and affirming the right of a citizen to defend his or her home against intrusion (this is known as the **castle doctrine**). Many local governments, however, continued to ban firearms from various areas within their jurisdiction, such as city buses, libraries, and senior citizen centers. In 2003, pro-gun groups persuaded the legislature to pass a law preempting local authority to regulate concealed weapons. Under this law, only the state can designate areas where weapons are banned.[24] The 1995 law was explicit in permitting citizens to defend their homes with deadly force. It was ambiguous, however, about the extent to which they might defend their property outside the home. In 2007, the legislature clarified this point. It passed a law extending the castle doctrine to defense against unlawful entry of a vehicle or workplace. During the 2015 session, the legislature passed a law allowing students and professors to carry weapons on campus with the hope that they might be a deterrent to campus violence. A number of professors objected to the law, arguing it might bring more gun violence to campus and was not protected by the Second Amendment to the U.S. Constitution because it didn't involve a "well-regulated militia," as required by that amendment. Their arguments were ultimately rejected by the 5th Circuit Court of Appeals in 2018.[25]

## Abortion

Since the famous Texas Supreme Court case of **Roe v. Wade** was decided by the U.S. Supreme Court in 1973, the issue of abortion has been, perhaps, first on the list of divisive and inflammatory political issues.[26] Supporters of legal abortion maintain that the issue is whether a

**castle doctrine** A law allowing Texans who have undergone ten hours of training to carry concealed handguns, and affirming the right of a citizen to defend his or her home against intrusion.

**Roe v. Wade (1973)** A U.S. Supreme Court decision that declared the restrictive Texas abortion law unconstitutional as a violation of a woman's right to privacy.

woman should have the right to control her own body. Opponents insist that the issue is whether the born should be allowed to kill the unborn. The passion of people on each side of the issue has rarely led to productive conversation, but rather has led to division, anger, and, occasionally, violence.

Building on the notion of a personal right to privacy that had been expanding since the mid-1960s—a right grounded in the freedoms granted by the First, Third, Fourth, and Fifth Amendments to the Constitution—the Court wrote in *Roe* that the Bill of Rights protected sexual privacy, including the right to have an abortion. All state antiabortion laws were overturned.

After the *Roe* decision, abortion became a common medical procedure, in Texas as elsewhere. About 55,287 legal abortions were performed in the state in 2015, a number more than 20,000 lower than in 2010.[27] Contributing to the diminished number of abortions is years of actions by the state legislature to make abortions less accessible to people seeking to terminate their pregnancies. *Roe* ignited an emotional national political debate that continues today. People who support the Court, who call themselves "pro-choice," argue that the decision to terminate a pregnancy should be made by the woman and her doctor; government has no business interfering. Those who disagree, styling themselves "pro-life," argue that to terminate a pregnancy is to commit homicide and that government has every obligation to prevent such a crime.

One of the arguments of the pro-choice forces is that no court, federal or otherwise, should have the authority to intervene in an area of public policy that impinges on such deeply held personal values as the nature and beginning of human life. Pro-life activists say that an "independent" judiciary that preempts the legislature—the people's representatives—from creating policy in an area of passionately felt moral opinions is short-circuiting democracy. Pro-life citizens therefore believe that in this area, unelected judges have no legitimacy. Pro-choice advocates, looking to the courts to protect what has become, to them, an important civil liberty, support the concept of an independent judiciary.

As we discussed in Chapters 3 and 4, the Texas Republican Party is strongly influenced by the Christian Right, which is intensely antiabortion. With large majorities in both houses of the legislature, therefore, its representatives have frequently enacted laws that place restrictions on abortion within the state.

**parental notification law** A law requiring that, before a girl under the age of eighteen could get an abortion, her physician must inform her parents. Parents could not stop the operation, but they would have forty-eight hours to counsel the girl about her choices.

The 1999 legislature passed a **parental notification law**, requiring that, before a girl under the age of eighteen could get an abortion, her physician must inform her parents. Parents could not stop the operation, but they would have forty-eight hours to counsel the girl about her choices.

Since 1999, the legislature has acted in virtually every session to place additional restrictions on abortion, befitting the fact that conservative Republicans have controlled the legislature completely since 2003. The 2003 legislature enacted two lasting laws discouraging abortion. First, the Women's Right to Know Act required that any woman must sign a statement at least twenty-four hours before the termination of her pregnancy affirming that she had been given access to photos of fetal development and information regarding the risks of abortion and pregnancy. Second, the Prenatal Protection Act amended the state's penal code to define an "individual" as beginning at the moment of fertilization and allowing criminal charges or civil lawsuits to be filed when an unborn child is killed.[28]

In 2005, the legislature passed a law that severely restricted the ability of doctors to perform abortions during the last three months of pregnancy, and required them to get the written permission of a girl's parents before performing an abortion on her at any stage of her pregnancy. In early 2007, Abbott rendered an Attorney General's opinion, stating that a doctor could not be charged with a capital crime for violating the state's abortion laws, which had been a possible consequence of the 2005 law.[29]

In 2010, the legislature added a sonogram requirement, meaning that any woman seeking an abortion would first have to view a sonogram of her fetus before the procedure could be done. The bill had 62 percent support among Texans.[30]

In 2013, after a filibuster by Senator Wendy Davis of Fort Worth staved off passage of a restrictive abortion law during what Governor Rick Perry called a second special session of the legislature. In the second session, the legislature passed one of the nation's most restrictive abortion laws. It banned abortions after twenty weeks of pregnancy, required that clinics performing legal abortions meet the same standards as other surgical facilities, and mandated that a physician who performs abortions have admitting privileges at a hospital within thirty miles. It also required oversight of women taking the "abortion pill" (RU 486) by a physician. The law did not restrict abortions necessary to save the mother's life. Effectively, the law had the impact of forcing all but a few clinics to close in the state. Opponents of the law immediately challenged it as violating the federal Constitution, but the Fifth Circuit Court of Appeals ruled that the law "on its face does not impose an undue burden on the life and health of a woman."[31]

The 2017 session yielded more restrictions: that fetal tissue be buried or cremated, regardless of whether it comes from a miscarriage or abortion, that a common procedure for second-trimester abortions, called "dismemberment abortions" by anti-abortion activists be banned, and that medical research on fetal tissue from abortions be banned along with further penalties for buying and selling fetal body parts. During a 2017 special session, more restrictions were added, including that abortion could not be covered under basic health care coverage packages under the federal Affordable Care Act.[32]

If a single lesson can be learned from the history of the abortion debate, it is that political conflicts that derive from strongly held, clashing moral convictions cannot be resolved by judges. Perhaps they cannot be resolved at all.

## Civil Rights

**civil rights** The constitutional claims all citizens have to fair and equal treatment under the law. Among the most important civil rights are the ability to vote in honest elections, to run for and serve in public office, and to be afforded a fair trial presided over by an impartial judge if accused of a crime. Civil rights refer to actions that government must take in order to ensure equal citizenship for everyone.

Broadly speaking, *civil liberties* refers to citizens' rights to be free of government regulation of their personal conduct, whereas **civil rights** refers to the claim that the members of all groups have to be treated equally with the members of other groups. Generally, if government harasses individual people because of something they have said or done, it may have taken away a civil liberty. If government oppresses groups of people because of some ethnic, gender, or other category to which they belong, it has violated their civil rights.

Historically, the domination of Texas by the traditionalist political culture inhibited state courts from actively protecting the civil rights of African Americans, Mexican Americans, women, and the LGBTQ (Lesbian, Gay, Bisexual, Transsexual, and Queer) community. Jim Crow laws, Black Codes, poll taxes, racial profiling, preventing women from serving on juries, and other infringements on rights and liberties existed undisturbed by the state judicial system for decades. These blights on democracy were overturned by federal, not state, courts.

### School Segregation

In 1954, the U.S. Supreme Court rendered one of the landmark decisions of its history. In a unanimous verdict, the Court ruled in *Brown* v. *Board of Education* that public schools that were segregated on the basis of race were in violation of the "equal protection of the laws" clause of the Fourteenth Amendment.[33] This decision was intensely disagreeable to the ruling Anglos in Texas and the sixteen other states that had segregated schools and, at first, sparked a great deal of obstruction and evasion.

In 1970, for example, Sam Tasby, an African American, sued the Dallas Independent School District (DISD) in federal court because his son was unable to attend a White school near his home. The DISD was in almost continuous litigation for more than thirty years thereafter, spending millions of tax dollars to draw up unsatisfactory desegregation plans and then contest the adverse rulings of the courts. In 2000, long after Mr. Tasby's son was grown and out of school, DISD officials decided that compliance was a better strategy than resistance. By 2003, U.S. District Judge Barefoot Sanders decided that "the segregation prohibited by the United States Constitution" no longer existed in DISD and ended federal court supervision. By that time, the composition of the district's students had declined from 59 percent White to 7 percent, the percentage of Hispanic students had risen to 59 percent, and the percentage of African Americans had held steady at a third of the population.[34]

Even after desegregation, schools occasionally still attempt to defy the federal courts by segregating their students within schools by ethnicity. For example, although North Dallas's Preston Hollow Elementary School was officially integrated, in practice the principal assigned White students to one set of classes, and minority students to another set. In 2006, a Hispanic parent sued. Federal judge Sam Lindsay found for the parent, writing that the principal was acting unconstitutionally by "in effect, operating at taxpayers' expense, a private school for Anglo children within a public school that was predominantly minority."[35]

Despite such attempts to bring back the Old South, the major problem today is not that school districts deliberately separate students, but that economic class separates them. Because poor people and middle-class people tend to live in different areas, and especially because the poorer tend to make their homes in the cities while the wealthier often live in the suburbs, citizens of different economic classes are served by different school districts. And because poorer districts cannot afford to supply adequate schooling, economic disparity is turned into educational inequality. Additionally, the creation of charter schools in public schools districts and the continually growing number of private elementary and secondary schools for those who can afford them, have created even more ways to segregate by social class. This is one of the major civil rights problems of the twenty-first century. For many states, Texas included, it has raised the question of whether education should be considered a civil right.

## Education: A Basic Right?

In 1987, Texas District Judge Harley Clark outraged the Texas political establishment by ruling in *Edgewood* v. *Kirby* that the state's system of financing its public schools violated the state constitution and laws. Clark's ruling referred to Article 7, Section 1, which requires the "Legislature of the state to establish an efficient system of public free schools," and part of Article I, which asserts that "All free men … have equal rights." Additionally, the Texas Education Code states that "public education is a state responsibility," that "a thorough and efficient system [is to] be provided," and that "each student enrolled in the public school system shall have access to programs and services that are appropriate to his or her needs and that are substantially equal to those available to any similar student, notwithstanding varying local economic factors."

At the time of that ruling, the state's educational system did not begin to offer equal services to every child. During the 1985–1986 school year, when the *Edgewood* case was being prepared, the wealthiest school district in Texas had $14 million in taxable property per student, and the poorest district had $20,000. The Whiteface Independent School District (ISD) in the Texas Panhandle taxed its property owners at $0.30 per $100 of value and spent $9,646 per student. The Morton ISD, just north of Whiteface, taxed its property owners at $0.96 per $100 evaluation, but because of the lower value of its property was able to spend only $3,959 per student.[36]

Gross disparities such as these made a mockery of the constitutional and statutory requirements, as well as the demands of democratic theory for equal educational funding. An estimated 1 million out of the state's 3 million schoolchildren were receiving inadequate instruction because their local districts could not afford to educate them. Democracy requires only equality of opportunity, not equality of result. But inequality of education must inevitably translate into inequality of opportunity. The courts were following the dictates of democratic theory in attempting to force the rest of the political system to educate all Texas children equally. (It is worth noting that since 1971, twenty state supreme courts have likewise held that their states' school funding systems unconstitutionally discriminated against poor districts.)[37]

The appropriate remedy was to transfer some revenue from wealthy to poorer districts. But, given the distribution of power in Texas, and especially the way it is represented in the legislature, this strategy was nearly impossible. As explained in Chapters 4 and 5, because of the lack of voting participation by the state's poorer citizens, its wealthier citizens are overrepresented in the legislature.[38] Despite the fact that a badly educated citizenry was a drag on the state's economy and therefore a problem for everyone, taxpayers in wealthier districts resisted giving up their money to educate the children of the poor in some other district. Their representatives refused to vote for some sort of revenue redistribution, regardless of what the court had said.

In 1989, the Texas Supreme Court unanimously upheld Clark's ruling that the system was unconstitutional, and told the legislature to fix it. After four years of stalling, the legislature passed a law that would take about $450 million in property taxes from ninety-eight high-wealth districts and distribute the money to poor districts. (The media dubbed this the "Robin Hood law," after the twelfth-century English bandit who allegedly robbed from the rich and gave to the poor.) In 1995, the Texas Supreme Court upheld the new law by a bare 5-to-4 majority, but that did not end the issue.

Wealthy citizens continued to complain about the Robin Hood law. Beginning in 2001, several school districts challenged the plan on the grounds that it violated the state constitution. In order to fulfill their obligations both to their own and to other districts' children, they argued, they were forced to peg their property-tax rates at the constitutional ceiling of $1.50 per $100 of assessed evaluation. Therefore, by in effect forcing all districts to tax at the same top rate, the Robin Hood law violated the constitution's ban on a statewide property tax.

In November 2005, the state supreme court declared the Robin Hood law unconstitutional on the narrow grounds that it forced school districts into a statewide property tax. The court did not address the larger issue of whether redistribution of wealth between rich and poor districts was itself constitutional.[39]

In a 2006 special session, the state's $10.5 billion surplus made it easy for the legislature to increase the amount of money the state would give to poor districts—the state's share of funding public education went up from 38 percent to about half—while cutting property taxes for wealthier citizens and reducing the amount that wealthy districts had to share. The whole agreeable scheme depended on the continued generation of a surplus by a roaring state economy, but the American recession beginning in 2008 made revenue insufficient to resolve the problem (see Chapter 12 for a detailed discussion of this issue). As the 2019 session began, there was continued concern about education finance with the large reliance on property taxes making Texas have among the highest property tax rates in the country. Proposals were introduced to use general funds from the state to allow for property tax relief.[40]

Nevertheless, more than two decades of litigation and political struggle have made one thing clear. The state judiciary, at least in this one area, has become the champion of the underdog. There never would have been a Robin Hood law in 1993 or a special legislative session in 2006 if the courts had not held the feet of the legislature and the governor to the fire. Although Texas courts are lagging on civil rights and civil liberties, they are ahead of the curve in educational equity. In this one area, Texas judges are attempting to force the people of Texas to live up to their democratic ideals.

## Civil Rights in Modern Texas: Jasper and Tulia

Even though the civil rights atmosphere in Texas is very different from what it was a few decades ago, there are still problems to overcome before everyone is treated equally under the law. In the not too distant past, two intense confrontations between the attitudes of the Old

South traditionalist culture and progressive racial policies occurred in the towns of Jasper, in 1998 and 1999, and Tulia, in the first years of the new century.

In June 1998, three White men chained an African American named James Byrd, Jr., by his ankles to the bumper of a pickup truck and dragged him three miles down country roads, leaving his mangled corpse by the gate of a traditionally Black cemetery. This horrendous murder in Jasper, Texas, which raised collective memories of the days when dozens of southern Black men were lynched every year, shocked the nation and attracted enormous media attention. For a few distraught hours, it almost seemed to people of goodwill that no progress had been made in Texas race relations in a century.[41]

Soon, however, the differences between old and new Texas became clear. Two days after the crime, three White men were arrested; they still had Byrd's blood on their clothing. All three men had poor education and criminal records. Two were avowed racists. Soon, the killers were convicted, two receiving the death penalty and the other a life sentence. Meanwhile, at James Byrd's funeral, citizens of every color had mourned together.

The Jasper murder and its aftermath underscored that although racism remains virulent in Texas, it is neither dominant nor respectable. The killers were on the fringes of society; indeed, two were virtually career criminals. Texas officials unanimously expressed outrage at the actions of the criminals, and in Jasper, no one attempted to defend them.

While the Jasper drama was unfolding, a different kind of civil rights outrage was beginning in Tulia, a small town between Amarillo and Lubbock. In January 1998, the Panhandle Regional Narcotics Task Force hired Thomas Coleman, a former law enforcement officer, as an undercover agent. Regional drug task forces, financed by federal money but answerable to the governor's office, are special law enforcement agencies that span jurisdictional boundaries and traditionally operate without much outside scrutiny. The members of this one did not discover that Coleman had left many of his jobs under an ethical cloud and that he was, as one journalist would later summarize, "a racist, a liar, and a thief."[42] Working with the Swisher County prosecutor's office, Coleman began conducting undercover "sting" operations in Tulia, looking for drug pushers.

In July 1999, police and sheriff's officers arrested forty-six people, most of them African American, but a few Hispanic, whom Coleman accused of having sold him illegal drugs. In a series of trials and plea bargains, by the spring of 2000, thirty-eight of these people had been convicted of drug charges. Several later explained that they had accepted plea bargains because, having seen the sentences handed down after the first convictions—60, 99, and 434 years—they were convinced by their lawyers that their best strategy was to plead guilty

Human trafficking can have devastating consequences. This semi-truck was used to smuggle people in to Texas from Mexico. It was found abandoned in San Antonio is 2017. Eight people had died in the trailer of suffocation. Thirty more people had to be taken to hospitals; 17 with life threatening injuries. See box on p.243 for discussion.

AP Images/Eric Gay

and accept a lesser sentence, even though they were innocent. Coleman's testimony was the only evidence against any of these people. He never produced any drugs or drug paraphernalia to substantiate his accusations, and no drugs were found when any of the defendants were arrested. Nevertheless, Coleman was named "Outstanding Lawman of the Year" by the Texas Narcotics Control Program.

Soon after the Tulia defendants went to prison, journalists and the NAACP began to raise public doubts. For one thing, it did not seem to make sense that Tulia, a town of about 5,000 residents, could support so many drug pushers. For another, investigations into Coleman's past turned up people willing to testify to his habitual disregard for the truth, his tendency to steal, and his hostility toward Black citizens. As the evidence mounted of something rotten in Tulia, the state's judicial system was persuaded to act.

In 2003, state judge Ron Chapman investigated the case. After hearing from many witnesses, including Coleman, the judge, prosecutors, and defense attorneys agreed that, in the words of Chapman's opinion, "Coleman's repeated instances of verifiably perjurious testimony render him entirely unbelievable under oath."

By the end of 2003, all the Tulia defendants had been released from prison and pardoned by Governor Perry. In March 2004, the city of Amarillo agreed to pay $6 million to

## ISSUE SPOTLIGHT:
### Thought-Crime or Emotion-Crime?

In the 1999 legislature, Senator Rodney Ellis, an African American from Houston, sponsored a bill that attempted to clarify Texas's 1993 hate crime law. Because of its vagueness, this law had been employed to prosecute criminals only twice since it had been passed, despite the occurrence of more than 300 hate crimes a year in Texas.

Supporters of the bill contended that the Byrd murder highlighted the need for additional measures to protect people from being assaulted because they happened to belong to an unpopular group. The bill passed the House, but failed in the Senate. Several arguments were made against the measure. Some critics pointed out that, without a new law, Byrd's killers had been swiftly brought to justice and given the ultimate penalty—why was another law necessary? Others expressed discomfort with the idea of punishing criminals for the thought behind their crime rather than for the crime itself. Still others argued that to punish criminals based on the identity of their victim would be to deny the equal protection of the laws to victims who were not included under the law's protection. Finally, some politicians refused to vote for a law extending special protection to homosexuals, asserting that such a consideration would be tantamount to endorsing their behavior.

By 2001, however, the temper of the state had changed. The legislature passed, and Governor Perry signed into law, the "James Byrd Jr. Hate Crimes Act" in May. It increased penalties for crimes that were motivated by hostility to race, color, disability, religion, national origin or ancestry, age, and gender and sexual orientation.

Competency Connection
**CRITICAL THINKING**

How well can the state determine the "thoughts," as opposed to the "actions," of people accused of crime?

Sources: Nathan A. Kracklauer, "The Crusade Against Hate: A Critical Review of Bias Crime Legislation," Plan II honors thesis, University of Texas at Austin, May 1, 2000; *Crime in Texas 1998* (Austin: Department of Public Safety, 1999), 61; Terence Stutz, "Hate Crimes Bill Fails," *Dallas Morning News*, May 14, 1999, A1; The Power of One Web site: www.powerofone.org/.

In 2017, the Texas Legislature passed a "sanctuary cities" bill requiring that cities not harbor undocumented residents from law enforcement agencies. Here, cartoonist Ben Sargent suggests that the sanctuary cities bill might jeopardize due process for undocumented immigrants or Hispanic citizens who might be profiled as illegally in the country.

Courtesy of Ben Sargent

**Competency Connection**
**PERSONAL RESPONSIBILITY**

Is it the responsibility of people of color to carry proper identification with them everywhere so that they can prove citizenship?

the forty-five Tulia defendants in return for their agreement to drop lawsuits (an average of $133,000 each). By the end of 2004, Tom Coleman had been convicted of aggravated perjury and imprisoned.[43]

In both Tulia and Jasper, eventually justice was done. For much of the history of Texas, crimes against minorities were everyday occurrences in the state. Texas officials did not concern themselves with injustices to African Americans or Latinos, and did not respond to accusations that their rights had been violated. In that sense, Jasper and Tulia show us how far Texas has progressed in granting equal rights to all its citizens.

But while open racism has been discredited, it has given way to other forms of more subtle discrimination. In Texas, and around the nation, patterns of discrimination in law enforcement show that progress yet needs to be made. For example, recent research reported by the *Austin American-Statesman* shows that Hispanics and African Americans are more likely to be searched pursuant to a traffic stop than are White Americans. In San Antonio, public records demonstrate that, although policemen do not use force in making arrests frequently, when they do, officers subdue Hispanics and African Americans at 78 percent higher rates than White suspects. One study, conducted by two criminal justice professors at the University of North Texas, suggests that this disparity may not be due to systematic racial profiling, but the study does admit that the disparity exists. Law enforcement professionals deny racial discrimination, but the patterns do exist. Might it be subtle, and might it not be intentional? Perhaps, but clearly patterns of racial disparity exist.[44]

## Civil Rights for Convicted Criminals

People convicted of crimes are still citizens, and although they lose many of their civil rights, they retain others. The Eighth Amendment to the U.S. Constitution forbids "cruel and unusual punishments," and most people probably agree that however much they fear and dislike criminals, there is something unseemly about subjecting them to torture or bestial conditions while they are incarcerated.

For most of the twentieth century, however, state prison systems, especially in the South, were places where criminals were subjected to treatment that, if not unusual, was certainly cruel. A number of states even passed laws declaring the inmates of correctional institutions to be legally dead during their confinement. They might sue the state for violation of their rights after being released—being returned to life—but the chances of receiving justice months or years after the fact were remote.

In the 1960s, however, as federal courts became more receptive to civil rights cases, literally hundreds of suits were brought in areas such as access to courts, mail censorship, medical care, solitary confinement, racial discrimination, work programs, staff standards and training, and a host of other aspects of a prisoner's existence. A glance at the legal record indicates that more cases were being filed against Texas jails and prisons than against those of any other state.[45]

The most important case of this type, and one that attracted national attention, began in 1972. An inmate brought suit against the Texas Department of Corrections (TDC), alleging cruel and unusual punishment of the 15,700 inmates in Texas prisons. In *Ruiz* v. *Estelle*, David Ruiz accused the TDC of violating prisoners' constitutional rights in the following five areas:

1. The physical security of prisoners
2. Living and working conditions
3. Medical care
4. Internal punishment administered by the TDC
5. Access to courts of law

Testimony in the case revealed horrific differences between the ideal system portrayed by top TDC officials and the actual conditions that existed within the prisons. Among the more chilling revelations was the fact that guards rarely entered the prisoners' cell blocks. Internal security was maintained by "building tenders"—privileged prisoners—who maintained order by terrorizing other inmates with lead pipes and other weapons.

Federal Judge William Wayne Justice ruled in favor of Ruiz, finding the TDC guilty of violating the Eighth Amendment. He ordered the organization to make a series of changes in its housing and treatment of prisoners. State officials reacted by "stonewalling"—denying that poor conditions existed, criticizing Judge Justice's "interference," and stalling on reform. The case dragged on for years before Governor Clements and other officials finally agreed to spend the money to make an effort to bring the TDC up to minimum standards.[46]

In 1992, Judge Justice approved a partial settlement of the Ruiz case, and the state was put back in charge of most of its prison functions. He warned Texas authorities, however, that the federal government would be monitoring its treatment of prisoners. In 2002, when David Ruiz was sixty years old, and the state prison system housed 145,000 inmates, Justice approved an agreement ending the lawsuit.[47]

As with any social change, the recognition that prisoners and others in state custody are human beings and have constitutional rights came about only with difficulty. The state resisted, and the federal courts had to step in. But much progress has been made. Official attitudes and programs today are more enlightened than those of the 1980s.

## Capital Punishment

**capital punishment** The execution of a convicted criminal, normally imposed only on murderers.

Texas is one of thirty-one states that imposes **capital punishment**—the death penalty—for specific types of murder. The state reserves the ultimate punishment of lethal injection for "capital felony"—criminal homicide associated with one or more of eight aggravating circumstances.[48] Some examples of those circumstances would be murder of a peace officer or firefighter, murder for hire, and murder of a child under six.[49]

Capital punishment is a highly controversial issue in Texas, in the United States, and internationally (see the "You Decide" box). The great majority of Texans approve of imposing the death penalty for criminals who have been convicted of a capital felony, but the trends show that Texans now have attitudes more similar to national trends than they used to be. Overall, 65 percent of Texans supported capital punishment in 2018, but that is a 10 percent decline compared to three years before. The decline is almost all among Democrats, where support for the death penalty dropped by 15 percent (from 61 percent to 46 percent) while among Republicans, support remained overwhelming and constant (dropping only slightly, from 88–85 percent). These numbers reflect the general polarization between the parties and reflect national party trends.[50] An ancient Greek definition of justice is "getting what one deserves." The majority of citizens believe that some people have committed crimes so terrible that they "deserve to die." Yet, many scholars and people of conscience argue that the death penalty does not deter crime and only adds a public, official murder to the private, unauthorized murder committed by the criminal. Both sides in the debate feel strongly. As with other emotional social issues such as abortion, the courts are not able to resolve the dispute.

## You Decide: Is Capital Punishment Justified?

Large majorities of citizens in the United States as a whole and in Texas in particular support capital punishment, but a vocal minority strongly opposes the practice. The arguments for and against capital punishment are both moral and practical.

### Pro

⬆ Executions are expensive because they are delayed by frivolous appeals. Eliminate those appeals and the cost will fall.

⬆ Not executing people costs lives. Convicts escape and kill, and they kill while in prison. No executed person has ever committed murder again. New scientific techniques, such as DNA testing, make the system less mistake-prone.

⬆ Social science studies are inconclusive as to whether capital punishment deters crime. Besides, a main purpose of capital punishment is retribution, not deterrence.

⬆ Forcing a murderer to pay for his or her crimes with his or her life is not wrong; it is justice.

⬆ The great majority of Americans believe that killing is sometimes justified, as in defense of the country or to punish murderers.

⬆ Statistical studies show that Black murderers are no more likely to be executed than White murderers.

### Con

⬇ It costs more than $2 million to execute a criminal, about three times the cost of imprisoning someone for forty years.

⬇ No matter how careful the judicial system, some innocent people are bound to be executed.

⬇ The death penalty does not deter criminal behavior.

⬇ Two wrongs do not make a right.

⬇ Killing is always wrong, whether done by an individual or the state.

⬇ The system of capital punishment is racially biased.

Sources: Thomas R. Dye, *Understanding Public Policy*, 8th ed. (Upper Saddle River, NJ: Prentice Hall, 2008), 86–87; Hugo Adam Bedau, ed., *The Death Penalty in America: Current Controversies* (New York: Oxford University, 1997), passim; Audrey Duff, "The Deadly D.A.," *Texas Monthly*, February 1994, 38; Jim Mattox, "Texas' Death Penalty Dilemma," *Dallas Morning News*, August 25, 1993, A23; Thomas Sowell, "The Trade-Offs of the Death Penalty," *Austin American-Statesman*, June 15, 2001, A15; "Death No More," editorial in *Dallas Morning News*, April 15, 2007, P1.

**Competency Connection**
**SOCIAL RESPONSIBILITY**

**Should the state of Texas ban capital punishment so that citizens cannot be complicit in erroneously putting innocent people to death? Explain?**

In 1972, the U.S. Supreme Court stopped the states from carrying out capital punishment because, it ruled, the death penalty was capriciously applied and, especially, racially biased. In 1976, after the states had taken steps to meet the Court's objections, it allowed executions again, subject to a number of rather stringent rules. The state must ensure that whoever imposes the penalty—judge or jury—does so after careful consideration of the character and record of the defendant and the circumstances of the particular crime. States are not allowed to automatically impose capital punishment upon conviction for certain crimes, such as murder of a peace officer. The capital sentencing decision must allow for consideration of whatever mitigating circumstances may be relevant. Capital punishment may be imposed only for crimes resulting in the death of the victim, so no one may be executed for rape, for example.[51]

Texas resumed executions in 1982. Of the states that allow capital punishment, it has been by far the most active in killing convicted criminals. Texas executed 559 people convicted of murder from 1982 through February 2019, far more than its share of those who were put to death nationally. Like the national trend, the number of executions per year in Texas is declining, and Governor Greg Abbott issued a stay of execution for death row inmate Thomas Whittaker in 2018, the first time a governor had commuted a death penalty in over a decade.[52]

Although capital punishment draws persistent criticism (see the "You Decide" box and the story of Cameron Todd Willingham in Chapter 9), its popularity virtually ensures that it will remain the law of the state. Within that overall truth are smaller issues that confront the state's policymakers. Until recently, one of these was the question of whether Texas should create a sentencing category of "life without parole." Until 2005, there were two possible sentences for those convicted of murder: life and the death penalty. Those sentenced to life were eligible for parole after having served forty years. Opponents of the death penalty thought juries would sentence more killers to life if they could be assured that the criminal would never be paroled; consequently, they supported the addition of the new sentencing category. Supporters of capital punishment shared that analysis, and consequently, they opposed the reform.

A related issue is whether a "life-without-parole" option should replace the death penalty. In each legislative session in the recent past, civil liberties groups, anti–capital punishment organizations, and some prosecutors endorsed a bill that would make the change in the state's laws. In each session, however, the bill also was strongly opposed by some big-city prosecutors and victims' rights groups, and failed.

Nevertheless, in 2005, the tide was running against the hard-line position on the death penalty. An awareness of the results of DNA testing, already discussed in Chapter 9, had tended to take the wind out of the sails of those who argued that states do not make mistakes in their judicial processes. Moreover, a series of Supreme Court decisions had made it clear that the justices were losing patience with state judiciaries that seemed too ready to ratify the results of sloppy court processes. As a result, in 2005 the legislature enacted a bill assuring that convicted murderers cannot expect to ever get out of prison. But they will probably be less likely to be sentenced to death.[53]

An issue that continues to create challenges to the death penalty in Texas has to do with the execution of mentally disabled people. Since 2002, it had been ruled unconstitutional for a state to execute a mentally disabled person, but states had been free to use discretion in defining mental disability. In the case of Bobby Moore, a Texas man sentenced to death nearly forty years ago for a Houston robbery and murder, the Texas Court of Criminal Appeals had ruled that Moore was competent to be put to death. But the U.S. Supreme Court overturned the decision, ruling in 2017 that the Court had used outdated standards in deciding on Moore's mental competence. The court again ruled against Moore, but the Supreme Court rejected its ruling again in 2019, saying that "We have found in its opinion too many instances in which, with small variations, it repeats the analysis we previously found wanting, and these same parts are critical to its ultimate conclusion." To reach its conclusion that Moore was not mentally disabled, the Court of Criminal Appeals had relied heavily on whether Moore's conduct showed leadership qualities and on whether he could "hide facts or lie effectively." The Supreme Court ruled those factors not to be grounded in prevailing medical practice.[54]

Another recent issue associated with the death penalty debate is the question of how young a killer must be before he or she is too young to execute. In the history of crime, people as young as six years old have purposefully killed other people, but no one argues that children who become murderers that young should be executed. At what age does a criminal become executable by the state? Traditionally, the official Texas answer was that people who become murderers at seventeen are mature enough to pay the ultimate penalty. In 2002, for example, three men who had committed murder at the age of seventeen were given lethal injections in Huntsville.[55]

Nevertheless, even many people who support capital punishment in general are reluctant to hold seventeen-year-olds to a mortal standard. In virtually every other area, state law has considered someone of that age to be a child and too immature to be trusted with the responsibilities of adulthood. In Texas, seventeen-year-olds are too young to vote, to buy alcohol, or to enter into a contract. To consider them mature enough to forfeit their lives for a crime seems to many people to be a large contradiction.[56]

Texas lawmakers and judges, fearing campaign criticism, seemed content to leave the seventeen-year-old minimum alone. The justices of the U.S. Supreme Court, however, not being under the necessity of defending themselves during election campaigns, had no such fear. In 2005, they struck down the execution of criminals who were younger than eighteen when they committed their crimes. The ruling in effect commuted the sentences of seventy-two convicted murderers nationwide—twenty-eight of whom were in Texas—to life imprisonment, and forbade the capital sentencing of others in the future.[57]

One remaining issue regarding the death penalty involves how the appeals are handled by the Texas Court of Criminal Appeals. In 2007, presiding Judge Sharon Keller decided to close the court at 5 P.M. rather than allow a last-minute appeal in the case of a man executed later that night. Judge Keller was reprimanded for her inaction. That reprimand was later overturned, though Keller's actions were deemed "not exemplary of a public servant."[58]

## Torts and Tort Reform

**tort** A private or civil wrong or injury resulting from a breach of a legal duty that exists by reason of society's expectations about appropriate behavior, rather than a contract. The injured party sues the alleged offender in order to receive compensation for his or her losses.

A **tort** is a private or civil wrong or injury resulting from a breach of a legal duty that exists by reason of society's expectations about appropriate behavior rather than a contract. The allegedly injured party sues the alleged wrongdoer to receive compensation for his or her losses. Because tort actions are civil, not criminal, the losing party does not go to jail, but must pay money to the injured party. The loser may also sometimes have to pay "punitive damages," compensation in excess of the actual damages. These are awarded in the case of willful and malicious misconduct. A doctor whose negligence causes health problems to a patient may be the object of a tort action, as may a company whose defective product causes injury to its customers, a city that fails to warn of a washed-out road, and so on.

Up to 1995, business in Texas had been complaining for years that it was being stifled by unjustified litigation. Doctors joined business leaders in asserting that "pain-and-suffering" awards in malpractice suits had gotten so out of hand that many physicians were being forced to stop treating patients. The tort reform movement thus originated in the opinion of important, wealthy interests that the Texas judicial system was dominated by the wrong values and had to be reined in. "Tort reform" is really "court system reform," in that it consists largely of taking power out of the hands of judges and juries, limiting their discretion, and denying them jurisdiction.

Meanwhile, lawyers and many consumers' groups argued that there was no "litigation crisis" and that the whole tort reform movement was the result of a business-physician political alliance that was misleading the public in order to get away with abuse of consumers. Tim Curtis, executive director of the Texas Citizen Action Network, argued,

"Remember that these defendants include: insurance companies who cheat their policy-holders; manufacturers of dangerous and defective products that have killed and maimed children; inexperienced, careless, or drug impaired doctors who commit medical mal-practice on trusting patients; even unscrupulous lawyers. . . . Legal concepts like joint and several liability and punitive damages have removed countless dangerous products from store shelves. Professionals who abuse their trust have been forced to change their prac-tices or leave the profession.[59]

The anti–tort reform coalition is thus pro-courts. Its purpose is to defend the power and discretion of judges and juries by endorsing the intelligence and justice of their actions in regard to civil litigation.

Whatever was the reality behind the clashing perceptions of the American, and Texas, litigation systems in the early 1990s, business (especially the insurance industry) and doctors launched a massive and well-financed campaign to persuade both state legislatures and Congress to enact comprehensive tort law reform. In Texas, the trend of history was on their side in this endeavor. Traditionally, business and doctors are part of the coalition of the Republican Party, while lawyers and consumer groups are part of the Democratic coalition (see Chapter 4). As Republicans partially took over Texas government in the 1994 election, and then wholly took it over in 2002, they became increasingly able to enact legislation that pleased their core constituency.

# ISSUE SPOTLIGHT:
## Hurry Up and Go Out of Business

At the same time that state lawmakers severely restricted the ability of patients to sue their doctors for malpractice in 2003, they created an institution that was supposed to protect and inform consumers about the behavior of health professionals. The Office of Patient Protection (OPP) was sup-posed to monitor thirty-five boards that oversee and regulate more than a half-million doctors, nurses, dentists, dieticians, and others.

But the OPP never got off the ground. By the time its first chair, Harry Whittington, had been appointed by the governor, rented an office, purchased furniture, hired a staff, created a Web site, developed a complaint form, and visited with the heads of the thirty-five boards under his authority, it was time for the 2005 legislature. Searching for ways to save the state money, and perhaps responding to the health professionals' doubts about regulation of their behavior by a state office, senators refused to fund the commission. It folded up and went out of business in August 2005, without having acted on a single consumer complaint. The extra five dollars that health professionals were made to pay for licensing fees, which was supposed to fund the OPP, now goes into general state revenue.

Source: Mary Ann Roser, "Patient Protection Office Shut; Fee Goes On," *Austin American-Statesman*, October 13, 2005, A1.

**Competency Connection**
**CRITICAL THINKING**

With severe limits in the amount of money that a victim of medical malpractice can recover in Texas, should the state establish an office of patient protection? Explain your answer.

Tort reformers wanted to change several aspects of Texas's laws regulating civil suits.

1. **Punitive damages.** Reformers wanted to change the law to make a litigant prove that not just "gross negligence"—the wording under the state's statute until 1995—but actual malice was involved before punitive damages could be awarded. Also, they wanted to limit the amount of punitive damages. Doctors were particularly determined to cap the size of any amounts that a jury could award a plaintiff beyond actual medical damages.
2. **Joint and several liability.** Under the law prevailing to 1995, anyone who participated in as little as 11 percent of the cause of the injury could be held liable for the actions of others. This meant that if company A was found to be 11 percent at fault, and the other companies were bankrupt or otherwise unreachable, company A had to pay 100 percent of the award to the plaintiff. Reformers hoped to eliminate this responsibility of the richest, most available company.
3. **Venue.** Attorneys filing tort cases had been able to "shop around" for a judge who was known to be sympathetic to plaintiffs. Reformers wanted to restrict filings to the geographical area where the injury occurred.
4. **Deceptive Trade Practices Act.** Texas's consumer protection act provided triple damages for things such as deceptive real estate or stock deals. Reformers wanted to make a consumer prove that a deceptive act occurred knowingly.

In 1995, with Republican Governor George W. Bush lobbying hard for tort reform, but Democrats holding on to shrinking majorities in both houses of the legislature, the result was a compromise. Highlights of new laws passed that year include the following:

1. Punitive damages were limited to the greater of $200,000 or the sum of two times economic damages, plus $75,000.
2. The joint and several liability rule was changed so that a defendant would have to be more than 50 percent responsible to be held liable for all damages.
3. To eliminate venue shopping, the legislature decreed that a business can be sued only in the county in which an injury occurred or in a county in which it has a principal office.
4. Judges were given more power to punish plaintiffs who file frivolous suits.
5. Plaintiffs who sue doctors or hospitals were required to post a $5,000 bond; if the claim proved baseless, the plaintiff was made to forfeit the bond.

In 2003, after achieving majorities in both houses of the legislature, Republicans continued to revamp Texas's tort laws. They limited citizens' ability to file class-action suits, conferred immunity from suits on companies whose products meet government standards, limited the fees of trial lawyers in some cases, established penalties for plaintiffs who rejected settlements before trial (even if they won the case), and capped "pain-and-suffering" awards in medical malpractice suits at $250,000. And in the 2017 session, they limited the rights of property owners to file lawsuits against insurance companies following natural disasters, meaning that "the number of lawsuits filed each month dipped significantly," even after the devastating Hurricane Harvey landed in Houston later that year.[60]

As a result of the tort reform movement, therefore, Texas civil courts are markedly less important, and have much less freedom of choice than they enjoyed prior to 1995.

Reactions to the legal changes have been predictably different from various sides of the political fence. Supporters of the 1995 and 2003 reforms argue that patients now have more access to health care because doctors who were leaving the state or retiring due to increasing insurance costs are staying in practice now that insurance rates have moderated.[61] Opponents of the reforms counter that malpractice insurance rates rose in the late 1990s and early 2000s, and fell after 2003, because of changes in the insurance market, and had nothing to do with tort reform. Meanwhile, patients who have been the victim of negligent doctors or dishonest hospitals have no recourse because they have been frozen out of the legal system.[62] Likewise, the pro-reformers boast that the "New Era of Pro-Business Leadership Is Good for Texas,"[63] while anti-reformers lament that the members of Texans for Lawsuit Reform "have remade the world in their image, one in which there is no recourse for wrongdoing, one in which the powerful simply get their way."[64] (For a discussion of the politics of tort reform during the 2011 legislature, see Chapter 3.)

Like the arguments over abortion, capital punishment, and other controversies discussed in this chapter, the disagreement over the value of tort reform will never die because, on the issue of lawsuits, there is a permanent conflict between people who are likely to sue and those who are likely to be sued. Unlike those other issues, however, torts do not involve constitutionally protected rights. As a result, on this subject, federal courts are reluctant to intervene in the Texas political process. Whatever the legislature, the governor, and the state Supreme Court endorse will be Texas law. Given the Republican alliance with antitort interests, and that party's ascendancy in state politics, Texas policymakers can be expected to remain hostile to "frivolous" lawsuits. For the time being, tort reformers have won, and as a result, the Texas civil justice system is greatly diminished in authority.

## Summary

**LO 10.1**   **Civil liberties have to do with the rights of individual citizens.**   Although there is an argument about whether citizens have a right to keep and bear arms, the frame of that issue has changed recently. The U.S. Supreme Court now has ruled gun ownership an individual right, but questions concerning which kinds of guns are protected remain unanswered. Although the national and state courts participate in struggles over social issues such as abortion, prayer in the schools, and personal expression, these issues provoke so much disagreement that they cannot be settled judicially.

**LO 10.2**   **Civil rights reflect the rights of groups of citizens to be treated equally.**   Though challenges remain, the school desegregation lawsuits that characterized Texas in the twentieth century are no longer being litigated. The Texas courts have courageously taken on the rest of the political establishment, especially the legislature, in ordering a more equitable distribution of school revenues. They have not completely succeeded in introducing educational equality into Texas public schools, but they have forced the legislature to make the educational system at least somewhat more equitable. Racial incidents in Jasper and Tulia reveal that though strife still exists in the state, much progress has been made. In Jasper, the whole community rose up against racial hatred, and in Tulia, racial injustice was overturned by the judicial system. Federal courts have mandated that conditions in prisons be made more humane over recent decades to comply with the ban against "cruel and unusual punishment" in the federal Constitution.

**LO 10.3**   **Texans strongly support the death penalty for murder, and as a result, Texas has put more people to death than any other state.**   Recently, the federal courts have said that Texas cannot put people who were under the age of eighteen when they committed a crime to death.

**LO 10.4**   **In recent years, many businesses became convinced that the outcome of Texas's tort laws was damaging the state's economy.**   They complained that the courts were too tolerant of frivolous suits that sometimes cost businesses so much money that they were forced to close down. In 1995 and 2003, the legislature, at the urging of Governors Bush and Perry, rewrote many of the tort laws so as to take discretion away from the civil judiciary. It is now much more difficult to file, and to win, a civil lawsuit in Texas. This change made consumer representatives unhappy, but as long as the Republican Party controls most state offices, the changes are not likely to be undone.

# Critical Thinking

1. Civil rights and civil liberties are two basic characteristics in American political life. Compare and contrast the ideas of civil rights and civil liberties. Explain why the liberties in the national Constitution's Bill of Rights now apply to the state of Texas. Describe an example of challenges that still exist in Texas regarding civil liberties and civil rights.

2. Texas has long been at the center of the abortion debate in the United States. Discuss the ruling in *Roe* v. *Wade*, explain how the Texas legislature has attempted to limit the right of abortion in Texas, and outline the differences of opinion regarding abortion expressed by the pro-choice and pro-life viewpoints. Why don't judicial decisions resolve the conflict between pro-choice and pro-life activists?

Natural disasters can challenge the capacity of local governments to provide basic services to citizens. This picture shows some of the devastation caused by Hurricane Harvey, a huge event that caused massive problems for local governments throughout southeast Texas.

*Scott Olson/Getty Images News/Getty Images*

# Local Government

**11**

## Learning Objectives

**LO 11.1** Describe the nature of county government in Texas and the relationship of counties to state government.

**LO 11.2** Discuss the nature of city government in Texas and the distinctions between home rule and general-law cities and among forms of government (especially council-manager and mayor-council).

**LO 11.3** Understand both the advantages and disadvantages of special district government in terms of democratic theory.

**LO 11.4** Recognize the fiscal and other challenges facing all local governments in Texas.

**LO 11.5** Understand leadership in local governments.

**W**hen the Texas Constitution was being written in 1875, the state was very rural in nature, with only 8 percent of the state's population living in urban areas. By the 2018 federal census estimates, Texas's population was 27.8 million of which about 85 percent lived in urban areas. Texas continues to lead the country in numeric population growth and includes six of the twenty largest cities in the United States with three of the top eight urban growth centers as of 2018 (Dallas–Plano–Irving, Fort Worth–Arlington, and Austin–Round Rock). Much of this population growth has been among people who have specific problems—Hispanics and the elderly in particular. The urban nature of Texas continues to be a challenge in a state that prides itself on its rural image and heritage. The **"empty space" politics** of Texas suggest some of the challenges to modern government, with county government still being the dominant force in rural areas but too inflexible to accommodate urban problems. Though Texas is among the nation's most urban states, many Texas political leaders harken to the time when cowboys and farmers dominated.[1]

Most of the urbanization has taken place since 1950, when the development of such industries as petrochemicals and defense began luring rural residents into cities. Like most American cities, Texas

ALL POLITICS IS LOCAL.
*Adage in American politics*

263

**"empty space" politics**  The idea that Texas often nurtures a rural mentality for governing in an urban state.

cities have grown with limited planning until recently, and even now, the legacy of unplanned growth can be seen. No better example can be found than the excessive flooding in Houston after Hurricane Harvey in 2017 due to limited planning in real estate development. Growth patterns have been determined by developers, who give little thought to the long-range effects of their projects on the total community. Only in the past forty years has community planning come to be taken seriously. In Texas and elsewhere, the nation's domestic problems—a clean environment, support for the impoverished, economic development, immigration and racial strife, and crime—seem to be focused in the cities. But before examining city government and its problems, this chapter steps back in time and looks at the first unit of local government: the county.

Local government is an especially rich field for exploring whether the tests of democratic government outlined in Chapter 1 have been passed. Americans have long viewed local government as the government that is closest and most responsive to them. As the opening quotation notes, "All politics is local." Political careers often begin in local politics; even national issues are translated into their prospective effect on the local community; local newspapers still provide critical in-depth information about local government doings. Local government in Texas reflects more of a moralistic culture than does the Texas state government, in that local government traditionally offers an array of tools for general citizen involvement and control. In looking at the organization, politics, and finance of Texas's local governments, this chapter closely examines whether citizens take advantage of the opportunity for involvement at the local level and whether differences exist between general-purpose local governments (cities and counties) and special-purpose local governments (special districts).

## Counties: One Size Fits All?

The county is the oldest form of local government in America. Today, 47 states are subdivided into 3,043 counties. Texas has the largest number of counties—254—of any state in the nation.

### Historical and Legal Background

Nationally, counties vary enormously in size and importance. The largest in area is San Bernardino County in California, with 20,131 square miles. Arlington County, Virginia, is the smallest, with only 2 square miles. The largest county in Texas is Brewster, with 6,028 square miles; the smallest is Rockwall, with 147 square miles. Even more striking contrasts exist in population size. The 2018 population of Loving County in West Texas was a grand total of 80 people, while Harris County, which includes Houston, had 4.7 million—a figure that represented continuing growth.[2]

In Texas, as in other states, the county is a creation of state government. In the days before automobiles, because citizens could not reasonably travel to the capital to conduct their business with the state, counties were designed to serve as units of state government that would be geographically accessible to citizens. Indeed, county size was limited so that a citizen could ride to the county seat on horseback in a single day. Until city police departments assumed much of the role, the county sheriff and the sheriff's deputies were the primary agents for enforcement of state law.

County courts still handle much of the judicial business of the state, and they remain integral to the state judicial system. State records such as titles, deeds, birth certificates, and court records, are kept by the county; many state taxes are collected by the county; and counties handle state elections. Counties also distribute large portions of the federal funds that pass through the state government en route to individuals, such as the funds for poverty assistance programs.

Thus, most dealings that citizens have with the state are handled through the county. Yet, strangely, state government exercises virtually no supervisory authority over county governments. They are left to enforce the state's laws and administer the state's programs pretty much as they choose.

County officials are elected by the people of the county and have substantial discretion in a number of areas. For example, they can appoint some other county officials and set the tax rate. The result is a peculiar situation in which the county is a creation of state government, administering state laws and programs—with a great deal of discretion on the part of its officers who are in no real way accountable to the state government for the performance of their duties. Not surprisingly, county officials view themselves not as agents of the state, but rather as local officials. One result is that enforcement of state law varies considerably from county to county.

## Organization and Operation of County Government

The Constitution of 1876, which established the state government, also set out the organization and operation of county government. The same concerns and styles are manifest for both governments, and there are close parallels in their organization and operation. For example, the decentralized executive found at the state level is reproduced at the county level in the county **commissioners court**,[3] the governing body in all Texas counties, and in semi-independent county agencies.

**Structure** Another distinctive feature of Texas counties is the absence of **home rule**, which allows local governments to adopt their own charters, design their organizations, and enact laws within limits set by the state. Texas had a county home-rule provision of sorts between 1933 and 1969, but it proved unworkable and was finally amended out of the constitution.

Because the county is the creation of the state and has no home-rule authority, the organization and structure of county governments are uniform throughout Texas. Tiny Loving County and enormous Harris County have substantially the same governmental structure. Unlike counties in many other states, Texas counties do not have the option of having a form of government with an appointed professional administrator, such as the council-manager type described later in this chapter. Nor can they choose a form of government with an elected chief executive similar to the strong mayor-council form of city government. Counties have often found themselves saddled with unnecessary offices, such as treasurer, school superintendent, or surveyor. In November 1993, Texas voters amended the constitution so that only residents of the county involved would need to vote to abolish an office.

Figure 11-1 illustrates the organization of Texas county government. The county is divided into four precincts, each of which elects a commissioner to the commissioners court. The presiding officer of the commissioners court is the county judge. The county commissioners and the administrative agencies constitute the executive branch of county government, but the commissioners court performs as a legislature as well. Figure 11-1 also illustrates that counties have a large number of elected officials, ranging from a sheriff to constables to an attorney.

Each of the four commissioners is elected from a precinct, but the county judge is chosen in an **at-large election**—that is, one in which all registered voters in the county are eligible to participate. County officials are chosen in partisan elections; that is, candidates run as Democrats, Republicans, or minor-party candidates.

**commissioners court** The administrative and legislative body of a county; in Texas, it has four elected members and is presided over by an elected county judge.

**home rule** The ability of cities with populations of 5,000 or more to organize themselves as they wish within the constitution and laws of Texas.

**at-large election** Elections in which each candidate for any given public office must run jurisdiction-wide—in the entire city, county, or state—when several similar positions are being filled.

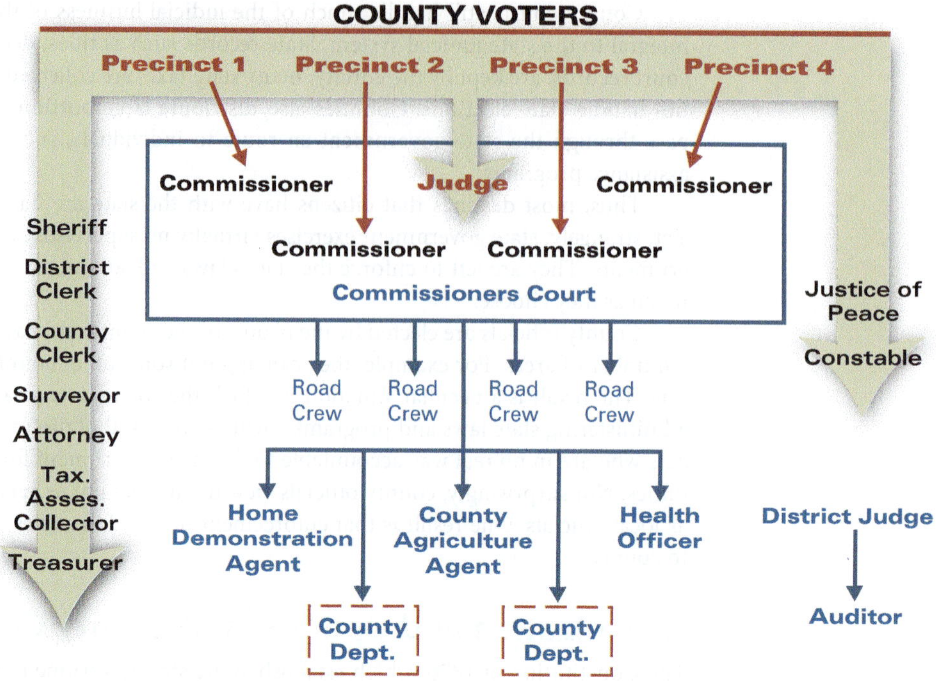

**COUNTY VOTERS**

Precinct 1    Precinct 2    Precinct 3    Precinct 4

Commissioner    **Judge**    Commissioner

Commissioner    Commissioner

**Commissioners Court**

Sheriff

District
Clerk

County
Clerk

Surveyor

Attorney

Tax.
Asses.
Collector

Treasurer

Justice of
Peace

Constable

Road Crew    Road Crew    Road Crew    Road Crew

Home
Demonstration
Agent

County
Agriculture
Agent

Health
Officer

District Judge

County
Dept.

County
Dept.

Auditor

Figure 11-1 Organization of Country Government in Texas

SOURCE: *Citizens' Guide to the Texas Constitution,* prepared for the Texas Advisory Commission on Intergovernmental Relations by the Institute of Urban Studies, University of Houston (Austin, 1972), 51.

**gerrymandering** The practice of drawing electoral districts in such a way as to advantage one party or one faction.

**Apportionment**   In the past, when county commissioners drew county precinct lines, they drew those lines on some basis other than population. County precincts were **gerrymandered** for the purpose of reelecting incumbent commissioners and dividing the county road mileage on an equal basis. Roads, many of which are maintained by county commissioners, were often more important than people. Not only were roads the lifeline for the state's rural population, which was once in the majority, but also contracts for roadwork represented the best opportunity for individual commissioners to wheel and deal. As a result, county commissioners often created precincts with great disparities in population.

In 1968, the U.S. Supreme Court, acting in a case against Midland County, ruled that all counties had to abide by the *one-person, one-vote* rule that had been applied earlier to the U.S. House of Representatives and to state legislatures (*Avery* v. *Midland County*, 88 S.Ct. 1114, 1968) (see Chapter 6). This rule requires that electoral districts must be roughly equal in population. After this ruling, some commissioners courts voluntarily redistricted on the basis of population; in other counties, federal judges ordered population-based redistricting. County apportionment has resurfaced as an issue in recent years in disputes over adequate opportunities for ethnic minorities to contend for county offices, in counties with substantial political party competition, and in urban counties with fast-growing suburbs.

**Commissioners Court**   The term *commissioners court* is a misnomer. It is not a judicial body, but an executive (policy-administering) and legislative (policymaking) body for the county. Although technically the county is nothing more than an administrative arm of the state, the commissioners court does have functional latitude in several areas. In addition to setting the tax rate for the county (a legislative function), it exercises discretion in the administration of state programs (an executive function). Some of these state programs are mandatory, but the county may choose among others and may determine the amount of money allocated to each.

For example, the state and counties are responsible for providing health care for the impoverished, including care for individuals who are not qualified for the federally funded Medicaid program, and counties must ensure that hospital service is provided. An individual county, however, may elect to operate a public hospital, pay a public hospital in an adjacent county for services, or pay a private hospital for care of the indigent. Counties also are responsible for building and maintaining county jails, generally for providing health and safety services in rural areas, and for subdivision regulation in unincorporated areas.

Perhaps the most important power of the commissioners court is that of controlling the county budget in most areas of county government. If it chooses, it can institute a variety of different programs, many of which are major undertakings, such as county hospitals, libraries, and various welfare programs. Counties are also active in economic development activity.

The county commissioners court has the responsibility for conducting general and special elections. The court also has the power to determine the precinct lines for the justice of the peace precincts, as well as for the precincts of the four commissioners themselves. This power is a potent political weapon that can be used to advance the cause of some individuals and groups, and to discriminate against others. When these lines are not drawn fairly and equitably, malapportionment results, as was the case in the Midland situation noted earlier.

**County Officials** The *county commissioners* also perform important functions as individuals. Each is responsible for his or her own precinct, including the establishment of road- and bridge-building programs, which represent a major expenditure of county funds. Since 1947, counties have had the authority to consolidate the functions of building and maintaining roads and bridges. About 10 percent of Texas's 254 counties have established a countywide unit system, enabling commissioners in those counties to take advantage of volume purchasing, share heavy road equipment, and so on. When she was a Travis County commissioner, former Governor Ann Richards led an unsuccessful campaign for statewide adoption of the unit system. In the other 90 percent of Texas's counties, commissioners still tend to roads and bridges in their individual precincts. One reason is the importance of these transportation facilities to residents in outlying areas, and thus the potential effect on reelecting the commissioner. Another reason is that individual commissioners simply like the patronage to hire personnel and award contracts for road and bridge work. They also like the political advantage to be gained from determining the locations of new roads and which existing roads and bridges will be improved.

The *county judge* performs many functions. As a member of the commissioners court, the judge presides over and participates fully in that body's decision making. As a member of the county election board, the county judge receives the election returns from the election judges throughout the county, presents the returns to the commissioners court for canvassing, and then forwards the final results to the secretary of state. In counties with a population of fewer than 225,000, county judges also serve in an administrative capacity as county budget officer. They have the authority to fill vacancies that occur on commissioners courts. They are notaries public, can perform marriages, and issue beer, wine, and liquor licenses in "wet" counties. Many citizens see the county judge as a representative of the people and ask him or her to intervene with other elected officials and county bureaucrats. Many county judges have strong countywide power bases and are influential politicians.

In small population counties, the county judge also presides over the county court, although the position does not require legal credentials other than "being well informed in the law." County judges devote time to such matters as probate of wills, settlement of estates, appointment of guardians, and in many counties, hearing lawsuits and minor criminal cases. However, in larger counties, the county commission usually relieves the judge of courtroom responsibilities by creating one or more county courts at law.

One of the most visible legal officers is the *county sheriff,* who is elected at large. The sheriff has jurisdiction throughout the county, but often also makes informal agreements involving a division of labor with the police of the municipalities in the county. Particularly where large cities are involved, the sheriff's office usually confines itself to law enforcement in the area of the county outside the city limits, though the sheriff often coordinates with city police and other law enforcement agencies to address pervasive problems such as illegal drug manufacturing and sales. The county sheriff has comprehensive control of departmental operations and appoints all deputies, jailers, and administrative personnel. In fact, the principal function of the sheriff is to serve as administrator of the county jail system. County jails house defendants awaiting criminal trial, individuals convicted of a misdemeanor and sentenced for a term up to a year, and felony (serious crime) convicts waiting to be transported to a state prison. Some counties have found it profitable to build larger jails than they require and rent space to the state and to other counties. Depending on the size of the county, the sheriff's department may be quite complex and may have a substantial annual budget—one often hotly disputed with the commissioners court. A 1993 amendment to the state constitution authorizes the legislature to impose qualifications on sheriffs, such as mandatory training as a peace officer.

Another prominent county official is the *county attorney,* often called the "district attorney" in large counties, also elected at large. As the head of the county's legal department, the county attorney provides legal counsel and representation of the county. The attorney also prosecutes misdemeanors in the justice of the peace and county courts.

Another of the important elective offices in the county is that of *county clerk,* who is also elected at large. The county clerk is the recorder of all legal documents (such as deeds, contracts, and mortgages), issues all marriage licenses, and is the clerk of both the county court and the commissioners court. Many of the responsibilities for the conduct of elections, which formally rest with the commissioners court, actually are performed by the county clerk. For example, absentee voting is handled by the county clerk.

The *assessor-collector of taxes* collects the ad valorem (general property) tax for the county—and, often, by contract, for other local governments in the county; collects fees for license plates, license renewal stickers, and certificates of title for motor vehicles; and serves as the registrar of voters. This last duty is a holdover from the days of the poll tax, which was a fee paid to register to vote (abolished by the 24th Amendment to the U.S. Constitution). The assessor-collector's job has been changed in recent years by the creation of the uniform appraisal system, to be discussed later in this chapter. In counties of 10,000 or more population, a separate assessor-collector is elected at large; in smaller counties, the sheriff serves as assessor-collector.

Other legal officers of the county are the *justices of the peace* (JPs) and the *constables.* In most but not all counties, there is at least one justice of the peace and one constable for each of the four precincts. Larger counties may have as many as eight JP districts. In the largest counties, numerous deputy constables assist the elected constables. The justice of the peace is at the bottom of the judicial ladder, having jurisdiction over only minor criminal cases and civil suits. The constable has the duty of executing judgments, serving subpoenas, and performing other duties for the justice of the peace court. Like the commissioners, the constables and JPs are elected for four years on a partisan basis by district.

Another elected official is the *county treasurer,* who is the custodian of public funds. Some counties have a *county school superintendent* to oversee rural schools.

The county has a number of other officers, some of whom perform important functions. In larger counties, a *county elections coordinator* is appointed to supervise elections. In counties with a population of more than 35,000, the state law requires that an *auditor* be appointed by the district judge having jurisdiction in the county for the purpose of overseeing the financial activities of the county and assuring that they are performed in accordance with the law. State law requires a *county health officer* to direct the public health program, and in most counties, the commissioners court appoints a *county agricultural agent* and a *home demonstration agent* for the purpose of assisting (primarily) rural people with agriculture and homemaking. The last two officers are appointed in conjunction with Texas A&M University, which administers the agriculture and home demonstration extension programs.

## County Politics

County politics is characterized by three interrelated qualities: partisanship, precincts, and a long ballot. With the exception of the professional appointments noted earlier, such as a home demonstration agent and health officer, all the county officials discussed earlier in this chapter are elected. The key electoral units are the four commissioners' precincts, which also serve as the electoral base for constables and JPs. All contenders run under a political party banner and are elected during general elections when major officials such as president, governor, and members of Congress are elected. Because the form of government is the same in all counties, so also are the electoral arrangements. Thus, to a great extent, a depiction of state parties and elections (see Chapters 4 and 5) also describes county politics.

## An Evaluation of County Government

When industrial firms experience problems, they call in teams of management consultants, who make a searching examination and a critical evaluation of the firm's operation. If one could arrange for a management consulting firm to make a thorough examination of county government in Texas, its report would very likely include the following topics.

**Structure and Partisanship** The county in Texas is a nineteenth-century political organization struggling to cope with the twenty-first century, a "one size fits all" design that might work well in rural areas, but does not allow for some innovation that might be preferable in urban areas. In many states, counties have the same flexibility as cities to choose a *form of government* that is appropriate for the size and complexity of that particular jurisdiction. In Texas, all county governments have the same structure, and the emphasis is on *party politics* because all officials are elected on a partisan basis. The positive aspect of partisanship is that the average voter can understand more clearly what a candidate's approximate political position is when the candidate bears the label Republican or Democrat than when there is no identifying tag.

Nationally, although most counties operate with a commission, urban counties serving the majority of the nation's citizens operate with a county manager or appointed administrator.[4] California, Florida, and North Carolina are examples of states in which counties are professionally managed. Though Texas does not provide formal authority for counties to vary the form of government, county judges in the largest Texas counties have hired professional local government managers to tend to administrative functions. Although the current structure is uniform and simple, it also makes it difficult to produce decisions for the benefit of all or most county residents because of the emphasis on precincts. Commissioners tend to see themselves as representing their precinct rather than the county as a whole. In turn, the precinct focus makes it difficult to enjoy economies of scale, such as purchasing all road-paving materials at one time.

The partisanship and restrictive structure can lead to governance problems. Commissioners often squabble over petty matters. Citizens have difficulty deciding whom to blame if they are dissatisfied with county government, because the commissioners serve as a collective board of directors for the county. For example, a troublesome sheriff or constable may be reelected while the voters blame the county commissioners for the law officer's behavior. Similarly, the voters may focus on the county judge, who has one vote on the commissioners court just like the other members, when other members of the court should be the object of attention. Such confusion can happen in any government, but the large number of elected officials—mirroring the state pattern—compounds the problem.

A plus for counties is that they are less bureaucratic than other governments; thus, the average citizen can more easily deal with a county office. One reason may be that, unlike the state government, county government does not have a clear-cut separation between legislative and executive branches and functions. The merger of executive and legislative functions, which is called a unitary system, also is found in some city and special district governments. It can sometimes produce a rapid response to a citizen problem or request.

One county judge assessed county government by noting that many county officials are highly responsive to public demands when they must face competitive elections. In fact, he argued that counties are the last true bastions of *grass-roots politics,* whereby government is close to all the people in the county. Although the court sets much of the policy and the tone for the conduct of county operations, it lacks the authority to give explicit orders to subordinate officials. Nevertheless, this county judge pointed out, by controlling the budget, the commissioners court can often dictate the behavior of other elected officials. Additionally, counties have the lowest tax rates of all the governments in Texas.[5] Another county judge put it this way: "We do meat-and-potatoes government . . . not flashy, press-release government, but good government."[6]

Thus, the evaluation of county organization and politics is mixed. The public and media often show little interest in what can be seen as the mundane politics of county government, and many of the functions of counties operate without much public attention. Yet, it is often highly democratic because commissioners must secure support for reelection. At the same time, however, the willingness of commissioners and other elected officials to attend to the needs of individuals and to deal with details can easily lead to corruption.

**Management Practices** County government in Texas is one of the last bastions of the **spoils system** in which people are appointed to government jobs on the basis of whom they supported in the last election and how much money they contributed. A spoils system may help to ensure the involvement of ordinary citizens in government by allowing a highly

**spoils system**
Appointing people to government jobs on the basis of whom they supported in the last election and how much money they contributed.

Texans enjoy roaming through historic Texas county courthouses, many of which have been restored to their nineteenth- and early-twentieth-century glory. The Presidio County Courthouse is in Marfa, in the Big Bend country.

iStock.com/DenisTangneyJr

diverse group of people to hold government jobs. When such a dispersion of jobs occurs, the result is *pluralism*—that is, a reflection in public employment and public policy of the cultural diversity in society.

However, a spoils system can also lead to the appointment of unqualified people, especially in jobs requiring specialized training. It can contribute to a high turnover rate if the county tends to usher new elected officials into office on a regular basis. For example, a common practice is for a newly elected sheriff to fire several deputies and bring in his or her own people. Finally, a spoils system may create not pluralism but *elitism;* those persons appointed to public office may represent only a narrow spectrum of society and reflect only the upper crust of the dominant political party.

Democratic government demands that citizens not only be willing to obey the law, but also be able to count on public officials being scrupulous in their own behavior, and not merely partisan. Also, political appointees may not be current on modern management practices; for example, elected officials may be reluctant to spend money to modernize computer systems as often as users would like. As one might expect, most experts think a spoils system has more risks than advantages.

From a management standpoint, a *civil service* or a *merit system* of recruitment, evaluation, promotion, and termination based on qualifications and a pay scale that would attract and hold competent personnel would help improve governmental performance. Such practices also would be fair to employees as recognition for their labors and to taxpayers as a return on their dollars. Some larger counties have made significant strides toward developing professional personnel practices, such as competitive hiring, merit raises, and grievance processes, but 90 percent of the counties have a long way to go. In a larger county, commissioners also appoint a wide array of professionals, such as a budget officer, personnel director, and economic development coordinator.

Two other features of county government illustrate its tendency toward inefficient management: decentralized purchasing and the road and bridge system. *Decentralized purchasing* means that each department and each commissioner make separate purchases, whether for office supplies or heavy road equipment. Quantity discounts, which might be obtained with a centralized purchasing agent, are unavailable on small-lot purchases. Also, the opportunity

## ISSUE SPOTLIGHT:
## Consequences of No County Ordinance Power

In unincorporated areas, the lack of county ordinance power manifests itself in many ways. Fireworks stands inevitably are erected a few feet outside a city's jurisdiction; contractors frequently take more liberties with sound construction principles in rural areas; and controversial establishments such as topless bars, noisy gun ranges, and polluting cement plants find homes in unincorporated county areas. In Williamson County, just north of Austin, a property management company even erected a 120-foot-high billboard that violated both state signage regulations and the rules of the homeowners' association for the apartments themselves. In all of these cases, counties are powerless to act.

**Competency Connection**
**CRITICAL THINKING**

Is the County Government model outmoded? Should the state replace counties so that it could have more power to remedy problems in rural areas?

for graft and corruption is real. To make sure that they will get county business, sellers may find themselves obligated—or at least feel that they are—to do a variety of favors for individual officials in county government. This situation is not unknown in the other governmental units, but becomes more widespread in highly decentralized organizations.

Unless a Texas county belongs to the elite 10 percent that have a *unit system for county-wide administration of the roads and bridges*, individual commissioners may plan and execute their own programs for highway and bridge construction and maintenance at the precinct level. The obvious result is poor planning and coordination and also duplication of expensive heavy equipment when efficiency is important. These inefficiencies are important because counties, like other local governments, must cope with taxpayer resistance to providing more funding for government.

**Lack of Ordinance Power** Texas counties have no general power to pass ordinances—that is, laws pertaining to the county. They do have authority to protect the health and welfare of citizens, and through that power, they can regulate the operation of a sanitary landfill and mandate inoculations in the midst of an epidemic. They can regulate subdivision development in unincorporated areas, sometimes sharing power with municipalities and, for flood control, the federal government. However, the lack of general ordinance power means that, for example, they cannot zone land to ensure appropriate and similar usage in a given area, and they have trouble guarding against rutted roads and polluted water supplies when land developers or gas drillers start to work.[7]

**Recommendations** Having reviewed Texas county government, contemporary management consultants probably would recommend the following:

▶ Greater flexibility in this form of government, particularly in heavily populated areas, to encourage more professional management of personnel, services, purchasing, and all other aspects of county government consistent with "crowded space" rather than "empty space" politics

▶ Taking advantage of economies of scale by centralizing purchasing and adopting a unit system of road and bridge construction and maintenance

▶ Cooperative delivery of services

However, they probably would not yet explore any of the forms of city-county cooperation that exist in areas such as San Francisco, Honolulu, or Nashville because counties in Texas are not yet ready to function as cities. The exceptions are El Paso County, where the county and city have explored consolidation, and Bexar County, where the county judge has advocated merger. The *Austin American-Statesman* has also urged some consideration of "government modernization" on the Travis County commissioners.[8]

**Prospects for Reform** Given the obvious disadvantages of the current structure, what are the prospects for changing county government in Texas? County commissioners, judges, sheriffs, and other county officers, acting individually, as well as through such interest groups as TACO (Texas Association of County Officials), are potent political figures who can and do exercise substantial influence over their state legislators. Unfortunately for the taxpayers, most county officials have shown little willingness to accept change in the structure and function of county government. The exceptions are usually county commissioners in more heavily populated counties, who have taken a number of steps to professionalize government, including the appointment of personnel and budget experts. They are outnumbered nine to one by commissioners in less populous areas. Thus, substantially more citizen participation will be necessary if change is to occur. If city residents, who tend to ignore county politics, were to play a much more active role, reform might be possible because of the sheer numbers they represent when approaching legislators.

Texas counties have no authority to pass general ordinances that could, for example, regulate land use in rural areas. The *colonias* on the outskirts of Texas cities along the Mexican border are an example of unregulated growth.

Courtesy of Ben Sargent

**Competency Connection**
**PERSONAL RESPONSIBILITY**

Can citizens be trusted to keep rural Texas clean, or should county governments have expanded powers to write laws or ordinances to regulate rural land usage?

# Cities: Managed Environments

Unlike the county, the city has a long history of independence and self-government going back to ancient Greece. In the Middle Ages, European cities received crown charters that established them as separate and independent entities. One of their major functions was to protect their citizens from external danger; for this reason, the cities of the period were surrounded by high walls, and the citizens paid taxes for this protection. Early American cities sought charters initially from the British crown and later from the state legislatures. In Texas, San Fernando de Béxar (now San Antonio) was the first city. Its settlement was ordered by the king of Spain and began with fifteen families in 1731.

State legislatures traditionally have been less than sympathetic to the problems of the cities, partly because of rural bias and partly because they wished to avoid being caught in the quagmires of city politics. Therefore, in the nineteenth century, the states (including Texas) established **general laws**—statutes that pertained to all municipalities—for the organization of the city governments, to which municipalities were required to conform. But these general laws were not well adapted to the growing problems of the cities, and around the turn of the 20th century, a movement toward *municipal home rule* emerged. The home-rule laws permitted the cities, within limits, to organize as they saw fit.[9]

In Texas, the municipal home-rule amendment to the constitution came in 1912. It provides that a city with a population of more than 5,000 is allowed—within certain procedural and financial limitations—to write its own constitution in the form of a city charter, which would be effective when approved by a majority vote of the citizens. A city charter is the local equivalent of a constitution. Home-rule cities may choose any organizational form or policies as long as they do not conflict with the state constitution or the state laws. General-law cities may organize according to any of the traditional forms of municipal government discussed later in this chapter, but with a number of restrictions due to the complex statutory categorization of general-law cities based on combinations of population and land area.

**general laws** Statutes that pertain to all municipalities that do not have home-rule status.

Traditionally, municipalities were organized into one of three major types of governments: *mayor-council*, *commission*, and *council-manager*, though each city would create its own unique organization. In the modern era, the commission form, once popular, has disappeared, but hybrid forms of government that combine mayor-council and council-manager are common, with at least seven modern forms of municipal government in use.[10] Thus, it is sometimes difficult to slot an individual city into a particular category.

In addition to home rule, two other important legal aspects of city government in Texas are *extraterritorial jurisdiction* (ETJ) and *annexation.* ETJ gives cities limited control over unincorporated territory contiguous to their boundaries, allowing them some control over what kind of development occurs just outside the city limits. The zone ranges from a half-mile in distance for cities under 1,500 in population to five miles for those over 100,000. Within these zones, municipalities can require developers and others to conform to city regulations regarding construction, sanitation, utilities, and similar matters. In this way, cities can exercise some positive influence on the quality of life in the immediate area around them.

Socially irresponsible individuals and businesses sometimes locate outside both city limits and a city's extraterritorial jurisdiction for the dual purposes of avoiding city taxes—usually higher than the county's—and city regulation, such as building codes. The lack of county ordinance power encourages such behavior, while ETJ helps to correct it.

Annexation power allows cities to bring adjacent unincorporated areas inside the municipal boundaries. Doing so helps prevent suburban developments from incorporating and blocking a large city's otherwise natural development. It also allows a city to expand its tax base. In the 1950s and 1960s, municipalities could make great land grabs without any commitment to providing services, but over the years, annexation powers have been limited. Annexation laws in Texas help prevent a phenomenon that is very common in other states' cities, such as Cleveland and Denver. There, more affluent residents have fled to upscale suburbs in what is often called "White flight" because most of the people who leave are Anglos. They leave the inner cities with inadequate tax revenues and decaying facilities. They no longer pay city taxes, but continue to use and enjoy such services as airports, libraries, utilities, and museums, which city residents pay taxes to support. When a city exercises its annexation powers, it can protect its tax base somewhat and preserve space for future development. Although Texas's larger cities are surrounded by suburbs, many of which are upscale, they have been somewhat successful in counteracting White flight and the erosion of their tax bases. In many cities, downtowns that were in decline a generation ago have experienced a renaissance in recent years. Houston is the best (or worst) example of a city using annexation to protect itself. In 1995, Houston, along with Austin, Nederland, and Longview, was the target of special legislation advocated by suburbanites to limit annexation power. Again, the cities prevailed. Houston is unusual in another sense because it is the only major American city without zoning ordinances that dictate what can be built where—homes, offices, factories, a unique arrangement that made the city particularly vulnerable to Hurricane Harvey, as mentioned at the beginning of this chapter.

## Organization of City Government

Texas municipalities are strongly drawn to professional city management. Of the 1,216 cities and towns,[11] 657 (54 percent) have either a city manager or city administrator. Among the 335 home-rule cities, 318 (95 percent) have council-manager government, and another 11 have a chief administrative officer; only 6 have mayor-council government. None has a commission form, though a few city councils are called "commission." Among the 881 general-law cities, 328 (29 percent) have a city manager or city administrator even though they operate under the less flexible general laws of the state. The basic forms of municipal government are described next,

# Texas Politics and You

Almost all cities, at least those of 5,000 or more population, have a Web page. Pick a city that is of interest to you and go to its Web page. Different communities use different social media to get information out to the citizens—through such sites as Twitter, Facebook, Podcasts, You Tube, Pinterest, and/ or Instagram. After a bit of searching, answer the following:

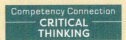

Competency Connection
**CRITICAL THINKING**

**What did you find? What's in the news for your city? What did some of your fellow students find out about their cities from using social media?**

with emphasis on the two most popular forms—council-manager and mayor-council—followed by a look at a hybrid form and a historical note on the commission form.

**The Council-Manager Form** San Antonio and Dallas are two of the largest cities in the country—along with Phoenix and San Jose—using this organizational model (Figure 11-2), but smaller cities such as Beeville, Gainesville, and Yoakum also operate with the *council-manager* form of government. Under this system, a city council of five to fifteen members is elected at large or by districts and, in turn, appoints a city manager who is responsible for the hiring and firing of department heads and for the preparation of the budget. A mayor, elected at large or by the council, is a member of the council and presides over it, but otherwise has only the same powers as any other council member.

Proponents of council-manager government, including many political scientists, traditionally have argued that this form of government allows at least some separation of politics

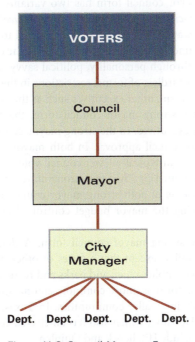

Figure 11-2 Council-Manager Form

Source: Adapted from *Forms of City Government* (Austin: Institute of Public Affairs, University of Texas, 1959), 23.

from administration. Under this system, the council is charged with making public policy. Once a decision is made, the manager is charged with administering policy. In reality, however, politics and administration cannot be separated: The city manager must make recommendations to the council on such highly political matters as tax and utility rates and zoning.[12] Nevertheless, the distinction between politics and policymaking on the one hand and administration on the other, has convinced many observers that it is the most efficient form of city government. States with a large number of council-manager cities include Texas, California, Florida, Maine, and Michigan, among others.

For all its efficiency and professionalism, council-manager government does have some problems. First, because council members are part-time and often serve short tenures, they may rely heavily on the manager for policy guidance. Because the manager is not directly responsible to the voters, this practice makes it more difficult for the average citizen to influence city hall, and many citizens react negatively to the perception, often with a bit of justification, that the city manager makes policy decisions even though the council must approve the managers decisions. Second, the comparison is frequently drawn between council-manager government and the business corporation because both involve policymaking "boards" and professional managers. When coupled with the emphasis on efficiency, this image of a professionally trained "business manager" also tends to promote the values of the business community. The result is that festering political problems, especially those involving ethnic minorities and the poor, have not always been addressed in a timely manner. However, district elections and direct election of the mayor in council-manager cities have reduced this problem somewhat, as representation on city councils has become more diversified. A review of the literature on city governance indicates that "evidence exists to support claims of improved performance of the council-manager form of government [over the mayor-council system]. The evidence is not as strong as many advocates likely expect, but progress has been made."[13]

**The Mayor-Council Form** In the *mayor-council* form of municipal government, council members are elected at large or by geographic districts, and the mayor is elected at large. "At large" means citywide. The mayor-council form has two variants: the *weak mayor-council* form and the *strong mayor-council* form. The words *strong* and *weak* are used in reference to a mayor's powers in the same way that the word *weak* is applied to the Texas governorship. The terms have to do with the amount of formal power given to the chief executive by the city charter. An individual mayor, through personality, political savvy, and leadership skills, can heavily influence local politics regardless of formal restrictions in the city charter.

In the weak mayor-council form, other executives such as the city attorney and treasurer also are elected, whereas in the strong mayor-council form, the mayor has the power to appoint and remove other city executives. In the strong mayor-council form, the mayor also prepares the budget, subject to council approval. In both mayor-council forms, the mayor can veto acts of the city council, but typically fewer council votes are needed to override the mayor's veto in a weak mayor-council city than in a strong mayor-council city. An individual city charter may combine elements of both strong mayor-council and weak mayor-council government—for example, giving the mayor budget control while also allowing for some other elected positions.

Figure 11-3 illustrates the strong mayor-council form. A diagram of a weak mayor-council form would be very similar, except that a series of other elected officials would be specified, such as the city attorney, police chief, and parks and recreation director.

The strong mayor-council form is most common among the nation's largest cities, whereas the weak form prevails in smaller communities. In Texas, the only large city with mayor-council government is Houston, which also has an elected controller to run the city's finances. Small-city examples include Hitchcock and Quinlan.

Because mayor-council government is what is called an "unreformed" or a "political" model,[14] it may experience more efficiency problems than a professionally managed city,

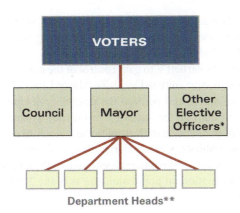

**Figure 11-3 Strong Mayor-Council Form**

SOURCE: *Forms of City Government* (Austin: Institute of Public Affairs, University of Texas, 1959), 10.

* In a number of strong mayor-council cities, the chief of police and some other department heads are elected, although that is not the case in Texas.
** Common departments are fire, police, streets and sanitation, utilities, and parks and recreation.

and have less ability to arrive at consensus on policy. To overcome some of its problems, mayor-council cities—particularly larger ones—often have a deputy mayor or chief administrative officer appointed by the mayor who tends to the internal business of the city, while the mayor tends to political matters.[15]

Many political scientists favor the strong mayor-council form of government because a strong mayor might provide the kind of leadership needed to cope with the growing problems of major urban areas, and it focuses on an elected, not an appointed, official. Another reason for this opinion is that the mayor and council members, especially in larger cities, are full-time paid officials who can devote their time to the development of public policy and oversight of government services. Thus, policy proposals come directly from elected officials. If these officials represent a broad public interest, as opposed to narrow interest groups, democracy is well served.

**The Mayor-Manager Form**  The *mayor-manager* form of government, also called the *chief administrative officer* (CAO) form, is growing in popularity nationwide.[16] This plan has generated interest because it combines the overt political leadership of a mayor-council plan with the professional management skills identified with council-manager government. Typically, it arises when the mayor recognizes a need for managerial assistance. In this form of government, the city manager reports only to the mayor, not to the council as a whole, and focuses on fiscal/administrative policy implementation. The mayor provides broad policy leadership in addressing major problems, such as crime and economic development.

In Texas, some smaller cities, such as Argyle and Mathis, use a city administrator plan, but often the smaller communities use the hybrid only until a charter election can be held to adopt council-manager government. Elsewhere, mayor-manager government is often practiced in consolidated city-county governments, such as Lexington-Fayette County, Kentucky, and some cities, such as San Ramon, California.

A variant of mayor-manager government is arising in larger municipalities. In Texas and across the country, large cities using the council-manager plan have seen disputes develop among the mayor, council members, and managers as assertive mayors try to carve out a larger role for themselves. The growing interest of big-city mayors in controlling both the political and the administrative aspects of city government is illustrated by events in Dallas. In 1987–1991, Mayor Annette Strauss imposed strong political leadership on the city with her "Honey, do it for Dallas" approach that masked behavior at times more reminiscent of a strong mayor than the mayor of a council-manager city. Then, in 1992–1993, Mayor Steve Bartlett, a former U.S.

congressman, and City Manager Jan Hart struggled for control, with Hart ultimately leaving in 1993 to enter the private sector. In 1997, Mayor Ron Kirk struggled more with the Dallas City Council, which resisted his bid for greater power, than he did with City Manager John Ware, but his intent was the same as Bartlett's: to gain control of the city's executive establishment. In 2002, a charter review commission initiated by Dallas Mayor Laura Miller began studying stronger formal powers for the mayor and perhaps the possibility of eliminating the city manager position. Two different elections on the issue of a strong mayor-manager form for Dallas were held in 2005; both resulted in retention of the traditional council-manager form. More cooperative mayor-manager relationships *can* exist in large cities, as, for example, in Fort Worth.[17]

Table 11-1 summarizes the form of government used in the nation's and the state's largest cities. It also provides information on population size as of the 2015 census estimates and the physical size of the cities.

**The Commission Form**  The *commission* form of city government is said to have originated in Galveston. In 1900, the city lost 7,200 persons in a disastrous storm surge that swept the Texas coast in the wake of a powerful hurricane. The city then applied for and received permission from the state legislature to adopt a commission form of government to meet its emergency needs.

Under this type of organization, the elected commissioners collectively compose the policymaking board and, as individuals, are administrators of various departments, such as

| TABLE 11-1 | Basic Facts about America's Ten Largest and Texas's Seven Largest Cities, as of the 2015 Census Estimate | | |
|---|---|---|---|
| **City with Rank in Population** | **2018 Population Estimate** | **Land Area in Square Miles** | **Type of Governance** |
| 1. **New York City** | 8,398,748 | 303.3 | Mayor-Council |
| 2. **Los Angeles** | 3,990,456 | 469.1 | Mayor-Council |
| 3. **Chicago** | 2,705,994 | 227.1 | Mayor-Council |
| 4. **Houston, TX** | 2,325,502 | 579.4 | Mayor-Council with elected Controller |
| 5. **Phoenix** | 1,660,272 | 474.9 | Council-Manager |
| 6. **Philadelphia** | 1,584,138 | 135.1 | Mayor-Council |
| 7. **San Antonio, TX** | 1,532,233 | 407.6 | Council-Manager |
| 8. **San Diego** | 1,425,976 | 324.3 | Mayor-Council with Chief Operating Officer (COO) |
| 9. **Dallas, TX** | 1,345,047 | 342.5 | Council-Manager |
| 10. **San Jose** | 1,030,119 | 175 | Council-Manager |
| 11. **Austin, TX** | 964,254 | 251.5 | Council-Manager |
| 13. **Fort Worth, TX** | 895,008 | 292.5 | Council-Manager |
| 20. **El Paso, TX** | 681,124 | 249.1 | Council-Manager |
| 50. **Arlington, TX** | 398,112 | 99.5 | Council-Manager |

NOTE: This information is for the city alone, not the metropolitan area, which may be double or triple the population size and several times the land area of the central city. The land area is as of 2005.

SOURCE: "Top 50 Cities in the U.S. by Population and Rank," *Infoplease.com*, found at https://www.infoplease.com/us/us-cities/top-50-cities-us-population-and-rank

Competency Connection
**COMMUNICATION SKILLS**

Most large cities have mayor-council forms of city government. Should Texas cities move to that model? What would be the advantages and disadvantages of such a change?

public safety, streets and transportation, finance, and so on. Although widely copied initially, the commission system lost favor because many thought that the commissioners tended to become advocates for their own departments rather than public interest advocates who act on behalf of the entire city. Also, the city commission had many of the same problems as the county commission, including corruption and unclear lines of responsibility.

Although some cities in other states still use the form, Texas home-rule cities have abandoned the commission form. Galveston itself became a council-manager city in 1961. A few general-law cities still use commission government.

**Forms Used in General-Law Cities** Texas has about 881 general-law cities—cities whose population is fewer than 5,000 or somewhat larger cities that, for one reason or another, have not opted for home rule. These cities can organize under any of three basic forms of government: aldermanic (a variant of the mayor-council type), council-manager, or commission. However, state law limits the size of the council, specifies other municipal officials, spells out the power of the mayor, and places other restrictions on matters that home-rule cities can decide for themselves.[18]

Because of their small size, most general-law cities have chosen the aldermanic model—basically, mayor-council government. The council-manager form, calling for the hiring of a professional city manager, challenges the budget of a small city, and trained city managers are rarely knowledgeable about small-town issues. However, some smaller cities, such as Morton, have designated the city clerk as the chief administrative officer without bothering to adopt council-manager government formally. A few have hired a part-time manager or have banded with other small communities to hire a "circuit-riding" city manager. Whatever their official title—city manager, city clerk, city secretary, or assistant to the mayor—administrators in smaller cities more than earn their salaries. They usually serve as general managers, personnel directors, tax assessor-collectors, and so forth because they are often the only full-time professional in the city's government.

**What Form Is Preferable?** The only clear answer is that city size seems to have some effect on the type of municipal government that works best. For small cities, all government structures can be equally successful. Smaller cities that can afford a city manager often do well

Local government is responsible for most police work. Here, a Houston mounted police officer directs traffic. Many sheriffs' offices also have mounted patrols.

James Nielsen/AFP/Getty Images

Competency Connection
**COMMUNICATION SKILLS**

Is having police mounted on horses an expensive extravagance for cities? Does it reflect an attempt to go back to the days of the Texas Rangers on horseback without really helping the quality of law enforcement?

with that form, but most use a mayor-council form, often relying on the city secretary to coordinate administrative affairs. Mid-size cities (from 25,000 to 250,000 in population) can afford to hire a manager, and because they tend to be suburban and relatively homogeneous in terms of class and ethnicity, they experience fewer intense political conflicts than larger cities. As a result, they often adopt the council-manager form of government because

## You Decide: Should the Largest Cities (Dallas, San Antonio, Austin, Fort Worth, for example) Abandon *Council-Manager Government in Favor of a Strong Mayor-Council Form?*

It is not uncommon across the country for cities to switch from council-manager government to mayor-council or mayor-manager (mayor-administrator) government once they near or exceed a half-million people in size. In Texas, Dallas has struggled bitterly with the issue of possible change, while El Paso moved from mayor-council to council-manager government. Yet, Houston is the only large mayor-council city in the state. What do you think the other very large cities in the state should do?

### Pro ☑

- Any large city should adopt a new municipal charter calling for a strong mayor-council form because:

- It needs a strong chief executive as leader, someone elected to provide the political and policy direction that supporters want.

- The mayor and the manager disagree publicly too much.

- The city has district council elections. Only the mayor can represent the whole city.

- City managers tend to favor business interests.

- It is too easy for the city manager and the rest of the bureaucracy to perform poorly without anyone knowing.

- More citizens would vote if the mayor's race mattered more.

- The city could address its out-and-out political problems better.

### Con ☒

- A large city that has council-manager government should keep its present governmental form because:

- A strong mayor would just divide the community because mayors must spend more time tending their electoral bases, to ensure that their friends win and their enemies lose, than focusing on making city government work efficiently and effectively for all citizens.

- The mayor can provide leadership even in a city manager form of government.

- The city manager is bound by a national code of ethics that requires him/her to stay out of politics and focus on making sure things run properly.

- The mayor and individual council members would be more likely to jockey for political position in a different form of government.

- Day-to-day operations are so complicated in a big city that a professional manager needs to be in charge of them.

- A strong mayor is more likely to "break the bank" in giving away political favors.

- Large cities with mayor-council or mayor-manager government still have major political problems.

**Competency Connection**
**SOCIAL RESPONSIBILITY**

Is the public interest better served by a professional city manager making decisions about basic services, or would the public be better served with leadership from a powerful elected mayor?

it allows for relatively efficient operation, and permits the city administration to maintain a distance from party politics and from state and national political issues. In big cities, however, where it is impossible to escape from class and ethnic tension, the overtly political mayor-council or mayor-manager form is often a better choice because of the need for the political focus provided by the elected mayor.[19]

## City Politics

The discussion of forms of city government has provided a framework for understanding the operations of the city, but has said little about how city government really works. Who gets the rewards, and who is deprived? Which individuals and groups benefit most from city government, and which groups bear the burdens?

The electoral system used by Texas cities is an indication of how the rewards and deprivations are distributed. Although the partisanship of candidates is well known in cities such as Beaumont and El Paso, all Texas cities hold **nonpartisan elections**. The irony is that the municipalities are surrounded by counties with highly partisan elections. In most Texas cities, municipal elections are held during the spring in a further attempt to separate city government from party politics.

**nonpartisan elections** Elections in which candidates bear no party label such as Republican or Democrat.

In this electoral setting, a private interest group such as a local realtors' association or homeowners may sponsor a slate of candidates for municipal office, just as a political party would, under the guise of a civic organization that purportedly has no goals of its own, except efficient and responsive government. Such a claim is misleading, however. These groups do have goals and are highly effective in achieving them. In some cities, a charter association or good government league exists; these organizations inevitably reflect the interests of conservative business elements in the community. In other cities, environmentalists or neighborhood advocates or antitax groups may launch well-organized single-issue campaigns. In addition, a number of more or less ad hoc groups usually appear at election time to sponsor one or more candidates, and in all Texas cities, independent candidates also come forth with their own campaigns to seek public office. Municipal organizations often have success on relatively small budgets because turnout in local elections tends to be very low, and with modern technology, voters who are likely to turn out can be identified easily.

Closely associated with nonpartisan elections is the system of electing candidates for the city council at large. All voters select all the members of the council and vote for as many candidates as there are positions on the council. In another practice widely followed in Texas cities, the **place system**, the seats on the council are designated as Place One, Place Two, and so on. In this type of election, candidates who file for a particular place run only against other candidates who also file for that place. Voting is still citywide. The at-large, by-place system predominates in smaller cities.

**place system** A form of at-large election in which all candidates are elected citywide, but the seats on the council are designated Place One, Place Two, and so forth, and each candidate runs only against others who have filed for the same place.

Increasingly, however, Texas cities with populations of 50,000 or more are amending their charters to provide for a district system, wherein candidates are required to live in a particular geographic area within the city and run against only those candidates who also live in the district. Voters choose only among candidates within their district, although the mayor is usually elected at large. In other cities, some council members are elected by district and some at large. Austin was long the major exception. In 2012, citizens voted to change the city charter from at-large, by-place elections to a **district system**, with only the mayor elected at-large, beginning in 2014.

**district system** A system in which a candidate is required to live in the particular geographic area in which he or she runs for office.

Often, the change to district elections came as the result of a successful court suit alleging discrimination against minorities, who were unlikely to win election in a citywide race. Running in districts costs less money and has the advantage of allowing minority candidates to concentrate their campaigning in neighborhoods with large numbers of individuals who share the candidate's ethnic background. Also, additional council seats are sometimes created when a city switches to district elections.

# ISSUE SPOTLIGHT:
## Urban Diversity

Changes in Texas politics are most evident in the major cities where leaders and interest groups reflect newer interests and where the sacrosanct principle of nonpartisanship is sometimes violated.

Austin, San Antonio, Houston, Dallas, El Paso, Fort Worth, and Galveston have had women mayors, as have more than 200 smaller communities. El Paso and San Antonio have elected Mexican American men as mayors, and Dallas and Houston have elected African American men. Austin, Houston, and Dallas have become the homes of large groups of politically active Lesbian, Gay, Bisexual, Transsexual, and Queer (LGBTQ) organizations. Houston elected Annise Parker, a lesbian, as their mayor in 2000.

In the big cities, the importance of neighborhood representation and ethnic representation has intensified to such an extent that it is difficult to gain a workable consensus for establishing public policy. Instead, individual council members sometimes advocate the needs of their districts to the exclusion of concerns about the city as a whole.

**Competency Connection**
**— CRITICAL —**
**THINKING**

At state and national government levels, males dominate decision-making. Yet, at the local level, there has been notable success for women in elected office. Why might that be the case?

Advocates of at-large and by-place elections argue that the council focuses on citywide concerns, but district elections result in a fragmented council whose members concentrate on only the problems of their electoral district. They also think district elections are incompatible with council-manager government, which predominates in the state's home-rule cities, because they make local elections "too political."

Advocates of district elections think the council is more representative when members are elected by wards or districts because diverse ethnicities, distinct neighborhoods, spokespersons for citizens' groups, and individuals without personal wealth have a better opportunity to be elected and will be more inclined to address "local district" problems. They believe government by its very nature is political, and so all political viewpoints should be represented.

Questions about the organization of elections and the nature of representation are at the heart of the democratic process. One measure of a city's democratic morality is the extent to which the council represents the city's ethnic, economic, and geographic diversity.[20]

Controversy also exists over whether elections should be nonpartisan. One argument is that nonpartisan elections rob the voters of the most important symbol that they have for making electoral choices: the party label. Without knowing whether a candidate is a Democrat, a Republican, or a member of some other party, how does the voter decide how to vote?

In answering this question, critics of nonpartisan elections say that voters depend on personalities and extraneous matters. For example, television personalities and athletes frequently win elections simply because they are better known than their opponents. These critics also think that nonpartisan elections rob the community of organized and effective criticism of the government in power. Because most candidates win as individuals rather than as members of an organized political party with common goals and policies, such criticism is sporadic and ineffectual, and meaningful policy alternatives seldom are stated. Another criticism is that nonpartisan elections encourage the development of civic organizations that are in essence local political parties whose purposes and policy proposals are not always clear to the voters.

Advocates of nonpartisan elections obviously disagree. They think the absence of a party label allows local elections to focus on local issues, and not on national issues about which the municipal government can do little or nothing—for example, whether President Obama's economic stimulus package was appropriate or whether President Trump's wall at the southern border will enhance safety in the community. They note that television personalities, athletes, and actors are also elected under party banners. Moreover, they point to the fact that local civic groups clarify, not confuse, local issues. Homeowners, taxpayers, and consumers have become political forces that stand in contrast to the traditional, business-oriented civic associations. As a result, participation is enhanced, although resolving political disagreements has become more difficult.

Local elections have had the salutary effect of allowing those who aspire to public service the opportunity to begin their careers in small and less partisan settings. The careers of women political leaders have often begun in city politics, as have the careers of minority candidates such as African Americans Ron Kirk in Dallas and Sylvester Turner in Houston or Hispanic Julian Castro in San Antonio. The election of Annise Parker, an openly gay person, in Houston, was yet another indicator of the opportunities for historically underrepresented persons in local politics.

At-large elections, nonpartisan voting, and holding elections in the spring apparently do contribute to low voter turnout. A municipal election in which as many as 25 percent of the eligible voters participates is unusual. Many local elections are decided on the basis of the preference of only 5–10 percent of the eligible voters. Moreover, statistics on voting behavior for all elections show that older, affluent Whites vote more frequently than do the young, the poor, and ethnic minorities. The structure of municipal elections in Texas, particularly when those elections are at large, tends to perpetuate the dominant position of the White middle-class business community. Thus, when one examines municipal government against the criteria for a democratic government, one finds some problems of participation, especially among the less affluent and ethnic minorities.

## Special Districts: Our Hidden Governments

For a state that advocates small government, Texas has a lot of governments. As previously discussed, Texas has 254 counties and 1,216 municipalities. It also has the second largest number of special district governments—3,679—in the United States, of which 1,079 are school districts. The number of counties has not changed in more than a century; the number of school districts is relatively stable, though occasionally small districts consolidate; the number of cities has increased slightly every ten years as housing developments incorporate as suburbs in the major metropolitan areas. Special districts just continue to grow, especially those created to provide utilities to new housing developments.[21]

### What is a Special District?

A special district is a unit of local government created to perform limited functions. Its authority is narrow and defined specifically. Special districts vary enormously in size, organization, function, and importance. A few early special districts were created by the constitution, but Texas statutes now stipulate that the legislature itself can create special districts, that counties and municipalities can create some types of special districts (especially for utilities, other basic services, and economic development), and that even state agencies can create some special districts (usually involving natural resources).

There are about two dozen different types of special districts in Texas. School districts and tax appraisal districts exist in every county. Approximately one fourth of the other special districts are housing and community-development districts, while another fourth are concerned with problems of water—control and improvement, drainage, navigation, supply, and sanitation (see Chapter 14 for additional information on water issues). Other frequently encountered types of special districts are airport, soil conservation, municipal utilities, hospital, fire prevention, weed control, public transportation, and community college districts.

No single state or county agency is responsible for supervising the activities or auditing the financial records of all these special districts. Such supervision depends on the type of district involved. For example, community college districts are supervised by the Texas Higher Education Coordinating Board and the Texas Education Agency. Average citizens, however, have a hard time keeping track of the many special districts surrounding them. The lack of uniformity and resulting confusion are caused in part by the various ways in which special districts can be created: through special acts of the legislature or under general laws, by general-purpose governments (cities and counties) in some instances, and even by state agencies.

## Why Special Districts?

Why does Texas have so many special districts? Are they really necessary?

**Inadequacy of Established Governments** First, our established governments—the cities and counties—are inadequate to solve many of the increasingly diverse problems of government. The problem of flood control and provision of adequate water supply can seldom be solved within a single city or county, for example; in fact, it frequently goes beyond state boundaries, thus requiring an interstate authority. Cities and counties lack funding to finance needed projects. Hospital and community college districts are sometimes created because the debt limitations on established governmental units make taking on a major new activity all but impossible. Special districts stem from antiquated government institutions designed for a low technology rural society fashioned nearly a century and a half ago that cannot address complex modern problems.

These inadequacies make the creation of a new unit of government an attractive solution. Perhaps nowhere does one see the need for, and advantages of, special districts more than in the various water supply districts. The Lower Colorado River Authority (discussed further in Chapter 14), for example, owns and operates six of the seven lakes in the Austin area. Another example of solving a problem through creation of a special district is the central appraisal district in each county that provides assessments of property value for all jurisdictions in the county.

**Ease of Organization and Operation** Part of the attraction of special districts is that they are *easy to organize and operate*. Political leaders of cities and counties frequently promote a special district as a solution to what might otherwise become "their problem," and the legislature is willing to go along. Creating a hospital district, for example, means that the city and the county do not have to raise their taxes. Indeed, the cost may be spread over several cities or counties included in the special district. Hunt Memorial Hospital District (Greenville and Commerce areas) is illustrative.

**Private Gain** In a few instances, *special districts have been created primarily for private gain*. Land speculators and real estate developers create special districts called municipal utility districts (MUDs) on the outskirts of urban areas to increase the value of their holdings. Once enabling legislation has been obtained from the state, it requires only a handful of votes in the sparsely settled, newly created district to authorize a bond issue for the development of water, sewer, and other utilities. This development increases the value of the property in the district to the benefit of the developers. Ultimately, of course, the taxpayers pay for the bonds, sometimes through very high utility rates. MUDs are a good example of the consequences of a lack of effective state regulation of special districts.

Economic development districts created by counties have the ability to collect taxes that are used mainly for private benefit. Examples include a district in Bexar County created to establish a golf course resort, one in Smith County that allowed a builder and his employees to constitute the board governing a district created to fund a truck stop, and a Hays County water control and improvement district that benefited only one California-based home builder.[22]

Denton County became so profligate in creating special taxing districts to help the developers of luxury housing additions that the attorney general in 2001 announced new rules for approving bond elections affecting such districts. However, a special district was created in 2010 by only two voters, although another district was dismantled.[23]

**Flexibility** *Special districts offer great flexibility to government organizations* and have the added attraction of rarely conflicting with existing units. A two-city airport such as Dallas–Fort Worth International is the result of a flexible airport authority.

**Apolitical Approach** With highly technical problems such as flood control, the *special district offers the opportunity to "get it out of politics."* In other words, it is possible to take a businesslike approach and bring in technical specialists to attack the problem. The Wise County Water Control and Improvement District 1 is an example. Such districts really are not apolitical, but they do allow the focus to remain on the task at hand. Of course, other types of special districts—most notably, those whose purpose is economic development—tend to be highly political.

## Assessment of Special Districts

Special districts other than school and appraisal districts are *profoundly undemocratic.* They are "hidden governments," with far less visibility than city or county governments. It is not an exaggeration to say that every reader of this book is under the jurisdiction of at least one special district, yet it will be a very rare reader who knows which districts affect her or him, how much they cost in taxes, who the commissioner or other officials of each special district are, whether they are elected or (as is more frequently the case) appointed, and what policies they follow. Special district government is unseen by and frequently unresponsive to the people. Thus, when one applies the test of democratic morality, one finds that special districts fail to meet the standards of participation and public input. Indeed, they are sometimes an unfortunate reflection of Texas's traditionalistic and individualistic political culture.[24]

Most special districts are small in size and scope. Therefore, they are *uneconomical.* Their financial status is often shaky, and so the interest rates that taxpayers must pay on the bond issues used to finance many types of special district projects are exceptionally high. Economies such as large-scale purchasing are impossible.

Finally, one of the most serious consequences of the proliferation of special districts is that they *greatly complicate the problems of government, particularly in urban areas.* With many separate governments, the likelihood is greater that haphazard development, confusion, and inefficiency will occur. No single government has comprehensive authority, and coordination among so many smaller governments becomes extremely difficult.

Texans have been reluctant to experiment with a comprehensive urban government. Their individualism demands retention of the many local units, although other states' metropolitan areas, such as Miami and Nashville, have succeeded with comprehensive government. Instead, Texans rely on one of the twenty-four *regional planning councils*, also known as *councils of governments* (COGs), to provide coordination in metropolitan areas. These voluntary organizations of local government provide such functions as regional land-use and economic planning, police training, and fact-finding studies on problems such as transportation.

Given the inadequacies of comprehensive planning and periodic revenue shortfalls at the local level, special districts will surely continue to proliferate. Under current conditions, they are too easy to create and operate as short-range solutions to governmental problems. Such continued proliferation, without adequate planning and supervision, will result not in solutions to, but rather in worsening the problems of, local and particularly urban government.

## School Districts

School districts are special districts, but they pervade Texas local politics and maintain a high local profile. School board members are publicly elected, their decisions are usually well publicized by local media paying careful attention to education decisions, and the public has considerable interest in and knowledge about school district politics. Indeed, although county or city public hearings sometimes fail to attract a crowd, as soon as a school board agenda includes a topic such as determining attendance districts—basically, who gets bused and who does not—or transgendered student bathroom access, the public turns out for the debate. Finally, although the local boards have a substantial amount of control over such matters as individual school management, location of schools, and personnel, the state is the ultimate authority for basic school policies and shares in the funding of public schools.

Public school finance has been a dominant issue in Texas politics at several points in the state's history, but particularly since 1987. The division of the state into more than a thousand school districts is one of the factors contributing to considerable unevenness in the quality of education provided from one district to the next. That unevenness in turn creates inequities in funding public education. School districts depend on two revenue sources: property taxes and state assistance. However, in Texas, state aid pays for only about half the cost of public education, thereby putting considerable pressure on the unpopular tax. The two largest differences in spending in richer versus poorer districts are in facilities (new buildings with adequate classroom size and modern technology versus decaying and cramped buildings) and enrichment activities (choir trips to Europe versus a poor-quality field for athletics and band). The issue of school finance, which is addressed throughout this book, is the ongoing source of political debate as Texas school funding overall is among the lowest in the nation, a fact that presents challenges to future economic growth. Moreover, wide variation in the tax revenue in local districts makes disparity in funding for schools a profound problem of equity.

# Local Government: Prospects for the Future

As trends toward urbanization and suburbanization continue, local government problems promise to become more acute. Yet local governments are absolutely vital components of the governance structure. What are the prospects for local governments in Texas under these circumstances?

## Finance

Local governments have issues involving both income and spending. Indeed, the long-term economic outlook and resource challenges are two of the mega-issues facing cities nationally.[25]

**ad valorem property tax** A tax based on the value of real property, and in some cases, the contents of structures, assessed at some cents per $100 of valuation.

**revenue bonds** Government debt that is sold to private investors and paid off by the revenue produced from services such as water sales.

**Revenue**  Local government finance closely parallels the state's economic and fiscal condition (see Chapter 12) in that lean times mean tight budgets and boom economies afford greater revenue and spending possibilities. However, local governments are more restricted in the ways they can attain revenue.

Across the country, the backbone of county, municipal, and school district finance is the **ad valorem property tax**, which is assessed against homes and commercial properties. All of these entities also borrow money to finance government operations, often with **revenue bonds**. For example, to build a new sewer system, a city might issue bonds that are then paid off with the revenue from wastewater collection fees. In other words, tomorrow's customers of the city's sewer services will be charged so as to reimburse the city for the costs of building the sewer today. Municipalities have more flexibility with regard to revenue sources because they can collect sales taxes, but counties and some special districts can also collect a sales tax under limited circumstances.

**user fees** A fee for a specific governmental service charged to the person who benefits from the service; a greens fee at a municipal golf course and college tuition are both user fees.

**intergovernmental transfers** Money granted to a lower level of government by a higher level of government for a specific use, for example, welfare dollars that are passed to the county from the state and the national governments.

**stimulus funds** To help in recovering from the recession of 2007–2009, the national government created a variety of funds to aid both the private sector (banks, insurance companies, automobile industry) and the public sector (local law enforcement, additional school teachers).

**mandate** Action that the national government requires state and local governments to take or that the state requires cities, counties, and special districts to take.

Governments also collect **user fees**. For example, a county will collect fees associated with court expenses; a water district will collect fees for the water it delivers; an airport district will collect landing fees from airline companies; a school district will collect admissions fees for athletic contents. Municipalities collect a number of fees, especially if they provide electric, water, wastewater, or drainage services or operate recreational facilities such as a golf course.

In addition, local governments receive **intergovernmental transfers**—money from a higher level of government such as the federal and state funds that flow to counties for welfare and indigent health care and the dollars that go to counties and cities to help with road and bridge construction. The most dramatic example is the funding of public schools.

**Spending** General-purpose governments, counties and municipalities, provide a wide variety of services to their citizens. Counties spend much of their budgets on roads and bridges, law enforcement, and welfare and health care for persons without private insurance. Municipalities also provide streets, law enforcement, and some social services, but in addition they provide parks, libraries, transportation, fire protection, and public utilities. Special districts are much more limited in the scope of their spending: the type of district determines the expenditures (schools, water, drainage, airport, utilities, and so on). For all local governments, revenue shortfalls make spending choices difficult.

**Fiscal Woes** Local governments gained fiscal support during the first stages of the recovery from the deep recession of 2007–2009 because of federal **stimulus funds** earmarked for local governments, but lost those funds as the national government faced its own financial crises for the 2012 budget year, though the 2019 session promises to provide increments in funding because of a growing economy. Moreover, both the national and state governments continue to **mandate** spending on certain programs whether or not the local governments want to provide those services.

As a high-growth state, Texas continues to have more and more residents, with proportionately less revenue to provide services. Local governments have sought creative solutions to the budget woes, including cooperating with one another and with the private sector, asking citizens to volunteer, seriously addressing productivity issues, and turning to contracting out services to the private sector (e.g., using private solid waste companies to pick up garbage). However, local fiscal problems, like state budget issues, will continue to grow for a number of reasons, such as public aversion to tax increases, the increasing inability of the state and national government to provide relief, and competition with one another, particularly over the property tax. In the election campaign of 2018, Lieutenant Governor Dan Patrick pledged to curtail local property taxes, the key revenue source for local governments.

## Other Issues

Several developments are worth noting. As urban problems and local finance problems become more acute, national and state governments are being forced to pay more attention to them. The legislature is becoming more "citified," though its capacity to act may be limited.

Until 1978, Texas had virtually no *mass transit* (trains, subways, buses) to relieve the congestion on the freeways. Beginning in Houston and Harris counties, mass transit has developed across the state, especially in the counties of a half-million or more population. It has long been obvious that the practice of virtually every person using his or her own motor vehicle for personal and business travel is incompatible with increasing urbanization. Smog, congestion, and even rush-hour gridlock do not make for a high quality of life. Mass transit systems must be established if the trend toward further urbanization is to continue, especially given the inability of the state to build roadways fast enough to move traffic at peak times or to clean the air sufficiently to meet federal standards. Cooperative discussions among urban mayors in Texas continue to examine ways to expand mass transportation, both within cities and between them. Another development is that of *strategic planning,* a type of planning that focuses on identifying a mission and pursuing it in an opportunistic manner by taking advantage of any favorable situation that comes along. For example, a community that strives to attract high technology might aggressively seek to persuade electronics plants to locate there, perhaps even ignoring some of their environmental problems.

A third area of concern for the future is *interlocal cooperation.* Councils of Government (COGs) are one example of an arrangement that allows the many kinds of local governments—counties, cities, special districts—to work together to solve their common problems. Cooperative ventures such as city-county ambulance service, city-school playgrounds and libraries, and multiple-city purchasing are other examples. Indeed, interlocal agreements are the most dynamic element of modern intergovernmental relations and can help overcome some of the negative effects of the growing number of governments.

A fourth area of concern is *ordinance-making power for counties.* The lack of ordinance-making power is developing into a serious problem for safety, environmental, and aesthetic standards, as well as other matters. For example, an issue of growing concern is the lack of control over adult bookstores and massage parlors that set up shop just outside a municipality, where control of them becomes a problem for the county. Counties want and need ordinance-making power, but have thus far been denied it, primarily because of the opposition of real estate businesses and developers, who can, for example, create developments in unincorporated areas outside the extraterritorial jurisdiction of the cities that do not have to meet rigorous city building codes.

A fifth major problem that will continue to plague local governments is *sprawl.* The demands on and costs of local government are not subject to economies of scale. In manufacturing, for example, producing more cars or soap bars results in a lowered *unit cost,* the cost of one car or bar of soap. This principle does not hold true for picking up more bags of garbage or cleaning more streets or teaching more children. Burgeoning populations that move farther and farther away from the central city make delivery of services more costly and more difficult.

## ISSUE SPOTLIGHT:
## Metropolitan Areas

Exactly what constitutes a metropolitan area is confusing because the U.S. Bureau of the Census categorizes metropolitan statistical areas (MSAs) in several ways. Texas has twenty-five or twenty-six metropolitan areas, depending on whether one looks at the combined Dallas–Fort Worth–Arlington MSA as one or divides it into Dallas–Plano–Irving and Fort Worth–Arlington MSAs. DFW and Houston are in the top ten nationally. The twenty-five recognized metropolitan statistical areas in Texas are, in descending order of population: Dallas–Fort Worth–Arlington, Houston–The Woodlands–SugarLand, San Antonio–New Braunfels, Austin–Round Rock, El Paso, McAllen–Edinburg–Mission, Corpus Christi, Killeen–Temple, Brownsville–Harlingen, Beaumont–Port Arthur, Lubbock, Laredo, Amarillo, Waco, College Station–Bryan, Longview, Tyler, Abilene, Wichita Falls, Midland Odessa, Sherman–Denison, San Angelo, Victoria, and Texarkana. Galveston is considered an urban cluster, lacking a few thousand people to be a metropolitan area.

Competency Connection
**SOCIAL RESPONSIBILITY**

Could the costs of government and quality of services be helped if some government functions were spread across metropolitan areas as a whole instead of having each city provide services, such as water, road maintenance, garbage collection, and police protection?

# Leadership in Local Government

Historically, genuine differences have existed between county leadership and the leadership of other local governments. Elected officials in county government hold full-time positions that pay decent salaries and represent starting points in party politics. In most other local governments, a strong tradition of amateurism prevails: the best elected officials are paid parking-and-lunch money and give of their time only as a public service.

The decentralized nature of county governments has often led to rural fiefdoms of commissioners or sheriffs, but in urban counties, candidates as diverse as ethnic minority candidates with major social agendas and young conservatives contemplating a lifetime in politics are beginning to seek county office.. In large cities, serving on the city council also can be a step into big-time politics, and mayors have gone on to both the state and national capitols. City councils and school boards are becoming increasingly diversified in terms of gender, ethnicity, and viewpoint.[26]

The Texas Association of County Officials continues to be dominated by rural interests, a modern example of the "empty space" politics of local governance. Municipalities are more consistently aided by the Texas Municipal League, which has divisions for both elected officials and professional personnel. In addition, a variety of specialized organizations, such as the Texas Public Power Association, address other local interests. All of these groups also lobby for local interests with the legislature.

A reader who would like to influence local government can get involved in many ways, perhaps beginning a path as a future leader:

▶ Attend a public hearing and speak out.
▶ Organize a petition drive on a matter of importance to you—saving the trees along a planned freeway route, for example.
▶ Attend a neighborhood meeting.
▶ Attend a meeting of the city council, county commission, or school board.
▶ Talk to the city clerk or the county clerk to find out how to volunteer for an advisory committee or citizen task force.
▶ Volunteer to work for a local candidate during an election.

## ISSUE SPOTLIGHT:
### Hurricanes, Hurricanes, Hurricanes

Texas cities have long been challenged by hurricanes. Galveston was devastated by a hurricane in 1900 which nearly wiped it off of the map and recovered in part through its new innovative city government system—the commission form discussed elsewhere in this chapter. Texas cities in 2005 and early 2006 were severely impacted by Hurricanes Katrina and Rita. The former resulted in tens of thousands of persons, especially from New Orleans, fleeing Katrina in favor of Houston, Dallas, and many other Texas cities, creating a long-lasting effect on law enforcement and social services, and for its generosity, Houston was named "Texan of the Year" for 2005 by the *Dallas Morning News*. Rita caused major damage to the Texas Gulf Coast, especially in the Golden Triangle (Beaumont–Port Arthur–Orange and surrounding towns) just as Hurricane Ike devastated Galveston in 2008. Then, in 2017, Hurricane Harvey caused massive flooding in all of southeast Texas, and challenged city government of Houston greatly, forcing a new discussion of the role of zoning and regulation in a city that has often eschewed both.

Competency Connection
SOCIAL RESPONSIBILITY

How might having zoning ordinances in Houston affect the city's susceptibility to flooding during a hurricane? And is such enhanced regulation a good idea?

## Summary

**LO 11.1** **Texas's 254 counties all have the same form of government, a commissioners court headed by a county judge.** County officials are elected on a partisan basis. The commissioners court is greatly limited by the lack of power to pass ordinances. Although about 10 percent of the counties have instituted modern management practices, counties have many aspects of nineteenth-century government. County governments are indispensable to the 3.6 million Texans who live in rural areas and very small towns, but the constitutional limits on the organization of government do not serve the needs of the twelfth most densely population state in the United States.

**LO 11.2** **In contrast to counties, cities are often professionally managed, and home-rule cities—those with 5,000 or more population—have considerable flexibility in how any given municipality is structured to provide both political accountability and managerial expertise.** Council-manager government prevails in home-rule cities, while mayor-council government is the usual form in general-law cities. Elections are nonpartisan.

**LO 11.3** **Texas is second only to Illinois in the number of special districts governments, which provide services for everything from water supply to airports.** These districts are created for a variety of reasons when counties and cities are just not sufficient to carry out a particular function, but they complicate decisions making and add a layer of taxation for citizens. Except for school districts, the public often knows little about special districts, which are largely hidden from view.

**LO 11.4** **Although Texas is a conservative state, citizens still expect local governments to provide many services.** A growing issue is finding adequate revenues, especially because property taxes are so unpopular. Local governments also share problems in terms of the need for strategic planning and better transportation. They try to help themselves through interlocal cooperation.

**LO 11.5** **A critical factor in the future success of local governments is the quality of the leadership.** Continuing issues include domination by the business community and the issues created by partisan elections in counties.

## Critical Thinking

1. Counties are constrained by the type of government the Texas Constitution provides for them. Discuss the structure of county government and explain the problems that result from it.

2. Explain why critics might argue that special district governments are not democratic. If they are not democratic, what arguments might be made to explain their existence? Describe how they exemplify the difference between democratic ideal and reality.

Many states reap a substantial portion of state
revenues from gambling, but conservative Texans
have protested against an expansion of gambling
in the state.

*AP Images/Harry Cabluck*

# The State Economy and the Financing of State Government

# 12

The *ability* of any government to generate the revenues needed to provide the programs and services that citizens want is directly tied to the economy. Are most people working? Are wages good? Are profits high? Is money available for loans to finance business expansion and home ownership? The *willingness* of a government to raise and spend money is determined by the state's political philosophy. In Texas, that is a previously traditionalistic-individualistic political culture. This chapter examines the Texas economy, how the state gets its revenue, and both its *ability* and its *willingness* to raise and spend money for public purposes. Looking at both aspects of fiscal policy allows us to compare the democratic ideal of providing adequate state services for citizens with the reality of the biennial budget.

Texas's political leaders have bragged for years about the state's ability to create jobs and the state's highly favorable (low-tax, few labor unions) economic environment. They have made the arguable assumption that all there is to having a robust economy is to recruit new business investment.[1] However, a sound economy includes helping existing businesses to grow and bringing as much diversity to the economy as possible. Furthermore, in industrialized nations, one expects the government to promote policies that create a good quality of life for all citizens and to manage the state's finances in such a way that the needs of tomorrow, as well as today, are considered.

> MOST OFFICEHOLDERS WOULD RATHER HANDLE RATTLESNAKES THAN VOTE FOR AN INCOME TAX.
>
> Dave McNeely,
> *Long-Time Writer on Texas Politics,
> in* State Legislatures, *2007*

Texas has a long history of a boom-or-bust economy. When oil and gas prices are high, the state has big surpluses. As the United States began to rely more on foreign oil, the state's revenue picture dimmed because Texas could no longer depend on energy sales to citizens in other states to fuel its budget needs even if prices went up. Consequently, it began to find that shortfalls were more common than surpluses. Particularly since a solution to the problems of public school finance (the largest share of the state budget) was supposedly fixed by changes in the business tax in 2006, the state has had problems because the structure of the tax was inadequate from day one. Not only has the state faced revenue problems since 2006, but also its population continues to grow.

Texas is a "pay-as-you-go" state. Unlike the national government, it cannot finance the short-comings of its revenue by accruing debt. The state has a boom-and-bust economy and big spending needs spurred by high population growth. At the same time, Texans would rather handle rattle-snakes than raise taxes. The result is a tendency to talk a good game when providing programs to meet ordinary people's needs but simultaneously be unwilling to fund such programs adequately.

Another major issue concerning the revenue system is its fairness. The poor in Texas pay a higher proportion of their incomes in taxes than do the wealthy, and the business tax has so many exclusions and exceptions that it will never meet revenue expectations. These facts raise questions about how democratic or equitable the state revenue system is.

The chapter evaluates how the state spends its money, including how elected officials struggle to agree on what the budget will be. Budgets are the best guides to policy priorities. They tell the story of how well citizens' interests are accommodated in state spending.

Texas grew from 17 million people in 1990 to more than 29.1 million people in 2019, and the population continues to grow at a rate much higher than the national average. During that same period, the state budget increased from $126.6 billion for **fiscal years** (FY) 1990–1991 to $216.8 billion for FY 2018–2019—an increase of 71.2 percent. When adjusted for population growth (more people require more services) and for **inflation** (i.e., increases in what things cost), the Texas budget has been relatively flat over nearly 30 years according to the Legislative Budget Board, as Figure 12-1 shows. Budget growth has

**fiscal year** The budget year for a government or a corporation; it may not coincide with a calendar year.

**inflation** A rise in the general price level, which is the same thing as a fall in the value of the dollar.

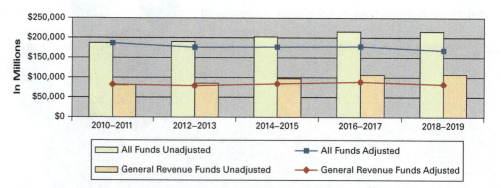

Figure 12-1 Trends in Texas State Government Expenditures, 2010–2019

SOURCE: Legislative Budget Board, Fiscal Size Up 2018–19, p. 24.

been less than 2 percent a year, below the population growth and inflation rates for the period as a whole. Meanwhile, the scope of government responsibilities continues to grow.[2]

# The Texas Economy

The Texas economy is characterized by cycles of boom and bust. The economic uncertainty is made worse by a tax code that doesn't provide much flexibility.

## Heart of the Economy

Historically, the Texas economy has been based on natural resources, chiefly oil, land, and water. Indeed, Texas has been characterized as the state where "money gushes from the ground in the oil fields and grows on the citrus trees in the irrigated orchards."[3] Texas is still an important producer of oil and gas, and listings of its principal products include petroleum, natural gas, and natural gas liquids.[4] Chemicals, cotton, and cattle also contribute their share of wealth, as do construction and manufacturing. The economy has diversified in recent years, but still relies on traditional resources disproportionally.

The state's fossil fuels are bountiful but not endless—that is, once used, they cannot be replaced. Furthermore, the Texas economy is shifting from one based on natural resources to one based on information and technology, including financial management. In 2017, the Texas gross state product was more than $1.645 trillion a year, with the highest growth rate in the country for much of 2018. Overall, the Texas economy ranked second only to California.[5] For perspective, Russia, with nearly five times as many residents as Texas, has an economy more than $400 billion smaller than the Lone Star State.[6] Although the economy has grown and diversified, the percentage of the state economy derived from agriculture still is second only to California. Moreover, Texas remains one of the top ten states for mining, which includes oil and natural gas production. Yet, one cannot ignore that the oil fields no longer represent the chief revenue source for the state. Indeed, gas drilling has shown more promise than oil.

Although the state's recent economy has moved away from one based solely on natural resources, it still has been subject to the ups and downs of resource-based components, such as oil and agriculture. Indeed, the erosion of the natural-resource-based economy has meant that employment rates fluctuate with the health of the energy-based economy. In December 2018, Texas had an unemployment rate of 4.0 percent, historically quite a low rate. Wages still have not attained the same level they had before the recession of 2008, and forecasts are that employment will remain stable and wages will be strong during the 2018–2019 biennium.[7] State government has worked to shore up the shaky economy by consolidating economic development programs, developing aggressive marketing campaigns for farm and ranch products, and selling the high-technology capability of the state through industry-university partnerships.

## Boom and Bust

In the spring of 2000, the high-tech sector of the U.S. economy began to plummet. The NASDAQ, the index that reflects technology stocks, lost almost three-quarters of its value; and large layoffs in telecommunications, computer, and Internet firms led to prolonged unemployment in "new economy" industries.

On September 11, 2001, terrorists attacked the United States by hijacking four airliners and using them as weapons. Two of these planes brought down the twin World Trade Towers in New York and a third destroyed a section of the Pentagon in Washington, D.C. The horror of lost lives and the surprise of the attack coupled with actual economic damages, particularly to the travel industry, further shook confidence in the U.S. economy. A series of corporate scandals made matters worse, especially because they involved the top corporate officers growing very rich while the pensions, and ultimately the jobs, of ordinary workers were squandered. The largest scandal of all was Houston-based Enron. Military action that began in Afghanistan in 2001 and Iraq in 2003 followed the 9/11 attack. Coupled with two national tax cuts, the costs of war sent the country into significant debt and rattled the economy further.

Texas and other states were in no way immune to these national and international events. Although Texas exports more products for sale than any other state, trade with Mexico was marred by both agricultural drought and fear of crossing the border into areas that were run by drug lords. Texans' confidence in the economy was steadily eroding due to the lack of job growth and the sluggish economy. The state had banked on high technology as an answer to the waning of the old natural-resource-based economy, but the high-technology crash led to tens of thousands of job layoffs and foreclosures on thousands of homes. The feeling of malaise was not improved by national news that some of the "new economy" jobs based on information and technology were being exported permanently to other countries with lower wage scales.[8]

However, some bright spots began to emerge. Houston's low unemployment rate signaled recovery in the oil and petrochemical industries. Texas also profited from heightened military activities because of its many defense contractors, even though individual families lost ground when reservists were called up from better-paying jobs into military service. Generally, however, higher unemployment rates cause a demand for more government services. The "bottom line" was that the legislature began its 2003 session with a $10 billion deficit, a situation not unfamiliar to those in other state capitals.

The 2005 and 2007 legislatures both began with surpluses as the economy improved. Thus, once again, the boom-and-bust cycle had made its will known. Texas reemerged as the number-one state in the country for corporate relocation and expansion.[9] By 2007, unemployment was down to 4.1 percent, and 239,000 jobs had been created in twelve months, in part due to robust foreign trade. Dallas–Fort Worth, Austin, and Houston ranked in the top thirty global cities in the country, which is a designation given to cities with a strong orientation toward international business. Texas had moved to number two in the country as a desirable retirement spot. Even agriculture was improving because the 2005–2006 drought had ended.[10]

By late 2008, Texans, like other Americans, were finding themselves mired in debt even to the point of losing their homes in foreclosures and lacking in basic protections such as health insurance. This situation was a product of the deep national recession of 2007–2009, although the Texas economy was not as bad as that of other states, and two years of prolonged drought in key agricultural areas of the state. The housing market continued to lag, and economy recovery did not include many new well-paying jobs. Although Texas boasted that it had created more new jobs than any other state, it also had the highest percentage (12.6 percent) of workers in the nation earning only the minimum wage.[11] A fully employed individual earning minimum wage would make only $14,616 a year.

In April 2011, the unemployment rate was 8.1 percent, better than the national 8.8 percent but still high, and concerns were growing about prospects for middle-class employment (highly skilled technical workers and minimally skilled service workers).[12] The legislature was forced to cope with a $27 billion shortfall in revenues needed just to maintain the level of service for the previous two years and pay leftover bills from FY 2011. Thus, the FY 2012–2013 budget saw many cuts in state services, especially education.

By the time the 2013 legislative session convened, Texas had returned to the boom cycle, producing more jobs than any other state, enjoying the revenue from taxes on oil and gas production, and taking full advantage of a "Texas is open for business" approach. By 2019, the budget continued to grow, employment rates were high and stable, and the short term economic forecast was strong.

## Creating a Favorable Business Climate

It is often said that the "bidness of Texas is bidness." Chapter 3 discussed the most powerful interest groups in the state, including energy and insurance. State policymakers have tried to create an environment in which business could easily expand and would want to locate in Texas. Indeed, in 2019, Texas was ranked fifteenth among all states in the best place to make a living and fifteenth among the states for a favorable business tax environment.[13]

State politicians like to brag that Texas has the most favorable tax environment for business; however, rating bureaus also consider the fairness of state taxes and whether they are adequate to fund state needs. The Texas revenue system, particularly its tax structure, lacks **elasticity**; that is, it is not easily adjusted to ups and downs in the economy, a problem made worse when the national government also cuts back payments to states. Whatever the system's limitations, the Texas tax structure is an overall plus for the business community.

So also are the state's stingy policies toward workers who find themselves unemployed or injured on the job. For a generation, the legislature has tinkered with legislation in these two areas in an effort to minimize costs to businesses and to provide them flexibility in the ways money must be set aside to pay for unemployment or injury. In Texas, a worker who loses his or her job can receive up to $465 a week, based on previous earnings, for up to 26 weeks unless the federal government extends the time period, as it occasionally does in times of recession. A worker who is injured or who develops a job-related illness can receive workers' compensation income and medical assistance. The rate is based on the wage rate of the person's previous thirteen weeks of employment, and the maximum number of weeks of support is 104.[14]

Texas has provided the governor with more than $600 million in incentives to lure technology companies and entrepreneurs to the state since 2004, although the appropriations have declined a bit in recent years. The state is loath to cut highway funds, regardless of other budget slashing, because of the importance of the roads to the movement of goods. However, the most serious shortcoming of the state's efforts to spur business development that provides better-than-minimum-wage jobs is its failure to understand the need for adequate support of its public education system. In a high tech world, an educated citizenry is required to attract business to any state. As business leaders noted during the 2011 legislative session, "School cuts are [a] risky business."[15] Indeed, one of the challenges to economic growth in Texas is the provision of an educated workforce.

## Where Does the Money Come From?

State finance consists of raising and spending money. For most of those involved in government, the budget is the bottom line, as it is for the rest of us. Policy decisions regarding state financing are made in the glaring light of political reality—what political scientist Harold Laswell called "Politics: Who Gets What, When, and How" back in 1911. Whenever money is raised, it comes from someone; whenever it is spent, someone gets it. Struggles over who will pay for the government and who will receive dollars from it are at the heart of politics in Texas, as elsewhere.

Part of the struggle over revenues comes from philosophical disagreements about revenue sources and who should bear the burden of taxation (see the later section titled "Who Pays?"). Both the traditionalistic and individualistic political cultures are antitax overall and in favor of regressive taxes when money must be raised. Figure 12-2 gives an approximate idea of the sources of state revenue for FY 2020–2021. Tax revenues account for the largest segment of revenue produced by Texas, with the sales tax bringing in 54.5 percent of revenue, other state taxes accounting for 33.8 percent, and other revenue sources producing 11.7 percent of revenue from within the state. In addition, about one third of all state revenue comes from the national government. Federal contributions have been relatively flat over the last several years. Much of

**elasticity** The flexibility and breadth of the tax system so that state revenues are not seriously disrupted even if one segment of the economy is troubled.

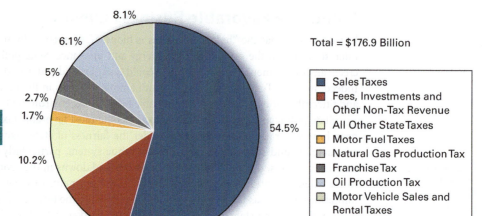

Total = $176.9 Billion

**Legend:**
- Sales Taxes
- Fees, Investments and Other Non-Tax Revenue
- All Other State Taxes
- Motor Fuel Taxes
- Natural Gas Production Tax
- Franchise Tax
- Oil Production Tax
- Motor Vehicle Sales and Rental Taxes

Percentages shown: 8.1%, 6.1%, 5%, 2.7%, 1.7%, 10.2%, 11.7%, 54.5%

**Figure 12-2 Comptroller Revenue Estimates 2020–2021, in Percentages (in Billions)\***

SOURCE: Glenn Hegar, Texas Comptroller of Public Accounts, Biennial Revenue Estimate, 2020–2021, January 2019.

**Competency Connection**
**CRITICAL THINKING**

The largest single source of revenue for the state is funding from the federal government? What are the advantages and disadvantages of states receiving funding from the national government?

federal aid comes in the form of grants and in specific budget areas, such as homeland security, Interstate highways, and Medicaid, it is not evenly spread across state needs and leaves some areas with sparse funding. Revenue sources fluctuate over time due largely to economic downtrends and uptrends, as well as changing federal budget priorities.

Oil and gas revenues once were the mainstay of Texas revenue. Both the severance tax—the tax on the production of oil, natural gas, and other minerals—and other energy-related income from land leases, equipment sales taxes, and even general sales taxes generated by energy industry employees remain important sources of revenues and have helped to forestall a state income tax. However, the energy business has its own booms and busts, thereby impacting the state revenues accordingly. Seeking to avoid tax increases, the legislature has frequently turned to charges such as the fees paid for professional licenses or college tuition to augment the state treasury. Over time, revenues paid directly by individuals—for example, licenses and fees—have steadily increased as politicians have attempted to offset the loss of severance tax dollars as an easy way to avoid unpopular taxes such as those on income or property. Always of importance is the proportion of state revenues generated by the general sales tax—the added cents on every purchase of clothing or restaurant meals—because this tax tends to hit the poor the hardest. The sales tax actually has erratically declined in percentage of revenues generated, although not in dollars, over the past thirty-five years because of the increase in nontax revenues and federal dollars.

Economic growth, higher and more expensive fees, and requiring local governments to fund some activities previously paid for by the state has allowed the state government to maintain programs without state tax increases, and a strong economic growth in 2018–2019 indicates optimism for more spending on a number of programs.

## Collection and Administration

State revenues are collected in many ways by many people. Monies from federal grants may be sent directly to the state agency responsible for administering the program being funded. The general retail sales tax is collected by retail merchants and then forwarded to the state comptroller. Other taxes, such as the inheritance tax, may be forwarded directly from the individual to the state comptroller. The two officials most concerned with state financial administration are the comptroller, who is responsible for tax collection, investments, and the safeguarding of public funds, and the auditor, who oversees state agencies to ensure the legality of their expenditures.

Once collected, state revenues are channeled into more than 5,000 funds, some of which are designated to supply monies for the general operation of government, while others are dedicated to (reserved for) specific services. Here are the five major funds in Texas:

1. The General Revenue Fund, which supports the majority of state programs
2. The Omnibus Tax Clearance Fund, which is allocated in part to two other funds, the General Revenue Fund and Available School Fund, and in part to such specific functions as the construction of farm-to-market roads, parks, and teachers' retirement
3. The Available School Fund, which underwrites public school textbooks and part of the Foundation School Program, the major source of state aid for local school districts
4. The Highway Motor Fuel Fund, one-fourth of which is allocated to the Available School Fund and the remainder to highways and roads
5. The State Highway Fund, which is used for highway and road construction and maintenance, right-of-way acquisition, and related purposes

Other funds set aside for particular purposes include those dedicated to federally funded programs, parks and wildlife, roads, and teachers' retirement.

## Nontax Sources of Revenue

The state has sources of revenue other than the checks oil producers write to the state comptroller and the pennies, nickels, and dimes that citizens dig out of their pockets to satisfy the sales tax. As discussed previously, these revenues include federal grants, borrowing, and several other sources, including fees such as college tuition.

**Federal Grants** The largest nontax source of money is federal grants. Beginning in the 1960s, state and local governments became heavily dependent on national budgetary policies that distributed monies to the treasuries of states, cities, and other local governments. Originally, these dollars came to states in the form of **categorical grants-in-aid** that could be used only for specific programs such as community health centers. **General revenue sharing** was then enacted; it was distributed by formula and could be used by state and local governments for whatever projects these governments wanted—police salaries, playground equipment, home care for the elderly. General revenue sharing ended for states in 1979 and for cities in 1986.

In addition, the federal government began to fund **block grants**, which ultimately became the principal vehicle for distributing dollars for general use in broad programs such as community development. States gained more control under block grants because many funds were no longer channeled directly to local governments, but rather "passed through" a state agency. This flexibility came at a price, however, as the amount of funding for many programs, especially those affecting the poor and urban development, was reduced. Nationally, block grants were often supported by Republicans. They reasoned that states could use money more efficiently if they were given flexibility. Accordingly, by using block grants, the total amount of appropriations for programs could be reduced without affecting the quality of programs. Democrats disagreed, arguing that the real agenda of the Republicans was to decrease government services. Ironically, one of the biggest conversions of a program from a categorical grant-in-aid to a block grant was done under President Bill Clinton, a Democrat, when Aid to Families with Dependent Children (AFDC) was converted to Temporary Assistance to Needy Families (TANF). As discussed in Chapter 13, the conversion led to the rapid decline of that program.

Initially, increases in federal funding were attributable to interstate highway construction and maintenance spending following the increase in the national motor fuels tax in 1983.

**categorical grants-in-aid** Federal funds that can be used only for specific purposes.

**general revenue sharing** A federal program that allowed state and local governments great flexibility in the use of federal funds. It expired in 1986.

**block grants** Federal funds that can be used for a broad range of programs; the state or local government recipient can determine specific uses within broad guidelines.

Subsequently, federal aid to the states increased because of the rising costs of social programs that are largely or completely funded by the national government, especially medical care for the poor, which is discussed in Chapter 13. National welfare reform legislation signed shortly before the 1996 presidential election resulted in the states' being asked to take over new responsibilities for health benefits for the poor and to emphasize job placements instead of cash assistance as the focus of welfare programs.[16] At the same time, the national government passed along funding to help support public assistance programs. However, critics of state policy processes have continued to chide Texas officials for not taking full advantage of national programs and even being willing to sacrifice considerable federal funds to avoid spending a smaller amount of state funds, a situation exemplified in 2011 when the legislature passed and the governor signed a request to the federal government to provide health funds as block grants and to cap the amount and in 2013 when the governor refused additional Medicaid funds. Also, some federal funds have been made available to help meet the requirements of post-9/11 homeland security and to help create jobs and improve infrastructure with economic stimulus funds. Altogether, the states and localities agree that costs of meeting the many federal mandates have exceeded the revenues provided. Nationally, the fiscal relationship between the national government and the states is seen as "fractured," indeed "at an all-time low."[17]

## Borrowing

Governments, like private citizens, borrow money for various reasons. Political expediency is one. Borrowing allows new programs to be implemented and existing ones to be extended without increasing taxes. A second reason is that borrowing allows future beneficiaries of a state service to pay for that service. Students who live in residence halls, for example, help pay off the bonds used to finance those halls through their room fees.

State government indebtedness is highly restricted in Texas, however. The framers of the state constitution strongly believed in "pay-as-you-go" government. A four-fifths vote of the legislature is needed to approve emergency borrowing, and the state's debt ceiling originally was limited to $200,000. A series of amendments has altered the constitution to allow the issuance of state bonds for specific programs, particularly land for veterans, university buildings, student loans, parks, prisons, and water development. In 2017, outstanding state indebtedness was just over $53 billion. This total is among the higher totals for states, but on a per capita basis it is among the lowest, with the total indebtedness per capita being around $1,700 dollars.[18]

## Other Nontax Sources

Because taxes are unpopular in Texas and elsewhere, government inevitably looks to nontax revenue sources whenever possible. The prospective budget deficits that began in 1985 have resulted in a pattern of raising money by increasing fees for almost everything, looking to gambling as a source of public revenue, and even manipulating state pension funds. An excellent example is college tuition, a type of **user fee**—that is, a sum paid in direct exchange for service.

Although current students may find this fact hard to believe, senior college tuition was only $4 per credit hour in 1984, plus about that much more in fees. Tuition and fees have risen steadily since 1984, as a reflection of both inflation and state policymakers' desire for students to pay a higher proportion of the costs of their own education. In 2004 boards of regents were given discretion to set tuition locally, and the governing boards took advantage of their new authority and raised tuition sharply. As a result, tuition and fees combined at state universities is now one hundred times the old $4 rate. Tuition is much higher for students in graduate

**user fee** A fee for a specific governmental service charged to the person who benefits from the service; college tuition is a user fee.

and professional schools and for out-of-state students. Each community college district sets its own rate because two-year colleges are financially supported not only by state revenues, but also by local taxes. Most community/junior colleges charge about 15 percent of the senior institution tuition. As discussed in Chapter 13, the rapidly increasing tuition rates in Texas, due in part to a decreasing portion of college costs being paid by the state, has led to calls for curbing tuition rate increases.

Other fees—for everything from driver's licenses and car inspections to water permits, from personal automobile tags to day-care center operator licenses—have continued to increase. Fines for various legal infractions have risen. Even the cost of fishing licenses has gone up.

Other nontax sources of state revenue include the interest on bank deposits, proceeds from investments, and sales and leases of public lands. Having a surplus increases investment income. The doldrums of the oil industry decrease income from land leases; higher prices encourage exploration and thus more leasing of land.

The 1987 legislature proposed a constitutional amendment, approved by the voters in November of that year, that permitted pari-mutuel betting on horse races and, in three counties, on dog races on a local-option basis. The state's revenue from pari-mutuel betting has not been a major income source.

After four years of proposals and debate, the state legislature placed a state lottery on the November 1991 ballot. Voters approved the lottery, which began in summer 1992. The largest lottery game at the time was Texas Lotto, but Texas joined the multi-state games Mega Millions in 2003 and Power Ball in 2010 to increase revenues. When the lottery was approved, the rationale was that revenues would go to public education. However, the legislature put the profits in "general revenue" for the state. Despite the fact that the lottery produces only a small fraction of the cost of education, critics have argued that the lottery was created under false pretenses. Casino gambling has been proposed during each legislative session, but none of those proposals has come close to passing to date.

## Taxation

Taxes are the most familiar sources of governmental revenue and the most controversial. Since colonial days and James Otis's stirring phrase "no taxation without representation," citizens have sought justice in the tax system. The conservative heritage of Texas has not always made justice easy to find.

Taxes are collected for two principal reasons. *Revenue taxes*—for example, the general sales tax—are the major source of government income. They make it possible for government to carry out its programs. *Regulatory taxes*—for example, the taxes on tobacco and alcohol— were originally designed primarily to control the individuals and/or organizations subject to them and to either punish undesired behavior or reward desired behavior. However, these taxes are easier to raise because any given regulatory tax affects only part of the population, and other citizens are willing to support the increase.

**tax equity** The inherent fairness of a tax. As the term is used in this book, ability to pay is a factor in fairness.

**revenue shortfall** A situation in which state revenues are not expected to be adequate to fund programs and services at current levels.

Although our discussion focuses on **tax equity** (fairness), another great concern with the Texas tax system is the lack of elasticity, which was discussed earlier in this chapter as one of the key factors resulting in periodic **revenue shortfalls**—insufficient funds to cover spending. A system based so heavily on sales and excise taxes runs into problems when the economy sours because the lower and middle classes, on whom such taxes depend, curtail their spending. With that curtailment comes a tailing off of tax revenues tied to consumer spending.

The tax policies of individual states reflect their economic resources, their political climates, and their dominant interest groups. Forty-two of the fifty states levy a personal income tax, although in two, the income tax is limited to interest and dividends. Forty-five states levy a corporate income tax. Texas has no personal income tax and, instead of a true corporate income tax, levies a complex business franchise (margins) tax that is based on the gross receipts of the business minus either the cost of goods sold or the total personnel costs—the individual business decides which each year. Smaller businesses with gross receipts under $1,000,000 are exempt. The franchise tax has been altered several times in recent legislative sessions to broaden the base and produce more revenue, most recently in the third called session of 2006,[19] but the 2009 legislature gave 40,000 additional small businesses an exemption from the levy. The state of Washington collects a similar tax. The tax will produce $7.4 billion in 2018–2019, less than it was forecast to yield in 2006.

Texas relies heavily on the general sales tax and other forms of sales taxes, such as the one paid at the pump for motor fuels. The result is a disproportionately high taxpaying burden on poor and middle-income taxpayers and an unevenness of the tax burden among different types of businesses. Each revenue shortfall brings with it debate over the need for a broader and more elastic tax system, but the state's traditionalistic/individualistic political culture cuts off discussions of raising taxes almost before they begin. Even in 2011 when the state faced a $27 billion shortfall, the only tax measures discussed were passing a sales tax exemption on luxury yachts and what proved to be a complicated measure that would tax sales if the only state presence of an Internet company was a warehouse.

Discussions about taxation, whether at the national, state, or local level, are seldom objective. One's own political philosophy and tax status inevitably color one's comments on the subject. Indeed, when government talks about taxes, its noble-sounding phrases such as "the public interest" do not always ring true. Today's citizens are sophisticated enough to realize that extensive campaigning, heated debates, and vigorous lobbying have formed our tax policies and that the public interest usually has been construed so as to benefit the influential. The American tax system generally favors those who are better off. Proposals to eliminate the federal income tax and move to a system of a very large (over 20 percent) national sales tax exemplify how tax systems can be made to benefit the wealthy, because such schemes include taxes on clothing, cars, and washing machines, but not on the purchase of stocks, bonds, or real estate investment trusts.

Texas professes fiscal conservatism and practices that philosophy by limiting state and local debt and by operating on a pay-as-you-go basis. The state budget reflects the political conservatism of Texas in its taxing and spending practices. An analysis of who pays, who does not pay, and who benefits from Texas taxes reveals not only the political and economic philosophy behind taxation in the state, but also which special interest groups most influence the legislature.

## Fairness and Equity in the Revenue System

Texas has prided itself on being a low-tax state, and political leaders have often pushed tax relief agendas—a popular short-term approach during a boom economy. Governor Rick Perry pressed hard for no new taxes even during serious budget shortfalls. Texas ranks forty-second in state tax collections per capita as of 2015, but in the absence of a state income tax, has among the higher sales tax (ranked twelfth) and property tax rates (ranked seventh) in the country.[20] The state ranks second in federal corporate income taxes and third in individual income taxes paid.[21] These measures suggest high rates of business activity (Big Oil is a major factor) and sizable personal wealth held by a minority of Texans.

One irony of the Texas tax situation is that the state does not fare well under many federal grant formulas that include tax effort—the tax burden already borne by citizens—as a criterion. The state does least well on matching grants for social services and welfare. Although Texas ranked third in individual and second in corporate income taxes paid, the state was ranked only forty-second in terms of per capita federal spending. In short, Texans contribute more in federal taxes to get back a dollar in federal grants than residents of most other states. Part of this is because Texas has turned down federal aid in some cases, most notably with regard to the extension of Medicaid under Obamacare.

The tax burden discussion raises two other issues. The first is ability to pay, and the whether both individuals and businesses really pay, and the second is who benefits from taxes paid. These two topics, and contemporary issues in taxation, are discussed in this section.

## Who Pays?

**progressive taxation**
A tax system based on ability to pay that requires wealthy people to pay taxes at a higher rate than poor ones.

A matter of some importance to taxpayers is whether the tax system is progressive or regressive. **Progressive taxation** is based on ability to pay. The idea is that those with higher incomes have more of an ability to pay than those with lower incomes. The only example of progressive taxes are income taxes, most notably the federal income tax, which progresses from relatively low rates for those with small incomes to increasingly higher rates for those with larger incomes. However, loopholes in the federal tax laws lessen the progressivity of the tax burden.

**regressive tax**
A flat-rate tax that is not based on ability to pay; as a consequence, the poorer the payer of the tax, the larger the percentage of income that goes to the tax.

A **regressive tax** requires lower-income earners to spend larger percentages of their incomes on taxable items. The best example of Texas's reliance on regressive taxes is the general retail sales tax. The general sales tax is assessed at 6.25 percent on a wide variety of goods and services at the time of sale, regardless of the income or wealth of the purchaser. Municipalities also can levy a 1 percent additional tax, as can mass transit districts and county economic development districts. Municipalities can also add sales tax percentages of a half percent each for economic development and in lieu of reduced property taxes. The result is that most Texans pay a sales tax of 8.25 percent.

The additional selective sales (excise) taxes—those levied on tobacco products, alcoholic beverages, and motor fuels, for example—also are regressive. The $25,000-a-year clerk and the $250,000-a-year executive who drive the same distance to work pay the same 20-cent-a-gallon tax on gasoline, but who is better able to bear the tax burden? The Institute on Taxation and Economic Policy, a Washington, D.C.–based nonprofit organization that studies state and national finance, reported in 2018 that in Texas, the poorest 20 percent of citizens pay 9.3 percent of their income in sales and excise taxes compared to 1.2 percent for the top one percent of citizens. Overall, the regressive burden of taxes in Texas,[22] unlike some states, does not yet tax "lifeline items"—food purchased at a grocery store, prescription medicines, and work clothes—and has a tax holiday in August to make it easier for parents to purchase school clothing for children. But, while in the aggregate Texas is a low tax state, the regressive nature of its tax structure means that it decidedly is not a low tax state for the poor.

The restructuring of the corporation franchise tax in 2006 produced greater equity in business taxes and closed the loopholes that allowed major corporations to escape paying the tax, but the legislature also has authorized more exemptions in subsequent years. Nevertheless, the state has passed a constitutional amendment making institution of a personal income tax very difficult. Yet, a fair tax system is a value associated with democratic government. Many observers believe that a progressive income tax would be fairer than the general sales tax and could replace all or part of it. But even the mention of an income tax is taboo among candidates for public office in Texas. Moreover, in the early years of the twenty-first century, resentment against the U.S. Internal Revenue Service and the federal income tax has carried over into state politics and has made tax reform virtually impossible. Texas cannot overcome the clash between democratic ideal and political reality.

**Taxes Paid by Individuals** A number of taxes are levied directly against individuals. Examples are the inheritance tax, which is collected at the time beneficiaries inherit estates and the motor fuels tax, paid each time a motorist buys gasoline. For many citizens, property taxes are among their highest, and they pay for local government. (The state ad valorem property tax was abolished by a 1982 constitutional amendment, but the property tax remains a mainstay for local governments.) Businesses also pay the motor fuels tax and local property taxes, of course, but by increasing prices they let their customers pick up the tab.

Some authorities would include all sales taxes in the category of taxes paid by individuals, on the assumption that businesses pass them on to the consumer just as they do local ad valorem and state vehicle registration taxes—whether that is the intention of the law or not. There are two types of individual sales taxes:

1. The *general sales tax* is a broadly based tax that is collected on most goods and services and must be paid by the consumer. It is illegal for a business to absorb the tax—for example, as a promotional device. This familiar tax was first adopted in Texas in 1961, with a 2 percent rate. Nationally, Mississippi was the first state to have a sales tax, but twenty-nine other states adopted the tax during the Great Depression of the 1930s. Originally, many exemptions existed, but these have become fewer and fewer with each legislative session except for an expansion of sales tax holidays that allow Texans to purchase school clothes and other items without paying a sales tax. Indeed, the tax is now paid on many services (lawn maintenance, for example), as well as goods (hamburgers, jeans).

2. *Selective sales taxes* (excise taxes) are levied on only a few items, comparatively speaking, and consumers are often unaware that they are paying them. These taxes are included in the price of the item and may not even be computed separately. Tobacco products, alcoholic beverages—tobacco and alcohol taxes are sometimes called "sin taxes"— automobiles, gasoline, rental of hotel rooms, and the admission price for amusements (movies, plays, nightclubs, sporting events) are among the items taxed in this category.

General and selective sales taxes account for over three-fourths of the state's tax revenue. Business initially pays about half of these taxes before recouping them in their pricing.

**Taxes Levied on Businesses** Taxes levied on businesses in Texas produce considerable revenue for the state, but are often regulatory in nature. One example is the *severance taxes* levied on natural resources, such as crude oil, natural gas, and sulfur that are severed (removed) from the earth. Their removal, of course, depletes irreplaceable resources, and part of the tax revenue is dedicated to conservation programs and to the regulation of production; thirty other states have similar taxes. Severance taxes once were the backbone of the state's revenue system, but have been subject to the familiar boom-and-bust economic cycle. For 2018–2019, they were expected to yield only 3 percent of the tax revenue.

The major Texas business tax today is the *franchise tax*, which is also known as the *margins* tax and the *business activity* tax. It is assessed against corporations, partnerships, business trusts, professional associations, business associations, joint ventures, holding companies, and other legal entities. Excluded are sole proprietorships and general partnerships. This tax is a revenue tax that reflects the cost of doing business in the state. Some people regard it as a type of corporate income tax because the business pays taxes based on its gross receipts. This tax was overhauled substantially in 1991, 2006, and 2009 to make it fairer. It originally emphasized taxes only on capital-intensive businesses, such as manufacturing, and collected little from labor-intensive businesses, such as computer software firms, financial institutions, and even the big downtown law firms. The 1991 version also left a loophole that let big corporations such as Dell, Inc. (the computer company) declare themselves to be partnerships and thus not covered by the tax. The more comprehensive version of the tax is expected to provide 3.3 percent of the tax revenue for FY 2018–2019.

In addition to the franchise tax, there are special *gross receipts taxes* levied on specific businesses, most notably utilities. Among other taxes levied directly on businesses in Texas is the *insurance premium tax,* levied on gross premiums collected by insurance companies. Miscellaneous *special taxes and fees* for such varied activities as chartering a corporation, brewing alcoholic beverages, and selling real estate also exist. Whenever possible, businesses pass these taxes along to consumers in the form of higher prices. Together, they account for about 5 percent of the state's tax revenue.

Because it is difficult to determine exactly what business taxes are passed on to consumers, one can only guess at who pays. Roughly 52.3 percent of the state's income comes from nontax sources. Of the revenue that comes from taxes, businesses directly pay at least 20 percent of the total. However, many taxes are paid by both individuals and businesses, making it difficult to assess what proportion of the taxes businesses and individuals actually pay. Examples of these latter taxes include those on motor fuels, motor vehicle sales and rentals, and utilities. Texas businesses actually contribute a higher percentage of state revenues than businesses nationally contribute to federal revenues. The federal corporate income tax, for example, produces slightly less than 8 percent of the national government's revenue. The most significant federal revenue sources are the personal income tax and the Social Security and Medicare taxes.

## Who Benefits?

To address the question of who benefits from taxation policies, we must consider the kinds of services the government provides. Nothing would seem more equitable than a tax structure resulting in an exact ratio between taxes paid and benefits received, and in Texas, some taxes are levied with exactly that philosophy in mind. The motor fuels tax, 20 cents per gallon on gasoline and diesel fuel, is paid by those who use motor vehicles, and three-fourths of the revenues from this tax are spent on maintaining and building highways and roads. The remainder goes to public schools. However, the example points out a problem with the "benefit theory" of revenue. People who do not own automobiles and who do not buy gasoline also benefit from those big trucks hauling goods to market over state highways.

Furthermore, we must consider not only *who* benefits, but *when* they benefit. For example, an entire economy is aided by educating children now, but it will not realize the benefit—or lack of benefit—of today's educational investment until today's children enter the workforce fifteen years from now.

One of the "sin taxes" collected by the state is on tobacco. This tax is based on the philosophy that those who subject their bodies to the damaging effects of tobacco may be discouraged from doing so and thus benefit if they have to pay more money for the privilege. Although the percentage of smokers is declining, the decline is not particularly due to this tax, which has become, in effect, a use tax. Those who smoke receive no special benefits from revenues from this tax, which are used for schools, parks, and general government functions. To conform to the benefit theory of taxation, the revenue from the tobacco tax would need to be spent primarily for cancer research, the treatment of lung diseases, and other programs related to the effects of smoking.

A strict benefit philosophy would have a disastrous effect on low-income citizens. For example, if all taxes were assessed on a pay-benefit basis, then the poorest citizens could not afford to educate their children, a situation that would only entrap them further in the cycle of minimal education, low-paying jobs, and marginal incomes. The extremely wealthy, on the other hand, could have their own police forces, four-lane roads to their weekend farms, and college classrooms with five-to-one student–teacher ratios. Society would hardly benefit from such a situation. Clearly, trying to apply a benefit theory of taxation, like all issues in taxation, is very difficult.

## Contemporary Issues

The history of economic and fiscal policy provides important background. However, new issues also confront state policymakers.

**Perspectives from the Past**  For a half-century, Texas relied on oil and gas production taxes as the major source of state revenue, with most of these being paid by out-of-state purchasers. How good were the good old days? "Texas went from 1971 to 1984 . . . without an increase in state tax

## You Decide: Should Texas Enact an Income Tax?

Texas is one of eight states without a personal income tax. Should the Texas legislature enact an income tax?

### Pro

⬆ The legislature should modernize the state tax structure and include an income tax because:

⬆ The present tax system is regressive; an income tax could make it less so.

⬆ An income tax would make billions of new dollars available for state services.

⬆ Legislative sessions would be less chaotic because the revenue stream would be more flexible.

⬆ The tax system would be fairer because it would be based on ability to pay.

⬆ The state would probably receive more federal funds because it could meet the "tax effort" test better.

### Con

⬇ The legislature should not consider an income tax because:

⬇ The tax would require a constitutional amendment except under a very limited circumstance. It would be impossible to get a majority from voters.

⬇ Texas does okay except when the economy is in a real slump.

⬇ It is fair for poor people to pay a higher percentage of their income in taxes because they demand more government services.

⬇ People can control how much they pay in sales taxes by how much they spend.

⬇ Texas needs to attract new businesses; a corporate income tax would drive away business.

**Competency Connection**
**SOCIAL RESPONSIBILITY**

Should Texas pass an income tax so that it will have adequate capacity to provide services to the citizens of the state even when the economic cycle is in a downturn?

---

rates, or new taxes" while the population was growing 42 percent.[23] After the world oil market crashed, Texans were ill prepared to develop a responsible and responsive revenue policy to provide funds for state services. The boom-and-bust cycle became the fiscal way of life in Texas.

**What's Next?**   Texas will be no different from other governments in its need to find adequate and equitable revenue sources to support the services needed by a rapidly growing citizenry and to make up for periodic revenue shortfalls that have a major effect on all states. One strategy that the state will pursue is *performance evaluation and management*, including cutbacks to funding that are recommended in the biennial Texas Performance Review (TPR) and in human service spending. The importance of the Texas Performance Review can only grow. The TPR originated with John Sharp when he was comptroller and was pursued relentlessly by his successor, Carole Keeton Strayhorn. Coupled with her refusal to certify the budget, Strayhorn's approach led the 2003–2004 legislature to reduce her powers and grant the performance review authority to the Legislative Budget Board. The performance evaluation/cutback approach is grounded in a national movement to "reinvent government."[24] This demand emerged from strategic planning and quality management movements in the private sector as sluggish industries had to downsize—or in the new terminology, "rightsize." In Texas, it has also been used to accomplish a political agenda, for example, in trying to force universities to divert attention from research to degree production.

Performance reviews speak not only to "smaller," but also to "smarter." Periodically, *Governing* magazine has examined management and/or fiscal policies in the states. The magazine published a fifty-state report on taxation early in 2003. The report began with the observation that "The vast majority of state tax systems are inadequate for the task of funding a 21st-century government."[25] A top rating was four stars. Texas got one star on the adequacy of its revenue, one on the fairness of the system to taxpayers, but three on management of the system. In 2005, *Governing* graded the states again to see how they had weathered national economic downtrends and responded to state needs. The reports have not been repeated since then, but authors of the reports suggested that political polarization in the last decade has made improving government performance often less important than politics itself. A majority of states are just "muddling through."[26] Those ratings gave Texas an overall grade of "B." In 2008, the Pew Center on the States graded the states, giving Texas these marks: "B" on money (finance, budget, for example); "B" on people (workforce, employee retention, for example); "B" on infrastructure (capital planning, maintenance, for example); and "A—" on information (strategic direction, managing for performance, for example).[27] Another strategy that all states and the national government will use is **privatizing**. Two examples are the private prisons that now serve the state—the state contracts them for services—and the increasing rate of tuition and fees paid by college students. The first is direct private provision of service; the second is passing along the cost to private citizens rather than burdening the revenue system.

**privatizing** Turning over public programs to the private sector to implement. For example, the state contracts with a private firm to operate some Texas prisons.

A third strategy is to *change the revenue structure* to avert the revenue shortfalls that plagued the state in the 1980s and early 2000s. Change would focus on making the system more elastic and better able to fund state services consistently. The major change to date is the restructuring of the corporate franchise/margins tax discussed earlier in this chapter. The dominant issue of the 1997 and 2005–2006 legislative sessions was revenue restructuring to lower school property taxes, but the lower property taxes did not stem entirely from a new revenue system. Instead, the difference between the revenues formerly raised by the school districts and what they raise now was to be made up by state surpluses, with uncertainties about what happens when there is not a surplus.[28] The Eighty-second Legislature in 2011 found that uncertainty meant massive cuts.

Another aspect of revenue structure is the competition among governments for tax sources. National and state governments both tax motor fuels, tobacco, and alcohol, for example, and both levels of government keep increasing tax rates. Both the state and local governments have general sales taxes. The upshot is that the combined tax rates begin to vex citizens after a while. Ironically, cuts in federal income tax rates since the 1980s enhance the state income tax as a logical new source of state revenue.

For tax restructuring to occur, state politics and citizen attitudes would have to change. Businesses, including partnerships, would have to accept some sort of business activity tax that functions as a true corporate income tax, whatever it is called. Ultimately, private citizens would have to be willing to accept a personal income tax. Businesses had to accept major changes in business taxes in 1991 and 2006, with the result that business taxes are broader and fairer than in the past, but the revenue is inadequate to fund state services. However, the mere advocacy of a personal income tax is a sure ticket out of office, as deadly as the rattlesnake bite alluded to at the beginning of the chapter.

Democratic theory recognizes the equality of the citizenry, and many people think that a revenue system that extracts more from people the poorer they are seriously compromises equality. Since 1991, business has paid a greater share of taxes, but as previously noted, the tax system in Texas is still regressive, placing a proportionately heavier burden on those with the lowest incomes. The reality is that without an income tax, the state will always have difficulty meeting its revenue needs in anything other than a booming economy. Historically, Texas attracted businesses because they found a favorable tax structure in the state. However, the experience of other states with economic development indicates that many modern industries are also concerned about the stability of state services. Such stability is difficult in the absence of a flexible tax structure.

The difficulty of revenue restructuring is illustrated by the 1997 legislature's failed debate over tax reform. Similar frustration occurred in the failure of the legislature to address school finance problems in the 2003 regular session or the fruitless special session of April 2004, postponing the solution until the last moment in a 2006 special session.

# How Are Budget Decisions Made?

Occasionally, an argument is heard in the state's legislative chambers that reflects serious concern about budgeting a particular program—who will benefit from it, whether it is needed by society, and how it will be financed. More generally, however, whether funds are allocated for a proposed program depends on which interests favor it and how powerful they are, who and how powerful the opposition is, and what the results are of compromises and coalitions between these and "swing vote" groups. The political viewpoints of the legislators, the governor, and the state bureaucracy also have an impact on budgetary decisions. In short, decisions about spending public money, like decisions about whom and what to tax, are not made objectively. Rather, they are the result of the complex relationships among the hundreds of political actors who participate in the state's governmental system. The biases of the political system are thus reflected in the biases of state spending. Rather than developing coherent public policy and seeking ways to fund programs and services, Texas allows the budget to determine policy priorities.

This section outlines the stages in the budgetary process, and then the following section describes the state's major expenditures. The budgetary process consists of three stages: planning and preparation, authorization and appropriation, and execution (spending).

## Planning and Preparation

**dual-budgeting system** A system in which both the executive branch and the legislative branch prepare separate budget documents.

Budget planning and the preparation of the proposed budget are functions of the chief executive in the national government and in forty-four states, but Texas has a **dual-budgeting system**. The constitution makes the legislature responsible for the state budget. The legislature is aided in this task by the Legislative Budget Board (LBB) and its staff, which prepare a draft budget. Four senators and four representatives compose the LBB, which is co-chaired by the lieutenant governor and the speaker of the House. Figure 12-3 depicts the workings of the LBB.

Modern governors have understood the importance of the budget as a political tool, and so, with the aid of the Budget, Planning, and Policy Division, the governor also prepares a budget. This duplicate effort is wasteful, and is in some ways analogous to the competitive budgeting done by the president's Office of Management and Budget and the Congressional Budget Office at the national level. It does allow different political perspectives on state spending to be heard. In 2003, the legislature took a most unusual approach to budgeting by involving the governor as an equal participant with legislators themselves. By 2007, legislators were trying to find ways around gubernatorial vetoes once again. In 2011, Perry's long tenure and newly elected ultraconservative legislators who shared his philosophy resulted in the budget he wanted. Governor Abbott has taken a more cooperative approach to building a state budget.

The two budgets agree in two respects. Both tend to be *incremental*—that is, both propose percentage increases or decreases for existing programs and the addition of new programs by way of feasibility studies and pilot programs. The recent emphasis on performance may at least give lawmakers a better picture of the real priorities of state agencies and how costs relate to benefits to the state. Additionally, both, like revenues, reflect the prevailing political sentiments of the state.

Budget planning ordinarily begins in the spring of the even-numbered year before the year in which the legislature meets in regular session. Since 1992, strategic planning has been

# Texas Politics and You

Liberals like Ben Sargent have compared the legislature's persistent refusal to raise taxes to meet the state's budget crisis to Emperor Nero's fiddling while Rome burned in A.D. 64.

Courtesy of Ben Sargent

Ben Sargent is an admittedly liberal editorial cartoonist, but he is also a shrewd observer of the Texas political scene. In this cartoon, he compares the legislature's persistent refusal to raise taxes to meet the state's program needs to Emperor Nero's alleged fiddling while Rome burned in A.D. 64.

Is Texas "burning"? Is the conservative legislature preventing Texas from achieving quality in its programs? Or, is the legislature doing a good job of "holding the lid" on expenses and managing the state's money?

Here are some comments from other college students regarding this cartoon:

"The Texas State legislature is sitting around while the state budget goes down, just like a rat on a sinking ship."

"The state legislature is fiddling to the popular tune of no new taxes while the state budget is burning. As opposed to enacting the necessary tax policy required to balance the budget, they are playing along with conservative popular opinion."

"The cartoon suggests that the guy fiddling is fat, and implies that the legislature fattens itself with money, but don't mind the people's business."

"The legislature needs to get votes based on the 'no tax' policies, but the state budget is in need."

"The state legislature feels very strongly about taxes and wants the government to do away with taxes and spending."

"This is written from a liberal point of view. Conservatives would argue that no new taxes help the economy and ultimately the state budget, since people have more money to spend."

**Competency Connection**
**PERSONAL RESPONSIBILITY**

**Much political science literature confirms that citizens will support tax increases when they think the government can be trusted to improve the quality of public life. Would you agree to pay higher taxes to improve public education or to modernize the highway system?**

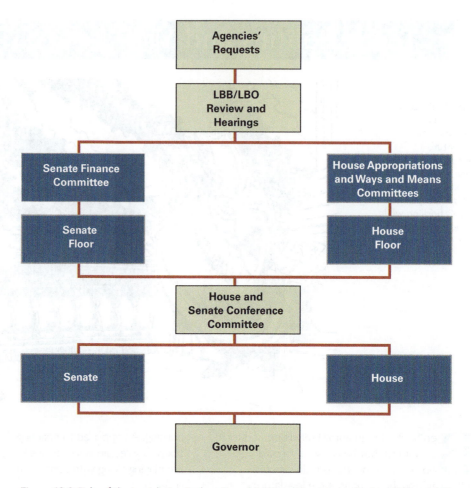

**Figure 12-3** Role of the Legislative Budget Board (LBB) and Legislative Budget Office (LBO) in the Texas Budget Process

integrated with budgeting so that the LBB, the governor's office, and the agencies have a compressed time period for preparing budget proposals. State agencies submit their requests for the next biennium on forms prepared jointly by the governor's and the LBB's staffs. Then, at joint hearings, the two staffs try to obtain sufficient information from agency representatives about agency needs to make adequate evaluations of the requests from the agencies. These hearings are usually held in the early fall and are the final joint effort of the two staffs. At this time, individuals and outside groups—the state's dominant interest groups—also provide input. Each staff then prepares a set of budget recommendations that reflects the priorities of its office. When completed, each document is almost two inches thick and provides summary information, as well as an agency-by-agency breakdown by specific budget categories. Both are submitted to the appropriate legislative committees for consideration.

Both budgets outline state expenditures for a two-year period. Completed in time for the opening of the legislature in January of one year (e.g., 2019), they must project state spending through August two years later (2021), regardless of any changes in the economic outlook that may take place during that thirty-two-month period. Consequently, shifts in the funding of state programs may be needed. Certainly, realizing that the constitutional directive for biennial legislative sessions means that the funding of state programs must be planned almost three years in advance, it is easy to understand why the state budget planners lean toward incrementalism rather than rationalism.

## Authorization and Appropriation

The authorization and appropriation stage consists of the authorization of programs to be provided by the state and the passage of a bill appropriating money—the state budget. The House Ways and Means (revenues), House Appropriations (spending), and Senate Finance (both revenues and spending) committees are the key legislative players. Agency representatives, the governor's staff, interest-group representatives, and private citizens testify on behalf of the particular agency or program of concern to them. There is considerable forming and reforming of coalitions as legislators, lobbyists, and committee members bargain, compromise, trade votes, and generally endeavor to obtain as much for "their side" as possible.

Past campaign contributions begin to pay off at this stage, and the relative power of different interest groups is reflected in the state budget. For example, political campaigns frequently include a call to "get tough on crime" and to build more prisons; in turn, prisons are typically well funded. The four main teachers' groups in the state expend considerable effort in trying to influence legislators, and schoolteachers usually get raises, albeit often small ones. The success of the business lobby is the most problematic, although to be sure, business interests are not monolithic. Small businesses often have somewhat different interests than large businesses, and international businesses are often in conflict with local businesses, for example. In 2003, the business lobby was so dominant that the visitors' gallery where corporate lobbyists sat while legislators were meeting was dubbed "the owner's box." In 2006, the business lobby accepted new taxes in order to fund public schools, and, in terms of fiscal policy, was virtually left alone in 2007 and 2009, except for additional franchise fee exemptions. In 2011, business mainly got more protection from lawsuits and greater highway funding. In the 2017 session, auto dealers were able to preserve the arcane laws which they helped draft that protect them in some ways more than other businesses.

The authorization and appropriation stage is a lengthy one, and the Appropriations and Finance committees submit their reports—the two versions of the appropriations bill—near the end of the session. Speaker Pete Laney and Lieutenant Governor Bob Bullock improved the process considerably, beginning in 1993, when they insisted on adequate time for review of the proposed state spending plan. The two versions are never identical; so, a ten-member conference committee composed of an equal number of senators and representatives carefully selected by the presiding officers must develop a single conference report on the budget, including adequate revenue measures to fund the proposed spending. The revenue stipulation is because Texas has a balanced-budget provision that requires the state comptroller to certify that expected revenues are sufficient to fund expenditures. The two houses must accept or reject the report as it stands. Usually, this approval comes fairly late in the session, often at the proverbial "eleventh hour." The approved appropriations bill then goes to the governor for signature.

The governor's line-item veto allows the striking of individual items from the appropriations bill if he or she disagrees with the spending provision. However, the governor cannot add to the budget or restore funding for a pet project that the legislature rejected.

## Execution/Spending

The actual disbursement of the state's income is rather technical and less interesting as a political process. It includes such details as shifting money into various funds, issuing state warrants and paychecks, internal auditing of expenditures by agency accountants, and external auditing by the state auditor's staff to ensure the legality of expenditures.

The major political issue involving budget execution has been efforts by several governors to gain greater control over spending between legislative sessions. In 1980 and 1981, voters defeated constitutional amendments that would have increased the governor's authority, but in 1987, the legislature gave the governor the power to slow down expenditures in economic slow times. Then, in 1991, the legislature created a new tripartite body—the governor, the lieutenant governor, and the speaker—to deal with spending and reallocation in order to rationalize the process between sessions.

A second political issue in budget execution concerns auditing. The state auditor, a legislative appointee, monitors state agencies and for many years has issued management letters directing agencies both to abandon and to implement different management practices. Although a legislative appointee cannot constitutionally tell an executive agency head how to run the agency, since 1991 the state auditor has been mandated to perform management audits.

## Where Does the Money Go?

Because the services delivered through state budget expenditures are of more interest to the average citizen than the technicalities of how the budget is executed, this section emphasizes a summary of spending on major state services. Figure 12-4 shows that health and human services plus education account for almost three-fourths of the 2018–2019 Texas budget of close to $250 billion.

## Education

Historically, a slight majority of the state's budget was spent on public schools and higher education. However, education's share of the state budget has been decreasing in the twenty-first century both because of education budget cuts and increases in the share health and human services take. For 2020–2021, the education share of the budget was 37.1 percent. The lion's share of the nearly $92 billion was for elementary and secondary schools in the state's independent school districts and for state schools for the deaf and visually impaired. The state provides textbooks as well as special services, such as programs for disabled children and vocational courses, the state achievement tests, school buses, operating costs, and teacher salaries. The state does not pay the total costs of public education, however. Local school districts actually fund more of the cost of education than does the state and also are responsible for buildings and other school facilities. Those that can afford it provide supplements to attract the best teachers, buy additional library books, develop athletic programs, and offer students enrichment opportunities.

**Competency Connection**
**COMMUNICATION SKILLS**

Looking at the chart, and assuming that the cost of health and welfare policy continues to rise in Texas over time, what might be the impact of such change on Texas education?

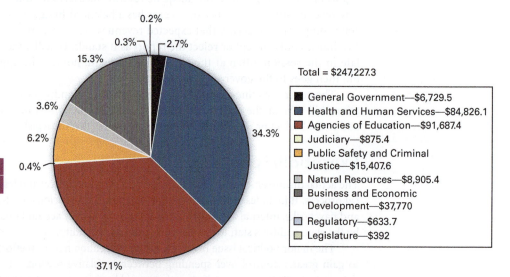

Total = $247,227.3

- General Government—$6,729.5
- Health and Human Services—$84,826.1
- Agencies of Education—$91,687.4
- Judiciary—$875.4
- Public Safety and Criminal Justice—$15,407.6
- Natural Resources—$8,905.4
- Business and Economic Development—$37,770
- Regulatory—$633.7
- Legislature—$392

0.2%
0.3%
2.7%
15.3%
3.6%
6.2%
0.4%
34.3%
37.1%

**Figure 12-4** LBB Estimate of Budget 2020–2021, in Percentages (in Billions)*

*TOTAL: $200.42 billion. All numbers are rounded.

SOURCE: "Legislative Budget Board, Summary of Legislative Budget Estimates 2020–2021 Biennium, January 2019.

Table 12-1 shows how the twelve most populous states spend their money for various major categories of state services and allows a comparison of Texas with the other eleven states. The figures are on a per capita basis, amount spent per person, except for education spending for which the measure is per pupil in the schools. In overall education expenditures Texas is ahead of only Florida in the dozen most-populated states.[29] The other large slice of the education dollar pie supports higher education: the operations of general academic institutions and community colleges, the technical college system, health science centers, and extension programs, plus retirement systems and debt payments on buildings. For both junior and senior colleges, a formula based on such factors as semester credit hours determines the basic level of state support, with the formula funding supplemented by special program funding and affected by performance norms originally adopted in 1992 and greatly simplified in 1997. The community/junior colleges also are supported by local districts. In 2003, the legislature deregulated university tuition, thereby permitting the institutions to begin charging whatever they needed to charge in 2004. Local tuition and fees account for a sizable portion of campus funding and were a matter of considerable debate in legislative sessions since 2007, as discussed in Chapter 13. Overall, the proportion of state funding for universities is declining. The remaining part of the education budget covers insurance, retirement, and various administrative expenses. One comparative measure of higher education in Texas is that the state ranks thirtieth in the number of persons age twenty-five or older who hold a bachelor's degree. Another measure is that, of all students enrolled in higher education, in Texas, 87.6 percent are in public institutions, considerably above the national average of 74.5 percent.

## Health and Human Services

Some $85 billion—34.3 percent of the budget—is allocated for human services programs, including welfare, unemployment compensation, employment services, workers' compensation, services for special groups such as the blind and the elderly, and health programs

Cartoonist Ben Sargent summarized the 2011 legislative session by pointing out that the legislature's solution to a major revenue shortfall was to slash the budget and ignore the implications for the future of the state. While some of the shortfalls were made up in subsequent budgets, Texas still lags behind many states in spending..

Courtesy of Ben Sargent

Is it the responsibility of adults in the legislature to make sure that government services will be available for future generations?

| TABLE 12-1 | Per Capita State Expenditures by Selected Function, Twelve Most Populous States, 2015, in Descending Order of Population | | | | | |
|---|---|---|---|---|---|---|
| State | Population | Total | Elementary and Secondary Education | Highways | Health and Hospitals | Public Welfare |
| California | 39,536,653 | 10,586 | 1,856 | 424 | 1,124 | 2,637 |
| Texas | 28,304,596 | 7,522 | 1,832 | 463 | 780 | 1,290 |
| Florida | 20,984,400 | 7,060 | 1,317 | 470 | 663 | 1,341 |
| New York | 19,849,400 | 13,033 | 3,228 | 568 | 1,079 | 3,110 |
| Pennsylvania | 12,805,537 | 8,873 | 2,123 | 724 | 658 | 2,094 |
| Illinois | 12,802,023 | 8,931 | 2,051 | 745 | 501 | 1,634 |
| Ohio | 11,658,609 | 8,210 | 1,936 | 510 | 791 | 1,730 |
| Georgia | 10,429,379 | 6,637 | 1,789 | 321 | 719 | 1,177 |
| North Carolina | 10,273,419 | 7,433 | 1,339 | 405 | 1,297 | 1,368 |
| Michigan | 9,962,311 | 8,062 | 1,687 | 368 | 859 | 1,650 |
| New Jersey | 9,005,644 | 10,112 | 2,951 | 512 | 467 | 1,940 |
| Virginia | 8,470,020 | 8,226 | 1,951 | 511 | 834 | 1,375 |
| United States | 327,167,434 | 8,845 | 1,904 | 525 | 825 | 1,900 |

SOURCES: World Atlas, The 50 US States Ranked By Population, https://www.worldatlas.com/articles/us-states-by-population.html; Tax Policy Center, "State and Local General Expenditures, Per Capita," October 17, 2017, https://www.taxpolicycenter.org/statistics/state-and-local-general-expenditures-capita

such as mental health and retardation programs, children's health insurance, treatment of substance abuse, contagious-disease control, and treatment for catastrophic illnesses such as AIDS, cancer, and kidney failure. About 60 percent of the funding comes from the national government. Chapter 13 will further discuss the health and welfare system.

Among the twelve largest states, Texas is ranked eighth in funding of hospitals and health and eleventh in public welfare, ahead of only Georgia. Texas continues to be a low service state compared to most others in the nation.

## Business and Economic Development

Texas's expenditures for business and economic development for FY 2020–2021 were $38 billion, or 14.7 percent of the total budget. This category includes transportation, economic development to promote the state's economy, the efforts of the Housing and Community Affairs Department on behalf of local governments, and employment and training services. Just under one-half of the expenditures in this category comes from federal funds, particularly highway matching funds to maintain and upgrade the 3,233 miles of federal interstate highways in Texas. In 1977, the legislature capped highway expenditures, with the result that the state has many poorly maintained roads and not enough highways. The third special session in 2013 was dedicated to creating a significant new fund for highway improvements. (See Chapter 14 for a more complete discussion.) Ranking states on highway expenditures is fraught with measurement problems. Texas is in the midrange of the top twelve states, but with so many miles of open road, it faces more difficult challenges in highway maintenance than many other states.

## Other Major Expenditures

The next largest category of expenditures is public safety, at just over $15 billion, or 6.2 percent of the total budget. This category includes law enforcement, prisons, and related programs. The category of natural resources, at $9 billion, constitutes 3.6 percent of the budget. It includes parks and agriculture support. General government, which includes the governor, legislature, and judiciary, accounted for $6.7 billion, or 2.7 percent, for 2020–2021. The remainder of the budget is a very small percentage of expenditures and funds regulatory agencies and general matters such as lawsuit settlements. This category also includes set-asides of any surplus for future expenditures.

## Summary

**LO 12.1** **Economic conditions, the political climate, and power plays are all part of the game of generating revenues for state government and determining how that income will be spent.** Both taxing and spending are usually incremental, with major changes rarely occurring. The Texas economy has long been built on natural resources, particularly oil and gas and agricultural production. More recently, the state has wooed high-technology companies and financial institutions. However, the state's boom-and-bust economy over the past thirty years has meant more tax and fee increases than usual and less budget growth. That "downer" scenario has periodically reversed itself when the economy is in the boom part of the cycle.

**LO 12.2** **The largest sources of revenue for Texas are the sales tax paid mostly by individuals and federal funds (the latter despite the state's disdain for the national government).** Texas has no personal and only an indirect corporate income tax (the franchise fee). It has long relied on oil and gas revenues to help fund the state budget. In recent years, it has added user fees and lottery proceeds to its revenue sources. Its borrowing capacity is restricted.

**LO 12.3** **In comparing Texas with other states, we find that the combined state and local tax burden is relatively low, with Texas ranked in the bottom fifth of all states.** These rankings are based only on taxes, not total revenues. The fundamental difference in the Texas revenue system from that of many other states is the disproportionate burden borne by the poorest citizens. This regressive system raises serious questions about how democratic the tax system is in the state.

**LO 12.4** **The Texas budget process differs procedurally from the ones used by most other states.** Those differences include the dual-budgeting system, the extraordinary dominance of the presiding officers in the appropriations process, and the virtually absolute veto power of the governor as a result of the short legislative session.

**LO 12.5** **Democracies are responsive to the citizenry.** The state's spending may not meet the needs of all its citizens, particularly when one considers that, in spite of spending more and more dollars, the state ranks in the bottom half of all states in every service category. However, Texas spending does match voter priorities, and the budget drives policy choices.

## Critical Thinking

1. If you had the power to overhaul the Texas revenue system, would you do so? What components would you either eliminate from or add to the revenue system? Why?

2. A state's spending policies reflect its political philosophy and reveal a great deal about how well the state budget provides for the needs of all its citizens. How effective are Texas spending processes? What philosophy do they represent? Overall, would you say that the budget reality reflects the ideal of democracy?

The face of Texas public education is changing. In the 2010–2011 academic year, Latino children became a majority of students in Texas public schools.

*Mario Villafuerte/Getty Images News/Getty Images*

# Public Policy—People

## Learning Objectives

This chapter provides a summary of Texas policies regarding the lives of citizens. Discussion of issues surrounding natural resources and the environment will follow in Chapter 14. For want of a better term, we refer to this chapter as dealing with "people policies," or policies having to do with the regulation of the health, welfare, and education of the citizens of the state. From the very beginning of our nation's history, these have been "police powers" of the state functions. Of course, as time has gone by, the responsibilities of states have grown dramatically, both because of the expectations of citizens and because of the growth of technologies. In rural cultures, governments were often far away and lacking in resources, while urbanization has created the situation where citizens are always in close proximity to government services. In the period before World War II, medical care was much more primitive and citizens had fewer expectations regarding care. With the development of antibiotics and modern medical screening technologies, both costs and expectations have increased. As the nation's economy has diversified and more and more jobs have come to require education as a prerequisite for employment, so too have pressures grown on the educational system. Finally, as governments have grown in complexity, the partnerships

**LO 13.1** Describe the importance of public policy, including mandates.

**LO 13.2** Identify the major social welfare and health care policies of the state and describe the redistributive nature of those programs.

**LO 13.3** Be introduced to the major issues of public education for the state.

**LO 13.4** Understand a number of issues facing higher education in state institutions.

**LO 13.5** Learn about the complex problem of immigration in Texas, along with the issue of sanctuary cities.

IF A NATION EXPECTS TO BE IGNORANT AND FREE, IN A STATE OF CIVILISATION, IT EXPECTS WHAT NEVER WAS AND NEVER WILL BE.

Thomas Jefferson,

among national, state, and local governments have often become convoluted and difficult to understand.

Some of these issues, such as poverty, health, and welfare, are favorites of progressives and liberals. Others have traditionally been of greater interest to conservatives, but are becoming more important for everyone. Still others, such as education, create widespread concern. Texans constantly have to assess whether they want to remain a "low-tax, low-service" state or provide greater government aid to residents of the state. That question applies equally to education and to social welfare policies. The struggle over priorities and social values has pitted Democrats against Republicans over their views of the proper role of government. This is a classic illustration of the struggle between competing sets of moral values—lower taxes to promote economic growth or higher services to assist opportunity for the poor.

The issues the state chooses to address and how state policymakers attempt to solve public problems permit another examination of how democratic the Texas political system is. Do policymakers try to deal with a wide variety of issues affecting all citizens? Or do they mainly look at issues placed on the agenda by political elites? Can they solve contemporary problems in the context of a conservative political culture when many of the issues stem from the needs of the "have-nots" of society, who traditionally have been supported by liberals? Do they consider alternative viewpoints? Can their policies be implemented effectively, or are they merely "smoke and mirrors" that only seem to address the problem?

Overall, Texas, when compared with other states, tends to rank toward the bottom in many service areas (see also Chapter 12). Also, the state is sometimes slow to respond to issues such as adult health care, failures of electric deregulation, and campaign finance.[1] However, state officials cannot proceed at a pace faster than that at which the public is willing to move and to fund. One of the awkward aspects of democracy is that following majority opinion does not always lead to wise or swift policy decisions.

## The Public Policy Process

Public policy is where government comes face-to-face with citizens. The things that government does, or chooses not to do, affect all of us as we live our daily lives. Like all other states, Texas faces important public issues that need to be addressed to regulate the health, safety, and welfare of its citizens. The issues that the legislature addresses during its session constitute the state policy agenda. The choices elected officials make to solve **public policy** problems establish priorities for programs that benefit the public. Because the choices involve billions of dollars and often deal with conflicting values of citizens, people even argue, sometimes intensely, about whether government should address some problems at all. Consequently, many controversial issues confront state policymakers, leading to impassioned democratic debate.

**public policy**
The overall purpose behind individual governmental decisions and programs. It is the result of public officials' setting of priorities by creating the budget, making official decisions, and passing laws.

### The Policy Agenda

In Texas, the backdrop of a traditionalistic/individualistic political culture that runs headlong into a newer moralistic culture among a vocal minority in the state often makes the disagreements over public policy issues sharp. Also, even when people agree that a particular problem needs to be addressed, they may disagree about the best way to deal with it. Furthermore, the fiscal health of the state can complicate the policy agenda considerably. The state never has enough money to fund all the desired programs at the same time, and so state finance itself becomes a major policy issue.

The development of public policy begins when decision makers identify a problem that needs to be addressed. When an influential public official, such as the governor or a legislator (see especially Chapters 6 and 7), recommends a government policy to deal with a problem, it is placed on the policy agenda, and the debates just mentioned may ensue. Often, gubernatorial and legislative viewpoints conflict. For example, in 2009, the legislature passed a bipartisan bill that would have provided full-day pre-kindergarten programs for high-risk Texas children. Governor Perry, without having objected to the bill during the session, vetoed it, explaining that the money appropriated for the program might be better used to expand existing programs.[2]

Similarly, interest groups and lobbyists often place items on the agenda by making known the priorities they think the state should set. These individuals and groups work through elected officials, the bureaucracy, and the media, but they are especially vigorous in pursuing legislative support for their policy emphases.

## Mandates

**mandate** Action that the national government requires state and local governments to take or that the state requires cities, counties, and special districts to take.

Another avenue for setting the policy agenda is through the complex relationships among federal, state, and local governments. Often, these relationships result in a **mandate**, a term that refers to an action of the national government that requires state and local governments to act in a certain way. National standards such as those required by the No Child Left Behind program in education that must be implemented by state and local governments is one major example. Mandates may be burdensome on state and local governments, which are required to act even though they receive no funding to help implement the new program. Nationally, the fiscal impact on the states is significant, with the federal Office of Management and Budget estimating the costs of unfunded federal mandates on the states at between $59 billion and $88 billion each year as of 2016.[3]

Mandates have several possible sources. These include the courts, administrative regulations, legislation, and/or highly publicized shifts in national priorities. For example, changes in Texas public school finance began in 1973 with a federal court order and continued with a 1987 state court order to provide a more equitable and "efficient" system of funding public schools.[4] The issue was not settled until 2006. Similarly, the state prison system was tied up in a long-running court suit that began in 1971, with the federal courts not relinquishing supervision until 2002.[5] The suit stemmed from historic problems, such as overcrowding, abuse of prisoners, and poor health care facilities.

The welfare system in Texas is a product of the state's emphasis on efficiency, national budget cutting, changing national priorities, and state efforts to gain administrative approval from the federal bureaucracy, as well as the traditionalistic/individualistic political culture. All states are struggling to provide adequate welfare and health care services in the midst of federal changes.

Another illustration of how public policy gets set is the intragovernmental example within the state-assisted higher education system in Texas. Like the Department of Human Services, a public university is a state agency. In 1997, the legislature enacted rules governing a number of business procedures universities had used to generate revenue, thus giving explicit instructions to executive branch agencies. The legislature also dictated diversity goals and called for greater excellence in higher education, but in doing so, it indirectly mandated that colleges and universities raise tuition sharply to generate funds to achieve curriculum, diversity, and excellence targets. By the twenty-first century, many legislators, ruing the increasing cost of education for the students, began to question the tuition rates that had been raised in part because of legislative mandates imposed on universities. In 2016, Governor Greg Abbott called for a policy that would control the costs of higher education and make a university education available to average Texans. Between 2003 and 2015, according to the Texas Higher Education Coordinating Board, the average cost of tuition and fees statewide rose 119 percent, from $1,934 to $4,229 a semester, for undergraduate students taking 15 credit hours.[6]

Although mandates cause difficulties, they are but one of many issues that contribute to society's problems. As society becomes more complex, the challenges of urbanization, business cycles, conversion from a manufacturing to a service economy, and the curtailment of federal funds to state and local governments are among other factors that cause difficulties. With new issues rising frequently, including the continuing growth of the Texas population, the policy agenda is constantly evolving.

## Poverty, Welfare, and Health Care

The most basic of human needs are food, clothing, shelter, and health care. The crucial question is whether the state should provide extensive services in these areas or be a "low-service state." Conservative agendas have long shaped Texas politics. In short, for reasons that were discussed throughout this book, the viewpoints of individuals in upper-income brackets often dominate public policy, and the predominant traditionalistic/individualistic political culture underlies this approach to politics. These political facts of life are particularly important when we examine the issues of poverty and welfare.

**redistributive public policy** Laws and government decisions that have the effect of taking wealth, power, and other resources from some citizens and giving those resources to others. Examples would be the graduated income tax and affirmative action programs.

Whenever the government attempts to improve the quality of life for the poor, it is producing **redistributive public policy**[7]—that is, policy that redistributes wealth from those who have the most to those who have the least. Inevitably, then, poverty, welfare, and health care politics produces strong emotions and sharp political divisions. In Texas, as elsewhere, some policymakers and ordinary citizens think that poor people could be more effective at helping themselves through job training, education, and looking for work. Even when compassion exists for those too ill or infirm to work, it does not spill over into sympathy for individuals deemed to be shirkers. Other people think that people are poor because they have never been given an opportunity to have a good education or relevant job training. Without question, the reasons for poverty are many. The task at hand is to determine how the state of Texas addresses poverty issues.

Any state's role in combating poverty and seeing to the welfare of its citizens is a mix of both state policy and federal programs. Because of changes in national policy, Texas, which has traditionally relied on federal funds for its welfare programs, has had to make changes in its own welfare system.

### Poverty in Texas

**poverty threshold** The level of income below which a family is officially considered to be poor. It is established annually as the basis for determining eligibility for a variety of social programs. Also called the federal poverty line.

The **poverty threshold** for a family of three in the lower 48 states was $21,330 for 2019, although it is somewhat higher in Alaska and Hawaii. This guideline is often stated for a family of three because a typical poor family consists of a mother and two children; an additional family member increases the line by $4,420.[8]

The problem of poverty in Texas is real, although rates of poverty have declined in recent years. The U.S. Census Bureau reports that the state's poverty rate for 2018 was 14.7 percent, down significantly from 18.5 percent in 2011. However, poverty rates are much higher, at 20.9 percent, among children. Poverty rates are three times as high for Hispanic or black children compared to white children in Texas. Counties in the Rio Grande Valley have poverty rates about twice as high as the state as a whole.[9] Even though Texas is a leader in the number of new jobs created annually, many of those jobs are low paying.

The National Center for Children in Poverty at Columbia University reports that 24 percent of all Texas children live in poverty—that is, the household income is below the poverty guideline—and another 24 percent are low-income, that is, their family income is less than 200 percent of the poverty threshold. At 48 percent living in poverty or low-income households, this exceeds the national average of 41 percent. Fourteen of the 100 poorest counties in the United States are in Texas, mostly in the counties in South Texas along the Rio Grande, states with high Hispanic populations.[10] The per capita income in Starr County in 2017 was only $13,167, substantially less than half of that for the state as a whole.[11] Statistics for Medicaid (the program that provides health insurance for the poorest individuals) enlighten the poverty figures. As of December 2018, of the 3,939,805 Texans receiving Medicaid assistance, 3,204,749 are under the age of 21. And another 384,704 children receive medical benefits from the Children's Health Insurance Program (CHIP).[12] Rural south and southwest Texas and the ghettos and *barrios* of the largest cities have the highest number of poor people.

One question that arises when the stark numbers of Texas poverty are stated is "what about the homeless?" Neither the state nor the national government has a very accurate measure of the number of homeless people because the homeless are a mix of people who sometimes have work and sometimes do not, and include a substantial number of mentally ill people. When adequate help is provided, the majority of homeless move into housing and find a job, according to the U.S. Bureau of the Census.[13] Homelessness is on the decline in the United States, and in Texas. However, there are still 23,548 homeless people in Texas as of the end of 2018. Of those, 2,200 were veterans and 1,318 were unaccompanied young adults (ages 18–24).[14] Given the population size of Texas and the entrenched poverty in some parts of the state, homelessness is likely to remain a stubborn problem.[15]

## The Players and the Major Programs

Texas has four departments that deal with the major social welfare issues in the state:

▶ Department of State Health Services (DSHS), which includes broad-based health services, health care information, mental health, and alcohol and drug abuse programs

▶ Department of Aging and Disability Services (DADS), which includes services for mentally challenged and community care, nursing home, and aging services

▶ Department of Family and Protection Services (DFPS), which includes child and adult protective services and childcare regulatory services

▶ Department of Assistive and Rehabilitative Services (DARS), which includes rehabilitation, services for the blind and visually impaired, services for the deaf and hard of hearing, and early childhood intervention

Each of these departments is headed by a commissioner who reports to the executive commissioner of health and human services, who in turn reports to the governor. A nine-member Health and Human Services Council assists the executive commissioner in policy development. In addition, the Health and Human Services Commission determines eligibility for and administers a number of significant programs that cut across the departments. These programs include accreditation, welfare, Medicaid/CHIP, and nutrition, among others. Employment services and benefits are handled through the Texas Workforce Commission.

To help assist those in poverty, state governments participate in two kinds of programs, in each case in a cooperative way with the national government: (1) income assistance programs and (2) health care programs. What makes assessing these programs at the state level alone difficult is that the programs are funded with high percentages of federal money, but are largely administered by state authorities.

More interestingly, the mix of costs and coverage of these kinds of programs has changed dramatically over the last two decades. Twenty-five years ago, the primary program for income assistance for families was a categorical grant called Aid to Families with Dependent Children (AFDC) and allowed families to receive benefits in an open-ended way as long as they could prove need. In 1996, AFDC was replaced by a block grant program called **Temporary Assistance for Needy Families**, a program allowing more flexibility at the state level in paying out benefits and capping the number of years a family can receive benefits at five years. As a result of this and other changes, income assistance "welfare" programs have been, relatively speaking, on the decline.

At the same time, both the advances in medical problems that can be treated and the costs of treating them have increased dramatically. Those increasing costs have meant that lower percentages of Americans have access to private health insurance and even middle-income families often lack health coverage. Indeed, because of the costs of health care coverage and hospitalization, nearly anyone lacking health care coverage is medically indigent. Texas remains the state with the highest rates of people without medical insurance, with the Texas Medical Association estimating the number of uninsured at 4.8 million—or about 17 percent of the population—in 2016.[16]

How dramatic is the shift? In December 2018, the Texas Department of Health and Human Services provided assistance to 59,770 clients through the TANF program. Appropriations for TANF cash assistance were $113.6 million, and amounts continue to decrease because of declining caseloads. This represents a large dollar amount, but a fraction of the health care costs. The cost of health care dwarfed traditional welfare spending. A total of $61.8 billion in All Funds ($25.7 billion in state funds, and $36.1 billion in Federal Funds) in Medicaid funding is appropriated across the HHS function for the 2018–19 biennium. Even the much smaller Children's Health Insurance Program (CHIP) cost several times what TANF did, with funding of $2.0 billion in All Funds, including $153.1 million in General Revenue Funds.[17]

Against this background, then, the national debate on health care reform has especially important consequences in Texas. Because none of these health or welfare programs are solely the responsibility of the state, the outcome of congressional action on health care may dramatically transform the state role in that area.

**Temporary Assistance for Needy Families (TANF)** A federal-state cooperative block grant program that provides cash assistance to indigent families with dependent children for a period of up to five years.

In this cartoon, Ben Sargent poses a dilemma concerning public education. Though Texans value public education, they continue to fund it at among the lowest levels of the states.

Courtesy of Ben Sargent

**Competency Connection**
**PERSONAL RESPONSIBILITY**

Should Texas spend more on education to make graduates of Texas schools more competitive for 21st Century employment?

**Medicaid** A jointly funded federal-state program to provide medical care to low-income families.

**Medicaid** is the program in the United States used to provide health care assistance for the needy in society. Before the 1960s, the provision of health care for the needy was almost entirely borne at the state and local levels, with county governments often having the lion's share of the responsibility. Beginning with the passage of Medicaid in 1965, the role of the national government increased dramatically and responsibility for administration centralized from county governments to the state, as the financial figures just cited demonstrate. Medicaid's principal programs are for children, the aged, the blind and disabled, and maternity care.

Expansion of Medicaid is one of the major aspects of the Patient Protection and Affordable Care Act ("Obamacare") passed by the U.S. Congress in 2010. Under Obamacare, states were to be required to expand Medicaid coverage, but in the U.S. Supreme Court decision upholding Obamacare as a whole, the Court ruled that Congress had overstepped its power in requiring states to accept an expanded Medicaid program. That provision would have unconstitutionally coerced states to either accept the expansion or risk losing existing Medicaid funding.

Republicans controlled the decision-making in the legislative session as Texas opted not to accept additional Medicaid funds. The fear among the majority in the legislature was that the initial incremental funding from the national government would fade away, leaving Texas to take over increased funding of medical care in only a very few years, which in turn might force higher taxes. Democrats argued that the refusal of funds was shortsighted, leaving federal money, drawn from Texans' taxes, to be distributed to other states at the competitive disadvantage of Texas. They also claimed that Texas must treat the indigent in emergency rooms of hospitals even without incremental funding and that the only people who would be hurt by remaining a low-service state would be the poor. Forgoing the expansion means Texas has passed up tens of billions in federal Medicaid dollars. The issue is especially important because Texas has a higher percentage of uninsured residents than any other state. Under the expansion, more than a million Texans not currently covered by Medicaid would have coverage.

However, Governor Rick Perry argued that under Obamacare, the costs of the new program, requiring states to pay 10 percent of the cost of increased coverage in the future, would be prohibitive. "Texas will not be held hostage by the Obama Administration's attempt to force us into the fool's errand of adding more than a million Texans into a broken system. Texas will not be participating in Medicaid expansion." Wendy Davis, a leading Democrat in the state senate, bemoaned the unwillingness of Texas to accept incremental federal funding for Medicaid. "The failure of Gov. Perry to lead on healthcare has left our state vulnerable," she said. "Instead of leveraging and investing $4 billion in federal funding to improve access to healthcare to Texans and to create hundreds of thousands of new jobs, he has stubbornly allowed other states to take advantage of our tax dollars."[18]

The CHIP mentioned earlier was originally passed by the national government in 1997 and provides for medical assistance for children even from families at above the official poverty level. With so many families without medical insurance, there was a priority given to making sure children had adequate health coverage. As Texas faced financial constraints in the early 2000s, the state restricted eligibility to the CHIP as a cost-saving device. In 2009, the legislature failed to expand coverage of the CHIP that would have provided assistance to 80,000 children.[19] Limited resources in the 2011 session precluded discussion of any expansion of benefits, and even with better economic circumstances since then, CHIP funding has remained virtually unchanged in 2019.

The national Social Security Administration provides direct case assistance for aged, disabled, and blind Texans through the Supplemental Security Income (SSI) program, and the U.S. Department of Health and Human Services channels funds to the consolidated Texas Health and Human Services Commission (HHSC) for the Temporary Assistance to Needy Families (TANF) program. TANF is a program for families with needy children under age eighteen who have been deprived of financial support because of the absence, disability, unemployment, or underemployment of both parents. The U.S. Department of Agriculture administers the Food Stamp Program, passing dollars through the HHSC.

All of these programs are designed to work with one another so that a person eligible to receive help from one program is *sometimes* eligible to receive help from one or more of the others, although the formulas determining eligibility vary with each program. Even though most states supplement these programs, Texas historically has chosen to provide "bare-bones" programs. Figure 13-1 illustrates trends in the receipt of Food Stamps (SNAP) and Temporary Assistance to Needy Families (TANF) over the time frame of 1995–2017. Over that time, assistance from TANF has declined and Food Stamp reliance, though fluctuating a bit, has increased. Even if families receive all of the Medicaid, Food Stamp, and TANF assistance that is available from the Texas government, they will fall far short of the poverty line. As a relatively low-service state, these data have not changed significantly over the last few years. Other social services include day care, foster homes, energy assistance for low-income persons (to help with heating bills), child protective services, and job training. Changing federal and state policy, economic conditions, and population changes contribute to the variations in the numbers from year to year, but overall the numbers indicate that Texas does not do a particularly good job in helping poor people. Texas for years has ranked in the bottom quarter of states with regard to social services. It is a state of contrasts between rich and poor, and although the stereotype of Texas is a state filled with rich oil tycoons, the state has large pockets of poverty and is perennially in the lower half of states in the nation in average per capita income.[20] Even at that, however, the rising costs of health and welfare programs are now almost equal to education spending, and in the future support for those programs may create pressure on adequate funding for education.

Another related service is unemployment compensation—that is, payments to unemployed workers. This program cuts across programs affecting business and those affecting the poor. It is administered by the Texas Workforce Commission, which also assists individuals in finding jobs and keeps records of employment in the state. Unemployment compensation is a joint federal-state effort. The basic funding method is a tax on wages paid by employers, plus

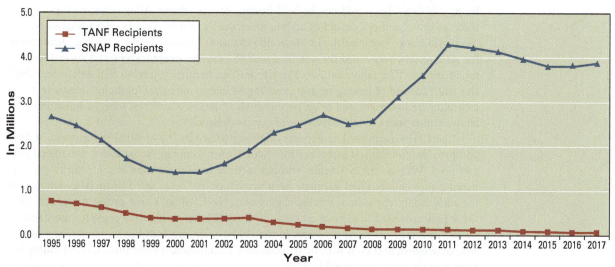

Notes: (1) TANF = Temporary Assistance for Needy Families; SNAP = Supplemental Nutrition Assistance Program. (2) Amounts shown for 2017 are estimated.

Figure 13-1  TANF and SNAP (Food Stamp) Caseloads, Fiscal Years 1995–2017

SOURCE: Legislative Budget Board, *Fiscal Size-up, 2018–2019 Biennium*, p. 189.

Explain the trends over time in spending on TANF compared to SNAP programs in Texas?

any surcharge needed to make the system fiscally sound, and reimbursements from governmental units for any unemployment benefits drawn by their former employees. If a state has its own unemployment compensation program and an agency to administer it, the employers can charge off most of the tax on their federal tax returns. If the federal government administers the program directly, employers cannot take advantage of the tax write-off. In Texas, unemployment benefits vary according to previous wage and disability status. In 2019, the maximum unemployment benefit was $465 per week. Benefits are payable for a period up to twenty-six weeks.

The 2009 session confronted one of the modern complications of federalism, the fiscal relationships between national and state governments. When the U.S. Congress passed a large economic stimulus package, it provided for increased coverage for unemployment compensation in difficult times, but insisted that coverage be broader than current Texas law allowed.[21] In order to gain access to millions of national government dollars, Texas had to provide coverage for workers not previously covered. Before reversing course and accepting the federal money, Governor Perry briefly considered not accepting national money because after the package has expired, Texas might be obligated to pay more for unemployment compensation in the future. The lesson here is that, although states are independent from the national government in many ways, the fiscal relationship between the two levels is complex and requires constant attention.

**workers' compensation** A program that provides medical, income, death, and burial benefits for workers who are injured, become ill, or are killed on the job.

**Workers' compensation** is a program to provide medical, income, death, and burial benefits for workers who are injured, become ill, or are killed on the job. The program has existed largely in its present form since 1917. The procedures and especially the costs of the program affect businesses of all sizes, from the local "Ma and Pa" diner to Exxon-Mobil Corporation, the largest corporation in the state. Texas is unique among the states in allowing employers to choose whether to provide workers' compensation, although public employers and employers who accept a public construction contract must provide workers' compensation. Employers who are not participants in the program must notify both the Texas Workers' Compensation Commission and all employees. These employers have a number of options as alternatives to the workers' compensation program, including private insurance and setting aside reserve funds ("self-insurance").

Generally, Texas has a history of having laws that are not as protective of workers' rights as other states. In addition to having a "right-to-work" provision, prohibiting union membership as a condition for employment, the workers' compensation laws have generally had rather high costs with low worker benefits. Texas has not been unique in its workers' compensation problems. Worker's compensation is related to workplace safety, and Texas often leads the nation in workplace fatalities, with 534 in 2017, a rate of 4.3 fatalities per 100,000 workers, compared to the national average of 3.5 and worker's compensation benefits remained among the lowest in the nation, with the maximum benefit as of 2019 being $938 per week.[22]

## Recent Policy Developments

**workfare** The concept that in order for poor citizens to qualify for welfare assistance, they must have a job or be actively seeking a job.

Early in the 1990s, many states, including Texas, had addressed the issue of welfare reform, all of them with emphasis on converting welfare to **workfare**, forcing "deadbeat" dads and moms to provide child support, and employing modern electronics to aid in tracking those in the welfare system. In 1996, the Personal Responsibility and Work Opportunity Reconciliation Act took effect. Fundamentally, this legislation followed the lead of the states in getting people off welfare and onto payrolls.

The *workfare* approach carried with it not only such positive values as helping welfare recipients regain their self-esteem by becoming better trained and gainfully employed, and freeing up money for other programs, but also such negatives as more rules and regulations.

The federal reform allowed five years of welfare support, but the time clock begins to tick from the first date a recipient receives a check even though the person might have extensive training to undergo. Texas provides for only three years of assistance, although the average time on welfare is less than two years. The federal requirement is that the individual be working within two years, without the flexibility of the earlier Texas plan that included job training, parenting or life skills training, and education or literacy training within the definition of work.[23]

In their concern for reducing welfare fraud, putting people to work, and generally moving one step away from Big Government, the politicians initially failed to address the fundamental reality of welfare reform—namely, that the legislation forces single mothers of dependent children to go to work and may deprive their children of health care coverage through Medicaid. Because workfare means that their children will be either left alone all day or placed in day care, this consequence would seem to contradict the much-touted "family values" espoused by many politicians. Less parental care is also likely to have the further consequences of more juvenile crime, poorer school performance, and thus, paradoxically, even more welfare dependency.

Welfare reform illustrates how complex social issues are. In trying to fix one set of problems, it is all too easy to create another set. This section has demonstrated that, while welfare costs have declined, the cost of health care has increased dramatically in this century. It is the cost of health care, through Medicaid and the Children's Health Insurance Program, that challenges the state budget.

The 1996 federal act created a "cafeteria-style" welfare system for the states, with each state receiving a block grant for welfare support, which it could apportion among programs that the state judged as having the highest priority. Proportionately less money now flows from Washington, and the states are allowed under the national legislation to slash their own welfare payments by 20 percent with no loss of federal funds.

By 2003, Medicaid expenses nationally were growing 7–8 percent a year, a major problem for Texas and many other states that were already facing deficits. State officials across the country found themselves having to decide among many well-deserving programs.[24] The opening ploy of the Texas legislative session was a House plan to deal with the budget shortfall via massive cuts in social services; part of this strategy was to pare back social services that House conservatives detested. That plan was unfeasible not only because it lacked Senate support, but also because cutting state services meant cutting federal dollars. Nevertheless, the combination of revenue shortfalls coupled with an unwillingness to raise taxes led to significant cuts, even though the cuts were not as deep as the House wanted.

The Seventy-ninth Legislature in 2005 moved to shore up the health and human services programs somewhat. Financial supplements were made to cover Medicaid and the CHIP costs, and the application and operations aspects of these programs were modified, although to the great confusion of clients. Some of the people cut from services in 2003 were restored to the rolls in 2005 and even more in 2007. However, as mentioned, CHIP has not notably expanded since then, even with 835,000 needy children still left without health care as of 2017.

In the face of large budget deficits in a state with a balanced budget amendment, Governor Perry suggested in late 2010 that Texas might simply opt out of Medicaid. At one point he even called it a "Ponzi scheme." However, because of the formulas where nearly two out of three dollars spent on Medicaid come from the federal government and the reality that nearly 3 million Texans require Medicaid assistance each month, the abstract thought of cutting state spending by slashing Medicaid never received serious consideration during the 2011 legislative session. The growing costs of Medicaid continue to challenge the legislature in 2019, and they are complicated further by the national opioid crisis.[25]

Texas has high levels of poverty and large numbers of citizens who need health care for their children, challenging programs such as the Children's Health Insurance Program. Texas is also visited from time to time by hurricanes, such as Hurricane Ike. The citizens pictured here are in need of basic necessities in the wake of the hurricane, testing the capacities of social programs in the state.

(Top) AP Images/Eric Gay.
(Bottom) Peter Turnley/Corbis News/Corbis

### Competency Connection
### SOCIAL RESPONSIBILITY

Hurricanes hurt everyone in their wake, but clearly they affect some people more negatively than others. What is the impact of natural disasters on people in poverty?

## Analysis

The off-again/on-again support for social services results in muddled signals. One reading is that despite a set of elected officials even more conservative than those of the past, the state has developed a social conscience with regard to the needy. An alternative interpretation is that the state is mainly interested in money—finding ways not to spend state dollars on the poor and finding ways to get a bigger piece of the federal welfare pie. Beyond dispute is the fact that Texas has a welfare problem that is tied to social divisions that rest on ethnic conflicts and struggles between the haves and the have-nots.

A combination of stringent qualifications for recipients and a booming economy resulted in one effect desired by state and federal welfare reformers—namely, a drop in the number of aid recipients. Several factors make it likely that social services will be a perennial issue in Texas politics. First, the economy swings between boom and bust, and when the economy is sluggish, the number of aid recipients increases at the same time that the state is less able to pay for the services. Second, the state's immigration rate is among the highest in the country, and many of the immigrants, especially those who are illegal, lack essential job skills. They often constitute the working poor, especially because they are willing to work for inferior wages.[26] Third, disparities between rich and poor seem to be growing, and that difference is exacerbated by a rapidly growing elderly population with more women than men.[27] National tax policy intensified the phenomenon of the rich getting richer and the poor getting poorer. Fourth, the conservatism of Texans became more evident early in the 2000s, and it continues after the results of the 2018 elections, though there was some moderating in the makeup of the legislature. One lingering issue in state politics is "the race to the bottom" phenomenon. In short, states would naturally find it advantageous if those who were neediest—in poverty, mentally disabled, and elderly, for example—would move elsewhere. Of course, no one would ever make such an argument explicitly, but the financial calculus is unarguable. As a result, states have incentives to limit their assistance to those in poverty.

## Public Education Policy

In many ways, the hopes and aspirations of American democracy are played out most centrally in the public schools. The founding fathers envisioned a society of educated citizens who could participate in informed discourse about their society and government and make informed choices in choosing their representatives in government, as the quote from Thomas Jefferson at the beginning of the chapter illustrates. Although public education in the United States as we now know it did not begin to develop until after the Civil War, it fits well with the aspirations of the Founders. As public education developed, it became far more than just a venue to teach, "reading, writing, and arithmetic," and took on other societal functions as well, including political and societal socialization, and the provision of equal opportunity to succeed.

A major example of the social agenda came with the forced integration of schools beginning in the 1950s with the U.S. Supreme Court case of *Brown* v. *Board of Education*. However important fulfilling the requirements of the U.S. Constitution's Fourteenth Amendment was, it illustrates the multiple goals of public education. (Discussion of issues of desegregation and equity in education can be found in Chapter 10.) Because of these varied goals, there has often been conflict in how to run a public school system.

One of the central functions of state and local governments is public education. In every state in the country, including Texas, the largest single expenditure of government is for public education. The cost is borne by both state and local government, with the largest portion being spent by local schools. In Texas, the system is complex, with some of the responsibilities for public education residing at the state level and others at the local level. The state has Local Independent School Boards that hire teachers, build school buildings, and make judgments about allocations of resources in their own local areas. But Texas also has a State Board of Education that makes broader decisions about what is required to gain an education in Texas and to graduate from a Texas high school. The interaction between these two levels, along with the national government, makes for ongoing political struggles.

The passage of the 1965 Elementary and Secondary Education Act marked the first major federal funding of public education in the United States. It was an attempt to bolster education and to focus especially on creating equal education opportunity for students in disadvantaged economic areas. The passage of the No Child Left Behind Act of 2001 (NCLB) expanded federal involvement in education by establishing requirements for annual testing of students in core subject areas, mandating the hiring of "highly qualified teachers," and allowing students in low-quality schools to transfer to more successful ones. This act has changed public education

## You Decide: Should Texas Find Ways to Pay for More Social Services?

### Pro

⬆ Many social service recipients are the working poor. They have full-time, but low-paying, jobs that are inadequate to support their families.

⬆ The biggest cuts have been in children's medical services, but it is far better to offer preventive programs to poor kids than to wait for a serious illness to strike them.

⬆ The mentally ill, including many homeless persons, were hit hard by the changes. These persons are basically helpless and deserve state assistance.

⬆ When good jobs are scarce and families are having a hard time making it economically, the state should provide even more social services, not fewer.

⬆ Human resources are the most important resources of all. It's good public policy to invest in them.

### Con ☒

⬇ Welfare recipients are lazy and must be forced to find jobs to support themselves and their families. It's not the role of the state to support them.

⬇ It is far more important to fund public education than to provide public funding for indigent children's health.

⬇ The most expensive medical programs are for mental illness and substance abuse. People get themselves into these messes. Let them get themselves out.

⬇ Citizens cannot afford to pay more state taxes and fees to support poor people. If public programs exist, they should be funded entirely by the federal government.

⬇ Privatization is a highly desirable public policy. If people need help, they should ask local charities.

**Competency Connection**
**SOCIAL RESPONSIBILITY**

Texas has always prided itself for being a low tax, low service state. Should it change its priorities to provide more services?

---

dramatically, though it has not been accompanied by funding necessary to accomplish its ambitious goals.[28]

Even with the federal programs, education programs are funded more than 90 percent by state and local funds, as discussed in Chapter 12. Passage of NCLB has made the purposes of public education seem even more complex, with competition among state, local, and national governments over controlling the nature and responsibility of public education. As a result of this competition, schools often seek to accomplish many different goals simultaneously.

In Texas, the conduct of education has met with mixed results. Without question, many graduates of Texas public schools are successful, and a number of schools and school districts are "exemplary." At the same time, Texas has had some notable challenges and has not always successfully met them. The Texas public school system is a large one, serving 5,399,682 students in the 2017–2018 school year, and it has grown by more than 15 percent over the last decade, more than six times the national average.

The number of economically disadvantaged students continues to grow within every ethnic group. By the 2017–2018 year, the number of economically disadvantaged students had risen to 58.7 percent of all students.[29] The growth of the Latino and other minority student population is especially noteworthy, with the makeup of Texas schools as follows: Latino (52.4 percent), followed by White (27.9 percent), African American (12.6 percent), Asian (4.4 percent), and multiracial (2.3 percent) students (see Figure 13-2).[30]

With the hyper-growth rates in schools and the challenges of ethnic and economic diversity, come another set of challenges, maintaining a high quality of public education. In

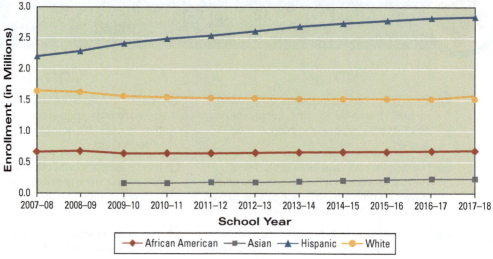

Figure 13-2 Enrollment by Race/Ethnicity, Texas Public Schools, 2007–2008 through 2017–2018

SOURCE: Enrollment in Texas Public Schools 2017–18, Texas Education Agency August 2018, p. 7.

terms of educational attainment, Texas ranks dead last among states, with one out of every six Texans not holding a high school degree. This places Texas at a competitive disadvantage in the workforce because more and more jobs require technical skills.[31]

## Education Reform

The history of modern education reform in Texas begins with the "No Pass, No Play" reforms of the mid-1980s. Under Governor Mark White, there was an emerging pressure to institute new standards to encourage high quality in education. A 1983 U.S. Department of Education study, *A Nation at Risk,* had found that the national education system had numerous deficiencies. What emerged from the legislature in 1984 were a number of reforms, including its most controversial recommendation that athletes not be able to participate in extracurricular programs if they were not passing all of their classes. Other reforms included higher attendance standards, a longer school year, and incentives for excellent teachers.

The 1984 reforms were but a first pass at educational reform that has been ongoing since. Beginning after the 2011 legislative session, a new evaluation tool called STAAR (State of Texas Assessment of Academic Readiness) was adopted. The new exams are designed to be more rigorous than their predecessors and are intended to encourage both academic performance and growth. By 2019, critics argued that the STAAR standards were actually set at above grade level standards, putting undue pressure on teachers and students alike. In the 2013 session, there was general agreement that under previous reforms, the state had begun to require far too much educational testing. As a result, testing was reduced dramatically. Under the 2013 law, students must pass five exams to earn a diploma: Algebra I, biology, English I and II, and U.S. history. The law also gives students more flexibility in course options to meet graduation requirements.[32]

## Nontraditional Education Proposals

**school vouchers**
A policy that would allow families who send their students to private schools to receive a tax deduction to cover a part of private school tuition. This has not been enacted in Texas.

To enhance the quality of education, critics of the education system argue that three innovations might help. The first is the idea of **school vouchers**, a policy that would allow families who send their students to private schools to receive a tax deduction to cover a part of private school tuition. Proponents of school vouchers argue that the system would create competition between private and public schools and give incentives for public schools to increase the quality of their offerings. They also feel that the tax adjustments would constitute a net savings for the state government, since students who attend private schools do not expend public funds. Vouchers have never been instituted in Texas, despite Governor Abbott pushing for them in the 2017 legislative session, because opponents have successfully claimed that a voucher system would result in top students abandoning the public schools, making it more difficult to maintain a healthy academic environment in the public schools. They further point out that even tax credits would not make private schools accessible to poor families and would give tax breaks to wealthy families who would perhaps send their children to private schools even without public assistance.

**charter schools**
Special public schools set up to provide unique educational opportunities for students who attend them.

A second nontraditional idea has met with much more success: **charter schools**, which are public schools set up to have a unique academic interest. The schools are begun from scratch and are founded, proponents argue, to provide competition that will encourage standard public schools to improve their performance. The legislature first approved the founding of charter schools during the 1995 legislative session, there are 707 open enrollment charter schools in the state as of 2018, serving more than 5 percent of all students. Charter schools have met with mixed success, and it remains unclear whether they can foster a more generalized improvement in public education. The failure rates for charter schools over the fifteen-year history of them have hovered around one-third, so challenges remain.[33]

The third innovation is the growth of home schooling in Texas. In recent years, a growing number of families have chosen to educate their children in a home environment rather than in public schools. In 1994, the Texas Supreme Court upheld a lower court decision that ruled that home schooling was protected just as private schooling was, making home schooling a viable option for education. Requiring education in public schools "deprived the home school parents of equal protection under the law," since their private schools in the home were unfairly discriminated against "on the sole basis of location in the home."[34] Recent estimates are that as many as 350,000 Texas students are being educated at home. Home schooling has little oversight, and the quality of instruction can vary widely.

## Texas Textbooks and Curricula

Texas is unique in some of the roles that are played by the State Board of Education (SBOE), an elected body with fifteen members. In Texas, school textbooks must be approved by the Texas Education Agency, overseen by the SBOE, to make certain that materials approved for classroom use cover the entire curriculum of an assigned course. Traditionally, the Texas process was perhaps the most politicized one in the country because of two factors—the conservative nature of the SBOE and the population of Texas. Conservatism led to charges by some that the process, rather than screening for academic excellence, became a method of guiding curricula to match the conservative agenda of state board members. The size of the Texas adoption forced textbook companies, in turn, to seek approval in Texas before they finished their textbooks. Because of the size of the Texas market, the process had a major impact not just in Texas but nationwide. As schools have gone to internet sources and e-readers, the process has gradually decentralized, and in 2011, the legislature changed the rules to allow local schools to select some of their educational materials.

The most recent example of the textbook adoption process came in the adoption of social studies standards by the SBOE in 2019. While the state board has traditionally set basic curricula requirements for high school graduation, they have not normally been involved in the day-to-day matters of what teachers cover in the classroom. However, in 2018, the SBOE briefly deleted Hillary Clinton and Helen Keller from the curriculum before reinstating them. Colin Powell and Oprah Winfrey were deleted, along with American Civil Liberties Union leader Clarence Darrow and Republican presidential candidate Barry Goldwater. John Hancock, whom second-graders were required to learn, was also cut. Eighth-graders no longer need to learn about John C. Calhoun, Henry Clay, or Daniel Webster.[35]

Texas has encountered a number of problems in education in the past several years. Particularly in the 2011 session of the Texas Legislature, the funding of public schools was vastly curtailed. Critics charged that the health of the Texas economy would be challenged because of reduced funding.

Courtesy of Ben Sargent

**Competency Connection**
**PERSONAL RESPONSIBILITY**

Do short term savings in education jeopardize the long term health of the quality of life in Texas?

The passage of the new curriculum came to counteract what members of the SBOE saw as a "liberal bias" among academics who write the books and classroom teachers. They wanted to show conservatism and Republican political philosophies in a better light. A conservative leader on the SBOE said that the only purpose was to "add balance" to the curriculum because "Academia is skewed too far to the left." In contrast, a Democrat on the board argued that the mission was nothing less than an attempt at "rewriting history." "The social conservatives have perverted accurate history to fulfill their own agenda."[36]

## Analysis

Texas public education, both at the elementary/secondary education level and the university level, has met with mixed results. Without question, Texas has some of the finest public schools in the country. But Texas also has some of the biggest challenges. The state ranks well below average among states in school funding and much higher than average in high school dropout rates. And even among those students who graduate, SAT score averages trail the national norms.

Although there is much to be happy with in Texas education, without question a continuation of current trends will not be sufficient to remain competitive nationally in the twenty-first century. One recent study showed that Texas was still spending less, by 20 percent, adjusted for inflation, in 2019 than it was spending before the recession of 2008.

## Texas Higher Education

Texas is fortunate to have a number of community colleges, four-year colleges, and major research institutions to encourage students to attain education beyond high school graduation. The institutions of higher learning vary from open admission community colleges—which are open to anyone holding a high school diploma or a GED and which have relatively low tuition fees—to highly selective research universities with higher tuition rates. In 2018, 1.54 million Texans were attending public state institutions of higher learning.[37] Unlike elementary and secondary education, higher education is not provided to all students free of charge, yielding a class bias involved in higher educational opportunity. Scholarships and other government programs can mitigate that bias.

## Issues

From the beginning of the state, there were funds set aside to ensure the creation and maintenance of state universities. The Permanent University Fund (PUF) stems from land set aside to build university campuses, granted to the state university system in the 1876 Constitution. Originally thought to be barren land with little value, the land proved to have huge oil deposits under it and has been, as a result, a continuing source of revenue for Texas higher education. As of 2017, the PUF owned 2,100,000 acres of land and had assets of $19.5 billion.[38] The funds are limited to the University of Texas and Texas A&M university systems and can be used only for capital investments (land acquisition, building construction and maintenance, capital equipment and library resources, for example), but they have been a huge boon to higher education in Texas from the beginning.

For many years, Texas was known nationally for its low tuition. But in recent years, as the state has sought to find ways to increase revenue streams and lower its financial responsibilities for higher education, tuition has increased rapidly. Tuition was once the same at all state universities, but in recent years, the legislature has allowed for variations among different campuses. Fees have always been variable from one school to the next. Beginning in 2003, the legislature authorized universities to set their own tuitions, though they were limited in the amount they could raise tuition in any given year. Tuitions went up by more than an average of 80 percent over the balance of the decade as universities sought to find resources to maintain their programs.

By 2011, there was great concern that college education was slipping from the grasp of low-income students, and Governor Perry proposed that universities come up with a $10,000 degree that would include all tuition, fees, and textbooks. Though Perry's proposal was not adopted, it pointed out the fact that college tuition continues to rise at rates higher than inflation, in part because Texas has continued to provide a smaller proportion of costs over time. Governor Abbott, too, has suggested that college costs need to be curtailed.[39] In addition to cost, another issue affecting universities has to do with giving access to members of ethnic minorities. In the latter half of the twentieth century, universities began to seek diversity in their student populations, bowing both to the political climate in the United States following the civil rights era and to the notion that diversity is a virtue unto itself, exposing students to people unlike themselves in some ways. Admissions programs that take race, gender, and ethnicity into account are known as **affirmative action** programs. Affirmative action was a controversial idea from its inception, with supporters arguing that it was necessary to make up for historical patterns of discrimination and detractors arguing that merit, rather than race and ethnicity, should determine college admission.

**affirmative action** Admissions program that takes race, gender, and ethnicity into account to attempt to make up for past patterns of discrimination.

In 1996, the case of *Hopwood* v. *Texas*,[40] challenged the Texas "ten percent rule," as it was called, which was designed to give access to students who graduated from urban minority schools to ensure that diversity would remain at state universities. Then, in 2008, University of Texas undergraduate Abigail Fisher sued to have the University's race-conscious admissions policy declared unconstitutional. In both cases the admissions policies were upheld, as discussed in Chapter 9.[41]

## Analysis

A national trend in public higher education is that more and more of the funding is coming from tuition and private sources as opposed to state funding. That trend is also taking place in Texas. Three decades ago, more than half the University of Texas budget came from the state. In 2017–18, the state contributed 12 percent of the budget. The consequences of such a trend are potentially going to change the nature of public higher education going forward. One result is that tuition costs will continue to rise or that students will find themselves attending "virtual universities" that offer discounted tuition for online learning.

In 2018–2019, the legislature was able to increase the total higher education budget to $20.2 billion, but the higher education system continued to grow at an even faster rate. As with other policy debates, there remains much to be decided. Cuts from the state challenge research productivity from state universities and raise questions about the need for the state to support academic research. Advocates for reducing investment in higher education argue that the central goal of universities is to provide education and that resources need to be redistributed for that purpose. The universities themselves argue that basic research from universities is key for a healthy society and for economic competitiveness.[42] This debate will continue to characterize funding of higher education in the foreseeable future.

## Immigration Policy

Since Texas became a republic in 1836, it has shared a border with Mexico along the Rio Grande, a border measuring 1,254 miles. The total border between the United States and Mexico is 1,954 miles in length, so roughly two-thirds of the total southern border is in Texas. For most of the history of the two nations, the border had little real regulation. People could traverse the river between Texas and Mexico without a passport, and few paid heed to the number of people crossing the border. The disparities between the economies of the two countries provided incentive for Mexicans to come to the United States. In addition, Texas was populated by "Texicans," and citizens of both nations shared friendships and family relations across the border. Many of the first citizens of Texas had been Mexicans before The Texas Revolution.

Texas had always had many undocumented people working in the state, largely in physically demanding jobs such as migrant workers in agriculture, construction, or housekeeping. Though Texas was aware of their undocumented status, there was little attempt to stop their employment. Texas was not always generous toward the undocumented, writing a law in 1975 denying children of undocumented Texans the right to public education. In 1982, in the case of *Plyler* v. *Roe*, the U.S. Supreme Court ruled that law unconstitutional, requiring that states, including Texas, allow children to attend schools. They wrote that, while the parents might have chosen to live in Texas illegally, "legislation directing the onus of a parent's misconduct against his children does not comport with fundamental conceptions of justice."[43]

The nature of immigration changed after the terrorist attacks of September 11, 2001, but Texas still had a moderate policy toward immigration and generally generous treatment of undocumented residents of the state. George W. Bush, the former governor of Texas, supported a moderate immigration policy for the United States in 2007, and supported a bill that would have given legal status and a path to citizenship for the 12 to 15 million undocumented immigrants living in the United States. In discussing the bill, Bush said: "We're . . . a nation of immigrants. And we've got to remember that proud tradition, as well, which has strengthened our country in many ways. These are not contradictory goals to remember our heritage and uphold our laws. America can be a lawful society and a welcoming society at the same time."[44]

When Governor Rick Perry ran for president of the United States in 2012, he made quite a ripple among conservatives nationwide by supporting the education of undocumented children and supporting in-state tuition at Texas colleges for undocumented residents, arguing "If you say we should not educate children who have come into our state for no other reason than they have been brought here by no fault of their own, I don't think you have a heart."[45] Perry's statement was consistent with the moderate politics of Texas immigration, but out of step with the conservative politics of the national Republican Party.

In 2014, Governor Perry took a more hawkish turn regarding immigration. Texas spent millions of dollars deploying 1,000 troops to the border when Central American immigrants were illegally crossing the border in large numbers. Perry justified the move as necessary when the federal government was being lenient regarding immigration.[46]

**sanctuary cities** Cities that welcome undocumented residents and generally do not report them to law enforcement as long as they are quiet and law abiding.

Conflict over immigration has greatly intensified since the presidential election of 2016 and the election of Donald Trump, including in Texas, and Texas politics regarding immigration have shifted to the right. In the 2017 legislative session, the legislature passed a law against **sanctuary cities,** cities that do not actively report undocumented citizens living within their borders. The law required law enforcement organizations to hold noncitizen inmates who are subject to deportation and allowed police officers to question a person's immigration status during routine stops. Governor Abbott declared that the law "banned sanctuary cities in the Lone Star State," but the Mexican American Legal Defense and Education Fund (MALDEF), blasted the law as "a colossal blunder" and promised to fight it.[47]

Building a wall along the Southern border of Texas is fraught with complications, both physical and legal. Because a river is the border, the problem in Texas is quite different than the one in other states where the border is across dry ground. That means that any barrier between Texas and Mexico would be inside Texas, and much of it would cross private land, an expensive and controversial process involving questions of eminent domain, the right of the government to take private land for public purposes with just compensation. The wall is a priority of President Trump, but all U.S. Representatives along the Texas border, including Will Hurd, a Republican who represents 820 miles along the Rio Grande, oppose it. The debate over building a barrier between Texas and Mexico promises to be a major topic in Texas politics for the foreseeable future.

## Summary

**LO 13.1** **Public policy debates involve making choices about the proper role of government and how government interacts with citizens.** Federal mandates require the Texas governments to implement programs to accomplish national goals, and can be funded by the national government or unfunded, that is, not funded by the national government. When they are unfunded, states complain, not surprisingly, about their unfairness.

**LO 13.2** **Human services, which present many challenges, have gone through fundamental changes recently in Texas and elsewhere.** Transformation of the welfare system into a workfare system is a national priority with which Texans can agree. However, the change in philosophy and the reduction in federal social spending are both boon and bane to Texas. While welfare programs have declined, health care programs have mushroomed, with those programs being the focal point of state human resource funding in the near future. In addition, the state probably will continue to have one of the highest proportions of poor people in the country for the foreseeable future, and also will continue to use cuts in social programs as a way to balance the budget in lean financial times.

**LO 13.3** **Challenges in public elementary and secondary education in Texas remain.** The state has some excellent schools, but the funding of public schools remains lower than the national average, while the need for high-quality education in an ever-increasingly technological world is self-evident. If Texas is to be competitive in attracting new business into the state in the years to come, a well-educated workforce will be required. The need for quality education, however, is made difficult to meet by the changing demographics of the state. With the majority of schoolchildren in Texas now being Latino, and many of them having English as a second language (if they speak English at all), the challenges of education become even more apparent. Moreover, with many children of minority status living in poverty, educational opportunity lags.

**LO 13.4** **In higher education, the largest challenge is allowing access to education among low-income students.** Tuition continues to rise while incomes do not. Governor Perry proposed a $10,000 college degree during his 2011 State of the State address as a way to address this issue of accessibility. However, many observers think that this aspiration is unreasonable. Nevertheless, the problem exists and requires consideration of ways to allow more Texans to receive a college education.

## Critical Thinking

1. Liberals and conservatives tend to have differing values regarding issues such as health care and welfare along with public education. Discuss the different perspectives expressed by liberals and conservatives about redistributive social programs. Similarly, assess the role of ideology on the State Board of Education regarding Texas schoolbook adoption.

2. The issue of immigration in Texas has been around as long as the state itself. Explain how Texans have traditionally viewed immigration and how immigration politics have changed in recent years.

Oil was the most important Texas energy source of the twentieth century. Wind may become the most important Texas energy source of the twenty-first century.

*mj007/Shutterstock.com*

# Public Policy—Resources

**14**

I t is in the nature of textbook-writing that the subject matter of this book has been about circumstances and events that will be in the past by the time students read about them. But the real value of any government textbook lies in its ability to enable its readers to understand their present circumstances so that they

**LO14.1**  Explain why the discussion of all types of policy conflict over resources takes place within the context of climate change, and recount the typical way in which Texas politicians have responded to the problem.

**LO14.2**  List at least two types of political conflict over water that can be expected to become more frequent in the near future in Texas, and discuss the reason why they will become more frequent.

**LO14.3**  Display an understanding of the metaphorical term "Faustian Bargain," and explain why it applies to the making of energy policy.

**LO14.4**  Give at least one advantage, and at least one disadvantage, for each potential source of energy for society.

**LO14.5**  List three themes that are important in Texas energy politics, and explain how each example offered in the text illustrates the theme.

**LO14.6**  Explain what historical theme in Texas environmental politics is illustrated by the story of Glenn Shankle and TCEQ.

**LO14.7**  Describe the most critical areas of air and water pollution in Texas.

**LO14.8**  Discuss the reason many people are concerned about the dependency of Texans on vehicles using the internal combustion engine, describe three general strategies for dealing with the problems caused by that dependency, and explain how public policy seeking to implement those strategies is faring.

---

"ONE HUNDRED YEARS AGO, TEXANS WERE CARRYING GUNS AND FIGHTING OVER WATER. NOT MUCH HAS CHANGED."

Pete Laney,
*Speaker of the Texas House of Representatives, to the membership of the House, during the 1990s.*

MEPHISTOPHELES (THE DEVIL): . . .
IF THROUGH LIFE YOU'LL GO WITH ME
IN THAT CASE I'LL AGREE . . .
I'LL BE YOUR SERVANT,
BE YOUR SLAVE!
FAUST: AND WHAT IN
TURN AM I
TO DO FOR YOU?

Faust,
*Epic poem by Johann Wolfgang von Goethe, German writer/naturalist, 1830s*

BUILD IT, AND THEY WILL COME.

Disembodied voice,
*To Kevin Costner's character, in the 1989 film Field of Dreams.*

can, by acting, have an effect upon the future. The purpose of Chapters 13 and 14 is to apply the understanding of Texas politics supplied in the first twelve chapters to policy problems that are troublesome now and will continue to challenge Texans in the future. Chapter 13 examined "people" policies, whereas this chapter focuses on "resource" policies. In both, the principles provided in the first twelve chapters are brought into play in the analysis of making and implementing Texas public policy.

Political scientists have spent many decades studying the inputs (citizen votes, public opinion, lobbying, media accounts), the processes (debates, legislative votes, calculations, hearings) and outputs (laws, rules, budget expenditures) of government, and have come up with a variety of "models," or systematic explanations, of how and why government produces the laws and actions that it does. One of the major conclusions of that literature is that there is not one single model that explains all types of policy outputs, or even how any one type of policy is handled from one policymaking episode to another. Therefore, we do not have a simple set of arguments to help us explain why Texas government produces one type of policy as opposed to another. In general, in these two chapters we are applying the sorts of explanations that we have used in earlier chapters of the book—the interaction of ideology and interests, the way the fragmented state system of institutions functions, and the maneuvering of Texas politicians within the larger context of American federalism. In addition, however, we will be bringing in some approaches that are more specific to the policy-making literature, particularly the analysis of economic costs-versus-benefits, and the portrayal of tradeoffs of advantages and disadvantages more broadly defined.

## Climate Change

In the first chapter of this book, we briefly discussed the death and damage wreaked on Texas by Hurricanes Rita in 2005, Ike in 2008, and Harvey in 2017. While it is tempting to remember such disasters as individual events, it would be more accurate to fit them into a larger global pattern. Indeed, not just deadly weather, but the policy problems of water supply, energy supply, environmental protection, and transportation are all aspects of a potential disaster that looms over the entire planet: climate change caused by human activity. We, not just as Texans, and not just as Americans, but as a species, are doing things that will make life on earth much more difficult for our children, grandchildren, and beyond.

For decades, scientists have been warning that the massive amounts of $CO_2$ gas the industrial economies have been pumping into Earth's atmosphere have caused a "greenhouse effect" that is causing the planet's climate to warm. The evidence is so voluminous, from hundreds of scientists in dozens of countries, that no fair-minded person can deny it. Besides melting ice caps in Greenland and Antarctica, thus raising planetary sea level, the hotter summers evaporate more water from the oceans, leading to heavier rainfall. What would have been merely a bad storm fifty years ago is now a cataclysmic event.[1]

The contribution of global warming to Hurricane Harvey's fury has by now been established by a slew of scientific studies. Investigators writing in *Environmental Research Letters* estimated that the storm's rainfall was 15 percent more intense than previous storms would have been, as a result of climate change. Another group of researchers, using a different methodology, and writing in *Geophysical Research Letters,* concluded that Harvey's downpours were "as much as 40 percent higher than rainfall from a similar storm would have been decades ago." In two papers published in the *Proceedings of the National Academy of Sciences,* the authors argued that human activity was making another Hurricane Harvey statistically more likely.[2]

Yet, for a generation, the entire ruling Texas conservative-Republican establishment has been consistently dishonest and irresponsible about the reality of global warming. Governor Greg Abbott, former Governor Rick Perry, Senator Ted Cruz, Senator John Cornyn, Representative Michael McCaul, Representative Lamar Smith, and many others farther down the line are all on public record repeatedly making statements on the issue that run from evasion to deception.[3] The most moderate Texas Republican pronouncements simply repeat the common, and untrue, assertion that there is no scientific consensus on what is causing the climate to warm. But a shockingly high percentage of these politicians' allegations combine misrepresentation of the nature of the problem with slanders of the scientists who are trying to warn the world of the perils of rising temperatures. A statement by Representative John Carter, from Texas 31st U.S. House district (running from north of Austin up to Temple) is not extreme, but actually typical:

> Global warming is simply a Chicken-Little scheme to use mass media and government propaganda to convince the world that destruction of individual liberties and national sovereignty is necessary to save mankind and that the unwashed masses would destroy themselves without the enlightened dictatorship of these frauds.[4]

The reason that the state's ruling party has so consistently denied the reality of climate change is easy to explain. As we recounted in Chapter 3, politicians often represent interests. In Texas, it has long been in the interest of the oil and gas industry to head off demands that government require Americans to change over from burning fossil fuels, which belch $CO_2$ into the atmosphere, to cleaner, renewable energy sources such as wind and solar. In order to protect their profits in the short run, those industries have bought off Republican politicians to become broadcasters of confusion and sophistry about global warming.[5]

Politics is always full of exaggeration and dishonest speech, and it is perhaps not alarming that the members of one party have wandered so far away from reality. But when Texans choose to live in the fantasy land of climate denial, it does not change the implacable reality of Nature. No matter how much rhetoric Texas politicians throw at it, the climate continues to warm, the summer seas become hotter, and storms become more destructive. As global warming continues apace into the future, catastrophic flooding events like Harvey will become more common. In the long run, Texas' denial of climate change will become self-destructive, and even suicidal. And the long run is almost here.

## Water Supply

For many people there is no mystery about where water comes from—turn on the tap in the kitchen or the bathroom, and out it flows. And it is easy, amidst the many economic, political, and personal troubles of daily life, to never realize that water supply is one of the most worrisome problems facing Texas. This problem existed long before our species' impact on the earth's climate began to be noticed. But it has become worse as global temperatures have risen over the past several decades. Indeed, while such high-profile problems as terrorism may never actually harm Texas, water supply is a difficulty that is absolutely certain to pose major challenges in the near future.

West of the **hundredth meridian** of latitude—the imaginary line that forms the eastern boundary of Texas's panhandle and extends south, crossing the Rio Grande not far northwest of Laredo—average rainfall drops off to fewer than twenty inches a year, making agriculture impossible without irrigation.[6] But the averages are not reliable indications of how much

**hundredth meridian** Of longitude; the imaginary north-south line that runs through Texas, west of which average rainfall drops off to fewer than twenty inches a year.

precipitation might fall at any place at any time, for Texas rainfall is notoriously fickle. Thus, at least parts of the state experienced droughts in 1996, 1998–2000, 2003, 2005–2006, 2007–2009, 2010, and more than 98 percent of the state was too dry in 2011.[7] A statewide drought was beginning to cause major problems in 2018 when an extremely rainy August and September filled most of the reservoirs and pushed the crisis back a few years. But it is a safe bet that the future will present many more dry periods.

There is now available for human use, in an average year in Texas, 17 million acre-feet of water from surface and underground sources (an **acre-foot** is the amount sufficient to cover an acre of land to a foot deep, or 325,851.4 gallons). But if the projections made by water professionals are accurate, at present usage rates the state will need an additional 9 million acre-feet by 2060.[8] So the question will become more urgent for Texans every year: are we going to get more water from somewhere, or are we going to use the supply we have more efficiently? If the population continues to grow, there is no third option.

Meanwhile, as the quotation from House Speaker Pete Laney at the beginning of this chapter illustrates, Texas has already experienced a variety of political conflicts over water. As the squeeze between water demand and water availability gets tighter, there are bound to be more frequent and more intense squabbles. These conflicts will be of several kinds.

## Urban Dwellers versus Farmers

One type of conflict that is certain to be more common can be termed "cities versus farmers." In the Western states, typically 70–80 percent of the water is used by agriculture for irrigating crops, but as urban populations grow, they demand more and more of the available liquid. Projections are that by 2040, Texas cities will use more water than Texas farmers.[9] Because the cities can afford to pay more for water than agricultural interests, they will inevitably crowd farmers out of the water market, unless farmers use their political influence to thwart the cities' desires. The situation faced by the Lower Colorado River Authority (LCRA) from 2009 to 2018 illustrates the sort of problems that will grow more numerous in the future.[10]

Although Texas water law, in general, favors landowners' use of the water on and under their property, if the state owns reservoirs, then the state and its institutions decide who gets what, and how much it will cost. The LCRA is a nonprofit utility established by the legislature in 1934 to govern the downstream half of the Colorado River, which rises in the Llano Estacado near the New Mexico line northwest of Lubbock, and flows 800 miles southeast to the Gulf. The LCRA manages drinking-water supply, makes electricity, tries to prevent floods, and governs wastewater for the Austin metropolitan area and many smaller cities along the river.

Outside the urban areas, however, and downstream of the Austin metro area, rice-farmers in Matagorda, Colorado, and Wharton Counties take a great deal of water, because growers flood the field to kill weeds. In 2009, the LCRA provided 370,000 acre-feet of water from Lakes Travis and Buchanan to about 350 rice-growers, and a further 70,000 acre feet from the run of the Colorado river, at a price of $5.39 an acre foot. Meanwhile, the LCRA was charging urban businesses $138.00 an acre-foot. If the utility had charged farmers what it charged the non-agricultural businesses for water, the farmers would have been unable to afford the expense and would have gone out of business.

In other words, as a matter of policy the LCRA was subsidizing agriculture at the expense of non-agricultural businesses. The subsidies could not be justified by the fear that if rice farmers disappeared, Texans would have no rice to eat. Many countries produce rice, and importing it is easy. Instead, the subsidies were based on an assumption that is rarely spoken—agriculture is such a wholesome activity that it should be supported by non-agricultural interests even if it is uneconomical.

---

**acre-foot** It is an amount of water sufficient to cover an acre of land to a foot deep, or 325,851.4 gallons.

But such assumptions tend to break down when water becomes scarce, as it did during a series of low-rainfall years that began in 2009. Faced with a serious drought, leading to rapidly falling lake levels, the people who govern the LCRA realized that they would soon not have enough water to satisfy the desires of farmers, urban businesses, and homeowners.

In 2009 and again in 2011, the LCRA threatened to cut off water to the farmers, but autumn rains temporarily relieved the pressure. Then, in another dry year, 2013, the utility did, in fact, vote to cut off the supply to downstream farmers. The farmers appealed to the Texas Commission on Environmental Quality, which caused a delay. In 2015, however, the ax fell; the TCEQ granted the LCRA the choice of how much water to send down river and how much to keep stored in the Highland Lakes. But a series of storms arrived just in time to partially refill the lakes, and the LCRA relented. As of 2018, the farmers were still receiving Colorado river water, but had been put on notice that they would be cut off the next time there was a water squeeze.

The day of reckoning for water users in central Texas has, thus, only been postponed. The next drought that hits the area will see a still greater population and still more businesses demanding to have their thirsts quenched. Given the exploding number of urbanites, and the small number of farmers, the farmers face a future in which they can no longer depend on enough water to sustain their rice crops. The politics of the next drought may include the elimination of one of Texas' traditional ways of life.

## Private Property Rights versus State Regulation

The conflict described above dealt with *surface* water—the kind available in rivers and lakes. But there are also disagreements about *underground* water—the kind that may have been enclosed in natural subsurface reservoirs, called "aquifers," for many thousands of years. Although water is pretty much the same stuff no matter where it is found, the law and politics of underground water in Texas is not quite the same as the law and politics of surface water.

For more than a century, Texas has relied on two contradictory principles for dealing with questions of the management of underground water.[11] The first principle, a legal doctrine known as the **Rule of Capture**, favors private ownership and use of such water. It holds that groundwater is more-or-less absolutely owned and controlled by the person who owns the surface land over the water. A landowner can pump all the water under her land that she desires, even if her neighbor's well runs dry, and even if the state has an interest in protecting underground water for future generations. The rule of capture, of course, is consistent with Texas's traditional emphasis upon private property rights.

The second principle, however, which is embodied in a series of laws passed by the legislature over the past several decades, recognizes that there is a public interest in the management of the state's underground water resources. The laws have established the Texas Water Development Board (TWDB) to try to coordinate the 98 locally controlled groundwater conservation districts, and in a loose sort of way given them all the authority to plan the drawdown of water to make it last as long as possible.

Thus, when it comes to underground water, for more than a hundred years, two ideals existed uneasily side-by-side: land-owners control whatever is under their property, but the state regulates it. The two systems co-existed because the individualistic, conservative perspective that is traditional in the state could not imagine that the two systems might come into conflict. That perspective did not see that what is good for the public interest, in the long run, might conflict with the interests of individual Texans in the short run.

But conflict was inevitable. Once the local groundwater districts started to tell land-owners how much liquid they could pump, someone was going to cry that the rule of capture deprived state authorities of the authority to do so.

**rule of capture**
A Texas legal principle under which a private landowner has ownership and control of all the water under his or her property.

And so, in the mid-1990s, the lawsuit of *Edwards Aquifer Authority v. Burrell Day and Joel McDaniel,* began to grind its way through the state judicial system. Day and McDaniel, two farmers, applied to the Authority for a permit to drill a well, and were denied. They sued, and the case slowly wound through the system.

In February, 2012, the Texas Supreme Court sided with the advocates of private property rights, ruling that although the state was, in general, entitled to regulate the use of groundwater, its rules in this particular case were unreasonable. The decision threw Texas water policies into chaos. Because the court did not leave any clear guidelines as to what kind of regulations were "reasonable," no public agency knew what it was now supposed to do.[12]

By 2019, the muddled conflict between the two conceptions of the public interest had still not been clarified. As one journalist remarked in reporting the court decision in 2012, "the decision could leave the state's . . . groundwater districts in a pickle."[13] The future of Texas water law thus promises to be confusing and unsettling.

## Economic Development versus Environment

A further problem created by Texans' growing need for the ungrowing resource of water is that it is not just human beings who need the liquid of life. Other creatures in the environment must have a certain amount of water to sustain them. When growing human populations demand more and ever more of the resource, sooner or later there comes a moment when people have to decide whether to allow other species to live, which will mean that humans have to use less, or to go on consuming more, which will mean that other species may cease to exist.

In California in 2007, for example, a federal court held that the state's agribusiness in the San Joaquin Valley was taking so much water that it was about to make some indigenous fish, including the delta smelt and the chinook salmon, extinct. The court ordered that water that had been intended to irrigate crops in the southern part of the valley must instead be left in the rivers. As a result, the smelt and the salmon are (barely) holding on, but much of the farmland in the southern valley has turned into a dust bowl.[14]

Water conflicts are not yet as bad in Texas as they are in California, but the writing is on the wall. A warning for the future can be seen in the recent conflict over water for whooping cranes.[15] These are large ("tall enough to peck your eyes out," as they are sometimes charmingly described) migratory birds that winter on the Gulf Coast near Aransas Pass, feeding and nesting in the **estuary** formed by the entrance of the Guadalupe River into San Antonio Bay. The cranes are one of those kinds of organisms that conservationists call "charismatic species," types of animals (tigers, grizzly bears, bald eagles; monarch butterflies) and plants (redwoods, bluebonnets) that involve people emotionally. Threats to charismatic species can energize the public to become interested in saving those species, and by extension, their whole habitats. They therefore have an effect upon public policy.

Such is the case with whooping cranes. The birds, which originally numbered in the many hundreds of thousands, had, by 1937, been reduced by the onslaught of human civilization to a total of 15 in Texas and 6 in Louisiana. In that year the federal government established the Aransas National Wildlife Refuge on the coast, to protect the birds during their winter breeding sojourn in Texas. In 1967, the birds were listed as endangered, and in 1973 the federal Endangered Species Act created a series of legal protections for all listed species. Partly because of the Act's shielding of such species from the threat of economic development, and partly because of the nurturing efforts of scientists and environmentalists, the crane population began to recover. By the first decade of the twenty-first century the birds numbered about 240 individuals.

Enter the **Texas Commission on Environmental Quality (TCEQ).** This state agency's mission is to strive to "protect our state's human and natural resources consistent with sustainable economic development."[16] The fact that there may sometimes be a conflict between

**estuary** An area of coastline where a river flows into the sea, mixing salt and fresh water.

**Texas Commission on Environmental Quality (TCEQ)** The state agency with authority to protect Texas's natural resources.

Endangered whooping cranes are vulnerable to water use by humans far upstream from their home on the coast.

Tom Uhlenbrock/MCT/Landov

environmental protection and economic development is not something that the people of TCEQ are prepared to admit. The agency is responsible for issuing air and water operating permits to businesses operating in Texas. Readers of preceding chapters in this book will not be surprised to learn that businesses that desire a permit are able to bring intense pressure to bear on the agency through political channels. In other words, science and the public interest are not the only concerns that determine TCEQ policy.[17] As a result, TCEQ has authorized so many permits for businesses to use Texas surface water that in years of scarcity many of the rivers come close to going dry.

The Fall of 2008 and the winter of 2009 saw insufficient rainfall in much of the southern half of Texas. By late winter, environmentalists noted with alarm that 23 whooping cranes, or 8.5 percent of the entire flock, had died during the previous few months. Although there is some attrition in the bird population every winter, this seemed to be a large and dangerous fluctuation. Scientists studying the cause of the die-off came to the conclusions that, because TCEQ had okayed so many permits for so many businesses to withdraw water from the Guadalupe River, the drought had caused fresh water amounts in San Antonio Bay to fall steeply. Blue crabs living in the Bay, which depend upon a certain mixture of fresh and salt water ("brackishness," in the vocabulary of those who talk about water), had found their environment too salty, and had either died in large numbers or moved somewhere else along the coast. The cranes, dependent upon the crabs for food, had discovered the pantry going bare. Without enough food to go around, an unusually large number of the cranes had either died of starvation, or, weakened by malnutrition, succumbed to disease.

When accused of having favored economic development over environmental protection, and thus of having caused stress on the crane population, TCEQ, in effect, answered that the problem was the drought, not its own policies. Environmentalists, of course, pointed out that Texas had endured occasional droughts for many thousands of years, and yet the whooping cranes had thrived. It was only when a (foreseeable) dry year had coincided with TCEQ's unrestrained granting of water-withdrawal permits that the recovery of the cranes was threatened. Naturally, TCEQ refused to agree that it shared any blame for the plight of the cranes.

People in the area around San Antonio Bay reacted to this problem by organizing, and founding the Aransas Project, a coalition of citizens, organizations, and local businesses "who want," according to its Website, "responsible water management of the Guadalupe River basin." In March, 2010, the Aransas Project filed suit in federal court, charging that TCEQ policies were in violation of the Endangered Species Act.[18] The plaintiffs asked the federal courts to force TCEQ to reduce the amount of water it permitted businesses to withdraw from the Guadalupe during low-rainfall years.

In March, 2013, a federal judge ruled that TCEQ had indeed managed the river's waters without concern for the survival of the birds, and forbade the agency to grant any new water-use permits until it could prove that such new withdrawals would not threaten the survival of the cranes. The judge, in other words, put a hold on development along the Guadalupe River until the state could figure out how to promote such expansion without threatening the crane's fresh water supply. For a brief time, it seemed that the environment had won a battle in Texas.[19]

But the victory was short-lived. In July, 2014, a federal appeals court reversed the pro-crane decision. The U.S. Supreme Court refused to hear the Aransas Project's appeal, and so the TCEQ was back in business, granting permits to use Guadalupe River water.[20]

And so "development" won that round against "environment." But the Aransas Project lawsuit, like the Edwards Aquifer lawsuit, brings issues to the courts that Texas' democratic political system has usually tried to avoid. Whatever the specific decisions in those cases, the conflicts they represent, and the philosophical dilemmas they pose, will be with Texans for a long time. The political system will soon be unable to continue avoiding those conflicts and dilemmas, and will have to face them squarely. The politics of water, like the rest of the state's politics, promises to be loud, colorful, and endlessly fascinating for observers of democracy.

# Energy Supply

All life on Earth depends upon achieving access to energy. Plants get it from the Sun, while animals get it by eating plants, or eating other animals that eat plants. At this most basic level, humans are animals and need energy to survive. But civilization, too, over and above its biologically human component, requires a steady supply of energy. Building a skyscraper, or driving a car from Beaumont to El Paso, or manufacturing a cell phone, or distributing paper napkins to a fast-food chain, or an uncounted number of other activities, would never exist if abundant energy was not available to be put to use. Where the future energy supply is going to come from, and how much it will cost, therefore, are questions of vital interest to all Texans, whether they are aware of it or not.

Although energy, like water, is at its most basic just one thing—the ability to do work—within the practical context of the technology, economics, and politics of energy it is split into a fantastic number of problems, controversies, and uncertainties. Even for the restricted area of one state, therefore, the general topic of energy supply is far too complex for a portion of one chapter in a textbook. Consequently, this section will not be a comprehensive treatment of the subject. First, it will give a brief overview of the advantages and disadvantages of various sources of energy supply, and second, go into detail on some aspects of energy politics in Texas.

## Sources of Energy

The political problem of energy supply starts at a philosophical level. Some people believe that economic market forces should be permitted to "decide" how energy is to be supplied. That is, the choices of individual consumers, responding to price cues, and the investment decisions of businesses, also responding to prices, should determine what sources of energy are used. In general, we have termed people who endorse this philosophy "conservatives." Other people think that public safety, or freedom from coercion by foreign governments, or avoidance of climate change, should take precedence over economic efficiency, and therefore that government should regulate and subsidize energy markets. We have termed people who endorse this philosophy "liberals." Always, however, when considering philosophical arguments, people tend to be swayed by their personal interests, so that public philosophies often become less important than private influence over decision-makers.

When discussing energy policy, one of the great epic poems of Western literature often supplies a grand metaphor to help us understand the situation. In the 1830s the German poet Johann von Goethe wrote "Faust," the story of a man who, in order to gain knowledge, love, and power, sells his soul to the Devil. Thus, Faust achieves all he wants in life, but is condemned (with the partial exception of a twist at the end), to suffer in Hell in the afterlife. Ever since, the notion that people can achieve desirable things, but only if they pay a terrible cost, has been known as a "**Faustian Bargain**." When it comes to energy policy, the notion of a Faustian Bargain is a useful one, because every energy option promises to supply Americans and Texans with much of what we need for the good life, but only at a price that increasingly looks terrible, no matter which alternative we choose.

**Faustian Bargain**
A metaphor for a type of decision opportunity in which every alternative offers great benefits but also comes at a terrible price.

Because people's philosophies disagree and because interests taint political discussion, it is impossible to give a completely objective summary of the Faustian Bargain inherent in each energy-supply option. But to the extent that the raucous public and scholarly arguments of the last century or so fall into clear patterns, the following account compiles the upsides and downsides of the main contenders for the title of "Texas' energy source of the future."

**Oil** For Texas, the twentieth century was the century of oil. The great Spindletop strike of 1901 permitted the creation of an industry that made many Texans individually rich, supported thousands of ordinary workers and their families, and raised the state as a whole from an agricultural backwater floundering in the aftermath of Civil War to an industrial, urbanized giant. As was to be expected for an industry that was the backbone of the state's economy for many decades, the oil industry was extremely powerful in Texas politics. Texas office-holders both in Austin and Washington almost considered it their duty to nurture the industry and give its representatives what they asked for in the way of laws and regulations (or lack of regulations).[21]

Starting in the early 1970s, Texas oil production went into a long decline, and by the year 2000 it seemed that the industry might be headed for irrelevance. But the arrival of several types of advanced technology dramatically increased the amount of the black liquid that was recoverable, and by 2018 the state was once again a titan in the world of oil. That year, the United States surpassed Russia and Saudi Arabia as the number one oil producing country, and Texas was by far the number one producer of all the states. The petroleum industry (oil and gas together) were responsible, directly or indirectly, for a third of the jobs in the state. At the same time, inevitably, Texas was the number one emitter of carbon dioxide, the worst "greenhouse gas."[22] Thus, the energy source that has made Texas prosperous, and dominates the state's politics, also makes the state the nation's worst contributor to global warming. Oil illustrates the Faustian Bargain at its most dramatic.

One major advantage of oil as a source of energy is that it has been crucial for so long that the state, like the nation, possesses a wealth of infrastructure and institutions to utilize it. Millions of vehicles relying on internal combustion engines sit in garages and clog roads. Gas stations dot every city and sit on lonely stretches of highway. Pipelines and refineries already exist. Moreover, of course, every time someone buys a gasoline-burning vehicle in one of the other forty-nine states, the purchase helps to create jobs for Texans. The state's citizens are well aware that, in a sense, modern Texas was built by the oil industry.

Oil has other advantages, too. Because it is a liquid, it is relatively easy and inexpensive to transport (through pipelines). The means of extracting and refining it have been developing for more than a century, and many of the experts on the subject live and work in Texas. Furthermore, it is ideal for the form of transportation that Americans in general, and Texans in particular, find most congenial—individually owned automobiles. Other sources of energy are easily used in such forms of transportation as trains and streetcars, but only oil has so far been manufactured into a convenient vehicle fuel. For this combination of reasons, oil has the greatest advantage of all: it is relatively cheap.

Oil will thus continue to be a very important source of energy for decades to come. But over the last forty years or so the world has learned that reliance on oil contains more than one Faustian downside. When the Organization of Petroleum Exporting Countries (OPEC) doubled the price in 1973, and at the same time Saudi Arabia shut in its wells to protest the support the United States had given to Israel within the international community, the double whammy threw all industrial economies into chaotic recession. Although Texans, who often worked for some facet of the industry, continued to cherish it, suddenly oil no longer seemed cheap and convenient to citizens of most other states. The prospect of another supply disruption—which in fact became a reality during the Iranian revolution of 1979—turned out to be a specter that has haunted the nation's consumers and policy-makers ever since.

The price of oil in a technical, short-term sense, then, is still low compared to the prices of other usable forms of energy. But the "price," in a broad, difficult-to-define, long-term sense is so high that there are major efforts being conducted, on the world stage, within the United States, and in Texas itself, to find a way to make a transition away from oil (and the other fossil fuels) toward a different energy base. Because a great many people in Texas still find employment in searching for, producing, transporting, and retail sales of oil, this effort within the state is more complicated and conflicted than it is in other states and countries that are not so dependent upon production of the black liquid.

**Natural Gas** A close cousin to liquid oil, and always found in the same underground reservoirs, petroleum in a gaseous state was for decades of little value. Towns located near oil fields began, during the 1920s, to use natural gas for lighting and heat, but because it was so hard to gather and transport, there was almost no other market for it. (In this textbook, "natural gas" refers to the stuff that comes out of the ground and is burned directly for fuel, as distinct from "gasoline," which is refined oil, and used as fuel for automobiles). In the late 1940s, however, producers began to find markets for their gas in the suburbs that sprang up around large cities—especially in the West and South—during the post-World War Two economic boom. By the middle 1950s, people in the business were searching for, and producing, natural gas in its own right, independently of any oil that might also be in the reservoir. Since that era there have been periodic booms and down-times in the gas industry, but the fuel as a whole is a major energy source for the country as a whole, and for the Lone Star State in particular. In 2018, Texas was the number one natural-gas producing state.[23]

The advantages and disadvantages of natural gas as an energy source are similar to those for oil, although there are also some important differences. Table 14-1 displays estimates by the federal Department of Energy (DOE) about the costs of generating electricity in hypothetical plants to be built that would come on line in 2022. Such estimates are always to be regarded

| TABLE 14-1 | Estimated Cost of New Electrical Generation by Resource, 2022 |
|---|---|
| **Energy Source** | **Cost Per Megawatt-Hour** |
| Coal | $95.1 |
| Natural gas | 48.3 |
| Nuclear | 90.1 |
| Wind | 48.0 |
| Solar photovoltaic | 59.1 |

Source: Wikipedia's summary of various calculations by the U.S. Energy Information Administration: https://en.wikipedia.org/wiki/Cost_of_electricity_by_source

Competency Connection
**SOCIAL RESPONSIBILITY**

Should Texans adopt a source of energy based solely on its price? Or should they take other factors into account?

with skepticism, partly because they rely on guesses about future fuel costs that may prove to be wildly unrealistic, and partly because they do not take into account such indirect costs as the price to a nation of health care that may be needed because of the pumping of pollutants into the air and water. Nevertheless, they give a good indication of the sorts of considerations that Texas policymakers must think about when they are trying to decide on public policy toward energy supply. The table shows that natural gas is, in general, an inexpensive source of electric power. The EIA (Energy Information Administration) economists did not include the costs of oil-generated power in their calculations, presumably because, although power plants can be built that burn oil, they never are these days, for a variety of reasons. Gas vies with wind for the title of cheapest source of fuel for electric utilities. Moreover, natural gas is a far cleaner source of energy than is coal. Although it produces greenhouse gases and other pollutants, gas emits many fewer noxious chemicals per unit of energy produced than coal.[24]

Further, during the 1990s, advances in the technology of producing gas opened up a vast reservoir that underlies the area around Ft. Worth, the Barnett Shale. By 2011, this field had become the largest in Texas and was on its way to becoming the most productive in the country. With this new supply, and others on the horizon, the future supply of natural gas in the United States looks secure. In other words, unlike the supply of oil, the supply of gas does not depend on the stability of international politics and the vagaries of international markets. Even more appealing to Texas politicians, the fact that the future supply will come out of the state means that their own policies will govern the industry, not the policies of a federal government they generally mistrust. All this makes gas an attractive choice for the future of Texas energy.

But natural gas is not exempt from the Faustian Bargain. It is extremely explosive, and always a danger whether it is being used by a single homeowner or a giant industrial complex. Leaking pipes, inexpertly-attached fittings, corroded metal casing, earthquake-ruptured containment vessels, careless smoking, terrorist bombs, and many other avoidable but inevitable occurrences can lead to instant destruction and tragedy wherever natural gas is being used. Although various foul-smelling chemicals are now added to gas as it is produced to alert people if there should be a leak, still, every year there are fatal explosions. In 2018, for example, a leaking pipeline caused a series of explosions in the Massachusetts towns of Lawrence, Andover, and North Andover, killing one person, injuring at least 25 others, and igniting fires in 60 to 80 homes.[25]

Moreover, although natural gas is cleaner than oil and much cleaner than coal as a fuel for electric power plants, it is still a hydrocarbon that releases greenhouse gases and other pollutants when burned. And like oil, its production from the ground can be filthy unless it is handled with great concern for the environment. Residents living near the 15,000 wells drilled in the Barnett Shale over the past decade and a half, for example, have registered many complaints about air and water pollution with federal and state regulators.[26] An investigation of documents produced by the federal Environmental Protection Agency and the Texas Commission on Environmental Quality by the *Dallas Morning News* reported that they "reveal a pattern of emissions of toxic compounds, often including cancer-causing benzene, from Barnett Shale facilities."[27]

So natural gas, like oil, is in many ways an unsatisfactory source of energy for Texas.

**Coal** Coal was the energy source of the nineteenth century, the substance that fueled the industrial revolution in the United States. It heated houses, powered factories, and made the railroad—the keystone technology of that time, as the computer is the keystone technology of our time—possible. Until quite recently, coal was a very important source of energy because it was cheap. It was cheap to mine (unless one took into account the lives lost in the process), cheap to transport (although not as cheap as oil and gas), and cheap to burn. Part of its cheapness was based on the fact that it does not explode like natural gas or melt down and release radioactivity like uranium. Furthermore, Americans who relied on burning coal for their energy never had to worry about having their supply disrupted by a hostile foreign government. Within the borders of the United States lay enough coal to power the country for centuries.[28] As Table 14-1 illustrates, however, for reasons that are beyond the scope of this textbook, coal has recently become much more expensive in relation to other power sources. Nevertheless, it is still a very important source of energy for generating electricity in the United States. It was used to power about 30 percent of the country's electricity generation in 2017.[29]

Nevertheless, coal's advantages are balanced by its very serious drawbacks. Eight coal miners were killed in accidents in 2016, and fifteen in 2017.[30] Meanwhile, about 700 are expiring each year from pneumoconiosis, or "black lung disease," which is caused by years of breathing coal dust in the mines.[31] If, instead of bringing up the coal from underground, companies instead choose to "strip mine," or remove the land over the coal with dynamite and bulldozers, what they gain in safety for their workers is lost in terms of the destruction of the ecosystem. As one article in *Time* magazine put it, in an area that has been strip mined, "Huge piles of gray debris . . . stand like gravestones over land so scarred and acidic only rodents can live there."[32]

But coal has an even worse impact on the environment when it is burned. It is by far the most polluting fuel. According the Union of Concerned Scientists, a typical coal-burning power plant generates, in a year's operation, 3,700,000 tons of carbon dioxide ($CO_2$), the major gas that is causing global warming, 10,000 tons of sulfur dioxide ($SO_2$), which causes acid rain, 10,200 tons of nitrogen oxide ($NO_x$), which causes smog, 170 pounds of mercury, 225 pounds of arsenic, 114 pounds of lead, and a variety of types of other noxious stuff in smaller quantities.[33] Various kinds of technology can be installed into boilers and onto smokestacks to clean these pollutants out of the factory's discharge before they reach the atmosphere, but all of them are expensive and raise the cost of coal-fired power. To make coal cleaner, therefore, is to progressively erase the reason people choose coal in the first place.

Almost all of the coal mined in Texas is lignite, the lowest grade (i.e., the type with the lowest yield of energy per ton burned). All of it is consumed within the state, generally by utilities that mine it and burn it onsite. Lignite's virtue is that, compared to other types of coal, it is relatively low in sulfur. It is still a major emitter of greenhouse gases, however. But Texas' appetite for coal is larger than its internal supply, so it imports many tons each year from mines in Wyoming.

In other words, embracing coal as a favored energy source is no way out of the Faustian Bargain for Texans.

**Nuclear Power**  Of all the possible sources of energy, nuclear power is the one that offers a Faustian Bargain in the starkest terms. For "atomic energy," as it used to be called, offers both the most tempting possibility for virtually unlimited clean power, and the most worrisome potential to exact a hellish price.

Nuclear power is not a viable option for fueling individual automobiles. Its value lies in its ability to produce vast quantities of electricity. Theoretically, at some point in the hypothetical future, that electricity could supply charging stations for millions of electric cars, thus freeing the United States from all dependence on oil. For the near-term, however, nuclear is an alternative for public utilities and the types of work that electricity does in modern American life.

Nuclear power works by boiling water, indirectly, with a controlled amount of heat from atomic fission reactors. The steam is then used to rotate turbines that produce electricity. The two nuclear plants in Texas, Comanche Peak, south of Ft. Worth, and the South Texas Nuclear Project, west of Houston, supply about 9 percent of the state's electricity.[34] The other 102 U.S. reactors produce about a fifth of the country's electric generation.[35]

As Table 14-1 illustrates, nuclear power is now about as expensive as coal power, but considerably more expensive than natural gas and renewables. Nuclear advocates argue that if the licensing process for new reactors could be streamlined and some of the political impediments to operation could be removed, nuclear power would become much cheaper.[36]

The potential cheapness of nuclear power, however, is less attractive that some of its other attributes. It does not release greenhouse gases into the atmosphere because it does not burn anything to produce heat. It therefore does not contribute to global warming, or to any sort of air pollution. Nuclear plants do cause "thermal pollution" because the water used to cool their reactors itself becomes heated in the process. If water is drawn from, say, an estuary on the coastline, and the organisms in that estuary are adapted to living at certain temperatures, and then hot water from a nuclear plant is dumped back into the ocean, the ecosystem will suffer grievously. This difficulty, however, can be overcome by allowing the water to sit in cooling ponds for a specified time, and the problem, at any rate, is not nearly as severe as the environmental stresses that nuclear power avoids. As a result, pro-nuclear advocates often argue that nuclear power is the environmentally responsible choice.[37]

Unlike the situation with, oil, the supply of nuclear power can be made stable. The uranium fuel is entirely available from mines within the United States, so that there is no potential for supply disruptions because of the vagaries of international politics.[38]

Nuclear power is therefore clean, affordable, and strategically secure. Its downside lies more in the realm of potential than in the realm of actual reality. But that potential is so grim that it gives many good citizens grave doubts about the wisdom of pursuing, or even continuing, the development of the energy source.

The first problem with nuclear power lies in the potential for a catastrophic accident. The temperature of the radioactive rods must be carefully controlled. Too little heat, and they will fail to accomplish their goal of producing steam. Too much heat, and they will literally melt each other and the factory in which they are housed. The danger is not that there could be a nuclear bomb-type explosion, but that a meltdown would allow large amounts of radioactivity to be released into the atmosphere, thus causing very severe health problems for the people living downwind. Given the human propensity to make mistakes, if enough people are engaged with enough technological complexity in enough nuclear power plants, the probability would seem to be very high that there will be errors made, and that some of those errors will be so bad that they will lead to a meltdown.

In fact, since the first edition of this textbook in 1979, there have been two very serious nuclear-power accidents around the world. The first was at Chernobyl, a city in the Ukraine, then a republic of the Soviet Union, in 1986. The second was in Japan, on its main island of Honshu, in 2011. Both accidents caused many deaths (by some estimates as many as a million at Chernobyl), billions of dollars of property damage, and releases of deadly radiation into the atmosphere.[39]

Nuclear advocates argue that both the Ukrainian and the Japanese experiences are not directly relevant to the United States in general or Texas in particular, because our reactors are better designed, or because our reactor operators are better trained, or because (specifically relevant to Texas power plants), the geological setting (with a very low probability of an earthquake) of our plants makes the Japanese comparison inappropriate.[40] They point out that in the only serious accident at a civilian installation in this country's history, at Three-Mile Island in Pennsylvania in 1979, no one was killed or injured and only a tiny amount of radioactivity was released into the air. Furthermore, they maintain that improvements have been made in the design of American reactors and in the procedures for operating them since 1979, so that another accident is very unlikely.

But these arguments come from experts, and ordinary citizens often do not have the education to enable them to judge the persuasiveness of technical arguments. But anyone could evaluate the televised images coming out of Japan during the spring of 2011, in which helicopters were frantically trying to drop loads of seawater onto damaged reactors, hoping to avoid a catastrophic meltdown. Such scenes have a powerful emotional impact, and stay in the memory a long time. There is therefore a strong dose of skepticism in public opinion about the safety of nuclear power.

## You Decide: Which Energy Source for Texas?

**E**very potential source of energy has something to recommend it. Every potential source has a serious downside. But policymakers cannot simply note that no choice is perfect and go on to something else. They have to decide among alternatives, all of which are costly in some way.

Pretend that you are a Texas official. Which energy source would you endorse? Start by ranking the various strengths and weaknesses of each source in terms of your own values. What is most important to you? Price? Safety? Environmental protection? Avoidance of climate change? What is next most important? And so on.

There is a large lesson to be learned from this exercise: governing is hard.

| Energy Source | Advantages  | Disadvantages  |
|---|---|---|
| **Coal** |  Abundant in U.S. <br> ⬆ Non-explosive <br> ⬆ Comparatively cheap | ⬇ Dangerous to mine underground; environmentally destructive to strip-mine <br> ⬇ Very polluting, including production of greenhouse gases |
| **Natural Gas** | ⬆ Abundant in U.S., especially in Texas <br> ⬆ Transportation infrastructure already in place | ⬇ Highly explosive <br> ⬇ Produces greenhouse gases <br> ⬇ Prices are notoriously volatile |
| **Nuclear Energy** | ⬆ Abundant in U.S. <br> ⬆ Does not produce greenhouse gases <br> ⬆ Does not produce air or water pollution | ⬇ Potential for catastrophic accident during production <br> ⬇ Problem of disposal of dangerous radioactive waste <br> ⬇ Thermal pollution of cooling water <br> ⬇ Good for producing electricity, but not for fueling individual transportation (unless electric cars become standard) |
| **Oil** | ⬆ Infrastructure in place <br> ⬆ Relatively inexpensive <br> ⬆ Good for fueling individual transportation | ⬇ Producing countries often unstable or hostile, leading to potential for supply disruption <br> ⬇ Produces greenhouse gases <br> ⬇ Potential for environmentally disastrous spills <br> ⬇ Even without a spill, can be highly polluting to groundwater |
| **Renewables (solar, wind)** | ⬆ Except for manufacture of equipment, non-polluting; especially, do not produce greenhouse gasses <br> ⬆ Do not rely on foreign supply <br> ⬆ Inexhaustible long-run supply | ⬇ Relatively expensive <br> ⬇ Infrastructure not in place <br> ⬇ Unreliable short-run supply (when sun does not shine or wind does not blow) <br> ⬇ Kill birds, disrupt fish migrations |

*(Continued)*

| Energy Source | Advantages  | Disadvantages  |
|---|---|---|
| **Conservation (efficiency)** | ⬆ No dependence on foreign supply<br><br>⬆ Large long-run cost savings<br><br>⬆ No additional pollution | ⬇ Requires coordinating the behavior of millions of people over a long period, either through command-and-control mechanisms or prices<br><br>⬇ Reliance on prices can be hard on the poor; reliance on command-and-control risks creating evasion, black markets, shortages, unintended consequences |

**Competency Connection**
**SOCIAL RESPONSIBILITY**

If you were a Texas politician, which energy source would you choose for the state? Why?

The second problem with nuclear power is the puzzle of what to do with the radioactive waste.[41] The power plants produce electricity with enriched-uranium fuel rods. After some years of service, the rods are no longer useful and must be discarded, but they remain radioactive, and therefore dangerous to human and all other life, for about 10,000 years. Since the 1960s the federal government has been trying to find a permanent place to put the spent rods so that they would not leak radioactivity into the environment, and especially the groundwater. Since 1983 the federal Department of Energy has spent more than $10 billion on research into ways to dispose of fuel. It has considered shooting it into outer space, sinking it to the bottom of the ocean, or finding ways to recycle it.

Researchers have concluded that it is technically possible to seal the rods in steel canisters and bury them in geologically stable areas of the country. But this technical solution always comes up against a political consideration, the NIMBY syndrome (for "Not in my back yard"). Everyone wants to find a solution to the problem of nuclear waste, but nobody wants it buried near them. Once the word "radiation" is used in public discussion, citizens react with fear and rejection. Surveys reveal that Americans would rather live near a chemical-waste landfill, an oil refinery, or a pesticide plant than near a nuclear-waste depository.

The NIMBY problem with nuclear power reveals a contradiction between the ideal and reality of democratic government, in Texas and elsewhere. Ideally, The People should speak about their policy preferences, through elections, and then elected officials should implement those preferences. But when the opinions of The People are self-contradictory—"Give us energy, but not if it is dangerous or expensive"—there is no rational way that politicians can implement them.

Thus, faced with intensely contradictory public attitudes, politicians at both the state and national levels are inclined to put off making decisions and leave the problem for someone else to take care of. The result of this political dithering is that, as of 2017, more than 90,000 metric tons of nuclear waste were sitting in "temporary" storage facilities in 39 states, a pile that was growing at the rate of 2000 tons a year.[42]

In summary, although the serious long-run problem of nuclear waste disposal may have a technical solution, its political aspects appear to be insoluble. Added to the crucial difficulty of the potential for a catastrophic accident, these two downsides of nuclear power are so severe that for many people they overbalance the otherwise great advantages of relying on nuclear power as an energy source. For much of the public, the price of that particular Faustian Bargain is too high.

**Renewables** The term "renewables" is applied to sources of energy that appear to come directly from Nature, without much intervention by human technology, specifically, power from wind and the sun. (In some states there is the possibility of power from geothermal sources and from hydropower, but they will not be discussed here because they are not relevant to the future of Texas). In both wind and solar energy, the Faustian Bargain is reversed from the way it structures the social choice of oil, natural gas, coal, and nuclear. In the traditional sources, the direct price is low but the "by-product price" in terms of pollution, danger, or both, is very high. In regard to wind and solar power, until very recently the by-product price was relatively low but the direct price was high. In just the last few years, however, the prices of wind and solar have been dropping. As Table 14-1 illustrates, wind power is now as cheap as electricity from natural gas. (It is worth repeating that these figures rest upon various assumptions that may turn out to be mistaken). Solar-generated electricity is still more expensive than gas, but cheaper than power from coal and nuclear.

Of the renewables, the cheaper, and therefore the more realistic short-term alternative, is wind. In fact, Texas farmers in the drier areas have been using windmills to pump water for their livestock since the nineteenth century. Currently there are more than 2,000 large wind turbines in West Texas alone, as anyone who drives along Interstate Highway 10 between Van Horn and Ozona can attest. Texas leads all other states in wind-power generation capacity, and utilities are building new mills all the time. Wind supplies 14.8 percent of all the electricity generated in the state, meaning that wind projects have the capacity to generate 20,000 megawatts—enough to supply power to about five million homes.[43]

But the Faustian Bargain applies to this natural energy source, also. Although the wind is free, operating a gigantic field of enormous spinning propellers exacts various kinds of costs. "Metal fatigue" tends to set in after a certain amount of time, so that the rotors have to be frequently tested for weakness. If they nevertheless fail, they can split and be hurled away from the mill, crashing into other mills and created damage that is expensive to repair. Further, windmills frequently have fatal consequences for birds migrating through the field of rapidly rotating propellers, a problem that will increase as the wind becomes more important as a source of power. Less obviously but just as stressful for wildlife, wind turbines situated offshore can disrupt the path of migrating fish.[44]

Solar power is the environmentalists' dream, the application of science that would directly harness sunlight to provide an energy source that is limitless and clean. But the technology to convert sunlight into electricity, while it has existed for decades and is steadily being improved, remains complicated and, as Table 14-1 illustrates, relatively expensive. The expense comes from the fact, that while the sun's power is direct and simple, the means to turn it into something usable by humans is labyrinthine. To generate enough power to make it worth a public utility's time and investment, either acres of land must be covered with photovoltaic cells that use chemicals to change sunlight into electric current, cells that themselves are the end product of a long manufacturing process that requires much energy input and several exotic minerals. Or tens of thousands of specially-fabricated mirrors must be precisely arranged so that they focus sunlight on a single point—a container in which water is boiled to turn turbines. In either case, the equipment must be constantly maintained. Dirty cells and mirrors do not function well, so that they must be frequently polished. It is also possible for individual homeowners to install solar collecting equipment on their roofs, but again, the equipment is so expensive that it may take decades for the owners to save enough on the "free" availability of sunlight to make the whole transaction economical.[45]

Furthermore, wind and solar energy share the considerable disadvantage that the supply is highly capricious—the wind may not blow for days, and the sun does not shine at night or on cloudy days. Therefore, both utilities and homeowners must have backup energy supply systems ready to kick in when the renewable source is not available. These systems, of course, add to the expense.

For those Texans who are seriously concerned about the contribution of the burning of fossil fuels to climate change, it is imperative that society make a transition to such "clean" energy sources as wind and solar. And, in fact, the state is making incremental but noticeable progress toward such a goal, especially in the area of wind. To people who are truly alarmed about global warming, however, the pace is intolerably slow, and much more needs to be done, much faster. Nevertheless, the relatively high cost of the clean energy sources, plus, as noted earlier, the obstinate denial of the truth of climate change by the state's ruling Republicans, are acting to obstruct more effective public policies. Texas government may, at some point, take action to help save us all from climate catastrophe, but so far its policies are only slightly encouraging.

**Efficiency** The more efficient use of resources would seem to be a way to avoid having to choose among the various unpleasant alternatives offered by diverse energy options. The value of increasing efficiency is easy to understand for automobiles. A late-model car with a hybrid engine may deliver an average of 45 miles per gallon, whereas an aging SUV gas-guzzler might achieve only fifteen. The hybrid is therefore three times more efficient than the SUV, and will use one-third the gasoline if driven the same number of miles. Scholars have calculated that if all US autos could be made to offer at least 35 mpg, the nation would save millions of barrels of imported oil each year, and each consumer would, after a certain number of years, save thousands of dollars on gasoline.[46] The same principle holds for every energy-using machine and appliance. More efficient refrigerators, more efficient light bulbs, more efficient air-conditioners and heaters, and so forth, could save the nation enough energy to make the problems of environmental pollution, climate change, dependence on international supply, and potential meltdowns very much less severe than they are now.

Energy efficiency, however, is a desirable *end*. The problem lies in deciding what *means* to adopt to achieve the end. There are two basic options. In the first, governments, state or federal, could rely on pricing, usually through targeted taxes, to persuade consumers and investors to change their behavior. For decades, for example, some economists have recommended taxing gasoline at much higher rates, thus changing consumer behavior across a wide spectrum of American life. If gasoline cost six or eight dollars a gallon, this reasoning goes, consumers would get rid of their old gas-guzzling vehicles, buy more fuel-efficient cars, make fewer and shorter trips to the store, support public-policy initiatives to construct public transportation instead of more highways, and so on. Similarly, if taxation would double or triple the cost of electricity, consumers would demand more efficient appliances and use those they already owned less. In fact, history has demonstrated that when international events have caused gasoline costs to spike, smaller, more-fuel-efficient cars have become more popular with consumers.[47] Thus, vast changes in public behavior, resulting in large reductions in the use of energy, could be achieved if governments were willing to tax energy use.

But both the moral and political objections to using tax policy to change mass behavior are formidable. Morally, the sorts of taxes that would discourage energy use are the types of levies—sales taxes—that are "regressive taxes" (see Chapter 12) that hit harder as people live farther down the income ladder. That is, hiking energy taxes would be hard on the middle class and very hard on the poor. (This principle, of course, applies equally to the problem of water supply. Higher utility taxes would induce people to use less water, but the wealth-drain would hit the poor most painfully).

Politically, the fact is that people resent taxes, and resent gasoline taxes especially. Many public-opinion surveys since 1973 have demonstrated that citizens in general vociferously oppose higher gasoline taxes, and are willing to punish any politician who supports them.[48] Therefore, while in economic theory higher gasoline and electricity taxes are the best strategy for creating an energy-efficient society, in political reality there is no immediate prospect that politicians—and especially Texas politicians—who have to face the voters will ever institute such taxes as public policy.

The second possible strategy for making American, and Texan, society more energy-efficient would consist of various command-and-control policies, as well as sundry types of subsidies for doing what the government wants done. The federal government, for example, has mandated in its Corporate Average Fuel Efficiency (CAFE) policy the average number of miles-per-gallon, for each car company, that all the vehicles produced and sold in the United States must have. When CAFE was first implemented in 1978, all the passenger cars offered by a given automaker had to average 18 miles per gallon. By 2014, the government had raised the average to 34.2 mpg, and the Obama Administration was planning to impose an average of 54 mpg. In 2018, however, the Trump administration announced that it was abandoning CAFE standards.[49]

As there are with market-based policies, there are serious problems with command-and-control policies. Suppose people resist acting in the ways the government is telling them to act, then what? Suppose, to continue the CAFE example, people do not buy the more fuel-efficient vehicles that would save the country many barrels of oil, what is the government to do? Should the government penalize car companies because consumers do not prefer the models the government wants them to prefer? Should the government penalize the consumers? If so, how? Such questions, if answered in the affirmative, would involve the government in a great deal of micro-managing of the economy, an activity that is certain to be unpopular with both business and consumers.

When such considerations are taken into account, the tendency of most politicians is to refuse to intervene to make companies and citizens behave in a way that uses energy more efficiently. (This is explicitly the policy of the Trump administration). But that neglect guarantees that the question of efficiency will be handled by the price system or not at all.

In practice, neglect has been the dominant—although not the only—strategy practiced by both U.S. and Texas politicians when faced with the challenge of making energy policy. As a result, the nation and the state have drifted toward greater and greater reliance on imported oil (although that trend has been reversed in recent years), and greater and greater emissions of greenhouse gases.

## The Politics of Energy in Texas

Although the politics of energy in Texas is magnificently complicated, some themes stand out. The first is "Texas versus the federal government."

As our discussion of the fight between Texas politicians and the federal Affordable Care Act ("Obamacare") in Chapter 2 illustrated, there is at the present time a ferocious determination among Texans to govern themselves in their own way, avoiding as much federal oversight and rule-making as possible. But this determination is not new. It is, in fact, almost a tradition for Texans to fight federal agencies over energy policy.

**pseudo (false) laissez-faire** A phrase referring to the tendency of entrepreneurs to oppose government involvement in the economy at the general philosophical level, but to seek government assistance for their particular business.

A second theme that is common in the politics of Texas energy is "**pseudo laissez-faire.**" "Laissez-faire" is a French phrase, loosely translated as "leave it alone." People who oppose government regulation of the economy often use this phrase, which has its roots far back in the history of economic thought. "Pseudo" is a word that means "fake" or "phony," and is based on the suspicion that some of the anti-government rhetoric is hypocritical.

As discussed in Chapters 1 and 4, the semi-official conservative ideology of the majority of Texans exalts the unregulated marketplace and disdains government interference in business decisions. Yet, in practice, many of the same conservative politicians who present themselves as small-government conservatives are happy to use tax money to subsidize and promote businesses they think are good for the state's economy.

For example, the state's subsidies and other encouragements for solar and wind power by electric utilities would not have been predicted by someone familiar with Texans' professed devotion to free-market, non-government policies. Indeed, when Rick Perry was governor, from 2000 to 2015, he was fond of repeating the philosophical position—this one from a speech on May 27, 2010—that "government's main job is to establish a positive climate for business development then get the heck out of the way so visionary leaders can do what they do best—generate innovative products and create jobs."[50] Yet Perry, perhaps surprisingly, was a strong advocate of subsidizing renewable energy.

In 1999, when Perry was Lieutenant Governor, the legislature passed, and Governor George W. Bush signed, a law to encourage the development of renewable energy.[51] The law established a complicated but workable system of rules that mandated electric utilities to steadily increase the proportion of their energy production that comes from renewable sources. The rules were to be enforced by the Electric Reliability Council of Texas (ERCOT). To compensate utilities for the expense of adding wind and solar capacity, the law, in effect exempted the part of their business devoted to renewable energy from the state's franchise tax (Texas's version of the corporate income tax, see Chapter 12). By thus depriving itself of income to encourage business to do something it would not do in the free market, the state has been indirectly subsidizing the building of wind and solar capacity by private industry. In 2005 and again in 2009, as Governor, Perry sponsored additional laws continuing and expanding the state's sponsorship of renewable power. As Perry's Website put it in 2011, "The Governor has made diversifying the energy mix of Texas's electricity one of his major priorities, and renewable energy . . . plays a key role in that diversification."

In other words, the Governor and the state legislature, though dominated by people who call themselves conservatives, have engaged in making energy policy that, under other circumstances, they might very well have denounced as "socialism." True free-market conservatives, watching this exercise in pseudo laissez-faire, have not been fooled. "The growth of windpower capacity in Texas is not the result of consumer choice and natural economics but mandates from the Texas legislature," complained Robert Bryce, a libertarian energy journalist, in 2009.[52] Exactly why such strong conservatives as Governor Perry and the members of the Texas legislature have been willing to contradict their own ideology is a question that has not been researched. Readers of this textbook might suspect that the answer might have something to do with the influence of utility-corporation lobbyists. But there is no evidence either way, so the conclusion must be that the making of energy policy in Texas is a good deal more complicated and unpredictable than it may at first appear.

A third theme in Texas energy policy is the "politics of regulation and deregulation."

All public utilities function under some sort of government regulation. Normally, public regulators permit utilities to charge more to their customers than they would be able to charge if they were under competition in a free market. In return for being able to charge more, regulators require that utilities keep a good deal of backup capacity. That is, utilities must have bigger plants, and more plants, than they need most of the time, so that under unusual circumstances, when there is a spike in the demand for electricity, the utilities can meet the demand. Further, authorities prevent competition in the utilities market, forbidding consumers to "shop around" for power from utilities that can offer cheaper electricity because they have invested in less backup generating capacity. In effect, the public authorities allow utilities to charge monopoly prices in return for making them invest in a large amount of surplus generating capacity that will sit idle most of the time. This policy is in line with modern liberal ideology: because competition in a free market forces companies to focus on short-run profits and neglect long-run potential problems, government must regulate in order to make everyone focus on the long-run public interest.

In 1999, however, Texas partially deregulated its public utilities. Government authorities no longer required utilities to keep a certain amount of backup capacity. Instead, they permitted consumers to shop around for service from electric utilities, and permitted the utilities to decide how much investment, if any, they would put into backup generating capacity. This policy of course, unlike the policy of subsidizing renewable energy, is in line with conservative economic ideology: government should get out of the way and let companies decide about investments, and consumers decide about purchases, within the free market. Faced with a new regulatory environment, consumers began to switch their public utilities in search of lower rates, and utility companies began to shed their excess capacity, becoming smaller so that they could compete by offering lower rates to consumers.

Although the state no longer regulates the prices that electric utilities charge their customers, it does manage and coordinate the way that the various companies allocate their product. Texas has its own, self-contained electric-utility network; it neither sends electricity to other states, nor receives electricity from them. This allows Texans to run their own power grid without interference from federal regulators. The institution that coordinates the activities of the state's 46,500 miles of transmission lines, and more than 550 generation units, is named ERCOT, for Electric Reliability Council of Texas. It is a non-profit corporation, overseen by both the Texas Public Utility Commission, and the legislature.[53]

Because of the 1999 price-deregulation, electric utilities in Texas are forced by market pressures to run with very little excess generating capacity—much less than the utilities in other states. Thus, functioning without much margin for error, they are vulnerable to sudden large increases in consumer demand. When such crises come, it is ERCOT's job to allocate the sharing of electricity all around the state so that no utility gets caught without enough power to deliver to customers. Such a system forces ERCOT, during very cold winters or very hot summers, to deal with the possibility of disaster.

When the unusually cold winter of 2011 caused Texans to turn up their electric heaters all over the state, a number of electric companies were unable to meet the demand, other utilities did not have enough spare generating capacity, and the whole system threatened to crash. ERCOT, therefore, had to step in and decree "rolling blackouts," during which thousands of homes went without power for six hours a day. This situation sparked citizen outrage, and caused an investigation by the legislature. There was ERCOT-bashing and finger-pointing, but the problem was not malfeasance by ERCOT; the problem was the deregulation of 1999.[54]

After the 2011 debacle, ERCOT and the electric utilities made adjustments to try to keep enough spare generating potential in the system. But they could not change the economic forces pressing utilities to run without excess capacity. And so, during the hot summer of 2018, the system was again close to failing. On July 19, basically every one of the state's generating capacity of 78 gigawatts was being used. If a single power plant had gone offline for maintenance, or because of a broken gas line, the grid would once again have been unable to meet consumer demand, and ERCOT would once again have had to decree blackouts.[55]

The electricity supply problems of 2011 and 2018 illustrate with unusual clarity the real-life consequences of ideological differences. Conservatives say that government should let free markets determine the supply and price of energy, and the result will be good for both business and consumers. Liberals say that only government regulation can insure that long-run considerations, rather than the short-run pursuit of profit, enters into the investment calculations of business and the buying calculations of consumers. In Texas, conservative ideology and conservative policies are dominant. Therefore, Texans enjoy an unusual amount of freedom in their energy markets, resulting in lower prices, but they are subject to occasional crises and disasters. When it comes to electricity supply, Texans have chosen liberty over security.

## Protecting the Environment

To discuss the environment is to discuss climate change. It is also to discuss energy, since the mining and burning of fossil fuels are among the most serious causes of environmental problems. But it is also to discuss transportation, because the purpose of much energy use is to permit automobiles and trucks to function. And it is to discuss water, because that liquid is one of the most important components of the human environment. Therefore, to focus on the environment, which is the subject of this section, is to engage in a certain amount of repetition.

## NIMBY and YBNIIMP

As we have emphasized in this book, the United States, and each of its individual states, is a democracy, which means that The People are the source of legitimate authority. But democracy faces an ironic difficulty, because when it comes to energy policy The People are sometimes part of the problem. Specifically, when queried about their views on energy in public-opinion surveys, citizens often express contradictory and sometimes absurd attitudes toward the various possible policies that government could pursue. When it comes to energy, therefore, governments cannot always give The People what they want, because what The People say they want does not make sense.

On the one hand, consistently, over several decades, at least two-thirds of Americans answer on the affirmative when they are asked if they consider themselves to be "environmentalists." Question number 1 in Table 14-2 illustrates the stability of citizens' positive attitude toward environmentalism. In addition, roughly nine and a half million citizens belong to a pro-environment interest group such as the Sierra Club, Environmental Defense Fund, Friends of the Earth, Greenpeace, or any of the more specialized organizations. It would seem, then, that there is a very strong base in public opinion for government policy to protect the environment.

On the other hand, the seemingly solid majority in favor of environmental protection sometimes melts away as soon as hypothetical policies are mentioned that might cause Americans to suffer inconvenience. In 2007, when Americans were asked if they would favor higher taxes on electricity to persuade people to use less of it, 79 percent were opposed. When asked if the government should increase taxes on gasoline so that people would either drive less or buy more fuel-efficient cars, 67 percent were opposed. In 2017, 61 percent of Americans told pollsters of the National Opinion Research Organization that climate change was "a problem that the government needs to address." But only half of those surveyed were willing to pay a monthly utility bill that was even ONE dollar higher.[56]

| TABLE 14-2 | U.S. Public Opinion about Environmentalism, 2016–2018 |
|---|---|

1. Gallup Poll 2018:

"...protection of the environment should be given priority, even at the risk of curbing economic growth:" 57%

"economic growth should be given priority, even if the environment suffers to some extent:" 35%

"Is the seriousness of global warming...

| | |
|---|---|
| generally exaggerated?" | 33% |
| generally correct?" | 25% |
| generally underestimated?" | 41% |

"Do you think the U.S. government is doing too much, too little, or about the right amount in terms of protecting the environment?"

| | |
|---|---|
| too much: | 9% |
| too little: | 62% |
| right amount: | 28% |

2. Pew Research Center, 2016:

"The country should do whatever it takes to protect the environment:" 74%
"The country has gone too far in its efforts to protect the environment:" 23%

Sources: Gallup Poll, 2018. https://news.gallup.com/poll/1615/environment.aspx; Monica Anderson, "For Earth Day, Here's How Americans View Environmental Issues" (April 20, 2017)—www.pewresearch.org/fact-tank/2017/04/20/for-earth-day-heres-how-americans-view-envoronmental-issues/.

Competency Connection PERSONAL RESPONSIBILITY

**What are your own answers to these questions?**

It would seem, therefore, that when it comes to environmental protection there is a special case of the NIMBY syndrome. This one might be called the YBNIIMP syndrome, for "Yes, But Not If I Must Pay." Environmental protection policy must be made within the paradox that such policies are popular in general but may be unpopular if there are specific costs attached that citizens perceive as falling on themselves. The opinion poll results in Table 14-2 are for U.S. citizens. Given the historical hostility that Texans have shown to paying taxes, however, it is a safe bet that they also will show a variation of the YBNIIMP syndrome when asked to judge environmental policies.

## Texas and Environmental Protection

Furthermore, that customary opposition to taxes has, historically, combined with various other aspects of Texas culture to make environmental protection an uphill climb. Texas' traditionalist-individualist culture, described in Chapter 1, places an emphasis on private, short-run exploitation of nature. Such legal doctrines as the Rule of Capture, described earlier in this chapter, officially reinforce the attitude that public interests should not interfere with private gain. The historical result has been that, well into the second half of the twentieth century, Texans were free to exploit and despoil their environment. As Tai Kreidler wrote in his survey of the relationship of Texans to their environment, "Hunting game to extinction occurred frequently . . . The east Texas black bear . . . vanished from the landscape . . . herons and snowy egrets were nearly wiped out . . . In the 1950s . . . 'indiscriminate clear cutting'" of forests began. "After cutting the larger trees, lumber crews bulldozed the remainder, eliminating any possibility for old forest regrowth . . . The expedient way in which the natural environment was used seemed to indicate that Texans believed the land and resources were inexhaustible."[57]

The awareness that resources are in fact limited, and that government action was needed to protect land, water, air, plants, and animals for the present and future public, advanced only slowly in Texas, and against grudging resistance. During the 1930s the Railroad Commission began to make rules to try to stop pollution of land and water, above and below-ground, by the oil and gas industries. The state first put into place quality standards for municipal water systems in 1945. In 1951 the Department of Health performed the first air-quality study. Two years later the legislature created the Texas Water Pollution Advisory Council, the first state agency with the direct responsibility to deal with pollution. In 1993 the legislature combined a variety of programs and agencies charged with protecting the environment into the Texas Natural Resources Conservation Commission (TNRCC) and gave it general responsibility for managing air, water, and waste programs. In 2002 TNRCC was reorganized, given slightly different responsibilities, and had its name changed to the Texas Commission on Environmental Quality (TCEQ). Officially, therefore, Texas now recognizes the need to protect the environment, and has a set of government agencies with authority to enforce laws that advance their mission.

## Public Policy and Private Interests

Although Texas now has a set of laws and institutions charged with protecting the environment, a principle discussed in Chapter 1, *private influence over public policy*, is powerfully relevant to TCEQ, the Railroad Commission, the Parks and Wildlife Department, and the other such state administrative agencies. Through interest groups and personal contacts (Chapter 3), through campaign contributions and the party system (Chapter 4), and through indirect pressure exerted through legislators (Chapter 7), people who will make more money if the government does not interfere with their plans to exploit nature have a powerful incentive to try to corrupt the system. In addition, such old-fashioned, pre-industrial legal doctrines such as the Rule of Capture often give private individuals an advantage over government servants trying to protect the public interest. These two tendencies do not always combine to thwart efforts to protect the environment. But modern environmental politics in Texas is always an ongoing struggle in which the environment is not necessarily the winner.

## ISSUE SPOTLIGHT:
### Distinctive but Not Unique

Although the laws creating Texas' environmental-protection agencies are in many ways similar to those in other states, and those passed by the federal government, in one important way they are different. Texas is one of fifteen states that explicitly commands its environmental regulatory agencies to take economic tradeoffs—that is, the cost of regulation—into account when regulating air, water, and waste pollution. As a result, those agencies, mission statements differ in tone from those of the other states and the national government. The Texas Commission on Environmental Quality mission statement, for example, tells the reader that the agency "strives to protect our state's human and natural resources consistent with sustainable economic development."

On the one hand, critics argue that such language encourages TCEQ and other state agencies to sacrifice environmental cleanliness when that goal comes into conflict with the need to make money. "What they think is better for the environment seems to be to do as little as possible," as one environmentalist put it. On the other hand, defenders of that sort of approach to environmental regulation argue that it is simply sensible government to take into account the costs of what one is doing. "Ignoring the cost of regulation is not good public policy," is the way one free-market advocate summarized the point of view.

Source: Asher Price, "Business Climate," *Austin American-Statesman*, April 3, 2011, D1.

**Competency Connection**
**SOCIAL RESPONSIBILITY**

Is it reasonable, in your opinion, to command an environmental-protection agency to take the costs of such protection into account?

---

One of the ways that private interests routinely make it easy for themselves to influence public policy in Washington, D. C. has become so common that political scientists have given it an informal name: the "revolving door."[58] As we discussed in Chapter 3, the name refers to the practice of wealthy special interests hiring government regulators as executives or lobbyists once they have finished their stint as members of the agency that is responsible for regulating that industry. Staff members, and the commissioners themselves, of the Federal Communications Commission, who retire from the commission are often quickly hired by the National Association of Broadcasters, for example. When it comes to the federal government, the revolving door has been much investigated. In state politics, however, scholars have not given a great deal of attention to the phenomenon. There are no statistics on how many regulators leave Texas agencies and are then immediately hired by the industry they used to oversee. The only thing available is a set of examples, such as the following.

Although there is no solution, as yet, to the problem of disposal of high-level nuclear waste, there is a storage site, in Andrews County in Texas (along the New Mexico border), that has been approved for storage of low-level waste. "Low-level" means less radioactive, and therefore less dangerous, and for fewer years. Low-level waste is still a threat to groundwater if it is handled carelessly, however. Therefore, the Dallas-based company that wanted to deposit it at the site, Waste Control Specialists, needed both a special law from the legislature and a permit from TCEQ. After years of lobbying and many dollars in campaign contributions, Waste Control Specialists received its law from the legislature in 2003. Its permit application then went to the Commission's technical staff in its Radioactive Materials Division. That Division employs the engineers and geologists, supposedly insulated from political concerns, who are charged with determining whether the waste might be a threat to the environment.

Much to the consternation of Waste Control Specialists, and, apparently, the Commissioners, these scientists concluded that, in fact, the waste was a threat to the groundwater under the high plains. They recommended that the permit be denied. But in 2007, the Commissioners, ignoring the experts on their own staff, granted the permit anyway. Outraged at this apparent indifference to the public health and environmental interest, and insult to their professional integrity, three of the scientists resigned.

The legal department of TCEQ then sent around a memo to the remaining scientific employees, addressing the question of whether it was unethical for them to continue working on a project they considered to be an ecological threat. The legal department's answer: "No, it is not unethical for a TCEQ professional to work on an application that is not in their opinion protective of human health or the environment." And just in case there was any remaining doubt, the memo continued, "Insubordination is expressly prohibited."

At this point, the obvious question to ask is, why did the Commissioners disregard their own staff recommendation and grant the permit? A possible answer arrived a year and a half after the permit was granted. In the middle of 2008, TCEQ Executive Director Glenn Shankle retired from the agency. In early 2009, he accepted a job as a lobbyist for Waste Control Specialists, which was to pay him at least $100,000 a year.[59]

There is no way to know how much the use of "the revolving door" enables private interests whose goals clash with the public interest to corrupt the functioning of the state agencies charged with protecting the Texas environment. All that can be said, on the basis of such examples as TCEQ, is that it does happen.

## The Problems Continue

Meanwhile, according to standards from the federal government, Texas is deficient in a number of measures of environmental health. As Figure 14-1 illustrates, many of the state's urban counties, including those where Houston, Dallas, San Antonio, Austin, Fort Worth, El Paso, Beaumont-Port Arthur, and Texarkana are located, were classified as "nonattainment" or "near nonattainment areas" by the federal Environmental Protection Agency in 2016, meaning that their air contained too much of one or more of the pollutants the EPA measures. Thus, people living in those areas were breathing some or all of the following: ozone, carbon monoxide, nitrogen dioxide, sulfur dioxide, particulate matter, or lead.[60]

The news is not much better for water. Although Texas does not seem to have the dirtiest rivers in the country—Indiana has achieved that dubious distinction—or the single filthiest waterway—the Ohio River wins the anti-prize—it still experiences enough pollution to place it second among the states in total volume of toxic discharges in 2014.[61]

A study in 2018 reported that almost half of the state's major industrial facilities had released illegal levels of pollution into rivers, lakes, and other waterways during the 2016–2017 period.[62] When asked about this finding, spokespeople for the Texas Commission on Environmental Quality blamed toxic spills from the impact of Hurricane Harvey in 2017 for most of the releases. Environmentalists disagreed, arguing that it was TCEQ's own lax oversight, not the vagaries of weather, that accounted for the poison in the state's water.[63]

The disagreement over what or whom to blame for toxic water in Texas is only the latest clash in what is a traditional conflict of traditions in the state. The conservative philosophy that dominates state policymaking through the reigning Republican Party is in general more favorable to industrial development than to environmental protection. Thus, Texas' vaunted "business climate," and its low unemployment rate are the result of that philosophy. So, however, are its problems keeping its air and water clean.

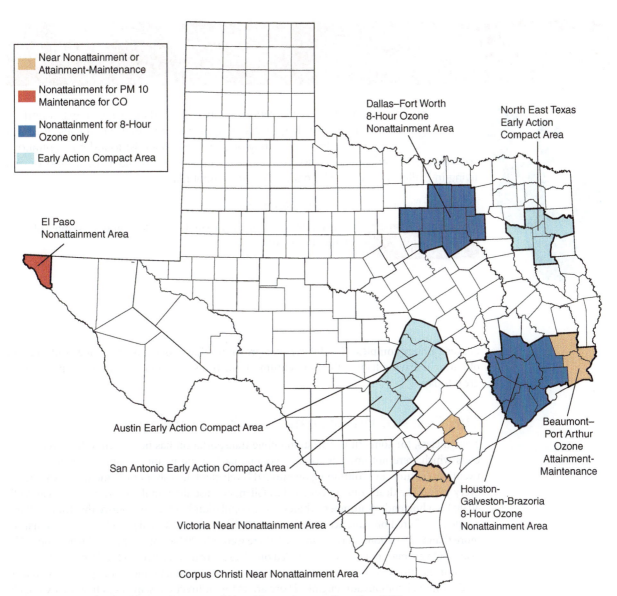

Figure 14-1 Air Quality Nonattainment and Near Nonattainment Counties, 2016.

Texas Commission on Environmental Quality

# Transportation

From the beginning of civilization, the most common form of transportation above mere human or animal muscle-power was to move a cart or box on wheels over some kind of road. From early in the twentieth century, the most popular form of transportation in the United States, and certainly in Texas, was to power the "box" with an internal combustion engine, a machine known as an automobile.

Texas is still an area in which most of the transporting is done with a box powered by an internal combustion engine, although some of those machines are now called trucks, sports-utility vehicles, pickups, and other, more exotic names. Such vehicles have the great appeal that they allow individual people to go where they please on their own schedule. Partly because of the freedom and romance this sort of transportation evokes, and partly

## ISSUE SPOTLIGHT:
## In Case The Bluegills Are Blue

The media frequently report strange and dangerous items found in waterways, including everything from industrial chemicals to birth control pills. In 2004, a Baylor University scientist found concentrations of Prozac, a medicine used to treat clinical depression, in bluegills, a type of fish living in Dallas' Pecan Creek near a water treatment plant.

Source: "Fish Pharm Redux," *Fly Rod & Reel*, March 2004, 14.

Competency Connection
**SOCIAL RESPONSIBILITY**

**Do you think that this is an isolated incident, or one example of a larger problem?**

because a huge complex of industries has grown up that is dependent upon a continuation of national driving habits, the momentum of our transportation choices of the past is very great today.

### The Costs of the Internal Combustion Engine

Nevertheless, for some time now automobile transportation has been seen to have very great costs which were not obvious when it became part of the national culture. For most of the twentieth century, and continuing on into 2017, vehicles killed about forty thousand Americans every year. (The death *rate*, of course, has fallen, because the population rises every year. Still, 40,000 is a horrendous number, whatever the population.)[64] Over and above the deaths, all the accidents suffered on American roads since 1900 have been estimated to have cost the nation more than $230 billion. In Texas in 2017, there were 14,299 "serious" road accidents, and 3,721 deaths. On average, one person was killed on a Texas road every two hours, 21 minutes.[65]

But the direct costs of car culture are only the most measurable of the problems created by the internal combustion engine. There are many indirect consequences that are extremely expensive, although hard to measure. Texas has 80,423 miles of pavement, from interstate highways to park roads, and that number does not include the amount of asphalt in parking lots, because no one keeps track of that number.[66] Each square foot of pavement is one square foot into which rain cannot soak, and on which vegetation cannot grow. The more paved roads, therefore, the less surface area for water to enter and replenish aquifers and springs, and the less room for plants to clean the air.

Furthermore, the air needs cleaning because the more than 22 million vehicles in Texas spew out roughly 200 million tons of carbon dioxide each year, plus huge amounts of other noxious gases.[67] Although there are no specific studies focusing on Texas, a 2013 M.I.T. study estimated that such vehicle emissions caused 53,000 early deaths a year in the United States.[68] Because, in 2018, Texas contained 8.7 percent of all the people in the country, that would translate to roughly 4,611 Texans a year dying from vehicle air pollution. And the number, of course, increases every year.

On top of this pollution is the fact that vehicle exhaust is a major cause of global warming. Put starkly, the internal combustion engine is both killing individual Texans and altering the climate of the planet.

Automobiles have always symbolized personal freedom to Americans in general and Texans in particular. When they become too numerous and concentrated, however, they stop being the servants of people, and become their masters. When that happens, they can become the symbols of servitude rather than of freedom.

Courtesy of Ben Sargent

Competency Connection
**PERSONAL RESPONSIBILITY**

Do you agree with cartoonist Ben Sargent's attitude, here? Or do you think that the virtues of the automobile outweigh its social cost?

In short, reliance on the internal combustion engine to move millions of people imposes steep costs on society and the environment. For this reason, concerned citizens and government officials have for some time been looking for ways to either create a different means of transportation, or mitigate the costs associated with the automobile.

## Which Way Transportation Policy?

At all levels of government, policymakers have a choice between three basic strategies for addressing transportation issues. They can build more roads, force cars to become cleaner and safer, or make available alternative forms of transportation.

**Strategy Number One: Build More Roads** Anticipating what was obviously the wave of the future, in 1917 the legislature created the Texas Highway Department to pave, build, and maintain, the state's roads.[69] It also set the state's vehicular speed limit at 25 miles-per-hour, and, in 1923, authorized its first gasoline tax, one cent a gallon. The agency would be reorganized and renamed several times, and both the speed limit and gas tax raised repeatedly. It is now known as the Texas Department of Transportation, or TxDOT, the speed limit is now 85 mph on some country highways, and the gas tax is now 20 cents a gallon. But the politics of transportation have not changed much in nine decades.

As its original name suggests, the mindset at TxDOT has always been to build roads. The people at the agency have traditionally tended to think in terms of accommodating the needs of the internal combustion engine. As journalist Griffin Smith wrote in his critique of the Highway Department mentality in 1974, the training of the agency's employees, and their socialization within its organizational culture, "have given Texas an established Highway Department bureaucracy of transportation professionals who think only roads . . . (whose) outlooks are routinely predisposed to favor highway transportation over rail mass transit and other modes." Further, since 1917 there has been a complex of interest groups in place—oil companies, cement-asphalt-and-tire dealers, bus and truck companies, road-building contractors, among others—who have had economic interests in building more roads, and who have organized and lobbied the legislature in favor of using state money for roads as opposed to other forms of transportation. As a result, despite the existence of climate change, a near-tripling of the Texas population since Smith wrote his exposé, and the movement of Austin, the Dallas-Ft. Worth Metroplex, Houston, and San Antonio into the ranks of the nation's most congested cities, the state's politicians still usually recommend more roads, as opposed to more public forms of transportation.[70]

Even though various public interest group spokespeople and policy scholars, as far back as the 1960s, were urging that public money be spent to try to move Texans in the faster, cleaner forms of transportation—high-speed trains, subways, monorails, and so on—that were in use in cities of the American Northeast and other countries in Europe and Asia, the state's mindset was resolutely oriented toward the internal combustion engine. It was not until the 1980s that some Texas politicians, especially the mayors of large cities, began to think in a serious way about the need to provide alternate means of getting their constituents to work.

Gasoline taxes have traditionally paid for new roads in Texas. But in recent decades such taxes have proven inadequate to finance the repairing all of the state's highways and the building of new ones. Further, federal funds for such purposes are falling victim to the national government's budget problems. The logical solution to the problem of building more roads with less available tax money is to build toll roads, raising money to finance road-building bonds by making motorists pay to use the highways. But it turns out that Texans detest the idea of traveling on pay-as-you-drive roads almost as much as they dislike the idea of paying taxes. Nevertheless, with gasoline tax revenue stagnant, a variety of interests and arguments have been backing the construction of toll roads, and slowly, against loud opposition, the state has been building them. As of 2018, there were 230 miles of such roads functioning in Texas, with planning ongoing for more.[71]

Nevertheless, an active and vocal sector of the Republican party, as represented by such interest groups as Texans for Toll-free Highways, puts great pressure on politicians to oppose all toll roads, period. Responding to such influence, in November, 2017, both Governor Greg Abbott and Lt. Governor Dan Patrick came out publicly in opposition to the Texas Department of Transportation's plan to spend four billion dollars, previously authorized by the voters, on more toll roads.[72] As a result, the prospect for any new such highways in the near future is very dim.

In summary, many Texans are stuck in traffic jams, and are demanding more roadways to relieve congestion. But they are demanding even more strenuously that they not be made to pay for them. This contradiction in public attitudes has slowed road construction in the state to near-paralysis. At the moment, "building-more-roads" does not seem to be a viable way out of the problems of transportation.

**Strategy Number Two: Make Cars Cleaner and Safer** The federal government has been the leader in making vehicles both cleaner and safer. In terms of cleaning the air, as mentioned earlier in this chapter, Congress passed a law in 1975 mandating that all cars and light trucks must have a certain Corporate Average Fuel Economy (CAFE). Similarly, in terms of safety, in 1977 the Department of Transportation issued a rule that by 1983 all vehicles sold must feature seat belts; air bags were made mandatory in 1994.[73]

A few states, notably California, have made independent efforts to provide that all the vehicles sold within their borders are as pollution-free as is practical. In 1990, California passed the first of what has come to be known as its "Clean Cars" laws. Together, these laws provide rebates to consumers who purchase low-emission vehicles, impose various penalties on cars that are heavy emitters of global-warming gases, and provide a variety of other incentives (such as specially-designated parking spaces) for cleaner vehicles. As of 2018, thirteen states and the District of Columbia have followed California in adopting some or all of its Clean Car policies. In regard to safety, most states impose mandatory seat-belt-wearing laws on drivers and passengers, and all have adopted some kind of rules to discourage drunk-driving.[74]

Texas was not at the forefront of efforts to make cars cleaner, but has recently begun to join the party. For decades, the ideal of everyone who worries about the filthy nature of automotive exhaust has been a car that produces no noxious emissions. The most practical way to realize such a dream is to build a vehicle that runs on electric power from a battery, one that is so useful yet cheap that consumers will want to buy it. Although such cars would not be "zero emission" in the large sense, because the manufacture of the vehicle itself and its battery requires power, which must come from a utility that probably burns fossil fuel, and because the electricity to recharge the battery must also originate in a utility, on overall balance such cars would be much cleaner than the internal-combustion-engine vehicles they replace.[75]

Practical electric vehicles, an ideal sought by both independent inventors and huge car companies during much of the twentieth century, tended to have a fatal drawback. They could not travel very far—generally about 40 miles—without needing to be recharged. Because commuters were leery about trusting their trip to and from work each day to a vehicle that might well run out of juice on the way home, none of these cars appealed to consumers.

In 2010, however, the Chevrolet Volt and the Nissan Leaf came onto the market. The Leaf got about 100 miles on a single battery charge. The Volt's battery only provided enough power to send it 40 miles, but the Volt featured a backup gasoline engine to fuel the car to the next charging station.

Even with significant subsidies from the federal, and sometimes state governments, the Volt and Leaf were only marginally successful in the marketplace. But as the frightening truths about climate change began to sink into the consciousness of government, business, and the public, both politicians and business executives moved to get serious about making pollution-free automobiles practical.

By 2017, every major automaker was offering electric vehicles, and some had announced their intention to phase out gasoline-powered cars in the future. That year, the government of Texas joined the party when the legislature instituted a $2,500 subsidy to consumers who bought an electric car. Combined with federal tax credits, Texas' program would lower the cost of a typical electric vehicle by up to $10,000. The state's politicians still had not admitted that they might be doing something to combat global warming, the reality of which most of them continued to deny. Instead, the program emphasized the contribution of electric vehicles to cleaning the smoggy air of the cities. The Texas Commission on Environmental Quality, which administered the program, dubbed it the "Texas Emissions Reduction Plan."[76]

Meanwhile, Texas cities were doing even more to encourage consumers to go electric. From the point of view of potential customers, one of the problems with buying an electric car was the lack of charging stations. Gas stations, of course, have blanketed the state for decades, so a motorist rarely has to worry about running out of fuel. But charging stations are relatively rare, so a consumer who is thinking about buying an electric car might hesitate because of the fear of running out of charge on the way home from work.

Led by Austin, however, Texas cities are attempting to allay such fears. In 2018, the city and its electric utility, Austin Energy, began to offer financial incentives to apartments, retailers, and employers to install "fast charging stations" on their property, so that consumers could recharge their electric vehicles in as little as twenty minutes. The city council had approved $1.5 million to build ten such stations in the downtown area.[77]

Thus, Texas governments are making progress when it comes to the obvious future of the automobile. The Electric Reliability Council of Texas has estimated that by 2031, there will be 1.6 million electric vehicles on the state's road, making up about 20 percent of all passenger vehicles. There is reason to hope, therefore, that the air will not be getting dirtier.[78]

In summary, unlike the case with road-building, there is forward movement on the Texas policy front in regard to encouraging citizens to acquire cleaner cars. This progress will not solve all the state's transportation problems, but it is at least addressing some of them.

**Strategy Number Three: Create Alternatives to Transportation by Automobile, and Persuade People to Use Them** Both of the previous policy strategies involved the automobile. But, for decades, many scholars have argued that the way to deal with both air pollution, and, more recently, climate change, is not to try to improve or accommodate the internal combustion engine. The way to deal with the problems caused by automobiles is to start relying more heavily on non-automobile transportation. Of the alternatives that have been offered, the most popular is to go back to technologically-improved versions of an old transportation system: railroads.

There are two types of rail transportation under discussion, high-speed heavy-rail between cities, and light-rail within cities. Here, we will discuss only one, the within-city alternative. **Light-rail metropolitan transit**, in which commuters get to work via subway, or monorail, or streetcars, or some other variation on the theme, is popular with urban planners partly because of studies that conclude that one person riding light rails instead of driving a car for one year reduces hydrocarbon emissions by nine pounds, nitrogen oxide emissions by five pounds, and carbon monoxide emissions by 62.5 pounds.[79] Light-rail also holds out the promise of lessening traffic congestion, relieving the city administration of supplying more parking downtown, and being more helpful than a bus system to poor citizens who do not own a car, although these expectations are controversial. But the promise of the alternate form of mass transit is so appealing that many city leaders have leant their money and prestige to efforts to persuade Texans, notorious for their love of automobiles and pickups, to support the construction of light-rail systems.

But progress has been slow, and not always satisfactory. The Dallas Area Rapid Transit (DART) authority began operating the first light-rail system in the American Southwest in 1996. Houston's MetroRail began running the first, 8-mile leg of its system in 2004. In 2009, Austin Capital Metro began offering commuter train service between the small town of Leander and the city's downtown convention center on a route that had the cost-saving virtue of running on an existing 32-mile freight line. Other Texas cities—San Antonio, for example—have not opted for light rail, relying instead on improved bus service. All the light-rail systems have experienced problems with cost over-runs, lower-than-projected ridership, management blunders, and a variety of other disappointments.[80]

Public transportation advocates argue that the problems are just growing pains, and that the kinks will be ironed out as time and experience progress. But many other observers differ, arguing that mass transit is inherently unsuited to the Lone Star State's cities.

Houston's light-rail system can be seen as an example of the problems common to all such transportation efforts in Southern and Western cities, which typically, having grown up with the automobile, have very low-densities. In the older, pre-auto-age cities such as those in the Northeast and Europe, any mass transit system is within the reach of very many potential riders per mile. In Houston, however, the city is so spread out, with people and buildings so far apart, that there are many fewer potential riders per mile. For example, New York City is almost exactly half as large, geographically, as Houston (305 square miles to 602), but contains almost four times as many people (8.2 to 2.1 million). In New York, therefore, there are eight times as many potential riders per square mile as there are in Houston. Since a new mile of track, and a new station, cost roughly the same in both cities, it is inevitable that Houston can expect fewer riders, and therefore fewer dollars in fares, per mile.

All urban transit systems run at a financial loss, and must be subsidized by tax money. But Houston's transit deficit must be systematically much greater than New York's. Yet the Bayou City is in tax-averse Texas, so its prospects of help from the state government are much worse than those of the Big Apple. It therefore faces a much more daunting funding situation.

Given this difficult fiscal reality, Houston's city leaders apparently decided that they had to cut corners. Whereas most light rail systems avoid running on city streets (using monorails,

**light-rail metropolitan transit** Within-city public transportation via subway, monorail, streetcar, or some other small railroad line.

subways, or tracks that in other ways somehow stay out of the way of vehicular traffic), Houston's politicians endorsed a plan that would run the trains down the already-congested avenues and boulevards. The result should have been foreseen, but wasn't. During the first test month before the line was opened to commuters in 2004, MetroRail trains collided with five passenger cars. The first year there were 62 accidents. Between 2004 and 2010, there were a total of 313 collisions between trains and automobiles or trucks. Houstonians took to mocking MetroRail with the nicknames "A Streetcar Named Disaster" (after a famous play by Tennessee Williams, "A Streetcar Named Desire"), and "Wham-Bam-Tram." MetroRail leaders blamed the auto drivers for these accidents, accusing them of running red lights or failing to look before turning left.[81] No doubt these observations were accurate, but they were also beside the point. The cheapskate design of the system, from the beginning, insured that the trains would be frequently crashing into cars. Moreover, even in the absence of accidents, the presence of additional large metal machines moving among and alongside automobiles has only increased congestion on the city's streets.

Attempting to cut down on the number of accidents, in 2017 the Houston Metropolitan Transit Authority started an aggressive enforcement program to keep drivers from turning in front of trains. But after months of warnings and tickets, trains were still hitting automobiles. In November, 2017, there were fifteen train-car collisions on the city's streets.[82] Given the initial design of the system, and the human propensity to make bad decisions, the future looked to be similarly full of accidental violence.

Trying to escape from the tyranny of the automobile, yet fated to work within the low-density of Texas cities, proponents of light-rail systems have apparently adopted the philosophy expressed in an iconic line from the 1989 movie, "Field of Dreams:" "Build it, and they will come."[83] Pro-rail advocates argue that once fully-functioning, efficient, cheap mass transit systems are in place, urban Texans will change their commuting habits in the short-run, and their living habits in the long run. As citizen behavior evolves, Texas cities will become denser, which will make for more financially viable public transit, which will lead to better service, which will cause still more modifications of citizen behavior, and so on in a virtuous spiral. Whether such a vision is a realistic blueprint for the future of Texas cities, or whether it is as much a fantasy as the movie that spawned its slogan, is a question to be considered in additional editions of this textbook.

Advocates of light-rail transit, such as this one in Houston, hope that Texans can be persuaded to leave their cars at home and "take the train" to work.

Stephen Finn/Alamy Stock Photo

## Summary

**LO14.1** **Discussions of water supply, energy supply, environmental protection, and transportation all take place within a context of changing world climate.** These discussions are complicated by the fact that the ruling Republican Texas politicians deny that such change is taking place.

**LO14.2** **Because the Texas population is growing, but the supply of water cannot be increased, economic—and thus, political—conflicts over the liquid are already intense and will become more so.** Examples of some of those present and future conflicts include urban-areas-versus-farmers and economic-development-versus-the-environment.

**LO14.3** **Policy questions about energy supply always involve a "Faustian Bargain," in that each potential source involves both great benefits and painful potential costs.**

**LO14.4** **We explain how the concept of the Faustian Bargain applies to oil, natural gas, coal, nuclear power, renewables, and efficiency.**

**LO14.5** **Three themes that are important in Texas energy policy are 'Texas versus the federal government,' 'pseudo laissez-faire,' and 'regulation versus deregulation.'**

**LO14.6** **Themes important to the politics of the environment are 'private influence over public policy,' and 'industrial development versus environmental protection.'**

**LO14.7** **We identify specific areas where Texas has failed to keep its air and water clean.**

**LO14.8** **Dependence upon automobiles for transportation is one of the main reasons that the air over Texas' cities is sometimes unbreathable.** We evaluate three potential strategies for solving transportation problems: "build more roads," "make cars run more cleanly," and "build public transportation, and persuade people to use it."

## Critical Thinking

1. Explain how the fact that the climate is growing hotter influences the policy problems of water supply, energy supply, environmental protection, and transportation.

2. Given the three possible strategies for dealing with the problem of transportation, discuss which strategy you would prefer, and why. Pay particular attention, in your answer, to the way that you think that the various options should be paid for.

# Notes

## Chapter 1

1. Sources: Two entries in the Texas State Historical Society Website: https://tshaonline.org/handbook/online/articles/yps01 and https://tshaonline.org/handbook/online/articles/fau14

2. Alwyn Barr, *Black Texans: A History of African Americans in Texas 1528–1995* (Norman: University of Oklahoma Press, 1996), 17.

3. Reported in *The Independent*, April 19, 1866, p. 4; accessed via www.the-american-catholic.com/2010/o4/30/Sheridan-hell-and-Texas

4. David Montejano, *Anglos and Mexicans in the Making of Texas 1836–1986* (Austin: University of Texas Press, 1986), 54, 58; Louis L'Amour, *North to the Rails* (New York: Bantam Books, 1971).

5. Jonathan W. Singer, *Broken Trusts: The Texas Attorney General versus the Oil Industry, 1889–1909* (College Station: Texas A&M, 2002), 5.

6. Barr, *Black Texans*, op. cit., 134–135; Montejano, *Anglos and Mexicans*, op. cit., 143–144.

7. "Texas a Net Loser from Falling Oil Prices, Economist Reports," *Energy Studies*, vol. 11, no. 5 (May/June 1986), 1 (newsletter of the Center for Energy Studies at the University of Texas at Austin).

8. Calculated from tables in p. 14 of *Crime in Texas 1992* (Austin: Texas Department of Public Safety, 1993).

9. Robbie Morganfield, "Texas Passes NY," *Houston Chronicle*, December 28, 1994, 1A.

10. Duwadi Megh, "Study: No. 2 'Cyberstate' Texas Lost the Most Jobs in Tech Bust," *Austin American-Statesman*, June 26, 2002, D1.

11. "Ike's Insurance Bill is Highest in State History," *San Antonio Express-News*, January 31, 2010, B6.

12. www.thebalance.com/hurricane-harvey-facts-damage-costs-4150087; Wikipedia.

13. David Shieh, "Major Storm on Coast Could Have Big Financial Impact Statewide," *Austin American-Statesman*, June 16, 2008, A1; Kelley Shannon, "Texas' Ike Insurance Tab Rising Rapidly," *Austin American-Statesman*, September 25, 2008, D1; Char Miller, "Ike's Wake," *Texas Observer*, October 3, 2008, 11.

14. Asher Price, "Hurricane Alters Debate on Coastal Construction," *Austin American-Statesman*, September 23, 2008, A1.

15. Dan Zehr, "Texas Jobless Rate Unmoved at 6.5%," *Austin American-Statesman*, July 19, 2013, B5; Erica Grieder, *Big, Hot, Cheap, and Right: What America Can Learn from the Strange Genius of Texas* (New York: PublicAffairs, 2013, 5, 10, 15, 16.

16. David Wilfong, "Texas 'firing on all cylinders' in first quarter of 2018," *Austin American-Statesman*, April 22, 2018, G1.

17. U.S. Census Bureau statistics, as analyzed in the blog bettertexasblog.org/2017/09/new-Texas-household-income-poverty-rate-census-numbers.

18. Information in the following account comes from Luke Darby, "Rick Perry and Texas Politicians Pressuring Mexico to Pay Its Water Debt," *Dallas Observer*, April 16, 2013; Julian Aguilar, "Federal Legislation Targets Mexico Over Water Treaty," *The Texas Tribune*, June 10, 2013.

19. Naveena Sadasivam, "Despite Trump, Water Agency Fosters Cross-Border Cooperation Between U.S. and Mexico," *Texas Observer*, April 18, 2018.

20. The following discussion is based on Daniel J. Elazar, *American Federalism: A View from the States,* 3rd ed. (New York: Harper & Row, 1984), 109–173; Ira Sharkansky, "The Utility of Elazar's Political Culture: A Research Note," 247–262; Robert L. Savage, "The Distribution and Development of Policy Values in the American States," 263–286, and Appendices A, B, and C, 287–294 in Daniel J. Elazar and Joseph Zikmund II, eds. *The Ecology of American Political Culture: Readings* (New York: Thomas Y. Crowell, 1975); for evidence that the Texas political culture continues to persist as originally described, see Paul Brace, Kevin Arceneaux, Martin Johnson, and Stacy G. Ulbig, "Does State Political Ideology Change Over Time?" *Political Research Quarterly,* V. 57, #4, December 2004, 529–540, esp. 534.

21. Sharkansky, "Utility," op. cit., 252.

22. Kathleen O'Leary Morgan and Scott Morgan, eds., *State Rankings 2017: A Statistical View of America* (Washington, D. C.: CQ Press, 2017), 525.

23. Aldan Quigley, "Texas Regains Ranking as No. 1 State for Business," *Austin American-Statesman*, July 11, 2018, B7.

24. http://chiefexecutive.net/best-worst-states-for-business-2013; accessed July 21, 2013.

25. Alicia A. Caldwell, "Census: More Than Half of Texans Are Minorities," *Austin American-Statesman,* August 11, 2005, B1.

26. Jay Root, "Census Data Shows Huge Hispanic Growth in Texas," *Associated Press Report*, February 17, 2011.

27. 1990 income figures from Steve Murdock, Steve White, Md. Nazrul Hoque, Beverly Pecotte, Xuihong You, and Jennifer Balkan, *The New Texas Challenge: Population Change and the Future of Texas* (College Station: Texas A&M, 2003), 7, and *Latinos in Texas: A Socio-Demographic Profile* (Austin: Tomas Rivera Center, 1995), 66, 84, 111; 2015 estimate from https://statisticalatlas.com/state/Texas/Household-Income

# Chapter 2

1. Morton Grodzins created the terms *layer cake* and *marble cake* as descriptions of federalism to help separate concepts of dual and cooperative federalism. See President's Commission on National Goals, "The Federal System," *The Report of the President's Commission on National Goals* (Washington, D.C., 1960).

2. Information on the fight over Medicaid expansion is from the following sources: Steve Clark, "Analysts: Texas Loses Big by Rejecting Medicaid Expansion," *Brownsville Herald*, June 8, 2013; Kenneth Artz, "Texas Medicaid Expansion Attempt Defeated," The Heartland Institute blog, June 7, 2013; Chuck Lindell, "Reform Bill Rejecting Medicaid Growth OK'd," *Austin American-Statesman*, May 22, 2013, B5; Umbereen S. Nehal and Angelo P. Giardina, "Arkansas Found a Medicaid Solution—So Why Can't Texas?" *Austin American-Statesman*, June 4, 2013, A7.

3. *National Federation of Independent Business et al.* v. *Sebelius*, 132 S. Ct. 603 (2012).

4. Martha Derthick, in "American Federalism: Half-Full or Half-Empty," *Brookings Review* (Winter 2000), 24–27, examines the status of federal-state relations at the beginning of the twenty-first century.

5. See www.constitution.legis.state.tx.us/ for the complete text of the Texas Constitution.

6. Texas was governed by Mexico from 1821 to 1836. Beginning in 1824, the Mexican Congress, acting under the Mexican Constitution, joined Texas and Coahuila, with Saltillo as the capital. That arrangement prevailed until independence in 1836. Thus, Texas was also governed by a seventh constitution, albeit as a colony, not as an independent nation or a state.

7. See, for example, Fred Gantt Jr., *The Chief Executive in Texas: A Study in Gubernatorial Leadership* (Austin: University of Texas Press, 1964), 24.

8. The Jacksonians supported slavery and the brutal treatment of Native Americans.

9. Jim B. Pearson, Ben Procter, and William B. Conroy, *Texas, The Land and Its People*, 3rd ed. (Dallas: Hendrick-Long, 1987), 400–405; *The Texas Almanac*, 1996–1997 (Dallas: *Dallas Morning News*, 1996), 499.

10. Historical perspectives are based on remarks of John W. Mauer, "State Constitutions in a Time of Crisis: The Case of the Constitution of 1876," Symposium on the Texas Constitution, sponsored by the University of Texas Law School and the *Texas Law Review*, October 7, 1989.

11. The Grange originated in Minnesota in the 1860s to air farmers' grievances about low prices and the actions of big business—namely, the railroads and the grain companies—with which they had to deal. The organization reached its peak of power and membership in the 1870s.

12. Wilbourn E. Benton, *Texas Politics: Constraints and Opportunities* (Chicago: Nelson-Hall, 1984), 51.

13. Because of its length, the entire Texas Constitution is rarely reproduced. However, the *Texas Almanac* included the full text with all amendments until the 2000–2001 edition, and continues to summarize proposed amendments and to track their passage. As previously noted, the complete document can be found online at www.constitution.legis.state.tx.us/.

14. A full discussion of poorly organized sections and provisions in conflict with federal law can be found in *Reorganized Texas Constitution without Substantive Change* (Austin: Texas Advisory Commission on Intergovernmental Relations, 1977).

15. The Alabama Constitution had approximately 376,000 words as of 2013. This and other comparative information can be found in *The Book of the States, 2013 Edition*, vol. 45 (Lexington, KY: Council of State Governments, 2013), 12.

16. The definitive study of the Texas Constitution is Janice C. May, *The Texas State Constitution, A Reference Guide* (Westport, CT: Greenwood Publishing Group, 1996), and *The Texas State Constitution* (New York: Oxford University, 2011).

17. Article 1, Section 4, stipulates acknowledgment of the existence of a Supreme Being as a test for public office; however, this provision is not enforced because it violates the U.S. Constitution.

18. As long as citizens were legally perceived to be citizens of the state first and of the nation second, state guarantees were vital. In recent years, state courts have begun to reassert themselves as protectors of rights because the federal courts have begun to be less assertive in their own decisions.

19. Article XV specifies the grounds for impeachment of judges, but not for the impeachment of executive officers; only the power to impeach the latter is given.

20. Margaret Ferguson, "Governors and the Executive Branch," in Virginia Gray, Russell L. Hanson, and Thad Kousser, eds. *Politics in the American States: A Comparative Analysis*, 11th edition (Thousand Oaks, CA: Sage/CQ Press, 2018), p. 252.

21. Even with all the modern cases dealing with the rights of the criminally accused, no national prohibition exists on the state's right to appeal in criminal cases. See *Palko* v. *Connecticut*, 302 U.S. 319 (1937), for the Supreme Court's position on the issue. Texas allowed no appeal by the state until 1987.

22. Contrary to popular opinion, a justice of the peace without legal training cannot become a judge on a superior (appeals) court. Qualifications for these courts include ten years as a practicing lawyer or a combination of ten years of legal practice and judicial service.

23. Some years ago, *Forbes* magazine reported that Texas and Alabama have the most expensive judicial elections in the country. With major amounts of money—as much as $2 million for a Texas Supreme Court seat—on the line, vote-getting skills become especially important. See Laura Casteneda, "D.C. Worst, Utah Best on Litigious List," *Dallas Morning News*, January 3, 1994, 1D, 4D.

24. Although many small school districts have consolidated, Texas continues to be among the national leaders in the number of special districts, second only to Illinois. The state had 3,679 special districts when the most recent Census of Governments was taken in 2012, more than three times the number of municipalities.

25. The National Municipal (now Civic) League of Cities State Constitutional Studies Project last produced its *Model State Constitution*, 6th ed., in 1968 (New York: National Civic League). Web searches reveal a variety of other "models,"

all of which seem to be partisan versions of constitutions from states where constitutional revision has been active.

26. A detailed analysis of the 1975 document is available in George Braden, *Citizen's Guide to the Proposed Constitution* (Houston: Institute of Urban Studies, University of Houston, 1975). The University of Houston served as a research and information center during the revision efforts and published numerous reports beginning in 1973. Scholars from across the state were involved in the Houston research. One, Janice C. May, published a book-length study, *Texas Constitutional Revision Experience in the 70s* (Austin: Sterling Swift, 1975). A summary of the general literature on the revision efforts and of voting behavior can be found in John E. Bebout, "The Meaning of the Vote on the Proposed Texas Constitution, 1975," *Public Affairs Comment*, vol. 24 (February 1978), 1–9, published by the Lyndon B. Johnson School of Public Affairs at the University of Texas at Austin.

## Chapter 3

1. Adam J. Newmark and Anthony J. Nownes, "Interest Groups in the States," in Virginia Gray, Russell L. Hanson, and Thad Kousser, eds., *Politics in the American States: A Comparative Analysis*, 11th ed. (Thousand Oaks, California: Sage, 2018), 113.

2. James A. Garcia, "Lobbying Group Subsidary Will Gather Insurance Data," *Austin American-Statesman*, August 27, 1996, B1; information updated by authors on August 1, 2013.

3. Information about 527s and 510c4 from Thomas M. Holbrook and Raymond J. La Raja, "Parties and Elections," in Virginia Gray, Russell L. Hanson, and Thad Kousser, eds, *Politics in the American States: A Comparative Analysis*, 10th ed. (Los Angeles: Sage/CQ Press, 2013), 73.

4. Ibid., 67.

5. http://www.opensecrets.org/states/donors.php?cycle=2012&state==TX, accessed July 31, 2013

6. Information on Simmons' fine from Wikipedia entry, accessed July 31, 2013.

7. Jim Vertuno, "Low-Level Nuclear Waste Site Gets OK," *Austin American-Statesman* March 23, 2012, B1; press release from J. F. Lehman, January 26, 2018, available at www.prnewswire.com/news-release/jf-lehman-company-acquires-waste-control-specialists-300589066.html

8. Compiled from data on the Texas Ethics Commission Website: www.ethics.state.tx.us/dfs/loblistsREG.htm#R2017.

9. Dave Mann, Eric Benson, and R. G. Ratcliffe, "Flush With Power," *Texas Monthly*, February, 2017.

10. Paul Burka, "Is the Legislature for Sale?" *Texas Monthly*, February 1991, 118.

11. Articles in the *Austin American-Statesman* are the source for this discussion of the telecom conflict: "Cable Industry Sues Again over Law," January 28, 2006, F2; Bruce Meyerson, "Sprint Joining Cable Providers to Battle SBC," November 3, 2005, B1; Claudia Grisales, "SBC Asks to Provide TV to San Antonio," October 11, 2005, D1; "Cable Firms Sue to Stop Telecom Law," September 9, 2005, C1; "Perry Approves Changes to Telecom Laws," September 8, 2005, C2; Bruce Mehlman and Larry Irving, "On Telecom, Texas Is Set to Bring on Competition," August 31, 2005, A13; Tim Morstad and Gus Cardenas, "Texas Needs to Stand Up to Big Phone Companies," August 18, 2005, A13; Claudia Grisales, "Phone Lobby Spent Big to Outmaneuver Cable Rivals," August 18, 2005, A1; Claudia Grisales, "Phone Companies Gain TV Win," July 18, 2005, B1; Phil King, "On Telecom, Legislature Lost a Chance to Help Consumers," June 30, 2005, A13; Jaime Martinez, "Bill Would Only Widen Digital Divide in Texas," May 17, 2005, A13; Claudia Grisales, "Legislative Battle over Television Looms," May 7, 2005, A1; Claudia Grisales, "Ad War Erupts in Fight over Telecom Reform," April 28, 2005, D1; Gary Chapman, "To Ensure Texas' Future, We Must Rewrite the Rules on Telecom," March 5, 2005, A15.

12. Asher Price, "Environmental Regulators Find Higher-Paying Jobs in Industry," *Austin American-Statesman*, January 18, 2009, A7.

13. Laylan Copelin, "Ethics Legislation Passes in Overtime," *Austin American-Statesman*, June 2, 2003, B1.

14. Texas Ethics Commission: "Promoting Public Confidence in Government," as revised September 15, 2015, on Website www.ethics.state.tx.us/guides/Go-e.htm#Bribery

15. Nownes and Newmark, "Interest Groups in the States," in Gray, Hanson, and Kousser, *Politics in the American States*, 11th ed., op. cit., 118.

16. Tom Craddick, "Reining In a Civil Justice System Gone Wild," *Austin American-Statesman*, August 29, 2003, A15.

17. Jake Bernstein and Dave Mann, "The Rise of the Machine," *Texas Observer*, August 29, 2003, 8; followthemoney.org/entity-details?eid=4625 Website, accessed September 3, 2018.

18. "History In The Making," *PR Newswire*, June 2, 2003, 1.

19. Dick Weekley, "Texas Ranks 'Best in the Nation in Tort Liability Index but Report Shows More Reforms are Needed" on Website of Texans for Lawsuit Reform, www.tortreform.com/dick_weekley_oped.asp; information taken from Pacific Research Institute, www.pacificresearch.org; both sites accessed September 23, 2006.

20. Lee Parsley, "HB: 1774: Where Are We Now?" on the TLR Website: www.tortreform.com/advocate/tlr-advocate-spring-2018/#25more; accessed September 3, 2018.

21. The information in this section is based on Mary Flood, "Doctors Orders: Medical Lobby Becomes a Powerhouse In Austin," *The Wall Street Journal*, May 19, 1999, T1; Osler McCarthy, "Doctor, Lawyer Groups Bury The Hatchet," *Austin American-Statesman*, February 28, 1999, J1; Laylan Copelin, "Influence Is Name of Game For An Army of Lobbyists," *Austin American-Statesman*, January 12, 2003, E3; "Texas Docs Led By Old Political Hand," *Modern Healthcare*, April 21, 2003, 32; R. G. Ratcliffe, "Perry Signs Prompt Pay Legislation," *Houston Chronicle*, June 18, 2003, A17; David Pasztor, "Doctors' Lobbying Stirs Concern," *Austin American-Statesman*, September 2, 2003, B1; news release, Texans For Public Justice, "Prop. 12 Proponents Gave $5.3 Million To Perry, Dewhurst and Lawmakers in 2002," August 29, 2003, 2; Embry, "Top-Spending PACs;" followthemoney.org Website, accessed August 7, 2013; YouTube discussion with TMA lobbyists about the organization's accomplishment during the 2017 state legislative session; www.youtube.com/watch?v=tOzWfplgEBg, accessed on September 4, 2018.

22. From the TMA's Website, www.texmed.org/, "Liability Reforms Bring More Care, More Doctors to Texans; TMA Survey Confirms: Prop 12 Was Good For Texas," accessed October 16, 2008.

23. The information in this section is based on William Martin, *With God on Our Side: The Rise of the Religious Right in America* (New York: Broadway Books, 1996); Chuck Lindell, "Pulpit To Polls Movement Gathers Steam," *Austin American-Statesman*, March 6, 1994, A1; Paul Burka, "The Disloyal Opposition," *Texas Monthly*, December, 1998, 117 Molly Ivins, "State Board of Obfuscation," *Austin American-Statesman* November 3, 1999, A17; Matt Curry, "In Texas, Appealing To Churchgoers Is an Integral Part of Campaigning," Associated Press news release, July 24, 2002, 1.

24. Hotze's Website quoted in Dan Quinn, "Steve Hotze's Conservative Republicans of Texas: A Cesspool of Extremism and Hate," Blog, Religious Right Watch, June 23, 2017; http://tfn.org/steve-hotzes-conservative-republicans-texas-cesspool-exremism-hate/

25. Patrick quoted in David R. Brockman, "The Christian Right's Politics of Cruelty," *Texas Observer*, August 10, 2018; accessed at www.texasobserver.org/Christian-right-politics-*of-cruelty*.

26. Quinn, "Steve Hotze's Conservative Republicans of Texas," op. cit.; Matthew Watkins, "Texas House Speaker Says He Will Not Seek Re-Election," *Texas Tribune*, October 25, 2017; Jonathan Tilove, "GOP Censures Straus for Obstruction," *Austin American-Statesman*, January 28, 2018, B1.

27. Chuck Lindell, "Court Blocks Texas' Fetal Burial Law," *Austin American-Statesman*, January 30, 2018, A1.

28. All figures from U. S. Bureau of Labor Statistics Website, accessed September 4, 2018; www.bls.gov/news.release/union2.nr0.htm

29. AFL-CIO Cope press release, February 1, 2018; www.texasaflcio.org/news/Texas-afl-cio-cope-posts-endorsements-congressional-legislative-seats-0.

30. A *secondary boycott* occurs when one union boycotts the products of a company being struck by another union. The *checkoff system* is a method of collecting union dues in which an employer withholds the amount of the dues from workers' paychecks. *Mass picketing* occurs when so many people picket a firm that traffic is disrupted and the firm cannot conduct business. A *closed shop* is in effect when workers must already be members of a certain union in order to apply for work in a given firm. A *union shop* is in effect when workers do not have to be members of the union to apply for work, but must join if they get a job.

31. Jeff Stein, "President Criticizes Union Chief in Tweet," *Austin American-Statesman*, September 4, 2018, A7.

32. The information in this section is based on Benjamin Marquez, *LULAC: The Evolution of a Mexican-American Political Organization* (Austin: University of Texas, 1993); Lori Rodriguez, "LULAC Turning Puerto Rican," *Houston Chronicle*, July 9, 1994, A25; James E. Garcia, "Latino Politics: Up To LULAC To Reform or Be Left Behind," *Houston Chronicle*, September 9, 1999, *OUTLOOK*, 1; Lori Rodriguez, "LULAC's Leaders Speech At Convention First Ever," *Houston Chronicle*, July 11, 2002, A1; Lori Rodriguez, "LULAC Role Evolves, But

Equity Still Focus," *Houston Chronicle*, July 23, 2002, A1; Amber Novak, "Up In Smoke," *Texas Observer*, May 23, 2003, 4.

33. Michael Phillips, "Why Is Big Tex Still a White Cowboy?" in Walter L. Buenger and Arnoldo De Leon (eds.), *Beyond Texas Through Time: Breaking Away from Past Interpretations* (College Station: Texas A&M University Press, 2011), 136–37.

34. Krissah Williams and Jonathon Weisman, "Latino Groups Play Key Role on Hill; Virtual Veto Power in Immigration Debate," *The Washington Post*, May 16, 2007, A04; and entry on bill in Wikipedia, accessed October 18, 2008.

35. Carlos Harrison, "In Voter ID Fight, Hispanic Advocacy Groups at Forefront," *Latino Politics (Huffington Post)*, September 11, 2012, at www.huffingtonpost.com/2012/09/11/voter-id-hispanic_n_1872628.html, accessed August 9, 2013.

36. Michael Barajas, "The Interview," *Texas Observer*, April/May, 2018, 10.

37. Perla Arellano, "Activists Furious over LULAC Chief's Letter Backing Trump Plan," *Austin American-Statesman*, February 2, 2018, B1.

38. Newmark and Nownes, "Interest Groups in the States," 118.

39. Kathleen O'Leary Morgan and Scott Morgan, eds., *State Rankings 2018: A Statistical View of America* (Los Angeles: Sage/CQ Press, 2018), 123, 142.

40. There is evidence suggesting that this suspicion is justified; see David F. Prindle, *The Politics of Evolution* (New York: Taylor and Francis, 2015), Chapters 3, 4, and 6.

41. Whiteker quoted in Jason Embry and Robert Elder, "Fed Up, Pro-Education Candidates Step Up," *Austin American-Statesman*, October 23, 2005, A1.

42. Information in this section is mainly based on these sources: "Summary of the 83rd Legislature: Power, Professionalism, Advocacy," Texas State Teachers Association, August, 2013; "Conflicts of the 2013 Legislative Session," Texas Classroom Teachers Association, August, 2013; both available from the organizations' Websites; accessed August 10, 2013; Arianna Prothero, "School Vouchers Don't Exist in Texas. Republican Opposition is the Reason," *Charters and Choice*, July 14, 2017, and numerous other media reports.

# Chapter 4

1. The customary assignment of liberals to the left side of the political spectrum and conservatives to the right side derives from the seating of parties in the French Parliament. Royalists, Gaullists, and others of a conservative persuasion always sit to the right of the center aisle, while socialists, communists, and others of more "progressive" persuasion sit to the left.

2. Source: Texas Lyceum Poll, conducted July 9 through 25, 2018: https://texaslyceum.org/resources/Poll%202018/Day%202%20218%20Texas%20lyceum%20Toplines%20(2).pdf

3. Robert S. Erickson, Gerald C. Wright Jr., and John McIver, "Political Parties, Public Opinion, and State Policy in the United States," *American Political Science Review*, vol. 83, no. 6 (September 1989), 729–750, especially 737.

4. Douglas E. Foley, *Learning Capitalist Culture: Deep in the Heart of Tejas* (Philadelphia: University of Pennsylvania Press, 1990), 110.

5. Quoted in Molly Ivins, "Political Writing—A State of Lazy Journalism," *Texas Humanist*, November–December, 1984, 14–15.

6. For a theoretical analysis of the evolution of party positions during the twentieth century, see Gary Miller and Norman Schofield, "Activists and Partisan Realignment in the United States," *American Political Science Review*, vol. 97, no. 2 (May 2003), 245–260.

7. Source: Texas Lyceum Poll, cited in endnote #2.

8. Dave McNeely, "Party Politics in the Precincts," *Austin American-Statesman*, March 4, 2000, A15.

9. Ken Herman, "Perry Not Standing on GOP Party Platform," *Austin American-Statesman*, June 12, 2002, A9.

10. Molly Ivins, "Texas Elephants Look to Ostracize the RINOs," *Austin American-Statesman*, June 12, 2002, A17; Jake Bernstein, "Elephant Wars," *Texas Observer*, July 5, 2002, 16.

11. Jonathan Tilove, "GOP Censures Straus for Obstruction," *Austin American-Statesman*, January 28, 2018, B1.

12. John F. Bibby and Thomas M. Holbrooke, "Parties and Elections" in Virginia Gray and Russell L. Hanson, eds. *Politics in the American States: A Comparative Analysis* * (Washington, D.C.: Congressional Quarterly, 2004), 74.

13. Gerald C. Wright and Brian Schaffner, "The Influence of Party: Evidence from the State Legislatures," *American Political Science Review*, vol. 96, no. 2, (June 2002), 376–377.

14. Dave McNeely, "Bipartisanship: The Road Not Taken in '03," *Austin American-Statesman*, January 4, 2004, H1.

15. Sean Theriault, "Party Polarization in the U.S. Congress: Member Replacement and Member Adaptation," *Party Politics*, July 2006. 12: 483–503.

16. Chuck Lindell, "GOP Changes Way Speaker is Selected," *Austin American-Statesman*, December 2, 2017, B1.

17. Dave McNeely, "For Incumbent Democrats, Some Heads Are Starting to Roll," *Austin American-Statesman*, March 10, 2004, A12; Ken Herman, "Wilson Pays Price for Siding with GOP," *Austin American-Statesman*, March 11, 2004, A1.

18. Laurie Goodstein, "Issuing Rebuke, Judge Rejects Teaching of Intelligent Design," *New York Times*, December 21, 2005, A1; W. Gardner Selby, "Perry: Add Intelligent Design to Classes," *Austin American-Statesman*, January 6, 2006, A1.

19. Source: Texas Lyceum Poll, conducted July 9–25, 2018: https://texaslyceum.org/resources/Poll%202018/Day%202%20218%20Texas%20lyceum%20Toplines%20(2).pdf

20. "Populist Party Platform," in Michael B. Levy, ed. *Political Thought in America: An Anthology* (Chicago: Dorsey Press, 1988), 356–359.

# Chapter 5

1. "White primary" laws and rules prevented voting in primary elections by anyone who was not Caucasian. Although the Fifteenth Amendment to the U.S. Constitution, passed in 1870, guaranteed the right of all citizens of any race to vote in general elections, it did not apply to primaries. The poll tax law required a citizen to pay a tax months in advance of election day in order to register. Unless registered, citizens were not legally qualified to vote. Poor people, of whom many were minority citizens, were often unable to pay the tax and thus became ineligible to vote. The U.S. Supreme Court invalidated Texas's white primary law in 1944 in *Smith v. Allwright*, 321 U.S. 649. The Twenty-fourth Amendment to the Constitution, adopted in 1964, forbid the poll tax in federal elections. Under threat of federal action, Texas repealed its state poll tax law in 1966 by amendment of its constitution. The state legislature, however, adopted a severe registration law that was, in effect, a poll tax under another name. A federal court struck down this law in *Beare v. Smith*, 321 F. Supp., 1100 (1971).

2. *Beare v. Smith*, 321 F. Supp., 1100 (1971).

3. Kathleen O'Leary Morgan and Scott Morgan, *State Rankings 2018: A Statistical View of America* (Thousand Oaks, CA: CQ /Sage, 2018), 522.

4. www.pewforum.org/religious-landscape-study/compare/party-affiliation/by/racial-and-ethnic-composition/among/state/texas/; the survey is from 2014.

5. National Pew Poll, "Trends in Party Affiliation Among Demographic Groups," conducted in 2017; www.people-press.org/2018/03/20/1-trends-in-party-affiliation-among-demographic/groups/.

6. Colleen McCain Wilson, "For Sanchez, More Wasn't Better," *Dallas Morning News*, November 7, 2002, A1; Laylan Copelin, "Costs Soar in Race to Be Governor," *Austin American-Statesman*, October 29, 2002, B1; Wyne Slater and Pete Slover, "For Sanchez, Perry, the Well Isn't Dry Yet," *Dallas Morning News*, October 13, 2002, A1; Pete Slover, "Political Checks and Balances," *Dallas Morning News*, January 16, 2003, A1.

7. Wilson, Ibid.; Laylan Copelin and David Elliott, "Williams Outspending Richards 2–1," *Austin American-Statesman*, October 30, 1990, A1.

8. Keith E. Hamm and Gary F. Moncrief, "Legislative Politics in the States," in Virginia Gray and Russell L. Hanson, eds., *Politics in the American States: A Comparative Analysis*, 9th ed. (Washington, D.C.: Congressional Quarterly, 2008), 165–166.

9. Texans For Public Justice, *Keeping Texas Weird: The Bankrolling of the 2006 Gubernatorial Race*, September, 2006, accessed on TPJ's Website on October 2, 2006: www.tpj.org/

10. Laylan Copelin, "Few Fans of Campaign Changes," *Austin American-Statesman*, April 22, 2007, B1.

11. Glenn quoted in Roger H. Davidson, Walter J. Oleszek, and Frances E. Lee, *Congress and Its Members*, 11th ed. (Washington, D.C.: CQ Press, 2008), 72.

12. Mike Ward, "65% of Politicians in Poll Favor Public Favor Public Financing of Campaigns," *Austin American-Statesman*, March 11, 1990, B8.

13. Quoted in Jeff South and Jerry White, "Computer Network Tracks Politicians' Funds," *Austin American-Statesman*, August 16, 1993, B1.

14. Laylin Copelin, "Ethics Panel's Future Hanging in the Balance," *Austin American-Statesman*, April 24, 2002, A1; Jake Bernstein, "A Dog Not Allowed to Hunt," *Texas Observer*, April 12, 2002, 3.

15. Laylan Copelin, "Ethics Panel Fines Legislator over Campaign Spending," *Austin American-Statesman,* November 7, 2008, B5; Laylan Copelin, "Ethics Commission Quietly Disciplines State's Politicians," *Austin American-Statesman*, June 19, 2008, B1.

16. Emma Platoff, "Appeals Court Revives Empower Texans Lawsuit Seeking to Gut the Texas Ethics Commission," *Texas Tribune*, August 3, 2018; Tim Eaton, "Ethics Commission Seeks to Force Empower Texans to Turn Over Records," *Austin American-Statesman*, June 11, 2015; Brian Sweany and Paul Burka, "The Skunk at the Garden Party," *Texas Monthly*, July 22, 2014; Brandon Rottinghaus, *Inside Texas Politics: Power, Policy, and Personality of the Lone Star State* (New York: Oxford University Press, 2018, 192.

17. "Keeping Ethics Panel Toothless," Editorial in *Austin American-Statesman*, April 5, 2013, A10; Mike Ward, "Weakened Ethics Bill Clears Both Houses," *Austin American-Statesman*, May 27, 2013, A8.

18. Julia Malone, "Campaigns Take Low Road," *Austin American-Statesman*, October 26, 2006, A7.

19. Donald Green, "Do Negative Political Ads Work?" *Scientific American*, 2018, available at www.scientificamerican.com /article/do-negative-political-ads-work/

20. Kim Fridkin Kahn and Patrick Kenney, "Do Negative Campaigns Mobilize or Suppress Turnout? Clarifying the Relationship between Negativity and Participation," *American Political Science Review*, vol. 93, no. 4 (December, 1999), 877–889; Stephen D. Ansolabehere, Shanto Iyengar, and Adam Simon, "Replicating Experiments Using Aggregate and Survey Data: The Case of Negative Advertising and Turnout," Ibid., 901–909.

21. Gary R. Orren and Nelson W. Polsby, *Media and Momentum: The New Hampshire Primary and Nomination Politics*, (Chatham, NJ: Chatham House, 1987).

22. The Texas Secretary of State oversees the activities of the county clerks in relation to primary elections. The rules are numerous and complicated; the SOS Website contains many helps for citizens and election officials trying to obey the law, which we accessed on September 29, 2018: www.sos.state.tx.us /elections/forms/teamview/help.shtml

23. Source: www.sos.state.tx.us/elections/candidates/guide/2012 /demorreppf.htm; accessed September 29, 2018. (Apparently, the rules and fees have not changed since 2012).

24. David Pasztor, "Millions Pour into Proposition 12 Fight," *Austin American-Statesman*, September 6, 2003, A1; Laylin Copelin and David Pasztor, "Limits on Damages Narrowly Approved," *Austin American-Statesman*, September 14, 2003, A1.

25. "Votes Are In, and Two-Thirds of Those in Texas Came Early," *Dallas Morning News*, November 12, 2008, A3.

26. "Judge Says Perry Took Ruling Out of Context in Ad," *Austin American-Statesman*, July 31, 2002, B3; Molly Ivins, "The Summer of Our Discontent," *Denton Record-Chronicle*, August 10, 2002, A6.

27. Ken Herman, "Perry Uses DEA Murder in New TV Ad," *Austin American-Statesman*, October 26, 2002, B1.

28. "Watkins: 'A New Day' in Dallas County," www.WFAA.com, accessed November 8, 2006; Dan Felstein and Chase Davis, "Warning For GOP in Harris County," *Houston Chronicle*, November 9, 2006, A1; Thomas Korosec, "Democrats Turn Dallas County a Shade of Blue," *Houston Chronicle*, November 9, 2006, B4; 29 W. Gardner Selby, "Though Democrats Made Gains, Looks Like GOP Has Hold On State," *Austin American-Statesman*, November 6, 2008, B1; "Democrats Enjoy Big Wins in Administrative, Judicial Races," *Dallas Morning News*, November 6, 2008, A17; Bob Moser, "Viva Los Republicanos," *Texas Observer*, December 10, 2010, 19; Dave Mann, "Knock, Knock, Who's There?" *Texas Observer*, August 6, 2010, 13.

29. Erica Grieder, *Big, Hot, Cheap, and Right: What America Can Learn from the Strange Genius of Texas* (New York: PublicAffairs, 2013), 197.

30. Matt Vespa, "Rock Bottom: Texas Democrats Have No Candidate for Governor," *Townhall*, August, 9, 2017.

31. Among the sources for this discussion of the 2018 election: Harry Enton, "Latest House Results Confirm 2018 Wasn't a Blue Wave. It Was a Blue Tsunami," *CNN Politics*, December 6, 2018; United States Elections Project, December 4, 2018: www.electproject.org/2018g; Ryan Murphy, "See the Results of the Texas 2018 Midterm Election Here," *Texas Tribune*, November 7, 2018: www.texastribune.org/series /texas-elections-2018/.

# Chapter 6

1. Locke, John, *Second Treatise of Government*, reprint (Indianapolis: Hackett Publishing, 1980) originally published 1690; Rousseau, Jean Jacques, *The Social Contract and Discourses* (New York: E. P. Dutton, 1950), originally published 1750.

2. Hamilton, Alexander, James Madison, and John Jay, *The Federalist* (New York: Random House, 1937), originally published 1787, pp. 141 (#22), 327 (#49), 336 (#51).

3. Ibid, 322 (#48).

4. Information on the legislatures of other states has been taken from *The Book of the States*, 2017 edition (Lexington, KY: Council of State Governments, 2017), Vol. 49, 47–51.

5. According to census estimates for 2013, Texas had a population of 26,050,203. Dividing that figure by 31 for senatorial districts and by 150 for house districts yielded the numbers in the text. Obviously, citizens move in and out of districts, so the numbers are never exact. The population in almost every district increases as the state's population grows.

6. A county was entitled to a maximum of seven representatives unless its population exceeded 700,000; then one additional representative could be districted for each additional 100,000 in population.

7. 369 U.S. 186 (1962).

8. 377 U.S. 533 (1964).

9. A multimember district is one in which two or more representatives are elected by all the people of the district. Each representative thus represents all the people of the district. Multimember districts tend to reduce the ability of ethnic

minorities to win elections, and the citizens tend to be confused as to which representative is truly theirs. See Steven Bickerstaff, "Legislative and Congressional Reapportionment in Texas: A Historical Perspective," *Public Affairs Comment*, V. 37, (Winter, 1991), 1–13, for a good review of early redistricting developments.

10. Keith E. Hamm and Nancy Martorano Miller, "Legislative Politics in the States" in Virginia Gary, Russell L. Hanson, and Thad Kousser, eds., *Politics in the American States: A Comparative Analysis*, 11th ed. (Thousand Oaks, CA: CQ Press, 2018), 206.

11. Alex Ura and Jolie McCullough, "Once Again, the Texas Legislature Is Mostly White, Male, Middle-Aged," *Texas Tribune*, January 9, 2017.

12. The media in Texas ran the 2003 redistricting story as a front page/lead item for weeks. Among the more useful sources are: Pete Slover and Matt Stiles, "Majority of AWOL Lawmakers Where You'd Least Expect: Oklahoma," and Christy Hoppe and Gromer Jeffers, Jr., "Angry over Redistricting, State Reps Deny Quorum," run as companion pieces under the banner "Democrats Disappear," *Dallas Morning News*, May 13, 2003, A1; Patricia Kilday Hart, "The Unkindest Cut," *Texas Monthly*, October, 2003, 44–52; Lee Hockstader, "Caught in the Crossfire," *Washington Post Weekly Edition*, October 6–12, 2003, 14.

13. *Book of the States*, 2017, 63.

14. "Report of the Judicial Compensation Commission" (Austin: JCC, 2018), 5; www.txcourts.gov/media/1442408/jcc-2018-report-final-pdf

15. Chuck Lindell, "Patrick Demotes Fellow GOP Senator," *Austin American-Statesman*, January 23, 2019, A1; Ken Herman, "Intrapartisan Fireworks at the Legislature," *Austin American-Statesman*, January 24, 2019, B1; Chuck Lindell, "Patrick Criticizes Seliger's Attitude, Lack of Teamwork," *Austin American-Statesman*, January 25, 2019, B1.

16. Hamm and Miller, "Legislative Politics," 218; H. Gardner Selby, "A Natural Long Shot," *Austin American-Statesman*, February 22, 2008, A1; Paul Burka, "Hello, My Name is Regular Joe," *Texas Monthly*, April, 2009, 128–131, 226–7, 232.

17. Johnathan Silver, "Bonnen Takes Bipartisan Approach to Assignments," *Austin American-Statesman*, January 24, 2019, A6.

18. Karl T. Kurtz, "Custodians of American Democracy," *State Legislatures*, July–August, 2006, 28–35.

19. See www.lrl.state.tx.us/sessions/billStatistics.cfm for a statistical summary of bills introduced, passed, and vetoed in each house in recent legislative sessions.

20. Alex Samuels, "With a Supermajority, Republicans Have Complete Control of the Texas Senate. That's at Risk This Election Cycle," *Texas Tribune*, September 13, 2018.

21. Ken Herman, "See If You Can Follow the Rules in the Texas Senate," *Austin American-Statesman*, May 5, 2011, A10.

22. Detailed information about the legislative process can be found at www.tlc.state.tx.us/gtli/legproc/process.html

23. Alexander Heard, ed. *State Legislatures in American Politics* (Englewood Cliffs, NJ: Prentice Hall, 1966), 3.

24. Salaries for legislators in California, Florida, Illinois, Massachusetts, Michigan, New Jersey, New York, Ohio, and Pennsylvania, obtained from *Book of the States*, 2017, 63–66.

25. Paul Burka and Patricia Kilday Hart, "The Best and Worst Legislators," *Texas Monthly*, July 2009; www.texasmonthly.com/2009-07-01/feature2.php

## Chapter 7

1. Two exceptions to this tradition were (1) Richard Coke, the first governor under the 1876 Constitution, who served only one term; and (2) Ross S. Sterling, who was not reelected in 1932. James E. Ferguson was reelected in 1916, but was impeached and removed from office in 1917. His wife, Miriam A. Ferguson, was later elected twice to nonconsecutive terms.

2. The constitution does spell out the grounds for removing judges, however. Other officials subject to impeachment include the lieutenant governor, the attorney general, the commissioner of the General Land Office, the comptroller, and appellate court judges. The grounds stipulated for impeachment of judges include partiality, oppression, official misconduct, incompetence, negligence, and failure to conduct the business of the court. See Fred Gantt, Jr., *The Chief Executive in Texas* (Austin: University of Texas, 1964), 123. Ferguson was impeached and convicted for mishandling public funds, conduct brought to light because funds for the University of Texas were involved.

3. "Comparison of Gubernatorial Salaries," Ballotpedia, https://ballotpedia.org/Comparison_of_gubernatorial_salaries; Adam Andrzejewski, "The Big Dogs of Texas Local Government: 18,000 Public Employees Make $100K+ Costing Taxpayers $2.1B," *Forbes*, Jan 16, 2019.

4. Hoinski, Michael, "Preservationists Watch as the Perrys Go Home Again," *New York Times*, July 28, 2012.

5. Allie Morris, "Gov. Abbott Pays Executive Staff Top Dollar—More than N.Y., Fla., Calif.," *San Antonio Express-News*, August 10, 2018.

6. The Web site of the Texas governor (https://gov.texas.gov/organization) provides an up-to-date list of the various divisions of the governor's office.

7. Brian McCall, *The Power of the Texas Governor* (Austin: University of Texas Press, 2009), 72–77.

8. An interesting assessment of the Clements years can be found in George Bayoud and James Huffines, "25 Years Later: Clements' Texas Legacy Stands Tall," *Austin American-Statesman*, November 6, 2003, A15.

9. For an excellent look at the career of Ann Richards, see Jan Reid, "Ann: An Appreciation," *Texas Monthly*, November 2006, 177–179, 278–280.

10. Term taken from a Richards's biography with that title: Mark Shropshire and Frank Schaeffer, *The Thorny Rose of Texas: An Intimate Portrait of Governor Ann Richards* (Birch Lane Press, 1994).

11. As of 2007, Texas claimed four former U.S. presidents—Dwight Eisenhower, who was born in the state; Lyndon Johnson, who was a lifelong resident; George H. W. Bush, who moved to Texas during an oil boom when he was a businessman, not a politician; and most recently, George W. Bush.

12. McCall, *The Power of the Texas Governor*, 126.

13. "The Big Winners and Losers of 1999: The Governor Had a Banner Year, While Local Education Lost Out," *Wall Street Journal*, December 29, 1999, T1.

14. Laylan Copelin and Jason Embry, "Lawmakers Rising Against Perry Policies," *Austin American-Statesman*, March 18, 2007, A1; W. Gardner Selby and Jason Embry, "Governor Says Texas Is One State That Could Leave Union, Though He's Not Pushing It," *Austin American-Statesman*, April 17, 2009; Christy Hoppe, "Perry Signs into Law Most Restrictive Abortion Law in Nation," *Dallas Morning News*, July 18, 2013, 1; Coral Davenport, "Rick Perry, Ex-Governor of Texas, Is Trump's Pick as Energy Secretary," *New York Times*, December 13, 2016.

15. John C. Moritz, "Texas Gov. Greg Abbott: Overcoming personal adversity shaped leadership in times of crisis," *Corpus Christi Caller Times*, January 4, 2019.

16. See the following bills passed in 2003: HB 2292, regular session; HB 7, third called session; and SB 2, third called session.

17. SB 2, Article 7, third called session, Seventy-eighth Legislature, exempts river authorities, junior college districts, agencies headed by one or more statewide elected officials, agencies with a majority of board members not requiring Senate confirmation, and agencies reporting to one or more elected officials. Purely local boards are also exempted.

18. This practice is most common with the licensing and examining boards in various health care fields.

19. See Paul Burka, "Behind the Lines: Altered State," *Texas Monthly*, July 2003, 6, 10, 12.

20. E. Lee Bernick, "Special Sessions: What Manner of Gubernatorial Power?" *State and Local Government Review* 26 (Spring 1994), 79–88, reports that special sessions tend to be cyclical and somewhat responsive to national events that force the states to enact new legislation. Bernick studied special sessions in all fifty states for 1959 through 1989.

21. Unlike the president, the governor does not have a "pocket veto." The governor must send a veto message to block a bill; laying a bill aside without a signature results in the bill's becoming law, even if the legislature adjourns.

22. Congress granted the U.S. president the item veto in 1996; the president used the power eighty-two times before the U.S. Supreme Court declared it unconstitutional in 1998.

23. Pat Thompson and Steven R. Boyd, "Use of the Item Veto in Texas, 1940–1990," *State and Local Government Review*, vol. 26 (Winter 1994), 38–45, provides perspective on the history of the item veto.

24. Dave Michaels and Robert T. Garrett, "Obama Wants to Speed Outflow of Stimulus Funds," *Dallas Morning News*, June 9, 2009.

25. James McGregor Burns, *Leader ship* (New York: Harper & Row, 1978), 42–45.

26. See, for example, Emma Platoff, "Potentially Expanding His Executive Power, Gov. Greg Abbott Orders Agency Heads to Run Proposed Rules by Him First, *Texas Tribune*, June 27, 2018.

## Chapter 8

1. The numbers in this paragraph are based on an actual count of entries in Appendix A, *Fiscal Size-Up, 2018–2019 Biennium* (Austin: Legislative Budget Board, 2018), 539–541.

2. See Josh Goodman, "The Second Best Job in the State," *Governing* (April 2009), 34–39.

3. See, for example, Grover Starling, *Managing the Public Sector*, 5th ed. (Fort Worth: Harcourt Brace, 1998), Chapter 7.

4. See "Bureaucracy" in *From Max Weber: Essays in Sociology*, translated, edited, and with an introduction by H. H. Gerth and C. Wright Mills (New York: Oxford, 1946), 196–244.

5. Emmette S. Redford, *Democracy in the Administrative State* (New York: Oxford, 1969), 3.

6. Governing, "States with Most Government Employees: Totals and Per Capita Rates," http://www.governing.com/gov-data/public-workforce-salaries/states-most-government-workers-public-employees-by-job-type.html.

7. An excellent study of bureaucratic power at the national level is Francis Rourke, *Bureaucracy, Politics, and Public Policy*, 4th ed. (Boston: Little, Brown, 1986). Rourke's framework is adopted here.

8. Paul Appleby, *Big Democracy* (New York: Alfred A. Knopf, 1945), 7.

9. See Alan J. Bojorquez, "New Open Government Legislation," *Texas Town & City,* October 1999, 11–14.

10. Ross Ramsey, It's looking like a cloudy day for sunshine laws in Texas, *Fort Worth Star Telegram*, February 7, 2018.

## Chapter 9

1. Professor Geoffrey C. Hazard, Jr., Quoted in Donald Dale Jackson, *Judges* (New York: Atheneum, 1974), 7.

2. "Gin, 'Barbed' Cases Make Morrison Fun," *University of Texas Daily Texan*, February 19, 1964, 1.

3. Dietz quoted in Arnold Garcia, Jr., "Do You Know Who Your Judges Are? Maybe You Should Find Out," *Austin American-Statesman*, September 14, 2002, A11.

4. Jackson, *Judges*, op. cit., 98.

5. Most of the information in this discussion comes from Bruce Hight, "Justices Bickering over Abortion Law," *Austin American-Statesman*, June 23, 2000, B1; the court case is *In re Jane Doe*, No. 00-0024 (Tex. Sup. Ct., June 22, 2000); on Owen's confirmation, see John Council and T. R. Goldman, "Senate Showdown Ends with Owen Confirmation," *Texas Lawyer*, vol. 20, no. 13 (May 30, 2005), 5.

6. In re Jane Doe 4, 19 S.W.3d 322 (Tex.2000).

7. Texas Attorney General's Office Website, https://www2.texasattorneygeneral.gov/opinion/ken-paxton-opinions, accessed February 3, 2019.

8. *Hopwood v. State of Texas*, 78 F.3d 932 (5th Cir. 1996).

9. Attorney General's Letter Opinion 97–001, February 5, 1997.

10. *Grutter v. Bollinger et al.*, 539 U.S. 306 (2003); *Gratz et al. v. Bollinger et al.*, 539 U.S. 244 (2003).

11. *Fisher v. University of Texas at Austin*, 133 S.Ct. 2411 (2013); Reeve Hamilton, "Appeals Court: UT-Austin May Use Race in Admissions," *Texas Tribune*, July 15, 2014; *Fisher v. University of Texas at Austin*, 136 S.Ct. 2198 (2016).

12. State Bar of Texas Membership: Attorney Statistical Profile (2018–19), https://www.texasbar.com/AM/Template .cfm?Section=Content_Folders&Template=/CM /ContentDisplay.cfm&ContentID=43800, Accessed February 3, 2019.

13. *Justice at the Crossroads: Court Improvements in Texas* (Austin: Chief Justice's Task Force for Court Improvement, 1972), 11.

14. Texas Courts: A Study by the Texas Research League, Report Two: *The Texas Judiciary: A Proposal for Structural-Functional Reform* (Austin: Texas Research League, 1991), xi.

15. *Annual Statistical Report for the Texas Judicial System, Fiscal Year 2018* (Austin: Office of Court Administration, 2019), 18, 26, 29–30, 33, 40–41, 53–54, 88–89, and 91.

16. Texas Constitution, Art. 5, Sec 15.

17. Crime in Texas 2017 http://www.dps.texas.gov/crimereports /17/citCh8.

18. Crime in Texas 1992 (Austin: Department of Public Safety, Crime Records Division, 1993), 14.

19. Crime In Texas 2017, http://www.dps.texas.gov/crimereports /17/citCh2.pdf

20. *Texas Tribune*, "Texas Prison Inmates," https://www .texastribune.org/library/data/texas-prisons, accessed February 8, 2019.

21. *Texas Crime, Texas Justice* (Austin: Comptroller's Office, 1994), 51.

22. Bruce Fein and Burt Neuborne, "Why Should We Care about Independent and Accountable Judges?" *Journal of the American Judicature Society*, vol. 84, no. 2 (September /October), 2000.

23. Melinda Gann Hall, "State Court: Politics in the Judicial Process," in Virginia Gray, Russell L Hansen, and Thad Kousser, eds., *Politics in the American States*, 11th ed., (Washington, D.C.: CQ Press, 2018), p. 290. For a complete survey of judicial selection systems, see National Center for State Courts, http://www.judicialselection.us/judicial_ selection/methods/selection_of_judges.cfm?state=

24. Brian Rogers, "Republican Judges Swept Out by Voters in Harris County Election," *Houston Chronicle*, November 10, 2018.

25. Emma Platoff and Jolie McCullough, "Texas Supreme Court Chief Justice Nathan Hecht Calls for Nonpartisan Judicial Elections, Bail Reform," *The Texas Tribune*, February 6, 2019.

26. See, for example, Chris W. Bonneau, and Melinda Gann Hall, *In Defense of Judicial Elections* (New York: Routledge, 2009).

27. Wynne quoted in Michele Mittelstadt, "Political Money Eroding Trust in Judicial System," *Dallas Morning News*, February 22, 2002, A6.

28. David B. Rottman and Roy A. Schotland, "2004 Judicial Elections," in *The Book of the States*, vol. 37 (Lexington, KY: Council of State Governments, 2005), 305–308.

29. Texans for Public Justice, Lowering the Bar, available on the TPJ Website, http://www.tpj.org/index.jsp.

30. TPJ Website, Ibid.

31. Adam Liptak and Janet T. Roberts, "Campaign Cash Mirrors a High Court's Rulings," *New York Times*, October 1, 2006, A1.

32. Mike Ward, "High Court Justice Leaves Case Involving Campaign Solicitor," *Austin American-Statesman*, April 13, 1996, B6.

33. Connie Mabin, "Suit Fails to Change Judicial Elections," *Austin American-Statesman*, September 28, 2000, B1.

34. Michele Mittlestadt, "Political Money Eroding Trust in Judicial System," *Dallas Morning News*, February 22, 2002, A6.

35. Debbie Nathan, "Wheel of Misfortune," *Texas Observer*, October 1, 1999, 22.

36. The Spangenberg Group, *A Study of Representation in Capital Murder Cases in Texas* (Austin: State Bar of Texas, Committee on Legal Representation for Those on Death Row, 1993), 157, 163.

37. Texas Fair Defense Project, https://www.fairdefense.org /right-to-counsel.

38. "Public Defenders Fight Back Against Budget Cuts, Growing Caseloads," *Pew Trust*, November 21, 2017, https://www .pewtrusts.org/en/research-and-analysis/blogs/stateline /2017/11/21/public-defenders-fight-back-against-budget- cuts-growing-caseloads.

39. From the Texas Department of Criminal Justice Website, https://www.tdcj.texas.gov/death_row/dr_gender_racial_stats .html, accessed February 13, 2019.

40. Innocence Project data, https://innocencetexas.org/our-work, accessed February 13, 2019.

41. Terri Langford, "Woman Fighting 1993 Murder Conviction Gets a Key Victory," *Houston Chronicle*, June 6, 2016; Anna Tinsley, "An Innocent Man Died in Prison. How His Legacy Helps the Wrongly Convicted in Texas," *Fort Worth Star Telegram*, May 17, 2018; Jennifer Emily, "Dallas Man Freed after 27 Years behind Bars for Rapes He Did Not Commit," *Dallas Morning, News*, May 12, 2011; Mitch Mitchell, "Lawyer: San Antonio Women Should Never Have Been Convicted," *Fort Worth Star Telegram*, November 23, 2016.

42. Robert Tharp, "Freedom Isn't Easy for Wrongly Convicted Man," *Austin American-Statesman*, August 5, 2006, D7; "Perry Pardons Man Wrongly Convicted," *Austin American- Statesman*, December 21, 2006, B3.

43. Information about the case of Cameron Todd Willingham comes from David Grann, "Trial by Fire: Did Texas Execute an Innocent Man?" *New Yorker*, September 7, 2009; Bob Ray Sanders, "Texas Forensic Science Commission Members Shine Light into Some Dark Places," *Fort Worth Star-Telegram*, September 21, 2010; John Schwartz, "Evidence of Concealed Jailhouse Deal Raises Questions About a Texas Execution," *New York Times*, February 27, 2014. Lara Solt/*Dallas Morning News*/Corbis News/Corbis

## Chapter 10

1. *Gitlow v. New York*, 268 U.S. 652 (1925).

2. Texas v. Johnson, 491 U.S. 397 (1989).

3. Avi Selk, Hannah Wise, and Conor Shine, "Eight Hours of Terror: How a Peaceful Protest Turned into the Dallas Police's Deadliest Day," *Dallas Morning News*, July 7, 2016; Manny

Fernandez, Richard Pérez-Peña, and Jonah Engel Bromwich, "Five Dallas Officers Were Killed as Payback, Police Chief Says," *New York Times*, July 8, 2016.

4. Anna M. Tinsley, "The Women's March Returns to Downtown Fort Worth on Sunday, Jan. 20," *Fort Worth Star Telegram*, January 17, 2019.

5. *McCreary County v. ACLU*, 545 U.S. 844 (2005).

6. *New Braunfels v. Waldschmidt*, 109 Tex. 302 (1918); *Ireland v. Bible Baptist Church*, 480 S.W.2d 467 (1972).

7. *Reynolds v. Rayborn*, 116 S.W.2d 836 (1938).

8. *Engel v. Vitale*, 370 U.S. 421 (1962).

9. *Abington School District v. Schempp and Murray v. Catlett*, 374 U.S. 203 (1963).

10. Jason Koebler, "Study: Catholic, Protestant Support for In-School Prayer Falls," *U.S. News and World Report*, January 3, 2013. A 2011 Rasmussen Poll reported that about 65 percent of Americans support prayer in school, with 73 percent of evangelicals supporting prayer in school.

11. Kim Sue Lia Perkes, "Survey: Texans Support Prayers in Public Schools," *Austin American-Statesman*, November 21, 1999, B1.

12. Susan Weddington, "A Referendum on Tradition," *Austin American-Statesman*, March 3, 2000; John Cornyn, "Free Speech Means a Right to Prayer," *Austin American-Statesman*, March 31, 2000; Paul Mulshine, "Whose Religion?" *Austin American-Statesman*, April 4, 2000, A1.

13. David Jackson, "High Court Rejects Pre-Game Prayer," *Dallas Morning News*, June 30, 2000, A1.

14. Lorenzo Sadun, "New Texas Pledge Creates More Divides among States," *Austin American-Statesman*, August 30, 2003, A21.

15. Jim Vertuno, "House Votes to Put 'Under God' in Texas Pledge," *Houston Chronicle*, May 4, 2007; *Croft v. Perry*, No. 09-10347 (Ct. App., 5th Cir., October 13, 2010).

16. Dudley Althaus and Katie Zezima, "As Border Wall Construction Moves Ahead in Texas, Judge Rules Feds Can Survey Church's Land," *Washington Post*, February 6, 2019.

17. Centers for Disease Control and Prevention, "Firearm Mortality by State," https://www.cdc.gov/nchs/pressroom/sosmap/firearm_mortality/firearm.htm, accessed February 17, 2019.

18. Federal Bureau of Investigation, Crime in the United States, 2017, accessed February 18, 2019, https://ucr.fbi.gov/crime-in-the-u.s/2017/crime-in-the-u.s.-2017/tables/expanded-homicide-data-table-15.xls

19. Ross Ramsey, "Parenting and Stricter Gun Laws Would Make Schools Safer, Texas Voters Tell UT/TT Poll," *Texas Tribune*, June 26, 2018, https://www.texastribune.org/2018/06/26/texas-poll-school-shootings-gun-control-parenting/, accessed February 17, 2019.

20. Christal Hayes, "After School Shooting, Texas Lt. Gov. Dan Patrick Says Guns are 'Part of Who We Are as a Nation'," *USA Today*, May 20, 2018, https://www.usatoday.com/story/news/politics/2018/05/20/texas-school-shooting-dan-patrick-guns/626990002/, accessed February 17, 2019.

21. Much of this discussion about the Second Amendment is based on information in Robert J. Spitzer, *The Politics of Gun Control* (Chatham, NJ: Chatham House, 1995).

22. *District of Columbia v. Heller*, 554 U.S. 570 (2008); *McDonald v. Chicago*, 561 U.S. 3025 (2010).

23. Virginia Gray ranks Texas as the forty-fifth most conservative (that is, most permissive of private gun ownership) among the states; see "The Socioeconomic and Political Context of States," in Virginia Gray and Russell L. Hanson, eds., *Politics in the American States: A Comparative Analysis*, 8th ed. (Washington, D.C.: Congressional Quarterly, 2004), 4, Table 1.1.

24. Robert W. Gee, "Gun-Rights Advocates Brace for Battle," *Austin American-Statesman*, August 30, 2002, B1; Michele Kay, "New Concealed Handgun Law Reverses Limits," *Austin American-Statesman*, June 21, 2003, B1.

25. "Governor Signs Off on Self-Defense Law," *Austin American-Statesman*, March 28, 2007, A11; Jeff Wentworth and Patrick Rose, "Criticism of Gun Bill Was Way Off-Target," *Austin American-Statesman*, March 28, 2007, A11; *Glass v. Paxton*, 900 F. 3d 233 (2018).

26. *Roe v. Wade*, 410 U.S. 113 (1973).

27. Texas Department of State Health Services, https://www.dshs.texas.gov/chs/vstat/vs15/t33.aspx, accessed February 22, 2019.

28. David Pasztor, "Senate Passes Bill That Defines a Fetus as an Individual," *Austin American-Statesman*, May 23, 2003, A1; Melissa Ludwig, "Law on Abortion Stayed for Now," *Austin American-Statesman*, August 5, 2003, B1; Rachel Proctor, "Your Right to Not Much," *Texas Observer*, August 20, 2003, 4.

29. Attorney General of Texas, Opinion Number GA-0501, January 24, 2007; we are grateful to Charlotte Harper of the AG's office for clarifying the meaning of this opinion for us.

30. Mike Norman, "Texas Pre-Abortion Sonogram Bill Short on Details," *Fort Worth Star-Telegram*, June 17, 2011.

31. Will Weissert, "Appeals Court Upholds Texas' Tough Antiabortion Rules," *Fort Worth Star-Telegram*, March 27, 2014; *Planned Parenthood of Texas Surgical Centers v. Abbott*, No. 13-51008 (Ct. App., 5th Cir., 2014).

32. Rachel Cohrs, "In Review: Abortion Restrictions in the 85th Texas Legislature," *Austin American-Statesman*, July 27, 2017.

33. *Brown v. Board of Education of Topeka*, 347 U.S. 483 (1954).

34. Joel Anderson, "Judge Ends School Desegregation in Dallas," *Austin American-Statesman*, June 6, 2003, B3.

35. Kent Fischer, "Public School, Private Club," *Dallas Morning News*, November 18, 2006, A1.

36. *Edgewood Independent School System v. Kirby*, 777 S.W.2d 391 (Tex. 1989).

37. Kenneth K. Wong, "The Politics of Education," in Grey and Hanson, *Politics in the American States*, op. cit., 368.

38. "Wealthy Make More Donations, Study Finds," *Dallas Morning News*, April 15, 2004, A3.

39. Jason Embry, "School Tax System Unconstitutional," *Austin American-Statesman*, November 23, 2005, A1; Maeve Reston, "Taxpayers' Lawsuit Challenges State's School-Finance System," *Austin American-Statesman*, April 6, 2001, B5;

Alberta Phillips, "School Finance Gives Robin Hood Bad Name," *Austin American-Statesman*, April 27, 2001, A15.

40. Aliyya Swaby, "Democrats Lay Out Their Priorities for Texas School Finance as Lawmakers Await Leadership-endorsed Bill," *The Texas Tribune*, February 21, 2019.

41. Most of the information in this account comes from Michael Berryhill, "Prisoner's Dilemma," *New Republic*, December 27, 1999, 18–23.

42. Information on the Tulia case is based on Adam Liptak, "Texas Cases Challenged over Officer's Testimony," *New York Times*, March 18, 2003, A20; Nate Blakeslee, "Free at Last?" *Texas Observer*, April 25, 2003, 10; David Pasztor, "In Infamous Tulia, 13 to Walk Free Today," *Austin American-Statesman*, June 16, A1; David Pasztor, "DA Faces State Bar Inquiry in Tulia Case," *Austin American-Statesman*, August 2, 2003, B1; Editorial, "District Attorney in Tulia Case Should Be Held Accountable," *Austin American-Statesman*, December 29, 2004, A10.

43. David Pasztor, "Amarillo to Pay $5 Million to 45 in Tulia Case," *Austin American-Statesman*, March 12, 2004, A1; Alan Bean, "A Letter from Tulia," *Texas Observer*, February 18, 2005, 29.

44. Eric Dexheimer, "DPS Searches Hispanics More, Finds Less, Statesman Analysis Shows," *Austin American-Statesman*, September 23, 2016; John Tedesco, "Analysis: SAPD Officers Use Force at Higher Rates against Minorities," *San Antonio Express-News*, May 28, 2016; University of North Texas, "Racial Profiling Analysis of the Texas Department of Public Safety," https://www.dps.texas.gov/director_staff/media_and_communications/2018/1213a_untSummaryFindings.pdf, accessed February 22, 2019.

45. See, for example, Frank S. Malone, *Correctional Law Digest 1977* (Toledo, OH: University of Toledo, 1978).

46. Frank S. Kemmerer, *William Wayne Justice* (Austin: University of Texas, 1991), 145–149; *Morales v. Turman*, 326 F. Supp. 577 (1971), 38; *Ruiz v. Estelle*, 666 F.2d 854 (1982); one of the authors of this text made several visits to the TDC units during the period of litigation and can personally attest to the accuracy of many of Ruiz's charges; see also Steve J. Martin and Sheldon Ekland-Olson, *Texas Prisons: The Walls Came Tumbling Down* (Austin: Texas Monthly Press, 1987); "Inside America's Toughest Prison," *Newsweek*, October 6, 1986, 48–61.

47. Mike Ward, "After 30 Years, Ruiz Is Ready for Case's Close," *Austin American-Statesman*, June 12, 2002, A1; Ed Timms, "30-Year Texas Prison Battle Ends," *Dallas Morning News*, June 9, 2002, A1.

48. http://www.deathpenaltyinfo.org/states-and-without-death-penalty, accessed April 15, 2014; *The Book of the States 2006* (Lexington, Ky.: Council of State Governments, 2006), 537–538.

49. Ken Anderson, *Crime in Texas: Your Complete Guide to the Criminal Justice System* (Austin: University of Texas, 1997), 73.

50. Ross Ramsey, "Led by Democrats and Young Adults, Most Texas Voters Want to Legalize Marijuana, UT/TT Poll Finds," *Texas Tribune*, June 27, 2018.

51. *Furman v. Georgia*, 408 U.S. 238 (1972); *Gardner v. Florida*, 430 U.S. 349 (1977); *Woodson v. North Carolina*, 428 U.S. 289 (1976); our summary of these death penalty rules is based on J. W. Peltason, *Understanding the Constitution*, 8th ed. (New York: Holt, Rinehart & Winston, 1979), 185.

52. Jolie McCullough, "Texas Sees Uptick in Executions, Death Sentences in 2018," *Texas Tribune*, December 13, 2018.

53. Robert Tharp, "Is Death Penalty Losing Capital?" *Dallas Morning News*, December 30, 2005, A; Mike Ward, "Life Without Parole Among 600 Laws Signed by Governor," *Austin American-Statesman*, June 18, 2005, A15.

54. Jolie McCullough, "After Texas' Second Supreme Court Loss in a Death Penalty Case, Reform Bill Lands Key GOP Support," *Texas Tribune*, February 20, 2019; Matthew S. Schwartz, "Supreme Court Blocks Texas from Executing Mentally Disabled Man," *NPR*, https://www.npr.org/2019/02/20/696178809/supreme-court-blocks-texas-from-executing-mentally-disabled-man, accessed February 23, 2019.

55. Alberta Phillips, "We Must Draw the Line at Executing Juvenile Offenders," *Austin American-Statesman*, September 1, 2002.

56. Alfred P. Carlton, Jr. (president of the ABA), "Executing Juveniles Demeans Our Justice System," *Austin American-Statesman*, August 27, 2002, A9; David Pasztor, "Global Review of Death Penalty," *Austin American-Statesman*, October 28, 2003, A1.

57. Mike Ward, "High Court Spares Juvenile Offenders," *Austin American-Statesman*, March 2, 2005, A1; the case is *Roper v. Simmons*, 543 U.S. 551, 125 S. Ct. 1183, 161 L. Ed. 2d 1 (2005).

58. Dave Montgomery, "Texas Court Dismisses Reprimand Against Judge," *Fort Worth Star-Telegram*, October 12, 2010.

59. Diane Jennings, "Keller Hearing Set for San Antonio," *Dallas Morning News*, June 18, 2009.

60. David Pasztor, "House Passes Bitterly Fought Tort Reform Bill," *Austin American-Statesman*, March 29, 2003; "Texas Tort Reform Group Says Post-Cat Lawsuits Have Dropped," https://www.insurancejournal.com/news/southcentral/2018/09/07/500490.htm, accessed February 23, 2019.

61. Howard Marcus and Bruce Malone, "2003 Reforms Helping Doctors Do Their Work," *Austin American-Statesman*, April 10, 2006, A9; Jon Opelt, "Contrary to What Study Says, Malpractice Lawsuits Drive Costs," *Austin American-Statesman*, March 18, 2005, A15.

62. Alex Winslow, "The Human Toll of 'Tort Reform,'" *Austin American-Statesman*, April 12, 2006, A11; Bernard Black, Charles Silver, David Hyman, and William Sage, "Hunting Down the Facts on Medical Malpractice," *Austin American-Statesman*, March 14, 2005, A9.

63. Bill Hammond, "New Era of Pro-Business Leadership Is Good for Texas," *Austin American-Statesman*, April 15, 2003, A11.

64. Mimi Swartz, "Hurt? Injured? Need a Lawyer? Too Bad!" *Texas Monthly*, November 2005, 258.

## Chapter 11

1. Discussion of county government in Texas relies in part on Robert E. Norwood and Sabrina Strawn, *Texas County Government: Let the People Choose* (Austin: Texas Research League, 1984). For a discussion of "Empty Space Politics," see Gail Collins, *As Texas Goes ...* (New York: Norton, 2012), pp. 26–40.

2. See "Population Data (Projections) for Texas Counties, 2018," *Texas Department of Health and Human Services*, available at https://www.dshs.texas.gov/chs/popdat/st2018.shtm

3. Although one often sees commissioners court written as commissioners' with an apostrophe, Chapter 81 of the Texas Local Government Code is explicit in the lack of an apostrophe.

4. Norwood and Strawn, op. cit., 157.

5. Bell County Judge John Garth, in a conversation with one of the authors on February 21, 1991.

6. Travis County Judge Bill Aleshire in "Elected County Officials—Unlike City—Actually Run Government," *Austin American-Statesman*, September 26, 1996, A15.

7. Robert Elder, Jr., and Brad Reagan, "Rural Counties Try to Stay One Step Ahead of Growth," *Wall Street Journal*, July 12, 2000, T1, T3.

8. Richard Oppel (editor of the paper), "Time to Ask Right Questions about County Government," *Austin American-Statesman*, September 22, 1996, E3; and Richard Evans, Liz Sumter, and Wayne Branscom, "County Governments Need More Power to Manage Growth," *Austin American-Statesman*, April 5, 2009, on the opinion page of the Statesman Web site and the editorial page of the print edition.

9. Provisions for how both home-rule and general-law municipalities can organize are found in Chapters 9 and 21–26 of the Texas Local Government Code. An extensive look at the concept of home rule both in Texas and nationally can be found in Dale Krane, ed., *Home Rule in America* (Washington, D.C.: CQ Press, 2000).

10. See Victor S. DeSantis and Tari Renner, "City Government Structures: An Attempt at Clarification," *State and Local Government Review*, vol. 14 (Spring 2002), 95–104.

11. Texas Almanac, 2019, https://texasalmanac.com/topics/facts-profile. The method of calculation may result in slight counting errors. Additional information on forms of government is available from http://webapps.icma.org /WhosWho/index.cfm?fuseaction=R2&State=Texas, "Who's Who: Recognized Local Governments," a directory accessible only by members of the International City/County Management Association. ICMA recognizes only 326 Texas cities as having a formal council-manager structure.

12. A thorough look at modern council-manager government can be found in John Nalbandian and George Frederickson, eds., *The Future of Local Government Administration: The Hansell Symposium* (Washington, D.C.: International City/County Management Association, 2002); in the monthly issues of *PM: Public Management*, published by ICMA; and the work of James H. Svara, for example, "Conflict and Cooperation in Elected-Administrative Relations in Large Council-Manager Cities," *State and Local Government Review*, vol. 31 (Fall 1999)

13. Jered B. Carr, "What Have We Learned about the Performance of Council-Manager Government? A Review and Synthesis of the Research," *Public Administration Review*, vol. 75 (September/October 2015), 686.

14. See Robert B. Boynton, "City Councils: Their Roles in the Legislative System," Municipal Year Book 1976 (Washington, D.C.: International City Management Association, 1976), 67–77, for a detailed discussion on the characteristics of the two models.

15. See Jane Mobley, "Politician or Professional? The Debate over Who Should Run Our Cities Continues," *Governing*, February 1988, 41–48, for an excellent discussion of the advantages and disadvantages of mayors versus city managers as executive officers of cities.

16. See *Model City Charter*, 8th ed. (Denver: National Civic League, 2003).

17. In 2014–2015, the International City/County Management Association began a new emphasis on leadership as having equal importance as managerial skill and a strong code of codes in effective local government management. Whether this emphasis will lead to more mayor-manager conflicts remains to be seen.

18. See *Texas Local Government Code*, Chapters 22–25.

19. See, for example, Robert B. Boynton, "City Councils: Their Role in the Legislative System"; Tari Renner and Victor S. DeSantis, "Contemporary Patterns in Municipal Government Structures," *Municipal Year Book 1993* (Washington, D.C.: International City/County Management Association, 1993), 57–68; Daniel R. Morgan and Robert E. England, *Managing Urban America*, 4th ed. (Chatham, NJ: Chatham House, 1996), 58–80.

20. John Nalbandian discusses local representation in "Tenets of Contemporary Professionalism in Local Government," in George W. Fredrickson, *Ideal and Practice in Council-Manager Government* (Washington, D.C.: International City/County Management Association, 1985), 157–171.

21. United States Census of Governments 2012, https://factfinder. census.gov/faces/tableservices/jsf/pages/productview. xhtml?src=bkmk.

22. Reese Dunklin and Brooks Egerton, "'Designer Districts' Benefit Developers," *Dallas Morning News*, July 3, 2001, 1A, 12A.

23. Peggy Heinkel-Wolfe, "Two Voters to Decide Taxing District," *Denton Record-Chronicle*, October 3, 2010, 1A; and "A Funeral with No Mourners," *Denton Record-Chronicle*, February 17, 2011, 4A. See also the Editorial, "The Emperor of Shiney Hiney," *Denton Record-Chronicle* online edition of May 5, 2010, available at http://www.dentonrc.com/sharedcontent /dws/drc/opinion/editorials/stories/DRC_Editorial_0505 .1a969c3d.html. The Denton paper carried news stories about Shiney Hiney through most of 2010 into early 2011.

24. See Jennifer Peebles, "Growing Governments: How 'Special Districts' Spread across Texas with Limited Oversight and Accountability—but with Plenty of Power to Tax," *Texas Watchdog*, available February 15, 2011, at http://www .texaswatchdog.org/2011/02/growing--governments-how-special-districts-spread-across-Texas-power-to-tax/1297796531 .story. Texas Watchdog investigates abuses of transparency in government.

25. Elizabeth Kellar, "5 Mega Issues Drive Local Changes," *PM: Public Management* (January/February 2011), 6–11.

26. See, for example, Edward C. Olson and Laurence Jones, "Change in Hispanic Representation on Texas City Councils between 1980–1993," *Texas Journal of Political Studies*, vol. 18 (Fall/Winter 1996), 53–74; Laurence F. Jones, Edward C. Olson, and Delbert A. Taebel, "Change in African-American Representation on Texas City Councils: 1980–1993," *Texas Journal of Political Studies*, vol. 18 (Spring/Summer 1996), 57–78.

# Chapter 12

1. Bob Bland, "Why Worry about Local Government Finances?" *Academic Matters*, a joint newsletter of the International City /County Management Association and the National Association of Schools of Public Affairs and Administration, June 2011, available at http://icma.org/en/article /101240/why_worry_about_local_government_ finances?pub=2&issue=&utc_source=academic+matters&utc_ medium=email&utc_campaign=. Although the article emphasizes local government, the point pertains to state government as well.

2. Fiscal Size-Up, 2014–2015 Biennium (Austin: Legislative Budget Board, 2014), 13, available online at http://www.lbb. state.tx.us/Documents/Publications/Fiscal_SizeUp/Fiscal_ SizeUp.pdf. Fiscal Size-Up is an excellent source of information about Texas state finance, and is published about six months after the close of each regular session of the Texas legislature (somewhat later if there are special sessions).

3. Wayne King, "Despite Success, Sun Belt Oil Patch Is Finding It's Not Immune to Recession," *New York Times*, June 9, 1981, 11.

4. See, for example, "Employment in Texas by Industry," *Texas Almanac, 2014–2015* (Denton: Texas State Historical Association, 2014), 619.

5. FRED Economic Data, Federal Reserve Bank of St. Louis, November 19, 2018, https://fred.stlouisfed.org/series/TXNGSP, accessed March 2, 2019.

6. Frank Holmes, "Which Has the Bigger Economy: Texas or Russia?," *Forbes Magazine*, April 17, 2018.

7. National Conference of State Legislatures, "State Employment Rates," http://www.ncsl.org/research/labor-and-employment /state-unemployment-update.aspx, accessed March 2, 2019; Legislative Budget Board, Fiscal Size Up, 2018–19 Biennium, p. 48.

8. Angela Shah, "Texans' Confidence in Economy Erodes," *Dallas Morning News*, March 17, 2003, 1D, 3D; "No Job Growth Seen," *Dallas Morning News*, March 7, 2003, 1D, 11D; Jonathan Weisman, "Jobs Gone for Good," *Washington Post National Weekly Edition*, September 15–21, 2003, 65; Greg Schneider, "Another Kind of Homeland Security," *Washington Post National Weekly Edition*, February 9–15, 2004, 18–19.

9. Angela Shah, "Texas Ranked No. 1 for Corporate Locales," *Dallas Morning News*, March 3, 2006, 1D, 5D.

10. Angela Shah, "Texas Jobless Rate Dips to 4.1%," *Dallas Morning News*, June 16, 2007, 1D; Brendan Case, "18% of Jobs Linked to Trade," *Dallas Morning News*, May 18, 2007, 3D; "Top Global Cities," *Dallas Morning News*, March 27, 2007, 3D; Bob Moos, "Texas Leaps to No. 2 as Place to Retire," *Dallas Morning News*, May 29, 2007, 1D, 6D.

11. "Movin' on Down," *Texas Observer*, June 3, 2011, 16. See also Robert T. Garrett and Brendan Case, "Much of Job Growth in Low-Wage Positions," *Dallas Morning News*, August 21, 2011, 1A, 32A.

12. See Brendan Case and Troy Oxford, "Punched in the Payroll," *Dallas Morning News*, February 14, 2011, 1D; Case and Oxford, "Working Better in Texas," *Dallas Morning News*, April 4, 2011, 1D; Paul W. Taylor, "Lone Star Vocation," *Governing*, April 2011, 8.

13. Jared Walczak, Scott Drenkard, and Joseph Bishop-Henchman, "2019 State Business Tax Climate Index," *Tax Foundation*, https://files.taxfoundation.org/20180925174436/2019-State-Business-Tax-Climate-Index.pdf, accessed March 2, 2019; "Best and Worst States to Make a Living, 2013: Full List," available at http://www.money-rates.com/research-center/best-states-to-make-a-living/2013-complete-list.htm, accessed April 2, 2014.

14. Texas Workforce Commission, "Benefit Amounts," available at http://www.twc.state.tx.us/ui/bnfts/eligibility-benefit-amounts.html#benefitAmounts, accessed April 2, 2014.

15. Brendan Case and Collin Eaton, "School Cuts Are Risky Business, Executives Say," *Dallas Morning News*, June 3, 2011, 1A, 5A. See also "Education," *Texas on the Brink* (Austin: Texas Legislative Study Group, 2011), 3, posted February 13, 2011, at http://texaslsg.org/texasonthebrink/?page_id=27.

16. See, for example, Carl Tubbesing and Sheri Steisel, "Answers to Your Welfare Worries," *State Legislatures*, January 1997, 12–19; Rob Gurwitt, "Cracking the Casework Culture," *Governing*, March 1997, 27–30; William McKenzie, "Texas Tries to Pick Up the Federal Burden," *Dallas Morning News*, May 20, 1997, 13A.

17. Carl Tubbesing and Vic Miller, "Our Fractured Fiscal System," *State Legislatures*, April 2007, 26–28, quotation on p. 26.

18. Texas Comptroller, https://comptroller.texas.gov/ transparency/local/debt/texas.php, accessed March 2, 2019.

19. See H.B. 3, Seventy-ninth Legislature, Third Called Session; Dave McNeely, "Texas-Style Tax Cut," *State Legislatures*, April 2007, 22–25.

20. Tax Foundation, "Facts & Figures: How does your state compare?", https://files.taxfoundation.org/20170710170127 /TF-Facts-Figures-2017-7-10-2017.pdf.

21. *Texas Fact Book, 2012*, 20, is the source for the impact of the comparative data on federal taxing and spending.

22. *Texas: Who Pays?* 6th Edition — ITEP, https://itep.org /wp-content/uploads/itep-whopays-Texas.pdf, accessed March 2, 2019.

23. "Bullock's Tax Speech Serves as a Warning for State," *Austin American-Statesman*, January 27, 1991, A8.

24. See, for example, David Osborne and Ted Gaebler, *Reinventing Government* (Reading, MA: Addison-Wesley, 1992), especially Chapter 5, "Results-Oriented Government"; Jonathan Walters, "The Cult of Total Quality," *Governing*, May 1992, 38–41; the many reports stemming from the Texas Performance Review and the National Performance Review. See also Julia Melkers and Katherine Willoughby, "The State of the States: Performance-Based Budgeting Requirements in 47 Out of 50," *Public Administration Review*, vol. 58 (January/February 1998), 66–73.

25. Katherine Barrett, Richard Greene, Michele Mariani, and Anya Sostek, "The Way We Tax: A 50-State Report," originally available at www.governing.com/archive/2003/feb/8p3intro. txt, quotation on p. 1; "Texas," from the Grading the States Summary, 2008, by the Pew Center on the States at http://www .pewcenteronthestates.org/states_card.aspx?abrv=TX.

26. Katherine Barrett and Richard Greene, with Zach Patton and J. Michael Keeling, "Grading the States '05: The Year of

Living Dangerously," *Governing*, available at http://governing.com/gpp/2005/intro.htm; Katherine Barrett and Richard Greene, "How Would Professors Grade the States?," *Governing*, April, 2017, http://www.governing.com/columns/smart-mgmt/gov-professors-grade-states.html, accessed March 2, 2019.

27. "Texas," from 2008 Grading the States Summary, published by the Pew Center on the States at http://www.pewcenteronthestates.org/states_card.aspx?abrv=TX.

28. Dave McNeely, "Texas-Style Tax Cut," *State Legislatures*, April 2007, 22–26.

29. World Atlas, The 50 US States Ranked By Population, https://www.worldatlas.com/articles/us-states-by-population.html; Tax Policy Center, "State and Local General Expenditures, Per Capita," October 17, 2017. https://www.taxpolicycenter.org/statistics/state-and-local-general-expenditures-capita"

## Chapter 13

1. See, for example, David Pasztor, "Low-Hanging Fruit," *Texas Observer*, January 26, 2007, 8–10, 20–21, for critical issues that the state legislature may continue to dodge.

2. Alan Greenblatt, "Federalism in the Age of Obama," *State Legislatures*, July–August 2010, 26–28.

3. 2017 Draft Report to Congress on the Benefits and Costs of Federal Regulations and Agency Compliance with the Unfunded Mandates Reform Act, https://www.whitehouse.gov/wp-content/uploads/2017/12/draft_2017_cost_benefit_report.pdf, accessed February 25, 2019.

4. *San Antonio Independent School District, et al. v. Rodriguez*, 411 U.S. 1 (1973), and *William Kirby, et al. v. Edgewood Independent School District, et al.*, 777 S.W.2d 391 (1989), are the appellate court opinions.

5. *Ruiz v. Estelle*, 666 F.2d 854 (1982) and 650 F.2d 555 (5th Cir. 1981).

6. Julie Chang, "Should Lawmakers Regulate Texas Tuition?," *Austin American-Statesman*, September 4, 2016.

7. See, for example, the policy discussion of Randall B. Ripley and Grace A. Franklin, *Congress, the Bureaucracy, and Public Policy*, 5th ed. (Monterey, CA: Brooks/Cole, 1991), Chapters 1 and 6.

8. U.S. Department of Health and Human Services, https://aspe.hhs.gov/poverty-guidelines, accessed February 25, 2019.

9. Alex Ura and Elbert Wang, "Poverty in Texas Drops to Lowest Levels in More Than a Decade," *The Texas Tribune*, September 13, 2018. "Per Capita Personal Income by State," http://bber.unm.edu/econ/us-pci.htm, accessed April 20, 2014.

10. See National Center for Children in Poverty, http://www.nccp.org/profiles/TX_profile_6.html, accessed February 27, 2019; U.S. Census Bureau, https://www.census.gov/library/visualizations/time-series/demo/census-poverty-tool.html 11, accessed February 27, 2019.

11. U.S. Census, Quick facts, https://www.census.gov/quickfacts/fact/table/starrcountytexas/SEX255217, accessed February 27, 2109.

12. Texas Health and Human Services, https://hhs.texas.gov/about-hhs/records-statistics/data-statistics/healthcare-statistics, accessed February 27, 2019.

13. "Study Provides Look at Homeless," *Dallas Morning News*, December 8, 1999, 3A. See also Joel Stein, "The Real Face of Homelessness," *Time*, January 20, 2003, 52–57; Wendy Cole and Richard Corliss, "No Place Like Home," *Time*, January 20, 2003, 58–61.

14. United States Interagency Council on Homelessness, https://www.usich.gov/homelessness-statistics/tx/, accessed February 27, 2019.

15. See Tasha Tsiaperas, "How Many Homeless Live on Streets? The Number Jumped 23% This Year," *Dallas Morning News*, March 22, 2018 for a look at homeless issues in one metropolitan center.

16. Texas Medical Association, https://www.texmed.org/TexasMedicineDetail.aspx?id=49562, accessed February 27, 2019.

17. Legislative Budget Board, *Fiscal Size-up 2018–19 Biennium*, pp. 179, 189.

18. *National Federation of Independent Business v. Sebelius*, 132 S. Ct. 2566 (2012); Sonia Smith, "Partisan Rift Over Medicaid Expansion Remains," *Texas Monthly*, April 2013; Anna Tinsley, "Tarrant Legislators Express Their Highs and Lows from the Session," *Fort Worth Star-Telegram*, June 1, 2013.

19. Peggy Fickac, "The Texas Legislature: Governor Says Session's Task Is Set in Stone," *Houston Chronicle*, June 29, 2009.

20. Suzannah Gonzales and Corrie MacLaggan, "Texas Is Fifth-Poorest State, Data Show," *Austin American-Statesman*, August 30, 2006, B1; recent census data place Texas as the twenty-first poorest state: http://www.census.gov/statab/ranks/rank29.html.

21. Kate Alexander, "To Get Stimulus Money, Texas Must Ease Rules on Unemployment Benefits," *Austin American-Statesman*, February 26, 2009.

22. U.S. Department of Labor, Bureau of Labor Statistics, https://www.bls.gov/news.release/cfoi.t05.htm, accessed March 1, 2019; Texas Department of Insurance, https://www.tdi.texas.gov/wc/employee/maxminbens.html, accessed March 1, 2019.

23. "Welfare Reform, Part Two: A Kinder, Gentler Plan for Texas," *Texas Government News*, September 23, 1996, 2. For an excellent explanation of the federal legislation and its consequences, see Carl Tubbesing and Sheri Steisel, "Answers to Your Welfare Worries," *State Legislatures*, January 1997, 12–19.

24. Scott Pattison, executive director of the National Association of State Budget Officers, in a joint meeting of two standing panels of the National Academy of Public Administration meeting on "Social Equity Implications of Local, State, and Federal Fiscal Challenges," held in Washington, D.C., Raleigh, N.C., and across the country via telephone conference on June 13, 2003.

25. Mitchell Schnurman, "Don't Opt Out of Medicaid," *Fort Worth Star-Telegram*, November 21, 2010.

26. See Daniel Gross, "Reeled In," *Dallas Morning News*, February 4, 2007, 1P, 5P.

27. Bob Moos, "The Gender Gap Endures, Even in Retirement," *Dallas Morning News*, June 18, 2006, 1A, 10A.

28. Kenneth K. Wong, "The Politics of Education," in Virginia Gray and Russell L. Hanson, *Politics in the American States* (Washington, D.C.: CQ Press, 2008), 352.

29. Texas Education Agency, Enrollment in Texas Public Schools, 2017–18, March 2014, ix.

30. Texas Education Agency, Enrollment in Texas Public Schools, 2017–18, March 2018, ix.

31. "Number of Texans Who Don't Have a High School Level Education Is Unacceptable," *Houston Chronicle*, January 11, 2018.

32. On the STAAR, see Mimi Swartz, "Are Texas Kids Failing? Or Are the Tests Rigged?" *Texas Monthly*, April 2019. Sue Armstrong, "Texas School Districts Reaching Point at Which They Can't Do More with Less," *Fort Worth Star-Telegram*, March 12, 2011; Terrence Stutz, "Legislature OKs Bills Expanding Texas Charter Schools, Cutting High-Stakes Tests," *Dallas Morning News*, May 27, 2013.

33. Texas Education Agency, Enrollment in Texas Public Schools, 2017–18, March 2018, ix.

34. *TEA, et al. v. Leeper, et al.*, No. D-2022 (Tex. Sup. Ct. 1994).

35. Lauren McGaughy and Brianna Stone, "John Hancock, Oprah, Confederate Figures Are Among 60 People Cut from Texas History Curriculum," *Dallas Morning News*, February 28, 2019.

36. James C. McKinley, Jr., "Texas Conservatives Win Curriculum Change," *New York Times*, March 12, 2010.

37. Enrollment Forecast, 2019–2030, Texas Institutions of Higher Education, January 2019, http://www.thecb.state.tx.us/reports/PDF/12102.PDF?CFID=94572891&CFTOKEN=13586376, accessed March 1, 2019.

38. Permanent University Fund, Texas Senate, http://www.senate.state.tx.us/75r/senate/commit/c535/20080625/062508_THECB_HEAF_PUF_Overview.pdf, accessed July 14, 2011.

39. Ralph K. M. Haurwitz, "Higher Education Agency Embraces Perry's $10,000 Degree," *Austin American-Statesman*, April 27, 2011; Benjamin Wermund, "Abbott Wants to Rein In College Costs," *San Antonio Express News*, March 7, 2018.

40. *Hopwood v. Texas*, 78 F.3d 932 (5th Cir. 1996).

41. *Fisher v. University of Texas*, 133 S. Ct. 2411 (2013).

42. Legislative Budget Board, *Fiscal Size-up 2018–19 Biennium*, p. 200.

43. *Plyler v. Doe*, 457 U.S. 202 (1982).

44. "Bush's Speech on Immigration," *New York Times*, May 15, 2006.

45. Sandhya Somashekhar and Perry Bacon, "Perry's Immigrant-Education Stand Draws Fire," *Washington Post*, September 23, 2011.

46. Leif Reigstad, "Trump to Deploy National Guard Troops Along the Border," *Texas Monthly*, April 4, 2018.

47. Patrick Svitek, "Texas Gov. Greg Abbott Signs "Sanctuary Cities" Bill into Law," *Texas Tribune*, May 7, 2017.

## Chapter 14

1. For reporting of scientific studies, and discussion of the issues, log onto the Website of the National Center for Science Education; see also Seth Borenstein, "Warm Water Boosted 2017's Hurricane Tally, Study Says," *Austin American-Statesman*, September 28, 2018, A11; Asher Price, "Harvey Report Warns of Changing Climate," *Austin American-Statesman*, December 14, 2018, A1; Coral Davenport and Kendra Pierre-Louis, "Climate Change May Shrink U.S. Economy," *Austin American-Statesman*, November 24, 2018, A1; Coral Davenport, "Climate Report: Crisis as Early as 2040," *Austin American-Statesman*, October 9, 2018, A1.

2. All four of these articles are discussed in Scott Waldman, "Global Warming Tied to Hurricane Harvey," *Scientific American*, December 14, 2017.

3. Brodesky, Josh, "In Harvey's Wake, Will Abbott Still Deny Climate Change?" *MySA*, September 2, 2017; Ellie Schechet, "'Whoa!' Climate Change Denying Politicians React to Hurricane Harvey," *The Slot*, August 28, 2017; Coral Davenport and Eric Lipton, "How G.O.P. Leaders Came to View Climate Change as Fake Science," *New York Times*, June 3, 2017; Asher Price, "Texas Oil Regulator: Science Not Settled on Global Warming," *Austin American-Statesman*, April 25, 2018, B5.

4. Carter quoted by the staff of *Motherboard*, "Texas' Climate Change Deniers," April 5, 2017.

5. Ari Rabin-Havt and Media Matters, *Lies, Incorporated: The World of Post-Truth Politics* (New York: Anchor Books, 2016), 34–57.

6. Stegner, Wallace, *Beyond the Hundredth Meridian: John Wesley Powell and the Second Opening of the West* (New York: Penguin, 1954), 214.

7. "Drought Caused Record Losses," *Austin American-Statesman*, March 22, 2012, B1.

8. Kirk Winemiller, "Understanding the Real Cost of Diverting More Water," *Austin American-Statesman*, February 21, 2013, A10.

9. Kathleen Hartnett White, "Water Supply," accessed at Texas Public Policy Foundation Website, December 30, 2009.

10. This account is based on the following sources: Mary Huber, "Parched Rice Farmers Rely on Highland Lakes," *Austin American-Statesman*, September 4, 2018, B1; "State's New Water Plan Favors Urban Residents," *Austin American-Statesman*, November 5, 2015, B1; Marty Toohey, "LCRA Board: Cut Rice Farms' Water," *Austin American-Statesman*, November 20, 2013, A1; Editorial, "Change Thinking, Policies on Water," *Austin American-Statesman*, July 23, 2013, A6; Asher Price, "Water Release Is Uphill Battle for Downriver Farmers," *Austin American-Statesman*, February 24, 2013, A1; "LCRA Decides Not to Release Water to Rice Farmers," *Austin American-Statesman*, March 3, 2016, B3; Editorial, "Rice Farmers May Be Up a Creek," *Austin American-Statesman*, November 16, 2009; LCRA Website.

11. The information in this section is based on Forrest Wilder, "Cash Flow," *Texas Observer*, September 3, 2010, 13; Joe Nick Patoski, "Playing By the Rule," *Texas Observer*, June 25, 2010, 10.

12. Court decision quoted in editorial, "Groundwater Ruling Potentially Unleashes Geyser of Future Cases," *Austin American-Statesman*, February 28, 2012, A8.

13. Chuck Lindell, "Court: Your Land? Your Groundwater," *Austin American-Statesman*, February 25, 2012, A1.

14. Dan Bacher, "Judge Upholds Pumping Limits to Protect Delta Smelt," *Alternet*, http://blogs.alternet.org/speakeasy/2010/02/11/1419/; "San Joaquin Dust Bowl Blamed on Water Fight," http://abclocal.gocom/kgo/story?section=news/assignment.

15. Information on this subject comes from Asher Price, "Whooping Cranes Are Subject of Likely Suit," *Austin American-Statesman*, December 9, 2009, B1; the Web Site of the Aransas Project, http://thearansasproject.org/; Forrest Wilder, "Whooping Cranes Rock the System," *Texas Observer*, March 30, 2010.

16. Mission Statement from the TCEQ Website, March 7, 2011.

17. For an illustrative example, see "The Science of Squelching," *Texas Observer*, February 5, 2010, 3.

18. *Aransas Project v. Shaw, et al.,* filed March 10, 2010.

19. Asher Price, "TCEQ Faulted in Bird Deaths," *Austin American-Statesman*, March 13, 2013, A1.

20. Asher Price, "TCEQ Wins Appeal in Crane Deaths," *Austin American-Statesman*, July 1, 2014, B1; Asher Price, "Feds Back Off Whooping Crane Death Statistics," *Austin American-Statesman*, January, 28, 2016, B6.

21. Robert Engler, *The Politics of Oil: Private Power and Democratic Directions* (Chicago: University of Chicago Press, 1961); Robert Engler, *The Brotherhood of Oil: Energy Policy and the Public Interest* (Chicago: University of Chicago Press, 1977); David F. Prindle, *Petroleum Politics and the Texas Railroad Commission* (Austin: University of Texas Press, 1981).

22. U.S. Energy Information Administration, "Texas," www.eia.gov /state/?sid=Texas; David Wilfong, "Oil Industry Needs Workers, Fights Image Problem," *Austin American-Statesman*, June 3, 2018, G1; Javier Blas, "Texas Poised to Create OPEC's Worst Nightmare," *Austin American-Statesman*, November 26, 2018, B5.

23. U.S. Information Administration, "Texas:" www.eia.gov /state/?sid=TX

24. U.S. Environmental Protection Agency, "Natural Gas," www .epa.gov/cleanenergy/energy-and-you/affect/natural-gas.html; Elisabeth Rosenthal, "Life After Oil and Gas," *New York Times*, March 23, 2013.

25. Bob Salsberg, "Officials Search for Cause of Gas Blast That Killed 1," *Austin American-Statesman*, September 15, 2018, A9.

26. Mike Lee, "EPA Still Working on Barnett Shale Air Pollution Problem, Agency Says," *Fort Worth Star-Telegram*, May 11, 2010.

27. Randy Lee Loftis, "Most Barnett Shale Facilities Release Emissions," *Dallas Morning News*, April 11, 2010.

28. B. Guy Peters, *American Public Policy: Promise and Performance*, 8th ed. (Washington, D.C.: CQ Press, 2010), 363.

29. U.S. Energy Information Administration, www.eia.gov/tools /faqs/faq.php?id=427&t=3.

30. John Raby, "U.S. Coal Mining Deaths Surge in 2017 after Hitting Record Low," *Chicago Tribune*, January 2, 2018.

31. Brenda Wilson, "The Quiet Deaths Outside the Coal Mines," April 6, 2010, from the National Public Radio Website, www .npr.org/templates/story/story.phpphp?storyid=126021059.

32. "Environment: The Price of Strip Mining," *Time*, March 22, 1971; www.time.com/time/magazine/article0,1971,904921.00 .html.

33. From the Union of Concerned Scientists Website: www.ucsusa .org.clean.energy/coalvswind.CO2c.html.

34. Nuclear Energy Institute, "The Economic Benefits of Texas' Nuclear Power Plants," 2015; www.nei.org/CorporateSite /media/filefolder/resources/reports-and-briefs/economic-benefits-Texas-nuclear-plants-201512.pdf.

35. Source: www.eia.gov/tools/faqs/faq.php?id=427&t=3.

36. John M. Sutton, "Nuclear Energy? Yes, It's Worth Considering," *Austin American-Statesman*, February 26, 2011, A13; see also the Web Site of Professor Bernard L Cohen: http://russp.org/info/inf75.html.

37. Ibid.

38. A great deal of information regarding the world's supply of uranium, broken down by countries, is available at: www .world-nuclear-org/information-library/nuclear-fuel-cycle /uranium-resources/supply-of-uranium.aspx; accessed January 8, 2019.

39. Wikipedia offers extensive information on both accidents.

40. Matthew Daly, "Nuclear Chief: U.S. Plants Safer Than Ever," *Austin American-Statesman*, March 11, 2013, A3; George Monbiot, "Why Fukushima Made Me Stop Worrying and Love Nuclear Power," *The Guardian*, www.guardian.co.uk, published March 21, 2011; John Horgan, "The Scientific Curmudgeon—Holding Firm on Nuclear Power," *The Stute*, March 25, 2011; http://media.www.thestute.com.

41. Information in this section comes from the following sources: Gary Taubes, "Whose Nuclear Waste?" *Technology Review*, vol. 105, no. 1 (January/February, 2002), 60–67; Bob Keefe, "Nuclear Plant Waste Disposal Is a Mountain-Size Problem," *Austin American-Statesman*, January 27, 2002, A5; Bob Keefe, "Nuclear Waste Consolidation Plan Angers Nevadans," *Austin American-Statesman*, January 27, 2002, A6; "Future Dim for Long-Planned Nuclear Dump," *Austin American-Statesman*, March 6, 2009, A7; Matthew Daly, "Court: Decide About Nuclear Waste Facility," *Austin American-Statesman*, August 14, 2013, A2.

42. Source: U.S. Government Accountability Office Website, "Disposal of High-Level Nuclear Waste:" www.gao.gov/key_issues/disposal_of_highlevel_ nuclear_waste/issue_summary.

43. Ryan Maye Handy, "How Texas Won Wind Power Crown," *Austin American-Statesman*, February 2, 2018, B6; "Texas Remains Tops in the Nation in Wind Energy," *Austin American-Statesman*, August 24, 2018, B6.

44. Ted Williams, "Wind Power Could Kill Millions of Birds Per Year by 2030," www.flyrodreel.com/blogs /tedwilliams/2011february/power-could-millions-birds; Ted Williams, "Wind Advisory," *Fly Rod and Reel*, January/February, 2006.

45. Severin Borenstein, "The Market Value and Cost of Solar Photovoltaic Electricity Production," Center for the Study of Energy Markets, Working Paper #176, January, 2008, www.ucei.berkeley.edu/PDF/csemwp176.pdf.

46. There are many such calculations, each using a slightly different set of assumptions; for example, see Roger Lippman, "The Prius Strategy: How to Displace Iraqi Oil with Energy Efficiency," at terrasol.home.igc.org/Prius.htm, dated August 6, 2006.

47. B. Guy Peters, *American Public Policy: Promise and Performance*, 8th. ed. (Washington, D.C.: CQ Press, 2010, pp. 360–61.

48. Texas A&M Transportation Institute, "2016 Texas Transportation Poll: Final Report," pp. 32, 36; https://static.tti.tamu.edu/tti.tamu.edu/documents/PRC-16-16-F.pdf; "Poll: Majority of Americans Oppose Gas Tax, New Energy Taxes in Wake of Gulf Oil Spill," Institute for Energy Research, July 7, 2010, www.instituteforenergyresearch.org/201007/07/poll.

49. Wikipedia, "Corporate Average Fuel Economy," https://en.wikipedia.org/wiki/Corporate_average_fuel_economy#2018-rollback-proposal.

50. "Governor Perry: Fox Executives Announce New Texas Production," from the governor's Website: http://governor.state.tx.us/news/speech/14686/.

51. Information in this discussion comes from the following sources: www.nationalwind.com/texas.wind.facts; "Expansion of Renewable Energy," Office of the Governor Website: www.governor.state.tx.us/priorities/infrastructure/energy/expansion-of-renewable-energy; Lisa Chavarria, "Wind Power: Prospective Issues," *Texas Bar Journal*, October, 2005, 832–841, at www.sbaustin.law.com/library-papers/Chevarria; Kate Galbraith and Asher Price, *The Great Texas Wind Rush: How George Bush, Ann Richards, and a Bunch of Tinkerers Help the Oil and Gas State Win the Race to Wind Power* (Austin: University of Texas Press, 2013).

52. Robert Bryce, "Texas Wind Power: Reality vs. Hype," August 24, 2009, www.masterresource.org/2009/08/texas-wind-power-the-numbers-versus-the-hype.

53. Wikipedia entry on ERCOT: https://en.wikipedia.org/wiki/Electric_Reliability_Council_of_Texas.

54. Brett Perlman, "Blackouts Raise Lots of Questions About Electricity Industry," *Austin American-Statesman*, February 10, 2011A 8; Ross Baldick, "ERCOT and the Historic Failure of Electric Generators," *Austin American-Statesman*, February 23, 2011, A6; Forrest Wilder, "Rolling Profits," *Texas Observer*, March 11, 2011, 2; Kate Galbraith, "Has Electric Deregulation Helped or Hurt Texas?" *Texas Tribune*, July 12, 2010, www.texastribune.org.

55. Bob Sechler, "ERCOT: Power Grid 'Healthy' for Fall, Winter," *Austin American-Statesman*, September 7, 2018, B6; Bernard Weinstein, "Power Consumption Puts Grid on Thin Ice During Hot Summer," *Austin American-Statesman*, September 9, 2018, E3.

56. The 2007 poll was from ABC News/Washington Post/Stanford University, and reported in the Website "Pollingreport;" 2017 information from "Most Americans Want Government to Combat Climate Change, Poll Finds," *UChicago News*, October 2, 2017.

57. Tai Kreidler, "Lone Star Landscape: Texans and Their Environment," in John W. Storey and Mary L. Kelley, eds., *Twentieth-Century Texas: A Social and Cultural History* (Denton: University of North Texas Press, 2008), 389, 393, 395.

58. See William T. Bianco and David T. Canon, *American Politics Today*, 2nd. ed. (New York: W. W. Norton, 2011), 320.

59. Forrest Wilder, "The Science of Squelching," *Texas Observer*, February 5, 2010, 3; Website of Senator Elliott Shapleigh, http://shapleigh.org/news/2992, accessed March 28, 2011; Forrest Wilder, "Radioactive Gifts," *Texas Observer*, April 8, 2001, 2.

60. Map source: www.arcgis.com/home/item.html?id=2f5ab5f5dfe640a8bd918c30340d32c3#visualize.

61. Gilad Edelman, "Texas Among Nation's Worst Water Polluters," *Texas Tribune*, June 19, 2014; www.texastribune.org/2014/06/19/texas-among-nations-worst/polluters/.

62. Kiah Collier, "Report: Major Texas Industrial Facilities Rank First Nationally in Illegal Water Pollution," *Texas Tribune*, March 15, 2018; www.texastribune.org/2018/03/15/report-texas-industrial-facilities-rank-first-illegal-water-pollution.

63. Naveena Sadasivam, "Too Big to Fine, Too Small to Fight Back," *Texas Observer*, February/March, 2018, 21.

64. Phil LeBeau, "Traffic Deaths Edge Lower, but 2017 Stats Paint Worrisome Picture," *CNBC Behind the Wheel*, February 15, 2018; www.cnbc.com/.../traffic-deaths-edge-lower-but-2017-stats-paint-worrisome-picture.html.

65. Texas Department of Transportation. http://ftp.dot.state.tx.us/pub/txdot-info/trf/crash-statistics/2012/01_2012.pdf; Texas Department of Transportation, "Texas Motor Vehicle Traffic Crash Facts, Calendar Year 2017"; https://ftp.dot.state.tx.us/pub/txdot-info/trf/crash_statistics/2017/01.pdf.

66. Stats from TexasHighwayMan.com.

67. Calculated from information in Matthew Philips, "The CO2 State," *Newsweek*, February 28, 2008, from Website; and wwwTXDMV.gov.about-us.

68. Richard Conniff, "The Pedestrian Strikes Back," *New York Times*, December 15, 2018.

69. Information on the politics of road-building comes from the following sources: Texas Department of Transportation Website: www.dot.state.tx.us/; Griffin Smith, "The Highway Establishment and How It Grew and Grew," in David F. Prindle, ed., *Texas Monthly's Political Reader*, 3rd. ed. (Austin: Texas Monthly Press, 1985), 69–80.

70. Texas A&M University, *Urban Mobility Report, 2012*, December, 2012; from Website; Bob Sechler, "Officials: Toll Roads May Be Key to Growth," *Austin American-Statesman*, March 29, 2018, B5.

71. Texas Department of Transportation, "Toll Road Operations," ftp://ftp.dot.state.tx.us/pub/txdot-info/sla/education-series/toll-roads.pdf.

72. Ben Wear, "GOP Asks: Should Toll Projects Get Public's Nod?" *Austin American-Statesman*, February 26, 2018, B1.

73. http://wikipedia.org/wik/Seat_belt#History.

74. https://en.wikipedia.org/wiki/United_States_emission_standards; www.ghsa.org/html/stateinfo/bystate/tx.html.

75. Roger Duncan, "It's Not Even Close: Electric Vehicles Emit Less Pollution," *Austin American-Statesman*, January 3, 2019, A11.

76. "With Nissan Leaf, Perks Keep Coming," *Austin American-Statesman*, October 23, 2010, E1; Brian Sloboda and Andrew Cotter, "Driveway Revolution," *Colorado Country Life*, March, 2011, 14; "No Fueling: All-Electric Vehicle Now Hums Along Austin Streets," *Austin American-Statesman*, March 25, 2011, B7; Fred Lambert, "Texas Brings Back its $2500 Electric Vehicle Incentives—Tesla is Still Out," *Electrek*, June 5, 2018, https://electrek.co/2018/06/05/Texas-electric-vehicles-incentives-tesla/; Chris Tomlinson, "Texas Rolls Out Cash Incentives for Electric Cars," *Chron*, May 31, 2018, www.chron.com/news/politics/Texas/article/Texas-rolls-out-cash-incentives-for-electric-cars-12957561.php.

77. Mary Huber, "Austin Is Going All In on Charging Stations," *Austin American-Statesman*, September 24, 2018, A1.

78. *Ibid.*

79. Thomas A. Garrett, *"Light-Rail Transit in America: Policy Issues and Prospects for Economic Development"* (Federal Research Bank of St. Louis, 2004), 9.

80. Bill King, "The Emperor's New Light Rail: Metro Expansion Plan Rests on Myths and Falsehoods," *Houston Chronicle*, March 20, 2010, from Web site; Garrett,"Light- Rail Transit," op. cit., 7 (on DART); Ben Wear, "Plan to Put Trains in Car Lanes on Half of Route is Unusual," *Austin American-Statesman*, April 4, 2011, B1; Wendy Siegle, "Houston Trains to Houston Drivers: We Are Bigger and Heavier Than You," KUHF, January 9, 2011, http://transportationnation.org/2011/01/19/Houston-trains-to-houston-drivers-we-are-bigger-and-heavier-than-you.

81. Phil Magness, "A Streetcar Named Disaster," *Houston Chronicle*, March 7, 2004, from Web site.

82. "Crashes Plague Light-Rail System, Trigger Traffic Enforcement Push," *Austin American-Statesman*, Wednesday, December 27, 2017, B4.

83. The line does in fact appear in public debate about Houston's light-rail line. See the response by Mike (no last name given) on July 28, 2008, to the blog "Inside Central Houston," sponsored by the *Houston Chronicle* Web site, http://blogs.chron.co/centralhouston/2008/07/is_commuter_rail_the_answer_to.html.

# Glossary

**527s** An organization that collects money and uses it to try to influence public opinion, mainly through the media, and mainly during election campaigns.

**510c4s** An organization that collects money and uses it to try to influence public opinion, mainly through the media, and mainly during election campaigns, but differs from "527s" in that it does not have to publicly reveal the names of its donors.

## A

**acre-foot** It is an amount sufficient to cover an acre of land to a foot deep, or 325,851.4 gallons.

**administrative discretion** The freedom that administrators (bureaucrats) have in implementing and interpreting laws.

**ad valorem property tax** A tax based on the value of real property, and in some cases, the contents of structures, assessed at some cents per $100 of valuation.

**affirmative action** Admissions program that takes race, gender, and ethnicity into account to attempt to make up for past patterns of discrimination.

**aggressive leader** A governor who uses the status of his office to try to dominate Texas politics despite the structural weakness of the office.

**appellate jurisdiction** The authority of a court to hear cases sent to it on appeal from a lower court. Appellate courts review only the legal issues involved and not the factual record of the case.

**appointment and removal powers** The governor's constitutional and statutory authority to hire and fire people employed by the state.

**at-large election** Elections in which each candidate for any given public office must run jurisdiction-wide—in the entire city, county, or state—when several similar positions are being filled.

## B

**bicameral** For a legislative body, divided into two chambers or houses.

**Bill of Rights** A section of a constitution that lists the civil rights and liberties of citizens and places restrictions on the powers of government.

**block grants** Federal funds that can be used for a broad range of programs; the state or local government recipient can determine specific uses within broad guidelines.

**bureaucracy** A type of organization that is characterized by hierarchy, specialization, fixed and official rules, and relative freedom from outside control.

## C

**capital punishment** The execution of a convicted criminal, normally imposed only on murderers.

**castle doctrine** A law allowing Texans who have undergone ten hours of training to carry concealed handguns, and affirming the right of a citizen to defend his or her home against intrusion.

**casework** A legislator's doing favors for constituents, such as troubleshooting or solving a problem.

**categorical grants-in-aid** Federal funds that can be used only for specific purposes.

**charter schools** Special public schools set up to provide unique educational opportunities for students who attend them.

**checks and balances** An arrangement whereby each branch of government has some power to limit the actions of other branches.

**civil liberties** Individual freedoms such as speech, press, religion, and assembly. The protection of these liberties is essential to a vital democratic society. Generally, the protection of civil liberties requires forbidding government to take certain actions.

**civil rights** The constitutional claims all citizens have to fair and equal treatment under the law. Among the most important civil rights are the ability to vote in honest elections, to run for and serve in public office, and to be afforded a fair trial presided over by an impartial judge if accused of a crime. Civil rights refer to actions that government must take in order to ensure equal citizenship for everyone.

**civil service system** A personnel system in a government administrative agency in which employees are hired, fired, and promoted based on merit.

**clientele group** The interest group or groups that benefit from or are regulated by an administrative agency.

**closed primary** An election held within a party to nominate candidates for the general election, in which only voters who are registered members of that party may participate.

**criminal jurisdiction** The authority of courts that handle offenses punishable by fines, imprisonment, public service, or death. These offenses include murder, rape, assault, theft, embezzlement, fraud, drunken driving, speeding, and other acts that have been defined as criminal by the state legislature or municipal authorities.

**coalition** A group of interests and individuals supporting a party or a candidate for office.

**commissioners court** The administrative and legislative body of a county; in Texas, it has four elected members and is presided over by an elected county judge.

**conservatism** A political ideology that, in general, opposes government regulation of economic life and supports government regulation of personal life.

**Constitution** The basic law of a state or nation that takes precedence over all other laws and actions of the government.

**constitutional amendment** A change in a constitution that is approved by both the legislative body, and, in Texas, the voters. National constitutional amendments are not approved directly by voters.

**constitutional revision** Making major changes in a constitution, often including the writing of an entirely new document.

**conference committee** A temporary joint committee of both houses of a legislature in which representatives attempt to reconcile the differences in two versions of a bill.

**cooperative federalism (marble cake)** A concept of federalism emphasizing cooperative and collective interaction between the nation and the states.

**cooptation** The process by which industries and their interest groups come to dominate administrative agencies that were originally established to regulate the industry's activities.

**cooperative leader** A governor who tries to be involved in decision-making at every stage through negotiation with legislative leaders.

**Court of Criminal Appeals** The highest state appeals court with criminal jurisdiction.

## D

**deferential leader** A governor who lets the legislature initiate policy, as the 1876 Constitution suggests.

**democracy** The form of government based on the theory that the legitimacy of any government must come from the free participation of its citizens.

**devolution** Redistributing power, responsibility, and funding from the national government to the states for many of the programs shared by the two levels of government.

**district system** A system in which a candidate is required to live in the particular geographic area in which he or she runs for office.

**dual federalism (layer cake)** A division of powers between the nation and the states that emphasizes each level operating independently.

**dual-budgeting system** A system in which both the executive branch and the legislative branch prepare separate budget documents.

## E

**economic issues** Disputes over government policy regarding regulation of business to protect workers and the environment, and types of and rates of taxes and support for poor people.

**elasticity** The flexibility and breadth of the tax system so that state revenues are not seriously disrupted even if one segment of the economy is troubled.

**election campaign** The activities of candidates and parties, trying to persuade citizens to vote for them, in the period of time before an election.

**"empty space" politics** The idea that Texas often nurtures a rural mentality for governing in an urban state.

**ethics Commission** A Texas government agency created by the 1991 Ethics Bill and charged with the task of enforcing the provisions of that bill.

**estuary** An area of coastline where a river flows into the sea, mixing salt and fresh water.

**Equal Protection Clause** The passage in the Fourteenth Amendment to the U.S. Constitution that guarantees all citizens the same rights as all other citizens.

## F

**faction** A group of citizens within a political party who differ in some important issues from the members of other groups within the same party.

**Faustian Bargain** A metaphor for a type of decision opportunity in which every alternative offers great benefits but also comes at a terrible price.

**federal system** A system of government that provides for a division and sharing of powers between a national government and state or regional governments.

**felony** A major crime, punishable by at least a year in prison upon conviction. Capital felonies may involve the death penalty.

**filibuster** An effort to kill a bill in a legislature by unlimited debate; it is possible in the Texas and U.S. Senates, but not in the Houses of Representatives.

**First Amendment** To the U.S. Constitution, containing a clause protecting the right of the people to "peaceably assemble, and to petition the government for a redress of grievances," among other protections.

**fiscal year** The budget year for a government or a corporation; it may not coincide with a calendar year.

**formal roles** Duties that the governor performs that stem from the Texas Constitution, including chief executive, chief legislator, commander in chief/top cop, chief of state, and chief intergovernmental diplomat.

**fringe benefits** Special considerations that the governor receives in addition to a simple paycheck.

## G

**general election** An election in which voters choose government officeholders.

**general laws** Statutes that pertain to all municipalities that do not have home-rule status.

**general revenue sharing** A federal program that allowed state and local governments great flexibility in the use of federal funds. It expired in 1986.

**gerrymandering** The practice of drawing electoral districts in such a way as to advantage one party or one faction.

**grand jury** A legal body of twelve or more individuals convened at the county seat. The grand jury considers evidence submitted by prosecutors and determines whether there is sufficient evidence to indict those accused of crimes.

## H

**hierarchy** Levels of authority in an organization, with the maximum authority on top.

**home rule** The ability of cities with populations of 5,000 or more to organize themselves as they wish within the constitution and laws of Texas.

**human trafficking** A form of modern day slavery, it is the exploitation of men, women, and children for forced labor or sex by a third-party for profit or gain.

**hundredth meridian** Of longitude; the imaginary north-south line that runs through Texas, west of which average rainfall drops off to fewer than 20 inches a year.

## I

**ideology** A system of beliefs and values about the nature of the good life and the good society, and the part to be played by government in achieving them.

**impeachment** The process of formally accusing an official of improper behavior in office. It is followed by a trial, and upon conviction, the official is removed from office.

**incorporation** The judicial rule that applies civil liberties in the national Bill of Rights to the states because of the due process clause of the Fourteenth Amendment.

**indictment** An official accusation that a person or organization has committed a crime, normally issued by a grand jury, and normally involving felonies rather than misdemeanors.

**individualistic** The culture, historically dominant in the middle tier of American states, in which citizens understand the state and nation as marketplaces in which people strive to better their personal welfare, citizen participation is encouraged as a means of individual achievement, and government activity is encouraged when it attempts to create private opportunity and discouraged when it attempts to redistribute wealth.

**inflation** A rise in the general price level, which is the same thing as a fall in the value of the dollar.

**informal roles** Duties that the governor performs that stem from the culture and traditions of Texas, including chief of party and leader of the people.

**interest group** A number of people who are organized to defend an interest they share or wish to promote; the interest can be narrow (e.g., rice growers) or broad (e.g., consumers).

**interest** Something of value or some personal characteristic that people share and that is affected by government activity; interests are important both because they form the basis of interest groups and because parties attempt to form many interests into an electoral coalition.

**intergovernmental transfers** Money granted to a lower level of government by a higher level of government for a specific use, for example, welfare dollars that are passed to the county from the state and the national governments.

**item veto** The governor's constitutional power to strike out individual items in an appropriations bill.

## J

**judiciary** A collective term referring to the system of courts and its judges and other personnel.

**judge** A public official who presides over a court.

**juvenile court** Special state court that handles accused offenders under the age of seventeen.

## L

**laissez faire** A French phrase loosely meaning "leave it alone." It refers to the philosophy that values free markets and opposes government regulation of the economy.

**legislative oversight** The legislature's supervision of the activities of state administrative agencies. Increasingly, the emphasis of oversight is on increasing efficiency and cutting back management—doing more with less.

**legitimacy** People's belief that their government is morally just, and that therefore they are obligated to obey its laws.

**liberalism** A political ideology that, in general, supports government regulation of economic life and opposes government regulation of personal life.

**light-rail metropolitan transit** Within-city public transportation via subway, monorail, streetcar, or some other small railroad line.

**lobbyist** A person who attempts to influence government policy through face-to-face contact.

**lobby** To try to influence government policy through face-to-face contact.

## M

**mandate** Action that the national government requires state and local governments to take or that the state requires cities, counties, and special districts to take.

**Medicaid** A jointly funded federal-state program to provide medical care to low-income families.

**message power** The governor's means of formally establishing his or her priorities for legislative action by communicating with the legislature.

**misdemeanor** A small or moderate crime, punishable by fines or, at maximum, a year in jail.

**moralistic** The culture, dominant in the northern tier of American states, in which citizens understand the state and the nation as commonwealths designed to further the shared interests of everyone, citizen participation is a widely shared value, and governmental activism on behalf of the common good is encouraged.

## N

**nonpartisan elections** Elections in which candidates bear no party label such as Republican or Democrat.

## O

**one-party system** A state that is dominated by a single political party, characterized by an absence of party competition, inadequate debate of public policy, low voter turnout, and usually conservative public policy.

**open primary** An election held within a party to nominate candidates for the general election, in which any registered voter may participate in any party's primary.

**original jurisdiction** The authority to hear a case first, usually in a trial.

**original trial courts** Courts having the authority to consider and decide both criminal and civil cases in the first instance, as distinguished from appellate courts.

# P

**parental notification law** A law requiring that, before a girl under the age of eighteen could get an abortion, her physician must inform her parents. Parents could not stop the operation, but they would have 48 hours to counsel the girl about her choices.

**permanent party organization** The small, fixed group of people that handles the routine business of a political party.

**picket fence** A refinement of the concept of cooperative federalism that also emphasizes the role of the bureaucracy and of private interest groups in policy implementation.

**place system** A form of at-large election in which all candidates are elected citywide, but the seats on the council are designated Place One, Place Two, and so forth, and each candidate runs only against others who have filed for the same place.

**plea bargain** The process in which an accused person agrees to plead guilty to a lesser crime and receives a lighter sentence. He or she avoids having to stand trial on a more serious charge, and the state saves the time and expense of a trial.

**plural executive** A system of organizing the executive branch that includes the direct election of multiple executives, thereby weakening the chief executive, the governor.

**plutocratic** Adjective describing a government that mainly functions to advance the interests of rich people; as a noun, this would be a "plutocracy."

**Political culture** A shared framework of values, beliefs, and habits of behavior with regard to government and politics within which a particular political system functions.

**political interest group** A private organization that attempts to influence politicians—and through them public policy—to the advantage of the organization.

**Political Action Committee (PAC)** A group formed by a corporation, trade association, labor union, or other organization or individual for the purpose of collecting money and then contributing that money to one or more political candidates or causes.

**political party** An organization devoted to winning public office in elections, and thus exercising control over public policy.

**political socialization** The process by which we learn information, values, attitudes, and habits of behavior about politics and government.

**poll tax** A tax levied on citizens before they are permitted to vote, forbidden by the Twenty-fourth Amendment to the U.S. Constitution in 1964.

**populist** Someone who believes in appealing to the political wishes of the common people, and that those people should be protected from exploitation by corporations, the elite, and government.

**populism** The political belief or mass movement based on faith in the wisdom and virtue of the common people, and on the conviction that they are being cheated by elites.

**poverty threshold** The level of income below which a family is officially considered to be poor. It is established annually as the basis for determining eligibility for a variety of social programs. Also called the federal poverty line.

**privately funded campaigns** A system in which candidates and parties must rely on private citizens to voluntarily donate money to their campaign chests.

**privatizing** Turning over public programs to the private sector to implement. For example, the state contracts with a private firm to operate some Texas prisons.

**progressivism** An alternative way of labeling the political ideology also known as "liberalism."

**progressive taxation** A tax system based on ability to pay that requires wealthy people to pay taxes at a higher rate than poor ones.

**prorationing** Government restraint, suppression, or regulation of the production of oil and/or natural gas resources, with the dual purpose of conserving the resources and propping up prices.

**pseudo laissez faire** A French phrase referring to the tendency of entrepreneurs to oppose government involvement in the economy at the philosophical level, but to seek government assistance for their particular business.

**publicly-funded campaigns** A system in which the government pays for the candidates campaign expenses, either directly or through parties.

**public policy** The overall purpose behind individual governmental decisions and programs. It is the result of public officials' setting of priorities by creating the budget, making official decisions, and passing laws.

# R

**realignment** A change in the standing decision to support one party or another by a significant proportion of the electorate, resulting in a change in which party has a "normal" majority on election day.

**reapportionment** To reallocate legislative seats by adding seats to areas with heavy population growth and taking away seats from areas without growth.

**redistricting** The designation of geographic areas that are nearly equal in population for the purpose of electing legislators—national, state, and local.

**redistributive public policy** Laws and government decisions that have the effect of taking wealth, power, and other resources from some citizens and giving those resources to others. Examples would be the graduated income tax and affirmative action programs.

**regressive tax** A flat-rate tax that is not based on ability to pay; as a consequence, the poorer the payer of the tax, the larger the percentage of income that goes to the tax.

**reinventing** A national and state movement in the 1990s to improve government performance; sometimes called "reengineering."

**representation** The capacity of one person to act in the interests of another person, a group, an ideology, or all the people in a legislative district; each representative in a legislative body acts in place of a large number of other people.

**reserved powers clause** Governmental powers reserved for the states and the people by the Tenth Amendment of the U.S. Constitution.

**revenue bond** Government debt that is sold to private investors and paid off by the revenue produced from services such as water sales.

**revenue shortfall** A situation in which state revenues are not expected to be adequate to fund programs and services at current levels.

**revolving door** Informal term used by political scientists to describe the process in which government regulatory agencies hire their personnel from within the industry being regulated; after leaving government, former employees are typically hired once more by the regulated industry.

*Roe* **v.** *Wade (1973)* A U.S. Supreme Court decision that declared the restrictive Texas abortion law unconstitutional as a violation of a woman's right to privacy.

**Rule of Capture** A Texas legal principle under which a private landowner has ownership and control of all the water under his or her property.

## S

**sanctuary cities** Cities that welcome undocumented residents and generally do not report them to law enforcement as long as they are quiet and law abiding.

**school voucher** A policy that would allow families who send their students to private schools to receive a tax deduction to cover a part of private school tuition. This has not been enacted in Texas.

**secular** A term that means "apart from religion." Public policies must serve a secular, as opposed to a religious, purpose to avoid establishing a religion.

**separation of powers** A system of assigning specific powers to individual branches (or departments, in Texas) of government. In reality, the powers of the branches overlap, so that "separate institutions sharing powers" would be a more accurate term.

**session power** The governor's constitutional authority to call the legislature into special session and to set the agenda of topics to be considered in that session.

**seniority** In a legislative body, the amount of time spent in continuous service in one house or committee.

**single-member district** A designated geographic area from which only one representative is elected.

**social issues** Disputes over government policy in regard to personal life, such as abortion, sexual behavior, and religion in public arenas such as the schools.

**spoils system** Appointing people to government jobs on the basis of whom they supported in the last election and how much money they contributed.

**stimulus funds** To help in recovering from the recession of 2007–2009, the national government created a variety of funds to aid both the private sector (banks, insurance companies, automobile industry) and the public sector (local law enforcement, additional school teachers).

**suffrage** The legal right to vote in public elections.

**sunset review** The process by which the legislature reviews the performance of administrative agencies, and then renews, reorganizes, or eliminates them.

**Sunshine Law** A law that provides for public access to the records of administrative agencies.

**Supreme Court** The highest state appellate court with civil jurisdiction.

## T

**tag** A means by which an individual senator can delay a committee hearing on a bill for at least 48 hours.

**tax equity** The inherent fairness of a tax. As the term is used in this book, ability to pay is a factor in fairness.

**Texas v. Johnson (1989)** A U.S. Supreme Court decision that ruled the Texas law against burning a U.S. flag in a political protest as an unconstitutional restriction of the freedom of speech.

**Temporary Assistance for Needy Families (TANF)** A federal-state cooperative block grant program that provides cash assistance to indigent families with dependent children for a period of up to five years.

**temporary party organization** The large group of people formed during election years to mobilize the party's potential electorate and win an election.

**Texas Commission on Environmental Quality (TCEQ)** The state agency with authority to protect Texas's natural resources.

**third party** A minor political party that fails to achieve permanence but frequently influences the major parties and, through them, public policy.

**traditionalistic** The culture, historically dominant in the southern tier of American states, in which citizens technically believe in democracy but do not encourage participation, and government activity is generally viewed with suspicion unless its purpose is to reinforce the power of elites.

**trial juries** Six to twelve persons who determine the legal guilt or innocence of defendants in a criminal trial or the liability of defendants in a civil trial.

**tort** A private or civil wrong or injury resulting from a breach of a legal duty that exists by reason of society's expectations about appropriate behavior, rather than a contract. The injured party sues the alleged offender in order to receive compensation for his or her losses.

**turnover** The proportion of the legislature that consists of first-term members because previous members retired, died, or were defeated at the polls.

## U

**user fee** A fee for a specific governmental service charged to the person who benefits from the service; a greens fee at a municipal golf course and college tuition are both user fees.

## V

**veto power** The governor's constitutional authority to prevent the implementation of laws enacted by the legislature. The item veto allows the governor to delete individual items from an appropriations bill.

**voter registration** The formal action, by government, of making an official decision as to who is legally eligible to vote.

**voter turnout** The proportion of eligible citizens who actually cast ballots in an election.

## W

**whistle-blower** Someone who "blows the whistle," that is, informs on a government official who is guilty of misdeeds or malpractice.

**Workers' compensation** A program that provides medical, income, death, and burial benefits for workers who are injured, become ill, or are killed on the job.

**workfare** The concept that in order for poor citizens to qualify for welfare assistance, they must have a job or be actively seeking a job.

# Index